The Believer and the Modern Study of the Bible

In memory of Belda and Marcel Lindenbaum

רְאֵה חַיִּים עִם אִשָּׁה אֲשֶׁר אָהַבְתָּ כָּל יְמֵי חַיֵּי הֶבְלֶךָ אֲשֶׁר נָתַן לְךָ תַּחַת הַשֶּׁמֶשׁ כֹּל יְמֵי הֶבְלֶךָ
כִּי הוּא חֶלְקְךָ בַּחַיִּים וּבַעֲמָלְךָ אֲשֶׁר אַתָּה עָמֵל תַּחַת הַשָּׁמֶשׁ
קהלת ט, ט

Enjoy happiness with a woman you love all the fleeting days of life that have been granted to you under the sun all your fleeting days.
For that alone is what you can get out of life and out of the means you acquire under the sun.
Ecclesiastes 9:9

The editors are grateful to Targum Shlishi, a Raquel and Aryeh Rubin Foundation for making the open-access publication of this book possible.

The Believer and the Modern Study of the Bible

Edited By Tova Ganzel, Yehudah Brandes, and Chayuta Deutsch

Boston
2019

Library of Congress Cataloging-in-Publication Data

Names: Ganzel, Tova, editor. | Brandes, Yehudah, editor. | Deutsch, Chayuta, editor.

Title: The Believer and the modern study of the Bible / edited by Tova Ganzel, Yehudah Brandes, and Chayuta Deutsch.

Other titles: Be-'ene 'Elohim ve-'adam English

Description: Boston : Academic Studies Press, 2019.

Identifiers: LCCN 2018055402 (print) | LCCN 2018056609 (ebook) | ISBN 9781618119520 (ebook) | ISBN 9781618119513 (hardcover)

Subjects: LCSH: Bible. Old Testament—Criticism, interpretation, etc. | Bible. Old Testament—Criticism, Redaction. | Bible. Old Testament—Commentaries. | Tradition (Judaism) | Faith (Judaism)

Classification: LCC BS1188 (ebook) | LCC BS1188. B4413 2019 (print) | DDC 221.601—dc23

LC record available at https://lccn.loc.gov/2018055402

© **Academic Studies Press, 2019**
ISBN 9781644692578
ISBN 9781618119520 (ebook)

Book design by Kryon Publishing Services (P) Ltd.
www.kryonpublishing.com

On the cover: "Tiferet," by David Rakia (1928-2012). Oil on canvas. Courtesy of Karin Rakia Simantov

Published by Academic Studies Press
28 Montfern Avenue
Brighton, MA 02135, USA
press@academicstudiespress.com
www.academicstudiespress.com

Table of Contents

Introduction	vii
Preface to the English Translation	xv
Acknowledgments	xvi
Annotated Anthology—"Wisdom and Knowledge Will be Given to You"	1
Yoshi Fargeon	

ARTICLES — 191

General Overview

Shawn Zelig Aster	A Personal Perspective on Biblical History, the Authorship of the Torah, and Belief in its Divine Origin	192
Yehuda Brandes	The Sages as Bible Critics	207
Marc Zvi Brettler	The Tanakh as History	228
Adiel Cohen	Kabbalah as a Shield against the "Scourge" of Biblical Criticism: A Comparative Analysis of the Torah Commentaries of Elia Benamozegh and Mordecai Breuer	245
Tamar Ross	Orthodoxy and the Challenge of Biblical Criticism: Some Reflections on the Importance of Asking the Right Question	263
Yuval Cherlow	Ask the Rabbi: "Biblical Criticism is Destroying my Religious Faith!"	288

The Theophany at Sinai and the Passages of Revelation

David Bigman	"I Shall Fear God Alone and Not Show Favor in Torah": A Conceptual Foundation for Wrestling with Biblical Scholarship	300
Benjamin Sommer	Revelation and Religious Authority in the Sinai Traditions	321

| Chezi Cohen | The Torah Speaks to People | 340 |
| Avraham Shammah | The Revelation Narratives: Analyses and Theological Reflections on Exodus, Deuteronomy, and Classical Midrash | 361 |

The Ethical Challenge

Chayuta Deutsch	The Binding of Isaac and Historical Contextuality	380
Hananel Mack	Manasseh, King of Judah, in Early rabbinic Literature: An Erudite, Unfettered, and Creative Biblical Critic	398
Amit Kula	Justification, Denial, and "Terraforming": Three Theological-Exegetical Models	412

The Bible in Historical Context

Yoel Elitzur	The Names of God and the Dating of the Biblical Corpus	428
Joshua Berman	Discrepancies between Laws in the Torah	443
Tova Ganzel	Between the Prophet and his Prophecy: Ezekiel's Visionary Temple in its Historical Context	463
Avia Hacohen	The Torah of Moses and the Laws of the Nations: A Study in the Teachings of Rabbi Tzadok ha-Kohen of Lublin	481
Yaakov Medan	Illuminating Inscriptions	498
Haggai Misgav	Archaeology and the Bible	515
Rivka Raviv	The Book of Daniel and the Twenty-First-Century Religious Bible Student	530
Index of Sources		547
Index of Names		557

Introduction

For thousands of years, the Bible was studied exclusively by people of faith who regarded it as a sacred text given by God. Considerable theoretical and practical importance was ascribed to this study and the literature it produced. Over generations, a worldview developed that this study required the reader to be totally committed to a belief in the integrity and sanctity of the text, and its consequent immunity from human error.

Sources that reflect critical thinking on the composition of the biblical corpus can already be found in classical rabbinic and medieval Jewish literature—for example, in the commentaries of Abraham Ibn Ezra and Rabbi Judah the Pious. However, these early articulations were not sufficient to challenge the basic traditional assumptions about biblical books, their origins, composition, and transmission. The appearance of critical biblical scholarship in the eighteenth century stunned religious readers of the Bible. For the first time, systematic use was made of scientific, analytical tools to study the Bible. Scholars presented methodological approaches and conclusions regarding the composition of the text that contradicted the naïve assumptions of preceding generations. Confronted with the cogency of biblical scholarship and cognizant of the challenges that this research entailed for them, those who believed in the divine origin of the Bible were forced to respond.

Bewildered believers confronted these challenges in several ways. One approach was to ignore the conclusions of this research or to utterly reject them, while scorning the world of science and ridiculing academic scholarship in general. This extreme conservative reaction to the challenge of biblical criticism reinforced a wholescale negation of the Enlightenment in these quarters. Proponents of this rejectionist approach, who eventually came to be known as Haredi Jews, isolated themselves from the surrounding culture and lacked any interest or ability in discerning between its positive and negative aspects. On the other extreme was the belief that the Enlightenment demanded the abandonment of religion, or at least its radical reform.

A third approach developed primarily in central Europe in the nineteenth century. Its proponents chose to study the conclusions of biblical research, to glean what could be accepted from a theological point of view, and to reject, with scholarly arguments, those positions that appeared to contradict Jewish faith, as they defined it. An outstanding example of this exegetical approach can be found in Rabbi David Zvi Hoffmann's Torah commentary and other writings. While this approach attracted many followers, it received criticism from both sides: the Haredi world objected to all contact with the Jewish Enlightenment and science, and the academic world doubted the intellectual integrity of those who approached biblical exegesis with preconceived assumptions about the nature of revelation and divine inspiration that limited their freedom of inquiry. Today, this approach—namely, the qualified acceptance of the conclusions of scientific research coupled with the rejection of those conclusions that do not conform to faith-based assumptions—is increasingly popular in the field of Bible education in modern religious circles.

A fourth approach has gained ground among religious intellectuals and academics, but it has yet to make a significant impact on the religious public. This approach recognizes the legitimacy of the questions posed by biblical scholarship. It accepts the underlying rational assumptions that are necessary to answer these questions, without perceiving this acceptance as a challenge to belief in God, acceptance of the Bible's sanctity, or commitment to observance of the commandments according to *halakhah*. This approach does deal directly with biblical criticism, yet it allows the possibility of engaging in academic research without *a priori* restricting potential conclusions. Proponents of this approach attempt to clarify—theologically, conceptually, and philosophically—how to live a religious life based on belief in God and the observance of the commandments, without basing that belief on factual knowledge that can be refuted by science—for instance, the historical authenticity of the various parts of the Bible, the integrity and unity of each of the biblical books, the date of composition of biblical literature, and the identity of its authors.

A famous example of this approach is the solution proposed by Rabbi Mordechai Breuer to the question of the unity of the Torah and its date of composition. Rabbi Breuer argued that the theory known as the documentary hypothesis, as propounded by classical biblical scholarship from the middle of the eighteenth century until today, should be accepted. The documentary hypothesis maintains that the Torah is a compilation of several disparate documents woven together to create a new text. However, in contrast to the original hypothesis, which holds that these documents were created by various literary schools active in the Land of Israel in ancient times, each of which related the events and the commandments found in the Torah in its own way, Rabbi

Breuer maintained that these disparate versions were all written by God, the author of the Torah, who relayed them to Moses after they had been combined.

The foundation of critical, scientific thinking is impartiality: preconceptions, faith-based or otherwise, cannot be allowed to direct research to certain conclusions. Thus, an archeologist, for example, should approach his excavation without any prior assumptions about the secrets buried in the earth or the conclusions that could be derived from them. Seeking the truth and rejecting any distortion or falsification are also the foundations of the fear of God. A God-fearing archeologist, who recoils from falsehood and distortion and is guided only by truth, should feel obligated, precisely because of his or her faith and religious commitment, to accept the facts as they emerge from the excavations and research. On this point, scientific method and the principles of faith converge. A nonreligious archeologist who distorts his or her research for extraneous reasons, such as political beliefs or the desire to find favor in academic circles by adhering to accepted opinions, betrays the principles of academic research. Likewise, a religious archeologist who allows adherence to accepted religious beliefs, or the opinions of the religious public, to influence the conclusions that he or she draws from his or her research betrays religious commitments.

It is therefore of upmost importance to develop religious approaches that free academic research from external coercion, and, at the same time, free the religious world from its fear of academic research. This development will contribute to the advancement of impartial research, as well as to the formulation of a clear, courageous, unbiased faith. Adherents of this faith will not fear the use of scientific methods, but will adopt them enthusiastically, recognizing that the search for truth is a religious obligation.

This is true in all academic fields, including Jewish studies. However, the challenge presented by the study of the Bible and its interpretation is especially great, as is the importance of developing new approaches that allow unbiased scholarly research of biblical literature and related fields. These approaches must entail, first and foremost, interpreting the text according to the contextual meaning (*peshat*); examining the processes of composition and transmission; studying the history and culture of the biblical world in order to examine the Bible in its own cultural context; understanding the beliefs and opinions expressed in the Bible; and analyzing the Bible's literary style and genres. Approaching the Bible from these perspectives, without rejecting belief in God and the obligation to observe the commandments, is one of the most pressing challenges of our time. Critical biblical scholarship is well known, well respected, and very convincing; it is impossible to ignore or reject it.

This book originated in a research seminar that took place at Beit Morasha in Jerusalem in 2009–2010, attended by both Torah scholars and university-based biblical scholars. In lively group discussions that were held, questions were clarified and potential solutions were examined. The participants took turns presenting their personal outlooks and ideas, which were then critically, congenially, and constructively analyzed by the group.

Professor Baruch Schwartz of the Hebrew University took an active part in directing the seminar and editing this book in its initial stages, and we would like to express our thanks for his important contributions. We also remember with admiration and affection, as well as with sadness at his untimely passing, our dear colleague, the late Professor Hanan Eshel. Hanan continued to participate in the discussion sessions until his final days, despite the pain and complications that he suffered from his illness. We learned a great deal from his wisdom and sensitivity during the seminar, but sadly did not merit his written contribution or his blessing upon the completion of the project. We would like to dedicate the fruits of our study to the memory of Hanan Eshel, a man of faith and truth.

During the seminar, we realized that a compilation of source documents from traditional Jewish literature, including commentaries and works of Jewish thought, was a necessity. These sources, scattered throughout rabbinic literature in a variety of contexts, are frequently cited in essays and polemics, but have never before been presented in an organized manner to an astute readership eager to delve more deeply into the subject matter. Dr. Yoshi Fargeon agreed to our request to compile and edit a selection of primary sources that form the basis for the discussions in the specific articles in this volume, as well as throughout the scholarly literature on the subject. He also carefully reviewed the English translation to ensure that it reflected the original source and was understandable to the reader. This anthology includes sources that span from the classical rabbinic period through the current era. These pertain to textual problems in biblical studies, historical questions, theological issues, innertextual contradictions, and questions about dating and editing. This compilation, the first of its kind, is a significant contribution to research, as well as an important tool for scholars and students, present and future, who are engaged in the study, teaching, and facilitation of public discussion on this subject. The anthology comprises the first section of the book.

The second section consists of a collection of articles that present a spectrum of opinions, approaches, and observations by religious thinkers, scholars, rabbis, and teachers engaged in the study and teaching of the Bible. Some of the participants in the original seminar contributed articles to this volume, but we have enlarged the group of contributors to include scholars in relevant fields from academic institutions throughout the world.

All of the authors accept the challenge posed by the encounter between the world of faith and the observance of the commandments, on the one hand, and the world of biblical scholarship, on the other. The writers attempt, each in his or her own way—focusing on the questions and topics most personally meaningful to them—to present a religious outlook that is committed to the Torah and its commandments, and, at the same time, capable of incorporating academic approaches from various fields of biblical scholarship. These approaches include the examination of surrounding cultures that influenced the development of Israelite religion, as well as the use of historical, archeological, and philological findings that often challenge a simplistic understanding of the Bible's historical authenticity.

The search for ways to "resolve the controversy" between the academic approach to the study of the Bible and religious belief does not entail the prima facie acceptance of any particular conclusions. The validity of certain academic approaches propounded by various schools of thought and the authenticity of specific findings raised in the research literature are outside the scope of this work. Nor is it our intention to decide among conflicting positions, or to reconcile them. The articles in this collection offer possible ways to reduce the tension between, on the one hand, belief in the sanctity of the Torah and the consequent obligation to observe the commandments, and, on the other, the intellectual obligation to impartial analysis, which is also a religious imperative. The purpose of these articles is not to engage in biblical criticism as such or to examine the conclusions of biblical research, but rather to define the meaning of belief in "Torah from heaven."

The articles have been divided into four sections:

Section One: General Overview

The articles in the first section address the religious response to biblical criticism from a general theoretical perspective. These articles address the fundamental questions that inspired this book:

Dr. Shawn Zelig Aster challenges the very existence of a direct conflict between faith and science.

Rabbi Dr. Yehuda Brandes demonstrates the affinity between modern biblical criticism and rabbinic midrash.

Professor Marc Zvi Brettler advocates a literary-mythological, rather than historical, approach to reading the Bible as a religious text.

Rabbi Dr. Adiel Cohen explains how two traditional Jewish scholars, Rabbi Elia Benamozegh and Rabbi Mordechai Breuer, assimilated the insights of modern scholarship into traditional, almost mystical, biblical commentaries.

Professor Tamar Ross suggests a new solution to the conflict between faith and biblical criticism based on subjective perceptions of God and revelation proposed by the later kabbalists.

Rabbi Yuval Cherlow shares a response he wrote to a letter received from a student experiencing a crisis of faith precipitated by the study of biblical criticism. Rabbi Cherlow explains how the study of biblical criticism can in fact strengthen religious faith and observance.

Section Two: The Revelation at Sinai and its Interpretation

The articles in the second section focus on the revelation of the Torah at Sinai.

Rabbi David Bigman demonstrates how stylistic variety within the biblical narrative attests to the multifaceted nature of the revelation and the biblical text itself.

Professor Benjamin Sommer suggests that the Bible should be considered oral law because it is composed in human language that develops and interprets divine command.

Rabbi Dr. Chezi Cohen emphasizes that the Torah is the word of God as given to man. Biblical exegesis must take into consideration the human nature of the Torah's recipients.

Rabbi Dr. Avraham Shammah compares the descriptions of revelation in Exodus and Deuteronomy, calling attention to philosophical and theological questions and identifying the significant and fundamental characteristics of each.

Section Three: Ethical Challenges

The articles in the third section discuss questions arising from the discrepancies between modern religious ethics and the ethical positions reflected in the simple meaning of the biblical text.

Dr. Chayuta Deutsch demonstrates that most of the interpretations of the Binding of Isaac are rooted in the cultural context of the commentator as well as in his basic system of beliefs, and argues that contemporary Bible readers have a moral and educational obligation to examine Abraham's response against the backdrop of the historical period in which he lived.

Professor Hananel Mack explains how Manasseh, King of Judah, whom the Bible portrays as a mass murderer and idolater, is depicted in rabbinic literature as a Torah scholar and biblical critic *avant la lettre* who asks challenging questions about the biblical text for which the rabbis must find answers.

Rabbi Dr. Amit Kula compares different explanations of divine providence with exegetical methods, and delineates three basic approaches: apology, denial, and "terraforming."

Section Four: The Bible in its Historical Context

The fourth section is comprised of articles that discuss the significance and challenges of examining the Bible in its historical and cultural context.

Professor Yoel Elitzur argues that the usage patterns of the names of God provide internal textual evidence for the authenticity of traditional biblical chronology.

Rabbi Dr. Joshua Berman compares biblical law to *The Code of Hammurabi*, and concludes that the laws in the Bible should be regarded as non-statutory.

Dr. Tova Ganzel delineates the influences of the surrounding Babylonian culture on Ezekiel's prophecy, including his vision of the future temple, and discusses the theological challenges posed by this discovery.

Rabbi Avia Hacohen examines the responses of Rabbi Tzadok ha-Kohen of Lublin and Rav Kook to the question of the connection between the Bible and ancient Near Eastern legal codes.

Rabbi Yaakov Medan argues that the use of critical analysis of ancient non-Jewish sources enhances our understanding of Jewish sources.

Dr. Haggai Misgav demonstrates how archaeological finds can be used to develop new exegetical methods and sophisticated understandings of the text.

Dr. Rivka Raviv surveys several central themes in the study of the book of Daniel where the religious approach conflicts with the conclusions of biblical criticism. She argues that these conflicts can inspire a thorough search for answers that leads to a deeper understanding of the biblical text and its classical rabbinic commentaries.

Neither the editors of this volume nor the contributing authors presume to offer a perfect solution, simple and easy, to the difficulties and disquiet engendered by the encounter between the traditional world of faith and academic research. Our goal is to share with our readers our questions, challenges, and search for potential solutions, as well as our realization that belief in the divine origin of the Torah is not threatened by the truth or by critical scholarship. As the spiritual leaders of Judaism have shown through the ages, religious Jews are more than capable of confronting the challenges posed by scientific advances and cultural changes in the outside world.

If this volume generates discussion, study, and creative output, our efforts will have been rewarded.

Preface to the English Translation

In translating the rabbinic sources that appear in the articles and anthology, we were aided by many preexisting translations, which we have adapted and revised to fit the specific context and to reflect current usage. An appendix of these works appears below.

As every translation is itself a commentary, the translations of the sources within the articles reflect their context and the individual interpretation of each author. As a result, the translations of the source documents as they appear in the articles do not necessarily correspond to the translations of the same sources elsewhere within the anthology.

All biblical quotations are from the *New Jewish Publication Society of America Tanakh* (1985), unless otherwise noted; though some verses have been modified to suit the context, all verse numbers refer to this edition. Citations of Maimonides' *Guide of the Perplexed* are from the translation by Shlomo Pines (Chicago: University of Chicago Press, 1963).

One of the greatest challenges facing the translator of biblical research is the rendition of the uniquely Hebrew and essentially indefinable terms, *peshat* and *derash*. In several articles, the Hebrew terms are used in transliteration, while in others, in which these terms occur less frequently, they were translated to suit the context.

Avi Staiman, CEO, Academic Language Experts (ALE)
Dr. Hannah Davidson (articles translator)
David Greenberg (anthology translator)
Dr. Samuel Thrope (English editor)

Acknowledgments

The editors would like to extend their heartfelt gratitude to Mr. Matthew Lindenbaum for his generous support of the English edition of this book. We wholeheartedly thank Rabbi Yitzchak Greenberg for his support at every stage of the project.

We would also like to thank the team at Academic Language Experts for their hard work in preparing the English text.

Annotated Anthology— "Wisdom and Knowledge Will be Given to You"

Yoshi Fargeon

Table of Contents

Introduction	1
Origins of the Torah	7
Scrolls from the Torah that Predated Moses	7
Moses' Role in the Composition of the Torah	17
Changes Made in the Torah after Moses' Days	42
Appendix: Reactions to Biblical Criticism	63
Origins of the Books of the Prophets and Writings	73
Origins of the Former Prophets	73
The Origins of the Latter Prophets	82
The Origins of the Writings	88
Books of the Prophets and Writings Nearly Suppressed by the Sages	110
The Text of the Bible through the Ages	116
Do Conflicting Orthography and Articulation Represent Unresolved Issues in the Scriptural Text?	116
Unresolved Textual Issues and the Existence of Multiple Versions	123
Scripture and Ancient Literature	146
Turning to Other Ancient Texts to Corroborate the Torah	147
Drawing on Ancient Texts to Understand the Diction and Narratives of the Torah	154
The Patriarchal Era in the Context of the Laws and Customs of the Ancient World	162
Ancient Laws and Customs as Context for the Commandments of the Tora	165

Wisdom and Knowledge Will be Given to You*

Introduction

In most cases, confusion results from nothing more than the fact that people make do with fixed, circumscribed views, and do not wish to trouble their intellectual abilities to drift about the entire expanse of an idea in its pristine state. Thus when they introduce, or are under the impression that they are introducing, some thought, they are unable to reconcile it in the least with fundamental things that have been passed down to the nation, and they then argue that the nation must inescapably be torn into factions, even as we see that the perfection of anything is achieved through its unity.[1]

—Rav Abraham Isaac Kook

The present anthology consists of a selection of sources from the time of the talmudic sages until some two generations ago that in some way parallel, resemble, or refer to the fields that figure principally in modern biblical scholarship.[2]

- The first two sections, on the origins of the Torah and of the books of the Prophets and Writings, correspond to the field known as higher, or literary-historical, criticism.
- The third section, on the evolution of the text of the Torah, is in dialogue with the field of lower, or textual, criticism.
- The fourth section discusses the relationship between Scripture and ancient literature, and corresponds to biblical scholarship pursued against the background of the literature of the ancient Near East.

It bears note that this anthology neither offers nor presumes to offer a complete and balanced picture of the views put forth in rabbinic literature on these subjects from the time of the sages until the recent past. Of course, the present compilation shares this problem with all other similar works simply because the vast trove of traditional Jewish literature through the ages far exceeds the bounds of a single anthology, whatever its length may be.

---

* This collection is dedicated to the blessed memory of my beloved brother Emmanuel Moshe (Ami) Fargeon, who studied the Torah with love and honesty all his life, and passed away at the age of 26.

Still, this collection of views is unusual because the sources that it contains have been selected neither for the role that they played in shaping a past or present religious consensus, nor for the esteem that they commanded among rabbinic scholars or the laity. Instead, lest there be any doubt as to the method employed, let it be said unequivocally that the selections within this anthology have been selected on the basis of two key requirements: First, the author of each source was considered to be a member of the rabbinical world (and in recent centuries, of the Orthodox rabbinical world). This criterion, with its emphasis on the identity of the speaker, may come as a surprise to some readers. However, in light of the fact that this anthology seeks to cast some amount of light on the borders of religious discourse, it is a necessary one. The second requirement is that each source correspond to a field of scholarship or to a commonly held view in modern biblical studies, which in turn has two ramifications that the reader should keep in mind. First, the views reflected in this anthology are not necessarily of greater service to religious faith or more plausible to the rational mind than are those views that have not been included.[3] Second, the opinions found here vary in the degree to which they have gained acceptance in the world of religious thought and exegesis. Some occupy a place at the very heart of the religious consensus (or at least enjoyed such a status at some time in the past) while others have earned both supporters and detractors, and still others defy (or once defied) tenets all but unquestioned in the religious community.[4]

The reader is further advised to take to heart that every selection presented here has been extracted from its original context and transplanted to a new setting. This shortcoming, too, is not unique to the present volume, as the very nature of an anthology is to remove sources from one context and insert them into another. Nevertheless, the problem warrants special attention in this work, with its focus on several of the topics most critical and most sensitive to Jewish biblical exegesis. Text removed from its original context, and sometimes truncated in the process, may lend itself to an imprecise understanding of the view of the scholar quoted; in more than a few instances, the larger context includes qualifications and provisos that are not clearly in evidence in the limited text presented in the anthology. This difficulty is still greater when the selection is placed among others authored by other sages, producing a new context in which the presence of many excerpts permits each to echo further than may have been intended. Thus, the reader would do well not to suffice with reading the selections presented here, but to supplement his knowledge of these scholarly views by studying them in the original context.

Finally, it must be said that the intended meaning of several sources included here is subject to debate, whether in the rabbinical world, between rabbinical scholars and academics, or within the academic sphere, and the mere inclusion of a given source in this anthology does nothing to settle any such dispute. Because the purpose of an anthology is to provide readers with the raw textual material, I have not seen fit to deprive the reader of the right (and the duty) that comes with studying this material and independently arriving at his or her own conclusions.[5]

Yet even with all these reservations, these selections make clear that many of the problems identified by academic scholarship of the Bible have been treated by the rabbis and sages throughout the generations, and that some solutions proposed by modern biblical scholars were previously considered, and even adopted, by traditional Jewish sages. It follows that we cannot excuse ourselves from confronting these difficulties, or the answers put to them, by arguing that they emerged only because of the penetration of the yeshiva by foreign influence,[6] or even as a result of heretical or antisemitic views.[7]

The path available to people of faith as they make their way toward religious truth is far broader than most are accustomed to thinking. Further, and of even greater importance, we see from the sources offered here that traditional Jewish sages neither now have a panacea for these difficulties, nor ever did. What our rabbis did have was a deep faith in God and His Torah that was uncompromised by their intellectual honesty, and a hunger for truth that was not lessened by their faith.[8] These two virtues together provide us with a range of interpretations from various eras offered by sages who exhibit a great deal of courage and an impressive degree of ingenuity, framed by humility and fear of God.

A few notes are in order with regard to the manner in which the sources are quoted. These texts have been collected from a long list of works authored in various periods, and the reader is advised to bear in mind that not all the information and exegetical proposals appearing in this anthology have withstood the test of time. Often enough, new discoveries and novel fields of study have altered the state of scholarship, or even revolutionized our understanding of the relevant facts. However, because the manner in which these sources contend with the questions that inspired them is of greater importance than any given point that they contain, they have been left in their original form.

The only changes that have been rendered to the sources are intended to facilitate the reader, and generally consist of adjustments to such matters as punctuation. These changes are not marked individually in the text.

The exegetical comments of Rashi, Pseudo-Rashi to Chronicles, Rabbi Joseph Kara, Rabbi Samuel b. Meir (Rashbam), Ibn Ezra, Rabbi Eliezer of Beaugency, Rabbi David Kimḥi (Radak), Rabbi Moses Kimḥi, Rabbi Menaḥem

b. Rabbi Simeon, Rabbi Joseph Bekhor Shor, and Nachmanides, unless otherwise noted, have been translated from the texts found in the online version of *Mikraot Gedolot ha-Keter* (http://mgketer.org).

Texts from Maimonides' *Guide of the Perplexed* are taken from the English translation by Shlomo Pines (Chicago: University of Chicago Press, 1963). Other works, unless otherwise noted, have been translated from the CD-ROM edition of the Responsa Project, version 22+ (Bar-Ilan University, 2014).

Endnotes

1. Rabbi Abraham Isaac Kook, *Li-Nevukhei ha-Dor* [For the perplexed of the generation], ed. Shachar Rachmani (Tel Aviv: Miskal, 2014), 259 (chap. 53); see also 124–126 (chap. 22).
2. The decision not to include material written in the last several decades certainly does not reflect a judgment of any sort as to the nature or importance of these sources or their authors. This choice was made strictly as a means of distinguishing between the debate now unfolding in the Orthodox community, and earlier sources that can enrich and deepen that discussion. Exceptions have been made only for a few sources produced in recent years, each of which is of clear relevance and does not play a role in the current debate.
3. Academic scholars have been known to portray views such as those collected in this anthology as "proto-critism" or "critical" interpretations. Such descriptions, however, are misleading. It is far from clear that these sources mark the start of a true linear process that begins with "proto-criticism" by rabbis and ends in modern biblical criticism. What is more, traditional exegetes were not normally *critical* in their spiritual posture (or perhaps better, their consciousness), at least in the usual sense of the term. Moreover, while in any number of cases the products of their work appear similar to those of modern biblical criticism, the exegetical tools that they deploy to reach those conclusions are utterly uncritical.
4. This anthology might be regarded as a counterbalance to the censorship sometimes brought to bear in modern editions of works by medieval and early modern traditional scholars to excise ideas deemed problematic. Let suffice as examples the censorship by ArtScroll of the commentary of Rabbi Samuel ben Meir (Rashbam) to Gen. 1 in the recent *Czuker Edition Hebrew Chumash Mikra'os Gedolos Sefer Bereishis* (New York: ArtScroll Mesorah Publications, 2014), concerning which see Marc B. Shapiro, "Self-Censorship in the *Arukh ha-Shulhan*, ArtScroll's Latest Betrayal, and Other Assorted Comments," *The Seforim Blog*, December 10, 2014, http://seforim.blogspot.co.il/2014/12/self-censorship-in-arukh-ha-shulhan.html; Shapiro, "ArtScrol's Response and My Comments," *The Seforim Blog*, January 14, 2015, http://seforim.blogspot.co.il/2015/01/artscrolls-response-and-my-comments.html. Similar examples are the censorship that editor Isaac S. Lange was forced to exercise in his second edition of the glosses of Rabbi Judah the Pious of Regensburg to the Torah (see note 86 below), and the omission of radical comments made by Rav Abraham Isaac Kook in a volume edited by the Rabbi Zvi Yehuda Kook Institute

(see note 106 below). Concerning the editing of works authored by Rav Kook, including criticism of the methods employed by the Rabbi Zvi Yehuda Kook Institute, see Meir Munitz, "Ḥug ha-Re'ayah va-Arikhat Ketavav shel ha-Rav Kook" (Rav Kook's circle and the editing of his writings), 2 vols. (PhD diss., Bar-Ilan University, 2008). See also Rabbi Eitam Henkin, "'Li-Nevukhei ha-Dor' mul 'Pinkas mi-Tekufat Boisk' [*For the Perplexed of the Generation* versus "Journal from the Bauska Period"], "Rav Tza'ir: Maḥshavot va-Ha-gigim mi-Shulḥano shel Rav Kehillah Matḥil" [Young rabbi: Thoughts and reflections of a beginner communal rabbi], http://ravtzair.blogspot.co.il/2010/06/blog-post_30.html; Henkin, "'Li-Nevukhei ha-Dor' shel ha-Re'ayah Kook: Mavo le-Ḥibbur she-Lo Hushlam" [*For the Perplexed of the Generation* by Rabbi Abraham Isaac Kook: Introduction to an unfinished work], *Akdamot* 25 (2009/2010): 171–188, especially 171–173.

5. Sources that are unintelligible without running commentary are not included in this anthology. The anthology therefore omits important and relevant discussions, such as the fierce debate over Maimonides' view of the prophecies of Moses and the emergence of the Torah. See Dov Schwartz, *Contradiction and Concealment in Medieval Jewish Thought* (Ramat Gan, Bar-Ilan University, 2002), 69–80; Micah Goodman, *The Secrets of the Guide to the Perplexed* (Or Yehudah: Dvir, 2010), 167–187; Alexander Even-Chen, "'I, the LORD, Make Myself Known to Him in a Vision; I speak to Him in a Dream. Not So with My Servant Moses . . .'? On Moses' Prophecy in Maimonides' Writings," in *"New Old Things": Myths, Mysticism and Controversies, Philosophy and Halacha, Faith and Ritual in Jewish Thought through the Ages*, ed. Rachel Elior (Jerusalem: Mandel Institute of Jewish Studies, Hebrew University, 2011), 1:181–214.

6. An extreme version of this approach is voiced by Harav Yosef Horvitz in "Whoever Accepts the Yoke of the Torah," a lecture published in the proceedings of a seminar on the addition of a rabbinical school to Yeshivat Midbara K'Eden:

> Only if one becomes loose in his attachment to this yoke [viz., of transcendence and fear of God] and thinks he is "fine," so to speak, that he has understood the Torah and is performing its obligations . . . then he suddenly has difficulty with the words of the Torah . . . and he asks himself, "Why is this section in this place?" According to (his) logic, it should not be. And why did this person do this and another person do that? If I had been in his place, I would not have! . . . A person who has that understanding—a person who accepts the yoke of the Torah and understands what Torah is—has no time or leisure to search for these bits of "wisdom," teasing out the meaning and significance of the words of the Torah according to the rules of style and keywords. He does not search the Torah to see whether it speaks as people do, thus lowering the Torah to the level of human language . . . but is constantly aware that we do not have a single moment to waste on these things, and everything has to be focused on instruction for the sake of the fear of heaven. This is what all the commentators throughout the generations, all the great sages of the Torah who toiled in their comments on the Torah, toiled to do: *to communicate to us these messages of the fear of God.* . . . The more we understand

the demands of the Torah, the less we are affected, at least while we are occupied with the Torah, by the imaginary duty to satisfy some human standard of conduct.

Rabbi Horvitz's complete comments appear as an appendix to Yoshi Fargeon, "Hora'at Sugyot ba-Mikra be-Aspaklaryat Sippur David u-Bat-Sheva" [Teaching issues in the Bible in view of the story of David and Bathsheba] (seminar paper, Herzog Academic College, 2003/2004), 69–71, http://www.herzog.ac.il/vtc/0075519.pdf.

7. Accusations that an opponent lacks religious commitment all too often take the place of material debate within the Orthodox community. It is not impertinent here to recall the comments of Rabbi Naphtali Tzevi Judah Berlin (Netziv), in his introduction to *Sefer Bereshit . . . im . . . Ha'amek Davar*, ed. M. Y. Kuperman (Jerusalem: M. Y. Kuperman, 2004/2005), 27–28:

> This is because—as explained in the discussion of the verse "The Rock!— His deeds are perfect. . . . True and upright is He" (Deut. 32:4), in the Song of Moses—God is praised as "upright" to acknowledge the righteousness of God's judgment in destroying the Second Temple, which was [during] a "crooked, perverse generation" (5), because they were righteous and pious and toiled with the Torah but were not upright *in their worldly conduct*. For this reason, due to the gratuitous hatred in their hearts for each other, they suspected those they saw not following their religious views to be Sadducees or heretics, and as a result came to shed blood . . . metaphorically speaking, and to do all other kinds of bad things, to the point that the Temple was destroyed. This was the reason for the acknowledgment of the righteousness of God's justice: that the Holy One, blessed be He, is "upright" and does not tolerate righteous people of this sort, but rather such as walk uprightly, not crookedly, in their worldly conduct *as well*, even if it [i.e., the unacceptable alternative] is intended for the sake of heaven.

8. This approach is eloquently expressed by Samuel David Luzzatto, *S. D. Luzzatto's hebräische Briefe, gesammelt von seinem Sohne Dr Isaias Luzzatto*, ed. Eisig Gräber (Przemyśl: typ Zupnik, 1882; Jerusalem: 1966/1967), 1:170: "As for me, just as I love truth and just as I fight my battles without favoring any person or persons, modern or ancient, so do I love the Torah of our God, which is a truthful Torah." Though Luzzatto figures prominently in discussions of the questions addressed by this anthology, his work is omitted in deference to Professor Shmuel Vargon, who ably presents the bulk of the relevant sources in his recent work *Shmuel David Luzzatto: Bikoritiut Minutah ba-Perush ha-Mikra* [S. D. Luzzatto: Moderate criticism in biblical exegesis] (Ramat Gan: Bar-Ilan University, 2013). See also Ephraim Chamiel, *Ha-Derekh ha-Memutza'at: Re'shit Tzemiḥat ha-Datiyyut ha-Modernit: Teguvot la-Modernah be-Hagut shel Maharatz Chajes, Rabbi S. Rabbi Hirsch, ve-Shadal* [The middle way: The emergence of modern-religious trends in 19th-century Judaism: Responses to modernity in the philosophy of Z. H. Chajes, S. Rabbi Hirsch, and S. D. Luzzato] (Jerusalem: Carmel, 2011), esp. 83–117; Yishay Lifshitz, "Haguto shel Shadal be-Parshanuto la-Mikra" [Luzzatto's philosophy and biblical exegesis] (master's thesis, Bar-Ilan University, 2013), especially 47–53.

Origins of the Torah

Scrolls from the Torah that Predated Moses

Our teacher Moses wrote this book of Genesis together with the entire Torah as dictated by the holy One, blessed is He. . . . It would have been appropriate for him to write at the beginning of the book of Genesis, "The Lord spoke to Moses all these words, saying." The reason it was written anonymously [i.e., with no such introductory phrase] is that our teacher Moses did not write the Torah in the first person . . . whereas our teacher Moses wrote the history of all previous generations and his own genealogy, history, and experiences in the third person. . . . Moses therefore is not mentioned in the Torah until his birth, and even then he is mentioned as if someone else were speaking of him. . . . Thus Moses was like a scribe transcribing an ancient book.

—**Nachmanides,** Introduction to Genesis

Nachmanides's words typify the mainstream rabbinical opinion regarding the composition of the Torah in general, and of Genesis in particular. Yet throughout the generations there were some who argued that the Torah had been given "in scrolls," each at the time most appropriate for its content to be revealed. The stories of Genesis, according to this opinion, were also given at their appropriate time, namely, that of the Patriarchs.[1] Moses then was not merely "like a scribe transcribing an ancient book," but literally used a preexisting text when writing the Torah.[2]

1

Rabbi Yoḥanan said in the name of Rabbi Banna'ah: The Torah was given in scrolls, as it says, "Then I said, 'Behold I have come, I am written about in the scroll of the book'" (Ps. 40:8). Rabbi Shimon b. Lakish says: The Torah was given as a sealed whole, as it says, "Take this book of teaching" (Deut. 31:26).

Babylonian Talmud, tractate *Gittin* 60a.

2

"Then I said, 'See I will bring a scroll recounting what befell me'" (Ps. 40:8)—[King David says:] Since the time the Torah was given, I have appeared in it. [In the verse regarding Lot's daughters who are saved from the destruction of Sodom it says,] "And your two daughters who are to be found" (Gen. 19:15). [They are saved] in the merit of David, who will descend from Ruth the Moabite and Naamah the Ammonite, mother of Rehoboam. Here is written, "who are to be found" (*ha-nimtza'ot*), and there is written, "I have found (*matza'ti*) David my servant" (Ps. 89:21). It therefore is called a "scroll": because first the scroll of Creation was written, then the scroll of Noah, then the scroll of Abraham, and thus David says, "I am written about" in the scroll of Abraham.[3]

Rashi, commentary to Babylonian Talmud, tractate *Gittin* 60a.[4]

3

Understand that if we posit that the Patriarchs were considered to belong to the sons of Noah, it may be said that the giving of the Torah began with Abraham, but Abraham was given [the commandment of] circumcision alone; to Jacob was added [the prohibition against eating the] sciatic nerve; in Egypt, the paschal sacrifice; at Marah, other commandments, and at Sinai the rest of the laws. It may be said that this understanding hinges on the debate between Rabbi Yoḥanan and Rabbi Shimon ben Lakish in the Babylonian Talmud, tractate *Gittin* (60a) concerning whether the Torah was given whole or in scrolls. ...According to the view of Rabbi Yoḥanan, it may be said that the giving of the Torah began with Abraham.

Rabbi Joseph b. Judah Engel, *Sefer Beit ha-Otzar* (Petrokov, 1902), 1:3.[5]

4

"That same day Pharaoh charged the taskmasters and foremen of the people, saying... 'Let heavier work be laid upon the men; let them keep at (it and not pay attention to deceitful promises)'" (Exod. 5:6,9)—This serves to teach us that they [i.e., the enslaved Israelites] possessed scrolls, in which they delighted each Sabbath, assuring them that God would redeem them because they rested on the Sabbath. Thus Pharaoh said to them, "Let heavier work be laid," and let them have neither delight nor rest on the Sabbath day.

Shemot Rabbah 5:18.[6]

5

"Then Moses returned to the Lord and said, 'O Lord, why did You bring harm upon this people?' (Exod. 5:22)—What is the meaning of the expression "O Lord, why did You bring harm"? Usually, if a person says to his friend, "Why did you do this?" he immediately becomes angry at him. Would Moses say to God, "Why have You brought harm [upon this people]"?

Rather, this is what he said: I took the book of Genesis and read it and saw the deeds of the generation of the Deluge and how they were punished, and it was just; and the actions of the generation of the Dispersion, and the Sodomites, and how they were punished, and it was just. Yet this people—what has it done to deserve to be enslaved more than all previous generations?

Shemot Rabbah 5:22.

6

"I took the book of Genesis" (*Shemot Rabbah* 5:22)—The implication is that the book of Genesis was already completely written . . . for he is of the view that the Torah was given in scrolls, and at the time of the giving of Torah, the entire book of Genesis [and the book of Exodus] until the matter of the giving of the Torah was already written.

Rabbi Ze'ev Wolf Einhorn,[7] commentary to *Shemot Rabbah* 5:22 (Vilna: Romm, 1844), 33.[8]

7

The Lord said to Moses, "Write this memorial in the book of the ancient elders, and put these words for Joshua to hear: that I will surely blot out the memory of Amalek from under the heavens."

Targum Pseudo-Jonathan to Exodus 18:14.

8

These are the prophets and sages who prophesied and received the Torah and transmitted it to one another. These are the prophets who prophesied to the world before the giving of the Torah: Adam, Noah, Shem, Ham, Japheth, and Eber, until Abraham, Isaac, and Jacob came. . . . In the times of our teacher Moses, there were written texts in which the Patriarchs, beginning with Adam, had recorded the chronicles from the beginning of time. . . . Adam transmitted it to Seth, Seth to Methuselah, Methuselah to Noah, Noah to Shem, Shem to Eber, Eber to Isaac, Isaac to Jacob, Jacob to Joseph and his brothers. . . . They told it to their children, and their children to their children, and those children to the next generation, because although our forebears were in Egypt, they always maintained a house of study, as we find in the *aggadah*, and this is the meaning of "Go and assemble the elders of Israel" (Exod. 3:16).

When our teacher Moses was at the point of writing the commandments, he thought it appropriate to write how Israel had received the Torah. Because he was already explaining what transpired in his time, he wrote the story that had brought them down to Egypt and the history of the Patriarchs from the beginning, looking in the books and writing based on them from the days of Creation. He did what he did with divine inspiration, "revealing to His people His powerful works" (Ps. 111:6). Yet although he wrote what he wrote, he did not write everything in entirety, but left most of the Torah as an oral tradition.

Rabbi Yeraḥmi'el b. Solomon,[9] "Seder Olam Nusaḥ Sheni," in *Sefer ha-Zikhronot: Hu Divrei ha-Yamim li-Yeraḥmi'el* (Memorial book: The Chronicles of Yeraḥmi'el), ed. Eli Yassif (Tel Aviv: Tel Aviv University, 2001), 368–369.

9

The midrash, in my view, makes an important statement in saying that they had scrolls in their possession, for it permits us to agree with the opinion that, prior to Moses, there were books or scrolls that told the stories of the earliest ancestors and the stories of the Torah were collected from them, just as passages are quoted from the Book of the Wars of the Lord and from the words of the bards.

Rabbi Elia Benamozegh, *Sefer Torat Hashem . . . ve-Nosaf alav Em la-Mikra . . . va . . . Em la-Masoret*[10] (Livorno: Defus Benamozegh, 1863), 5:151b–152a (Notes and Omissions to Exod. 4:10).[11]

10

The scrolls recounting events that preceded the giving of the Torah were written for Israel before, as noted in *Shemot Rabbah* (5:18, 5:22). . . . We thus see that the book of Genesis appears to have been written earlier, each story in its generation, and for this reason the midrash refers to it as "scrolls": because each one wrote a scroll in his generation. And thus it went, in order, the story of Joseph, the story of Jacob's descent to Egypt, the story of Moses until the giving of the Torah. At the time of the giving of the Torah, God selected which scrolls to tell Moses to write in the written Torah, which to retain as oral law, and perhaps which to conceal due to their falsehoods, while those that were true endured as part of the Written and Oral Law. . . .

Since the scrolls were written in their time, there is no reason to wonder about the formulation of "who are coming" (*ha-ba'im*), in the present tense, as opposed to "who came" (*asher ba'u*), in the past tense, because it truly was written then, at that time, in the present tense. And it is not outlandish to think thus, based on the statement of the midrash to Mikkets: "Rabbi Yehudah b. Simon said: Joseph himself knew that his brothers were descending to Egypt to purchase food. What did he do? He assigned guards to all of the entrances and told them: See to it that for everyone who enters to purchase food, you write his name and the name of his father,"[12] as with the convention of passports in our day, which Joseph appears to have been the first to conceive.... Thus this remained the case even after Joseph revealed himself to his brothers. This scroll, from "These are the names of the Israelites, Jacob and his descendants, who came to Egypt" until "all these persons numbered sixty-six" (Gen. 46:26), was written by the guards at the gates, and Manasseh was present and took receipt of the notes, as is stated in the midrash (4), and he added the verses "And Joseph's sons who were born to him in Egypt, etc." (27).... God commanded Moses to insert this scroll into the Torah, as with the other true scrolls. Therefore, there is no need to be surprised by the fact that they are written thus.

Rabbi Chaim Hirschensohn,[13] *Sefer Nimmukei Rashi: Ḥiddushei ha-Raḥah 'al Nimmukei ha-Ḥummash le-Rashi* [Novellae of Rabbi Chaim Hirschensohn on Rashi's explanations of the Bible] (Seini: Jakob Wieder, 1929), 1:83b (Sec. 274, commentary to Gen. 46:8).[14]

11

"Moses went and repeated to the people all the commands of the Lord and all the rules, and all the people answered with one voice, saying, 'All the things that the Lord has commanded we will do!'" (Exod. 24:3)—It is already clear from our previous remarks that "the rules" are those found in *parashat* Mishpatim, which Jethro had previously suggested and God agreed to have recorded in the written Torah.[15] Yet what "commands of the Lord" were there aside from those rules that Moses wrote? Though it is not explained in the present section, these undoubtedly are the divine commands found in the written Torah, for it says, "Moses then wrote down [all the commands of the Lord]" (4). These appear to be the verses in *parashat* Mishpatim that God added to the words of Jethro, e.g., "You shall not ill-treat any widow or orphan. If you do mistreat them, I will heed their outcry as soon as they cry out to Me, etc." (22:21–22) ... and perhaps other, similar verses scattered among the passages of the Torah, which are not arranged chronologically. . . .

Perhaps the reason for scattering the passages of the Torah is to prevent us from giving precedence to the commandments of one covenant over those of another, because ultimately covenants were made with regard to all the commandments of the Torah. . . .

However, in the account of what was repeated to the nation, it is written, "Moses went and repeated to the people all the commands of the Lord and all the rules,| while in the account of Moses' writing, it is written, "Moses then wrote down all the commands of the Lord," with no mention of the rules, because these had already been written by Jethro. The statement "These are the rules" (21:1) indicates that he transmitted something organized and already written. Thus here he wrote only "the commands of the Lord." When God commanded Moses to include the story of Jethro and his rules in the written Torah, God commanded that they be written together with "the commands of the Lord" in a single passage . . . for the book of Genesis also had been previously written in its entirety, as is stated in the midrash[16] . . .

However, these were written in the Torah only when God commanded so, when the Torah was given "whole." At this juncture, he had as yet been commanded to write down in the Torah only these "commands of the Lord," and the people appear as yet to have willingly accepted only that spoken by God, for they said, "All the things *that the Lord has commanded* we will do," and similarly said, "All that the Lord has spoken we will faithfully do!" They had not yet accepted the rules, until God commanded that they be written in the Torah.

Further, God appears not to have commanded that anything be included in the written Torah without first revealing this to the nation and obtaining their consent and acceptance, or entering a covenant with regard to it. The truthful Lord God, whose seal is truth, deferred to the honor, cognizance, and acceptance of the people, as well as their faith and intellect, and the Torah speaks in the language of human beings in order to ease their ability to apprehend.

Rabbi Chaim Hirschensohn, *Elleh Divrei ha-Berit* [These are the words of the covenant] (Jerusalem: Defus Ivri, 1927), 2:34–35.

12

The Israelites were not eyewitnesses to the [events of] the book of Genesis, from "When God began to create" until the birth of Moses, but merely heard it from their predecessors. True, Adam saw himself alone in the Garden of

Eden, and saw the snake and heard the decree of Heaven, and from him, the oral tradition was passed on to Shem, until Amram and Moses. Because it is a well-established principle among the sages that fathers do not bequeath lies to their sons, it is considered as if we had seen it all with our own eyes. . . . The Jewish people were eyewitnesses not only to those things heard and done from the early days of Moses until his death, but we are eyewitnesses to the stories in Genesis as well, because fathers do not bequeath lies to their sons. . . . Because prior to his death, Jacob said to his sons, "Come together that I may tell you" (Gen. 49:1), and what he said would come to be fulfilled, it is as if we had seen all the book of Genesis with our own eyes.

This is the meaning of what Rabbi Hamnuna says in tractate *Sukkah* of the Babylonian Talmud (42a): "What is Torah? 'When Moses charged us with the Torah as the heritage of the congregation of Jacob' (Deut. 33:4)." When Moses called Israel "the congregation of Jacob," he taught us that we had heard all the book of Genesis from the mouth of Jacob, who had heard it from Shem and who told it to Amram, and Amram to Moses. It therefore is as if we had seen another part of Torah, namely Genesis, with our own eyes, and therefore we are grooms of Genesis.[17] Our relationship to the part of the Torah called Genesis is like that of a groom coming forth from the chamber, rejoicing to greet his betrothed with bonds of love.

Rabbi Solomon Tzevi b. Nathan Schick,[18] *Sefer Torah Shelemah: Be'ur u-Perush 'al Ḥamishah Ḥumshei Torah* [*Torah Shelemah:* An elucidation and commentary on the five books of the Torah] (Sathmar: Defus Z. Schwartz, 1909), 1:83a–84b.

Endnotes

1. See, e.g., Menachem M. Kasher, *Torah Shelemah,* part 19 (*Parashat* Mishpatim, part 3) (New York: Ha-Va'ad le-Ma'an ha-Torah Shelemah be-Eretz Yisra'el, 1960), 345–362; Amnon Bazak, *Ad ha-Yom ha-Zeh: She'elot Yesod be-Limmud Tanakh* [Until this day: Fundamental questions in Bible teaching] (Tel Aviv: Yediot Books, 2013), 34–38.
2. The effort to identify the scrolls that lay before Moses as he wrote Genesis comprised one of the earliest stages of the development of the critical approach to Bible study, and in fact served as the foundation for the composition of *Conjectures Sure les Memoires Originaux Dont il Paroit que Moyse S'est Servi Pour Composer le Livre de la Genese: Avec Des Remarques Qui Appuient Ou Qui Eclaircissent Ces Conjectures* [Conjectures regarding the original notes that seemed to have served Moses in writing the book of Genesis: With remarks supporting or clarifying these conjectures] (Brussels, 1753), by Jean Astruc (1684–1766), court physician to Louis XV and the father of the documentary hypothesis. See M. Soloweitschik

and S. Rubascheff, *Toledot Bikkoret ha-Mikra* [The history of Bible criticism] (Berlin: Dwir-Mikra, 1924), 65–67.

3. Rabbi Barukh Epstein (1860–1942; son of *Arukh ha-Shulḥan* author Yeḥi'el Mikhel Epstein; nephew and brother-in-law of Naftali Berlin of Volozhin) takes a similar approach in *Torah Temimah* to Gen. 19, n. 4, in explaining the interpretation of Ps. 40:8 advanced by Rava in *Yevamot* 77a: "I [i.e., King David] said when anointed king: 'Now I have come to greatness, and only now have they conferred this on me, and I did not know that this already was written about me in the times of Abraham in the scroll,'" that is, the Torah, as has been explained. The Torah is called a scroll according to the opinion in *Gittin* 60a: "The Torah was given in scrolls." For a discussion of the comment by Rashi and its ramifications, see Kasher (note 9 above), 346.

4. Rabbi Solomon b. Isaac (Rashi; ca. 1040–1105) is considered the greatest Jewish biblical and Talmudic exegete. For a biography, see, e.g., Avraham Grossman, *Ḥakhmei Tzarefat ha-Ri'shonim: Koroteihem, Darkam be-Hanhagat ha-Tzibbur, Yetziratam ha-Ruḥanit* [The early sages of France: Their lives, leadership, and works] (Jerusalem: Magnes, 2001), 121–253; as well as the version written by the same author for popular consumption: *Rashi: Rabbeinu Shelomoh Yitzḥaki: Gedolei ha-Ruaḥ ve-ha-Yetzirah ba-Am ha-Yehudi* [Rashi: *Rabbeinu Shelomoh Yitzḥaki*: Spiritual and creative giants of the Jewish people] (Jerusalem: Zalman Shazar Center, 2006). For a discussion of Rashi's comment excerpted here, see Kasher (note 9 above), 345–350. A similar approach to Rashi's is that taken by Yehuda Kiel in his commentary to Genesis; see especially *Da'at Mikra*, Genesis, vol. 1 (Jerusalem: Mosad Harav Kook, 1997), 8–22.

5. Rabbi Joseph Engel (1859–1919), born in the Galician city of Ternopol, presided over the Krakow rabbinical court and spent the end of his life in Vilna. For a detailed biography, see Aharon Sorsky, *Marbitzei Torah me-Olam ha-Ḥasidut ba-Dorot ha-Aḥaronim* [Disseminators of Torah from the Hasidic world in recent generations] (Benei Berak: printed by author, 1986), 2:217–245. The excerpt printed here is a small section of a larger discussion of the subject by Engel; see *Sefer Beit ha-Otzar*, 1:1–26.

6. Cf. *Midrash Tehillim*, ed. Buber, to Psalms 119:92: "'Were not your Torah my delight'—Israel said: Were it not for your Torah, which was with me and was my delight, I would be lost in my suffering, and thus did Moses say: 'When I am filled with cares, your assurance soothes my soul' (94:19), and thus does Pharaoh say: 'Let heavier work be laid upon the men; let them keep at it and not pay attention to deceitful promises' (Exod. 5:9). They possessed books in which delighted each Sabbath, and therefore it says: 'Were not your Torah my delight.'"

7. Rabbi Ze'ev Wolf Einhorn (Maharzu; ?–1862), of Grodno and later Vilna, authored one of the central commentaries to *Midrash Rabbah*.

8. Rabbi Einhorn writes similarly in his commentary to *Bereshit Rabbah* (Vilna) 16:2 (74): "Ḥavilah did not yet exist: Although one might say that when Moses wrote the Torah, Ḥavilah and all the other cities already existed, the view of the sages is that the book of Genesis had already been written." In his comments to *Shemot Rabbah* (Vilna) 5:18 (32), Einhorn writes: "The scrolls comprise the entire content of the book of Genesis, scrolls of

the stories of Adam, Noah, the Deluge, the Dispersion, the stories of the Patriarchs and all of the prophecies and promises made."
9. Rabbi Yeraḥmi'el b. Solomon, who flourished in eleventh-century southern Italy, is the scholar generally credited with this work. See the introduction by editor Eli Yassif, 23–31, and additional sources cited there.
10. The book's byline reads: "Including new comments, research and explanations based on philology, critical study, and archaeology, the history of Babylonia, Assyria and the like, and the beliefs and practices of the ancient nations, as well as sharp judgment regarding some of the opinions and theories of contemporary scholars."
11. Rabbi Elijah Benamozegh (1823–1900) of Livorno was an innovative thinker and biblical exegete. Concerning his life and thought, see Mordechai Agmon, "Eliyyah Benamozegh: Kavvim li-Demuto ki-Mefaresh ha-Mikra" [A sketch of the figure of Elijah Benamozegh as a biblical exegete] master's thesis, Hebrew University, 1971; Yair Yarbachti, "Rabbi Eliyyahu Benamozegh ve-Hagut ha-Renaissance" [Rabbi Elijah Benamozegh and Renaissance thought], master's thesis, Bar-Ilan University, 2008. On the debate provoked by Benamozegh's commentary in the Aleppo community, see the above sources and Yaron Harel, "Ha'ala'at *Em la-Mikra* al ha-Moked: Ḥalb 1865" [The edict to destroy *Em la-Mikra*: Aleppo 1865], *Hebrew Union College Annual* 64 (1993): 27–36. Rabbi Dr. Eliyahu Zini has been toiling in recent years to publish a new edition of Rabbi Benamozegh's writings, while emphasizing the great importance this writing has for our particular generation.
12. *Bereshit Rabbah*, 91:6.
13. Rabbi Chaim Hirschensohn was an original halakhic authority and thinker, and among the first to join the ranks of the Mizrahi movement. For a summary of Hirschensohn's biography, see the introduction by editor David Zohar to the new edition of *She'elot u-Teshuvot Malki ba-Kodesh* (Jerusalem: Hartman Institute and Schechter Institute, 2006), 1:13–38. On Hirschensohn's approach to the challenges of biblical criticism, see Eliezer Schweid, *Demokratyah va-Halakhah: Pirkei Iyyun be Mishnato shel ha-Rav Chaim Hirschensohn* [Democracy and *halakhah*: Studies in the thought of Rabbi Ḥayyim Hirschensohn] (Jerusalem: Hebrew University, 1997), 130–143; David Zohar, *Meḥuyyavut Yehudit be-Olam Moderni: Ha-Rav Chaim Hirschensohn ve-Yeḥaso el ha-Modernah* [Jewish commitment in a modern world: Rabbi Chaim Hirschensohn's relationship with modernity] (Jerusalem: Hartman Institute, 2003), 261–293.
14. Rabbi Hirschensohn takes a similar exegetical approach elsewhere. See, for instance, *Sefer Nimmukei Rashi*, 1:71 (Gen. 38:11), 73b (on Gen. 39:11); vol. 2 (Seini: Jakob Wieder, 1929), 141a (on Exod. 24:4); *Elleh Divrei ha-Berit*, 2:70–71, 75.
15. Rabbi Hirschensohn's view is that most of the commandments in *parashat* Mishpatim were communicated by Jethro; see source 218.
16. See sources 4–5 above.
17. The groom of Genesis (*ḥatan Bereshit*) is the individual honored on Simḥat Torah with the first reading of the new Torah cycle. The term is used here for rhetorical effect.

18. Rabbi Solomon Tzevi b. Nathan Schick (Rashban; 1844–1916), rabbi of the city of Karcag, Hungary, was the author of many books, among them *Siddur Rashban* [The prayer book of Rashban] and *She'elot u-Teshuvot Rashban* [Responsa of Rashban]. On his biography and works, see Moshe Hershko, *Toledot Kehillat Karzag u-Kehillot Meḥoz Nagykunsag* [The history of the community of Karcag and the communities of the district of Nagykunsag] (Jerusalem: Karcag Society, 1977), 11–30; Yitzḥak Yosef Cohen, *Ḥakhmei Hungarya ve-ha-Sifrut ha-Toranit Bah* [The sages of Hungary and its Torah literature] (Jerusalem: Jerusalem Institute, 1997), 155–158, 441–443; Adam S. Ferziger, "The Road Not Taken: Rabbi Shlomoh Zvi Schick and the Legacy of Hungarian Orthodoxy," *Hebrew Union College Annual* 79 (2008), 107–140 (esp. 110–112).

Moses' Role in the Composition of the Torah

It is a commonly held view that Moses, far from having any part in writing the Torah, was "like a scribe transcribing an ancient book and writing . . . from God's mouth to Moses' ears."[1] Yet some sources imply that Moses had a limited active part in the creation of the Torah. Does this tarnish the impeccable reliability of Moses as the messenger of God? The following source expresses the complexity of this matter in a fascinating way.

13

"And the Lord said to Moses: Write down these commandments, for in accordance with these commandments I make a covenant with you and with Israel" (Exod. 34:27)—The angels began saying before the holy One, blessed be He: You permit Moses to write down anything he wishes, so that he may then say to Israel, "I have given the Torah to you, and it was I who wrote and gave it to you"?! But God replied: Far be it from Moses to do such a thing, and even if he does, he can be fully trusted, for it says, "Not so with My servant Moses; he is trusted throughout My household" (Num. 12:7).

Shemot Rabbah, 47:9.

Moses' Role in the Composition of the First Four Books of the Torah

Various Jewish sages throughout history have emphasized the role played by Moses in formulating sections of the Torah, with an emphasis on narratives such as those in Genesis. To some, the implicit position of these sources is that Moses formulated the narrative sections of the Torah.[2] Other sources, however, suggest that Moses was an active party to the writing of halakhic passages as well.

14

Why were [the laws of forbidden foods that appear in Leviticus (11)] repeated in Deuteronomy (14)? Among animals—for the cleft hoof; among birds—for the kite. This teaches you that a person should not be embarrassed to say, "I forgot," for if Moses, the sage of sages, the greatest of great men, the father of prophets, was not embarrassed to say, "I forgot [to write these laws in Leviticus]," then surely one who is unequal even to the most miniscule fraction of one of his students certainly should not be embarrassed to say, "I forgot."

Midrash Tanna'im al Sefer Devarim, ed. D. Hoffmann (Berlin: Z. H. Itzkowski, 1900), 1:75, 14:12.

15

"Then the Lord said to Moses, 'Go to Pharaoh. For I have hardened his heart and the hearts of his courtiers, in order that I may display My signs among them, and that you may tell your sons and of your sons' sons how I made a mockery of the Egyptians'" (Exod. 10:1–2)—God revealed to Moses the plague that He would bring upon them, and Moses in his record alluded to it with the words "that you may tell your sons." This is a reference to the plague of locusts, as it is said: "Tell your children about it" (Joel 1:3).

Shemot Rabbah, 13:4.

16

"The Lord God planted a garden in Eden ... with the tree of life in the middle of the garden, and the tree of knowledge of good and evil" (Gen. 2:8–9)—Rabbi Pinḥas b. Ya'ir said: Before Adam ate of this tree it was simply called a tree. Once he had eaten of it and transgressed God's decree, it was called "the tree of knowledge of good and evil." The pious Moses prematurely called it "the tree of knowledge of good and evil" because of what happened in the end, just as we find that many other things are discussed with reference to what happened with them in the end, such as "subdued all the territory of the Amalekites" [referring to an event preceding the birth of Amalek].

Midrash Bereshit Rabbati: Nosad al Sifro shel Rabbi Moshe ha-Darshan (*Midrash Bereshit Rabbati:* Based on the book of Rabbi Moses ha-Darshan[3]), ed. Chanoch Albeck (Jerusalem: Mekize Nirdamim, 1940), 52–53 (2:9).

17

At the time the Holy One, blessed be He, gave the Torah to our teacher Moses on Mount Sinai, when the Holy One, blessed be He, said, "Remember the Sabbath day and keep it holy . . . for in six days the Lord made heaven and earth, etc." and "and He rested on the seventh day" (Exod. 20:8, 11). He told him the whole story of Creation from beginning to end, and our teacher Moses arranged the entire story of Creation in a book and wrote, "the sixth day" (Gen. 1:31)—the day when the creation of the world was completed—and so it says, "But on the sixth day, when they apportion what they have brought in" (Exod. 16:5). Thus here too, he stated, "the sixth day," meaning, the sixth [day] of Creation.

Rabbi Toviyyah b. Eliezer,[4] *Midrash Lekaḥ Tov* (*Pesikta Zutarta*), Gen. 1:31.[5]

18

"Rabbi Yehudah argued: 'Was not the sciatic nerve prohibited from the time of the sons of Jacob, and at that time unclean animals were still permitted to them?' They replied: 'This law was ordained at Sinai but was written in its proper place'"—The prohibition [against eating the sciatic nerve (Gen. 32:33)] was stated on Sinai, and until Sinai they were not enjoined concerning it, but after it was stated on Sinai, it was written down in the appropriate place. When Moses wrote and organized the Torah, he wrote this verse adjacent to the event [of Jacob's injury]: the Children of Israel therefore were later enjoined against eating the nerve.

Rashi, Commentary to Talmud, *Ḥullin* 100b.

19

This entire section, concerning the six days of creation, also was written by Moses out of anticipation, with the purpose of explaining to the reader what the holy One, Blessed be He, said when He gave the Torah (Exod. 20:8–11): "Remember the Sabbath day and keep it holy . . . for in six days the Lord made heaven and earth and sea, and all that is in them, and rested on the seventh day." This is reason why it is written: "There was evening and there was morning, *the* sixth day" (Gen. 1:31)—that same sixth day, the end of the creation process, of which God spoke when He gave the Torah. That is why Moses related [the story of Creation] to Israel: to inform them that what God said was true, [as if saying:] "Do you think that this world has existed forever as you now see it, filled with all good things? This is not the case. Rather, 'When God began to create.'"[6]

Rashbam,[7] Commentary on Genesis 1:1–2.[8]

20

"God called the light Day" (Gen. 1:5)—Following the plain meaning of Scripture, consider: Why would God have to call the light Day as soon as it was created? Rather, [one is to understand that] our teacher Moses wrote that whenever we find that God uses the terms *day* and *night*, for example, "day and night shall not cease" (8:22), He is referring to the same light and darkness that were created on the first day. [This verse serves to indicate that] it is these that God regularly calls "day" and "night." The same is true of all instances of the phrase "God called" written in this section. . . .

"There was evening and there was morning" (1:5)—The text reads not "there was 'night' and there was 'day,'" but "there was evening"—that is, the light of the first day subsided and darkness fell—"and there was morning"—the morning at the end of the night, when dawn broke. At that point, "one day" of those six described by God in the Decalogue (Exod. 20:11) was complete. The second day then began when God said, 'Let there be an expanse.'" (Gen. 1:6).

Rashbam.

21

Now the text states: "These are the generations of Jacob" (Gen. 37:2)—that is, his seventy descendants and how they were born. . . . Our teacher Moses had to record all this because he would exhort them, saying: "Your ancestors went down to Egypt seventy persons in all" (Deut. 10:22).

Rashbam

22

"The sixth day" (Gen. 1:31)—It says only "a first day" or "a second day" in all cases except the sixth and seventh days, where it says "the sixth" and "the seventh" (Gen. 2:2), because these were specifically singled out. When our teacher Moses was writing the Torah for Israel, upon reaching the sixth day, he told them, "This is the sixth day, on which God gives you a double portion," and when he reached the Sabbath, he said, "This is the seventh day, which God has commanded to honor and observe."

Rabbi Yosef Bekhor Shor,[9] Commentary to Genesis 1:31.[10]

23

Moses wrote his book and the passage of Balaam . . . and the passage of Balaam, though written in God's Torah, was nevertheless written by the hand of Moses. Because he [i.e., Balaam] was of the prophets of the nations of the world, it was not written by God Himself.

Rabbi Jacob b. Joseph Reischer,[11] *Iyun Ya'akov: Ve-Hu Ḥiddushei Aggadot al kol Ein Ya'akov* [Aggadic novellae on the complete *Ein Ya'akov*] (Wilhemsdorf: Tzvi Hirsch ben Ḥayyim, 1728), 78a (*Bava Batra* 15).

24

"Moses wrote his book and the passage of Balaam and Job" (Babylonian Talmud, tractate *Bava Batra* 14b)—Perhaps Job was a separate book that Moses wrote, but why should the passage of Balaam, which is a part of the Torah, be considered separately? It is included in the statement "Moses wrote his book," that is, the five books of the Torah!

It seems that the Torah is called the Torah of Moses because he wrote the words of regular people: the words of Laban, of Esau, of Hagar, and the like, and these were turned by him into words of Torah and his book [thus] is called the Torah of Moses.[12] . . . It thus states that he wrote the passage of Balaam, which is not included in the statement that "Moses wrote his book," because, in this instance, our teacher Moses, of blessed memory, had no need to turn the words of regular people into words of Torah, because that passage consisted of the words of God.

Rabbi Tzadok ha-Kohen of Lublin,[13] *Peri Tzaddik* to *parashat* Yitro, sec. 4.

Moses' Role in the Composition of the Book of Journeys (Num. 33:1–49)

The end of the book of Numbers contains a list recording the travels of the Israelites during the forty years of wandering in the desert, prefaced with the words: "Moses recorded the starting points of their various marches as directed by the Lord" (33:2). The emphasis on the status of Moses as the writer occasioned a discussion of the role that he played in the composition of this passage.

25

Why were the journeys recorded? Moses said to himself: If I do not write the journeys from the Exodus from Egypt until this day, then tomorrow the nations of the world will say that during all of the forty years that Israel were in the desert, they had no rest, but walked night and day because they were lost in the desert. He thus recorded all of the journeys, so that the nations of the world, knowing that it is impossible for a person to wander for forty years in the places named—and all the more so for 600,000—would know that the only reason Israel tarried in the desert for forty years was because of what had happened to them. Moses therefore recorded all of the journeys.

However, Moses did not know to write the journeys until God alluded as much to him in the two tablets that he brought down from Mount Sinai, upon which were forty-two engravings, an allusion to the forty-two journeys. From where do we learn that God approved of his doing so? From the statement: "And Moses recorded the starting points of their various marches as directed by the Lord" (Num. 33:2).

Midrash ha-Gadol: Be-Midbar II (Jerusalem: S. Fisch, 1963), 339–340 (Mas'ei, sec. 33)

26

"Moses recorded the starting points" (Num. 33:2)—We must understand what the text is coming to tell us with this statement. If it is to tell us that Moses wrote it—all of the Torah, including the journeys written in the Torah, was written by Moses!...

It appears that the text seeks to relate to us the manner in which the journeys were recorded: that they were written not in a single day, but rather in this order: Moses began writing in his notebook at the command of the King [God] on the day they left Egypt. Thus on the day they left Egypt, he wrote the verse "The Israelites set out from Rameses [and encamped at Succoth]."... He thus recorded each journey at the time until they reached the plains of Moab. Afterwards, God instructed him to arrange them in the Torah as he had written them, and this is what is intended when the text says: "Moses recorded the starting points," referring to the day they left Egypt, meaning the two verses beginning with "They set out from Rameses."...

The term "of their marches" indicates the sequence of their journeys from the day they left Egypt until the end of their travels. The phrase "as directed by the Lord" indicates that the original record was by God's word: He told Moses to write as they went. The phrase "Their starting points," indicates that these are the very journeys that Moses recorded according to their starting points, each in its time and place, and this is a transcription of it.

Rabbi Ḥayyim b. Moshe Ibn Attar, *Or ha-Ḥayyim.*[14]

27

There is an important point here regarding the history of literature that is unknown to most scholars of the Bible but was known to the sages, namely that expressed in Babylonian Talmud tractate *Bava Batra* 14b: "Moses wrote his book and the passage of Balaam and Job." A child is accustomed to explaining, "Moses wrote his book" as referring to the Torah. Yet this is a mistake, for the Torah contains the passage of Balaam as well, so that it need not say, "his book and the passage of Balaam."...

Rather, this tradition refers not to the Torah of Moses, but to the book of Moses, for in addition to the Torah communicated to him from the mouth of God, he wrote for himself a journal of daily occurrences and happenings. However, God did not instruct him to write the contents of this book in the Torah. Nevertheless, the Torah mentions it, and this is the meaning of the verse: "Moses recorded the events according to their journeys as directed by the Lord," meaning everything that had happened to them during their journeys by the word of the Lord. God did not tell him to write the contents of this book in the Torah, and it remained a separate book called the book of Moses: his memoir. What God instructed him to write in the Torah was only the sequence of the journeys, not all of the events, and these are recorded in *parashat* Mas'ei, "These are their journeys according to the happenings"— the journeys according to the events that transpired. But the events according to their journeys were not recorded in the Torah as they were in the book of Moses.

Moses similarly wrote the passage of Balaam, including Balaam's poems, his parables, how he was forced to say the opposite of what he thought to say, and the entire delightful story. God did instruct him to write the contents of this book in the Torah, God dictating and Moses repeating and writing it. Moses also composed the book of Job . . . but God did not instruct him to write this in the Torah, and it remained a separate book. To our chagrin, however, we have lost the book of "events according their journeys," to which the sages were referring when they said that Moses wrote his book, the book of "events according to their journeys." . . . To our chagrin, we have lost this precious book, like many of the books of the prophets and the chronicles of the kings of Israel and Judah.

Rabbi Chaim Hirschensohn, *Sefer Nimmukei Rashi: Ḥiddushei ha-Raḥah al Nimmukei ha-Ḥummash le-Rashi* [Novellae of Rabbi Chaim Hirschensohn on Rashi's explanations of the Bible] (Seini: Jakob Wieder, 1933), 4:120a.

Moses' Role in the Composition of Deuteronomy

It is commonly believed that there was no difference between the composition of one book of the Torah and any other, and that all were received by Moses from God.[15] The difficulty posed by this view is that Deuteronomy appears to describe Moses, not God, as the speaker.[16] The sages and their successors throughout the generations thus differentiated between the books, as we see in their writing. The central approaches seek to make a sharper distinction between speaking—by Moses—and writing—by divine command—or else between speaking and writing, by Moses, and the inclusion of this material in the Torah, at the command of God.[17] This cooperative effort by God and Moses is the basis for viewing Deuteronomy as a book that lies at the intersection between the divine and the human, and perhaps even a foundation of the Oral Law that is embedded within the Written Law.[18]

Moses' Role in the Composition of the Curses and Blessings (Deuteronomy 28)

28

Abaye said: This rule [against interrupting the reading of the Torah] was only taught concerning the curses in Leviticus (chap. 26), but in the curses in Deuteronomy (chap. 28) a break may be made. What is the reason? In the former, Israel are addressed in plural form and Moses relays the words of the Almighty; in the latter, Israel are addressed in the singular, and Moses utters them in his own name.

Babylonian Talmud, tractate *Megillah* 31b.

29

Rabbi Levi said: Come and see [how] the Divine disposition differs from that of mortals. The Holy One, blessed be He, blessed Israel with twenty-two [letters] and cursed them with [only] eight. He blessed them with twenty-two, from "if [you follow] my laws" (Lev. 26:3) to "[made you walk] erect" (13),[19] and he cursed them with eight, from "but if you do not obey Me" (14) to "and spurned My laws" (43).[20]

Moses our teacher, however, blessed them with eight and cursed them with twenty-two. He blessed them with eight, from "now, if you obey" (Deut. 28:1) to "to the worship of [other gods]" (14),[21] and cursed them with twenty-two, from "but if you do not obey" (15) to "but none will buy" (68).[22]

Babylonian Talmud, tractate *Bava Batra* 88b–89a.

30

"The skies above your head shall be copper" (Deut. 28:23)—These curses were stated independently by Moses,[23] while those at Mount Sinai were stated by the Holy One, blessed be He, as implied by the text. There it says, "but if you do not obey *Me*" (Lev. 26:14), "And if you remain hostile toward *Me*" (21), and here it says "[but if you do not obey] *the Lord your God*" (Deut. 28:15), "*The Lord* will make [pestilence] cling to you" (21), "*the Lord* will strike you" (22).

Moses made his curses less harsh by stating them in the singular.[24] He also made this curse less harsh, for in the first curses it says, "your skies like iron and your earth like copper" (Lev. 26:19), meaning, the skies will not perspire, just as iron does not perspire, and there thus will be drought in the world, and the earth will perspire, as copper perspires, and cause the fruits to rot, but here it says, "your skies like copper and your earth like iron," meaning, the skies will perspire, and although they will not pour forth rain, there nevertheless will not be a cataclysmic drought in the world, and the earth will not perspire just as iron does not perspire, so that the fruits will not rot. In any case, however, it is a curse. Whether like copper or iron, the earth will not bring forth fruit, and the skies will not pour forth rain.

Rashi.

Moses' Role in the Arrangement of Passages in Deuteronomy

31

Even the authority who does not expound on textual adjacency in the rest of the Torah does so in Deuteronomy,[25] because the rest of the Torah was stated by the Almighty and it is not in order, but Moses, who arranged Deuteronomy one passage after another, arranged it as he did only for the purpose of exposition.

Rabbi Eliezer b. Nathan, *Even ha-Ezer*, Responsa sec. 34.[26]

32

Even the authority who does not expound on textual adjacency in the rest of the Torah does so in Deuteronomy, because Deuteronomy consists of the words of Moses. Though all were stated by the Almighty, because they have been stated in one sequence and he now repeats them in another sequence, surely when he juxtaposes matters, they are juxtaposed for the purpose of exposition, for they are not ordered in their original sequence.

Shittah Mekubbetzet, *Berakhot* 21b.

33

It being acknowledged that two given matters in the Torah are not in a particular order, how can we expound on textual adjacency? In truth, this is no challenge at all. It is acceptable to expound on textual adjacency based on the logic of universal application: if the passages were communicated to Moses by God in juxtaposition, then certainly we can expound on this, and if they were not communicated to Moses in juxtaposition and it was Moses who juxtaposed them contrary to the sequence in which they were communicated by God, then this itself proves that we should expound on textual adjacency, because it is for this reason that Moses changed the sequence from that in which they were communicated to him by God: to teach us to expound on textual adjacency.

In fact, one may say that this is why Rabbi Yehudah does not interpret textual adjacency: because the Torah is not in order, we do not know whether the juxtaposition was made by God, and Rabbi Yehudah is of the view that we are not to expound on a juxtaposition made by Moses, but rather only on one made by God.

Rabbi Joshua b. Nahum Baumol, *She'elot u-Teshuvot Emek Halakhah,* 2:34.[27]

Moses' Role in the Composition of Deuteronomy as a Whole

34

Before he was privileged to receive the Torah, Scripture writes of Moses: "I am not a man of words" (Exod. 4:10). Yet after he was privileged to receive the Torah, his speech was cured and he began to speak words. Whence do we know this? From what we have read in the passage under comment: "These are the words that Moses spoke" (Deut. 1:1).

Devarim Rabbah (Vilna), 1:1.

35

"These are the words" (Deut. 1:1)—Rabbi Tanḥuma said: This may be compared to a man who had some purple wool for sale and would call out, "Here is purple wool!"

The king peeked out and heard his cry. He called him and asked him, "What have you for sale?"

He replied, "Nothing."

[The king] said, "I heard you calling out, 'Here is purple wool,' and you say that you have nothing!?"

He replied, "Sire, true, it is purple wool, but to you it is as nothing."

So it was with Moses. Before God, who created the mouth and the power of speech, he declared, "I am not a man of words" (Exod. 4:10), but when he spoke with Israel, it is written of him: "These are the words."

Devarim Rabbah (Vilna), 1:7a.

36

"So, too, with the Avvim who dwelt in villages in the vicinity of Gaza: the Caphtorim, who came from Crete, wiped them out and settled in their place" (Deut. 2:24)—What need did Moses have to write this verse? Because Abraham had sworn to Abimelech that his children would not take any of his land as long as his son and grandson were alive, and since his grandson was still alive, the Holy One, blessed be He, decreed that people would come from Crete and destroy the Avvim, who were of the Philistines, and reside in their land, and then Israel would come and take it from the Caphtorim.

Midrash Aggadah, ed. Buber, Deut. 2:23.[28]

37

"You will be passing through the territory of your kinsmen, the descendants of Esau, who live in Seir. Though they will be afraid of you, be very careful not to provoke them.] For I will not give you of their land so much as a foot can tread on; I have given the hill country of Seir as a possession to Esau" (Deut. 2:5–6)—And thus [a similar idea] is expressed concerning the Moabites, "Do not harass the Moabites or provoke them to war" (9), and about the Ammonites, "Do not harass them or start a fight with them" (19). Moses needed at this particular point to communicate all of these exhortations to the Israelites lest their courage falter and they say, "If God truly wishes to bring us to our Promised Land and He has the ability to do so, why has He not defeated for us all of those nations that we passed along the way?" Moses thus told the Israelites now that God had not wanted [them to capture these regions], because God had allocated these regions to those nations, as is written regarding them all: "I have given Mount Seir as a possession to Esau [Edom]" (5), "I have assigned Ar as a possession to the descendants of Lot [Moab]" (9), and also concerning the Ammonites, "I have assigned it as a possession to the descendants of Lot" (19). [God assigned these regions to those peoples] in Abraham's honor, for they were his relatives, just as He did for Israel.

Furthermore, Moses wrote these [stories about the other nations] to teach the Israelites that they had no reason to worry: if God assigned territories to these nations solely to honor our forefathers, how much more certainly will God fulfill His promise "to give them the heritage of nations," as He promised the Patriarchs!

Rashbam.[29]

38

Scripture mentioned two things here: It stated "that Moses addressed the Israelites in accordance with the instructions that the Lord had given him for them" (Deut. 1:3), this being an allusion to the commandments that he would tell them in this book and that had not been mentioned thus far in the Torah. And it says that these commandments were "in accordance with the instructions that the Lord had given him" (ibid.); he did not add to or subtract from what he had been commanded. This statement is necessary because the phrase "the Lord spoke to Moses, saying" is not said before them, and therefore Scripture included them now, that they were all according to what he was commanded from the mouth of the Holy One, blessed be He. It is further stated that, "Moses began explaining this law" (Deut.1:5), this being an allusion to the commandments that had already been given: he would repeat them in order to clarify them further and to give additional instruction about them. And the meaning of the expression *ho'il Moshe* is that Moses wished to explain the Torah to them. This is mentioned in order to indicate that Moses saw fit to do so of his own accord; God had not commanded him regarding this. The word *ho'il* is related to the expressions *ho'el na ve-len* ("won't you stay overnight" [Judg. 19:6]); *va-lu ho'alnu va-neshev* ("if only we had been content" [Josh. 7:7]); and many other, similar expressions.

Nachmanides, Commentary on Deuteronomy 1:1–3.³⁰

39

It is possible that after he wrote the poem "and taught it to the Israelites" (Deut. 31:22) one by one, according to their tribes as he had them brought before him to the *beit midrash*, he wrote it in the Torah and commanded the priests: "Take this book of Teaching," meaning that the poem, too, should remain in the Ark with the Torah, for it is part of the Torah since it is there as a witness. Then Moses told them to assemble before him again, all the elders of the tribes and the officers, and that the people should join them, as it says at the end, "And Moses came and spoke all the words of this poem in the hearing of the people" (Deut. 32:44). Now the priests did so and they assembled the entire people before him, and he called heaven and earth to witness against them in assembly, in the hearing of the priests and all the people. Then God, blessed be He, told him, "Ascend these heights of Abarim" (49). This he was bound to do immediately, and so he stood up and blessed them *parashat* Ve-zo't ha-berakhah (Deut. 33), and wrote it at the end of the book that he gave to the priests. Then the priests did as he commanded them, and placed the complete book by the side of the Ark of the Covenant.

Nachmanides, Commentary on Deuteronomy 31:24–25.

40

I asked and considered whether the *mishneh Torah*, "that Moses set before the Israelites" (Deut. 4:44), that is, the book of Deuteronomy, was from God, of heavenly origin, and if Moses spoke the words in it from the Almighty's mouth, just like the rest of the Torah from Genesis to "before all Israel" (Deut. 34:12), that these and these are the words of the living God without any change or substitution; or, was this *mishneh Torah* spoken by Moses, who composed it and said it on his own, explaining the commandments based on what he understood of God's intentions, as the verse states, "Moses undertook to expound this Teaching" (1:5), in the manner of experts and learned men who explain everything that is difficult in a book, things which the Ancient One concealed... . However, the true essence of this book is that our teacher Moses, of blessed memory, said these things, and explained the commandments mentioned here to Israel, in parting from them. And the Holy One, blessed be He, after Moses finished saying them, desired that it all be written in the Torah, as Moses said it. And perhaps the Almighty added explanations and other things at the time of writing. Thus, although these words were said to Israel by our teacher Moses, of blessed memory, he did not cause them to be written down in the Torah. For he, [Moses] of blessed memory did not write these things on his own accord; for how could he write something on his own in God's Torah?! Rather, all this was written from the mouth of the Almighty, like all of the words of the Torah, because the Holy One, blessed be He agreed with him, and the words of the trustworthy leader were right in his eyes (cf. Prov. 25:13).... Thus, the Holy One blessed be He dictated the entire Torah, including Deuteronomy, and Moses wrote what he heard and received ... and therefore this book is one of God's books just like the others. And anyone who says that Moses wrote a verse by himself is counted among those intended by "because he has spurned the word of the Lord" (Num. 15:31), because the writing was from God, and not Moses.[31]

Rabbi Isaac Abravanel, Preface to the book of Deuteronomy.[32]

41

You ought to know the difference between Deuteronomy, which also contains the second set of the Ten Commandments (Deut. 5:6–18), and the rest of the Torah. . . . This does not mean, God forbid, that Moses said something of his own accord, even a single letter. Rather, the difference between Deuteronomy and the rest of the Torah is that the Torah that God gave Israel has two aspects: The first aspect is God's side, the giver of the Torah. The second aspect is Israel's side, who receives the Torah. . . . Therefore it is fitting that the aspect of the giver is predominant in the Torah, except for Deuteronomy, the fifth and final book. For the recipient receives in the end; when the giver finishes his words, and then the recipient receives. That is the reason why it is called *mishneh Torah*, as if it were something unique that is from the recipient's side. And there is an aspect of the recipient's side, as it says in Deuteronomy, "Moses undertook to expound his Teaching" (1:5), for the recipient needs more commentary and explanation. This is the difference between the Torah and Deuteronomy. Therefore, each statement in the Torah, despite the fact that Moses said it, it was as if God was speaking . . . so it was with each word Moses spoke, God put the words into his mouth. But in Deuteronomy, Moses spoke on his own, like a messenger who has been commanded by he who sent him. This is the meaning of the sages' statement, "Moses spoke the curses in Deuteronomy in his own name."[33] That is, God did not place the words into his mouth, for the purpose of Deuteronomy was only to receive the Torah, and receiving is done by someone close to the recipient, for the recipient is primary in Deuteronomy. Therefore, it was done by our master Moses, of blessed memory, who was close to the recipient . . . and therefore the words are according to what is appropriate for the recipient, for the recipient is primary there, that is . . . to explain more, as is appropriate for the recipient. This is a great principle. And in this way, all of the changes and substitutions in the second set of commandments are explained.

Furthermore, you should know that the Torah is the covenant between God and Israel who receive the covenant. The covenant binds together the one who makes the covenant with the one who receives it. And anything that binds two things together is close to one of them on one side, and close to the other on the other side. Therefore, the Torah, which is the covenant between God and Israel, is close to God who made the covenant, on one side, and on the other side, is close to those who received the covenant, Israel. Therefore, God Himself, who made the covenant, spoke the entire Torah to them, except for Deuteronomy. But Deuteronomy, which is at the end of the Torah, is the second side, close to Israel who receive the Torah. Therefore, they heard Deuteronomy from the mouth of Moses, because he is close to Israel, the recipients. . . .

Furthermore, the entire Torah that God spoke, God spoke to man, because man has intellectual capacity. Therefore, all of the statements were made in a way appropriate to an intellectual man, who does not require much explanation and interpretation. But Deuteronomy is at the end of the Torah, and the receiving of the Torah is not by way of the intellect, but rather by a physical recipient, and, in this way, it is appropriate to human beings, not to angels. Therefore, in Deuteronomy Moses, a human being, spoke to Israel as human recipients, and therefore more explanation was necessary.

Rabbi Judah Loew b. Rabbi Betzalel (Maharal), *Tiferet Israel,* chap. 43.[34]

42

"Moses wrote his book and the section of Balaam" (Babylonian Talmud, tractate *Bava Batra* 14b)—It seems that Rashi's opinion is that "Moses wrote his book" refers to Deuteronomy, which is called by Moses' name, as it says, "Be mindful of the Torah of my servant Moses" (Mal. 3:22), as opposed to the rest of Torah, which preceded it by two thousand years, as the book of Numbers concludes, "These are the commandments and regulations that the Lord enjoined upon the Israelites, through Moses" (Num. 36:13), and Deuteronomy begins, "These are the words that Moses addressed to all Israel" (Deut. 1:1) [without "that the Lord enjoined"]. (And this answers the question of the *Pesikta de-Rav Kahana*, mentioned in the *Yalkut Shimoni* at the end of the book of Malachi: "'Be mindful of the Torah of my servant Moses'—But it is God's Torah, as it says 'The Torah of God is perfect' (Ps. 19:8)."

Rabbi Jacob b. Joseph Reischer, *Iyun Ya'akov,* 78a (*Bava Batra* 1:16).

43

"These are the words" (Deut. 1:1)—"These" excludes what preceded them, meaning that because it adds "that Moses addressed," these are his own words, because the whole book is made up of rebukes from Moses at those who transgress God's word. And the sages said, "Moses spoke the curses in Deuteronomy in his own name,"[35] and he was not even commanded to review and explain God's earlier statements, but rather he reviewed matters of his own accord. Scripture was careful not to imply that, just as Moses said these matters of his own accord, so too were previous statements made in his own name. Therefore it says, "*These* are the words," meaning only here did Moses speak his own words, but in all the previous four books not even speak a single letter was of his own accord; there the words came from the Commander in their precise form, without a single letter added or subtracted.

Rabbi Ḥayyim b. Moshe Ben Attar, *Or ha-Ḥayyim.*[36]

44

I asked our saintly, pious teacher and rabbi, the *Ga'on* Rabbi Elijah of Vilna: What is the difference between the holy Torah and Deuteronomy? He told me that the first four books were heard from the Holy One, blessed be He,

Himself, through the throat of Moses. On the other hand, Israel heard the book of Deuteronomy just as they did the words of other prophets after Moses: the Holy One, blessed be He would speak to the prophet on one day, and the next day the prophet would go and relate the vision to Israel. Thus when the prophet [Moses] spoke to Israel, the Divine word was already cut off from him. Thus was the book of Deuteronomy heard by Israel from our master Moses' own mouth.[37]

Rabbi Jacob Kranz (the Maggid of Dubno), *Ohel Ya'akov al ha-Torah: Sefer Devarim* (Jerusalem: Yerid Sefarim, 2011), 20.[38]

45

For Moses spoke Deuteronomy of his own accord, and the Divine Presence did not speak through his throat as with the rest of the Torah. Thus in the rest of the Torah, Moses was not the speaker at all, and for this reason the fact that he was "slow of speech" (Exod. 4:10) did not bother him, but in Deuteronomy, if his tongue had not been healed he would not have been able to deliver the speech.

Rabbi Samuel b. Rabbi Abraham Borenstein, *Shem mi-Shemuel*, Exodus, *parashat* Va-'era' (1911).[39]

46

Since it says, "As God commanded," this implies that all [the Torah] is the words of God spoken through Moses' throat. So why does it say, "The Lord our God spoke to us at Horeb" (Deut. 1:6), as if he [Moses] is speaking on His behalf? . . . It seems reasonable to say that immediately after defeating Sihon in Tishrei, he [Moses] decided to pronounce all of Deuteronomy as it is written before us in his own words; God had not commanded him, and he prepared the words in his heart . . . and then . . . when he came to say what he had prepared, the Divine Presence spoke through his throat the very things that Moses had prepared during all those days, in his own exact formulation, and the Holy One, blessed be He, did depart from the language that Moses had prepared for himself. . . .

Rabbi Moses Sofer, *Ḥatam Sofer al ha-Torah*, ed. J. N. Stern (Jerusalem: Ma'ayan ha-Ḥakhmah, 2006), Deuteronomy 1, 4.[40]

47

From the way in which the sages singled out the section of Balaam, it seems that when they said that "Moses wrote his book," they were not at all referring to the entire Torah, since the section of Balaam is also in the Torah. If he wrote all of the Torah, he certainly also wrote the section of Balaam; why would the Talmud need to inform us that he wrote it as well? Rather, the only explanation is that this specific *baraita* considered only Deuteronomy as "Moses' book." For apart from the first five verses and the last nine sections, it is all undoubtedly Moses speaking for himself. . . . And it makes sense to call this "Moses' book." . . . From the plain meaning of the language of the rest of the words of the Torah, at least for the superficial reader, it seems that an editor wrote all of Moses' words in a book. However, regarding the last eight verses in the Torah, Rabbi Yehudah said, and some say it was Rabbi Neḥemiah, that they were written by Joshua.[41] But as for the rest of the sections and verses mentioned, they did not inform us of the name of the writer, or they had no tradition regarding it; in any case, they did not let us know their opinion on the matter. . . . But the rest of the Torah, according to the majority of sages, was wholly written by Moses . . . with the exception of this *baraita* in Babylonain Talmud, tractate *Bava Batra* [15a] that I cited above: "Moses wrote his book," which seems to suggest that he only wrote the book of laws and statutes of Deuteronomy, along with its introductions and summations, as well as the section of Balaam. . . . But the rest of the Torah was written and arranged from "the great book of Torah"—all the words of Torah from God's mouth by Moses' hand.

Rabbi Ḥayyim Hirschensohn, Sefer Malki ba-Kodesh [*Sefer malki ba-kodesh*: Queries and responsa], ed. David Zohar (Jerusalem: Shalom Hartman Institute, 2012), 2:479–480 (responsa 6, 4).

48

In *Ba-midbar Rabbah* 19:33 [it says:] "'Then shall Moses [sic: Israel] sing' (Num. 21:17)—This is one of the three things that Moses said before the Holy One, blessed be He, and He responded, 'You have taught me!' . . . The second was when the Holy One, blessed be He, said to him, 'He visits the iniquities of parents upon children' (Exod. 34:7)—Moses said, 'Master of the world, if wicked people gave birth to righteous people, they will partake of the sins of their fathers?' The Holy One, blessed be He, said to him, 'You have taught me! By your life, I will cancel my words and uphold yours, as it says, "Parents shall not be put to death for children, nor children be put to death for parents" (Deut. 24:16), and by your life, I will write it in your name, as it says, "in accordance with what is written in the Book of the Teaching of Moses, where the Lord commanded, 'Parents shall not be put to death for children'" (2 Kings

14:6). The third was when the Holy One, blessed be He, told Moses to make war with Sihon: even if he does not wish to war with you, instigate a war with him, as it says, 'Up! Set out across the wadi Arnon' (Deut. 2:24). But Moses did not do so, but rather, as it is written, 'Then I sent messengers' (Deut. 2:26). The Holy One, blessed be He, said, 'By your life, I will cancel my words and uphold yours, as it says, "When you approach a town to attack it, you shall offer it terms of peace" (Deut. 20:10).'"[42] . . . As mentioned above, Deuteronomy is specifically called "Moses' book," and this is what the midrash is referring to when it says, "By your life, I will write it in your name, as it says, 'in accordance with'" (2 Kings 14:6). The sages are hinting at what is said explicitly in Babylonian Talmud, tractate *Megillah*, that Deuteronomy was said by Moses on his own, with divine inspiration, and God agreed that it be written in the Torah, and Moses merited that it be called by his name, "Moses' book."

Rabbi Menachem Mendel Kasher, *Torah Shelemah* (New York: Torah Shelemah, 1960), 341–342 (19, Mishpatim 3).[43]

Deuteronomy as the Foundation of Oral Law

49

"These are the words" (Deut. 1:1)—This book is different from the first four books in various ways, as is known, and above all, since it is an explanation and elaboration on some of the commandments that are mentioned in the earlier books. And I say that it is the beginning of the writing of the Oral Law, according to the needs of the time. . . . In this book, Moses is the writer, and not God, even though he is writing prophetically. But nevertheless, he is writing "in his own name," that is, as the leader of sages and prophets, unlike the first four books, in which he was like a vessel in the hands of the blessed Creator, and he wrote everything He commanded him from His mouth.

Rabbi Elia Benamozegh, *Sefer Torat Hashem*, 3a.

50

And they came to be in the plains of Moab, and this Moses said this of his own accord, as it is stated.[44] Although it was the word of God, it was included among the Writings that were composed with divine inspiration, and this is already the beginning of the Oral Law, which even though they are the words of the living God, are composed with divine inspiration . . . and this divine inspiration is considered to be akin to the Writings, just as the holy Ari (Isaac Luria) said about King David that he was the master of all those divinely inspired, and his words are part of the Writings.

Rabbi Zadok of Lublin, *Peri Tzaddik,* Leviticus, Behar 1.[45]

51

In the first tablets, which were given to the completely righteous, [the fifth commandment] did not say "good" ... it was explained that the good feeling from the Torah's light comes from the understanding of the Oral Law; from novel interpretations of the Torah one tastes the pleasant sweetness of the words of Torah, when one discovers an understanding which was previously hidden ... but this is not found in explicit revelations of the text. Therefore, in the first [set of tablets] it does not say "good" at all. In the second set, which were received on Yom Kippur, after that incident [the sin of the golden calf], when they had begun learning Torah and forgetting it, which comes from the breaking of the tablets ... by forgetting words of Torah, the extrapolations of the Oral Law were created ... and therefore, the second tablets were said in Deuteronomy, which Moses said on his own but is nevertheless part of the Written Torah. Aside from the commandments themselves, which he had already received at Mount Sinai from God's mouth, even the words that came from him of his own accord, which are not preceded by "The Lord spoke to Moses, saying" before them, are also part of the Written Torah. For all of his words are also part of the perfect Torah, like the conversations of our forebears and other similar matters that are discussed in the Written Torah. But the statement "These are the words" (Deut. 1:1), which are his own words, is the root of the Oral Torah, what the sages say in their own name.

Rabbi Zadok of Lublin, *Peri Tzaddik, Kedushat Shabbat,* article 7.

52

And by this statement, we can understand the holy words of my honorable, holy father [Rabbi Avraham Borenstein of Sochaczew], that Deuteronomy is situated between the Written and Oral Torah. Since Moses said it of his own accord, and it is not exalted and separated from Israel like the four previous books. Therefore in Deuteronomy, the interpretations are more apparent, and even sages who did not rise to the level of Rabbi Akiva, interpreting mountains of laws from every single jot and tittle, found it easier in Deuteronomy to discover what was implied and to understand from the text the details of the laws that were explained orally. It was similarly easier for the sages to find words of *aggadah* and the esoteric secrets of the Torah in Deuteronomy, and so too are words of ethical guidance from Deuteronomy able to pierce more deeply into the Jewish heart, and to be more inspiring. As the Yid Hakodosh [Yaakov Yitzchak Rabinowicz] of Pshischa said, the greatest book of *musar* is Deuteronomy, and he would constantly instruct his students to study Deuteronomy in order to inspire them. The reason is that the more belonging and closeness there is in a person, the more the words enter his heart and the more open his ears are to hear *musar*. Therefore, Deuteronomy is considered as a middle stage between the opaque Written Torah and the revealed Oral Torah.

Rabbi Samuel b. Rabbi Abraham Borenstein, *Shem mi-Shemuel,* Deuteronomy, *parashat* Devarim.

Endnotes

1. As written by Nachmanides in his introduction to Genesis.
2. See Bazak (note 9 above), 38–47; see also articles listed in the notes to the remainder of this chapter.
3. Rabbi Moses ha-Darshan was a Provençal Jewish sage of the eleventh century. His work is cited by Rashi, among others. On the little known about him and his teachings, and skepticism concerning the unsound attribution of the homilies of *Bereshit Rabbati*, see Ḥannanel Mack, *Mi-Sodo shel Moshe ha-Darshan* [The mystery of Rabbi Moshe Hadarshan] (Jerusalem: Bialik Institute, 2010).
4. Rabbi Tobijah b. Eleazar was a Greek Jewish preacher who lived in the final third of the eleventh century. For the little known about him and a comprehensive characterization of *Midrash Lekaḥ Tov*, see Israel Moshe Ta-Shma, "Midrash Lekaḥ Tov: Rik'o ve-Ofyo" [*Midrash Lekaḥ Tov*: Its background and character], in *Knesset Meḥkarim* [Collected studies] (Jerusalem: Bialik Institute, 2006), 3:259–294. On the structure of the work and editions, see Anat Raizel, *Mavo la-Midrashim* [Introduction to the midrashim] (Allon Shevut: Tevunot, 2011) 370–377.
5. Concerning this source, see Jacob Elboim, "'*Yalkut Sekhel Tov: Derash, Peshat ve-Sugyat ha-'Sadran'*" [The anthology *Sekhel ṭov: Derash, peshaṭ* and the issue of the redactor (the *sadran*)], in *Davar Davur al Ofnav: Meḥkarim be-Parshanut ha-Mikra ve-ha-Qur'an bi-Yemei ha-Beinayim Muggashim le-Ḥaggai Ben Shammai* ["A word fitly spoken": Studies in medieval exegesis of the Hebrew Bible and the Qur'an presented to Ḥaggai Ben-Shammai], ed., M. M. Bar Asher et al. (Jerusalem: Yad Ben-Zvi, 2007), 93–95. On the relationship between Tobijah's approach and the collection of Byzantine exegesis, see Gerson Brin, *Re'u'el va-Ḥaverav: Parshanim Yehudiyyim mi-Bizantin mi-Sevivot ha-Me'ah ha-Asirit la-Sefirah* [Re'u'el and friends: Jewish Byzantine exegetes from around the tenth century] (Tel Aviv: Tel Aviv University, 2012).

6. See also Rashbam's comment on Gen. 1:27.
7. Rashbam (Samuel b. Me'ir, 1080?–1160?) was a grandson of Rashi and a biblical and talmudic exegete. Concerning him and his exegetical method, see Eliezer Touitou, *"Ha-Peshatot ha-Mithaddeshim be-Kol Yom": Iyyunim be-Perusho shel Rashbam la-Torah* ["The new explanations discovered each day": Studies in Rashbam's commentary to the Torah] (Ramat Gan: Bar-Ilan University, 2003).
8. Regarding this and similar sources, see, for instance, Touitou, *Ha-Peshatot ha-Mithaddeshim be-Kol Yom*, 112–121; Eran Viesel, *"Da'to shel Rashbam bi-She'elat Ḥelko shel Moshe bi-Ketivat ha-Torah"* [Rashbam's opinion regarding Moses' part in writing the Torah], *Shnaton: An Annual for Biblical and Near Eastern Studies* 22 (2013): 167–188. However, see also Mordechai Sabato, *"Perush ha-Rashbam la-Torah"* [Rashbam's commentary to the Torah], *Maḥanaim* 3 (1993): 110–125 (esp. 116–117); Itamar Kislev, *"Va-Ani le-Faresh Peshutan shel Mikra'ot Ba'ti"* [But I have come to explain the plain meaning of Scripture], *Shnaton: An Annual for Biblical and Near Eastern Studies* 15 (2005): 315–330 (esp. 321).
9. Rabbi Yosef Bekhor Shor (twelfth century; b. circa. 1140 according to some views) was a tosafist, biblical exegete, and poet who flourished in Orleans. For a short biography and an expansive description of his exegetical methodology, see the editor's appendix by Shemu'el Avraham Poznanski, "Mavo al Ḥakhmei Tzarefat Mefareshei ha-Mikra" [Introduction to the French Bible exegetes], in *Peirush al Yeḥezke'l u-Terei Asar le-Rabbi Eli'ezer mi-Belgentzi* [A commentary on Ezekiel and the Twelve Minor Prophets by Rabbi Eliezer of Beaugency] (Warsaw: Mekize Nirdamim, 1913), LV–LXXV; Yehoshafat Nevo, *Parshanut ha-Mikra ha-Tzarefatit: Iyyunim be-Perushei ha-Mikra shel Parshanei Tzefon Tzarefat bi-Yemei ha-Beinayim* [French biblical exegesis: Studies in the biblical commentaries of the medieval exegetes of northern France] (Reḥovot: Mikhlelet Moreshet Ya'akov, 2003), 76–180.
10. For additional sources from the commentary of Yosef Bekhor Shor and a comparison of his method with that of Rashbam, see Raphael Harris, "Muda'ut la-Arikhat ha-Mikra etzel Parshanei Tzefon Tzarefat" [Awareness of the editing of Scripture amongst northern French exegetes], *Shnaton: An Annual for Biblical and Near Eastern Studies* 12 (1999): 289–310 (esp. 301–305).
11. Rabbi Jacob b. Joseph Reischer (ca. 1670–1733) was a rabbi and presiding judge of the rabbinical court in the communities of Ansbach, Worms, and Metz, and among the most prominent sages of Central and Western Europe at the end of the seventeenth century and the beginning of the eighteenth. Among his best known works are *She'elot u-Teshuvot Shevut Ya'akov* (a collection of response for which he is known eponymously), *Iyyun Ya'akov al Ein Ya'akov*, and *Ḥok Ya'akov al Shulḥan Arukh, Hilkhot Pesaḥ*. Regarding the author, see Shemu'el Shiloh, "Ha-Rav Ya'akov Reischer Ba'al ha-Sefer *Shevut Ya'akov*: Ha-Ish bi-Zemano, li-Zemano-ve-li-Zemanenu?" [Ya'akov Reisher, author of the *Shevut Ya'akov*: The man in his time for his time—and for ours?], *Din, Musar va-Yosher ba-Mishpat ha-Ivri: Kovetz Ma'amarim* (Jerusalem: Hebrew University, 2006), 303–324.
12. Compare Zohar, 3:149b.

13. Rabbi Zadok ha-Kohen Rabinowitz (Rubenstein) of Lublin (1823–1900) was the second rebbe of the Hasidim of Lublin. Although he wrote extensively, he did not allow anyone to see his writings during his lifetime. He hinted before his death that he wished for his writings to be published, but most were burnt when his study hall was destroyed during the Holocaust. Among his published works are *Tzidkat ha-Tzaddik, Peri Tzaddik, Kometz Minḥah, Resisei Lailah*. For brief biographical notes and extensive discussions of his thought, see, for instance, Sarah Friedlander ben Arza, "Torah she-bi-Khetav ve-Torah she-be-al Peh ve-Ifyunei Gilluy ve-He'lem be-Kitvei Rabbi Tzadok ha-Kohen mi-Lublin" [Written and Oral Torah, and elements of revelation and hiddenness in the writings of Rabbi Tzadok ha-Kohen of Lublin], master's thesis, Hebrew University, 2003; Amirah Lever, "Torah she-be-al Peh be-Kitvei Rabbi Tzadok ha-Kohen mi-Lublin" [Oral Torah in the writings of Rabbi Tzadok ha-Kohen of Lublin], doctoral dissertation, Hebrew University, 2006; Eitan Abramowitz, "Migdal Poreaḥ ba-Avir: Zehut Yehudit be-Kitvei Rabbi Tzadok ha-Kohen mi-Lublin" [A tower floating in mid-air: Jewish identity in the writings of Rabbi Tzadok ha-Kohen of Lublin], doctoral dissertation, Bar-Ilan University, 2013.
14. Rabbi Ḥayyim b. Moshe Ibn Attar (1696–1743) was a kabbalist, commentator and halakhic authority who flourished in Morocco, Algeria, and, at the end of his life, in the Land of Israel. He is renowned chiefly for his eponymous commentary to the Torah, *Or ha-Ḥayyim*. Concerning him and his work, see Eliezer Touitou, *Ḥayyim b. Attar u-Perusho "Or ha-Ḥayyim al ha-Torah"* [Ḥayyim Ibn Attar and his commentary *Or ha-Ḥayyim al ha-Torah*] (Jerusalem: Ministry of Education and Culture, 1997).
15. As we saw above, there are different opinions among the sages regarding the composition of Genesis and some other passages in the Torah as well.
16. This difficulty is described well in Rabbi Yom Tov Lipman Muhlhausen, *Sefer Nitzaḥon*, facsimile of the Hackspan edition (Altdorf-Nirenberg, 1644), with an introduction by Ephraim Frank Talmage (Jerusalem: Dinur Center, 1984), 73–74 (Deut., sec. 123):

> "Moses undertook to expound this Teaching" (Deut. 1:1)—This poses a difficulty for the Sadducees. How can they understand the explanation of Deuteronomy? If they say that the matter is to be understood according to its plain meaning, and our master Moses, of blessed memory, gave his own explanations to matters not fully explained earlier and explained further here, how can he introduce in his explanation entirely new commandments not mentioned prior to Deuteronomy? . . . What sort of an explanation is it to add a new matter? And if they say that Deuteronomy was also from the mouth of God, then they have already falsified our Torah, because this is not implied by the plain meaning in any place; just the opposite, it is implied that our master Moses, of blessed memory, recited Deuteronomy of his own accord, as it says: "Moses undertook to expound this Teaching."

17. Pseudo-Rashi to 2 Chron. 34:14 writes, "the book of God's Torah given by Moses found in the Temple by Hilkiah the Priest is *mishneh Torah*." Based on this, Viesel understands that "for a certain time, the Israel's Torah did not include five books, but at the most, four"; see Eran Viesel, "Takdim Yehudi le-De Wette: Ha-Sefer she-Matza Ḥilkiyyahu ha-Kohen be-Beit ha-Shem ba-Perush ha-Meyuḥas le-Rashi le-Sefer Divrei ha-Yamim" [A Jewish precedent for De Wette: The book Hilkiah the Priest found in the house of the Lord in the commentary of Pseudo-Rashi to Chronicles], *Shnaton: An Annual for Biblical and Near Eastern Studies* 17 (2007): 103–112 (quote from 106). Viesel's interpretation is possible; however, Pseudo-Rashi's comments are too laconic to serve as a reliable foundation for such radical conclusions (compare Sforno to Deut. 31:26).
18. On this point see, for instance, Kasher (note 9 above), 342–343; Abraham Joshua Heschel, *Torah min ha-Shamayyim be-Aspaklarya shel ha-Dorot* [Heavenly Torah: As refracted through the generations] (London and New York: Defus Shontsin, 1964), 181–219; Rabbi Yehuda Cooperman, *Peshuto shel Mikra: Al Mikomo shel Peshuto shel Mikra ba-Shelemut ha-Torah u-ba-Kedushatah* [The simple sense of Scripture: On the place of the simple sense of Scripture in the wholeness and sanctity of the Torah] (Jerusalem: Jerusalem College, 2007), 1:97–144, see also 2:309–318; and see further Moshe Greenberg, "Tefisot Yehudiyot shel ha-Gorem ha-Enoshi be-Nevu'ah" [Jewish conceptions of the human factor in prophecy], in *Sefer ha-Yovel le-Rav Mordechai Breuer* [Mordechai Breuer Jubilee Volume], ed. Moshe Bar-Asher (Jerusalem: Akademon, 1992), 1:63–76 (esp. 66–68).
19. The words quoted begin with the first letter, alef, and end with the twenty-second, tav.
20. Beginning with the sixth letter, vav, and ending with the fourteenth, mem.
21. Also beginning with vav and ending with mem.
22. Beginning with vav and ending with heh, thus encompassing the entire alphabet.
23. See Babylonian Talmud, tractate *Megillah* 31b.
24. See Babylonian Talmud, tractate *Megillah* 31b.
25. Babylonian Talmud, tractate *Yevamot* 4a: "Rav Yosef said: Even one who does not expound on textual adjacency in the rest of the Torah does so in Deuteronomy, for Rabbi Yehudah generally did not expound [textual adjacency], but in Deuteronomy he did."
26. Rabbi Eliezer b. Nathan (Ra'avan; ca. 1090–1170) is considered the greatest of the rabbis of Ashkenaz. His best-known work is *Even ha-Ezer* (also known as *Tzafenat Pa'neaḥ* and *Piskei Ra'avan*).
27. Rabbi Joshua b. Nahum Baumol (1880–1948) served as the dean of the yeshiva of Viznitz during his youth and gained renown as one of the greatest rabbis in the United States after immigrating.
28. See also *Midrash Aggadah*, ed. Buber, Deut. 3:6.
29. See also Rashbam to Deut. 32:31.
30. Nachmanides (1194–1270) was one of the greatest Biblical exegetes, an important commentator on the Talmud, a halakhic authority of great stature, a philosopher, and one of the greatest kabbalists of his generation. On his life, see, for example, Rabbi Ḥayyim Dov Chavel, *Rabbeinu Moshe ben Naḥman: Toldot Ḥayyav, Zemano, ve-Ḥibburav* [Rabbi Moses

b. Naḥman: His life, times, and works] (Jerusalem: Mosad Harav Kook, 1967). On his commentary on the Torah, see Yosef Ofer and Jonathan Jacobs, *Tosafot Ramban le-Peirusho la-Torah she-Nikhtevu be-Eretz Yisrael* [Nachmanides' Torah commentary addenda written in the Land of Israel] (Jerusalem: Herzog College, 2013). On his thought, see Haviva Pedaya, *Ha-Ramban: Hit'alut: Zeman Maḥzori ve-Text Kadosh* [Nachmanides: Cyclical time and holy text] (Tel Aviv: Am Oved, 2003).

31. Similar interpretations can be found in the work of Rabbi Isaac Karo, uncle of Rabbi Joseph Karo (1458–1538?) author of the *Shulḥan Arukh*, in his *Toldot Yitḥak* on Deuteronomy 1:1. Rabbi Meir Wisser (Malbim) proceeds in a similar direction in his commentary on Deuteronomy 1:1–3. In this context, see also the supercommentary by Rabbi Nissim of Gerona (Ran) on Rabbi Isaac Alfasi's (Rif) interpretation of Babylonian Talmud, tractate *Megillah* 11a.

32. Rabbi Isaac Abravanel (1437–1508) was an important Jewish leader, wealthy statesman, biblical commentator, and philosopher. Benzion Netanyahu wrote extensively on Abravanel's character in his *Don Isaac Abravanel: Statesman and Philosopher* (Philadelphia: JPS 1953). On the critical aspect on Abravanel's thought (especially as it relates to the gap between his approach in the prophetic books and his approach in the Torah), see Yair Hass, "Seti'ot Metodologiot shel Abravanel be-Feirusho la-Torah, le-Or Tefisato et Mahut ha-Torah" [Methodological inconsistencies in Abravanel's commentary on the Torah in light of his understanding of the essence of the Torah], master's thesis, Bar-Ilan University 2001.

33. Babylonian Talmud, tractate *Megillah* 31b.

34. Rabbi Judah Loew b. Rabbi Betzalel, the Maharal of Prague (1512?/1522?-1609), was a *Rosh Yeshiva*, halakhic authority, kabbalist, exegete, and one of the greatest thinkers of the period of the *Aḥaronim*. His renown was due mostly to his profound works of Jewish thought. For further information about his history and philosophy, see Avraham Gottesdiener ha-Kohen (Ovadiah), *Ha-Ari she-be-Ḥakhmei Prague: Toldotav, Rabbanotav, u-Mishnato shel Rabbi Yehuda Loew b. Rabbi Betzalel, ha-Maharal mi-Prague* [The lion of the sages of Prague: The history, teachers, and thought of Rabbi Yehuda Loew, the Maharal of Prague] (Jerusalem: Mosad Harav Kook, 2001); see in particular the articles in Elchanan Reiner (ed.), *Maharal—Akdamot—Pirkei Hayyim, Mishna, Hashpa'ah* [Maharal: Overtures: Biography, doctrine, influence] (Jerusalem: Zalman Shazar Center, 2015).

35. Babylonian Talmud, tractate *Megillah* 31b.

36. See also Rabbi Mordechai Kohen, *Siftei Kohen al Ḥameshet Ḥumeshei Torah* (Warsaw: Yitzḥak Goldmann, 1883), 5:3.

37. For a discussion of this source, see Kuperman (note 44 above), 1:116–117.

38. Rabbi Jacob Kranz, the Maggid of Dubno (1741–1804) was considered the most outstanding Lithuanian *darshan* of the eighteenth century. His major work, published posthumously, is *Ohel Ya'akov al ha-Torah*.

39. Rabbi Samuel b. Rabbi Abraham Borenstein (1856–1926) was the second Rebbe of Sochaczew. His most popular book is the commentary *Shem mi-Shemuel* on the Torah and the festival readings.

40. Rabbi Moses Sofer (1762–1839), rabbi of the city and region of Pressburg, and head of its yeshiva, was one of the greatest, most influential Torah scholars of recent generations. His major works are the collection of reponsa *Hiddushei Torat Moshe (Hatam) Sofer*, and the commentaries *Hiddushei Hatam Sofer* on the Torah and *Torat Moshe* on the Torah, the five *megillot*, and the Passover Haggadah. For a biography and description of his thought, see Rabbi Eliezer Katz, *Ha-Hatam Sofer: Rabbi Moshe Sofer—Hayyav ve-Yetzirato* [The *Hatam Sofer*: Rabbi Moses Sofer, his life, and works] (Jerusalem: Mosad Harav Kook, 1963); Maoz Kahana, "Mi-Prag le-Pressburg: Ketiva Hilkhatit be-Olam Mishtaneh, me-ha-Nod'a bi-Yehuda el ha-Hatam Sofer 1730–1839" [From Prague to Pressburg: Halakhic writing in a changing world, from Yechezkel ben Yehuda Landau to the Hatam Sofer, 1730–1839], PhD. diss., Hebrew University, 2010.
41. See source 53 below.
42. Up to this point, the author quotes from the midrash.
43. Rabbi Menachem Mendel Kasher (1895–1983) founded and led the *Sefat Emet* yeshiva of the Gur Hasidic dynasty. After two years, he resigned from the yeshiva in order to dedicate himself full time to religious writing. His most famous work is the uncompleted *Torah Shelemah* commentary on the Pentateuch, a monumental work which collects and organizes rabbinic statements by biblical verse, and includes comprehensive discussions on the fundamental questions which arise in this area.
44. Babylonian Talmud, tractate *Megillah* 31b.
45. See also Rabbi Zaddok's comments in *Peri Tzaddik*, Exodus, 15 Shevat, 2; Leviticus, Be-hukkotai 11; Deuteronomy, Va-ethannan 1; Ki Tavo, 14; and more.

Changes Made in the Torah after Moses' Days

The common belief is that Moses received the entire Torah through prophecy, from the beginning of Genesis until the end of Deuteronomy. However, there are several verses in the Torah whose ascription to Moses raises difficulties. In some instances, there is a chronological problem with verses describing events or concepts that only came to be after Moses' death; in others, a stylistic problem arises from verses formulated in ways that are not befitting of Moses. The sages, and following them some of the *Rishonim* and *Aḥaronim*, noted these difficulties, and concluded that there are, indeed, verses in the Torah that were not written by Moses, but by Joshua, later prophets, and even by the men of the Great Assembly.[1]

The Description of Moses' Death

Ascribing the last verses of the Torah to Moses is especially difficult. Not only do these verses explicitly discuss Moses' death, they also describe events that clearly occurred after Moses had died. Indeed, there is a dispute between the sages and later rabbis whether Moses wrote the last eight (or even twelve) verses in the Torah.

53

Our rabbis taught . . . "And who wrote them [the book of the Bible]? Moses wrote his book, the section of Balaam, and Job. Joshua wrote his book and the eight [final] verses of the Torah." . . . The master said, "Joshua wrote his book and the eight verses of the Torah." There is an oral tradition that agrees with the one who said, "There are eight verses of the Torah that Joshua wrote," as the tradition states: "'Moses the servant of the Lord died there' (Deut. 34:5). Can it be that Moses had died [variant preferred by *Masorat ha-Shas*: "was alive"] and wrote, 'Moses died there'?[2] Rather, until here, Moses wrote; from here on, Joshua wrote." Thus Rabbi Yehudah; others say it was Rabbi Neḥemiah. Rabbi Shimon said to him, "Can it be that the Torah scroll was missing a single letter when it is written, 'Take this book of the Teaching' (Deut. 31:26)? Rather, until here, the Holy One, Blessed be He, spoke and Moses spoke and wrote;[3] from here on, the Holy One, Blessed be He, spoke and Moses wrote with tears, as it is stated elsewhere, 'He answered them, "He himself recited all those words to me, and I would write them down in the scroll in ink"' (Jer. 36:18)." Which view is taken by the statement by Rabbi Yehoshua bar Abba, citing Rav Gidel, citing Rav, that "Eight verses of the Torah are read by a single person"? Is it correct to say that this (is the view of Rabbi Yehudah) and is not the view of Rabbi Shimon? You can say even that this is the position of Rabbi Shimon: since they are different (in their written), they are different (in how they are read).

Babylonian Talmud, tractate *Bava Batra* 14b–15a.

54

"The wise shall obtain honor" (Prov. 3:35)—This refers to Joshua, who inherited honor from our master Moses. . . . Moses wrote the Torah, as it is stated, "Moses wrote down this Torah" (Deut. 31:9), and so too Joshua: "Joshua recorded all this in a book of the Torah of God" (Josh. 24:26).

Midrash Tanḥuma (Warsaw), Tetzavveh 9.

55

"Joshua recorded all this in a book of the Torah of God" (Josh. 24:26)—Rabbi Yehudah and Rabbi Neḥemiah disagreed over this. One said, "the [final] eight verses [of the Torah]"; the other said, "cities of refuge." In accordance with the one who said, "the eight verses," it is written, "in a book of the Torah of God." However, according to the one who said, "cities of refuge," what is meant by the words "in a book of the Torah of God"? It means this: "Joshua recorded all this," which is written "in a book of the Torah of God," in his book [i.e., in Josh. 20, which discusses cities of refuge].[4]

Babylonian Talmud, tractate *Makkot* 11a.

56

Eight verses of the Torah are read by a single person. That is, the person who reads the verses before them is not permitted to conclude the Torah, because he then would be reading what was written by Moses along with what was written by Joshua. Instead, he stops, and another person comes up and reads these verses alone, so that it will be obvious that not Moses, but Joshua, wrote them.

Another interpretation: "Are read by a single person"—that is, and he may not stop between them, so that it will not be obvious that it is Joshua who wrote them. [Thus] Rabbi Joseph Ibn Megas.

Shitta *Mekubbetzet* on Babylonian Talmud, tractate *Bava Batra* 15a.

57

"Ten verses of the Torah are read by a single person"—Meaning, there are eight verses at the end of the Torah, from "So Moses [the servant of the Lord] died" until the end, that are read by a single person, since they are not to be joined to the previous verses. This is because they are not part of the Torah. Joshua wrote them.

Rabbi David ben Levi of Narbonne, *Sefer ha-Mikhtam al Massekhet Megillah,* ed. Moshe Yehudah Blau (New York: M. Y. Blau, 1996/1997), 485.[5]

58

"Moses went up" (Deut. 34:1)—It is my view that Joshua wrote from this verse on,[6] because once Moses had gone up, he did not come down, and he [i.e., Joshua] wrote it prophetically. The evidence: "the Lord showed him" (1), as well as "the Lord said to him" (4), as well as "He buried him" (6).

Rabbi Abraham Ibn Ezra.[7]

59

"To this day" (Deut. 34:6)—The words of Joshua. It may be that he wrote this toward the end of his life.

Rabbi Abraham Ibn Ezra.

Accounts of Events Following Moses' Death

Is the view that Joshua wrote the conclusion of the Torah an exception relevant only to these verses, or is it a paradigm for other verses that it is difficult to imagine Moses wrote? Most traditional scholars have strongly subscribed to the first possibility,[8] but a number of sages throughout the generations have preferred the second, suggesting (if sometimes hesitantly or obscurely) that those verses that seem to postdate Moses were indeed added to the Torah in later times.

60

"These are the kings" (Gen. 36:31)—Aside from the chieftains, for the kings came from various places and ruled Edom "before any king reigned over the Israelites" (ibid.), from the time the Edomites became numerous until the reign of Saul son of Kish over Israel. The compiler[9] wrote them together in order to conclude the discussion of the straw and hay, to remove them from the grain, as it is said, "How can straw be compared to grain?—says the Lord" (Jer. 23:28).

Rabbi Menahem ben Solomon, *Midrash Sekhel Tov,* ed. Solomon Buber (Berlin: H. Itzkowski, 1900), 210.[10]

61

"These are the kings" (Gen. 36:31)—Rashbam explains that this section was written in the era of the Judges. However, this is problematic. Is it possible for a Torah scroll to be incomplete, and still attributed to our master Moses, as asked in the *Sifrei*? Also problematic is that there are any number of verses that our master Moses wrote in accordance with future circumstances, as Rashi comments in *parashat* Bere'shit: "Cush and Ashur did not yet exist, but the terms were written in Scripture in accordance with future circumstances"?

Rashbam (Rabbi Samuel ben Meir), according to MS Paris 260 *(in Moshav Zekenim: Perushei Rabbotenu Ba'alei ha-Tosafot (Moshav Zekenim: The Tosafists' commentaries),* ed. David Solomon Sassoon [London: Defus Ḥayal, 1958]).[11]

62

This is the meaning of "in accordance with the instructions that the Lord had given him for them" (Deut. 1:3) [and] "on the other side of the Jordan.—Through the wilderness, in the Arabah" (1). If you understand the secret of the twelve,[12] as well as "Moses wrote" (31:22), "The Canaanites were then in the land" (Gen. 12:6),[13] "One presents himself on the mountain of the Lord" (22:14), and "His bedstead, an iron bedstead" (Deut. 3:11), then you will perceive the truth.[14]

Rabbi Abraham Ibn Ezra, Commentary on Deut. 1:2.

63

"The Canaanites were then in the land" (Gen. 12:6)—It may be that the Canaanites seized the Land of Canaan from others. If it is not so, then a secret pertains,[15] and let one who is discerning be silent.

Rabbi Abraham Ibn Ezra.

64

["'The Canaanites were then in the land. (Gen. 12:6)' It may be that the Canaanites seized the land of Canaan from others"]—The meaning is this: It is known that the word "then" indicates a definite time in the future or in the past, so that its meaning is similar to "at that time." He therefore needed to explain that the Canaanites were in power at that time, because they were in the process of taking it from others.

"If it is not so, then a secret pertains, and let one who is discerning be silent"—The meaning is this: If the word "then" does not indicate that they then were taking it from others, then the meaning is a problematic, opaque one that is best obscured. He alludes to the relevant secret at the beginning of *parashat* Devarim (Deut. 1:2), and the meaning is this: How could he have used the word "then" here, meaning that "they were then in the land, but they are there no longer"? Is it not the case that Moses wrote the Torah, and in his time the land was in the possession of the Canaanites? It is implausible that Moses said "then," because logic dictates that the word "then" was written at a time when the Canaanites were not in the land, and we know that the Canaanites departed it only after the death of Moses, when Joshua conquered it. It therefore seems that Moses did not write this word here, but Joshua or another of the prophets wrote it. We similarly find in Proverbs (25:1): "These too are proverbs of Solomon, which the men of King Hezekiah of Judah copied." Why is Hezekiah, who was born only some generations later, mentioned in the book despite the fact that Solomon composed it? Because this [i.e., Proverbs] was an oral tradition transmitted to one person from another going back to Solomon, and on that basis it was committed to writing; it was as if Solomon had written it. This is true here as well. Since we must believe in tradition and prophecy, of what significance is it to me if Moses or another prophet wrote it, given that all of them spoke truly and prophetically?

If you object that it is written, "do not add to it" (Deut. 13:1), the answer is this: Know that Rabbi Abraham himself explains this in *parashat* Va-'etḥannan (5:5): words are like bodies and rationales are like souls; thus, there are sections that appear twice or even three times in the Torah, and each contains something additional that the others do not and [therefore] is not considered extraneous. He further says in his first recension to *parashat* Lekh Lekha (Gen. 12:4) that "do not add to it" refers only to the commandments, meaning that the Torah's admonition "do not add to it" applies only to the number of commandments and their essence, not the words. Thus, if a prophet inserted one or more words to explain a given matter based on the tradition he had received, this is not an addition. The proof of this is that the elders who translated the Torah to Greek for King Ptolemy, as I noted in *parshat* Noaḥ, altered thirteen things, as it is written in Mishnah tractate *Soferim* 1:9 and Babylonian Talmud tractate *Megillah* 9a.... Since they were not concerned by any of these things, it is clear that they were permitted to add words of explanation, and all the more so, a prophet is permitted to add an explanatory word to the work of another prophet. This is certainly the case in material that is not a commandment, but only a story about things past. It therefore is not considered an addition.

You might further object that our sages said in *perek* Ḥelek of Babylonian Talmud tractate *Sanhedrin* (99a) that even if a person said that the entire Torah is of heavenly origin except a certain verse, which the Holy One, Blessed be He, did not say but Moses said of his own accord, Scripture says of him: "Because he has spurned the word of the Lord" (Num. 15:31). One can reply that this is the case regarding the commandments, as we said above, but not stories. Why linger further on the point when Rabbi Yehudah and Rabbi Neḥemiah expounded in *perek* Elu Hem ha-Golin of Babylonian Talmud tractate *Makkot* (11a), "'Joshua recorded all this in a book of the Torah of God' (Josh. 24:26)—one said [that he recorded] eight verses of the Torah, and the other said, 'the cities of refuge'"? . . .

It is best not to tell people this secret so that they will not make light of the Torah, because an individual who is not discerning cannot distinguish between verses that contain commandments and verses that contain narrative, as well as because of the nations that tell us, "Your Torah was truthful, but you changed and altered it." He therefore says, "and let one who is discerning be silent," because an individual who is discerning knows that this is not harmful; only fools would find fault in it.

Joseph ben Samuel Bonfils, *Perush al Raba al ha-Torah*, ed. David Herzog (Kraków: Joseph Fischer, 1911), 1:91–93.

65

[The sense of "One presents himself on the mountain of the Lord" (Gen. 22:14) is given in *parashat* Devarim.]

Meaning, at the beginning of the parashah (Deut. 1:2). He takes the view that the mount of the Lord is Mount Moriah, on which the Temple was built, as it is written in 2 Chronicles 3:1. Moses did not write in the Torah which mountain this was, but wrote only "the site that the Lord your God will choose" (Deut. 12:5), indicating that he did not know which mountain it was, because the Lord did not reveal it until the time of David. How then could he have said here, "One presents himself on the mountain of the Lord," which would indicate that Moses knew which it was? Further, he said, "whence the present saying" (Gen. 22:14), which is equivalent in meaning to saying: "This is what people in our generation now say when they go on pilgrimage—'One presents himself on the mountain of the Lord.'" In other words, one goes on pilgrimage to celebrate the holiday in Jerusalem, and prostrate oneself on the mount of the Lord. They cannot have said such a thing in the time of Moses. Moses thus did not write this verse, but the later prophets did so.

Joseph ben Samuel Bonfils, *Perush al Raba al ha-Torah*, 1:112.

66

"This is the meaning of 'in accordance with the instructions that the Lord had given him for them' (Deut. 1:3) [and] 'on the other side of the Jordan.—Through the wilderness, in the Arabah' (1)"—The meaning is this: He takes the view that these verses, from the beginning of the section to "The Lord our God spoke to us" (Deut. 1:1–6), are interconnected, as if it they read, "These words—in the following sections—previously were said by Moses to Israel in accordance with the instructions that the Lord had given him for them in the places mentioned, namely, 'through the wilderness, in the Arabah.'"

"If you understand the secret of the twelve, as well as 'Moses wrote' (Deut. 31:22), 'The Canaanites were then in the land' (Gen. 12:6), 'One presents himself on the mountain of the Lord' (22:14), and 'His bedstead, an iron bedstead' (Deut. 3:11), then you will understand the truth"—The meaning is this: Know that the twelve are the twelve verses at the end of the Torah (Deut. 34:1–12). He says there (Ibn Ezra's commentary to 34:1,6) that in his view, Joshua wrote from the verse "Moses went up" (1) to the end of the Torah. We can infer from this his view regarding the other verses. I shall explain each of them.

"The secret of the twelve"—The meaning is this: He explains there that once Moses had gone up, he did not come down, and it was necessary therefore to explain that Joshua wrote them [i.e., the twelve verses] prophetically. This is the simple sense. As for the explanation given by our Rabbis that Moses wrote them with tears, know that it is debated in *perek* Ha-Golin of Babylonian Talmud tractate *Makkot* (11a) . . . and there is one who says what Rabbi Abraham says.

"As well as 'Moses wrote'"—The meaning is this: In *parashat* Va-yelekh it is written, "Moses wrote down this Teaching and gave it to the priests" (Deut. 31:9), and the words "wrote" and "gave it" prove that it already had been given when this verse was written. . . .

"His bedstead"—The meaning is this: "Is not his bedstead, an iron bedstead, now in Rabbah of the Ammonites?" serves to testify to them that it is in Rabbah of the Ammonites. However, it is known that Moses did not enter the land of the Ammonites, because it is said, "But you did not encroach upon the land of the Ammonites" (Deut. 2:37). Given that he did not go there, how did he know that Og's bedstead was there? It is known that the Israelites did not enter Rabbat until the time of David, on whose orders Joab captured the land of the Ammonites, and then they knew that Og's bedstead was in Rabbah. This is evidence that the verse was written in the Torah afterward, and Moses did not write it, but one of the later prophets did so.

"You will understand the truth"—The meaning is this: If you understand the secret of these verses, which Moses did not write, then you will understand that those five verses from the beginning of this section until the beginning of "The Lord our God spoke to us" (Deut. 1:6) were written not by Moses, but by one of the later prophets. And that the verse "The Lord our God," which is the beginning of the matter, is linked to the verse, "These are the commandments and regulations," which is the conclusion of the book of Numbers (36:13). One who carefully considers these verses will understand the truth, as evidenced by the fact that all five verses speak in the style of an onlooker, as if spoken by a narrator. If you object that the entire Torah speaks in the style of an onlooker, then know that this case is different, because these verses indicate the places where these commandments were stated, these indications being: "Through the wilderness, in the Arabah," etc. Had Moses written them, he would not have needed to include such indications, because all the Israelites were there and they were familiar with the places mentioned. Given that they were so familiar with the places where they had been, what need did he have to indicate these to them?

Joseph ben Samuel Bonfils, *Perush al Raba al ha-Torah*, ed. David Herzog (Berlin, 1930), 2:65–66, Commentary on Deut. 1:2.

67

"Away from Elath and Ezion-geber" (Deut. 2:8)—You might ask, how did they travel to Etzion Geber, as it is said in *parashat* Mase'ei: "They set out from Ezion-geber" (Num. 33:36)? Did it not belong to Edom, as it is said in Chronicles: "At that time Solomon went to Ezion-geber . . . on the seacoast of the land of Edom" (2 Chron. 8:17)? My father [i.e., Rabbi Judah the Pious] says that Etzion Geber did not belong to Edom. Rather, the king of Edom married Mehetabel daughter of Matred (Gen. 36:39), and she brought him as dowry Etzion Geber, through which they would bring gold from the kingdom where it originated, as with Marseille and Pandya, where it is brought for withholding purposes. They thus could not have gone in pursuit of gold without first going to Etzion Geber. This is the meaning of *bat mei zahav* [literally, "daughter of gold water"] (Gen. 36:39): she brought him as dowry a city from which they travel by sea to the gold. This happened not in the time of Moses, but "before any king reigned over the Israelites" (31), meaning, before Saul reigned; it happened after that point, but prior to the time of Solomon. [They therefore wrote it in the Pentateuch in the time of the Great Assembly, so that you would not wonder how Etzion Geber had come into the possession of Edom, as it is written in 2 Chronicles 8:17.][16]

Rabbi Judah the Pious, *Perushei ha-Torah,* ed. Isaac S. Lange (Jerusalem: Daf Ḥen, 1974/1975), 198.[17]

68

"You shall not omit the salt of your covenant with God from your meal offering" (Lev. 2:13)—The sages[18] said that "this refers to the salt of Sodom," regarding which is written, "to enter into the covenant of the Lord your God ... with its sanctions" (Deut. 29:11). And what is written there? "All its soil devastated by sulfur and salt" (22). Then, the continuation of the verse: "just like the upheaval of Sodom and Gomorrah." Thus Rabbi Isaac of Russia told me in the name of my father [i.e., Rabbi Judah the Pious]. Yet this seems problematic to me: was this not said at the end of Moses' life? The correct answer seems to be ... perhaps there originally was a different text here[19]: "You shall not omit salt from your meal offering," without further detail. And after our master Moses wrote that in *parashat* Nitsavim, they added to the text as follows: What is indicated by "salt"? "The salt of your covenant with God."

Rabbi Judah the Pious, *Perushei ha-Torah,* 138.

Diction and Style Inconsistent with Mosaic Authorship

A few traditional exegetes commented on verses that do not necessarily describe events that occurred after the time of Moses, but exhibit diction or style that seems to indicate a different author.

69

"Thus he put Ephraim before Manasseh" (Gen. 48:20)—My father [i.e., Rabbi Judah the Pious] explained: This refers not to Jacob, but to Moses. Moses put Ephraim before Manasseh, at the lead of a division, because Jacob had said, "Yet his younger brother shall be greater than he" (19). This was written by Joshua or the men of the Great Assembly, because if you say that Moses wrote it, he should have said, "Thus I put Ephraim before Manasseh," just as the text later says, "And now, I assign to you one portion more than to your brothers" (22). My father explained that Moses wrote during the fortieth year [of the wandering the desert]. Since Moses knew that Jacob had said, "Ephraim and Manasseh shall be mine no less than Reuben and Simeon" (5), [he said] I have given them—the half-tribe of Manasseh—the kingdom of Og, whom Moses killed, in Bashan. For whatever part of the land Ephraim took technically should have belonged to Ephraim and Manasseh, and the total part taken by Manasseh should have been greater than that of Ephraim, due to the birthright. However, Moses said, I already began fulfilling the commandment and gave the half-tribe of Manasseh what I gave it; I have therefore instructed Joshua and the twelve officers who will divide the land to give Ephraim a portion equivalent to that of any of the tribes and to give the half-tribe of Manasseh its due.

Rabbi Judah the Pious, *Perushei ha-Torah,* 64–65.

70

The meaning of the name Azazel is comparable to "wilderness," and this is the meaning of the verse "to send it off to Azazel" (Lev. 16:10). And what is Azazel? "The wilderness" (ibid.), as a wilderness is called *azazel* in Aramaic. . . . Do not be overly surprised by the fact that the Torah contains an Aramaic term, because he [Moses] did not write this verse. This is the secret mentioned here: Moses did not author this verse, but another person wrote it. Do not be overly surprised by my saying that another person wrote it, because there are other such cases in the Torah, meaning that there are many that our master Moses did not author, such as "Moses went up" (Deut. 34:1) until "before all Israel" (12),[20] and " [his bedstead] is now in Rabbah of the Ammonites?" (Deut. 3:11). Moses certainly did not write that, because when Moses authored this verse, he had not gone to Rabbah of the Ammonites, so how would he have known? On the contrary, it definitely was written by another person.[21] You might object, "Although Moses was never in Rabbah of the Ammonites, he could have prophesied with divine inspiration and written, 'is now,' etc., so why then do you say that Moses did not write it?" It can be said in reply: About what sort of topic could he have prophesied and expressed himself with divine inspiration? About something for which there was a need. However, he did not experience divine inspiration for something unnecessary like this verse "is now," etc. Since he did not experience divine inspiration, and he never was in Rabbah of the Ammonites, how could he have known? Rather, Moses certainly did not write it. The same is true of "The Canaanites were then in the land" (Gen. 12:6), regarding which the eminence [i.e., Ibn Ezra] comments on *parashat* Lekh Lekha: "It may be that the Canaanites seized it from others. If it is not so, then a secret pertains, and let one who is discerning understand and be silent," meaning that if the Cannanites [did not] seize it from others, then another person wrote this.

Rabbi Solomon ben Samuel of Würzburg, supercommentary to Ibn Ezra.[22]

Scribal Emendations

It is widely believed that once Moses had written the Torah, no person made, or was permitted to make, any change to it. However, several traditions in midrashic literature, and a number of later rabbis who adopted them, state that scriptural expressions judged disrespectful of God (and in one case, Moses) were subjected to "scribal emendation," understood by some to indicate that later scribes adapted the text.

71

Because the Israelites are cherished like the pupil of the eye of the Holy One, as it is stated, "Whoever touches you touches the pupil of his own eye" (Zech. 2:12). These are the scribes and sages who established this bulwark.

Shemot Rabbah, 30:15.[23]

72

"Whoever touches you touches the pupil of his own eye" (Zech. 2:12)—It should have said, "My eye," but Scripture emended it, meaning, that it refers, as it were, to [God] above. However, Scripture euphemized it, a scribal emendation by the men of the Great Assembly.... Similarly, "while Abraham remained standing before the Lord" (Gen. 18:22), [should refer to God], but Scripture euphemized it. Similarly, "If You would deal thus with me, kill me rather, I beg You, and let me not see my evil!" (Num. 11:15). Similarly, "Let her not be as one dead, who emerges from our mother's womb with half our flesh eaten away" (12:12), but Scripture euphemized it . . . the men of the Great Assembly euphemized these verses. For this reason, they were called *soferim* [meaning "counters" and "scribes"], because they would count and expound on all of the letters of the Torah. Similarly, "and thrust the branch to My nostrils," but they emended as "to their nostrils" (Ezek. 8:17).

Midrash Tanḥuma (Warsaw), Be-shallaḥ 16.

73

There are eighteen words that are scribal emendations, as follows: "while Abraham remained standing before the Lord" (Gen. 18:22); "let me not see my evil" (Num. 11:15); "with half his flesh eaten away" (12:12) . . . These eighteen are emendations by the scribes, and they are to be commended for their precise renderings. Cursed be any who reprehend them!

Masorah Parva, in *Sha'ar ha-Shem he-Ḥadash (Mikra'ot Gedolot)*, ed. Jacob ben Ḥayyim (Venice, 1524), beginning of Numbers.[24]

74

There are eighteen scribal emendations, as described in *Midrash Yelammedenu*.... "Whoever touches you touches the pupil of his own eye" (Zech. 2:12)—in the original books, it is written as "the pupil of My eye."

Rabbi Nathan ben Yehiel of Rome, *Arukh ha-Shalem* with *Musaf he-Arukh* by Benjamin Mussaphia, ed. Alexander Kohut (New York, Pardes: 1954), 4:181, s.v. *kabbed*.[25]

75

"Remained standing" (Gen. 18:22)—But is it not true that he did not go to stand before Him, but rather that the Holy One, blessed be He, came to him and told him, "The outrage of Sodom and Gomorrah is so great" (Gen. 18:20)? He should have written, "while the Lord remained standing before Abraham"! The answer is that this is a scribal emendation [see *Bereshit Rabbah* 49:7]: our Rabbis changed it to read this way.

Rashi.[26]

Changes to the Song of the Ark

The Song of the Ark (Num. 10:35–36) is both preceded and followed by an irregularly formed letter nun.[27] One opinion has it that these glyphs foretell a future change to the text of the Torah, with the section moved from its present location and inserted where it truly belongs. Another view regards these characters as evidence of a past change to the Torah (whether in Moses' time or later) and posits that these verses are the remnant of a longer book that was hidden away. A third position is that these marks imply that the two bracketed verses were authored not by Moses, but by Eldad and Medad.[28]

76

Our Rabbis taught, "'When the Ark was to set out, Moses would say' (Num. 10:35)—the Holy One, blessed be He, made marks before and after this section to say that this is not its place.... Rabban Shimon ben Gamaliel says, "This section is destined to be uprooted from here and written in its place. Why then did he write it here? To create a break between the first calamity and the second calamity." ... Where is its place? Rav Ashi said, "In [the passage of] the standards."[29]

Babylonian Talmud, tractate *Shabbat* 115b–116a.

77

"When the Ark was to set out" (Num. 10:35)—Dotted both before and after. Rabbi [i.e., Rabbi Yehudah the Patriarch] said, "It was a separate book and it was hidden away."

Midrash Mishlei, ed. Solomon Buber (Vilnius: Romm, 1893), 100, 26:24.[30]

78

There are two verses marked by inverted nuns and appended to the Torah, signifying that these verses come from the prophecy of Eldad and Medad. And the meaning of that prophecy was unknown until it was expounded by Ezekiel, as it is stated, "Thus said the Lord God: Why, you are the one I spoke of in ancient days through My servants, the prophets of Israel" (Ezek. 38:17). There are some who say, "It teaches that there was a book there that was hidden away."

Midrash Ḥaserot vi-Yeterot 98, in *Battei Midrashot,* ed. S. A. Wertheimer, 2nd ed. (Jerusalem: Mosad Harav Kook, 1952/1953), 2:274.

79

A scribe must mark the section "When the Ark was to set out" (Num. 10:35) with two inverted nuns; this also is our tradition. . . . There are a few other homilies in which they give another reason. They say: Why did the sages add inverted nuns to "The people took to complaining" (Num. 11:1)? The answer is that the sages said, the entire Torah consists exclusively of the prophecies of Moses, with the exception of two verses prophesied by Eldad and Medad. He therefore bracketed them with a bent nun, and it was thus added to the Torah.

Rabbi Judah ben Barzillai al-Bargeloni (attributed), *Ginzei Mitzrayim: Hilkhot Sefer Torah* (An eleventh-century introduction to the Hebrew Bible), ed. Elkan Nathan Adler (Oxford: Hart, 1897), 37.[31]

Psalm 136: Once a Part of the Torah?

80

"Then Israel sang this song" (Num. 21:17)—My father and teacher explained: This refers to the Great Hymn [i.e., Psalm 136], because this poem was composed after they were saved from Sihon and Og and they crossed the Wadi Arnon. It was written in the Pentateuch, but King David removed all of Moses' untitled psalms (i.e., without superscriptions or attributions) from the Pentateuch, and included them in his book of Psalms. Know that they said, "Who gives food to all flesh" (Ps. 136:25) regarding the manna, and he mentioned Sihon and Og as well, so that he mentions, "Sihon, king of the Amorites, His steadfast love is eternal. . . . Who gives food to all flesh, His steadfast love is eternal. Praise the God of heaven, His steadfast love is eternal" (19, 25–26), meaning that He rained down bread for them in the wilderness. Joshua came and added to it a second, similar psalm, "who stand in the house of the Lord" (135:2). He included only one novel thing: "and all the royalty of Canaan" (11), meaning that this came to pass because of a miracle. Then, when David conquered Zion, he also added a line: "Blessed is the Lord from Zion, He who dwells in Jerusalem. Hallelujah" (21).

Rabbi Judah the Pious, *Perushei ha-Torah,* 184–185.[32]

The Incorporation of the Book of Balaam in the Torah

81

"When God began to create" (Gen. 1:1)—It is a universal Jewish practice to call the individual who completes the Torah reading [on Simḥat Torah] the *ḥatan Torah* (groom of the Torah), the individual who begins reading the Torah the *ḥatan Bereshit*, and the individual who completes [the reading] with the sacrificial section the *ḥatan maftir*. What is the reason and the basis for these three titles and honorees?

Regarding the reason for and source of this practice and the honorees' titles, I say as follows: The Torah may be divided into three parts. The first part consists of the Torah and commandments given at Sinai before the eyes of all Israel and the signs and portents performed before the eyes of all Israel, as well as the commandments communicated to the Israelites through Moses; since they themselves had seen the signs and portents that Moses had performed before the eyes of all Israel in Egypt, at the sea, and in the wilderness, they had faith in Moses. All of this, from the book of Exodus to the end of the Torah, is as if the sixty myriad Israelites [of the time] had written the Torah, because there is no doubt about the truth of these things. The second part is the book of Genesis, from "When [God] began to create" (Gen. 1:1) until the birth of Moses, which the Israelites had not themselves seen, but only heard from the ancients.... The third part includes the section of Balak and Balaam and the incident of the donkey, for which we have no eyewitnesses, but only the testimony of Moses, who wrote it in a separate book. He, Moses, did not include these things in the Torah scroll that he gave the Israelites before his death, as described in Babylonian Talmud tractate *Bava Batra* 14b—"Moses wrote his book and the section of Balaam"—as well as in tractate *Sotah* in the Jerusalem Talmud, chapter 5: "Moses wrote the five books of the Torah and then wrote the section of Balak and Balaam." Since our master Moses wrote this as a separate book, we must determine who inserted the story of Balak and Balaam in the Torah, and when. Second, we must determine why Moses did not include these sections in the Torah.

In fact, our master Moses gave the Israelites only those things that they and their ancestors had themselves seen, to which they had been eyewitnesses, which is to say the first two parts. He did not give the third part, which neither they nor their ancestors had witnessed, to the general Israelite community, so that they would not cast doubt on what he had written. He wrote it as a separate book and gave it to the elders, just as he gave the elders the Book of the Wars of the Lord mentioned in *parashat* Ḥukkat (Num. 21:14), and similarly wrote the book of Chronicles with which the greatest *Rishonim* yet were familiar.[33] And in fact, after Moses died and the Israelites arrived in the land that, as Genesis recounts, the Lord had promised their ancestors, when they personally saw the absolute, precise realization of everything that Moses had said and what he had written in the Book of the Wars of the Lord concerning the borders of the land and the places within it, which is beyond human intellect—for how can a mortal man say in advance what will be in a land he never has visited?—then all the Israelites clearly understood that the spirit of the Lord had spoken through Moses' throat. They came to ascribe holiness to everything that he had said, spoken, or written in a book, and they endorsed its sanctity as if they had personally witnessed even the incident of Balak and Balaam. The elders and prophets then decided to include the section of Balak and Balaam among the *pashiyot* of the five books of the Torah.

With this, we emerge from gloomy darkness to bright light and can explain the statement in Jerusalem Talmud tractate *Bava Batra* (8:2) that "Rav Hoshaya said, 'Wherever the term "heritage" is used, it indicates uncertainty.' ... But is it not written, 'When Moses charged us with the Torah as the heritage of the congregation of Jacob' (Deut. 33:4)?" Is there any doubt about the Torah with which Moses charged us? He then answers, "Yes, at first—uncertainty, but when he toils at it, he attains it all." Who can help but be astounded by the statement that there at first were doubts about the Torah of Moses? . . . Since our master Moses knew that the term "heritage" has two senses, he did well to write, "When Moses charged us with the Torah as the heritage of the congregation of Jacob" because it was in doubt whether they would treat the Torah he had given them as a true inheritance, inheriting it and passing it down, or else turn their backs on the Torah, so that their children after them would neither inherit it nor pass it down. . . . This is why they said to him, "But is it not written, 'as the heritage of the congregation of Jacob'?" Did Moses think that all of Israel could—heaven forfend—repudiate the entire Torah? To this he responded, "Yes, at first—uncertainty." Here we have clear proof that Moses initially doubted whether everything he said, which the Israelites had not themselves seen, would be believed. This is decisively proven by his use of the word "heritage," which alludes to doubt. For this reason, he proceeded to write about the inheritance of the land and the incident of Balak and Balaam in a separate book. In fact, they later arrived in the land and fought the wars that Moses had prophesied, and they clearly saw that Moses had been truthful. They then earnestly decided that his Torah, too, was truthful, and they accepted as well the third part of the Torah of Moses, which he had written in a separate book, as part of the Torah of Moses. The Torah of Moses was then complete; this is the meaning of "but when he wearies himself over it, he attains it all." . . . This is precisely what Rabbi Ḥiyya meant by his homily in Babylonian Talmud tractate *Pesaḥim* 49b: "'When Moses charged us with the Torah as the heritage of the congregation of Jacob'—Read not *morashah* (heritage), but *me'orasah* (betrothed)." In our day, when we wholeheartedly believe in the entire Torah and have no doubts as to its truthfulness, we can declare that our relationship with the Torah that Moses charged to us is like that of a woman betrothed to a man, in that they are inseparable and are bound together by cords of love.

When the Israelites were in Babylonia, at which time they had the complete Torah and were bound with fierce love to the Torah of the Lord, which is perfect and renews life, they instituted the practice that on the day they finished reading the Torah, in which they believed without any doubt at all, one of the elders of the community, representing the entire community, rose and said aloud, "We are grooms of the Torah! Like a groom who happily comes out from his wedding canopy to meet his bride who was betrothed to him, we today are happy and rejoice over the Torah of Moses, which is like our betrothed because we are eyewitnesses to everything contained in the Torah: it all came true before the eyes of all Israel."

After him, a second elder of the community rose and stated that not only were all Israel eyewitnesses to what had been heard and done during Moses' lifetime until his death, but we are eyewitnesses even to the stories told in the book of Genesis, because parents do not pass down lies to their children. . . . Therefore, it is as if we had seen the second part of the Torah, namely creation (*ma'aseh Bereshit*), with our own eyes, and so we are grooms of *Bereshit*. With regard to the part of the Torah called *Bereshit*, we are like a groom coming out from his wedding canopy and happily going to meet the woman betrothed to him with cords of love.

After him, a third elder of the community would rise to testify in the name of all members of the community that they believed as well in the third part of the Torah of Moses, which he had written in a separate book—the book of Balak and Balaam—and the Book of the Wars of the Lord. They rejoiced and were happy over this part of the Torah like a groom coming out from his canopy to meet his betrothed, because after our ancestors came to the land, which they apportioned according to the borders set by Moses, and then clearly saw that all he had written there had been shown to be true and all that he had said had been realized. This is why on the day the Torah is finished we read from Joshua [as a *maftir* reading] the account of what happened after the death of Moses and of their arrival in the land. The individual who reads the *maftir* section is called ḥatan *maftir*, because the creation of the world *ex nihilo*, the miracles and wonders performed in Egypt, at the sea, and in the wilderness, and the arrival in the land are interconnected and inseparable. The ḥatan *Torah*, corresponding to the part consisting of the Torah and the commandments that we received from Moses, who received them at Sinai, corresponds to creation, symbolized by the ḥatan *Bereshit*, and the part consisting of the Torah and creation corresponds to the inheritance of the land and the arrival there, symbolized by the ḥatan *maftir*, in accordance with the inclusion in the *haftarah* reading of matter concerning the inheritance of the land and the arrival there. The word of the Lord is forever upheld by the testimony of these three witnesses.

Rabbi Salamon Schück (Rashban), *Sefer Torah Shelemah* (Szatmár: Defus Z. Schwartz, 1908/1909), 1:83a–84b (§4).[34]

Endnotes

1. On this topic, see Rabbi David Zvi Hoffman, *Sefer Devarim*, trans. Zvi Har-Shefer (Tel Aviv: Netzach 1960–1961), 577–582; Heschel (note 44 above), 381–393; Bazak (note 9

above) 49–65; Rabbi Elḥanan Samet, *Iyunim be-Parashat ha-Shavua: Sidra Shlishit* [Studies in the weekly portion: Third series] (Tel Aviv: Yediot Sefarim, 2015), 2:530–546.

2. The discrepant versions of this sentence are reflected in other midrashic traditions as well, e.g., *Sifrei Devarim* 357:5: "Can it be that Moses had died and wrote, 'Moses [the servant of the Lord] died there'?"—voicing the logical argument that a dead man cannot write; *Midrash Tanna'im* to Deut. 34:5: "You say, 'Can it be that Moses was alive and wrote, "Moses [the servant of the Lord] died there"?'"—a theological protest that Moses cannot have written in the Torah anything untrue, such as writing that he had died when he still was alive. For textual variants of the talmudic passage as it appears in manuscript, see Raphaelo Rabbinovicz, *Sefer Dikdukei Soferim: Bava Batra* (Munich: H. Roesl, E. Huber, 1880/1881), ad loc. (66).

3. According to Rabbinovicz, *Sefer Dikdukei Soferim: Bava Batra*, 66, the version in all manuscripts is "and Moses wrote."

4. Abraham J. Heschel, *Heavenly Torah: As Refracted through the Generations*, ed. and trans. Gordon Tucker with Leonard Levin (New York: Continuum, 2006), 620–622, suggests that the reference here to cities of refuge originally referred to Deut. 4:41–43, which describes Moses in the third person as designating cities of refuge.

5. Rabbi David ben Levi of Narbonne was a mid-thirteenth-century talmudic commentator and halakhic authority. His best-known composition is *Sefer ha-Mikhtam*, a work on the Babylonian Talmud.

6. Ibn Ezra, expanding on the view of the Rabbis, attributes even the first four verses of the chapter to Joshua. He is not alone in this approach; a comparable opinion is that of the Tosafot to the Babylonian Talmud, tractate *Megillah* 21b, s.v. *tana mah she-ein kein ba-Torah*: "One person reads them alone. Two readers may not interchange in the reading of these *eight verses*, starting with '[Moses] went up,' because it is the beginning of the passage." The Tosafists thus in practice apply the discussion of "eight verses" to the twelve verses of the final chapter of the Torah.

7. Rabbi Abraham Ibn Ezra (1089–1164) was a poet, philosopher, linguist, and astronomer, as well as one of the foremost Jewish exegetes of the straightforward meaning (*peshat*) of Scripture.

8. Abravanel (in his comments to Num. 21:1–9) notably castigates Ibn Ezra and Nachmanides because he misconstrues their comments as implying that the account of the Israelite campaign against Arad was written in the time of Joshua: "The master [i.e., Nachmanides] is brought to shame by writing that Joshua wrote this. He left the point vague, saying that Scripture had completed it, but did not state who wrote it, because it was not Moses, may he rest in peace. This view in general was taken by Ibn Ezra from the Karaites, who in their commentaries on the Torah agreed that Moses did not write this, and Nachmanides followed Ibn Ezra. It is astonishing that he, a person perfect in Torah and holiness, would have said that the Torah contains anything not written by Moses, and in doing so, they placed themselves among those who have 'spurned the word of the Lord.'"

9. The identity of this "compiler" is unclear. It may refer either to Moses or to some later compiler.
10. Rabbi Menachem ben Solomon was a twelfth-century Italian Jewish preacher and the author of the 1139 work *Midrash Sekhel Tov*.
11. The version of Rashbam's commentary in standard printed editions, based on the now-lost Breslau manuscript, contains a different explanation: "'Before any king reigned' (Gen. 36:31)—Before Moses, who saved the Israelites. All rulers of nations may be called kings." See Jonathan Jacobs, "The Text of Rashbam's Commentary on the Torah According to MS Breslau and Other Sources," in *Zer Rimonim: Studies in Biblical Literature and Jewish Exegesis Presented to Professor Rimon Kasher*, ed. Michael Avioz et al. (Atlanta, GA: Society of Biblical Literature, 2013), 468–488, especially 476–480. Ibn Ezra, in his commentary to Gen. 36:31, refers to an interpretation by "the Isaacite" reminiscent of the one attributed to Rashbam quoted above: "The Isaacite wrote in his book that this section was written in the time of Jehoshaphat, and he interpreted the generations as he wished. He was rightly named Isaac: everyone who hears will laugh at him . . . and perish the thought that the truth is as he said concerning the time of Jehoshaphat. His book is fit to be burned." Concerning attempts to identify "the Isaacite," see Uriel Simon, "*Yishaki*: A Spanish Biblical Commentator Whose 'Book Should Be Burned', According to Abraham Ibn Ezra," in *Minhah le-Nahum*, ed. Marc Brettler and Michael Fishbane (Sheffield: JSOT Press, 1993), 300–317.
12. Ibn Ezra here apparently refers to the final twelve verses of the Torah (Deut. 34:1–12), which were written by Joshua rather than Moses (see source 58 above). For a detailed exposition of the secret, see Rabbi Joseph ben Eliezer, sources 64–66 below.
13. Ibn Ezra appears to refer to the same secret to resolve the difficulty posed by the words, "The Canaanites and Perizzites were then dwelling in the land" (Gen. 13:7); see his comments on that verse. This case seems to be a clearer one than Gen. 12:6, where the non-critical approach is implausible.
14. For an explanation of Ibn Ezra's secret, see Rabbi Joseph ben Eliezer, source 66 below.
15. See Ibn Ezra's commentary to Deut. 1:2.
16. The bracketed text was omitted from the second edition by the editor.
17. Rabbi Judah the Pious of Regensburg (d. 1217) is considered to have been the most salient member of the Ashkenazic Pietists of the eleventh and twelfth centuries. His glosses on the Torah were posthumously recorded by his son Rabbi Moses Zaltman. Ostensibly problematic sections in the commentary of Rabbi Judah the Pious were expunged by the editor, Isaac S. Lange, in the second edition of this work due to pressure brought to bear by Rabbi Moses Feinstein and others; see Feinstein, *Iggerot Moshe: Yoreh De'ah* (New York, 1981/1982), vol. 3, responsa 114–115. Miriam Weitman, "Hedei Parshanuto shel Rabbi Yehudah he-Ḥasid be-Kitvei Talmidav: Hemshekh mul Tzimtzum" [Echoes of the exegesis of Rabbi Yehuda he-Ḥasid in the writings of his disciples: Continuity versus reduction], *Megadim* 55 (2013–2014): 53–89, demonstrates that the glosses of Rabbi Judah the Pious

are quoted in works by a number of sages over the generations that followed him, including the Torah commentary attributed to Rabbi Eleazar of Worms; *Paneaḥ Raza*, by Rabbi Isaac ben Judah of Sens (thirteenth century); a manuscript attributed to Rabbi Avigdor Katz of Vienna (thirteenth century); *Sefer Tziyyoni: Perush ha-Torah al Derekh ha-Emet*, by Rabbi Menahem Tziyyoni of Speier (fourteenth century). The sentences that explicitly argue for the post-Mosaic authorship of these words are absent from the remarks attributed to Rabbi Judah in several sources. Weitman views the omission as evidence that some of these authorities were wary of the exegetic approach taken by Rabbi Judah, but further study would do well to ascertain whether the more radical material was expunged by copyists even before that point.

18. Babylonian Talmud, tractate *Menaḥot* 21a.
19. This explanation is that of Rabbi Moses Zaltman, not Rabbi Judah the Pious.
20. See source 58.
21. See source 62 above.
22. Rabbi Solomon ben Samuel of Würzburg (1160–ca. 1240), a native of France, migrated as a young man to Speier, where he studied under Rabbi Samuel ben Kalonymos of Speier, his sons Rabbi Judah the Pious and Rabbi Abraham, and others. For a biographical sketch, see Israel M. Ta-Shma, "Al Bikkoret ha-Mikra be-Ashkenaz bi-Yemei ha-Beinayim" [On biblical criticism in medieval Ashkenaz], in *Studies in Medieval rabbinic Literature* (Jerusalem: Mosad Bialik, 2004), 1:273–281, especially 274–278; the quoted matter appears on 276–277. Ta-Shma, "On Biblical Criticism," 278, notes that "the excerpts quoted here by the Ashkenazic pietist are not his own commentary to the remarks of Ibn Ezra, but quoted almost verbatim from the supercommentary of Moses Ibn Tibbon (Provence, 1200–1283), glosses now lost that are preserved in the few quotations found in the work of Rabbi Judah Mosconi."
23. See Berman Ashkenazi, *Perush Mattenot Kehunnah*, to *Shemot Rabbah* ad loc., as well as to *Bereshit Rabbah* (Vilnius: Romm, n.d.), 201, 49:7, cf. *Shemot Rabbah*, ed. Avigdor Shinan (Tel Aviv: Dvir, 1984), 13:1.
24. List 168 of *Okhlah ve Okhlah*, ed. Salomon Frensdorff (Hannover: Hahn, 1863/1864), 113, begins with the words: "Eighteen words were emended by Ezra."
25. Rabbi Nathan ben Yehiel of Rome (1035–1106) served as the dean of a yeshiva in that city. His best-known work is *Sefer he-Arukh*, the first still-extant Hebrew dictionary of difficult and foreign words in rabbinic literature. His opus earned the esteem of traditional scholars for both the original contributions and the ancient knowledge that it encompasses.
26. See also Rashi, commentary to Num. 11:15; commentary to Mal. 1:13; commentary to Job 32:3.
27. The form of these characters varies widely across different traditions; see, e.g., Menachem M. Kasher, *Torah Shelemah* (Jerusalem, 1977/1978), 29:124–132. Concerning the relationship between these marks and the antisigma (inverse sigma, ἀντίσιγμα), see Lieberman, *Yevanit vi-Yevanut be Eretz Yisrael* [Greek and greekness in the Land of Israel] (Jerusalem: Mosad Bialik, 1962), 38–46.

28. See, e.g., Solomon ben Jehiel Luria, responsum 73, in (Maharshal, ca. 1510–1574), *Shut Maharshal*; Heschel, *Heavenly Torah*, 642–646.
29. Understood as referring to either Num. 2:17 or 10:21.
30. Lieberman (*Yevanit vi-Yevanut be Eretz Yisrael*, 41n28) explains, "It appears that the Rabbi alludes to the apocryphal book of Eldad and Medad . . . an excerpt of which was allegedly attached to the Bible."
31. Scholars have suggested several different figures as the author of this book; see Shraga Abramson, "Hilkhot Sefer Torah ('Ginzei Mitzrayim')" [Laws of Torah Scrolls ("Hidden Treasures of Egypt")], *Sinai* 95 (1983/1984): 197–208; *Sinai* 98 (1985/1986): 1–21; *Sinai* 99 (1985/1986): 193–214; *Sinai* 105 (1989/1990): 212–219, who gives a lengthy and thorough rebuttal of the then-prevailing view, and proposes that the author was Rabbi Joseph Rosh ha-Seder, a younger contemporary of Maimonides.
32. This interpretation is also credited to Rabbi Judah the Pious by Rabbi Menahem Tziyyoni (d. ca. 1410), *Sefer Tziyyoni* (Lemburg, 1882), on *parashat* Ḥukkat, 64b. After his crusade against the publication of the commentary of Rabbi Judah the Pious, Rabbi Moses Feinstein called for similar treatment of the work of Tziyyoni (see notes 82, 87 above).
33. Apparently a reference to the *Chronicles of Moses*, a late aggadic work that Rabbi Schück attributes to Moses.
34. Several of the sentences omitted here appear in source 12 above.

Appendix: Reactions to Biblical Criticism

The almost universal Orthodox reaction to the arrival of biblical criticism was to label all of its arguments as forbidden and odious, and to set both them and the scholars responsible for them squarely beyond the pale. However, some sages took up the challenge and formulated more calibrated responses to the difficulties biblical criticism raised. Some sought to distinguish between the critics, who yet might be brought back into the fold, and their criticism, which was to be rejected (or interpreted such that it was made irrelevant). Others, meanwhile, distinguished between problematic and admissible aspects of biblical criticism. Finally, some tried to find religious meaning in the findings of the critics while preserving the traditional bounds of the faith.

82

The true foundation is the Oral Torah, whose basis is the entirely indisputable national tradition. Here we need not construct abstract homilies, but must only ask, "Are you one of us or are you our enemy?" For this reason, the Written Torah too was imbued with the sanctity of the Oral Torah. This took place in the days of Ahasuerus, when they "undertook and irrevocably obligated themselves" (Esther 9:27), thus affirming a general agreement to observe the Torah in practice throughout the generations, and reflecting the inner recognition that it is the foundation of our lives. . . . We may be thus excused from the many considerations of disquieting heretical deceit, because historical things do not require any testimony or philosophizing. This is the lowest, bottom level. From it one rises to the higher level of recognizing the excellence of the Community of Israel. . . . This will give the scholar and investigator strength and splendor to ascend the degrees of sanctity and faith, to enter the council of the Written Torah, whose divine truth and veracious testimony are fully manifest to all despite the passage of time. . . . There is no longer any fear of those white scorpions in the guise of donkeys that surrounded Mount Sinai, as recounted by Rabbah b. Bar Ḥannah. Even if vain comments and calumnious thoughts, contesting the time of the Torah's composition and the arrangement of its sections, are as many as the sands of the sea, this cannot in the least compromise our faith that our Torah is a Torah of truth and is an eternal source of unceasing life for us. For we all recognize, both generally and in a natural, internal manner—in addition to the testimony transmitted by our fathers concerning the revelation of the divine presence, and we desire thus to live and to be the nation of the

Lord, our God—we recognize that we can have absolutely no other existence in this world.... In any case, the covenant of the Oral Torah that emerges from the general power of the nation eternally abides as a bulwark for the Torah, sparing us any need to engage an Israelite heretic by offering some argument premised on fragile investigations, and permitting us instead to declare that we wish to live by the Torah alone. We therefore love it as we love the Lord, may He be blessed, and we love all the deeds, the studies, and the opinions that foster its love and glorification. It follows that we must hate those who hate it and revile those who revile it, these being the same individuals who hate and revile us. It is therefore enough to respond to an Israelite heretic who comes to aggravate us by briefly stating the national consensus. But to a gentile heretic we can put forward intellectual and logical arguments and proofs, because he is not obliged to be a party to our consensus. However, it is in any case appropriate to correct him, too, so that he will perceive the grandeur and divinity of the Torah, and thus become receptive to the general influence that it has on all mortals created in the image of Adam. When the need for intellectual arguments ceases to be a practical matter, because the foundation of the Oral Torah suffices, then the intellect is liberated and can freely and leisurely arrive at the truth of love. After much profundity and inquiry, it will arrive at those cogent conceptions that are the principle of the Torah.

Rabbi Abraham Isaac Kook, *Li-Nevukhei ha-Dor***,** 215–220.[1]

83

Indeed, all instruments of war require intellectual strength. The intellect thus has the opportunity to consider and to comprehend, to study and to learn, until it apprehends the error. Yet for one basic heresy in our day, it is necessary to find a cure, a means of saving individuals from it, even in a lowly way such that individuals may then proceed to ascend from one level to the next. This lowness is the denial, accompanying the criticism of the Holy Scripture, of the heavenly origin of the Torah. It unsettles every feeble or weak individual who is estranged from the Torah and knowledge of the Lord. For as long as the Torah is considered to have been written by our teacher Moses, may he rest in peace, and in his time, all the wonders within it can provide that individual with support, but if he decides—though it is impossible to imagine such a thing if the Torah is studied truthfully—that the entire Torah (perish the thought) was written at a later date, then the entire premise of the obligations that must be fulfilled falls away, and he stumbles more and more. For this malady there is no recourse other than to follow the way of our teachers the *Rishonim* Maimonides and [Baḥya Ibn

Pakuda, author of] *Ḥovot ha-Levavot*[2]—the latter authority in particular, who contended with several heretical views by exclusion as well as by agreement, which is to say that he clarified that the yoke of the Torah must be shouldered even if the heretics' view (perish the thought) achieves consensus. Then, when throwing off the yoke is no longer possible, the wandering ceases, the light of truth appears in all its radiance, and illumination brings repentance.... Thus, we must demonstrate the obligation to observe the Torah and its sanctity in a way that would be effective even if all the erroneous arguments of the critics of the Holy Scripture were to be accepted. In any case, it is fitting to consider sacred whatever emerges from the spirit of the Israelite nation, which has done so much to make the name of the Lord, blessed be He, known to the world by dint of its very existence and which continues to abide ... and this certainly is the wish of the supreme One, and a supreme and beneficial ethical behavior. That we feel this way is clear from the fact that we ascribe sanctity even to rabbinic enactments, and even to Israelite customs with no connection at all to rules received by Moses at Sinai.... When an Israelite arrives at perfection in this respect, he fulfills the Torah and the commandments with much love, and because the presumed cause for throwing off the yoke is annulled, he comes closer to the Torah and its study. He then recognizes the great truth: that the word of the Lord is with us, and that historical truth in its entirety consists of His works, whose understanding is perfect (Job 37:16), who in His grace has done great things for us, redeeming us in His love and compassion (see Isa. 63:9). The host of erroneous and false thoughts will consequently leave his heart; and he will recognize and know the truthfulness of the Torah and its ways; and his spirit will become holy, able to tell him what is recorded in the book of truth (Dan. 10:21); and wisdom will enter his mind and knowledge will delight him (see Prov. 2:10); and the light of the Torah of the Lord, blessed be He, and complete faith will be his stronghold, coming from a heart full of love: "Faithfulness to Your charge is [his] wealth, wisdom and devotion [his] triumph, reverence for the Lord—that is his treasure" (Isa. 33:6).

Rabbi Abraham Isaac Kook, "Pinkas 4 (Pinkas 13: Rishon le-Yafo)" [Journal 4 (journal 13: Jaffa journal 1)], in *Pinkesei ha-Re'ayah* [Journals of Rabbi Abraham Isaac Kook] (Jerusalem: The Rabbi Zvi Yehuda Kook Institute, 2007/2008), chap. 87a, 1:250–252.

84

Heresy draws on four spurious arguments: first, that shouldering the yoke of the Torah and commandments causes—so it fancies—gloom and sadness;

second, the differences of opinion stemming from the existence of different religions, each of which claims to be true, due to which faith altogether grows weak among them [i.e., heretics]; third, because of the new sciences, which appear to conflict with the depiction of creation in the Torah and the like; fourth, due to criticism of the Holy Scripture, which weakens—perish the thought—the principle of the heavenly origin of the Torah.

 The answers to them are these: Regarding the first claim, in reality the wholesomely righteous and truly wise are full of strength, happiness, and might. . . . As for the second, in reality every religion contains some value and some divine spark—even paganism contains a good spark on account of the little morality within it—but there are various levels, one higher than the last . . . from the nadir of a little note of some moral tendency to the completeness of the prophecy of the master of the prophets, may he rest in peace, and there are many levels between the two. There is no contradiction at all here, and in reality most religions can be good, depending on the state of their nations. . . . As for the third, one must accurately understand the nature of prophecy. We must know that it is entirely unconcerned with the sciences that can be investigated over the course of time by the human intellect: everything in the Torah seeks to convey what the listener is capable of assimilating, according to the knowledge that is available at a given time, so as to enhance moral behavior. . . . As for the fourth, the truth is entirely in keeping with our tradition, because no hand has been put to the Torah, which has always been guarded with great care. Yet even according to the meritless view that some sections were written at a late date, or some scribal errors—perish the thought—crept in, this has no bearing on the basic nature and observance of the Torah. For observance of the Torah writ large is dependent on national acceptance, and the nation accepted and continues to accept it with love; the nation has made the Torah and its commandments in their present state the symbol of its faithful covenant with God. An individual thus cannot simply excuse himself from the group . . . because the individual cannot introduce a change against the will of society. If he does nevertheless introduce a change, he does violence to himself . . . and because there is no possibility of serious disruption, even if the worse views are to be granted, again, there is no possibility at all that they will prevail. And when Israel observes the Torah, there is such pure and fine sentiment and the connection to the Torah is so great that they gain true insight, in the form of inner knowledge, that there is no place at all for those objections. They perceive that the arm of God is outstretched above them, and that He has performed wonders for us from time immemorial until now, so they cling to Him with love.

Then, having perceived the greatness of the Torah, they perceive its divinity, until all the misgivings entirely disappear and Israel prospers, and the Torah of the Lord is its stronghold.

These are the four roots of heresy, from which each and every branch of heresy stems. They are thus clearly vain things that cannot weaken any holy bond or positive deed. In reality, what gives the covenant force is national tradition, which is the foundation of the Oral Torah, and this is the gate to the Lord. For when the power of the Oral Torah abides, it leads one to the power of the Written Torah. . . . What is more, the words of the calumnious heretics are fundamentally words of dream and bluster that cannot truly withstand upright, free criticism. The truthfulness of the Torah in the simplest sense—that it was written by a faithful shepherd as spoken by the Lord—is a self-evident truth that is Israel's crown and glory, alongside the values of the practical obligations, which are steadfast and enduring and cannot in any way be moved even a hairsbreadth by any gust in the world.

Rabbi Abraham Isaac Kook, Pinkas "Rishon le-Yafo" [Jaffa journal 1], in *Kevatzim mi-Ketav Yad Kodsho* [Unpublished works from manuscript] (Jerusalem: The Rabbi Zvi Yehuda Kook Institute, 2007–2008), § 91a.[3]

85

Indeed, the belief that Moses himself wrote and completed the entire Torah . . . in accordance with the comment by Nachmanides at the beginning of Genesis that Moses wrote the entire Torah as dictated by the Lord, "like a copyist transcribing an ancient book" . . . and the doubts regarding this expressed by some, who think . . . that it was written by another man of truth who narrates everything that the Lord spoke to Moses—this question does not in any way fall under the rubric of "one who denies the Torah" or "has spurned the word of the Lord." It falls only under the rubric of faith in the sages: Our duty to have faith in the words of our masters the talmudic authorities and their view of the matter. And they said, "Moses wrote his book, the section of Balaam, and Job. Joshua wrote his book and eight verses of the Torah."[4] However, where practical *halakhah* is not concerned, one is permitted to interpret differently from the talmudic authorities . . . one therefore would not be guilty of any sin for saying that Moses did not write the book of Job, because this is neither a religious principle nor a legal or halakhic matter. The question of the writing of the Torah, however, you might call a religious principle, or at least ascribe to it the value of a halakhic principle. Even if it does not answer to these definitions, any person who deviates from the view of the sages, even where practical *halakhah* is not concerned, must provide appropriate evidence.... But all the words of the sages, whether expressed singly or together, are words of the living God, and their inquiries into the truth and debates over it belong to the back-and-forth of Torah study and the debate over what is true and what false, but not (perish the thought) denial of the Torah or spurning the word of the Lord.

The author of the liturgical poem *Ani Ma'amin* ["I Believe"] ... produced a vernacular adaptation ... of the thirteen principles written by Maimonides in his commentary to the first *mishnah* of *perek* Ḥeleq [i.e., chapter 11 of Mishnah tractate Sanhedrin]. The poet was imprecise in writing that the entire Torah "now in our possession" is that which was given to our master Moses. He should have written instead that the entire Torah written by our master Moses was given to him by the Lord or dictated to him by the Lord.... How different are the words of the poet who authored *Ani Ma'amin*, which was written injudiciously, from those of Maimonides, which were written with great precision! For an individual who does not believe in our master Moses, all of whose words are truth, is described as denying the Torah, like the deniers of Moses' time who challenged his statements until he said, "By this you shall know that it was the Lord who sent me [to do all these things]; that they are not of my own devising!" (Num. 16:28).... Thus faith in the Torah is equivalent to faith in the Lord and in Moses, who was His servant and was trusted throughout His household. A denier who says that Moses was deceitful regarding any one thing, and that, of his own accord, Moses said in the name of the Lord something that He had not said, denies the entire Torah, because he casts doubt on the trustworthiness of Moses, which causes everything to collapse.... The author of *Ani Ma'amin*, a righteous man who lived according to his faith, believed in the truth of the words of our master Moses [Maimonides] just as he did as in the words of our master Moses. He fancied that he understood the words of our master Moses without carefully studying them ten times over, and without contemplating them with deep attentiveness. Thus, in his haste, he wrote as a principle for the entire nation, "I wholeheartedly believe that the entire Torah now in our possession ...," and he did not understand what he was doing, because he was a righteous man who lived according to his faith. One who shares his faith is fortunate, and so are his sons, disciples of the Lord. However, he should have taken care not to cause the death of thousands of righteous individuals with this poem; it causes them to be considered unbelievers by the people, because in their wholesomeness and search for truth, they reviewed the words of Moses our master [Maimonides] more than ten times, and gained a better understanding of his deeper meaning. They therefore do not know to be careful to avoid becoming sinful and deserving of blame in the eyes of the people. And the hands of the people are first against them to put them to death, although they have not sinned in the least against the Lord and His Torah, but rather the people of the Lord spread about (*ma'avirim*) such a thing. The word *ma'avirim* is spelled defectively [so that it might be vocalized *ma'aviram*, "he causes them to exceed"] because they cause them to go beyond their understanding and the law of their Creator by bringing bad reports of "it is no favorable report" (1 Sam. 2:24), such that the ignoramuses of our people hold their heads high but they stumble.

Rabbi Chaim Hirschensohn, *Sefer Malki ba-Kodesh*, ed. David Zohar, responsa 6:4, 2:478–488.[5]

86

Any intellectually competent person can understand from the preceding that we cannot lump together all those who engage in such studies, termed *Bibelkritik* (biblical criticism), and call them all "deniers of the Torah and individuals who spurn the word of the Lord." . . . Rather, as with every halakhic matter, different rules apply. Just as the laws of the Sabbath recognize different classes of action—an individual who is guilty of committing forbidden acts, another who is exempt although his actions were forbidden, and still another who is exempt and has acted permissibly—and just as they encompass both the commandment of "Remember [the Sabbath day]" (Exod. 20:7) and that of "Observe [the sabbath day]" (Deut. 5:12), so too is the case here.

One who is guilty of spurning the word of the Lord

This is he who says that Moses said in the Lord's name things that he had fabricated. . . . If a person says that Moses fabricated even a single statement, even a single word, and that Moses falsely said that he had arrived at it through his aforementioned discernment although he in fact had not, then that person mocks the father of the prophets, and denies not only that particular word or statement, but the entire Torah. . . .

One who is exempt, although his actions were forbidden, is the higher biblical critic

If he says nothing against Moses, the servant of the Lord, but only denies a few pericopes, which he says found their way into the Torah from elsewhere and were not written by Moses. It is forbidden to say such a thing, because he thus denies our tradition and what is sacred to our nation and desecrates the sanctity of Israelite nationhood, whose sanctity is its Torah. However, he does not deserve to be cut off, because he has said nothing against the Lord or His servant Moses, and he is not among those who have no part in the world to come. The same is true of the lower biblical critic, and of all the things previously described ... in regard to which we decide as a matter of *halakhah* to follow the majority of books.[6] Though he is permitted to study according to his method, he is forbidden to write accordingly in a Torah scroll ... and if someone came and said that all of our Torah scrolls were defective, we would neither give heed nor assent, not even if it were Elijah himself....

One who is exempt and has only done something permissible

This means studying all these things ... with the intention not of changing anything in a Torah scroll, but of understanding the meaning of Scripture by drawing on evidence from *targumim*, midrashim, and the two Talmuds, or according to his own intuition, and discovering the soul of Scripture. Even where higher criticism is concerned, if one studies it as any other wisdom, not as a matter of faith, and especially with the intention of knowing how to respond to heretics, as Maimonides studied Greek philosophy ... though it is certainly forbidden to teach the youth, secondary school students for instance, anything that due to their limited intellectual accomplishments would cause them to view sacred things as profane, older people, such as university students, may go down to that nut grove (Songs 6:11), eat the inside and discard the shell, and thus learn how to respond to heretics. Fundamentally, it depends on the teacher or educator, on how he teaches and what his aim is, and in this respect there is no difference between the study of higher biblical criticism and the study of philosophy or any other theoretical knowledge....

An Obligation and a Duty

One of our duties to the Torah is to magnify and glorify it, and to take action so that it will not be forgotten by Israel. On seeing that there is a part of the Torah that might be forgotten, it is incumbent on us to spare no effort to ensure that it will not be forgotten.... This part is that of the Masorah. Our sages of blessed memory gave their lives for it.... And yet, the long exile caused us to neglect this part entirely. Books on the Masorah were written in many generations, but they were not read. Gentile scholars who study biblical criticism have gathered the remaining hundreds of manuscript fragments from repositories, and safeguarded them above all else in libraries. Yet which rabbis—in our generation, we almost could say, which Jews—are aware of them? Jacob is nearly brought to shame and his face made pale when the biblical critics say to us: You oppose biblical criticism? You have not safeguarded the greatest shield against lower criticism—the Masorah—and it is only we who safeguard it above all else, and we have made it an important part of our biblical criticism studies! It is a duty and an obligation that a chair of this discipline be established at the Hebrew University!

Rabbi Chaim Hirschensohn, *Sefer Malki ba-Kodesh*, responsa 6:6, 2:496–504.

87

We all know that the Bible offers two accounts of the creation of man. We are also aware of the theory suggested by Bible critics attributing these two accounts to two different traditions and sources. Of course, since we do unreservedly accept the unity and integrity of the Scriptures and their divine character, we reject this hypothesis which is based, like many other Biblico-critical theories, on literary categories invented by modern man, ignoring completely the eidetic-noetic content of the Biblical story. It is, of course, true that the two accounts of the creation of man differ considerably. This incongruity was not discovered by the Bible critics. Our sages of old were aware of it. However, the answer lies not in an alleged dual tradition but in dual man, not in an imaginary contradiction between two versions but in a real contradiction in the nature of man. The two accounts deal with two Adams, two men, two fathers of mankind, two types, two representatives of humanity, and it is no wonder that they are not identical.

Rabbi Joseph B. Soloveitchik, "The Lonely Man of Faith," *Tradition: A Journal of Orthodox Jewish Thought* 7:2 (Summer 1965): 10.[7]

Endnotes

1. Rabbi Abraham Isaac Kook (1865–1935) played a central role in establishing the Chief Rabbinate of Palestine and served as its first Ashkenazic chief rabbi. He was an accomplished master of all fields of traditional Judaism, and is widely considered the most important twentieth-century religious thinker in the Land of Israel.
2. Section 3:4.
3. This section appears in the edition published by the Rabbi Abraham Isaac Kook Publications Center (132–135) but was expunged from the edition of the Rabbi Zvi Yehuda Kook Institute. (Concerning censorship of the works of Rabbi Abraham Isaac Kook, see note 4 above.)

4. Babylonian Talmud, tractate *Bava Batra* 14b.
5. Rabbi Hirschensohn's view is echoed by Rabbi Mordechai Breuer in an work published toward the end of the latter's life, *Limmud ha-Torah be-Shitat ha-Behinot* [Studying the Torah according to the theory of aspects] (Jerusalem: Masorah Foundation, 2004/2005), a piece seemingly unfamiliar to most students of his work:

> I am simply unable to understand why they [i.e., religious scholars] have a problem with the accepted understanding of faith in a heavenly Torah ... but matters of faith and opinion are difficult to argue. I take it as a given that faith in a heavenly Torah, simply defined, is truly within the grasp of religious people of science in our day, and they are therefore compelled to give this belief a new meaning that our Rabbis did not imagine. According to this understanding, it is self-evident that Moses did not write the Torah, because science has proven that the Torah includes various and contradictory documents, all of which no single person could possibly have written. Yet despite this firmly held scientific view, they do not say so explicitly, but generally keep it secret, in the sense that "the heart does not reveal it to the mouth," because they know that according to Judaism, Moses received the Torah at Sinai, and this is considered one of the fundamental principles of the faith, a principle whose rejection places a person outside the bounds of Judaism. However, I will be a gossip and reveal a secret—and I am willing to say out loud what they generally do not dare say in public: If a person cannot believe that God gave Moses the precise current text of the Torah, then there is no reason for him to say that Moses wrote the Torah. On the contrary, he is entitled to say that the documents of the Torah were written by various prophets in a process that spanned centuries, and only at the end of the First Temple Period or the beginning of the Second Temple Period did a prophetic redactor collate them as a single book, as already proven by biblical critics. By adopting this understanding as such, they did no violence to any belief espoused by Judaism, because nowhere is it stated that a person who says there is no Mosaic Torah has no part in the hereafter: it is stated only that a person who says there is no heavenly Torah has no part in the hereafter. Indeed, they also say that the Torah is heavenly in origin and was written by prophets with the spirit of prophecy!

6. See source 180 below.
7. Rabbi Joseph B. Soloveitchik (1903–1993) was one of the foremost leaders of American Jewry in the twentieth century.

Origins of the Books of the Prophets and Writings

Compared to the question of how the Torah took shape, the origins of the books of the Prophets and Writings is of only secondary importance in Jewish thought. The principal reason for this is that this question does not impinge on the basic tenets of traditional Jewish faith. All prophets other than Moses are considered to have occupied roughly the same plane, and thus there is nothing fundamentally troubling about the idea that one completed the work of another. A further reason for the relative lack of concern is that several sources record rabbinic debates about the identity of these books' authors, an indication that the sages lacked an unambiguous tradition about the authorship of these works.

Origins of the Former Prophets

The four books of the Former Prophets detail the history of the Israelites from their arrival in the Land of Canaan until the exile to Babylonia. References in a given book to events from a later time generally were explained not as reflecting prophetic knowledge on the part of the author, but as evidence of the late date of the book's authorship or redaction. The fact that these books contain descriptions of historical events extending across periods that exceed a single human lifespan was sometimes understood to show that the prophets had made use of compositions that predated them, adapting and reworking these earlier works into the scriptural books. The following excerpt describes the origins of the books of the Former Prophets.

88
Indeed, with regard to the way those books were composed, and how the prophets were aware of previous developments that they recorded, the prophets doubtless found things that had been written in those times in

the chronicles mentioned in the book of Kings. These things were there in writing dating back to that previous time, whether written by the judges, the kings, or other pious individuals of those generations and scribes. Some of them were scattered and dispersed in any number of places, and they contained things that had been written out of personal inclination rather than because they were true, and they included extraneous things, because it is the way of authors and chroniclers to praise and deprecate to excess, according to their affinities and aversions. They contained true things mixed with false and extraneous things mixed with the indispensable. The spirit of the Lord therefore rested on those prophets, and He commanded them to compose books containing the whole, truthful versions of these stories. They gathered all of those documents, and the Lord, blessed be He, prophetically told them how to supplement those things, informed them of the true and correct version, and taught them how to separate true from false and the indispensable from the dispensable.

Don Isaac Abravanel, Preface to the Former Prophets, in *Perush al Nevi'im Rishonim* [Commentary to the Former Prophets] (Jerusalem: Torah ve-Da'at, 1975/1976), 8.

Origins of the Books of Joshua and Judges

89

"Joshua wrote his book"—But is it not written, "Joshua son of Nun, the servant of the Lord, died" (Josh. 24:29)? Eleazar finished it. But is it not written, "Eleazar son of Aaron also died" (33)? Phineas finished it.

Babylonian Talmud, tractate *Bava Batra* 15a.

90

"Caleb dislodged from there" (Josh. 15:14)—After the death of Joshua, as Hebron was not captured during Joshua's life, as said in the book of Judges (1:10). This was written here only because of [its relevance to] the division.

Rashi.[1]

91

"To the kings of Judah" (1 Sam. 27:6)—Although we see (Josh. 15:31) that the Children of Judah took possession of Ziklag during the conquest of the land, it is possible that this was recorded there [i.e., in Joshua] to reflect what

would happen at a later time [viz., that the tribe of Judah acquired the city in the time of David].
Rabbi David Kimḥi.

92

Indeed, with regard to the worker—that is, the individual who wrote and composed these books—our sages of blessed memory considered the matter in general terms in the first chapter of Babylonian Talmud tractate *Bava Batra*, where it says, "And who wrote them? . . . Joshua wrote his book and eight verses of the Torah. Samuel wrote his book." However, when I considered the verses, I found the view that Joshua had written his book highly implausible. Not because it says, "Joshua [son of Nun, the servant of the Lord,] died" (Josh. 24:29) in the conclusion (which is the only conundrum mentioned by the Gemara), but because of the verses that clearly attest that Joshua did not write them. When the rocks are set up in the Jordan, it says, "they have remained there to this day" (4:9); and concerning the circumcision, it says, "So that place was called Gilgal, as it is to this day" (5:9); and regarding Achan, "That is why that place was named the Valley of Achor—as is the case to this day" (7:26); and regarding the Gibeonites, it is said, "That day Joshua made them hewers of wood and drawers of water—as they are to this day—for the community and for the altar of the Lord" (9:27); and it says, "Thus Hebron became the portion of Caleb son of Jephunneh the Kenizzite, as it is to this day" (14:14); and regarding the inheritance of the Children of Judah, it says, "But the Judites could not dispossess the Jebusites, the inhabitants of Jerusalem; so the Judites dwell with the Jebusites in Jerusalem to this day" (15:63); and it is similarly said regarding the inheritance of Ephraim, "the Canaanites remained in the midst of Ephraim, as is the case to this day. But they had to perform forced labor" (16:10). If Joshua wrote all this, how could he have said, "to this day"? The recording of these events would immediately have followed them! Rather, the strength of the words "to this day" necessarily signifies that it was written long after these events happened! You find as well regarding the inheritance of the Children of Dan that it says, "But the territory of the Danites slipped from their grasp. So the Danites migrated and made war on Leshem" (19:45), which is known to have happened in the days of Micah's idol, toward the end of the time of the judges. This is decisive evidence that these words were written only many years after the death of Joshua, and proves that Joshua did not write his book. . . . Because of all this, I have concluded that Joshua did not write his book, but Samuel the

Prophet wrote it, as well as the book of Judges. For this reason, you do not find in the book of Joshua that Joshua wrote it, as the Torah attests concerning our master Moses, may he rest in peace, saying that "Moses wrote down this Teaching" (Deut. 31:9), and that "It was when Moses had put down in writing the words of this Teaching to the very end" (24). Further, Scripture states at the end of the book of Joshua that he recorded all the things he had said to the people. If he had written his book, how could Scripture not have attested to this as well? To the contrary, it is as I said: Scripture attested that Joshua had written what he had, and Scripture did not attest that he had written what he had not. It is because the book of Joshua was written by Samuel that it says the things I have noted . . . because the things described were in the distant past by the time the book was written. . . . Do not be surprised by my disagreement with our sages regarding this, because even in the Gemara they do not agree about the matter; they debate there whether Moses wrote the book of Job and whether Joshua wrote eight verses of the Torah. Since our sages themselves entertained doubts regarding some of that tradition, it is not unthinkable for me as well to take a more correct and appealing approach to some of it, according to the nature of the verses and a straightforward reading of them. . . . If you prefer to say that Joshua wrote his book, so as to be in agreement with our sages, then for these reasons say also that Jeremiah, or else Samuel, gathered those materials [that Joshua had written] and arranged them as a book, and he is the one who added to them the information that God granted him.

Don Isaac Abravanel, Preface to the Former Prophets, 7–8.

93

But I, Jerahmeel, found in *Jossipon* that Samuel wrote the book of Judges; there are those who say that Ezra wrote the book of Judges and Hezekiah wrote Proverbs and the book of Kings.

Rabbi Yeraḥmi'el ben Solomon, "Seder Olam: Nusaḥ Sheni," 382.

Origins of the Book of Samuel

94

"Samuel wrote his book"—But is it not written, "Samuel had died" (1 Sam. 28:3)? Gad the Seer and Nathan the Prophet finished it.

Babylonian Talmud, tractate *Bava Batra* 15a.

95

"For the prophet of today was formerly called a seer" (1 Sam. 9:9)—What we of later generations call prophets, earlier generations called a seer. . . . From the fact that it says, "for the prophet of today was formerly called a seer"— what this generation calls a prophet, earlier generations called a seer—you can understand that when this book was written, they already had returned to calling a seer a prophet. This indicates that this book was not written in the time of Samuel, because if you search all of Scripture, you will find a prophet call a seer only here, when he says, "where is the house of the seer?" (1 Sam. 9:18). You understand from this that "formerly in Israel" indicates Samuel's generation, and this was a later generation than Samuel's, and about this generation it says, "For the prophet of today." However, our rabbis said on the contrary that Samuel wrote his book.[2] May He who illuminates the land so too turn our darkness to light and the rough places into level ground (cf. Isa. 42:16).

Rabbi Joseph Kara.[3]

96

The verses similarly indicate that Samuel did not personally write his book. It is said there concerning the Ark, which in his day was in the land of the Philistines, "That is why, to this day, the priests of Dagon and all who enter the temple of Dagon do not tread on the threshold of Dagon in Ashdod" (1 Sam. 5:5); and it is said as well that the Philistines returned the Ark: "As for the golden mice, their number accorded with all the Philistine towns that belonged to the five lords—both fortified towns and unwalled villages, as far as the great stone on which the Ark of the Lord was set down, to this day, in the field of Joshua of Beth-shemesh" (6:18). Had these things happened during the time of Samuel, how could he have said "to this day," which indicates a long time? You find as well that when Saul came to him to inquire about the donkeys, it says, "Formerly in Israel, when a man went to inquire of God, he would say, 'Come, let us go to the seer,' for the prophet of today was formerly called a seer" (9:9). This verse necessarily demonstrates that Samuel did not write it, because Saul lived at the same time, so how could he have said of him, "Formerly in Israel . . . for the prophet of today was . . . called a seer"? To the contrary, this necessarily and clearly demonstrates that it was written long after the death of Samuel, when mores had changed. . . . It similarly says regarding David, "At that time Achish granted him Ziklag; that is how Ziklag came to belong to the kings of Judah, as is the case to this day" (27:6), but there were no kings during the time of Samuel who ruled only Judah. It says concerning Uzzah, "David was distressed because the Lord had inflicted a breach upon Uzzah; and that place was named Perez-uzzah, as it is called to this day" (2 Sam. 6:8). It is impossible that Nathan the prophet or Gad the seer wrote this, because it happened in their time, so how would either of them have said "to this day"? Meanwhile, everything I have written indicates that Samuel, too, did not write his book. . . . Who then wrote the book of Samuel? Aside from what our sages wrote (as I have noted), it is said in Chronicles regarding David's death, "The acts of King David, early and late, are recorded in the history of Samuel the seer, the history of Nathan the prophet, and the history of Gad the seer" (1 Chron. 29:29), which indicates that Samuel wrote his book, and Nathan and Gad completed it, as they [i.e., the sages] stated I am astounded that our sages did not cite this verse to corroborate their view. What seems correct to me in this matter is that Samuel recorded those things that happened in his day, Nathan the Prophet similarly wrote a separate document, and Gad the Seer similarly wrote another separate document, each writing all the things that happened in his time, and Jeremiah the Prophet gathered and combined these documents and arranged the entire book based on them. Otherwise, who would have compiled those materials, which were written by several transitory people? After all, Scripture did not say that these prophets sequentially wrote their works [in the same book], but that each wrote a separate book. It seems that when Jeremiah set out to write the book of Kings, he prepared[4] the foregoing book of Samuel, compiled the works of the prophets mentioned in the book, and doubtless explanations of that material as he saw fit, which is evidenced by his saying "to this day." And it is illustrated by what he wrote, "Formerly in Israel . . . for the prophet of today was formerly called a seer" and the other verses I have noted that indicate a late date. All of these were the work of the editor and compiler, may he rest in peace.[5]

Don Isaac Abravanel, Preface to the Former Prophets, 7–8.

The Origin of the Book of Kings

97

If it is true that Jeremiah the Prophet, fulfilling a divine command, sought to recount all of the affairs and happenings of the kings in this book—the book of Kings—then why did he not give a complete account of their affairs, and instead suffice with telling some and omitting others? Do you not see that in telling the story of every one of the kings of Judah and the kings of Israel, Scripture says that "the other events of" the given king "and his actions and the exploits he performed are recorded in the Annals of the Kings of Israel" or "the Kings of Judah," indicating that they were in possession of the annals in which the affairs of all the kings, both of Israel and of Judah, had been recorded. When the prophet wrote the book of Kings, he took some of these things from it and left others. That is why at the end of its account, Scripture says that the other affairs of a given king, which the prophet did not record, are recorded in the annals. One might therefore wonder, if all of these things were written in those earlier annals, then why did the prophet needlessly write the book of Kings? Further, if divine wisdom deemed it appropriate to record the affairs of the kings in a book written by a prophet, why were all of them not recorded, but only some and not others? . . . When this question stirred me, I swore—and I will make good—to resolve it and provide an answer here. The most correct solution is that it doubtless was the practice among the Israelites (as it is still today among the nations) to keep a written record of the affairs and actions of kings. . . . Among these stories and tales were indispensable things, as well as those that solely served the narrative purpose of creating a written record of all the things done by the kings from one day to the next. They also contained things written out of personal inclination, as it is the way of authors writing a chronicle to praise and deprecate to excess, according to their affinities and aversions. When the Holy One, blessed be He, wished to command a prophet to record the affairs of the kings, the purpose was not like that of the tales of the annals, but simply to give an account of how the generations advanced and the kings followed one another, and to give an account of their righteousness or wickedness and the reward that they received from the Lord for their actions or the punishment meted out to them, all according to the prophetic truth and divine revelation. This being the prophet's purpose in this book, he omitted many things from the annals concerning tales and actions of the kings and their exploits and the construction of cities, because all of these things, while relevant to the events of the time, were not appropriate or indispensable to this book, whose fundamental and foremost purpose was to give an account of how the kings followed one another, their righteousness and their wickedness, their reward and their punishment, and nothing else.

Don Isaac Abravanel, Preface to the book of Kings, in *Perush al Nevi'im Rishonim,* 428.

98

Scripture stated that "the other events of Solomon's reign, and all his actions"—meaning, actions other than those noted here—"and his wisdom"—meaning, an account of the areas of his knowledge and its extent—"are recorded in the book of the Annals," that they created in his time to give a detailed account of Solomon's affairs. It was the practice among kings to instruct a wise man, skilled in producing appealing sayings and recording genuine truth, to produce a written record of all the affairs and actions in his time, composing from one day to the next and one night to another (cf. Ps. 19:3). This is the book that is described here as the book of the Annals of Solomon. It is similarly written regarding other kings "in the book of the Annals of the Kings of Israel" or "the Kings of Judah," because they all recorded their stories. The prophet took from these stories what was most significant and useful for his purpose, and prophetically recorded them here, in the book of Kings, and left out other things, because telling them would have been needless and of no use. Ezra the Scribe later drew on these original Annals in creating another book, which is why Ezra's Chronicles contains stories that are not mentioned here [i.e., in Kings]: because Ezra obtained them from those books. As Maimonides wrote in his treatise on medicine, "let one who chooses choose for himself"; in other words, let a person who chooses to derive rules from the works of earlier authorities exercise his discretion in selecting the best and most helpful elements, one person preferring this story and another that story, as I wrote in the preface to this book. . . . Indeed, it says in Chronicles, "The other events of Solomon's reign, early and late, are recorded in the chronicle of the prophet Nathan and in the prophecies of Ahijah the Shilonite and in the visions of Jedo the Seer concerning Jeroboam son of Nebat" (2 Chron. 9:29). The meaning is that two books were produced giving accounts of Solomon's actions, one on the early things (his nature, virtues, and achievements), written by Nathan the Prophet as all these things occurred, and another book on the late things: those that happened in his old age, concerning his love of women, his heart's straying after them, their pagan activities, the divine prophecies and statements that arrived through the prophets as punishment for him, the enemies who rose against him in his old age, and the adversities that they brought upon the Israelites. This second book was written by Ahijah the Shilonite in his account of Solomon's sins and the debacles that came in his old age. Such things were included as well in a book by Jedo the Seer in which he wrote of Jeroboam son of Nebat, because he needed to include there some matters concerning Solomon that involved Jeroboam. These three prophets—Nathan, Ahijah, and Jedo—thus did not jointly write a single book . . . but each composed his own book, as I have described. The commentators understood the matter differently, in a way I find incorrect, and I have therefore discarded it.

Don Isaac Abravanel, Commentary to 1 Kings 11:41, in *Perush al Nevi'im Rishonim*, 550–551.

Endnotes

1. See also Rashi, commentary to Josh. 19:47; Rabbi David Kimḥi, commentary to Josh. 19:47; and more vividly, Gersonides, commentary to Judg. 1:10.
2. Babylonian Talmud, tractate *Bava Batra* 14b.
3. Rabbi Joseph Kara (eleventh and twelfth centuries), a student and colleague of Rashi, was one of the greatest masters of the *peshat* interpretation of Scripture.
4. This reading accords with the first printed edition (Pesaro: Soncino, 1511).
5. More than any other traditional source of which I am aware, Abravanel's view that the book of Samuel came into being as an amalgamation of three preexisting compositions combined by a redactor who added his own glosses recalls the development of the first four books of the Torah described by the classical documentary hypothesis (which posits sources E, J, and P, combined by a redactor, R).

The Origins of the Latter Prophets

The Origins of the Book of Isaiah

Did the prophet Isaiah in fact author all of the prophecies in the book of Isaiah? This question has been a bone of contention between secular scholars and the rabbinical establishment for many years. Most biblical scholars subscribe to the hypothesis that Isaiah contains the work of two prophets, if not more. First was Isaiah son of Amoz, whose prophecies (from the beginning of the book until about chapter 39) belong to the events of the eighth century BCE, when he lived. The second figure, termed "Deutero-Isaiah" for the sake of convenience, is an anonymous prophet of the sixth century BCE whose work (beginning with chapter 40) concerns the final years of the Babylonian exile and the dawn of the return to Zion. The rabbinical establishment tends to reject this hypothesis outright, but there are a few traditional sources that do not assume that the entire book of Isaiah was written by its namesake.[1]

99

Rabbi Simon said, "Beerah recited two verses of prophecy and they were insufficient for a book, so they were appended to Isaiah. The verses are: 'Now, should people say to you, "Inquire of the ghosts and familiar spirits"' (Isa. 8:19), and its counterpart (20)."

Va-yikra Rabbah, ed. Mordechai Margaliot, 6:6.

100

"Comfort, oh comfort" (Isa. 40:1)—This section is appended here because he previously (39:6–7) stated that all the king's treasures, as well as his sons, would be exiled to Babylonia. These words of comfort therefore come afterward. According to Rabbi Moses the Priest, these first words of comfort, beginning at the middle of the book, concern the Second Temple [Era]. It is my view, however, that it all concerns our exile, though the book also contains material about the Babylonian exile, in recognition that it is Cyrus who released the exiles, and the material at the conclusion of the book concerns the future, as I shall explain [see commentary to 52:1]. Know that the transmitters of the commandments [i.e., the sages] stated that Samuel wrote the book of Samuel, which is true to the verse "Samuel died" (1 Sam. 25:1).[2] Let Chronicles (1 Chron. 3:19–24) prove it, because it has one generation after another of the sons of Zerubbabel.³ The evidence: "Kings shall see and stand up; nobles, and they shall prostrate themselves" (Isa. 49:7).⁴ One may counter that [they will do so] when they hear the name of the prophet, though he is gone, and let one who is discerning be silent.

Ibn Ezra.⁵

101

As it is said, "For this to Me is like the waters of Noah" (Isa. 54:9). Do not object that this verse, "as I swore" (ibid.), was said by Isaiah.... Prophets were divinely inspired to use verses that had been passed down in the continuation of their work. *Va-yikra Rabbah* 6 goes still further.⁶ ... Thus it was a received tradition that these two verses had predated Isaiah, and he then had come along and been divinely inspired to add them to his book.... This is why a number of aggadic homilies explain the verses ... [as composed] by earlier generations: because it was a received tradition; or else they understood, in their wisdom, that a particular verse should have been written in a different manner given its context. However, the received tradition ... of old had been precisely suited to that context when that verse had first emerged, and it then had been passed down. Then, in later generations, they said and wrote it in the accustomed manner in a contemporary context.... This appears to be the source of a number of instances in the Prophets and the Writings where the vocalized and written text differ: because there was a certain accepted version, and when the time came to write it in a certain context, there was a need for some modification of the verse, while the old version was given as the written one. Both versions are to be expounded, because both were issued with divine inspiration.

Rabbi Naphtali Tzevi Judah Berlin (Netziv), *Mekhilta de-Rabbi Yishma'e'l im ... Birkat ha-Netziv*, rev. ed. (Jerusalem: Yeshivat Volozhin: 1996/1997), 200–201 (Jethro 1).⁷

102

Letter to Rabbi Chaim Hirschensohn by Rabbi Aaron Hyman: ⁸

It is a source of grief to my very heart that they study the teachings of Isaiah with untaught boys, but teach them that there were a Deutero-Isaiah and a Trito-Isaiah....

Response by Rabbi Hirschensohn:

In truth, though his honor the Torah sage, may he live long and prosper, takes it as a sin to study Deutero-Isaiah [as such], I consider this not biblical

criticism, but a matter of "the order of Scripture."[9] There is nothing illicit about calling him [i.e., the author of the second part of Isaiah] the Comforter of Zion.
Rabbi Chaim Hirschensohn, *Sefer Malki ba-Kodesh* (Seini, 1928), 5–6: 203–208.

Origins of the Book of Jeremiah

103

It is my humble opinion that the Book of Jeremiah is comprised of several books, each of which contained an introductory statement. There are three principal books . . . (a) his prophecies during the time of Josiah; (b) his prophecies from the time of Jehoiakim until the eleventh year of the reign of Zedekiah; (c) those that he prophesied after exile from the land. The introduction of the third book appears in its rightful place: "The word that came to Jeremiah from the Lord, after Nebuzaradan, the chief of the guards, set him free at Ramah" (Jer. 40:1). However, the first two books, whether accidentally or purposely, became intermingled, each becoming intermixed with the other, and the two introductions thus appear together at the beginning of the book. This resolves all of the contradictions. . . . In the introduction to the first section, we truly can see that things are intermixed: its introduction is intermixed with that of the second book of Jeremiah, which begins in chapter 17 or 18 . . . and the introduction of this second book is intermixed with that of the first book, from the time of King Josiah son of Amon of Judah. . . . . The first book, inclusive of all its parts, had the introductory statement: "The words of Jeremiah son of Hilkiah, one of the priests at Anathoth in the territory of Benjamin. The word of the Lord came to him in the days of King Josiah son of Amon of Judah, in the thirteenth year of his reign. The word of the Lord came to me: Before I created you in the womb" (Jer. 1:1–2,4–5). The second book had the introduction: "The words of Jeremiah son of Hilkiah from the days of King Jehoiakim son of Josiah of Judah until the end of the eleventh year of King Zedekiah son of Josiah of Judah, when Jerusalem went into exile in the fifth month" (1:1,3). And all . . . of these introductory statements came to be jumbled together and intermixed, and became a single mass.

However, the introductions to these books did not come to be connected to each other due to an omission by copyists. Rather, the very scribes who arranged the books, who gathered the holy scriptures scroll by scroll and combined them in a book on the basis of some connection, though not precisely in chronological order. . . . In truth, the fact that the verses are jumbled together resulted from an omission by copyists and the emendation of the text itself, for in the body of the book, as prepared by those who arranged the Holy Scripture, was written, "The words of Jeremiah son of Hilkiah, one of the priests at Anathoth in the territory of Benjamin. The word of the Lord came to him *from the days* of King Jehoiakim son of Josiah of Judah until the end of the eleventh year of King Zedekiah son of Josiah of Judah, when Jerusalem went into exile in the fifth month," and then the introduction to the first book: "It was in the days of King Josiah son of Amon of Judah in the thirteenth year of his reign. The word of the Lord came to me: Before I created you in the womb, I designated you; before you were born, I consecrated you."[10] However, the copyist omitted "from the days of [King] Jehoiakim" until "in the days of [King] Josiah," and all this resulted from confusion between "from the days" and "in the days."[11]

Rabbi Chaim Hirschensohn, *Sefer Yamim mi-Kedem, Hu ha-Chronologyah ha-Biblit* [The biblical chronology] (Jerusalem: Zuckermann, 1908), 151–162.

Origins of the Book of Ezekiel

104

"I saw visions of God" (Ezek. 1:1); "Lo, a stormy wind" (4)—This is the extent of what Ezekiel originally wrote—he did not even give his name—because he was to explain the subject of his book later, as in "Ezekiel shall become a portent for you" (24:24). He therefore allowed himself to be brief, as I have told you (in the preface) regarding the "thirtieth year" (1:1), [the precise meaning of which] is proven by the content of the book. However, the scribe who compiled his work added explanatory remarks to supplement what he had left unexplained and terse in these two verses.

Rabbi Eliezer of Beaugency.[12]

105

On examining the book of Ezekiel, we see that he himself wrote or at least arranged the entire book, as attested by the verses that appear in most sections of the book: "The Lord said to me" (e.g., 3:1); "The word of the Lord came to me" (e.g., 21:1).[13] . . . However, it contains two verses, one of which was certainly written not by Ezekiel, but by the men of the Great Assembly, and the other of which is in doubt. These are the two verses: "On the fifth day of the month—it was the fifth year of the exile of King Jehoiachin—the word of the Lord came to the priest Ezekiel son of Buzi, by the Chebar Canal, in the land of the Chaldeans. And the hand of the Lord came upon him there"

(Ezek. 1:2–3). But the men of the Great Assembly inserted these verses in Ezekiel's narration. For the natural order of the verses is: "In the thirtieth year, on the fifth day of the fourth month, when I was in the community of exiles by the Chebar canal, the heavens opened and I saw visions of God. I looked, and lo, a stormy wind came sweeping out of the north." (1:1,4). Between these continuous verses, the men of the Great Assembly inserted those two verses (2–3) to indicate who had said this and when. Meanwhile, it seems most likely that verse 3—"On the fifth day of the month—it was the fifth year of the exile of King Jehoiachin"—is the work of Ezekiel himself, who always gives the date according to the exile of King Jehoiachin. The proper order then is: "In the thirtieth year, on the fifth day of the fourth month—it was the fifth year of the exile of King Jehoiachin, when I was in the community of exiles by the Chebar Canal—the heavens opened and I saw visions of God," but by some chance this was omitted from the main text and an emender wrote it below, indicating that its proper place was at "in the fifth month." A copyist then mistook it for a discrete verse and inserted it in the body of the text in the wrong place. In any event, the third verse—"the word of the Lord came to [the priest] Ezekiel son of Buzi"—undoubtedly was not written by Ezekiel, and in the view of our sages of blessed memory, it undoubtedly was added by the men of the Great Assembly to indicate the name of the book's author.

Rabbi Chaim Hirschensohn, *Sefer Yamim mi-Kedem,* 192–194.

Endnotes

1. The notion was rejected even by such scholars as Samuel David Luzzatto (see, e.g., Shmuel Vargon, *Shmuel David Luzzatto: Bikoritiut Minutah ba-Perush ha-Mikra* (S. D. Luzzatto: moderate criticism in biblical exegesis) [Ramat Gan: Bar-Ilan University, 2013], 285–307). In recent decades, however, there has been some movement in attitudes to this question; see, e.g., late chief rabbi of the British Empire J. H. Hertz (1872–1946), ed., *The Pentateuch and Haftorahs: Hebrew Text, English Translation and Commentary* (London: Soncino Press, 1968), 941–942, who accepts the idea as religiously conceivable but rejects it on exegetic grounds; Mordechai Zer-Kavod and Yehudah Kil, ed., *The Bible: Proverbs with the Jerusalem Commentary,* trans. Albert Milton Kanter and Yocheved Engelberg Cohen (Jerusalem: Mosad Harav Kook, 2014), lxxx (introduction to chap. 22) and 296 (commentary to 25:1), whose comments imply partial agreement with the theory; Amos Hakham, *Da'at Mikra: Sefer Yesha'yahu* [Da'at Mikra: The book of Isaiah] (Jerusalem: Mosad Harav Kook, 1984), 1:13–17; Rabbi Yuval Cherlow, *Yir'eh la-Levav: Al Yi'ud ha-Nevu'ah ve-Tokhnah ha-Penimi* [Yir'eh la-levav: On the purpose and essence of prophecy] (Tel Aviv: Miskal, 2007), 246–247 n. 52; Rabbi Avia Hacohen, "Ha-Omnam Eḥad Haya Yesha'yahu?" [Was there really only one Isaiah?], *Derekh Efratah* 9–10 (2000/2001): 79–88; Rabbi Yoel Bin-Nun and Rabbi Binyamin Lau, *Isaiah* (Tel Aviv: Miskal, 2013), 30–31; Amnon Bazak, *Ad Ha-Yom Ha-Zeh* [Until this day] (Tel Aviv: Miskal, 2013), 161–172.

2. Babylonian Talmud, tractate *Bava Batra* 15a.
3. Though Chronicles is generally attributed to Ezra, the genealogy to which Ibn Ezra refers extends to the third generation after Ezra. Thus Ezra could not have written it (unless he is assumed to have prophetically obtained such knowledge), and a later author must have finished the composition of Chronicles (see source 142 below).
4. Ibn Ezra understands the quoted verse as a promise to the prophet that kings and nobles will prostrate themselves before him after seeing the realization of his prophecies about Cyrus. This prophet therefore must be not the eighth-century BCE Isaiah, but a prophet who was active during the Babylonian captivity and the return to Zion.
5. See also Ibn Ezra's commentary to Isa. 49:7–8 and 53:12. For an explanation of the cryptic content of these sources and an account of Ibn Ezra's understanding of how the book of Isaiah came into being, see Uriel Simon, "Ibn Ezra between Medievalism and Modernism: The Case of Isaiah 40–66," *Vestus Testamentum Supplements* 36 (1985): 257–271.
6. See source 99 above. Regarding this midrashic tradition, Rabbi Naphtali Tzevi Judah Berlin (Netziv) writes in his *Sefer Bereshit . . . im . . . Ha'amek Davar*, 739 (additional comments of the *Harḥev Davar* to Gen. 49:10): "There are many cases such as this in the Prophets and the Writings."
7. Rabbi Naphtali Tzevi Berlin (1817–1893), the dean of the yeshiva of Wołożyn, was one of the foremost Torah sages of the nineteenth century. See furher Rabbi Naphtali Tzevi Judah Berlin, *Sefer Devarim . . . im . . . Ha'amek Davar* [The book of Deuteronomy . . . with a commentary entitled *Ha'amek Davar*], ed. M. Y. Kuperman (Jerusalem: M. Y. Kuperman, 2010/2011), to Deut. 6:4 (114–115); Berlin, *She'iltot de-Rav Aḥai Ga'on . . . im . . . Ha'amek She'alah: Be-midbar-Devarim* [The queries of Rav Aḥai Ga'on . . . with . . . a commentary entitled *Ha'amek She'alah*: Numbers and Deuteronomy] (Jerusalem: Mosad Harav Kook, 1952/1953), 166:5 (285–286).
8. Rabbi Aaron Hyman (1863–1937) was a scholar of the talmudic period. Among his best known works are *Torah ha-Ketuvah ve-ha-Mesurah* [The written and transmitted Torah] and *Toldoth Tannaim Ve'amoraim, Comprising the Biographies of All the Rabbis and Other Persons Mentioned in rabbinic Literature.*
9. An allusion to Rabbi Hirschensohn's book *Seder la-Mikra*.
10. Rabbi Hirschensohn writes in a note to the original, "That the words 'I selected you' (*yeda'tikha*) [as in the masoretic text] and 'I designated you' (*yi'adtikha*) were confused is proven by the second half of the verse: 'Before you were born, I consecrated you.'"
11. Rabbi Hirschensohn here gives a lengthy and detailed description of how the copyist's error occurred.
12. Rabbi Eliezer of Beaugency was one of the sages practicing the simple, *peshat* interpretation of Scripture who were active in northern France in the twelfth century. He may have been a disciple of Rabbi Samuel ben Meir (Rashbam). It is believed that Rabbi Eliezer wrote commentaries on the entire Tanakh, but only his glosses on Isaiah, Ezekiel, and the Twelve Prophets, as well as selected remarks on Job, are extant.
13. Later in this same chapter (194–197), Rabbi Hirschensohn considers when Ezekiel wrote the book and his intention in doing so. He concludes that Ezekiel compiled the book thirty-five years after the exile of Jehoiachin, and thirty years after the beginning of his prophetic career. Rabbi Hirschensohn attempts to resolve the problem as follows: "We do not know from what time the thirty years to which Ezekiel refers in his vision by the Chebar Canal (Ezek. 1:1) are counted. . . . It is impossible to ascertain with what point Ezekiel's thirty years are associated" (191).

The Origins of the Writings

The Origins of the Book of Psalms

Rabbi Se'adyah Ga'on, in his preface to the book of Psalms, writes that "the entire book consists of prophecies by David, for the entire nation concurs in calling it the Songs of David, and it is thus attributed to him in many places."[1] His view, which many share to a greater or lesser degree, is not a little problematic. The superscriptions that introduce the psalms attribute only about one-half of them to David, while others are explicitly described as the work of other poets. What is more, a number of psalms describe events that postdate King David by several centuries. In point of fact, many traditional sages through the ages viewed David as the greatest of the psalmists, and some even as an editor of the book, but did not consider him the author of every psalm. In the opinion of some of these commentators, psalms that appear to have been composed at a later date, in this view, were written not by David, but by prophets and poets whose time extended to the age of Ezra.

106

"Built *le-talpiyyot*" (Songs 4:4)—What does *le-talpiyyot* mean? A book spoken by many mouths (*piyyot*). Ten people composed the book of Psalms: Adam, Abraham, Moses, David, Solomon—there is no dispute about those five. Who are the other five? Of Rav and Rabbi Yoḥanan, Rav said, "Asaf, Heman, Jeduthun, the three sons of Koraḥ, and Ezra"; Rabbi Yoḥanan said, "One by each of Asaf, Heman, and Jeduthun; the three sons of Korah (one); and Ezra."

Shir ha-Shirim Rabbah 4:4.[2]

107

There is a great debate amid the commentators between those who say that the entire book is by David and that he was a prophet . . . and those who say that the book contains no prophecy regarding the future, and for this reason, the ancients[3] arranged it alongside Job and the [Five] Scrolls.[4] The proof: "psalm" and "song" and "prayer." They said that "By the rivers of Babylon" (Ps. 137) was composed by a poet in Babylonia. They said thus: every "psalm of the Korahites" is by one of the poets living in Babylonia who were descended from Heman, and their work refers to exile, while no such thing is to be found in the works of David. They further said that Asaf similarly is the name of a poet who lived in Babylonia and this is not Asaf the Conductor who lived in the time of David [see Ps. 75:1; 1 Chron. 6:24]. Thus Ethan the Ezrahite [see Ps. 89] composed a psalm when the Davidic monarchy was crushed in the time of Zedekiah. In the case of those psalms to which no name is appended, the individuals who arranged this book of praises did not know the name of the author, and "of the Korahites" thus refers to one of his [i.e., Korah's] descendants whose name is unknown, and "Happy are those whose way is blameless" (Ps. 119) is the work of a young Israelite who was treated with honor by the kings of Babylonia. The proof: "How can a young man keep his way pure?" (9), "I am belittled and despised" (141), "Though princes meet and speak against me" (23). I am inclined to agree with the view of the ancients, of blessed memory, that this book in its entirety was composed with divine inspiration.[5]

Ibn Ezra, First commentary on Psalms.

108

"Make [Zion] prosper" (Ps. 51:20)—A certain sage from Spain said that these two verses were added by a pious person living in Babylonia who would fall before the Lord and recite this psalm in prayer.[6] He was compelled to say this because Zion was known to be the chosen place only in David's old age. It is preferable to say that they were composed with divine inspiration.

Ibn Ezra, First commentary on Psalms.

109

"A song of ascents" (Ps. 120:1)—According to the simple sense of the verse, when they would ascend [on pilgrimage] during the time of David and Solomon, whether in [the era of] the First Temple or the Second, they would compose a song for the occasion of the ascent, and from then on these songs were regularly said at the Temple. Some were composed when Ezra and his entourage ascended from Babylonia. This is proven by these psalms, since you find either all of Israel, "Zion," or "Jerusalem" mentioned in all of them—other than the first and the fourth, because those two were composed during the Babylonian exile, when the city had not yet been rebuilt. But in the others you find "Jerusalem," all of Israel, and "Zion," because they would ascend on pilgrimage and gather in Jerusalem.

"From treacherous lips" (Ps. 120:2)—When they would ascend on pilgrimage in the time of Ezra, they were afraid that the gentiles around them would come to plunder their homes and capture their cities. . . .

"A song of ascents. To You ... I turn" (Ps. 123:1)—They composed this [psalm] during the Babylonian exile, when the exiles ascended to rebuild Jerusalem. They came not together, but in small numbers, one group followed by another, as it is written in the book of Ezra.[7] They would beseech [God] to show mercy and let their brothers still in exile also be ingathered.

"O Israel, wait" (Ps. 130:7–8)—This entire psalm discusses the forgiveness of sins. It was composed during the Babylonian exile. For exile results from the sins of a generation, and they therefore plead that He forgive their sin and they thus be freed from exile.

Rashbam (Rabbi Samuel ben Meir), Commentary on Psalms, in Aharon Mondschein, "Al Gilluy ha-Perush ha-Avud shel Rashbam le-Sefer Tehillim u-Pirsum Mukdam shel Perusho le-Mizmorim 120–136" (On Rashbam's rediscovered 'lost commentary' on Psalms), *Tarbiz* 79 (2010): 130–138

110

The men of the Great Assembly arranged the Prophets and Writings. In Psalms, which David composed with divine inspiration, they arranged as well other praises and thanks to God, blessed be He, that other people had composed with divine inspiration, and they wrote the name of its author at the beginning of each one, as in "A psalm of Asaph," "A prayer of Moses," and the like.

Rabbi Elijah of Vilnius, *Be'ur ha-Gera: Proverbs,* ed. Meir Yehoshua Katznelbogen, rev. ed. (Jerusalem: Mosad Harav Kook, 2012/2013), 283 (24:23).[8]

111

As long as the spirit of the Lord traversed the world and glory rested on His prophets and seers, upon those who merited good understanding and generous spirit to speak or compose verse with divine inspiration, the gates of this treasury were never closed, for the elders of one generation after another continued filling its granaries with the yield of the generations, placed amidst the shoots of times past ... until the prayers that they established during the Babylonian exile concerning the burning of the Temple and the exile, until the Lord brought back those who returned to Zion in the time of Cyrus (Ps. 137, 85).

Rabbi Wisser comments:[9]

Do not think this interpretation strange, because you find such things in the works of our sages ... as well as in the works of the early commentators who always interpreted [the authorship of Psalms] according to the simple, *peshat* sense of Scripture. I write this to free of us the arguments of those who mock us, asking how it could be that in the time of David, while the kingdom was still at its height, the Israelites were in their land, and the decree had not yet been decreed, they already sang on the platform of the end of the monarchy and the exile of Zedekiah in chapter 89, and their dwelling by the rivers of Babylonia and cursing Babylonia and the Edomites, who had not yet committed any sin or wickedness, and other such arguments. I therefore have given an interpretation that follows the simple, *peshat* sense, to shut the mouths of the instigators and agitators. For even according to the sages' statement that this book was composed by ten elders, among them the Korahites and Asaf, while they disagreed regarding Jeduthun, it need not all have been in the time of David. As long as there was prophecy among the Israelites, until the final prophet, Malachi—who was Ezra—the channel was open and the Levite poets had divinely inspired visions, and what they said is sacred; until Ezra, who completed the Holy Scripture. Since then nothing has been added to them. All this follows the *peshat* sense, whose path we have taken in this commentary, in which I set myself the goal of directing my arrows against the pack of expounders whose purpose is to degrade the Holy Scripture. Among us, however, it is believed that there are seventy facets to the Torah, and according to the homiletic, allusive, and mystical paths, all of these psalms were envisaged in the vision of the prophets and the poets, the Korahites and Asaf, in the time of David. They were kept hidden and concealed by men of spirit through the generations until each given matter came to be, and then they were proclaimed from the platform, each at its time.... However, understanding the verses based on their *peshat* sense and poetic nature, whether they were composed by a man of spirit of the Levites in the time of David or in the time of Hezekiah or the like, does nothing to detract from the verses' grandeur and power. For the spirit of the Lord and His word in those days circulated with invariable sacred glory, until the vessel was shattered at the spring and the light was taken away in the time of the final prophets, when her [i.e., Zion's] prophets received no vision from the Lord.

Rabbi Meir Leibush Wisser (Malbim), Preface to the commentary on Psalms.[10]

112

"For the leader. Of David" (Ps. 14:1)—This psalm appears twice in this book [see Ps. 53] with some changes. It seems clear to me that David composed the psalm on the occasion of a miracle that was performed for him, when he was saved from an enemy that had harmed and oppressed the Israelites. Then, when the miracle of Sennacherib happened in the time of Hezekiah, they found that this psalm was appropriate for giving thanks for that miracle as well. They adapted it with a few additions, and they attributed it to David, because he had composed it.

Rabbi Meir Leibush Wisser (Malbim).[11]

Origins of the Book of Proverbs

Common belief holds that King Solomon was the author of the book of Proverbs, as suggested by the opening verse of the book: "The proverbs of Solomon son of David, king of Israel."[12] A consideration of other verses in the book, however, raises substantial difficulties with this approach. The book is conspicuously divided into a number of discrete collections, each with its own introductory statement, one of which reveals the identity of the copyists: "These too are proverbs of Solomon, which the men of King Hezekiah of Judah copied" (Prov. 25:1).[13] Meanwhile, several of the collections are attributed not to Solomon, but to other sages, as with "The words of Agur son of Jakeh" (30:1), and "The words of Lemuel, king of Massa" (31:1). Surely enough, many traditional sages were of the view that, although Proverbs was based on the work of Solomon, he had not personally written the book, and a number of commentators believed as well that the book included proverbs authored by sages other than Solomon.

On the Compilation and Redaction of the Wisdom of Solomon

113

"Too" (Prov. 25:1)—This verse was authored by the scribe—possibly Shebna, because he was the royal scribe [see 2 Kings 18:18]—and in it he described the transcription. The word "too" refers back to those that appeared earlier. It means that they gave instructions for these proverbs to be copied from his books as a single collection. This section begins with "It is the glory of God" (2).

Rabbi Moses Kimḥi.[14]

114

I say that if a person writes a book, then his name ought to appear in it. This serves to inform the masses whether he is a wise person of great intellect and people can rely on what he has written, and to indicate his purpose in writing it. This was the intention of the writer of this book, who wrote, "The proverbs of Solomon" (Prov. 1:1), giving his name as evidence of the greatness of its content and indicating that he was a renowned sage and intellectually great. He wrote as well the purpose of the author of the book, whose intent was for it to benefit people who wished to hear his ethical remarks.

Rabbi David Kimḥi, Preface to the commentary on Proverbs.

115

Here ends the writing of the individual who transcribed the book, and here the author of the book begins writing: "The fear of the Lord is the beginning of knowledge" (Prov. 1:7).

Rabbi David Kimḥi, Commentary on Proverbs 1:6.[15]

116

"These too are proverbs of Solomon, which the" sages who lived in the time of Hezekiah copied (cf. Prov. 25:1). It would seem that the reason these proverbs were separated from the others is that these were collected from his proverbs by the aforementioned sages, while the proverbs that appear earlier were found verbatim in the works of Solomon.

Gersonides.[16]

117

"These too are proverbs of Solomon" (Prov. 25:1)—This, too, is a witness, for Solomon did not write the entire book as it is arranged, but would state or write his dicta at intervals, some on a certain day and some a year or two later. Subsequently, perhaps during his lifetime and perhaps later, the men of Jerusalem copied his dicta. However, they did not copy these latter ones until the time of King Hezekiah of Judah, for he was a great sage. It appears that they searched with his men in his treasuries, and found and copied this book, which they appended to the preceding.

Rabbi Joseph Ibn Kaspi.[17]

118

King Solomon, may he rest in peace, composed the book from its beginning to this point as it is arranged, and the sages of the generations from Solomon to Hezekiah, who wrote it down and added it to the Holy Scripture, knew it by heart. . . . However, contemporary sages did not know the fourth part of Proverbs [i.e., from chap. 25] by heart. Rather, this sage knew one proverb and that sage another proverb.

Alternately, King Solomon wrote it in the form of allusions scattered and dispersed among his treasuries. When King Hezekiah succeeded him and found these proverbs too, dispersed among his treasuries, he instructed Shebna the Scribe and he copied them and he included them with his original work. . . . The verse "These too are proverbs of Solomon" (Prov. 25:1) was written by the scribe; the proverbs begin with "It is the glory of God to conceal a matter" (2).

Rabbi Joseph Ibn Naḥmias, *Perush al Sefer Mishlei* (Commentary to Proverbs), ed. M. L. Bamberger and Samuel Poznański (Berlin: Ḥevrat Mekitsei Nirdamim, 1911), 141–142.[18]

119

"These too are proverbs of Solomon" (Prov. 25:1)—Because he interrupted to include material by other sages, he says here, "These too are proverbs of Solomon."

"Which [the men of King Hezekiah of Judah] copied"—For the men of the Great Assembly compiled and arranged all of the Prophets and Writings, and they found this material by Solomon that had been copied by the men of King Hezekiah, who had rehabilitated the Torah after the death of Ahaz.

Rabbi Elijah of Vilnius, *Be'ur ha-Gera: Proverbs*, ed. Meir Yehoshua Katznelbogen, rev. ed. (Jerusalem: Mosad Harav Kook, 2012/2013), 288.

Redactional Censorship of the Wisdom of Solomon

120

"These too are proverbs of Solomon" (Prov. 25:1)—In the two previous sections, it does not say "too." . . . However, the words "These too are proverbs of Solomon," according to the ancient masters of the tradition, are added here because when Hezekiah's men were copying the proverbs of Solomon and arrived at this point, they found things that were not appropriate to write because they were so profound that they appeared to discourage fear of heaven. It therefore was appropriate to remove those things from here and to append the remainder of the proverbs that they were copying. By saying, "These too are proverbs of Solomon," it means to equate them to the prior ones copied by the men of King Hezekiah of Judah. The words "It is the glory of God to conceal a matter" (2) were juxtaposed to it for this reason: because the concealment of those things that they concealed was to the glory of God. Similarly given here is the proverb "The dross having been separated from the silver" (4), because all the Proverbs of Solomon are like refined silver, while those that they removed and did not copy were like the dross of silver.

Rabbi Joseph Kimḥi, commentary to Prov. 25:1–2.[19]

121

"These too are proverbs of Solomon, which the men of King Hezekiah of Judah copied" (Prov. 25:1)—For Solomon in his wisdom wrote many books, as it is said, "He discoursed about trees" (1 Kings 5:13), but they were not written in Scripture, and these things that the men of Hezekiah copied are written in those books. Seeing that they [i.e., those proverbs] were about fear of heaven, they copied them from there and wrote them here, while they hid away the other books, which were not about fear of heaven.

Rabbi Isaiah di Trani.

The Book of Proverbs: Inclusion of Authorities Other than Solomon

122

Agur, who lived during the time of Solomon, followed an upright path, was great in knowledge, and was esteemed by his contemporaries. King Solomon therefore collected his wise sayings in his book.

Rabbi Moses Kimḥi, Commentary on Prov. 30:1.

123

Agur son of Jakeh was the name of a great sage, who said these things to his students Ithiel and Ucal. Because they were said with divine inspiration, as reflected by the use of the word "pronouncement," they appended them to the work of Solomon, may he rest in peace.

Rabbi Joseph Ibn Naḥmias, *Perush al Sefer Mishlei,* 179 (30:1).

124

"The words of Agur son of Jakeh" (Prov. 30:1)—For the men of the Great Assembly arranged in each book all that had been composed with divine inspiration on its subject … and in the book of Proverbs, they similarly arranged all ethical proverbs that had been composed. This passage was authored by Agur son of Jakeh, these being his name and that of his father; this is the meaning of "The words."

"To Ithiel, to Ithiel and Ucal"—These were the names of two great men who sent to Agur to request that he teach them mysteries of wisdom of divine ways, and this was his response to them.

Rabbi Elijah of Vilnius, Be'ur ha-Gera: Proverbs, 328–329.[20]

125

"These also are by the sages" (Prov. 24:23)—The proverbs of Solomon end at this point. From here until the end of the chapter is a collection of remarks by other sages.

Rabbi Meir Leibush Wisser (Malbim).

The Origins of the Book of Job

126

"Eliphaz the Temanite" (Job 2:11)—Of the family of Teman son of Eliphaz son of Esau [see Gen. 36:11]. It is most probable that this was close to the time of Moses, because he would have been traced to Teman only after a number of generations, and our sages said that Moses wrote the book of Job.[21] It seems to me most probable that this is a translated book; this is why its meaning is difficult to determine, as with any translated book.[22]

"The Shuhite"—Of the children of Keturah wife of Abraham: "Ishbak, and Shuah" (Gen. 25:2).

"The Naamathite"—We do not know whether his surname refers to his country or to his family.

Ibn Ezra.[23]

Origins of the Song of Songs

127

"The Song of Songs, by Solomon" (Song of Sol. 1:1)—The scribe tells us that Solomon composed this song. This was not written by Solomon; the book begins with the words "Oh, give me of the kisses" (2). Similarly, "The words of Koheleth" (Eccles. 1:1) was written by a scribe, and "The proverbs of Solomon son of David" (Prov. 1:1) similarly was written by a scribe, with the meaning that the person telling the proverbs in this book is Solomon, while the beginning of the book is as appears afterward. The meaning of "Song of Songs" is that this is one of the many songs that Solomon composed, as it is said, "his songs numbered one thousand and five" (1 Kings 5:12). Why was this one, of all of them, written down? For this reason: because it had become beloved by all.[24]

"Oh, give me of the kisses of your mouth" (2)—According to the simple sense of the verse, Solomon had a certain wife he loved more than all his other wives, and she cherished him, and he composed this song about her: how much she loved him, and a certain incident that had taken place, as he tells below. The verses below corroborate the idea that he had one [wife] he loved more than all the others, as it is said below, "There are sixty queens, and eighty concubines, and damsels without number" (6:8), all of whom he married, but "Only one is my dove" (9), whom I love more than all the others.

Rabbi Joseph Kara.

128

"The Song of Songs" (Songs 1:1)—This means that there was a certain young woman who was not of royal or aristocratic descent, but a shepherdess, who fell passionately in love with King Solomon, and in her love for him and her passion, she composed many songs for him, and this song was the finest of them, or else her beloved Solomon composed it for her.

Rabbi Isaac Arama,[25] *Sefer Akedat Yitzhak al Hamishah Humshei Torah ve-al Hamesh Megillot* (*Sefer Akedat Yitzhak* on the Pentateuch and the Five Scrolls), ed. Joachim Joseph Pollack (Pressburg: V. Kittseer, 1849), 3:163b.

The Origins of Ecclesiastes

129

These two verses—"The words of Koheleth" and "Utter futility" (Eccles. 1:1–2) were authored not by Koheleth, but by the person who arranged the material in its current state.

Rashbam (Rabbi Samuel ben Meir).

130

"Utter futility" (Eccles. 12:8)—Now the book is finished. Those who had arranged it speak from here on, saying, "All the accustomed events of this world are utter futility," said Kohelet.

Rashbam (Rabbi Samuel ben Meir).[26]

The Origins of the Book of Chronicles

As described by the midrash, the book of Chronicles, and especially the complex genealogies it contains, poses pronounced challenges to biblical commentators: "When Rabbi Shimon ben Pazi would begin lecturing on Chronicles, he would say this: 'All of your words are bewildering—but we know how to expound them!'"[27] Three further, interconnected problems arise from the tendency of the book to reiterate information already provided by previous books: When Chronicles is in agreement with an earlier book, the exegete must justify the repetition. If Chronicles omits material that appears in another book, then a reason must be found for the omission.[28] Finally, when Chronicles contradicts a previous book, the exegete is required to reconcile the conflicting verses. In sum, such a commentator finds himself attempting to contend with a book that contains glaring difficulties but is not of any obvious use, and it therefore is not surprising that most of the traditional commentators declined to extend their efforts to Chronicles, while those few who did so voiced a surprising degree of skepticism.

Traditional Exegetes' Limited Treatment of Chronicles

131

This book contains very obscure things and information that contradicts the books of Samuel and Kings. Because the book is a historical narrative, it is not often taught, and I have not found that any of the commentators exerted himself to interpret it. I do not know who wrote those commentaries to the book that I have found here in Narbonne, and I have seen that they generally take a homiletical approach. A certain sage from Girona, one of the disciples of my father and master, asked me to interpret it, and I saw fit to do as he asked. I wrote not verse by verse, but only on verses that require explanation.

Rabbi David Kimḥi, Preface to the commentary on Chronicles.

132

Why did Ezra the Scribe repeat in the book of Chronicles what already was written here, in the book of Samuel? What purpose did he see in repeating these things? What is stated here [i.e., in Samuel] need not have been written there [i.e., in Chronicles] and if he saw fit to include there all of these matters even though they are stated here, then why did he include some and omit others?[29] ... All of these significant matters that appear in the book of Samuel are not mentioned by Ezra in the book of Chronicles, although he included there a verbatim account of other stories that do appear in Samuel, and in others altered a few words and names. The question then is, what purpose did Ezra the Scribe see in all of this and of what benefit was it to him? ... All this cannot have been done for no reason! These are the central conundrums raised by this profound question. In searching for an answer and solution, I am left all alone: there is no man entertaining these matters with me. I have found nothing—little or great, good or bad—relating to this inquiry that was written by our sages of blessed memory, neither the early ones, who authored the Talmud, nor the later ones, with their books and commentaries. Not a single one took any note of this conundrum, and not a single one of them proffered a way to solve it. Indeed, the Lord adds misery to my pain in that among us, in this land, there is no commentary to Chronicles other than scant remarks of Rabbi David Kimḥi, but those are idle things and he did not explore the matter in any depth. Further, that book, Chronicles, is not commonly used by the Jews in their homiletics. I must make mention today of my offenses: I never studied it and never delved into it at any time until now. I am left here with only the force of logic and the intellectual ability to analyze the simple, *peshat* sense of the verses, and the grace of the God who girds me with might. May He prosper my way.

Don Isaac Abravanel, Preface to the book of Samuel, in *Perush al Nevi'im Rishonim*, 163–164.[30]

Material in Chronicles That Postdates Ezra

133

"Ezra wrote his book[31] and the genealogy of Chronicles until himself"[32]—This corroborates Rav, since Rav Yehudah, citing Rav, said, "Ezra did not ascend from Babylonia until he had written his genealogy; then he ascended." And who finished it? Nehemiah son of Hacaliah.

Babylonian Talmud, tractate *Bava Batra* 15a.

134

How could Ezra have given the genealogy of generations that followed him? Were Zerubbabel and Ezra not contemporaries, and were there not ten generations from Zerubbabel to Anani? . . . Judah Ben Quraysh says that at the end of the Second Temple [Period], they determined their genealogy based on the memoirs of the kings. For they would make a record of genealogical matters and deeds, as it is said regarding Ahasuerus, "[he ordered] the book of records, the annals, to be brought" (Esther 6:1). I respond to them: certainly the sages were correct in saying, "Ezra wrote his book and the genealogy of Chronicles until himself." . . . From the beginning of the Torah to its end, prophets read and write what they have not seen and never have been told.

Perush al Divrei ha-Yamim Miyuḥas le-Eḥad mi-Talmidei Se'adyah Ha-Ga'on, A commentary to Chronicles attributed to a disciple of Se'adyah Ha-Ga'onъ, ed. Raphael Kirchheim (Frankfurt de Main: F. W. Breidenstein, 1874), 16 (to 1 Chron. 3:24).[33]

The Limits of the Knowledge of the Chronicler and His Dependence on Preexisting Documents

135

"The sons of Naphtali: Jahziel" (1 Chron. 7:13)—The reason for not tracing this genealogy further is as explained at the conclusion of Jerusalem Talmud tractate *Megillah*[34]: "Ezra found three books, each containing some of the genealogy.[35] What he found, he wrote, and what he did not find, he did not write, and he did not find any more about the Naphtalites." This is why this entire genealogy is jumbled and disordered: because he skipped from one book to another and combined them, and what he was not able to write in this book, he wrote in the book of Ezra. You know that this is true because after this section it says, "All Israel was registered by genealogies; and these are in the book of the kings of Israel. And Judah was taken into exile in Babylon" (1 Chron. 9:1). Meaning, if you wish to know the genealogy of the ten tribes, then go to Halah, Habor, the Gozan River, and the towns of Media [see 2 Kings 17:6], because their chronicle was exiled with them, but as for the Judeans, I found their book in Babylonia, and what I found, I have recorded.

Pseudo-Rashi.[36]

136

"The father of Gibeon dwelt in Gibeon" (1 Chron. 8:29)—This section, until "All these were the sons of Azel" (38), appears twice in this book, as do the sections "The first to settle in their towns, on their property" (9:2), and the section "Of the priests: Jedaiah, Jehoiarib" (10). The same is true of the book of Ezra, where it is written, "These are the heads of the province" (Neh. 11:3).[37] The explanation for this is found at the conclusion of Jerusalem Talmud tractate *Megillah*[38]: "Ezra found three books, the book of *Me'onim*, the book of *Za'atutei*, and the book of *Ha-Aḥim*, and they rejected what was in one and accepted what was in two." They similarly found many genealogies. When they found three or five, they rejected the minority and accepted the majority, but when there was an even number, as with "The father of Gibeon dwelt in Gibeon," he needed to write two versions, because the genealogies are not the same. He similarly found "The first to settle" (1 Chron. 9:2) in an even number of conflicting sources, so they wrote it twice: here, and in his book.

Pseudo-Rashi.

137

"Carmi, Hur, and Shobal" (1 Chron. 4:1)—Carmi is Caleb. That his name is altered here is no cause for surprise, for we find in the Jerusalem Talmud that Ezra found three books and did not know what to do—meaning, which [one's version] to write—so he would accept two and reject one. We similarly find in tractate *Megillah*, "'Against the leaders of the Israelites?' 'Against the young men of the Israelites?' It is because he found three books." Here too, he found that two books read Celubi and one read Carmi and did not know where to write it, so he wrote it here.

Pseudo-Kara.[39]

138

"All Israel was registered by genealogies. . . . The first to settle in their towns" (1 Chron. 9:1–3)—These two verses written in this book are the work of Ezra the Scribe. . . .

"All Israel was registered by genealogies; and these are in the book of the kings of Israel" (1)—This was written by the compiler so that you would not be surprised by the incomplete record of the tribes' genealogies, the omission of the genealogies of Zebulun and Dan, and the inclusion of Judah at greater length than the other tribes. For this reason, he said: "All Israel was registered by genealogies"—but I have less knowledge of the genealogies of the other tribes, because they were exiled earlier. They have their genealogies in the Annals of the Kings of Israel, and when Sennacherib and the kings of Assyria exiled them to Halah, the [River] Habor, the River Gozan, and the towns of Media [see 2 Kings 17:6; 18:11], they brought their books with them, so I do not have them. That you find some of their genealogies here is due to the fact that I found some of their genealogies, and I have written what I found.

"And Judah was taken into exile in Babylon because of their trespass" (2)—This provides some explanation for the fact that you find the genealogy of Judah given here at greater length than the other tribes. For the Children of Judah were taken into exile in Babylonia, and I, the compiler, was with them in exile and found some information regarding their genealogy in three books. However, they were not the same as each other, so where I was able to reconcile them, I wrote the information in this book, and where I was unable to do so, I wrote it in my book, in Ezra.

Pseudo-Kara.[40]

139

"A refutation"—Meaning, you can understand from this that they already had been exiled and confused in the time of Sennacherib. However, this seems problematic to me. Did Ezra not write the book of Chronicles, as is said in the first chapter of tractate *Bava Batra*?[41] He lived many generations after Sennacherib confused [the nations]. How could he have written "to this day" in his books? They did not live there during his lifetime! A possible answer is that Ezra copied Chronicles from a number of books that he found, as I wrote there. Therefore the genealogy is not given in order and there are many contradictions within it and between Chronicles and the book of Ezra, because he found one version in one book and another version in another book, and he copied according to what he found. One might alternately say that he found an ancient book that had been written before Sennacherib confused [the nations] in which it was written, "And some of the Simeonites went ... and they live there to this day," and he copied this as he found it written and did not want to change it.

Rabbi Aryeh Leib Gunzberg, *Gevurat Ari* commentary to Babylonian Talmud, tractate *Yoma* 54a.[42]

140

"The sons of Carmi" (1 Chron. 2:7)—Keep this rule in mind throughout this book: Ezra copied his book from the great genealogical work that contained the pedigree of every family, shoots and branches, from beginning to end. Ezra copied only what was needed and only certain people. There it was written, "The sons of Zimri," and then a list of all the sons of Zimri, of whom there were many including Carmi, and afterward were written all the sons of Carmi including Achan. Ezra, however, skipped what was unnecessary and copied only "The sons of Carmi," then skipped to Achan, and copied, "Achar, the troubler of Israel." He therefore wrote "sons," in the plural, as it was written in the genealogy, which referred to many sons. . . .

"The sons of Ethan"—All of the sons of Ethan, of whom there were many, appeared in the great genealogical work, followed by the genealogy of the other sons of Ethan. Ezra skipped all of them while including only the first son, Azariah, and skipping the others. But he wrote "sons" in the plural, as he wrote in the genealogy, as though it said, "The sons of Ethan were Azaria, etc.," or "and so forth," as you find in Ezra (4:17; 7:12), where he used the word *shelam* [here understood as "and so on"] or *gemir* [etc.]. For Ezra did not copy the entire genealogical work, but only a rubric and only what he required. For this reason, "the sons of" often appears regarding a single son, because in fact there were many that he did not mention here (as noted on the prior verse). Similarly with the verses, "The sons of Dan were Hushim" (Gen. 46:23) and "The sons of Pallu were Eliab" (Num. 26:8), they later had other sons, but only those required for the purpose at hand are included, because Hushim was among those who arrived in Egypt, and of [the sons of] Eliab he wanted to list Dathan. This is a universal rule.[43]

Rabbi Meir Leibush Wisser (Malbim).[44]

Discouragement of Overly Rigorous Analysis of Chronicles

141

However, let me tell you a rule: it is not right to scrutinize this book as closely as that written by our master Moses, which is from heaven. For this one consists only of summaries and selections by its author, who thus omits and alters as he likes. Do you not see that he jumbles the order of the tribes? He also notes the death of Er but not of Onan (1 Chron. 2:3) and abridges the incident of Tamar, in addition to the many other changes in this book. Each book ought to be scrutinized according to the virtues of its author. As this book clearly contains important matters as well, it was included in the Holy Scripture.

Rabbi Joseph Ibn Kaspi, commentary to 1 Chron. 1:5.

The Fallibility of the Author of Chronicles

142

Chronicles (1 Chron. 28:17) erroneously has "basins" instead of "bowls," and instead of "ladles," "bowls," while it lists the jars unchanged, and instead of "jugs" says "forks"; all of these were golden [utensils] for use with the table. Perhaps they were other vessels that David commanded be placed on the tables that Solomon would make, but the table in the Tent of Meeting was not so.

Ibn Ezra, long commentary to Exod. 25:29.

143

Indeed, the statements in Chronicles regarding Jehoshaphat's partnership with King Ahaziah of Israel, "He joined with him in constructing ships to go to Tarshish; the ships were constructed in Ezion-geber" (2 Chron. 20:36), and "The ships were wrecked and were unable to go to Tarshish" (37), are very problematic, because Scripture attests that Etzion Geber is on the shore of the Red Sea and Tarshish was on the Mediterranean Sea, that is, Tyre. . . . It then is impossible that they traveled there from Etzion Geber, because the Red Sea has no Mediterranean outlet. Perhaps Ezra found it written that Jehoshaphat constructed, and misunderstood this verse as indicating that these ships were to travel to Tarshish. However, this is incorrect. To the contrary, they were to travel to Ophir, while the words "Tarshish ships" refer to their type. If so, this is an error committed by Ezra the Scribe.

Don Isaac Abravanel, commentary to 1 Kings 10:22, in *Perush al Nevi'im Rishonim*, 543–544.

Endnotes

1. *Tehillim 'im Targum u-Perush ha-Ga'on Rabbenu Se'adyah ben Yosef Fayyumi* (Psalms with the Translation and Commentary of Rabbi Se'adyah ben Joseph Ga'on of Fayum), ed. Joseph Kafiḥ (Jerusalem: American Academy of Jewish Research, 1965/1966), 28 (first preface). In his second preface to Psalms (53), Rabbi Se'adyah ascribes this opinion to "the faithful transmitters of the tradition," i.e., the Rabbis, but it actually is an exceptional view rather than the rule. Concerning the approach taken by Rabbi Se'adyah in his commentary to Psalms, see Uriel Simon, *Four Approaches to the Book of Psalms*, trans. Lenn J. Schram (Albany: State University of New York Press, 1991), 1–57.
2. A less radical account is given in the Babylonian Talmud, tractate *Bava Batra* 14b–15a: "David wrote the book of Psalms together with ten elders: with Adam, with Melchizedek, with Abraham, with Moses, with Heman, with Jeduthun, with Asaf, and with the three sons of Korah." The role played by these elders is described by Rabbi Meir ben Todros Abulafia in

his *Yad Ramah* commentary to tractate *Bava Batra* 14b: "The tradition that 'David wrote the book of Psalms together with ten elders' means that these ten elders composed hymns that appear in the book of Psalms, one composing a single psalm and another writing more, and David compiled them and wrote them in the book of Psalms."

3. Babylonian Talmud, tractate *Bava Batra* 14b.
4. Ibn Ezra here alludes, on the one hand, to Rabbi Se'adyah Ga'on, in his commentary to Psalms (*Tehillim im Targum u-Perush*, 24, 28), and, on the other, to the eleventh-century Spanish biblical exegete and grammarian Rabbi Moses Ibn Chiquitilla. This latter allusion is indicated by Ibn Ezra's comments in the first inquiry of the preface to his second recension to Psalms. Concerning Ibn Chiquitilla and his approach to exegesis of the Psalms, see Simon, *Four Approaches*, 113–144. Simon concludes, "Ibn Giqatilah found a Babylonian background in psalms attributed to the sons of Koraḥ (42, 47, 84, 85, and 87); to Asaph (78, 79, and 81); to Ethan (89); and to anonymous poets (43, 102, 106, 119, 126, and 137), but not to any psalm attributed to David (composed by or about him). This also applies to the historical background later than David but antedating the destruction of the First Temple; this too he found only in psalms that are not by David—one by the sons of Koraḥ (46) and one by Asaph (76)" (136–137).
5. Babylonian Talmud, tractate *Pesaḥim* 117a.
6. See note 139 below.
7. Mondschein here (n. 33) comments, "The commentary on Psalms 106:3, above, explains: 'He composed this [psalm] during the Babylonian exile, as stated at the conclusion of the psalm: "and gather us from among the nations" (47), for even in the time of Cyrus, those coming to Jerusalem would come not together, in a single group, but one group followed by another, and they needed to beseech [God] to show mercy and let them all be ingathered there . . . .'" Compare, e.g., Ezra 1:5."
8. Rabbi Elijah ben Solomon of Vilnius (1720–1797), known as the Ga'on of Vilnius, is regarded as one of the greatest Jewish intellectuals since the close of the Middle Ages. He was famed for his unflagging devotion to study and his erudition in Torah knowledge both conventional and esoteric.
9. This remark, which is absent from the first edition of Rabbi Wisser's commentary (Warsaw, 1867/1868), apparently was added in response to criticism from conservative circles. This sequence of events is corroborated by his commentary to 1 Chron. 2:6–8, where it seems unlikely that the true objective is to engage in polemics with the nonreligious.
10. Rabbi Meir Leibush Wisser (1809–1879, known as Malbim) was a leading Torah scholar and one of the greatest traditional biblical commentators in recent times. He served as rabbi in various communities, but time and again was compelled to leave his pulpit after earning the ire of the *maskilim*, with whom he was in recurrent conflict, as well as once because of the Hasidim, who accused him of betraying enlightenment influences in his exegesis.
11. For a similar exegetic approach, see source 80 above.
12. Among the sources that take this position is *Shir ha-Shirim Rabbah*, ed. Saloman Buber (Vilnius: Romm, 1924/25), 1: "He wrote three books: Proverbs, Ecclesiastes, and the Song of Songs."
13. This verse appears to have made itself felt in the rabbinic attribution of not only Proverbs, but also the other works of Solomon and even the book of Isaiah, a prophet who was active in the time of Hezekiah, to "Hezekiah and his entourage." See, for instance, Babylonian Talmud, tractate *Bava Batra* 15a: "Hezekiah and his entourage wrote Isaiah, Proverbs, the Song of Songs, and Ecclesiastes."
14. Rabbi Moses Kimḥi (d. ca. 1190), a biblical exegete of Narbonne (in Provence), was the son and student of Rabbi Joseph Kimḥi and the elder brother and teacher of Rabbi David Kimḥi

(Radak). Among his works are commentaries to Proverbs, Job, Ezra, and Nehemiah and the linguistic compositions *Sefer Mahalakh Shevilei ha-Da'at* and *Sefer Sekhel Tov*.
15. For a similar explanation, see source 131 below.
16. Rabbi Levi ben Gershom (Gersonides, 1288–1344) of Provence was a philosopher, mathematician, astronomer, and eminent biblical exegete. For the little known of his life and a survey of his approach to various areas of knowledge, see Seymour Feldman, *Gersonides: Judaism within the Limits of Reason* (Oxford: Littman Library of Jewish Civilization, 2010).
17. See also Ibn Kaspi, primary commentary to Prov. 25:1, as well as similar remarks by Rabbi Menahem ha-Meiri, commentary to Prov. 25:1; Rabbi Moses Alsheikh, commentary to Prov. 25:1. Rabbi Joseph ben Abba Mari Ibn Kaspi (b. 1279, d. after 1340) was a biblical commentator, philosopher, and grammarian in the Provençal locale of L'Argentière (which was the source of his Hebrew surname, meaning, *of silver*). Lists prepared by Ibn Kaspi indicate that he authored nearly thirty works, but not all have been preserved.
18. Rabbi Joseph Ibn Naḥmias (Toledo, fourteenth century) was a disciple of Rabbi Asher ben Yehiel and an exegete of both the Hebrew Bible and the Oral Torah; for the little known of his life, see A. Neubauer, "Joseph ben Joseph (Jose) Naḥmias," *Jewish Quarterly Review* 5: 4 (1893): 709–713. See also, correcting Neubauer, Gad Freudenthal, "Le-Havḥanah bein Shenei Rabbi Yosef ben Yosef Naḥmias: Ha-Eḥad Mifaresh, ha-Sheni Itstagnin" [The distinction between two Rabbi Joseph b. Joseph Naḥmias: The Commentator and the Astrologer], *Qiryat Sefer* 62:3–4 (1987/1988–1988/1989): 917–919.
19. Rabbi Joseph Kimḥi (1105?–1170?), principally of Narbonne, in Provence, was a biblical exegete, grammarian, and poet, as well as the father and teacher of Rabbi Moses Kimḥi and the father of Rabbi David Kimḥi (Radak). Among his surviving works are his commentaries to the Torah, the Prophets, Proverbs, and Job, and two books, *Sefer ha-Zikkaron* and *Sefer ha-Galuy*, combining grammar and rabbinical exegesis. For similar interpretations, see Rabbi Joseph Ibn Naḥmias (fourteenth century), *Perush al Sefer Mishlei*, 141; Rabbi David ben Solomon Ibn Yaḥya (1440–1524), *Perush Sefer Mishlei ha-Nikra Kav ve-Naki* [Commentary to the book Proverbs entitled Kav ve-Naki] (Lisbon: Defus Eli'ezer Toledano, 1491–1492), 25:1 (pages unnumbered).
20. See also Rabbi Elijah of Vilnius, *Be'ur ha-Gera*, 283–284 (commentary to 24:23). A similar explanation is given by Rabbi Meir Leibush Wisser (Malbim), commentary to Prov. 30:1.
21. See Babylonian Talmud, tractate *Bava Batra* 14b.
22. Ibn Ezra's identification of many of the main characters in the book as non-Jews may be linked to his suggestion that the book of Job was written in a language other than Hebrew and only subsequently translated.
23. Samuel Davide Luzzatto appears initially to have favored a similar explanation but ultimately reversed himself; see Vargon, *S. D. Luzzatto: Moderate Criticism*, 329n40.
24. A similar explanation is given by the anonymous commentator to the Song of Songs in the fragment discovered by Eppenstein, "Fragment d'un commentaire anonyme du Cantique des Cantiques tire d'um MS de la Bibliotheque de l'Universite de Turin," *Revue des Études Juives* 53 (1907): 242–254:

> The Song of Songs. The unique song of all the songs of Solomon, for there were many, as it is written (1 Kings 5:12), "his songs numbered one thousand [standard editions add: "and"] five," and this is one of them. One might say that of those songs, these men of wisdom selected these songs and connected them in order to teach about the Holy One, blessed be He, and the community of Israel, and this is what it

means to say: the song created from the Songs of Solomon, for they took several of his songs and compiled this one, arranging it to tell about the Holy One, blessed be He, and the community of Israel, and they left the others, because this one, being the most sacred, was composed with divine inspiration and written among the Holy Scripture, for the men of wisdom arranged the works of Solomon, as it is written, "These are proverbs of Solomon, which the men of King Hezekiah of Judah copied" (Prov. 25:1). Further, from his proverbs—as it is written, 'Solomon composed two thousand proverbs' (1 Kings 5:12)—they arranged Proverbs and Ecclesiastes, which teach wisdom and reverence of Heaven.

25. Rabbi Isaac Arama (ca. 1420–ca. 1493) was a noted preacher of philosophical inclination who was active in Castile and Aragon during the time that immediately preceded the expulsion from Spain. His best-known work is *Akedat Yitzḥak*, a work on the Pentateuch with additional discourses on the Five Scrolls. This interpretation is perhaps cast in a softer light by Arama's remarks in his preface to the Song of Songs.

26. This translation reflects the insights of Sara Japhet and Robert B. Salters, eds. *The Commentary of Rabbi Samuel ben Meir, Rashbam, on Qoheleth* (Jerusalem: Magnes, 1985), 212. A similar explanation is given by Rashbam's brother Rabbi Jacob ben Meir of Ramerupt (known as Rabbenu Tam), *Sefer ha-Hakhra'ot*, § 69, in Gedalia Lasser, "Ḥibbur ha-Hakhra'ot shel Rabbenu Tam bein Menaḥem ben Saruk le-Dunash ben Labrat: Hahadarat ha-Ḥibbur u-Beḥinat Shitato shel Rabbenu Tam be-Perush ha-Mikra al Pi Ḥibbur Zeh" [Rabbeinu Tam's resolution treatise on the confrontation between Menahem ben Saruq and Dunash ben Labrat: Editing the composition and analyzing the exegetical method of Scripture of Rabbeinu Tam based upon this composition], PhD diss., Bar-Ilan University, 2011, 2:198–199 (see also Lasser's explanation, *Rabbeinu Tam's Resolution Treatise*, 1:100). Their older contemporary Rabbi Joseph Kara shared this view; see source 127 above. For similar explanations, see Rabbi Meir ben Abraham Shapiro of Kovno, *Megillat Kohelet im Perush Imrei Shefer* [The book of Ecclesiastes with the commentary Imrei Shefer] (Wilno: Bi-defus Y. L. Mats, 1903), 29a; Rabbi Reuben Margulies, *Ha-Mikra ve-hu-Masorah* [Scripture and tradition] (Jerusalem: Mosad Harav Kook, 1963/1964), 27; Rabbi Shlomo Aviner, *Yotzer Or: Berur Shorshei ha-Emunah* [Yotzer Or: An inquiry into the fundamentals of faith] (Beit El: Sifriyat Ḥava, 2005/2006), 331–332.

27. *Yalkut Shimoni* 2:1074 (for an alternate version, see Babylonian Talmud, tractate *Megillah* 13a). Still more cutting is the rabbinical dictum recorded in *Va-yikra Rabbah*, ed. Margaliot, 1:3: "Rabbi Simon, citing Rabbi Yehoshua ben Levi and Rabbi Ḥama father of Rabbi Hoshaya, citing Rabbi, said, 'The book of Chronicles was given only for homilies.'" This statement appears mainly to be a reaction to the genealogical lists in the book, but the wide variety of problems that Chronicles poses to those who would interpret it brings Rabbi Yaakov Korzvail to suggest that the principle be extended to the entire book: "There is nothing to be gained from contemplating the simple sense of the verses, because 'the book of Chronicles was given only for homilies.'" See his "Lo Nittan Sefer Divrei ha-Yamim Ella le-Hiddaresh" [The Chronicles were presented for no other reason than to be expounded], *Hama'yan* 52:2 [2011/2012]: 123.

28. The first two aspects of this difficulty are highlighted by Don Isaac Abravanel, preface to the book of Kings in *Perush al Nevi'im Rishonim*, 428: "The second conundrum regarding Ezra the Scribe is that he included in his book of Chronicles stories about the kings contained in

this book, and in some of these stories neither added nor detracted anything. Thus this part of his work was superfluous and futile, because he described what the prophet already had recorded in this book, with neither addition nor omission. However, in treating some other kings, he omitted many things written by the prophet here, and in treating still others, he added stories that do not appear in this book, and we do not know whether to believe what the prophet wrote in the stories of the kings and consider the additional things that Ezra wrote about them to be untrue, or to believe that the prophet failed to write what should have been written and Ezra completed it."

29. The inclusion of the words "and if he saw fit to include there" is according to Don Isaac Abravanel, *Perush ha-Nevi'im le-Rabbenu Yitzḥak Abravanel* [The commentary to the prophets], ed. Yehuda Shaviv (Jerusalem: Horev, 2009), 2:4.
30. See also Abravanel, Preface to the book of Joshua, 9; Preface to the book of Kings, 428–429 (note 156 above).
31. Many sages through the ages took the view that Haggai, Zechariah, and Malachi had assisted Ezra in the composition of Chronicles; for a survey, see Eran Viezel, "Haggai, Zechariah and Malachi and Their Role in the Composition of Chronicles: The Origin of an Exegetical Tradition," *Journal of Jewish Studies* 60:1 (2009): 5–17; Viezel, *Ha-Perush ha-Meyuḥas le-Rashi le-Sefer Divrei ha-Yamim* [The commentary on Chronicles attributed to Rashi] (Jerusalem: Magnes, 2010), 222–231.
32. On the meaning of the expression "until himself," see Eran Viezel, "*Ezra katav sifro veyaḥas shel divrey ha-yamim 'ad lo ... uman 'askeh? Neḥemiah ben-Ḥakalya*: On the Author of Chronicles in *Bava Batra* 15a," *Jewish Studies Quarterly* 16:3 (2009): 243–254.
33. The author of this commentary, who moved in circles close to the disciples of Rabbi Se'adyah Ga'on, lived in the late tenth or early eleventh century. He is believed to have been a native Arabic speaker, though the commentary appears to have been written in France or Germany. See further Eran Viezel, "Ha-Perush ha-Anonimi le-Sefer Divrei ha-Yamim ha-Meyuḥas le-Talmid shel Resag: Mekomo be-Toledot Parshanut ha-Peshat ha-Yehudit" [The anonymous commentary on the books of Chronicles attributed to a student of Se'adyah Ga'on: Its status in the history of the Jewish *peshat* exegesis], *Tarbiz* 76:3–4 (2006/2007): 425–434.
34. In standard contemporary editions, the quoted passage appears in tractate *Ta'anit* 4:2, 68a. Viezel (*Ha-Perush ha-Meyuḥas le-Rashi*, 27–28) suggests that Pseudo-Rashi simply confused the two tractates. Yoshi Fargeon alternatively suggests that the word *megilah* could refer to a "scroll" of the Jerusalem Talmud.
35. The author of this gloss appears to have referred to a somewhat different version of the homily excerpted in source 169 below; see Viezel, *Ha-Perush ha-Meyuḥas le-Rashi*, 27–28, 234–238.
36. Though many editions identify the author of this commentary as Rashi, it was written by a student of Rabbi Eleazar ben Meshullam of Speier and of Rabbi Joseph Kara. For a detailed inquiry into the identity of the exegete, see Viezel, *Ha-Perush ha-Meyuḥas le-Rashi*, 303–333.
37. Traditional sources refer to Nehemiah as a part of the book of Ezra.
38. On this erroneous reference (the passage actually appears in tractate *Ta'anit*), see note 162 above.
39. This is a central exegetic principle in the work of Pseudo-Kara; see also his commentary on 1 Chron. 6:8,44; 8:30,31; 9:4,7,8,9,11,12,13,14; 11:11,27; 13,9; 21:4; 24:20; 27:16. The identity of the author of this commentary, once thought to be the work of Rabbi Joseph Kara, is unknown, but it is almost certain that he was a disciple of the anonymous Pseudo-Rashi to Chronicles; see Viezel, *Ha-Perush ha-Meyuḥas le-Rashi*, 272–291. In preparing

excerpts from Pseudo-Kara, I was greatly aided by the work of the scholars participating in the Mikra'ot Gedolot Haketer project of Bar-Ilan University, who are in the process of refining the text of this commentary. Many thanks to them for providing me access to this unfinished material. Because their work on the text has not yet reached its conclusion, I have allowed myself to give an eclectic version of these comments based on available manuscripts.

40. See also Pseudo-Kara to the remainder of this verse, as well as his commentary to 1 Chron. 7:13.
41. Source 133 above.
42. Rabbi Aryeh Leib Gunzberg (1695–1785), best known for his work *Sha'agat Aryeh*, was among the leading rabbinic thinkers of the eighteenth century. He served as the rabbi of Wołożyn and later of Metz, in France.
43. Explaining unusual textual phenomena in Chronicles by reference to a presumed version in the writer's sources is not unacceptable in traditional exegesis. However, the fact that Rabbi Wisser includes two examples from the Torah, and then establishes that "this is a universal rule," can hint at the surprising possibility that, according to Rabbi Wisser, the writer of the Torah too had an earlier source from which he copied his text.
44. See also Rabbi Meir Leibush Wisser (Malbim), commentary to 1 Chron. 2:31,46–47; 4:11; 6:13.

Books of the Prophets and Writings Nearly Suppressed by the Sages

Many believe that the books of the Bible were regarded as sacred from the time of their composition and immediately joined the canon. Rabbinic sources, however, demonstrate that the process of canonization was arduous and complex, and concluded only after numerous generations of debate and vacillation. Among the books whose sanctity and suitability for the canon were debated by the sages are Ezekiel, Proverbs, Ecclesiastes, the Song of Songs, Esther, and possibly Ruth.

The Sages' Intent to Suppress the Book of Ezekiel

The book of Ezekiel presents two challenges. Not only is Ezekiel the only prophet other than Moses who gives a significant number of commandments, but a number of these instructions contravene or modify those of the Torah. Because of these contradictions, the Rabbis sought to suppress Ezekiel. Another source of their apprehension was the Vision of the Chariot contained in the book, which they were concerned might make mystical secrets accessible even to spiritually immature children.

144

Rabbi Yehudah said, "That man truly is well remembered, and his name was Hananiah ben Hezekiah. If not for him, the book of Ezekiel would have been suppressed, because its words contradicted words of the Torah. What did he do? They brought up three hundred bottles of oil for him, and he sat in his attic and expounded it."[1]

Our rabbis taught, "It happened that a certain child was reading the book of Ezekiel in his rabbi's house and had an understanding of *ḥashmal*, so fire came out of *ḥashmal* and incinerated him. Because of this, they wanted to suppress the book of Ezekiel. Hananiah ben Hezekiah said to them, 'If this one was wise, is everyone wise?'"

Babylonian Talmud, tractate *Ḥagigah* 13a.[2]

The Sages' Intent to Suppress Proverbs, Ecclesiastes, and the Song of Songs

The books attributed to King Solomon presented even greater difficulties for the sages. Those posed by the book of Proverbs were relatively minor: it has the appearance of a collection of mere mortal knowledge and contains internal contradictions.³ A more formidable challenge is the Song of Songs, which describes the romantic relationship between a man and a woman (whose conduct in this relationship does not necessarily ascribe to rabbinic standards of modesty), and contains not a single mention of God's name. Most troubling of these books is Ecclesiastes, whose numerous internal contradictions are accompanied by messages that worried the sages because they encourage (or tend toward) heretical beliefs.

145

All of the holy scriptures impurify the hands.[4] The Song of Songs and Ecclesiastes impurify the hands. Rabbi Yehudah says, "The Song of Songs impurifies hands; Ecclesiastes is a matter of debate." Rabbi Yosi says, "Ecclesiastes does not impurify the hands; the Song of Songs is a matter of debate." Rabbi Shimon says, "[The status of] Ecclesiastes is one of those matters where the School of Shammai was lenient and the School of Hillel was strict."[5] Rabbi Shimon ben Pazi said, "I have a tradition from seventy-two elders from the day they seated Rabbi Eleazar ben Azariah at [the head of] the yeshiva that the Song of Songs and Ecclesiastes impurify the hands." Rabbi Akiva said, "Perish the thought! No Israelite questioned whether the Song of Songs impurifies the hands, for the entire world cannot compare to the day the Song of Songs was given to Israel, because all the scriptures are sacred, but the Song of Songs is most sacred![6] If they debated the matter, then they debated only Ecclesiastes." Rabbi Yoḥanan ben Yehoshua son of the father-in-law of Rabbi Akiva said, "As Ben Azzai said. Such was the debate and such was the conclusion."

Mishnah, tractate *Yadayim* 3:5.

146

Rabbi Shimon ben Menasya says, "The Song of Songs impurifies the hands, because it was composed with divine inspiration. Ecclesiastes does not impurify the hands, because it belongs to the wisdom of Solomon."

Tosefta, tractate *Yadayim,* ed. Moses Samuel Zuckermandel (Jerusalem: Wahrman, 1974), 2:14.

147

"What real value is there for a man in all his toils beneath the sun?" (Eccles. 1:3)—Rabbi Benyamin bar Levi said, "The sages wished to suppress the book of Ecclesiastes, because they found in it things that encourage heretical beliefs. They said, 'Should Solomon have said, "What real value is there for a man in all his toils beneath the sun?" Perhaps this includes even the toil of the Torah?!' They later said, 'Had he said "in any toil" and nothing more, we would say that it included even the toil of the Torah. By saying, "in all his toils"—his toils do not avail him, but the toil of the Torah does avail him.'" Rabbi Shmuel ben Rabbi Yitzḥak said, "The sages wished to suppress the book of Ecclesiastes, because they found in it things that encourage heretical beliefs. They said, 'Should Solomon have said, "O youth, enjoy yourself while you are young! Let your heart lead you to enjoyment in the days of your youth. Follow the desires of your heart and the glances of your eyes" (11:9)?! Moses said, "so that you do not follow your heart and eyes" (Num. 15:39), and Solomon said, "Follow the desires of your heart and the glances of your eyes"?! The rein has been released? There is no law and there is no judge?!' But once he had said, 'but know well that God will call you to account for all such things' (Eccl. 11:9), they said, 'Solomon spoke well.'"

Pesikta de-Rav Kahana, ed. Dov Mandelbaum, 135 (8:1).

148

Rav Yehudah bar Rav Shmuel bar Sheilat, citing Rav, said, "The sages wished to suppress the book of Ecclesiastes, because it contradicted itself. And why did they not suppress it? Because it begins with words of Torah and ends with words of Torah. It begins with words of Torah, as it is written, 'What real value is there for a man in all his toils beneath the sun?' (Eccles. 1:3), and the members of the School of Rabbi Yannai say, 'It is "beneath the sun" that there is not, but before the sun, there is.' It ends with words of Torah, as it is written, 'The sum of the matter, when all is said and done: Revere God and observe His commandments! For this applies to all mankind' (12:13). . . . The sages wished to suppress the book of Proverbs as well, because it contradicted itself.[7] And why did they not suppress it? They said, 'Did we not consider the book of Ecclesiastes and find that there was reason to it? Let us consider this too.'"

Babylonian Talmud, tractate *Shabbat* 30b.[8]

149

"Be patient in justice"—In what way? This teaches that one should be unhurried in doing justice, because whoever is unhurried in doing justice has composure in doing justice, as it is stated, "These too are proverbs of Solomon, which the men of King Hezekiah of Judah copied" (Prov. 25:1)—not that they copied (*he'tiku*), but they were unhurried (*himtinu*). Abba Shaul says, "Not that they were unhurried, but that they interpreted. At first they would say, 'Proverbs, the Song of Songs, and Ecclesiastes are suppressed,' because they had said, 'They are aphorisms and not scripture,' and had proceeded to suppress them, until the men of the Great Assembly came and interpreted them."[9]

Masekhet Avot de-Rabbi Natan, version A, 1:4, in *Aboth de Rabbi Nathan, Edited from Manuscripts with an Introduction, Notes, and Appendices,* ed. Solomon Schechter, 2nd ed. (New York: Feldheim, 1945), 2.

Impediments to the Canonization of the Book of Esther

The book of Esther occupies a key place among the Writings. Not only is the holiday of Purim tightly linked to Esther, but the book is unique among the Prophets and Writings (as opposed to the Torah) in that there are specific halakhic requirements governing the way it is written. The book and its holiday ultimately merited an entire talmudic tractate, namely, *Megillah*, but the sources clearly attest that Esther's canonization was no smooth process. In considering the book, the sages were compelled to confront several questions: Was the authorship of the book divinely inspired? Is it permissible to commit the content of the book to writing? Does the document communicate ritual impurity to the hands of one who touches it? Doubts concerning the sanctity of the book of Esther persisted as late as the third generation of *amoraim*.

150

Rav Shmuel bar Yehudah said, "Esther sent to the sages, 'Establish me for all generations.' They sent to her, 'You are arousing jealousy of us among the nations.' She sent to them, 'I already appear in the chronicles of the kings of Media and Persia.' . . . Esther sent to the sages, 'Write me down for all generations.' They sent to her, '"Indeed, I wrote down for you a threefold lore" (Prov. 22:20)—threefold, but not fourfold,' until they found a verse for it written in the Torah: 'Inscribe this as a reminder in a document' (Exod. 17:14). 'Inscribe this'—what is written here and in Deuteronomy. 'As a reminder'— what is written in the Prophets. 'In a document'—what is written in the Scroll [of Esther]." . . .

Rav Yehudah, citing Shmuel, said, "Esther does not impurify the hands."[10] Is that to say that Shmuel believed that Esther was not composed with divine inspiration? Did Shmuel not say, "Esther was composed with divine inspiration"? It was composed to be recited; it was not composed to be written. . . . Rabbi Shimon says, "[The status of] Ecclesiastes is one of those matters where the School of Shammai was lenient and the School of Hillel was strict, but Ruth, the Song of Songs, and Esther impurify the hands."[11]

Babylonian Talmud, tractate *Megillah* 7a.

151

Rabbi Shmuel bar Naḥman, citing Rabbi Yonatan, [said], "Eighty-five elders, including more than thirty prophets, were perturbed by this. They said, 'It is written, "These are the commandments that the Lord gave Moses" (Lev. 27:34): these are the commandments that Moses instructed us to observe. Moses told us this: from this time on, no prophet will give you anything new—but Mordecai and Esther want to give us something new?' They did not move from there, debating the matter, until the Holy One, blessed be He, illuminated their eyes and they found it written in the Torah, the Prophets, and the Writings. It is as written: 'Then the Lord said to Moses, "Inscribe this as a reminder in a document"' (Exod. 17:14). 'This'—the Torah. . . . 'A reminder'—these are the Prophets. . . . 'In a document'—these are the Writings: "And Esther's ordinance validating these observances of Purim was recorded in a document" (Esther 9:32).

Jerusalem Talmud (Venice), tractate *Megillah* 1:5 (70d).

152

Levi bar Shmuel and Rav Huna bar Ḥiyya were fitting the wraps of the books at the study house of Rav Yehudah. When they reached the Scroll of Esther, they said, "This one [Esther] does not need a wrap."

Babylonian Talmud, tractate *Sanhedrin* 100a.[12]

Endnotes

1. Rashi, commenting on Ezekiel 45:22, writes, "but because of our sins, what he expounded has been lost." It may be that the homily in *Sifrei Devarim* 294 attributed to Eleazar ben Hananiah ben Hezekiah ben Garon is a surviving fragment of this tradition.
2. Compare Babylonian Talmud, tractate *Shabbat* 13b; tractate *Menaḥot* 45a.
3. There are clear parallels between the book of Proverbs and non-Jewish wisdom literature; see, e.g., Nili Shupak, "The Instruction of Amenemope and Proverbs 22:17–24:22 from the Perspective of Contemporary Research," in *Seeking Out the Wisdom of the Ancients*, ed. Ronald L. Troxel et al. (Winona Lake, IN: Eisenbrauns, 2005), 203–220.
4. The nature of the impurity communicated by biblical books is explained in the Babylonian Talmud, tractate *Shabbat* 14a: "And why did our rabbis decree that books would be a source of impurity? Rav Mesharsheya said, 'Because they used to put away *terumah* foodstuffs

[which were to be given to priests] with Torah scrolls, saying, 'This is holy and this is holy.' When they saw that they were becoming damaged, our rabbis decreed that they would be a source of impurity.'" Rashi (ad loc.) explains that "mice would be attracted by the food and damage the book."

5. See Mishnah, tractate *Eduyyot* 5:3.
6. See Saul Lieberman, "Mishnath Shir ha-Shirim," in Gershom G. Scholem, *Jewish Gnosticism, Merkabah Mysticism, and Talmudic Tradition* (New York: Jewish Theological Seminary of America, 1965), 118–126 (appendix D).
7. Compare *Va-yikra Rabbah*, ed. Margaliot, 28:1; *Kohelet Rabbah* 1:4, etc.
8. A number of authorities refer to this source to explain the practice of not reciting a blessing on the recitation of Ecclesiastes; see Samuel Löw, *Maḥatzit ha-Shekel* to *Oraḥ Ḥayyim*, 490.
9. Editor Solomon Schechter suggests that the proper reading is not "the men of the Great Assembly," but "the men of King Hezekiah of Judah."
10. See note 176 above.
11. This formulation may be evidence that the status of Ruth also was subject to debate. However, no extant source clearly attests to such a question.
12. Rabbi Samuel Eliezer ben Judah Edels (Maharsha, ca. 1555–1632), in his novellae on non-legal matter in the Talmud, comments, "It is possible that they were of the view of the one who said in the first chapter of *Megillah*, 'The Scroll of Esther does not impurify the hands and was not composed with divine inspiration so as to be written' [see source 145 above], so that it does require a wrap as the other holy scriptures do."

The Text of the Bible through the Ages

Modern Torah scrolls, and to a lesser extent other biblical books, are believed by many to contain the original text precisely as it was given; indeed, many view any challenge to this idea as incompatible with the fundamentals of traditional Judaism. Yet the countervailing assumption, unlike many matters of religious faith, can be subjected to some degree of empirical verification, because textual witnesses from various periods and places have survived to the present. The manuscripts and early editions do corroborate the belief that the books of the Bible were transmitted with remarkable consistency, but also betray the existence of variants in not a few of their finer details.[1] It is a matter of record that these discrepancies historically were known to traditional sages, and many of these figures—including individuals who undertook inquiries into the biblical text for both theoretical and practical halakhic purposes—describe a complex reality in which doubts persists, uncertainties remain, and the text of the Hebrew Bible may even contain errors of some consequence.[2]

Do Conflicting Orthography and Articulation Represent Unresolved Issues in the Scriptural Text?

As a rule, the *kerei*, or prescribed manner of reading words in Scripture, is in full agreement with the *ketiv*, the way they are written. Nevertheless, in a significant number of cases (the different counts range from 800 to 1,566), the two vary. The startling fact of two different versions coexisting in the same text attracted the attention of past sages, who offered a number of explanations. Of these, one of the most surprising is that the *kerei* and the *ketiv* reflect doubts that arose with regard to the text.

I shall also provide an interpretation for both the words that are written and pronounced differently, written but not read, or read but not written, when

I can give a reason for both, each in its place. These words seem to be given in this way because during the first exile, the books were lost and dispersed, and the sages who were knowledgeable in Scripture died, but the men of the Great Assembly restored the Torah to its previous state. When they found a discrepancy between books, then followed what they judged to be the majority view, and when they were unable to arrive at a conclusion, they wrote one version and left it unpointed, or wrote it in the margins and not in the main text, and so they wrote it one way in the main text and another way in the margin.

Rabbi David Kimḥi, Preface to his commentary on Joshua.[3]

154

The reason for the discrepancies between the books is as we began to explain: That in the era of the first exiles, the books were lost, the sages were displaced, and the experts on Scripture perished and expired. Then, when the men of the Great Assembly came and the Lord instilled in their hearts the courage to restore the Torah to its original form, they found that there were discrepancies between the books and followed the majority opinion. . . . When there was no majority to follow, they accepted the version that in their opinion seemed best. When their intellect did not suffice, they wrote the text one way and read it a different way, writing the version to be written in the main text and the version to be read in the margin. In some places in Scripture they added text that was to be read but not written, or written but not to be read, but these two are absent from the Torah of Moses. Later, differences of opinion emerged between grammarians, as you know regarding the debates of Ben Asher and Ben Naftali and those of the Westerners [i.e., Palestinians] and the Easterners [i.e., Babylonians]. There are those who say that they instituted differences between the written and the articulated text because they considered the text [in such instances] to be distasteful, but this does not seem correct, because the holy tongue contains no term for any base instrument or base action, as the master, the righteous teacher, wrote, and they said that the word *yishgalenah* (to have intercourse) is derived from *shegel* (young woman), as Maimonides wrote.[4]

Rabbi Menahem ha-Meiri, Preface to *Kiryat Sefer*.[5]

155

Decay and confusion already began to overtake them during those seventy years of the Babylonian captivity, as people despaired of them. Having taken note of this, the impeccable one, the head of the scribes, the priest and scribe

Ezra roused himself and made every effort to correct whatever had been corrupted, as did all the scribes who came after him; those scribes made corrections to the extent possible. . . . and where decay and confusion had overtaken them, they left [alternate text: "he rendered"] discrepant vocalized and written versions, because what he had found had left him in doubt. Indeed, this decay appears to have set in even in the time of the [First] Temple, because people studied them so little and were so mindless of them—it is written even of the Torah that the High Priest Hilkiah found it by chance.

Profiat Duran, *Sefer Ma'aseh Efod,* ed. Jonathan D. Friedland and Jakob Kohn (Vienna, 1864/1865), 40.[6]

156

Indeed, with regard to the second skill, namely, eloquence in poetry and excellence of language, I believe that Jeremiah was not especially adept in literary arrangement and poetic artistry, as were Isaiah the Prophet and other prophets. You therefore find in the work of Jeremiah many verses that all commentators agree omit one or more words, although I shall try to explain them as they are. You very, very often find in his work the word *al* used instead of *el*, masculine instead of feminine, feminine instead of masculine, plural instead of singular, singular instead of plural, past instead of future, future instead of past, and a single statement sometimes using the second person and sometimes the third person. You find in his work as well things belong earlier in a passage placed toward the end, and things that belong later placed toward the beginning. . . . Although such anomalies exist in [the works of] the other prophets as well, there is a great disparity in quantity: in [the works of] other prophets, you find this on occasion, but in the work of Jeremiah, such things tend to be far more common than is the case with other prophets. I believe that the reason for this is that Jeremiah was only a young man when he began prophesying, so that he was not yet fully versed in the ways of language, its arrangement, and poetic artistry, and this in fact is what he intended when he said, "I don't know how to speak, for I am still a boy" (Jer. 1:6). This is to say that while Isaiah was of royal descent and, having grown up in the court of the king, had sweet speech and comely locution, and the other prophets prophesied after becoming practiced in worldly affairs and activities and doing business with people, and so knew how to arrange their words, Jeremiah was one of the priests at Anathoth and prophecy came upon him while he was young, before he had accustomed himself to speaking and become proficient in its ways, and he was compelled to use his accustomed style of speech to express what the Lord commanded him.

Indeed, also with regard to proficiency in the third skill, namely, writing accurately and with precision, I believe that Jeremiah was not fully adept, for the reason I have described: he was young when he began prophesying and therefore did not obtain an appropriate education in grammar and writing. This is indicated by discrepancies between orthography and articulation, words that are written but not articulated, and words that are articulated but not written, which you find in his book more than those of the other prophets. To illustrate, you find that the book of Jeremiah is similar in length to the part of the Torah that begins with Genesis and continues to the beginning of *parashat* Bo'; the book of Jeremiah is also similar in length to the books of Joshua and Judges. If you check, you will find that the aforementioned part of the Torah contains twenty-one discrepancies between articulated and written text, whereas the book of Jeremiah, which is similar in length, contains eighty-one such instances. In the books of Joshua and Judges, you find forty-one such instances; the book of Jeremiah contains double as many.

To prove how very correct this argument is, I see fit to explain here the phenomenon of discrepancies between articulated and written text: why there are words that appear a certain way in the books of the Torah, the Prophets, and the Writings but are given differently in the margins, although a prophet or individual speaking with divine inspiration doubtless expressed himself in a single way, not two. . . . The truth of the matter in my view is that Ezra and the men of the Great Assembly found the books of the Torah in their perfect and pristine state, as they had been written, and before Ezra took it upon himself to add points, cantillation marks, and verse endings, he contemplated Scripture, and when he saw things that seemed strange to him based on the nature of the language and the intent of the story, he decided that this was due to one of two reasons. The writer might have intended by these strange things to refer to any of the secrets of the mysteries of the Torah, each according to the degree of his prophecy and the depth of his wisdom, and he [i.e., Ezra] therefore refrained from extending his hands to erase anything from the books of God . . . and thus left them written in the main text as they had been written, though in the margin he placed a vocalized version, an explanation of the strange written version, according to the nature of the language and the simple explanation for a given matter. All of the discrepancies that you find between articulated and written text in the Torah belong to this category . . . . When he subsequently pointed the text, similarly in order to explain it, he therefore set the points to the vocalized text, which reflects the truth of any given matter. Also possible, thought Ezra, is that the Holy Scripture contains letters and words that had been written strangely not because of any specific reason, but because the person who had expressed them had not done so as precisely as he should have, due to insufficient knowledge of Hebrew or because of insufficient knowledge of the particulars of properly ordered, correct writing. This would have been done by the prophet or individual speaking with divine inspiration, an error committed by the master. He therefore needed to explain the truth of the given words based on the story, and this is the sense of the vocalized version that he placed in the margin, because the holy scribe was afraid of doing any violence to the words spoken or written by individuals who had divine inspiration. He did this—added an explanation of the given word—of his own accord, and he placed it in the margin as an explanation that he had given of his own accord, and he doubtless received this tradition from the prophets and the sages of the preceding generation. When you study the book of Jeremiah and the nature of the discrepancies between vocalized and written text in it, you will find that most of them are of this category: Jeremiah wrote them this way by mistake and by accident, and Ezra came and provided explanations, which he wrote in the margin according to [proper] language and spelling. . . . When you look through all of the discrepancies between vocalized and written text in the book of Jeremiah, you will thus find that it serves to provide explanation, and was added because the language and writing were not precise, as I have described. . . . You can thus conclude that in the books where this is a common occurrence, it is because the speaker was lacking in the second skill, namely, knowledge of the ways of language, or the third, namely, knowledge of how to write with precision. . . . However, in the divine Torah, given entirely by the Almighty—even though it is nearly four times the length of the book of Jeremiah—there are only a few discrepancies between vocalized and written text—sixty-five—and all of them, based on context, were written as they were purposely and with great wisdom, not in the least by mistake or error (perish the thought).

Don Isaac Abravanel, Preface to the book of Jeremiah, in *Perush al Nevi'im Aḥaronim* [Commentary to the latter prophets] (Jerusalem: Torah ve-Da'at, 1948/1949), 298–300.

Endnotes

1. The *JPS Hebrew–English Tanakh* (Philadelphia: Jewish Publication Society, 1999), much as some other editions, contains two major departures: Joshua 21:35 is followed in the Hebrew text by two verses that do not exist in conventional modern Hebrew editions, and a note is

included after Nehemiah 7:67 stating that some texts here include an additional verse, which appears in parentheses in the English translation but is absent from the Hebrew.
2. Rabbi Mordechai Breuer, whose text has been adopted in many modern editions of the Tanakh, memorably remarked,

> The fact that there also were other versions of Scripture that were different from the version made sacred by masoretic transmission was known to the sages of Israel in all eras.... Therefore, if a person today sets out to prove that the biblical books of the Second Temple period, or those dated to after the destruction of the Temple, differed from each other in their letters or words, then he is making much of nothing. I would describe such a person with the words of Job: "Who does not know all these?" True, the sages of Israel in previous generations had no way to understand the extent of the problem. They may not have had any inkling of the number of textual variants or the extent of the difference between some versions. But this is not fundamentally important.... Another question is, does the technique of rendering decisions based on a majority bring us to the "correct" text of Scripture? And here, serious doubts do arise, because everyone knows what a disparity there can be between the view of the majority and the truth. It indeed is quite easy to solve the entire problem with the familiar tool of compartmentalizing: the correct reading of Scripture is the one put forward by the various scientific hypotheses, but this nonetheless is a halakhically invalid reading.... Ultimately, we would be conducting public readings of a halakhically impeccable book, but we would be wary of that book when we set out to study Torah: every page is full of errors ... but this still is only half the truth ... because the rational mind cannot make its peace with it, since this solution only perpetuates the split personality typical of all such solutions.... What should a God-fearing researcher who wishes to study Torah do in all those places where his scientific awareness alerts him to errors? ... How does one "learn" errors? ... And if there is an error and "learning" it is a source of religious merit, what meaning should it have to a person who studies it? ... We previously mentioned the *mishnah* that describes the transmission of the Torah from God up to the men of the Great Assembly. This *mishnah* ... expresses both aspects of the Torah, which is both the Torah of God and the Torah of man.... The partnership between the divine giver of the Torah and its recipients does not find expression on the practical plane alone ... rather we wholeheartedly believe that the view of the sages is nothing short of Torah.... Even if science could prove that the majority had made a mistaken determination here or there—which we have no reason to believe cannot happen—this would not do the slightest damage to the sanctity of this version. That "error," once adopted by the majority of the sages of Israel, itself becomes Torah, and it too must be studied. It is in all ways equivalent to true Torah, ... and we wholeheartedly believe that all of these things bear interpretation in the way of the Torah, through all those devices used to interpret the Torah.

See further Rabbi Mordechai Breuer, "Emunah u-Madda be-Nusaḥ ha-Mikra" [Faith and science in the text of scripture], *De'ot* 47 (1977/1978): 102–113. Professor Menachem Cohen, series editor of the *Mikraot Gedolot Haketer* published by Bar-Ilan University, advocated a similar approach in an article in the same issue of that journal: "Ha-Idea bi-Devar Kedushat ha-Nusaḥ le-Otiyyotav u-Bikkoret ha-Tekst" [The idea of the sanctity of the biblical text and the science of textual criticism], 83–101. Cohen, however, sees less value in the study of what he regards as errors. For a wide-ranging survey of rabbinical literature on this topic, see Rabbi Shlomo Zalman Havlin, *Masoret ha-Torah she-be-'al Peh: Yesodoteha, Ekronoteha ve-Hagdaroteha* [The tradition of the Oral Torah: Foundations, principles, and definitions] (Jerusalem: Orot College, 2011/2012), 251–282.
3. See also Kimḥi's commentary to 2 Sam. 15:21, 21:9; and 1 Kings 17:14.
4. The reference is to *The Guide of the Perplexed*, 3:8.
5. Rabbi Menahem ben Solomon ha-Meiri (1249–ca. 1315) was a leading talmudic commentator from Provençe, as well as the author of halakhic compositions, scriptural commentaries, liturgical poetry, and other works. For a similar explanation, see ha-Meiri, *Beit ha-Beḥirah* to Babylonian Talmud, tractate *Nedarim* 37b.
6. Profiat Duran (Rabbi Isaac ben Moses ha-Levi, ca. 1350–ca. 1415) was a Catalonian philosopher, grammarian, and poet, and an active party to Jewish–Christian polemics. Among his works are *Ma'aseh Efod*, a grammatical work, and *Perush Afodi* to Maimonides' *Guide of the Perplexed*.

Unresolved Textual Issues and the Existence of Multiple Versions

Much has been made of the stunning phenomenon that despite the millennia that have passed since the Torah was given, the vast distances between Diaspora communities, and the traumas that befell them, no more than nine letters separate the versions of the Torah maintained by different segments of the Jewish people—variants considered to result from the travails of exile. The success of the Jewish people in guarding the text of the Torah truly is an incomparable achievement. In reality, however, these nine letters were the crux of discrepancies between competing versions specifically in the age of the printing press, when the possibility of improved proofreading, the production of entire batches of identical copies, and, of course, efforts by leading scholars to correct printing errors became the order of the day. Nevertheless, prior to the invention of the printing press, the text was transmitted through manuscripts that substantially diverge from each other, particularly with regard to whether various words were spelled defectively or in plene.[1] Many sages through the ages were aware of the existence of divergent versions of the text and attempted to provide answers to the weighty questions that they raise. When multiple versions exist, how is the correct one to be identified? What should be done when a question concerning the biblical text goes unanswered? Is it admissible to utilize a non-standard version for the purpose of explaining the text?

157

Three books were found in the Temple courtyard: that of *me'onim*, that of *hi hi*, and one called the book of *za'atutim*. One contained the text, "The ancient God is a *ma'on* (refuge)," and two contained the text, "The ancient God is a *me'onah*" (Deut. 33:27). The sages rejected the one and accepted the two. One contained nine instances in which *hi* was spelled with a yod, and two contained eleven such instances. The sages rejected the one and accepted the two.[2] One contained the text, "He designated some *za'atutei* (young men among) the Israelites" and "Yet He did not raise His hand against *za'atutei* (the young men of) the Israelites," and two contained the text, "He designated some *na'arei* (young men among) the Israelites" (Exod. 24:5) and "Yet He did not raise His hand against *atzilei* (the leaders of) the Israelites" (11). The sages rejected the one and accepted the two.

Sifrei Devarim 356.[3]

158

Similarly: "Concealed acts concern the Lord our God; but with overt acts, it is *lanu* (for us) and *u-le-baneinu* (for our children) *ad olam* (forever) to apply all the provisions of this Torah" (Deut. 29:28)—the words *lanu* and *u-le-baneinu* and the ayin of *ad* are dotted. Why? Ezra said thus: If Elijah comes and asks me, "Why did you write this?" I can tell him, "I have dotted them," and if he tells me, "You have written appropriately," then I will remove the dots from them.[4]

Avot de-Rabbi Natan, version A, chap. 34.

159

This second version of the Ten Commandments is that of the second tablets, and all of the changes and additions in it are as God wrote on them, while the first [in Exod. 20] is the text of the broken tablets. Rabbi Se'adyah Ga'on said that they are two different communications [i.e., revelations]. This is his view as well regarding the psalms that recur with changed wording, and regarding differences between the Babylonian Masoretic authorities and those of the Land of Israel. . . . He says that this proves that this and other prophecies containing changes were communicated twice, and both versions were preserved as communicated. However, I believe that this change happened during copying. Without a doubt, some members of the nation copied it in the name of the prophet in certain words, and others in other words, and both transcriptions were preserved. In my view, this is also the reason for the differences of opinion between Ben Asher and Ben Naphtali: each of them found a text, each of them found a text that was in accordance with his view and declared it the authoritative one while disregarding the other, and the same goes for all of the differences of opinion between the Westerners [i.e., Palestinian masoretic authorities] and the Easterners [i.e., Babylonian masoretic authorities], as explained by the ancients [i.e., the Rabbis].

Rabbi Judah Ibn Balaam, Commentary on Deut. 5:6–21.[5]

160

There are those who interpret this as meaning "who makes peoples (*ammim*) subject to me," but in a precisely written book the text is amended to "my people (*ammi*)," and the masoretic comment regarding it is, "There are three [words] that one would presume should be 'peoples' (*ammim*) but are read as 'my people' (*ammi*)." The masoretic comment regarding the words "subject to me (*taḥtai*)" states: "Read as *taḥtav*" [standard contemporary texts have *taḥtai* as both the written and the spoken version].

Rashi, commentary to Psalms 144:2.

161

"They set out *vayyitztayyaru*" (Josh. 9:4)—[Meaning that] they disguised themselves as envoys sent by the people of their homeland, as described in this passage: "So our elders and all the inhabitants of our country instructed us as follows, 'Take along provisions for a trip, and go to them'" (11). There are books that say *vayyitztayyadu* (they took provisions), meaning that they made "all the bread they took as provision . . . dry and crumbly" (5), as though they had come from a distant land. These and those give evidence for their respective readings, but neither have succeeded in besting the others. Here, too, it is impossible for anyone but our God to ascertain which is correct, but based on context, I am inclined to favor the books that have the reading *vayyitzdayyadu*, because such a thing is indicated in several places: Why did they prepare such provisions? So that what they had to say would be believed, so the people would see their provisions and this would make clear that they were far from them. This is as it is written, "The men took [their word] because of their provisions (*tzeidam*)" (14). It further explains in the passage, "This bread of ours, which we took from our houses as provision (*hitztayyadnu*), was still hot when we set out to come to you; and see how dry" (12)—every statement refers back to the provisions (*tzeidah*).

Rabbi Joseph Kara.[6]

162

"Saul was . . . years old when he became king" (1 Sam 13:1)—He said: This indeed is truncated [i.e., Saul's age is omitted], just as is the statement, "He laid a fine on the land of 100 silver talents and gold talents" (2 Chron. 36:3), the meaning of which is "and 100 gold talents" or some other number. We already have given numerous examples of this in the first section.[7]

Rabbi Tanḥum of Jerusalem.[8]

163

Regarding your difficulty with the matter in tractate *Avodah Zarah* (29b), that Rabbi Yishmael said to Rabbi Akiva, "Brother, how do you read 'For your love (*dodekha* or *dodayikh*) is more delightful' (Songs 1:2)?" How is it possible that as great a sage as Rabbi Akiva stumbled in saying a verse that the children know, unless we say that their books were unpointed? . . . Response: Even if their books were pointed, whether Rabbi Akiva made a mistake in saying this verse does not pose a problem, because it is possible that there was a discrepancy regarding this word between their books, as there is today regarding many words between the Westerners [i.e., Tiberian masoretic authorities] and Easterners [i.e., Babylonian masoretic authorities], or between Ben Asher and Ben Naphtali.[9] Is it not correct that there were differences between books even to the point of divergent words, and the sages remained in doubt and had to follow the majority, as we learn in tractate *Soferim*: "Rabbi Shimon ben Lakish said, 'Three books were found in the Temple courtyard'"?[10]

Rabbi Isaac Perfet, responsum 284, in *Shut ha-Rivash* (Responsa by Rivash).[11]

164

If a person says that one word in the book now before us in the Ark was not given by the Lord, should he be called "one who denies the Torah" and "has spurned the word of the Lord"? Clearly every upstanding, virtuous person who is not one to think very deeply will have no doubt at all that indeed he is. Yet that very upstanding, virtuous person, if he thinks deeply about this question, will find that even the talmudic authorities themselves entertained doubts regarding a few words in the Torah, and they said that even Ezra the Scribe, the great scribe of the Torah, had doubts regarding them . . . regarding whether the words had been communicated by the Holy One, blessed be He, or had not. There are three words that are written in our contemporary Torah scroll only because of the principle that one is "to favor the majority," even though it is possible that Moses wrote *ma'on* and *za'atutei*, and in ten instances wrote *hi* with a yod.[12] If Ezra had had all thirteen Torah scrolls that Moses wrote and gave to the respective tribes . . . then perhaps the majority would have had *za'atutei*, *ma'on*, and ten instances where *hi* was spelled with a yod. Ezra then would have rejected the readings *me'ona* and *na'arei* and that *hi* should be spelled with a yod eleven times on their account due to the same rule, that one is "to favor the majority."

I know that a person so inclined could argue that those cases mentioned by the Rabbis were in doubt, but they settled the matter based on the majority, in accordance with the rule of the Torah that one is "to favor the majority," but there is no doubt regarding the remainder of the Torah and a person who entertains doubts regarding any word other than these is designated one who "has spurned the word of the Lord" and denies the Torah. In reality, though, this is no answer at all. Once we know that it was possible for the text to become subject to question and there were entire words that seem virtually superfluous because they are not in agreement with the rule, such as, "Speak to the Israelite people, saying: When any of you or of your posterity who are defiled by a corpse or are on a long (reḥokah) journey would offer a passover sacrifice to the Lord" (Num. 9:10). According to the law, [the same rule applies] even if one is merely at the threshold of the [Temple] courtyard or beyond, as a mishnah states in tractate *Pesḥahim* 93b: "What is a 'long journey'? . . . Rabbi Eliezer says, 'From the threshold of the courtyard and beyond.' Rabbi Yosi said to him, 'Therefore the heh (of the word *reḥokah*) is dotted [in Torah scrolls].'" Rashi explains, "'The heh is dotted'—in *reḥokah*, and any dot serves to detract, indicating 'remove the word from here' [i.e., read the verse without it for exegetical purposes]," following the tradition in *Avot de-Rabbi Natan*.[13] . . . in any event, in his view [i.e., that of Rabbi Yosi], the word *reḥokah* is entirely superfluous in a Torah scroll, and in the view given in *Avot de-Rabbi Natan*, it [i.e., whether it should be written] is in doubt, how then did Ezra and Rabbi Yosi the Galilean or ben Ḥalafta, or both, entertain doubts? They all are beloved, all outstanding, all individuals whose righteousness undergirds this world—and they entertained doubts regarding the Torah scroll they had before them, with halakhic implications?

Perish the thought that these fathers of the world erred—perish the thought—and became guilty of spurning the word of the Lord! . . . Since doubts and confusion can set in, even if we maintain our ancestors' faith that no doubt or confusion has set in regarding any other aspect of the Torah before us, we cannot consider a person who points out what he considers to be another jumbled or interpolated word to be a denier of the Torah, particularly because we know that even after Ezra and after the toil of the masoretic authorities, who counted the letters of the Torah, words of the Torah have been omitted, added, or changed due to scribal oversights. . . . Indeed, Ezra did not wish to rely at all on the books of the common people, which were full of errors and interpolations, and instead relied only on three authenticated books in the Ark, but even in them there were thirteen objects of doubt, ten of which he was not able to settle even by majority, apparently because the question pertained to all three of them, and so he was compelled to insert dots for Elijah, who would examine his work. If this is the case, even if we consider there to be no other questions, it is not right to consider as a heretic and a denier of the Torah a wholesome person who has apprehensions concerning another word or words, regarding which he feels a question set in even before Ezra or after his time, since there are places in the Talmuds that foster such thoughts.... Since the words of our sages themselves allow space for such doubts, it is clear that as long as the truth has not been ascertained, he is not punished for these doubts, and his questions are considered to be in fulfillment of the commandment to study Torah.[14] For not only religiously deficient individuals such as the biblical critics, but even righteous people living by their faith, great luminaries of Israel, such as the Tosafists, wrote that "our Talmud is in conflict with our books."[15] ...Would one open his mouth to defame these great People of Israel by saying that they had erred (perish the thought) and sinfully "spurned the word of the Lord"? Can a man rake embers into his bosom without being burned by the coals of these sages, pillars of the Torah?... It is not only questions of letters and words that these great *Rishonim* are known to have noted... but even regarding the Torah scroll itself, guarded like the apple of the eye, and the sacred names written in holiness, purity, and deliberate concentration to sanctify the name [of God], the *Rishonim* believed that there were textual variants.... Indeed, it cannot be doubted that an error can creep into the books because of a scribal error, because even the scribal family is of this world and they are liable to err as are all mortals. We know that there are debates between the Ben Naphtali family and the Ben Asher family and between the sages of the Talmud and the masoretic authorities regarding whether words should be spelled defectively or in plene, and in practice we follow the masoretic authorities in writing Torah scrolls.... Rabbi David Ibn Abi Zimra... cites a responsum by Rabbi Solomon Ibn Adret stating that where the sages derived a rule from the text, it is written according to the view of the sages of the Gemara. Yet we nevertheless write *karnot*, *totafot*, and *ba-sukkot* defectively, in accordance with the view of the masoretic authorities.... Is it then we or Ibn Adret whose Torah scrolls are defective?! The truth is that both our Torah scrolls and those of Ibn Adret are fit for use, due to the reason given by Ibn Adret himself... that whenever the text of the books is in doubt, we are to follow the majority of books... and when we follow the majority of books, our Torah scrolls are legally fit for use... and his [i.e., Ibn Adret's] Torah scroll nevertheless also was fit for use where he lived. Any rabbi of a place who has the authority to rule according to his discretion has the authority to rely on the view of Ibn Adret and designate it fit for use.... One way or another, not one of Ibn Adret, Nachmanides, Rashi, the Tosafists, the [author of] *Mar'eh Panim*, the [author of] *Mattenot Kehunnah*, Rabbi Akiva Eger, or our sages was guilty (perish the thought) of spurning the word of the Lord or saying that "no heavenly Torah exists." One who properly considers what they said about the words "he has spurned the word of the Lord" in the passage in tractate *Sanhedrin* 99a, and in Maimonides' comments in chapter 3 of the Laws of Repentance in the *Mishneh Torah* will understand that these things were not by any means intended to refer to a person who entertains doubts about whether a single word or even a single verse belongs to the true text of the Torah of Moses, even if he is mistaken.

Rabbi Chaim Hirschensohn, *Sefer Malki ba-Kodesh,* 2:450–475 (responsa 6:1–3).

Well-Known "Irregular" Variants

In the world of the Rabbis, two Torah scrolls were famed for the many irregularities they contained: the scroll of Rabbi Meir, and a scroll kept in the Synagogue of Severus in Rome, called thus in honor of the emperor of that name. Though most of the sources describe these variants without commenting on the challenge raised by their very existence, one text obliquely alludes to the problem in its hopeful concluding remark: "May the righteous teacher come soon in our lifetime and tell us."[16]

165

In the Torah of Rabbi Meir, they found written, "and found it very good, and found death was good."[17]

Bereshit Rabbah, ed. Theodor and Albeck, 67–74 (§ 9).

166

"The Lord God made garments of skins (*'or*) for Adam and his wife, and clothed them" (Gen. 3:21)—In the Torah of Rabbi Meir, they found written, "garments of light (*'or*)."

Bereshit Rabbah, ed. Theodor and Albeck, 196 (§ 20:21).

167

In the Torah of Rabbi Meir, they found written instead of "Dan's sons: Hushim" (Gen. 46:23), "Dan's son: Hushim."

Bereshit Rabbah, ed. Theodor and Albeck, 1171–1185 (§ 94).

168

"He has made (*vaysimeni*) me a father to Pharaoh" (Gen. 45:8)—Because I am like a creditor to him. . . . In the scroll of Rabbi Meir, it is written, "He has made me a creditor (*vayyasheni*) like a father," as it is said, "that he claims (*yasheh*) from his fellow" (Deut. 15:2).

Bereshit Rabbati, Based on the Work of Rabbi Moses the Preacher, **ed. Chanoch Albeck (Jerusalem:** Mosad Harav Kook, 1966/1967), 209 (45:8).

169

These are the verses written in the Torah scroll found in Rome, secreted and sequestered in the Synagogue of Severus, in which letters or words are altered:[18]

"God saw all that He had made, and found it very good (*me'od*)" (Gen. 1:31)—it said, "death (*mavet*) [was good]."

"Garments of skins [for Adam and his wife], and clothed them (*kotnot*)" (3:21)—it said, *kotnod*.

"Whether they have acted altogether according to its outcry that has reached Me (*tza'akatah*)" (18:21)—it said, "their outcry" (*tza'akatam*).

"I said: O Lord, God of my master Abraham [... and from my native land] (*u-me-eretz*)" (Gen. 24:7)—it said, *u-me-ara*.

"And he sold his birthright to Jacob (*bekhorato*)" (25:33)—it said, "his sale" (*mikhrato*).

"I am old now [and do not know on what day I shall die (*yom moti*)" (27:2)—it said, *yomamoti*.

"Ah, the smell of my son is like the smell of the fields (*sadeh*) [spelled with the letter sin]" (27)—it said, *sadeh* [with the letter samekh].

"Jeush" (*Ye'ush*) in the verse of "Oholibamah bore" (36:5)—it said, *Ye'ish*. Similarly, in the verse of "And these were the sons of [Esau's wife Oholibamah] ... Jeush (*Ye'ush*)" (14)—it said, *Ye'ish*.

"They made their way down to Egypt (*mitzrayma*)" (43:15)—it said, *mitzrayim*.

"Eliphaz, the son of [Esau's wife] Adah (*ben adah*)" (36:10)—it said, *ben'adah*.

"He has made me a father to Pharaoh (*le-far'oh*)" (45:8)—it said, *par'oh*.

"I buried her there (*sham*) [spelled with the final form of the letter mem]" (48:7)—it said, *sham* [spelled with the usual form]...."[19]

May the righteous teacher come soon in our lifetime and tell us. Appendix of textual variants, in MS Paris 31 (1404).[20]

Discrepancies between the Masoretic Text and Citations in rabbinical Sources

Since early post-talmudic times, sages have remarked on the not-infrequent quotation in rabbinic literature of verses that differ from the text in contemporary books,[21] a circumstance that raises the question of which variant ought to appear in new Torah scrolls (as well as other biblical volumes). A still more delicate problem pertains in those cases where the Rabbis based a halakhic rule on a version of the text that is at odds with current convention. Should the passages of the Talmud then be corrected to conform to current volumes? Should existing books be emended to reflect the talmudic reading? Or perhaps are we compelled to acknowledge the existence of both variants, and to refrain from rendering changes to either the homilies of the Rabbis or the masoretic text?

170

We are in need of an answer from our master [i.e., Rabbi Hai Ga'on] concerning verses found in the Talmud that do not exist in Scripture, so that they appear (perish the thought) to contradict each other. We write here the following two so that we might gain knowledge of an explanation of them:[22] First, in tractate *Berakhot*: "'Hug her to you and she will exalt you; she will cause you to sit *bi-negidim* (among nobles).' Read not *bi-negidim*, but *bein negidim*." However, we find only "if you embrace her."[23] We learn as well in tractate *Megillah*: "The wording is precise as well, as it is written, 'Asa strengthened'" However, nowhere have we found anything but "constructed"(2 Chron. 14:5). Let our master clearly explain to us the answers to these.

Response:
Know that the sages committed no error concerning the verse, for how greatly did they toil with [memorizing] their mishnaic pericopes, so that the teaching of one sage would not become confused with that of another, with each of them taking pains to recite according to the language used by his teacher—how much more so the Torah and Scripture! Rather, you must examine every question you have and determine its essential nature: whether it is an error by a copyist, or the conversational flow of unseasoned students who lacked expertise, or words not originally intended as a verse. The matters regarding which you have asked are straightforward. First, while Rabbi Shimon ben Shetaḥ was seated between the king and queen, the king asked him, "You see what honor we have given you?" and Shimon ben Shetaḥ responded, "You did not give it to me: the Torah gave it to me, as it is written, 'Hug her to you and she will exalt you; she will bring you honor if you embrace her.'" This is our reading of the entire verse—the entire verse appears thus in our texts as well—and afterward we read, "among nobles," meaning that this is an explanation of that. We do not have the reading, "Read not *bi-negidim*," but *bein negidim*. . . . As for your writing, "The wording is precise as well, as it is written, 'Asa strengthened,'" this

too is not our reading . . . but we have researched what you wrote and found that among the versions that have developed there is one that erroneously says, "But it is logical that Asa built them, since it is written, 'Asa strengthened fortified cities in Judah'?" However, this is not the text of the verse, as with many errors that reflect the casual conversation of the unseasoned, especially that of those students from the villages who were not well-versed in Scripture . . . but it is not so, for our rabbis are meticulous, while those who consider a tradition but do not continue to study it to the point of fluency recited the word as "constructed" from the beginning.

Rabbi Hai Ga'on, Responsum 78, in *Teshuvat Ha-Ge'onim: Ge'onim Kodmim*) Responsa by the *Ge'onim*: early *Ge'onim*).[24]

171

As for your question: Our rabbis taught, "The Torah is comprised of 8,888 verses.[25] The book of Psalms exceeds it by eight, Chronicles is exceeded by it by eight." According to what reckoning? We see they are not so! You rightly found this problematic. Certainly they are not so! The Torah is comprised of 5,884 verses, the book of Psalms of 2,524 verses, and Chronicles [in fact] of 1,970. In answer, we have thus heard from the early sages: they composed this oral tradition in tractate *Soferim* [?][26] regarding the Torah scroll they discovered in Jerusalem that was unusual in its writing and the number of verses it contained, and so with the book of Psalms, and so with the book of Chronicles. Now, however, the Torah is only thus, and Psalms only thus, and Chronicles only thus.

Rabbi Hai Ga'on, Responsum 3, in *Teshuvot ha-Ge'onim*.

172

"The last syllable of *ma'avirim* is spelled defectively"—Our Talmud conflicts with our books, in which the word *ma'avirim* is written in plene. We similarly find in the Jerusalem Talmud regarding Samson, "'He led Israel for forty years.' This teaches that the Philistines were as afraid of him twenty years after he died as they had been during his life." Yet all of our books say "twenty years" (Judg. 16:31).

Tosafot to Babylonian Talmud, tractate *Shabbat* 55b, s.v. *ma'avirim*.[27]

173

Question: Is a Torah scroll invalid if it contains defective or plene spellings that run contrary to the Masorah? I say that masoretic books are not better than the books of the Talmud, according to which *pilagshim* [concubines], *va-asimem* [and appointed them], *kelot* [finished], and *karnot* [horns of] are spelled defectively, while our books have *pilagshim* spelled with a yod, *va-asimem* with a yod, *kelot* with a vav, and *karnot* with a vav, contrary to what the sages said, and we do not concern ourselves with emending the scrolls based on the books of the Talmud, because this is what I learned from you. How could we concern ourselves with the masoretic books, new ones, which came but lately? I can provide evidence of this teaching from the first chapter of tractate *Kiddushin*, which says that in the time of Rav Yehudah and Rav Yoseph, they were not well-versed in whether to spell words defectively or in plene. And we how much the more so! As for those who based homilies on the words *pilagshim*, *va-asimem*, and *kallot*, we can say that this is how they found those words written in their books. We, however, need not concern ourselves with them, and we shall maintain our books as they are. Now, I am not bothered by verses on which aggadic homilies are based, as we have said, but I am concerned by the two defective appearances of *karnot*, because the school of Shammai and the school of Hillel agree regarding them, while they disagree only as to whether "the reading has primacy" or "the tradition [i.e., vocalization] has primacy," and both arrive at legal conclusions from defective or plene spelling. I was inclined to emend them, but I am afraid of doing so, and I shall wait until your word arrives and provides us instruction. . . .

Answer: It is my view that this is correct, that we do not make additions and deletions throughout the books based on the masoretic tradition or aggadic homilies, because they reflect the disagreements of sages from various places and countries who were well-versed in defective and plene spellings. . . . In any event, if anything appears in the Talmud as the crux of a law, such as the two defective appearances of the word *karnot*, . . . then we certainly should emend (the minority),[28] and in every matter, even whether words should be written defectively or in plene, we should thus emend the minority based on the majority, because the Torah explicitly says, "to favor the majority."

Rabbi Solomon Ibn Adret, responsum 232, in *Shut ha-Rashba ha-Meyuḥasot le-Ramban* (Responsa by Rabbi Solomon Ibn Adret Previously Attributed to Nachmanides).[29]

174

All things are established according to the principle that one is "to favor the majority." Therefore we do not introduce any new thing based on the Masorah if introducing such a new thing might cause [Torah scrolls] to be invalidated. Rather, we follow the books of the majority of scribes, who are worthy of our trust, and general practice. Know that it is so, for in the Gemara and the midrashic works they said that the word *kallot* (Num. 7:1), *pilagshim* (Gen. 25:6), and *va-asimem* (Deut. 1:13) are written defectively, but in the Torah scrolls in our possession, they all are written in plene; it has not happened that [anyone] emended them, and it cannot be that the Masorah is greater than the Gemara and Midrash. The sages grounded their comments about emending books on this law of the Torah: that one is "to favor the majority." They said in tractate *Soferim*, "Rabbi Shimon ben Lakish said, 'Three books were found in the Temple courtyard . . . and they accepted the two and rejected the one.'"[30] Therefore we do not depart from the path taken by the majority of books.

Rabbi Moses ben David Halawa, Responsum 144, in *Shut Maharam Ḥalawa* (Responsa by our teacher Rabbi Moses Halawa).[31]

175

As I previously apprised you, wherever the Gemara or the Midrash is in disagreement with the Masorah as to whether a word should be spelled defectively or in plene, we follow the Masorah—not only if there is an aggadic homily [based on the word] . . . but even where a law is derived from it. . . . Nachmanides was asked about this in no. 232 of his responsa . . . and he responded that for all purposes, even whether words should be written defectively or in plene, we should emend the books in the minority based on the majority, because the Torah explicitly says, "to favor the majority."[32]

Rabbi Jedediah Solomon Raphael Norzi, *Minḥat Shai on the Pentateuch*, ed. Zvi Betzer (Jerusalem: World Association of Jewish Studies, 2004/2005), 236–237, on Lev. 4:34.[33]

176

I have been asked by scribes who write Torah scrolls and authenticate copies of the Torah of our God concerning the case of a Torah scroll found to contain an additional letter or to lack a letter, such that when they open another Torah scroll, they find its text to be contrary to the first scroll. Thus the given word is spelled in plene in one scroll and defectively in another. What ought they do: ought they accept this one or that one?

Response: As we know from the tradition transmitted by the *Rishonim*, as we have heard with our ears and seen with our eyes, according to the Torah, one [i.e., a minority] is disregarded in the presence of two [i.e., a majority].... Thus if we find that the text in one book is in plene, with a yod, and in two books is defective, without a yod, we reject the single one based on the two and correct the single one, and so on and so forth.... This is straightforward throughout the Torah except those few instances, well-known to the scribes, regarding which there are unresolved disagreements among grammarians, where the law has not been settled to reflect either view. Whichever course one takes is acceptable: if we find that one Torah scroll contains an aleph and another contains a heh, we do not reject one on account of the other, but they are to be left as they were found and no hand must be put to them. Such a matter is much the same as the disagreement between Rashi and Rabbenu Tam, and this is self-evident.

Rabbi Samuel Vital, responsum 27, in *Responsa Be'er Mayim Ḥayyim,* ed. Ephraim Fishel Hershkowitz (Tel Aviv and Benei Berak: Defus Eshel [Shalom Freidman], 1965/1966), 64–65.[34]

Writing a Torah Scroll with Available Knowledge of Matres Lectionis

A Torah scroll containing an error, even a defective or plene spelling, is halakhically unfit for use. However, as early as talmudic times, the Rabbis acknowledged that they were not sufficiently aware which words were to include, and which to omit, such letters. In practice, some manuscripts conflict with each other in this regards in hundreds of cases, leaving halakhic sages to wrestle with a number of formidable questions, such as: How it is possible to write a Torah scroll if we are unsure of the correct text? And, even, must all Torah scrolls in use in fact be regarded as defective?[35]

177

The ancients were called *soferim* [meaning, "counters" and "scribes"] because they would count all of the letters in the Torah, saying that the vav of *gaḥon* ("belly," Lev. 11:42) marks the midpoint of the Torah by letters; *darosh darash* ("inquired," 10:16) marks the midpoint by words; and *vehitgallaḥ* ("shall shave himself," 13:33) by verses.... Rav Yoseph asked, "Is the vav of *gaḥon* in the first half or the second half?: He said to him, "Let us bring a Torah and I'll count them." Did Rabbah bar Bar Ḥannah not say, "They did not move from there until they brought a Torah and they counted them"? He said to him, "They are well-versed in defective and plene spellings, but we are not." Rav Yoseph asked, "Is *vehitgallaḥ* in the first half or the second half?" Abbaye said to him,

"Let them at least count the verses!" "We are not well-versed in the verses either: when Rav Aḥa bar Ada came, he said, 'In the West [i.e., the Land of Israel], they divide this verse into three: "And the Lord said to Moses, 'I will come to you in a thick cloud [in order that the people may hear when I speak with you and so trust you ever after.' Then Moses reported the people's words to the Lord]" (Exod. 19:9). Our rabbis taught, "The Torah is comprised of 5,888 verses. Psalms exceeds it by eight, Chronicles is exceeded by it by eight."

Babylonian Talmud, tractate *Kiddushin* 30a.[36]

178

Now give your attention to the precise renderings of the scribes and the forms of the letters. Because we are not entirely well-versed in syntax, as Rav Yoseph says at the conclusion of the first chapter of tractate *Kiddushin*, "They are well-versed in defective and plene spellings, but we are not," and "it is a time to act for the Lord." Thus ours [i.e., our Torah scrolls] also are fit for use.

Rabbi Jacob ben Meir of Ramerupt (Rabbenu Tam), "Hilkhot Sefer Torah ve-Signon Sefer Torah Me'ulleh" (Laws of Torah scrolls and superior technique for Torah scrolls), in *Maḥzor Vitry,* § 517.

179

"They are well-versed in defective and plene spellings, but we are not"[37]—and all the more so because in our iniquities we have seen the fulfillment of the verse, "Truly, I shall further baffle that people with bafflement upon bafflement; and the wisdom of its wise shall fail, and the prudence of its prudent shall vanish" (Isa. 29:14). We might seek to rely on the authenticated books that we have, but they too diverge in many cases, and if not for the masoretic traditions created as a bulwark for the Torah, one would be virtually unable to make heads or tails of the discrepancies. Even the masoretic traditions are themselves not free of these discrepancies. On the contrary, there are discrepancies between them in quite a few places, although not as many as with the discrepancies between the books of the Torah. If one were to resolve to write a Torah scroll as the law requires, it would contain omissions and superfluities. One would be groping about like a blind man in the dark of the discrepancies, and neither succeed in one's intention nor fulfill one's wish; even if a sage should desire to resolve them, he would not be able to do so. When I, Meir the Levite son of Rabbi Todros the Levite of Spain, saw what a fate had befallen all the books and traditions with regard to defective and plene spellings—for time had breached their fence and occluded their source—I hastened to the vanguard to examine and inquire into the authenticated, carefully written books and the syntactical traditions and to comprehend their discrepancies, to forsake new books that only lately came, and to follow the old, dependable ones and the majority of them. For, in any case of conflict, we are commanded in the Torah to follow the majority, as it is said, "to favor the majority." Perhaps I can restore the fence of the Torah with regard to defective and plene spellings so that one will be able to write a Torah scroll as the law requires, following the majority.

Rabbi Meir Abulafia (Ramah), preface to *Sefer Masoret Seyag la-Torah* (Berlin, 1760/1761), 3a.[38]

180

The fact that we find corrections made by scribes on which we rely in writing Torah scrolls—those are only based on what they found in books that are presumed precise, not because the matter is so clear. Therefore I am inclined to act leniently in this regard and not to designate a Torah scroll defective for such a reason, because this was said only with regard to matters in which we have expertise. Even masoretic books should not be entirely trusted, and neither should midrashic traditions—indeed, we find discrepancies between midrashic traditions and the books of the Masorah . . . except that the Ge'onim agreed regarding this: because it is found in the Talmud as the basis of a [halakhic] rule . . . we rely on the Talmud in those cases. However, those that are found in aggadic contexts and are not the basis of any rule . . . should not be used to render decisions and are not grounds for designating anything defective. You thus learn that, because we lack expertise, if any word is spelled defectively or in plene, but no letter is clearly missing or added, it is not appropriate to be so particular as to designate the Torah scroll defective—even if the Masorah, the reference books, or even the midrashic traditions attest to the case, because they are known to contradict each other. I am of the same view regarding *parshiyot* that begin on new lines and those that do not, in any case where we lack expertise and we have found there to be a difference of opinion.

Rabbi Menahem ha-Me'iri, *Beit ha-Beḥirah* to Babylonian Talmud, tractate *Kiddushin* 30a.[39]

181

"If an error is found in a Torah scroll during reading, another Torah scroll is taken out"—Another is taken out only if an unambiguous error is found.

However, another should not be taken out because of defective or plene spelling, because our Torah scrolls are not so precisely written that we can say the other is any better.

Rabbi Moses Isserles (Rema), gloss to *Shulḥan Arukh, Oraḥ Ḥayyim*, 143:4.[40]

182

Question: Let our master teach us regarding Maimonides' statement at the beginning of the tenth chapter of the Laws of Torah Scrolls in the *Mishneh Torah* that if any of twenty things applies to a Torah scroll, then it does not have the sanctity of a Torah scroll and may not be read in public. One of the twenty things that he lists is an omission by the scribe of even one letter or inclusion of even one additional letter. This seems problematic, because today we do not have any proper Torah scroll meeting all the requirements that is just as it was given at Sinai. Even the sages of the Talmud in their time did not have a single proper Torah scroll, as is stated in the first chapter of tractate *Kiddushin*.[41] ... Now, if the sages of the Talmud who came before us, when some trace of the ancients still remained, were not well-versed in defective and plene spellings, what can we say at this late date, when we have been displaced time and again and intellects are not what they once were? If this is correct, then Maimonides at least should have said that this is the law according to the Torah, but in the present we do not have any Torah scroll that meets all requirements, is precise in defective and plene spellings, and that can be considered admissible, because this is simply impossible.

Response: We find in tractate *Soferim*, "He found three books in the Temple courtyard."[42] They acted according to the law in disregarding one in favor of the other two, because, according to the Torah, one is to follow the majority in all matters, even though it might be found that we have not acted in accordance with the truth. ... The words of Maimonides are thus correct: because it is possible to inquire and ascertain the origin of each book—to be sure that it was not copied from another—we can settle conflicts between them according to the majority. We consider a book whose text is carefully rendered in this way as if it were as given at Sinai, and any text containing a defective or plene spelling that runs contrary to it is absolutely inadmissible according to the Torah and entirely lacks the sanctity of a Torah scroll. ... Now, based on the preceding, it is possible to gain a more precise understanding of Rabbi Jacob de Castro's comments in his glosses to section 143 of *Shulḥan Arukh, Oraḥ Ḥayyim* concerning the rule that if an error is found in a Torah scroll, then the reading begun in the scroll containing an error is completed in one that is admissible . . . "because of the questions that crept into the traditions over the course of the exile. . . . Who knows which is as it was given at Sinai, without a single letter added or missing? Therefore, after the fact, when they already have read, they should not recite the blessing a second time, as previously stated." To put a fine point on the preceding, given his view that we have no Torah scroll that meets all the requirements, we should deal leniently even a priori with any error, whether it relates to defective or plene spelling, words, or verses; it is impossible to do otherwise. Why then should we distinguish between one defect and another, more and less numerous, after the fact and a priori, since even without this error the scroll is inadmissible? Its very deficiency is the cause of its rehabilitation! As we have written elsewhere, there is no good reason in such a case to distinguish between what already has been read and what is yet to be read. Rather, logic dictates that in the case of an active deed [as opposed to passive omission], one should not act contrarily to the view given by Maimonides in his work, as his rationale is cogent. However, one should not be so strict about what already has been read, because then no active deed is required. Furthermore, there is an authority who is of the view that no Torah scroll should be disqualified for use in public reading due to an error. The preceding suggests that in general, the scribes who preceded us, who pored over the traditions . . . followed the majority of books that were fit to be followed in majority . . . one therefore should neither add to nor detract from the emendations that have been rendered to our books, which were rendered by those who preceded us: we consider it as if this were our tradition from Sinai. If any conflict is found now with the convention instituted by the scribes who preceded us, even differences of defective or plene spelling involving a single, small letter, then we avoid using such a scroll for public readings, and consider it as nothing more than a text of the Torah not meant for ritual use.

Rabbi Abraham ben Mordecai, *Responsa Ginat Veradim* to *Oraḥ Ḥayyim* 2:6.[43]

183

In any event, I can argue for an exemption from another commandment—the commandment to write a Torah scroll—in our day, because, even in the time of the *amoraim*, they were not well-versed in which words to write defectively and which words to write in plene. Thus Rav Yoseph said to Abbaye in the first chapter of Babylonian Talmud tractate *Kiddushin* 30a: "They are well-versed in defective and plene spellings, but we are not." Yet a Torah scroll that is missing even one letter or has even one extra letter is defective! We therefore cannot fulfill this commandment. . . . In any event, it is clear that there is a rabbinic requirement to write a Torah scroll in our day for a different reason: otherwise the Torah would be forgotten by Israel . . . and because it is in any case obligatory to write the five books of the Torah, it is fitting to write them entirely in accordance with the laws that govern the sanctity of a Torah scroll.

Rabbi Aryeh Leib Gunzberg, *Responsa Sha'agat Aryeh,* responsum 36.

Endnotes

1. In his preface to *Mikra'ot Gedolot Haketer (Joshua and Judges,* Jerusalem, 1992, *4–*5) series editor Menachem Cohen characterizes the scant affinity between medieval Hebrew manuscripts and the directives of the Masorah thus:

   > On inspection of some one hundred complete medieval manuscripts of the Tanakh written in the principal centers of transmission over the course of approximately five hundred years, it became clear from the degree to which the letters in these versions conformed to the directives of the Masorah that, although a sizable majority of these manuscripts are adorned with the notes of the Masorah Parva and Masorah Magna, only fifteen to one hundred can be placed in the category of the "masoretic text." . . . A sizable majority of the manuscripts belongs to two different groups. Those in the larger group (roughly 50% of the manuscripts) are far removed from the masoretic text, with over 75% inconsistency between their text and masoretic notes, while the second group (about 35% of the manuscripts) is consistent with the Masorah in 25% to 75% of cases. . . . The precise text of no complete manuscript of the Tanakh from Ashkenaz that has been discovered to date may be defined as masoretic.

   However, notes Cohen, this description is not exhaustive:

   > A distinction must be drawn in this respect between the text of the Torah and the other parts of Scripture. It arises from a survey of the data that there is a far greater convergence with the masoretic text in the text of the Torah . . . and the above numbers do not accurately reflect this aspect of the textual reality. Still, even with regard to the text of the Torah, the leading sages of Ashkenaz were aware that the text in their region was far from reflecting that of the Masorah (*92n7).

2. In the Torah, the word *hi* (she) generally is spelled heh–vav–aleph, with the vav left unvocalized, while in a minority of cases (either nine or eleven), it is spelled with a yod instead of a vav.
3. This tradition appears in several other sources in various versions; see, e.g., *Avot de-Rabbi Natan,* version B, chap. 46 (65 in the Schechter edition); Jerusalem Talmud, tractate *Ta'anit* 4:2 (68a); Mishnah tractate *Soferim* 6:4. Concerning the relationship between the discrepant versions, see Havlin, *Masoret ha-Torah,* 256–258; Kasher, *Torah Shelemah,* 29:102–103.
4. The parallel in chap. 37 of version B of *Avot de-Rabbi Natan* suggests that such uncertainty exists wherever a word is dotted in the Bible, as indicated as well in *Ohlah ve Okhlah,* list 96

(96): "Ezra dotted ten [words] in the Torah, four in the Prophets, and one in the Writings." Hezekiah ben Manoah, *Ḥazzekuni*, similarly comments on Gen. 16:5, "Ezra the Scribe harbored doubts concerning all of the dotted words in the Torah." See also Lieberman, *Yevanit vi-Yevanut be Eretz Yisrael*, 43–46; Kasher, *Torah Shelemah*, 29:133–136.

5. Rabbi Judah ben Samuel Ibn Balaam of Spain was a scriptural exegete, grammarian, and halakhist of the latter half of the eleventh century. His commentary to Numbers and Deuteronomy appeared in Maravi Perez, "Perush li-Bemidbar u-Devarim (min Kitab al-Targhib) li-Yehudah ben Shemu'el Ibn Bil'am im Tirgum Ivri, Mavo ve-He'arot" [Commentary on Numbers and Deuteronomy (from "Kitab Al-Targhib") by Jehuda b. Shmuel Ibn Balaam with Hebrew translation, introduction and notes], master's thesis, Bar-Ilan University, 1970. For a survey of Ibn Balaam's approach to contradictions in Scripture, including the present excerpt, see Maravi Perez, "Darkhei Yishuv Setirot ve-I-hatamot ba-Mikra be-Perushei Rabbi Yehudah Ibn Bilam" [Methods of resolving scriptural contradictions and incompatibilities in the glosses of Rabbi Judah Ibn Balaam], *Millet: Meḥkarim be-Toledot Yisra'el u-be-Tarbuto* [Milet: Everyman's university studies in Jewish history and culture] 2 (1983/1984): 253–274. The text of the excerpt given here is based on the revised translation in "Methods."
6. See also Kara, commentary to Jer. 25:13; Rabbi Joseph Ibn Kaspi, commentary to Prov. 1:3.
7. That is, in Rabbi Tanḥum's book *Al-Kulliyyat*, the general introduction to his biblical commentary.
8. Rabbi Tanḥum ben Joseph of Jerusalem (d. 1291) was a biblical exegete and lexicographer. His two best-known works are *Kitab al-Ijaz wal-Bayan* [The book of simplification and elucidation], or simply *Kitab al-Bayan* [The book of elucidation], a collection of his glosses to the Tanakh, and *Al-Murshid al-Kafi* [The sufficient guide], a companion glossary to Maimonides' code. This translation is from the work of Dr. Shalom Sadik, whose Hebrew translation is of the Arabic transcription in Theodor Haarbruecker, *Commentarium Arabicum ad Librorum Samuelis et Regum: Locos Graviores e Codice Unico Oxoniensi (Pocok. 314) Secundum Schnurreri Apographum* (Lipsiae: F. C. G. Vogel, 1884). Whether Rabbi Tanḥum here intends textual corruption or some other phenomenon is unclear. Among the scholars who have adopted his explanation is Yehuda Kiel, *Da'at Mikra: Sefer Shemu'el* [Da'at Mikra: The book of Samuel] (Jerusalem: Mosad Harav Kook, 1981), 1:113: "Most compelling is the explanation by Rabbi Tanḥum of Jerusalem that the number of years came to be omitted, so that the sense of the verse is, 'Saul was . . . years old when he became king.'" A similar interpretation is that of Isaac Reggio, *Iggerot Yashar el Eḥad mi-Meyuda'av* [Letters of Isaac Reggio to a friend] (Vienna: Defus Anton Dleyr von Schmidt, 1834), 1:34: "And I in my innocence do not understand what damage or misfortune or heresy will result if we say that one of the ancient copyists omitted one word . . . and that perhaps the ancient version read 'twenty years old' or 'thirty years old,' because such an error, of omitting one word, easily happens to any copyist."
9. Rabbi Aaron ben Moses Ben Asher and Rabbi Moses ben David Ben Naphtali, both tenth-century scions of families of masoretic scholars and prominent sages in their own right who lived in Tiberias, disagreed regarding various masoretic questions.
10. See source 174 above.
11. Rabbi Isaac ben Sheshet Perfet (Rivash, 1326–1408) was one of the greatest halakhic authorities of Spanish Jewry. He served as the rabbi of several Spanish communities prior to his migration to Algiers, where he served as rabbi and as chief justice of the local rabbinical court. See further Rabbi Abraham M. Hershman, *Rabbi Yitzḥak bar Sheshet (ha-Rivash): Derekh Ḥayyav u-Tekufato* [Rabbi Isaac bar Sheshet (Rivash): his life and times] (Jerusalem: Mosad Harav Kook, 1955/1956).

12. See source 157 above.
13. *Avot de-Rabbi Natan*, version B, chap. 34, source 158.
14. For a stronger statement of this idea, see Hirschensohn, *Sefer Yamim mi-Kedem*, 23–24:

    Let the reader take this is as an important rule in this and other books of mine: Wherever I emend the text of Scripture, my intention is not (perish the thought) to alter Scripture as it appears in the book in the ark (perish the thought), but only for purposes of studying the Oral Torah, which is considered to include all of the books that exist today other than the twenty-four [biblical books]. If a person dared alter a book in the ark, one of the twenty-four, even slightly, I would rule the book defective, and I would rule it forbidden to possess by virtue of being one that had not been authenticated, because the books are sacred to us just as they are written, and as they are written, so they are read when we [publicly] read Scripture. However, in order to learn and inquire and arrive at the soul of Scripture, it is right for us to alter and correct commensurately with the gift of wisdom that God bestowed on man. Only in this way is it possible to ascertain the true intention of the Torah, and anyone who preserves a single soul of Scripture is to be regarded as if he had preserved an entire world. This is the truthful path trodden by our sages of blessed memory, but they hid the way a little so that it would not lie wide open before all trespassers—beasts, humans, and animals—which are prone to foul it with their excrement and waters.

15. See source 172.
16. See David Samuel Löwinger, "Sefer Torah she-Hayah Ganuz be-Beit Keneset Sevirus be-Roma: Yaḥaso el Megillat Yesha'yahu mi-Midbar Yehudah ve-el 'Torato shel Rabbi Meir'" [The Torah scroll secreted in the Severus Synagogue in Rome: Its relationship to the Dead Sea Isaiah Scroll and the "Torah of Rabbi Meir"], *Beit Mikra* 15 (1969/1970): 237–263.
17. "Derashat ha-Ramban al Divrei Kohelet" [Sermon by Nachmanides on the words of Kohelet], in *Kitvei Rabbenu Mosheh ben Naḥman* [The writings of our rabbi Moses ben Naḥman], ed. Charles Ber Chavel (Jerusalem: Mosad Harav Kook, 1962/1963), 1:184:

    They said, "In the Torah scroll of Rabbi Meir we found written, 'and found it very good, and found death was good.'" "For Rabbi Meir was a scribe, and while writing a certain Torah scroll he was thinking to himself that 'and found it very good'" must refer even to death and every sort of cessation, and his hand followed his mind and he accidentally wrote in the Torah scroll "and found it very good, and found death was good," as he had been thinking to himself.

18. The history of this scroll is described in greater detail in *Midrash Bereshit Rabbati*, 209 (45:8): "This is one of those words written in the Torah that was plundered from Jerusalem and brought to Rome, and kept secreted in the Synagogue of Severus." The list of variants given by Albeck (209–212) is significantly different from that in the present source and probably corrupt.
19. The list proceeds to enumerate some twenty variants in the remaining four books of the Torah.

20. This list is given by Löwinger, "Sefer Torah she-Hayah Ganuz," 243–245. For a complete annotated version, including disparities between the masoretic text and the standard text assumed by the author of the list, see Nathan Rabbi Jastram, "The Severus Scroll and Rabbi Meir's Torah," in *The Text of the Hebrew Bible*, ed. Elvira Martín-Contreras and Lorena Miralles-Maciá (Göttingen: Vandenhoeck & Ruprecht, 2014), 137–145.
21. Some twenty such textual variants are given by Rabbi Akiva Eger (1761–1814), *Gilyon ha-Shas* to Babylonian Talmud, tractate *Shabbat* 55b. A considerable list of sources appears in Rabbi Isaiah Berlin (Pick), *Hafla'ah she-ba-Arakhin* (*Be'ur he-Arukh*) [Exposition of the Arukh] (Vienna: Leib Sulzbach & son Hirsch, 1859), § *me'ah*, 2:4b-5b. An even more comprehensive compilation is provided by Samuel Rosenfeld, *Sefer Mishpaḥat Soferim* (Wilno: Romm, 1883). As early as the title page, he notes that "the changes given here from our sages of blessed memory regarding the twenty-four books of the Holy Scripture number 1,381, of them 556 in Moses' Torah alone."
22. Shraga Abramson, *Ba-Merkazim u-ba-Tefutzot bi-Tekufat ha-Ge'onim* [In the centers and the diasporas during the gaonic period] [Jerusalem: Mosad Harav Kook, 1965], 130–132), published this responsum according to the Cambridge manuscript, in which the two examples given here are joined by a third: "We learn as well in tractate *Berakhot*: 'Elkanah rose and went after her,' but we have found only 'Then Elkanah went home to Ramah' (1 Sam. 2:11)."
23. The most similar known verse to that in the Talmud is Proverbs 4:8: "Hug her to you and she will exalt you; she will bring you honor if you embrace her."
24. Rabbi Hai Ga'on (939–1038), the dean of the yeshiva of Pumbedita, was the last and one of the greatest of the Ge'onim of Babylonia.
25. Standard contemporary editions of the Talmud have a five in the thousands place (see source 194 below) but there are multiple variants of the figure; see Havlin, *Masoret ha-Torah*, 275n65.
26. The intended reference is unclear; see Havlin, *Masoret ha-Torah*, 275n66.
27. Rashi ad loc. prefers to emend the text of the Talmud according to the accustomed biblical text. See also Tosafot to Babylonian Talmud, tractate *Niddah* 33a, s.v. *ve-ha-nose*.
28. Yeshayahu Maori, "Midreshei Ḥazal ke-Edut le-Ḥillufei Nusaḥ ba-Mikra: Toledot ha-Meḥkar ve-Yissumo be-Mahadurat 'Mif'al ha-Keter'" [rabbinic midrash as evidence for textual variants in the Hebrew Bible: history and implementation in the Haketer edition], in *Iyyunei Mikra u-Parshanut: Sefer Zikkaron le-Moshe Goshen-Gottstein* [Studies in Bible and exegesis], ed. Moshe Bar-Asher et al. (Ramat Gan: Bar-Ilan University, 1992/1993), 3:283–284, describes the parenthetical text ("the minority") as an inauthentic addition.
29. Rabbi Solomon Ibn Adret (1235–ca. 1310) was among the leading talmudic and halakhic authorities of medieval Spain.
30. See source 163 above.
31. Rabbi Moses ben David Halawa, a student of Rabbi Solomon Ibn Adret, was a halakhic authority and talmudic commentator from fourteenth-century Barcelona.
32. See source 188 above. The responsum, actually penned by Rabbi Solomon Ibn Adret, was erroneously attributed to Nachmanides by Norzi and other sages due to a corruption in its text (see note 245 above).
33. Rabbi Jedediah Solomon Raphael Norzi (b. 1560, d. after 1626) was a community rabbi in Mantua. His opus *Minḥat Shai* (which he titled *Goder Peretz*) substantially influenced the standard text of modern masoretic editions.
34. Rabbi Samuel Vital (b. 1598, d. after 1676) presided over a yeshiva in Damascus and later in Egypt. His teachings were heavily influenced by those of his father, Rabbi Ḥayim Vital, the

leading disciple of the kabbalist Rabbi Isaac Luria. Concerning the significance and ramifications of this responsum, see Jordan S. Penkower, *Nussaḥ ha-Torah be-Keter Aram-Tzova: Edut Ḥadashah* [New evidence for the Pentateuch text in the Aleppo Codex] (Ramat Gan: Bar-Ilan University, 1992), 81–90.

35. See Havlin, *Masoret ha-Torah*, 273–279.
36. The numbers given here are not consistent with any of the texts of the Torah now prevalent; see source 187 above. Rabbi Jacob Schor, *Mishnat Rabbi Ya'akov* (Petrokov: Defus H. Palman, 1929/1930), 8–9 (4:3), aptly writes,

> I then thought, and acted accordingly, to count all of the letters and words of the Torah with great precision, and I thus counted them as they are written in the Torah scroll. I found and saw that the number of letters in a Torah scroll is . . . 304,805 . . . so that half of the number of letters in a Torah scroll is . . . 152,402.5. I then counted the letters from *bereshit* (Gen. 1:1) until the vav of *gaḥon*, and I found and saw that there are . . . 157,236. Therefore, if in the time of the ancients the vav of *gaḥon* was the midpoint of the Torah by letters, then the total number of letters in their Torah scrolls necessarily was . . . 314,472. . . . Yet more astounding, I found and saw that the total number of words in a Torah is . . . 79,980 [while there are four fewer in the text given in the Vilnius edition], so that half of the number of words in a Torah is 39,990, yet when I counted the words from *bereshit* until *darosh [darash]*, I found and saw that there were 40,921. Therefore, if in the time of the ancients the words *darosh [darash]* were the midpoint of the Torah by words, then their Torah scrolls, including all the words of the Torah, necessarily must have contained 81,842, and that number . . . is 1,862 more words than in our Torah scrolls, so that we are missing them. . . . Instead of the vav of *gaḥon*, for the midpoint of a Torah scroll by letters, it should give "the vav of *hu*," because the midpoint of the Torah by letters is in *parashat* Tsav (Lev. 8:28): the vav in the word *hu* of *isheh hu le-Adonai* ("it was an offering by fire to the Lord"), and the word [sic] *yesod ha-mizbe'aḥ vaykaddeshehu* ('the altar. Thus he consecrated it') there (8:15) is the midpoint of the Torah by words.

> Concerning the number of verses in the Torah, Rabbi Aaron ben Moses Ben Asher, the greatest of the masoretic authorities, writes in *Sefer Dikduk ha-Te'amim*, ed. Yitzhak Baer and Hermann Leberecht Strack, reprint ed. with introduction by David Samuel Löwinger (Jerusalem: Makor, 1969/1970), 55, § 68, "The number of verses in the five books of the Torah is 5,845," a total that falls forty-three short of that reported in the Gemara (but see also the number of words and of letters) and places the midpoint of the Torah by verse at Leviticus 8:8. Reacting to the disparity, Rabbi Jedediah Norzi, *Minḥat Shai* to Leviticus 8:8, laments, "I find it difficult to understand the statement in the first chapter of Kiddushin that 'The ancients therefore were called *soferim*.' . . . Also difficult to understand is the tradition recorded there that 'our rabbis taught, "The Torah is comprised of 8,888 verses"'. . . . The number of verses in our texts is hundreds and thousands below this count! . . . How did such a great disparity come about? We can say that we are not well-versed in how the verses are to be divided, as is stated there in *Kiddushin* . . . but I still am not comfortable with this, because the disparity is so great . . . so let Ezra explain."

37. Babylonian Talmud, tractate *Kiddushin* 30a.
38. Rabbi Meir ben Todros Abulafia (ca. 1165–1244) was one of the greatest Jewish sages of early thirteenth-century Spain. Concerning Abulafia and his part in the Maimonidean controversy, see Bernard Septimus, *Hispano-Jewish Culture in Transition: The Career and Controversies of Ramah* (Cambridge, MA.: Harvard University Press, 1982).
39. See also ha-Me'iri, preface to *Kiryat Sefer*.
40. Rabbi Moses Isserles (ca. 1530–ca. 1572), a community rabbi and dean of a yeshiva in Kraków, was the preeminent Ashkenazi halakhic authority of the sixteenth century. He is best known for his glosses to Rabbi Joseph Karo's *Shulḥan Arukh*.
41. See source 183 above.
42. See source 174 above.
43. Rabbi Abraham ben Mordecai (b. ca. 1650, d. after 1704, possibly 1710 or 1712), one of the leading authors of responsa in the modern period, served as a rabbi, and presided over a rabbinical tribunal in Egypt. His best-known work, whose title is widely used as his sobriquet in traditional scholarship, is *Responsa Ginat Veradim*, which was one of the most comprehensive works of responsa to date. His other published works include a number of brief pamphlets (*Milḥemet Mitzvah, Ya'ir Nativ, Gan ha-Melekh*); most of his works have not been printed.

Scripture and Ancient Literature

Can the texts of the ancient Near East—a body of typically pagan works—play a role in Torah scholarship? At first blush, the answer may appear to be negative, even emphatically so, given the Torah's contempt for idol worship and its eagerness to distance its audience from pagan teachings and behaviors. Nevertheless these works sometimes prove valuable, whether by corroborating the Torah, contributing to our understanding of the environment in which it was given, or allowing us to form a more accurate understanding of the Torah's commandments and values. Should the study of these sources be repudiated even in these cases? This question calls for a more nuanced response than the previous one. One answer offered by the sages is as follows:

184

"You shall not learn to perform the abhorrent practices of those nations" (Deut. 18:9)—Can it be that you are not permitted to learn in order to instruct and understand? The text says, "to perform": you may not learn in order to perform them, but you may learn in order to instruct and understand.

Sifrei Devarim, 170.

It would be a mistake to conclude from this source that the sages often studied foreign works. On the contrary, such scholarship in tannaitic times was mainly the province of judges, who had a practical need for the relevant knowledge, and sages who were in close contact with non-Jews. In the generations that followed, as the pagans who had lived in proximity to Jewish populations dwindled and disappeared, the practical feasibility, as well as the potential benefits, of studying their texts waned accordingly. Even at this point, however, some Jewish scholars found it expedient to refer to these sources for one reason or another. Beginning in the nineteenth century, as discoveries from the ancient Near East began to appear, the interest of rabbinic authorities in this subject was rekindled. This time, the academic community that heralded the return of these sources was perceived as more dangerous than the discoveries themselves, with the ironic outcome that the findings became a means of corroborating the Torah in the face of arguments leveled by academics in other fields.

Turning to Other Ancient Texts to Corroborate the Torah

The most elementary religious link between the Torah and other ancient texts lies in those instances where material in the latter corroborates and reinforces the content of the Torah. Though rabbinic sages were generally loathe to appeal to non-Jewish sources, which lacked traditional authority, in order to buttress individuals' faith in either the Written or the Oral Torah, some were willing to employ such texts to shield their religious community from attacks in times of heightened polemical activity.[1]

185

A certain heretic said to Rabbi Ḥanina, "Do you have a tradition of how old Balaam was [at the time of his death]?" He said to him, "It is not written, but based on the words 'those murderous, treacherous men; they shall not live out half their days' (Ps. 55:24), he was thirty-three or thirty-four years old." He said to him, "You have spoken well. I saw the ledger of Balaam, and it said, 'Lame Balaam was thirty-three years old when the bandit Phineas killed him.'"

Babylonian Talmud, tractate *Sanhedrin* 106b.

186

Therefore the Book of the Wars of the Lord speaks of "Waheb in Suphah, and the wadis: the Arnon" (Num. 21:14)—The simple sense of "the Book of the Wars of the Lord" is that in those generations there were wise men who would record the events of the great wars—since it is so in all generations. The authors of these books were called "the authors of parables" (27), because they would compose parables and poetics about them, and they would attribute the victories they found spectacular to the Lord, because in truth they are His. They found the exploits of Sihon in Moab spectacular, and so they recorded them in a book and composed poetics about them.

Nachmanides.

187

The words "For the Arnon is the boundary of Moab, between Moab and the Amorites" (Num. 21:13) mean that the Israelites inherited the Arnon because they were between the Arnon and the Amorites, and the Amorites had taken it from the Moabites, since they had extended their border to the Arnon Wadi. The Israelites then were told, "Up! Set out across the wadi Arnon!" (Deut. 2:24), on the inside of the border of the Amorites. "See, I give into your power Sihon the Amorite, king of Heshbon, and his land. Begin the occupation: engage him in battle" (ibid.). He cites as evidence an excerpt from the Book of the Wars of the Lord, which is a book that existed among the nations that contained records of the wars that occurred throughout the world and attributed them to the Lord, because all is from Him and in His hand. Those who recounted these events would do so with parables and fine riddles. It is said there about the war waged by the Amorites and their conquest of the Land of Moab, "Waheb in Suphah, and the wadis: the Arnon with its tributary wadis, stretched along the settled country of Ar, hugging the territory of Moab" (Num. 21:14).

Don Isaac Abravanel, Commentary on Num. 21:10.

188

Of all the creation myths, that of the Babylonians [namely, the Enûma Eliš] in certain respects bears the greatest resemblance to the scriptural account. . . . Gunkel views as of particular importance the agreement of the Hebrew and the Babylonian tradition on the point that most defines them: the world comes about as a result of the division of the primordial sea. From this he deduces that the earliest texts of Genesis chapter 1 and the Babylonian myth were in fact different variants of a single tradition. Strack, however, rightly points out that the differences between the two traditions are far greater than their similarities. In the Babylonian version, the gods are afraid of Tiamat, Marduk must furnish himself with an array of armaments, and only after a taxing battle does he succeed in splitting Tiamat in two. Conversely, the book of Genesis features a single God standing outside and above all matter. He speaks, and His word is carried out. The book has nothing to say of any sort of conflict. The abyss is not described as a primordial monster; in fact, it is mentioned only a single time (Gen. 1:2), after which the text invariably refers only to water. Though Rahab (Job 9:13; 26:12) and Leviathan (3:8) appear elsewhere in the Bible, we would do well to bear in mind that these names were alien to the Babylonians, and prove nothing about the account of Creation in the present book. The few similarities that exist between the pentateuchal and the other accounts of Creation are resolved by the assumption that there was an ancient tradition shared by all humanity, a tradition that among the ancestors of the Israelite nation was more precisely passed down from generation to generation, until divine revelation arrived in the Torah and committed it to writing in a definitive form and in accordance with the actual progression of events. The comparable elements shared by the pentateuchal account of the Deluge and that in the Babylonian myth are more numerous.[2] ... The similarity between the pentateuchal account of the Flood and the Babylonian accounts is conspicuous. Yet still more conspicuous is the profound contrast between the two accounts. As noted by Holzinger, the heathen gods in the Babylonian account are genuinely heathen in their lies, in their command to the people to lie to each other,[3] in their craving for sacrifice, in their rivalries, in the arbitrariness of their relations with humankind, and in the fickleness of their moods. How different from them all is the God of the Torah—a God who approaches man with justice and judges him with righteousness, a righteousness that innermost man is compelled to acknowledge! We would further add, and emphasize, that God's justice visits man not, for instance, because he has insulted his God, but only "because the earth is filled with lawlessness" (Gen. 6:13). Indeed, it is not impertinent to refer to the image elsewhere conjured by Stade.... "The relationship of the biblical to the Babylonian account is that of the pristine mountain spring to the turbid, squalid village puddle." The notion that the scriptural account is dependent upon the Babylonian account can occur only to a person for whom the stories of Genesis are not historical truth, but mere myth. But we argue with certainty that the stories of Genesis are historical truth, for the Torah expressly demands that we view as historical truth all that is unfolded within it, just as it demands, for instance, that we sanctify the Sabbath in remembrance of Creation. If the Flood truly took place, then it is only natural that the memory of that awful event was preserved by the nations, and most reliably by those who earliest committed it to writing [i.e., the Babylonians]. Yet the tradition can be considered historically reliable in its entirety only where divine inspiration enlightened and guided the writer. It is self-evident that two writers telling of the same historical event will produce much the same description of the objective facts, but no less self-evident is that they will diverge in their subjective assessment of the causes, reasons, and outcomes of these events, not least when they belong to different nations. Indeed, the biblical and the Babylonian accounts of the Flood are in agreement with regard to the following: (1) a great deluge laid waste to humanity and animals, and only a handful of people were saved; (2) this salvation was effected through the construction of a large ship; (3) they were granted this salvation by God (or a particular pagan deity); (4) the survivor's ship landed on a mountain when the turbulence of the water subsided; (5) the passengers on the ship sent various birds to determine whether the earth had in fact become dry; (6) the leader of those saved, after exiting the ship, sacrificed offerings to God (or pagan deities). All the above are facts that a tradition has no difficulty at all preserving, but it is clear that the details of the dimensions of the ship, the duration of the deluge, the name of the mountain on which they landed, and the names of those saved are quickly forgotten, and even the different Babylonian myths indeed diverge not a little on these points. In any event, there is no grounds for the assumption that the Hebrews received the story of the Flood from the Babylonians. What is more, it is quite difficult to establish when this tradition could have made its way from the Babylonians to the Hebrews. The transmission cannot be dated to the Babylonian exile, because even in the view of the biblical critics, the present story was authored far earlier. . . . Only one who argues that the book of Genesis contains no historical truths, but only legends, is compelled to search for dubious, improbable answers, while the resemblance of the different accounts can so easily be explained, as we have demonstrated.

Rabbi David Zvi Hoffmann, *Genesis,* ed. and trans. Asher Wasserteil (Benei Berak: Netzaḥ, 1968/1969), 1:199–204n40.[4]

189

Most of the recent critics (Wellhausen . . . and others) date Leviticus 26 to the Babylonian exile or the period that followed. However, their principal proofs, predicated on [prophetic] premonition of the exile and its bitter outcomes, are deemed to be of value only by those who believe that it was impossible in the time of our master Moses, or some other time in antiquity when the state of Israel was still established and in full bloom, to prophesy anything of the exile and all its terrors. To these doubters, it is in order to note as follows: *The Code of Hammurabi,* like (to a limited extent) the laws of the Torah, is accompanied by an exhortation that promises anyone who fulfills its commandments happiness and prosperity, while fiercely cursing those who violate the code. Here we shall excerpt a few verses from that exhortation . . . :

> If a succeeding ruler considers my words, which I have written in this my inscription, . . . then may Shamash lengthen that king's reign . . . that he may reign in righteousness over his subjects. . . . If this ruler do not esteem my words . . . if he despise my curses, and fear not the curse of God, if he

destroy the law which I have given . . . may the great God . . . withdraw from him the glory of royalty, break his scepter, curse his destiny. May Bel, the lord, who fixeth destiny . . . ordain the years of his rule in groaning, years of scarcity, years of famine, darkness without light, death with seeing eyes be fated to him . . . the destruction of his city, the dispersion of his subjects. . . . May Belit, the great Mother . . . turn his affairs evil before Bel, and put the devastation of his land, the destruction of his subjects, the pouring out of his life like water into the mouth of King Bel. May Ea, the great ruler . . . shut up his rivers at their sources, and not allow corn [or sustenance] for man to grow in his land. . . . May Adad, the lord of fruitfulness . . . withhold from him rain from heaven, and the flood of water from the springs, destroying his land by famine and want. . . . May Ishtar, the goddess of fighting and war . . . strike down his warriors . . . deliver him into the hands of his enemies, and imprison him in the land of his enemies. . . . May Nin-karak . . . cause to come upon his members in E-kur high fever, severe wounds, that can not be healed . . . until they have sapped away his life. . . . May the great gods of heaven and earth . . . altogether inflict a curse and evil upon . . . his land . . . his subjects, and his troops. May Bel curse him with the potent curses of his mouth that can not be altered, and may they come upon him forthwith.[5]

Thus wrote Hammurabi some centuries before our master Moses lived. Please, let them weigh these admonitions against the cautions and curses of Leviticus 26 and Deuteronomy 28, and ask themselves whether there is any definitive reason for opposing the view that our master Moses wrote these verses, aside from the lone argument, albeit a significant one for those deniers of prophecy, that the curses uttered by our master Moses were manifestly realized against the Israelites.

Rabbi David Zvi Hoffmann, *Leviticus,* trans. Zvi Har-Shefer and Aharon Lieberman (Jerusalem: Mosad Harav Kook, 1976), 2:247.[6]

190

The recently accelerated search through hidden treasures has provided much material for research into antiquities, especially matters related to studies of our Torah and ancient matters closely related to us, namely Assyriology, [the study of] the cradle of our early ancestors and the location of the earliest events connected to those matters detailed in the Torah. Indeed, what happened to intellectual studies when they encountered the Torah has happened to this sensory, searching quest. As with the intellectual studies—those characterized by upright intellect and healthy logic—they became an elixir of life for those who apply them properly, contributing to the development of their intellectual ability to truly and purely understand matters of the Torah. But for those who apply them improperly, they became a deadly poison: either they ultimately reject intellectual activity and run from any examination or inquiry into the wisdom of God and the ways of His Torah, which is a great and terrible wrong, or (perish the thought) they cease following the Lord and join those who deride His word and breach His command, this being a fire that consumes both collective and individual to the point of annihilation.... Indeed, what has unsettled many hearts and brought others to absolute heresy with regard to the heavenly origin of the Torah, and then to ruination of [religious] practice and repudiation—just as bad roots naturally branch out—is the comparison of a number of narratives as written in the Torah and as inscribed in ancient tablets containing Babylonian and Assyrian antiquities, such as the Flood, the division [of languages], and so forth. Although there these matters appear differently, scholars concluded that they were common legends among the ancient nations, and were written in the Torah in a somewhat different style, according to the character of the nation and its spirit. Yet when we contemplate this, we find that this is proof capable of lending courage to anyone who seeks the truth. For it is clear even without any searching that the matters that appear in the Torah as true stories could not by any means have failed to be transmitted by the ancients to all the nations of antiquity. What's more, imaginative and erroneous elements could not in any way have failed to become mixed into these narratives. Indeed, is the power of prophecy writ large not a divine power that reveals profound things amid darkness, fully penetrating primordial truth just as it fully penetrates final [i.e., eschatological] truth? Certainly the prophecy of the master of prophets, which was communicated orally, plainly and not in riddles, separated the wheat from the chaff and accurately transmitted the truth to us in the Torah of truth.... Indeed, it is the view of Maimonides and many early sages of Israel that the account of Creation contains both historical and allegorical narrative elements. Those that are allegorical certainly have a significant relationship to the historical elements, but the greatness and purity of the allegory's power depends on the greatness and purity of the spirit. Thus it is amply clear that the allegories that emerged from these primordial narratives among the nations, which had intellectually and morally descended to the depths of the filth of paganism and all the abominations that accompany it, came to be full of vanities and intermixed with such imaginary things, because, as they were explained and developed, they accumulated false imaginativeness and fools' morality. Thus just as pure prophecy in the spirit of the Lord and the word of His mouth, blessed be He, separated out the narrative from deceit and lies, so did it separate out the allegory from that mixture of nothingness, wickedness, and folly. Those subjects that were appropriate to express allegorically were transmitted in divine legislation by a faithful shepherd as spoken by the Lord, so as to be a source of life from which to draw holy, exalted morality and pure, eternal divine wisdom—fit to be a light to the world and a source of joy for every generation.

Rabbi Abraham Isaac Kook, *Li-Nevukhei ha-Dor,* 170–172 (chap. 33).

Endnotes

1. One of the earliest and most wide-ranging descriptions of this approach is provided by Titus Flavius Josephus (37/38–ca. 100 CE); see his remarks in, e.g., *Against Apion,* trans. John M.G. Barclay, vol. 10 of *Flavius Josephus: Translation and Commentary,* ed. Steve Mason (Leiden: Brill, 2007), 3–88 (book 1, especially chap. 1–21).
2. Namely, the flood account in the eleventh tablet of *The Epic of Gilgamesh.* Rabbi Hoffmann was familiar as well with one form or another of the *Atra-Hasis,* a myth that includes another version of the story of the Flood.
3. According to the Babylonian flood myth, Enki commands the hero to trick his fellows.
4. Rabbi David Zvi Hoffman (1843–1921), a preeminent leader of German Jewry, was the rector of the rabbinical seminary of Berlin. His best-known works are a commentary to the Torah and the polemical *Decisive Evidence against Wellhausen.* Rabbi J. H. Hertz, *The Pentateuch and Haftorahs,* 193, 196–198, voices a similar argument as that presented here. Hertz makes liberal use of sources from the ancient Near East to prove the ancient origins of Scripture and refute critical theories; see *The Pentateuch and Haftorahs,* 199–200, 398–399, 404–406, 555 (following Hoffman in source 208), 941.
5. "The Code of Hammurabi," trans. L. W. King, The Avalon Project: Documents in Law, History, and Diplomacy, Yale Law School, 2008, http://avalon.law.yale.edu/ancient/hamframe.asp.
6. See also Hoffman, *Leviticus,* 260.

Drawing on Ancient Texts to Understand the Diction and Narratives of the Torah

The world in which the Torah was given disappeared into the mists of time long ago, and many things that were self-evident to those who lived in that era are an enigma to later generations who wish to study the Torah.[1] Traditional sages mainly tended to the timeless messages of the Torah, and, if bothered by questions of history, found answers in midrashic literature. However, a few saw fit to avail themselves of ancient texts or to conjecture about the culture or language of ancient races in order to arrive at a more precise understanding of the historical reality in which the Torah made its appearance.

191

Moses' name is a translation to the holy tongue from Egyptian; his name in Egyptian was Monios. This is as written in the agricultural books translated from Egyptian to the language of the Kedarites [i.e., Arabs], as well as in the books of the Greek scholars.

Ibn Ezra, long recension to Exod. 2:10.[2]

192

It is well know that *Abraham our Father*, peace be on him, was brought up in the religious community of the Sabians,[3] whose doctrine it is that there is no deity but the stars. When I shall have made known to you in this chapter their books, translated into Arabic, which are in our hands today, and their ancient chronicles and I shall have revealed to you from through them their doctrines and histories, it will become clear to you from this that they explicitly asserted that the stars are the deity and that the sun is the greatest deity. They also said that the rest of the seven stars are deities, but that the two luminaries are the greatest of them. You will find that they explicitly say that the sun governs the upper and the lower world. They say it in these very terms. And you will find that they mention in those books and those chronicles the story of *Abraham our Father*.... They do not mention what is related in our true traditions, and the prophetic revelation that came to him. For they tax him with lying because of his disagreeing with their corrupt opinion. I have no doubt that in view of the fact that he, may peace be upon him, disagreed with the doctrine of all men, these erring men reviled, blamed, and belittled him. Accordingly, because he bore this for the sake of God, may He be exalted, and preferred truth to his reputation, he was told: "I will bless those who bless you and curse him that curses you; and all the families of the earth shall bless themselves by you" (Gen. 12:3). ... However, when *the pillar of the world* [i.e., Abraham] grew up and it became clear to him ... that the fables upon which he was brought up were absurd, he began to refute their doctrine and to show up their opinions as false; he publicly manifested his disagreement with them and called *in the name of the Lord, God of the world* (Gen. 12:33)—both the existence of the deity and the creation of the world in time by that deity being comprised in that call.

In conformity with these opinions, the Sabians ... built temples, set up the statues in them, and thought that the forces of the planets overflowed toward these statues and consequently these statues talked, had understanding, gave prophetic revelation to people—I mean, the statues—and made known to people what was useful to them. Similarly they said of the trees, which were assigned to the various planets, that when one particular tree was set apart for one particular planet, planted with a view to the latter, and a certain treatment was applied to it and with it, the spirit of that planet overflowed toward that tree, gave prophetic revelation to people, and spoke to them in sleep. You will find all this set forth literally in their books, to which I shall draw your attention. These were *the prophets of Baal and the prophets of Asherah* that are mentioned in our texts; among them these opinions became so firm that *they forsook the Lord* (Isa. 1:4) and called: "O Baal, answer us!" (1 Kings 18:26). All this came about because of these opinions being generally accepted, ignorance being widespread and the world then often being given to raving concerning imaginings of this kind. Accordingly such opinions developed among them that some of them became *soothsayers, enchanters, sorcerers, charmers, consulters with familiar spirits, wizards, and necromancers* (Deut. 18:10–11). We have already made it clear in our great compilation, *Mishneh Torah*, that *Abraham our Father* began to refute these opinions by means of arguments and feeble preaching, conciliating people and drawing them to obedience by means of benefits. Then the Master of the prophets received prophetic inspiration; thereupon he perfected the purpose in that he commanded killing these people, wiping out their traces, and tearing out their roots.

Maimonides, *The Guide of the Perplexed*, 3:29.[4]

193

We would do well to direct our attention to resolving a profound conundrum that arises in this story and many other stories in the Torah. Namely, in light of the perfection of the Torah, there should be no repetitions or anything superfluous in it. Here, however, we see that there is seemingly needless repetition, because it would have been sufficient to say, "Bezalel son of Uri son of Hur constructed the Tabernacle as the Lord had commanded Moses. At his side was Oholiab son of Ahisamach." We already have seen such repetition in numerous places in the Torah, and to this day we have not found a reason that suffices to explain the general phenomenon. Perhaps we might say that the accepted practice when the Torah was given was to tell stories in this way, and prophets speak according to convention.

Gersonides, Commentary on Exod. 40:2.

194

However, I will not refrain from saying that, in my view, this story has the same purpose as the many stories of the Torah whose purpose is to eliminate false beliefs and valueless stories, conceived by priests of the false gods during the dark ages, that spread among the nations during antiquity. Something remains of their mythology even today: if anyone developed some given craft, then they ascribed godly power to that person. For instance, they would say that a given god had developed the pursuit of nomadic shepherding, another god had developed the playing of music, another god had developed military tactics and the craft of iron and instruments of war, while another god had conceived the construction of cities and political mores. They would tell wondrous things about the birth and godliness of each of these demigods, and call on people to worship them at set times and designated festivals. The Torah therefore gave notice: Do not believe in these misleading falsehoods. Know that the individual who conceived the construction of cities, political mores, and civic association was Cain, the first murderer. Those who developed the craft of shepherding, commerce, the playing of music, and the craft of iron and metals were the sons of Lamech, a descendant of Cain. The woman of whom they told such great things in their mythology, placing her on a lofty pedestal, was Naamah, the sister of Tubal-Cain. They all were mortal humans, not demigods. These messages were greatly needed in those days, when these stories had spread among all the nations, with whom they remained current until the destruction of the Second Temple, as is well known.

Rabbi Meir Leibush Wisser (Malbim), Commentary on Gen. 4:22.[5]

195

"The divine beings saw" (Gen. 6:2)—Because the language of the masses already had begun to deteriorate by the time Chronicles was written, and a good number spoke the language of Ashdod, etc.,[6] they needed to define the old word "cherubim," not because they had insight into the nature and function of the cherubim, but because after the exile, they did have a clear understanding of their form. . . . He therefore clarified what he had said with the words *ma'aseh tza'atzuim* (2 Chron. 3:10), meaning that they resembled children. It was not so in the time of our master Moses, may he rest in peace, for in the Torah written by the master of prophets, he did not need to explain very much. . . . Aside from the proofs from the Holy Scripture, we can learn from another source: the Egyptian cult. It is no wonder that things they later used for sacred purposes previously had been in use by the Egyptians, if we correctly understand what the kabbalists informed us regarding the words "they stripped the Egyptians" (Exod. 12:36) [meaning that the departing Israelites took with them the traces of holiness found in Egypt]. . . . Thus we have found that in the worship of their idols, the Egyptians used various vessels not dissimilar in style and form to the sacred vessels. Hear what is said by the author of *Shevilei Olam*, in the section on Africa: "Amid the ruins of the temples, recent travelers have found carved stones exquisitely carved with forms and images similar to those of the Ark, the tent, the Tabernacle, cherubim, the showbread, and the other sacred vessels, as the Lord commanded Moses." If it is our wish to view the form of the cherubim in Egypt, then we should praise and thank the Lord that a good and fitting place to inspect and fully appreciate it has been preserved: when we look at the faces of the forms drawn in Champollion's book on Egypt, and our eyes behold that they have the form of children, in agreement with the tradition received by our sages.[7] This is an extraordinarily precious discovery that brings vision to sightless eyes, and, in truth, it is not only in the forms of the cherubim and the vessels that the Egyptians and the Jews accorded, but also in the form of the temple and its style, as well as its vestibules, its chambers, and all its divisions, as correctly noted by Champollion.

Rabbi Elia Benamozegh, *Sefer Torat Hashem . . . ve-Nosaf alav Em la-Mikra . . . va . . . Em la-Masoret,* 1:16a-b (Gen. 3:24).

196

This is the entire result of the proposals that we have offered to this point: they have prepared a good and fitting place for our hypothesis, predicated upon correct inquiry, spreading the radiance of its glory atop the tradition of our forefathers, setting splendor and magnificence upon it, by placing in our hands a truthful sign and unequivocal signal that, even more than our rabbis taught us, their words are veracious and correct. They—even they—did not fully appreciate the extent of the proofs corroborating their words and potential inquiries into them, which are becoming manifest and observable only to our eyes today, as we gain knowledge of customs unknown to our forefathers. They simply proceeded according to the wholesomeness of their hearts. Knowing that they would neither lie nor deceive, they did not balk at arranging before us the tradition they had received, even if it was alien to its audience, and they did not drop back out of fear of the blasphemers and mockers, knowing that a sage speaks truth. They also did not fail to buttress their words in all ways at their disposal, by appeals to logic and Scripture. If due to great distance of time and place, they were not cognizant of the original and primary reason, then this is to their glory and splendor; they did not forsake their traditional truth even though they had forgotten its rationale. Despite the fact that it was thoroughly alien to them, they did not balk at proclaiming it aloud. This hypothesis is based on our knowledge of the customs of the Egyptians, among whom our forefathers were reared and grew up, and from whom they learned numerous customs both good and bad, and it is to those who left Egypt that the Torah was given. If, as our rabbis stated, the Lord, blessed be He, did not balk at speaking to his children in Egyptian in saying, "I (*anokhi*) the Lord am your God" (Exod. 20:2), then it certainly should not go unstated that the expressions, laws, and rules of the Torah can be understood based on the conventions familiar to those who left Egypt (where they do not contradict divine law), as today has been verified by study and inquiry into the writings of the Egyptians.

Rabbi Elia Benamozegh, *Sefer Torat Hashem . . . ve-Nosaf alav Em la-Mikra . . . va . . . Em la-Masoret,* 4:90b (Num. 29:11).

197

"Ordain them" [literally, "fill their hands"] (Exod. 28:41)—The term "to fill the hands" always refers to investiture, when a person permanently takes on a new role. In a foreign language [French], when they appoint a person [to a position, the ruler puts in his hand a leather glove called a *gant*, which symbolizes the fact that he is placing him in that position, and this act of transmission is called *rewestir*. This is what *to fill the hands* means.]

Nachmanides tartly criticized Rashi for these comments, saying that he had drawn on fools for evidence. Yet it is here that we see Rashi's greatness, as they [i.e., the sages] said: "Who is wise? One who learns from all people." What the scholars of the nations today learn from excavations and inquiries and from examining antiquities, learning the origins of ancient practices from such sources in order to gain an understanding of the words of the sages and their riddles, Rashi understood this as he sat on a stone chair, cloistered in his little study hall in Worms [the location of his ostensible study hall], and he excavated and toiled and found in the letters of the Torah a basis for practices early and late. He did not wish in the least to state that the Torah had learned from their *gant*, but he is in agreement with the view of Nachmanides.

Rabbi Chaim Hirschensohn, *Sefer Nimmukei Rashi* (Seini: Jakob Wieder, 1929), 2:166b (§ 593).

198

When Jacob wrestled with the supernatural man while he was crossing the ford of the Jabbok, and the man was unable to defeat him, he said to him, "Your name shall no longer be Jacob, but Israel, for you have striven with beings God and humans, and have prevailed" (Gen. 32:29). Any person who has a sense for such things understands that he called him this not merely because of the two letters shin and resh [contained in both the word for striving (*sarita*) and the name Israel], but based on the name of a well-known person of their time who had famously achieved many feats and triumphs with God and humans, and at the time was well known as Israel. The individual who wrestled with Jacob said to him: A man of such valor (cf. Judg. 8:21) ought to be known by the name Israel. . . . Yet who was this man Israel by whose name Jacob was to be called? . . . In fact, it seems that . . . Israel is the name of the famous tribe and nation of Jacob's family, to which he traced himself, and this pedigree served to earn him the respect of all the inhabitants of the land of Canaan. Yet which nation, esteemed throughout the land, was it in whom Israel would take pride even before we, the children of Jacob, had become a nation, also called by the name Israel? This is a riddle that has escaped all the writers of history, and one that we now seek to solve. . . . If we contemplate the history of the world during the five hundred years from Reu until Joseph . . . we know that in the time of Reu or Serug, the Hyksos kings began their rule of Egypt, and as we are told by Egyptian historical works, these Hyksos came from descendants of Eber and Arab. . . . The Hyksos, like all those living in Egypt, accepted the god Osiris, to whom all of the souls that are not judged and sentenced for destruction return. The Hebrews referred to this god as Asir, a name that is widely found in Phoenician inscriptions . . . and the Hyksos undoubtedly referred to Osiris as Ashur, the name used by the people of Eber, and to its greatest members by the name Asriel, albeit we have not found this name in Hyksos inscriptions. However, sufficient evidence is provided by the name Asriel used in Egypt, including among the Jews there, and particularly among the children of Manasseh, the firstborn son of Joseph. He was reared in the king's palace, and his son, who was the father or brother of Machir, was named Asriel, as it is said, "The sons of Manasseh: Asriel, whom his Aramean concubine bore; she bore Machir the father of Gilead" (1 Chron. 7:14). A son of Machir was also called Asriel, as it is said, "[of] Asriel, the clan of the Asrielites" (Num. 26:31).... Anyone who contemplates the soul of those assimilated or semi-assimilated among our brothers in the countries of Europe and America, who give their children names according to the lands where they live and the nations that live there, understands that human beings throughout the world, with all the changes in time and status, are animated by a single spirit. In those days, when the Hyksos were esteemed throughout the land and among all its esteemed residents, the name Asriel was a glorious and honorable one. As the different syllables of the name were transposed among the tribes of the east, it also took the form as well of Israel. ... This name apparently was given to elders, who were the leaders of their families, when they had already obtained a deed or guarantee from the priests that, once they had died, their souls would migrate to the divine abode to unite with Osiris, as was their belief.... This was the actual reason for calling Jacob Israel: so that he would be traced to this family in Egypt.... With this, we can understand the verse, "These are the names of the Children of Israel, Jacob and his descendants, who came to Egypt" (Gen. 46:8), which indicates that Jacob as well was considered to be one of the Children of Israel.... This is the sense as well of the verse, "These are the names of the Children of Israel who came to Egypt with Jacob" (Exod. 1:1), meaning that there were other Israelites as well in the land, but these came with Jacob ... albeit some were not sons of Jacob, but descendants of his distant ancestors, dating to Reu and Serug.... When God instructed Moses to take the Israelites out of Egypt, Moses asked, "'When they ask me, "What is His name?" what shall I say to them?' and God answered him, 'Thus shall you say to the Israelites, "Ehyeh sent me to you."' And God said further to Moses, 'Thus shall you speak to the Israelites: The Lord, the God of your fathers, the God of Abraham, the God of Isaac, and the God of Jacob, has sent me to you'" (3:14–15). This was said in duplicate for the benefit of these two families. To the earlier Israelites, he said, "Ehyeh sent me to you," because they knew a similar name, Ea, from the Assyrians, as the names of the Assyrian gods were pronounced. For their sake, he referred to the true God with a name that sounds similar in order to appeal to their little understanding and limited spirit. However, to the Israelites who had come with Jacob—to the descendants of Abraham, Isaac, and Jacob—he said, "The Lord, the God of your fathers, [the God of] Abraham." ... This is the sense as well of the verse, "Thus shall you say to the house of Jacob and declare to the children of Israel" (19:3) and many similar verses in the Torah, the difficulty of which is thus resolved.

Rabbi Chaim Hirschensohn, *Sefer Yamim mi-Kedem,* 28–35.[8]

Endnotes

1. See, e.g., *Perush Rabbenu Avraham ben ha-Rambam za"l al Bere'shit u-Shemot* [The commentary of Rabbi Abraham Maimonides to Genesis and Exodus], ed. Ernest Wiesenberg (London: Defus ha-Ḥinukh, 1957/1958), 132 (Gen. 36:39).
2. For other explanations of the name Moses, see Rabbi Meir Leibush Wisser (Malbim), commentary to Exod. 2:10; Rabbi Naphtali Tzevi Judah Berlin, *Sefer Shemot ... im ... Ha'amek Davar* [The book of Exodus ... with ... a commentary entitled Ha'amek Davar], ed. M. Y. Kuperman (Jerusalem: M. Y. Kuperman, 2006/2007), 18 (Exod. 2:10); Rabbi Elia Benamozegh, *Sefer Torat Hashem ... ve-Nosaf alav Em la-Mikra ... va ... Em la-Masoret,* 2:7b (Exod. 2:10).
3. Translator Shlomo Pines notes: "The term 'Sabians,' as used by Maimonides, designates the pagans."
4. Rabbi Moses Maimonides (ca. 1138–1204) is famed as one of the greatest Jewish halakhic authorities and philosophers of all time. His most renowned halakhic work is the legal code *Mishneh Torah* (also known as *Yad Ḥazakah*), and his best-known philosophical treatise is *The Guide of the Perplexed.*
5. A similar explanation is given by Samuel Davide Luzzatto, *Perush al Ḥamishah Ḥumshei Torah* [Commentary to the Pentateuch], ed. Pinhas Schlesinger (Tel Aviv: Dvir, 1969), 35 (Gen. 4:20, 22). Rabbi Wisser not infrequently draws on mythological materials as a means of understanding the Bible; see his comments to Gen. 6:24; 12:14–16; 1 Kings 1:12, 28; Isa. 9:7–9; 14:13–14; 19:5 (in note); 43:9–10; Ezek. 7:20 (in glossary); 32:2,7; Hos. 8:14; Jon. 1:8; Ps. 5:5; 78:2–4.
6. See Neh. 13:24.
7. Jean-François Champollion (1790–1832), regarded as the father of Egyptology, was the first scholar to decipher Egyptian hieroglyphics.
8. See also Hirschensohn, *Elleh Divrei ha-Berit,* 2:57–60 (chap. 3, § 1).

The Patriarchal Era in the Context of the Laws and Customs of the Ancient World

Numerous Jews subscribe to the belief that the Patriarchs fully observed the Torah despite the fact that it had not yet been given (see, e.g., Babylonian Talmud, tractate *Yoma* 28b), an idea that informs the traditional tendency to interpret the actions of the Patriarchs in light of the laws of the Torah. The problem with this approach is that clear examples of commandments observed by the Patriarchs are difficult to identify, while there are a number of instances in which the conduct of the Patriarchs departs from that prescribed by the Torah. Some sages therefore preferred to interpret the behavior of the Patriarchs as reflecting the laws and practices of the ancient world in which they lived.

199

She [Tamar] acted lawfully [toward Judah], because, before the Torah was given, all male relatives—even the father of the deceased—were eligible for Levirate marriage, and because Shelah had not fulfilled the obligation toward her, it was left to Judah to do so. Later, the Torah was given and a new law was introduced limiting Levirate marriage to paternal brothers, but, nonetheless, even after the Torah was given, they extended the practice to relatives other than paternal brothers who were permissible to the woman, as Boaz did with Ruth (Ruth 4:10)....

"She is with child by harlotry" (Gen. 38:24)—Because as long as she was waiting for a levir, they considered her a married woman.

"And let her be burned" (ibid.)—Such was the law in their practice before the Torah was given.[1] Our rabbis said that she was the daughter of a priest, the daughter of Shem—Melchizedek—who was a priest, and the [adulterous] daughter of a priest is punished by burning [see Lev. 21:9].[2]

Rabbi Joseph of Orleans, Commentary on Gen. 38:13, 24.[3]

200

My father's father[4] [reasoned] that this is because, in ancient times, the brothers were preferred for the role of Levirate marriage, but if they did not perform it, it passed to the father or other relatives. When Tamar saw that she had not been married to Shelah and the idea of tricking Judah occurred to her, she exploited the opportunity to do so, and when she had performed that trick and achieved her goal by becoming pregnant from Judah, [she left]. Judah thought that she was pregnant from a nonrelative, and he therefore commanded that she be executed for committing adultery while bound to a levir. When he learned that he was the father, he excused her from death on the grounds that she was not guilty because he was a potential levir. My father and teacher found this approach sensible and considered it decisive.

Rabbi Abraham Maimonides, *Perush Rabbenu Avraham ben ha-Rambam za"l al Bere'shit u-Shemot* (The commentary of our master Abraham Maimonides to Genesis and Exodus), ed. Ernest Wiesenberg (London: Defus ha-Ḥinukh, 1957/1958), 144 (Gen. 38:11–12).[5]

201

In the laws of life and customs regulating conduct of family and society, Abraham and his children after him, until the time the Torah was given, followed the laws that prevailed in the lands of the East: *The Code of Hammurabi.* Abraham and Sarai's treatment of their maid Hagar before Abraham married her and afterward, and Jacob's treatment of his wives and concubines, all correspond to examples contained in the code. Reuben says to Jacob, "You may kill my two sons if I do not bring him back to you" (Gen. 42:37), which is based on law 235 of the code. We discussed in the previous chapter the sentence issued by Jacob: "Anyone with whom you find your gods shall not remain alive!" (Gen. 31:32). The death sentence set down by Joseph's brothers for whoever had stolen the goblet similarly was based on prevailing practice.[6] Tamar permits herself to perform her deed at the entrance to Enaim and has no qualms about [the prohibition of] exposing the nakedness of a man's son's wife because Er and Onan had had unnatural intercourse with her, and she was not considered according to their laws to have been acquired by them. Hammurabi thus requires punishment for [intercourse with] one's son's wife only given prior intimate relations, and Judah, for the same reason, did nothing to her despite the fact that he had called for her to be burned for unmitigated adultery. Amram similarly marries his aunt Jochebed, and so forth. In reality, the importance of the Patriarchs lies in the fact that they injected the light of their souls into the laws of these Noahides, and invested them a part of their spiritual richness and grace. They restored the concepts of monotheism to their pristine state, inculcated the hearts of humanity with moral feeling, and imparted greater richness to the laws of righteousness and justice governing interpersonal relations.[7]

Rabbi Saie Reicher, *Torat ha-Rishonim: Yesodot ha-Torah she-be-al Peh ve-Hitpatteḥutah ha-Ḥiyyunit ba-Ḥayyim u-ba-Sefer ba-Dorot ha-Rishonim*

[The Torah of the ancients: the foundations of the Oral Torah and its indispensable development in the praxis and theory of antiquity] (Warsaw: Jeshurun, 1935), 1:26.⁸

Endnotes

1. Following a survey of opinions regarding Judah's sentencing of Tamar to burning (Gen. 28:24), Rabbi Menachem M. Kasher, *Torah Shelemah*, 7:1468–1469n96–98, comments,

   > It is intriguing that the three aforementioned practices are echoed in *The Code of Hammurabi*, which was in force four thousand years ago. In *The Code of Hammurabi* . . . section 110, the burning of a woman who has been disloyal. In such cases, the husband is entitled to forgive his wife, and this is exclusively dependent on him (ibid., sec. 129). In specific cases, they ruled that a mark was to be made on the forehead of an offender (ibid., sec. 126). . . . And it is explained in [the commentary of] Nachmanides that this was the law in those days, as it was in his lifetime in Spain: that if a woman was disloyal to her husband, then she was presented to her husband and he ruled whether she live or die, as he wished, and they considered Tamar to have the status of a married woman. We find such a thing as well in *The Code of Hammurabi*, section 129, that the husband is entitled to forgive his wife in such a case.

2. *Bereshit Rabbah*, ed. Theodor and Albeck, 1039 (§ 85:10).
3. For a similar interpretation, see Nachmanides, commentary to Gen. 38:8–9,24; see also Rabbi Joseph of Orleans, commentary to Exod. 22:2.
4. Editor Ernest Wiesenberg remarks (note 17 in the original), "This term is dotted in the manuscript, possibly indicating that the text contains a scribal error and should read, according to the proofreader, 'my father and teacher' rather than 'my father's father.'"
5. Rabbi Abraham Maimonides (1186–1237) was an exegete and succeeded his illustrious father, Rabbi Moses Maimonides, as a thinker, the leader of Egyptian Jewry, and a physician. He was a renaissance man at home in the worlds of halakhic jurisprudence, scriptural exegesis, philosophy, and medicine. For a comparable explanation to that presented here, see Gersonides, commentary to Gen. 38:26.
6. "Hammurabi rules, 'If anyone is committing a robbery and is caught, then he shall be put to death.' . . . Thus Jacob pronounced a death sentence for the individual who had stolen an object and concealed the crime—'anyone with whom you find your gods shall not remain alive!' (Gen. 31:32)—and his sons pronounced a similar sentence for the one in whose possession the goblet might be found." (13)
7. For a comparable explanation, see Rabbi Chaim Hirschensohn, *Sefer Nimmukei Rashi*, 1:71a (to Gen. 38:11).
8. Rabbi Saie Reicher (1879/1880–1942/1943), the rabbi of the community of Izmayil in Bessarabia, Romania (then Ukraine), was the author of several books and articles on Jewish subjects. He was deported during the Holocaust with his family to a work camp in Transnistria, where he was murdered.

Ancient Laws and Customs as Context for the Commandments of the Torah

The height of divine revelation in the Torah lies in its laws, commandments commonly introduced by the words "The Lord spoke to Moses, saying." Traditional Judaism has long emphasized the everlasting nature of the divine code: not only is it compulsory for all time, but it also lies beyond the limits of time and space. For this reason, it is no wonder that there have been scholars who balked at the very idea of a comparison between the sacred and eternal word of God, and laws conceived by mortal man. Yet more than once, the Torah, explicitly or not, refers to the historical context of a given commandment. Many sages, including figures who were eager to emphasize the eternity of the Torah, therefore addressed themselves to the religious and legal reality in which the Torah was given.

Pentateuchal Polemics against Contemporary Laws and Customs

Theologically speaking, the most direct link between the commandments of the Torah and the laws, beliefs, and customs of the ancient world is biblical polemics that seek to accentuate the goodness of the Torah's commandments and the contrasting negative aspects of the laws and practices of other peoples. Such an approach is explicit in several commandments, such as the commandment to the Israelites, "You shall not copy the practices of the land of Egypt where you dwelt, or of the land of Canaan to which I am taking you; nor shall you follow their laws. My rules alone shall you observe, and faithfully follow My laws: I the Lord am your God" (Lev. 18:3–4). It would be difficult not to agree that the commandments of the Torah refer to a concrete normative and legal reality that it seeks to repudiate. This reality, however, is not always detailed in the Torah, leaving to scholars the attempt to reconstruct it using written polytheistic sources, by building on their familiarity with ancient customs, or based on acquaintance with societies judged to be primitive (and thus to maintain practices reflective of prior ages).

202

"Parents shall not be put to death for children" (Deut. 24:16)—The ancients [i.e., the Rabbis; see, e.g., Babylonian Talmud, tractate *Sanhedrin* 27b] interpreted this homiletically as referring to testimony, meaning that the testimony of relatives about each other and themselves is invalid. The simple sense of the verse is that it is prohibited to punish the father for the sins of the son, or the son for the sins of the father. For you see that this is so, as it is written, "But he did not put to death the children of the assassins, in accordance with what is written in the Book of the Teaching of Moses, where the Lord commanded, 'Parents shall not be put to death for children, nor children be put to death for parents'" (2 Kings 14:6)? Rabbi Se'adyah did well in saying that the verse made sure to include this even though it is intellectually obvious, for the Arabs judged in such a manner during their time of *jahiliyyah* [i.e., ignorance: the pre-Islamic era]. One relative would be put to death due to another, and the Lord exhorted that this not be done. Do not object that the words of the ancients regarding the received meaning are contrary to the simple sense of the verse, because it is not unknown in their work [i.e., they frequently diverged from the simple sense].... It similarly was necessary to include, "You shall not bring the fee of a whore" (Deut. 23:19) even though the intellect finds such a thing reprehensible, for here, in several of the Indian islands, women debauch themselves with wayfarers, and sacrifice to their idols whatever consideration they receive.

Rabbi Judah Ibn Balaam.

203

I shall now return to my purpose and say that the meaning of many of the laws became clear to me and their causes became known to me through my study of the doctrines, opinions, practices, and cult of the Sabians, as you will hear when I explain the reasons for the *commandments* that are considered to be without causes. I shall mention to you the books from which all that I know about the doctrines and opinions of the Sabians will become clear to you so that you will know for certain that what I say about the reasons for these laws is correct....

All the books that I have mentioned to you are *books of idolatry* that have been translated into Arabic. But there is no doubt that they are but a very small part of this literature if compared to the writings that have not been translated and are not even extant, but have perished and been lost in the course of the years. However, the books extant among us today contain an exposition of the greatest part of the opinions and the practices of the Sabians; some of the latter are generally known as present in the world. I mean the building of temples, the setting-up in them of images made of cast metal and stone, the building of altars and the offering-up upon them of either animal sacrifices or various kinds of food, the institution of festivals, the gatherings for prayer and for various kinds of worship in those temples in which they locate highly venerated places that are called by them the temple of the intellectual forms, as well as the setting-up of images *upon the high mountains, and so on* (Deut. 12:2), the veneration of those *asheroth*, the setting-up of *monumental stones*, and other matters of which you will learn in the books to which I have drawn your attention. The knowledge of these opinions and practices is a very important chapter in the exposition of the reasons for the *commandments*. For the foundation of the whole of our Law and the pivot around which it turns, consists in the effacement of these opinions from the mins and of these monuments from existence.

Maimonides, *The Guide of the Perplexed,* 3:29.

204

The commandments comprised in the second class are those *commandments* that we have enumerated in *Laws concerning Idolatry*. It is manifest that all of them have in view deliverance from the errors of *idolatry* and from other incorrect opinions that may accompany *idolatry*, such as belief in *soothsayers, enchanters, sorcerers, charmers* (Lev. 5:5; 16:21), and others belonging to the same group. When you will have read all the books I have mentioned to you, it will become clear to you that the magic of which you hear consists in actions that used to be performed by the Sabians, the Chasdeans, and the Chaldeans; most of them were also found among the Egyptians and the Canaanites....

After these premises, which you will find valid upon reading such books of theirs as are at present in our hands and as I have let you know, hear my discourse: Inasmuch as the intent of the whole Law and the pole around which it revolves is to put an end to *idolatry*, to efface its traces, and to bring about a state of affairs in which it would not be imagined that any star harms or helps in anything pertaining to the circumstances of human individuals—this in view of the fact that such an opinion leads to star worship—it follows necessarily that all magicians must be killed.... And inasmuch as in all these practices the condition is posed that for the greater part they should be performed by women, it says: "You shall not tolerate a sorceress" (Exod. 22:17).... Inasmuch as the magicians deemed that their magic was effective, that by means of these practices they drove away harmful animals like lions, serpents, and so forth, from the villages; and they also deemed that by means of their magic they warded off various sorts of damage from plants.... because of these things that at that time were generally known, it is stated among other things in the *words of the covenant* (Deut. 28:69) that it is because of *idolatry* and of the magical practices by means of which you think that these kinds of harm can be kept away from you that these calamities will befall you.... To sum up the matter: Having in view all the devices used by the *idolaters* to perpetuate their cult through suggesting to people that thereby certain kinds of harm may be warded off and certain kinds of benefits obtained, it is included in *the words of the covenant* that through their cult these kinds of benefits are lost and these kinds of damage come about. Thus it has already become clear to you, you who engage in speculation, what Scripture intended in these particulars of the *curses* and the *blessings* contained in *the words of the covenant*, singling out them rather than the others for statement. Know likewise the extent of the great utility of this.

In order to keep people away from all magical practices, it has been prohibited to observe any of their usages, even those attaching to agricultural and pastoral activities and other activities of this kind. I mean all that is said to be useful, but it is not required by speculation concerning nature, and takes its course, in their opinion, in accordance with occult properties. . . .

We have already explained in our great compilation that the shaving of *the corner of the head and of the corner of the beard* has been forbidden (Lev 19:27) because it was the usage of *idolatrous priests*. This is also the reason for the prohibition of *mingled stuff* (Deut. 22:11), for this too was a usage of these *priests*, as they put together in their garments vegetal and animal substances bearing at the same time a seal made out of some mineral; you will find this set forth literally in their books.

This is also the reason for its dictum: "A woman must not put on man's apparel, nor shall a man wear woman's clothing" (Deut. 22:5). You will find in the book of Tumtum[1] the commandment that a man should put on a woman's dyed garment when standing before [the planet] Venus and that a woman should put on a cuirass and arms when standing before Mars . . .

If then you study carefully one by one all the *commandments* dealing with *idolatry*, you will find that the reason for them is manifest and consists in putting an end of these corrupt opinions and turning people to another direction far away from them.

Among the things to which we shall draw attention belongs the following point: Those that set up these false opinions, which have no root or any utility, in order to fortify belief in them, use the device of spreading among the people the opinion that a certain calamity will befall those who do not perform an action perpetuating this belief. Now this may happen by accident someday to a certain individual, and consequently he will seek to perform the action in question and to follow that belief. Now it is known that it is the nature of men in general to be most afraid and most wary of losing their property and their children. Therefore the worshippers of fire spread abroad the opinion in those times that everyone who would not *make his son or his daughter to pass through the fire* (Deut. 18:10) would die. And there is no doubt that because of the strong pity and apprehension felt with regard to children and because of the trifling character of the action and its ease, for it simply consisted in making them pass through fire.... Therefore the Law is strongly opposed to this action, an opposition that is affirmed in such terms as are not used with regard to other kinds of *idolatrous* practices: "and so defiled My sanctuary and profaned My holy name" (Lev. 20:3). Thereupon the truthful one [i.e., Moses] makes known in the name of God, may He be exalted, and says: Whereas you perform this action so that the children stay alive because of it, God will cause him who performs it to perish and will exterminate his descendants: he says "I Myself will set My face against that man and his kin [and will cut off from among their people both him and all who follow him in going astray after Molech]" (5)....

The *idolaters* have acted in a similar way with regard to property. They have made the ordinance that one tree, namely, the *asherath*, should be consecrated to the object of their worship and that its fruits should be taken, part of them serving as an offering while the rest should be eaten in an *idolatrous temple*, as they have explained in the laws concerning the *asherath*. They have also prescribed that the first fruits of every tree whose fruits are edible should be used in the same manner, I mean that a portion of them should serve as an offering while the rest should be eaten in an *idolatrous temple*. They have also spread abroad the opinion that if the first fruits of any tree whatever were not treated in this manner, the tree in question would wither or its fruits would drop or its produce would be small or some calamity would befall it; just as they have spread abroad the opinion that every child that was not passed through the fire would die. Inasmuch as men were afraid for their property, they likewise hastened to perform these practices. Accordingly the Law opposed this opinion, and He, may He be exalted, commanded that everything produced in the course of three years by a tree whose fruits are edible should be burnt. For some trees bear fruit after one year, other bear their first fruits after two years, and others again after three.... And He has commanded to eat the *fourth-year fruit of planting before the Lord* (Lev. 19:24) as a substitute for eating the *first products* [of trees] in an *idolatrous temple*, as we have explained.

The ancient *idolaters* also mention in "The Nabatean Agriculture" that they let certain things mentioned by them putrefy, looking out in this connection for the sun's entering into a certain sign of the Zodiac, and performing many magical operations. They thought that this thing should be prepared by everybody and that whenever one planted a tree bearing edible fruit, one should scatter around it or at its very place a portion of the thing that has been made to putrefy, in order that the tree should grow more quickly and that it should bear fruit in a way contrary to what is usual, within the shortest possible period. They mentioned that this is a wondrous method that is of the same character as the talismans and that it is the most wondrous of the methods of magic in regard to increase in rapidity in the production of the fruit of all trees that produce fruit. We have already explained to you and made known to you that the Law eschews all these magic operations. Therefore the Law forbids all that is grown by trees bearing edible fruit within the period of three years from the day they were planted. Accordingly there is no need, contrary to what they thought, to increase their rapidity in producing fruit. After three years, however, the produce of most of the trees in Syria bearing edible fruit attains its perfect state according to the course of nature, and there is no objection in resorting to the generally known magical operation that was employed by them. Understand this wondrous thing too.

One of the opinions generally known in those times and perpetuated by the Sabians was expressed by their statement concerning the grafting of a tree of one species onto another tree. They said that if this is done when a certain star is in the ascendant and if certain fumigations are made and certain invocations pronounced at the time of the grafting, that which is produced by the graft will be a thing that, as they believe, will be very useful. The clearest point concerning these things is the one mentioned in the beginning of the "Agriculture" concerning the grafting of the olive tree onto the citron tree. In my opinion it must indubitably be true that the *book of medicaments* that *was suppressed by Hezekiah* belonged to this group. They also mention that when one species is grafted upon another, the bough that is meant to be grafted ought to be held in the hand of a beautiful girl and of a man who has come into her in a disgraceful manner that they describe and that the woman must graft the bough upon the tree while the two are *performing* this act. There is no doubt that this was generally adopted and that no one remained that acted otherwise, especially in view of the fact that in this custom pleasure of sexual intercourse is joined to the desire for the benefits in question. Therefore the *mingling* [of diverse species], I mean the *grafting of one tree upon another* is *forbidden*, so that we shall keep far away from the causes of *idolatry* and from the *abomination* of their unnatural kinds of sexual intercourse. It is with reference to *the grafting of a tree* that is has been forbidden to join together any two species of *seeds*, even if only putting one near the other. . . .

They also state explicitly in the "Agriculture" that it was they custom to sow barley and grapes together, for they thought that a vineyard could only propser through this practice. Consequently the Law has forbidden the [sowing of] *a vineyard with diverse seeds* and has commanded burning all such things. For all *the customs of the nations* that were thought to have occult properties were prohibited, even if they did not at all smack of *idolatry*; just as we have explained with reference to their dictum: *It is not [allowed] to hang it upon a tree, and so on*. All these, I mean *their customs*, which are called *Amorite usages*, have been forbidden because of their leading to *idolatry*. If you consider their customs in agriculture, you will find that in certain kinds of agriculture they turn toward the stars, in others toward the two luminaries.... Consequently all these *customs of the nations* have been forbidden in a general way, and it says: "You shall not follow the practices of the nation [that I am driving out before you. For it is because they did all these things that I abhorred them]" (Lev. 20:23). That among them which was more generally accepted and widespread or that which contained an explicit reference to some kind of *idolatry* was the object of various particular prohibitions—for instance, those regarding the *first products* [of trees], the *mingling* [of diverse species], the [sowing of] *a vineyard with diverse seeds*. I wonder at the dictum of Rabbi Josiah, considered as a *legal decision*, concerning [the sowing of] *a vineyard with diverse seeds*, according to which one has committed no transgression *unless one sows together, in one throw of the hand, wheat, barley, and pips of grapes*. Doubtless he had learned that this custom had its origin in the *Amorite usages*.

Thus it has been made clear to you, so that there can be no doubt about it, that *mingled stuff*, the *first products* [of trees], and the *mingling* [of diverse species] were forbidden because of *idolatry*, and that *their customs*, which have been referred to, were forbidden because they lead to *idolatry*, as we have explained.

Maimonides, *The Guide of the Perplexed*, 3:37.[2]

205

In the case of most of the *statutes* whose reason is hidden from us, everything serves to keep people away from *idolatry*. The fact that there are particulars the reason for which is hidden from me and the utility of which I do not understand, is due to the circumstance that things known by hearsay are not like things that one has seen. Hence the extent of my knowledge of the ways of the Sabians is drawn from books and is not comparable to the knowledge of one who saw their practices with his eyes; this is even more the case since these opinions have disappeared two thousand years ago or even before that. If we knew the particulars of those practices and heard details concerning their opinions, we would become clear regarding the wisdom manifested in the details of the practices proscribed in the commandments concerning the *sacrifices* and the form of *uncleanness* and other matters whose reason cannot, to my mind, be easily grasped. For I for one do not doubt that all this was intended to efface those untrue opinions from the mind and to abolish those useless practices, which brought about a waste of lives *in vain and futile things* (Isa. 49:4). . . . Accordingly every commandment or prohibition of the Law whose reason is hidden from you constitutes a cure fro one of those diseases which today—thank God—we do not know anymore.

Maimonides, *The Guide of the Perplexed*, 3:49.

206

What seems more correct in this regard is that it was the practice of pagans at their gathering to do this—i.e., to cook kids in milk at harvest time—which they believed would cause their gods to favor them, come nearer to them, and bless their endeavors. As it is said, "that they may offer their sacrifices no more to the goat-demons" (Lev. 17:7). Shepherds in particular were certainly accustomed to doing this when they gathered to perform their rites and rituals, when they would eat kids cooked in milk and all sorts of other cooked dishes of meat and milk. This practice exists to this day in the kingdoms of Spain, where all of the shepherds gather twice each year to consult and create regulations concerning shepherds and sheep, a gathering called "mixing" in their language. We have investigated the matter and found it to be true that at this gathering they indeed eat meat and milk. Kid meat is their preference in this dish. I have inquired and probed and learned with certainty that even among those at the edge of the earth, in the land known as England, where there are more sheep than anywhere else, this is the established practice. I truly believe that this is why God, blessed be He, admonished them, when they gathered on Sukkot, not to cook kids and milk, as the non-Jews do. He forbade eating, deriving benefit from, and cooking such food, as they [i.e., the sages] stated, in order to distance them as much as possible from pagan practices.

Don Isaac Abravanel, Commentary on Exod. 23:19.[3]

The Preservation of Good Laws that Preceded the Giving of the Torah

Nachmanides, writing of the greatness of the Torah, bleakly describes the state of the ancient world before it was given: "First and foremost, you must know that all things known and understood by created beings are direct or indirect products of the Torah. If not for the Torah, there would be no difference between a person and the donkey he rides. . . . He has no notion of meritorious deeds or sin, no intellect and no ability to reason, and he does not view any deed as better or more favorable than another. . . . All things thus are equal to him, just as he is equal to the animals. . . . All the nations initially were this way, as it is said, 'Or what great nation has laws and rules as perfect as all this Teaching that I set before you this day?' (Deut. 4:8)."[4] The ancient world was a disarray of irrationality and nothingness, and the mission of the Torah was to wage an unrelenting war against all human practice that had preceded it.

Nachmanides' view may be notionally more agreeable to the ears of Orthodox Jews, but it presents formidable challenges on a more practical level. Descriptions in Genesis of local nations suggest not utter anarchy, but a social order characterized by laws and ethical principles. This difficulty is compounded by the ancient legal codes revealed by archaeological excavations. These codes include laws with some level of similarity to those of the Torah. Sure enough, some Jewish scholars throughout history took quite a different approach: not only did neighboring nations have certain commendable laws and practices before the Torah was given, but some of these conventions were good enough for the Torah to endorse or even adopt!

207

"My laws, and My teachings" (Gen. 26:5)—Most correctly, according to the simple sense of the verse, all of the obvious [i.e., rationally explicable] commandments, such as those concerning theft, forbidden sexual relations, coveting, monetary law, and hospitality, were in force before the Torah was given, but they were then reinstituted and expounded to the Israelites, and they entered a covenant to observe them.

Rashbam (Rabbi Samuel ben Meir).

208

As for the reason for the *levirate*, it is literally stated [in Scripture] that this was an ancient custom that obtained before the *giving of the Torah* and that was perpetuated by the Law.

Maimonides, *The Guide of the Perplexed*, 3:49.

209

A sudden transition from one opposite to another is impossible. And therefore man, according to his nature, is not capable of abandoning suddenly all to which he was accustomed. As therefore God sent *Moses our Master* to make of us "a kingdom of priests and a holy nation" (Exod. 19:6)—through the knowledge of Him, may He be exalted ... and as at that time the way of life generally accepted and customary in the whole world and the universal service upon which we were brought up consisted in offering various species of living beings in the temple in which images were set up, in worshipping the latter, and in burning incense before them—the pious ones and the ascetics beings at that time, as we have explained, the people who were devoted to the service of the temples consecrated to the stars—: His wisdom, may He be exalted, and His gracious ruse, which is manifest in regard to all His creatures, did not require that He give us a Law prescribing the rejection, abandonment, and abolition of all these kinds of worship. For one could not then conceive the acceptance of [such a Law], considering the nature of man, which always likes that to which it is accustomed. At that time this would have been similar to the appearance of a prophet in these times who, calling upon the people to worship God, would say: "God has given you a Law forbidding you to pray to Him, to fast, to call upon Him in misfortune. Your worship should consist solely in meditation without any works at all." Therefore He, may He be exalted, suffered the above-mentioned kinds of worship to remain, but transferred them from created or imaginary and unreal things to His own name, may He be exalted, commanding us to practice them with regard to Him, may He be exalted. Thus He commanded us to build a temple for Him: "let them make Me a sanctuary" (Exod. 25:8); to have an alter for His name: "Make for Me an altar of earth" (20:21); to have the sacrifice offered up to Him: "When any of you presents an offering to the Lord" (Lev. 1:2); to bow down in worship before Him; and to burn incense before Him. And he forbade the performance of any of these actions with a view to someone else: "Whoever sacrifices to a god [other than the Lord alone] shall be proscribed" (Exod. 22:19), "for you must not worship any other god" (34:14). And He singled out *Priests* for the service of the *Sanctuary*, saying: "let them serve Me as priests" (28:41). And because of their employment in the temple and the sacrifices in it, it was necessary to fix for them dues that would be sufficient for them; namely, the dues of the *Levites* and the *Priests*. Through this divine ruse it came about that the memory of *idolatry* was effaced and that the grandest and true foundation of our belief—namely, the existence and oneness of the deity—was firmly established, while at the same time the souls had no feeling of repugnance and were not repelled because of the abolition of modes of worship to which they were accustomed and than which no other mode of worship was known at that time.

Maimonides, *The Guide of the Perplexed,* 3:32.

210

"That which was torn by beasts" (Gen. 31:39)—After Jacob, may he rest in peace, recounted how virtuous and loyal he had been while living with him [i.e., Laban], he proceeded to describe Laban's ignominy and the false arguments that he had made against him in business. He would make him pay what the law did not require, meaning that he would require him to pay for livestock killed by an animal in circumstances where the event was caused not by any action of his, but by force majeure. The Judge of the world, blessed be He, thus righteously included in the laws of guardians the decree that "If it was torn by beasts, he shall bring it as evidence; he need not replace what has been torn by beasts" (Exod. 22:12).

"Whether snatched by day or night" (Gen. 31:39)—Meaning, both any sheep stolen during the day, which the shepherd is required to repay with his wage—as the Lord, may He be exalted, said, "[But] if it was stolen from him" (Exod. 22:11)—and any unavoidably stolen during the night, for which shepherds are not liable. As the transmitters explained, with respect to the laws of an unpaid guardian, he is exempt from paying for that which is carried off as he is for that which is injured or dies. Laban in his ignominy would require him to pay for livestock stolen at night, for which he was not legally liable, just as for livestock stolen during the day, for which he was liable. Jacob, may he rest in peace, did not describe all this in full because this is the law that customarily applied to guardians in ancient times, as indicated by this statement. You already know that Levirate marriage, although it is one of the commandments of the Torah, was an ancient custom, and the Torah left it as it was. The same doubtless is true of some other commandments.

Rabbi Abraham Maimonides, *Perush Rabbenu Avraham ben ha-Rambam za"l al Bereshit u Shemot,* 100b.[5]

211

The birthright was considered legally binding by the ancients, and they similarly set a few natural matters as law before the Torah was given. Once the Torah had been given, those things it found to be good, such as birthright and Levirate marriage, it left as they were, and those things that it did not find to be good, it superseded, as they said: "the Torah was given and a new law was introduced."

Rabbi Ibn Mansur al-Damari, *Midrash Ner ha-Sekhalim.*[6]

212

"For he will turn your children away from Me" (Deut. 7:4)—our sages said that "your son from a gentile woman is called her son." We know from the beliefs and ordinances of the Egyptians that they considered children from a maidservant to be legitimate, because they did not consider the mother to be of any consequence for the pedigree of the offspring. This view was accepted by the Greeks as well. . . . This is one of the proofs that the giver of the Torah neither accepted nor rejected the laws of Egypt, contrary to the views of some scholars, both Jewish and gentile. There are those who have said that the laws of Israel adhered in every respect to those of the Egyptians, among whom we grew up . . . and there are those who have said that the exclusive purpose of the Torah was to oppose the ordinances of Egypt. Yet neither is the truth. To the contrary, the Torah was unafraid to hew marvelously close to the Egyptians in numerous respects, while in not a few others it went to the opposite extreme. This is the well-founded truth according to both scholarly inquiry and faith.

Rabbi Elia Benamozegh, *Sefer Torat Hashem . . . ve-Nosaf alav Em la-Mikra . . . va . . . Em la-Masoret*, 5:33a–b.

213

"Who on hearing of all these laws" (Deut. 4:6)—the sage Samuel Davide Luzzatto, in his *Ha-Mishtadel*, struggles to extrapolate from this verse that the laws of the Torah cannot have been taken from the Egyptians or other nations. Yet how can this rescue us when, in comparison, we see that the laws of Egypt and the laws of the Torah are similar, as any student can correctly prove? Equally unhelpful is his further comment, "For we must at least acknowledge that the divine Torah separated out the good from the bad?" This statement contradicts itself, and is unacceptable! How would it be divine if it had managed only to separate out the good from the bad? How could their valueless articulations be the master or teacher of our perfect Torah? There is some truth to his latter comment, but only if we understand it according to the kabbalists' view regarding the other separation [i.e., as referring to the Israelites' extraction of the traces of holiness found in Egypt], which is superior to the separation in *Ha-Mishtadel*. From this, understand that the word of the Lord that they spoke is true, for although the kabbalists neither knew nor understood—as we recently have come to understand—that the laws of Egypt and the laws of the Torah are quite similar, they formulated a solution even before that problem arose, putting forth the secret of extraction while there was not yet pressure to find a justification.

Rabbi Elia Benamozegh, *Sefer Torat Hashem . . . ve-Nosaf alav Em la-Mikra . . . va . . . Em la-Masoret,* 5:175a.[7]

214

"Next day, Moses sat as magistrate among the people" (Exod. 18:13)—Rashi interprets this verse as does the *Mekhilta*,[8] "the day after the Day of Atonement." Thus the section of the giving of the Torah begins with Jethro. The holy Zohar[9] says that it was necessary to capture the king and priest of the shell in order for the Torah to be given. This follows the opinion that Jethro came before the giving of the Torah.[10] This is the difficulty that the holy Zohar is attempting to resolve: Why is Jethro, the priest of Midian, mentioned here? It answers that the preparation for the giving of the Torah included the capture of the priest of the shell: Jethro's conversion (as explained in essay 3). However, we must understand why this passage, which all agree took place after the Day of Atonement, as Rashi writes, appears before the giving of the Torah. As the holy Zohar (69a) states, "Pharaoh had three counselors: Jethro, Job, and Balaam." The main goal of the Egyptian captivity was for them to "go free with great wealth," meaning that they would free their holy, living sparks, as it says, "they stripped the Egyptians" (Exod. 12:36), making it like a fort without grain, like deep waters without fish, the root and mainstay of life (as has been explained on several occasions), and the Israelites thus merited that they be given the Torah. Pharaoh was the crown of the shell, the mystery of the great crocodile, as reported in the Zohar,[11] and they freed from him all the life force and words of Torah that had been held by him in captivity. Pharaoh's three counselors and advisors had inside them other words of Torah, and they needed to free these from them as well. . . . Before the Torah was given, once they had freed all of the words of Torah that had been in captivity in the wisdom of the Egyptians . . . they needed to free the holy sparks and words of Torah from Pharaoh's three advisors. Jethro joined the Israelites and converted, and Job is considered a pious gentile,[12] unlike Balaam, and Balaam's words of Torah therefore were established among the Israelites only forty years later. The words of Torah that were in Jethro are the passage about judges . . . but he spoke on the level of his simple intellect and did not understand what he was saying, which really was words of Torah. They freed them from him before the Torah was given, and this was preparatory for the giving of the Torah, but it was established among the Israelites at its proper time. Scripture therefore placed this passage before the giving of the Torah, despite the fact that it took place after the Day of Atonement, because the act of freeing the words of Torah from him, as described, was preparatory for the giving of the Torah. The words of Torah taken from Pharaoh's three advisors correspond to wisdom, insight, and knowledge. . . . After our master Moses obtained the words of Torah from Pharaoh's three advisors, the Israelites merited the giving of the Torah, but [the contribution of] each was established as words of Torah among the Israelites at its proper time, as described.

Rabbi Zadok of Lublin, *Peri Tzaddik*, Exodus, Yitro 4.[13]

215

"This is the record of the generations of humanity" (Gen. 5:1)—this is the major principle of the Torah, said the sages of blessed memory.[14] It truly is felicitous to recognize how exalted and lofty the human spirit is, and that any lofty and sublime idea has already been conceived by the collective intellectual power of humanity. Just as the select among the ancient ones were remarkable in physique—in the state of their physical abilities—they were distinguished as well in their spiritual state and the depth of their spiritual sensitivity and outlook. But the masses, who steadily declined with time because they were inculcated with bad things and incapable of assimilating the knowledge of the great ones among them, corrupted the great ideas of those ancients.

Therefore it is logically necessary, as well as a mark of the splendor of the Torah of truth, that all great, universal ideas and beliefs, which became corrupted among the pagan masses into any number of vain and imaginary versions, be found in the Torah in their untainted form. The Torah restored them to their original form, seeking to heal the harm done to humanity by the fall of the masses and many of its capable rulers who were brutal and wild, and to uplift humanity to that exalted level that is the natural place of humankind—the level occupied by the most distinguished among them in ancient times. Thus even many virtues, religious requirements, and customs can emerge from pure divine insight. True, they became degraded over the course of time by the foulness of the bad, contemptible views with which the masses erred, but the Torah restored them to their original grandeur and purity.

It is mere idleness to think that if we find things in the Torah, whether views, depictions, or commandments, the likes of which are found among the most ancient nations, then it should disincline the heart to believe in the sanctity of the Torah. Perish the thought! Just as the civilized nations of the world certainly subscribed to the intellectually comprehensible commandments—and the Torah divinely restored those that had been compromised and weakened, among these the better part of the Ten Commandments—thus many traditional commandments, which certainly are intellectually comprehensible at their core, previously had a place in the sacred guidance provided by the most eminent of ancient generations, among whom were divine sages as well as prophets and sacred ministers. Whatever divine wisdom found fit to set in the crown of the Torah was set as an eternal witness, as a law of Israel. This gives any true sage much greater affection for the power of the commandments and [appreciation of] their divine splendor, for they were hidden away in the council of the pure wisdom of God before the atmosphere of the world was defiled by fabulists and tyrants, before the purity of the human spirit was displaced. The hand of the Lord, through the perfect, supreme prophecy of the master of the prophets, selected all those pieces fit to remain, and added whatever was fit to add in light of new developments: namely, the arrival of Israel and its activity on behalf of both itself and the world.

Thus the recently expanded search through lost works of the antiquities of nations, and the similarities identified between them and the content of the Torah give light and joy to anyone who truly seeks the Lord. It is right to amplify and aggrandize this vigorous scholarship and teach understanding to those spiritually lost: how to use it to serve the purpose of truth, to show all the nations of the world that the foundation of the Torah is pure humanity, without which it steadily degenerates over time....

Those who think it implausible for any bit of the sanctity and splendor of the Torah to be found in the spirit and inherent talents of humanity fail to recognize the splendor of the image of God, in which the Creator of man created him.

Rabbi Abraham Isaac Kook, *Pinkas mi-Tekufat Boisk* [Journal from the Bauska period], in *Pinkesei ha-Re'ayah* [Journals of Rabbi Abraham Isaac Kook] (Jerusalem: The Rabbi Zvi Yehuda Kook Institute, 2009/2010), 2:118–119 (chap. 32).[15]

216

Similarly, when Assyriology emerged, disquieting many due to the similarities in views, morality, and practice that its groundless hypotheses identified between our holy Torah and things in cuneiform documents ... with regard to similarities in practice, has it not been established since the time of Maimonides—and even earlier, in the remarks of our sages of blessed memory—that prophecy interacts with human nature, because one's nature and proclivities must ascend in accordance with divine guidance, because "the commandments were given only to purify humankind"? The divine Torah thus left alone whatever had been inculcated in the nation and the world prior to the giving of the Torah, so long as it had some moral foundation and could be raised up to eternal, refined moral status. Viewed more clearly, this is the true foundation of the positive cultural consciousness rooted deep in human nature, such that "this is the record of the generations of humanity" (Gen. 5:1) is the underlying principle of the entire Torah—a principle even greater than that of "Love your fellow as yourself," as posited by Rabbi Akiva. Any thinking person first considering the matter ought to arrive at these and other such insights: there was no reason at all for that factitious heresy to appear, spread, and gain strength due to these developments.

Rabbi Abraham Isaac Kook, "Ra'yonot le-Toledot ha-Ga'on Adderet" (Thoughts on the biography of the great Elijah David Rabinowitz-Te'omim), *Eder ha-Yeqar ve-Ikvei ha-Tzon* (Jerusalem: Mosad Harav Kook, 1966/1967), 42–43.[16]

217

It is clear that those who challenge the jabbering of Professor Delitzsch identifying a similarity between the laws of the Torah and the laws of Hammurabi thoroughly fail to understand that once Moses, with his fine, divinely inspired intellect, had studied all the laws of contemporary nations, or those in historical works of nations and the world, that he found good and right, he did not write them in his Torah until the wondrous intellectual understanding metaphorically known as divine speech came to him. Then, only then, did he record them in the book, because once that wondrous understanding had come to him, he knew that his thoughts contained nothing twisted or crooked, and he recorded these things as instructed by the Lord.

Rabbi Chaim Hirschensohn, *Sefer Malki ba-Kodesh*, 2:497–498 (responsum 6:6).[17]

218

Any person with a healthy intellect can understand the truth of my statement when I note that the words "The Lord spoke to Moses, saying" do not appear at all in *parashat* Mishpatim, which I have arranged [chronologically, in the present work] after the words of Jethro. . . . The crux of the matter is as I previously wrote, that this is a continuation of what Jethro said: "You shall also seek out . . . and these are the rules that you shall set before" these elders (Exod. 18:21, 21:1). . . . It cannot be doubted that

Jethro said this regarding the rules that he [i.e., Moses] ought to set before the officers of the people and before the elders who would judge the people at all times.

With this now understood, it is no surprise that there is a similarity between these rules and *The Code of Hammurabi* with which Delitzsch astounded the world, because we have no reason to be surprised if Jethro used some ancient laws as examples. I find plausible as well the view of my close friend, the scholar Dr. Rubin, who believed that the sense of "When you acquire a Hebrew slave" (Exod. 21:2) extends to all the children of Eber, rather than Israel alone. For the advice given by Jethro was asked of a Midianite sage, [and he thus counseled] preferential treatment of the children of Edom and Ishmael, and those of Keturah, Ammon, and Moab. This similarly is the meaning of the verse "If you lend money to My people," that is, to the Kenites and Midianites, or "to the poor among you, do not act toward them as a creditor" (Exod. 22:24). For the same reason, we find the phrase "I will set for you a place to which he can flee" (Exod. 21:13), because Jethro was well-versed in all the wadis and valleys of the wilderness and its cities. So he said that he would find him a suitable place to which someone who had killed a person unintentionally might flee. According to the simple sense of the verse that *God* told him this *parashah*, He should have said, "you will set for yourself," as it is said, "Then Moses set aside three cities on the east side of the Jordan" (Deut. 4:41). However, the words "from My very altar" appear as they do [i.e., in the first person] because God already had instructed him regarding this [and modified the original wording], as Jethro said to Moses, "and if God so commands you," as it is said: "Moses went and repeated to the people all the commands of the Lord and all the rules" (Exod. 24:3) Indeed, Jethro's remarks included the words "you shall take him from an altar" because for the ancients, grasping the altar was akin to fleeing to a city of refuge, as Jethro said: "you shall take him from my very altar" (Exod. 21:14). Among the Arabs until today, a person who flees to the Kaaba shrine in Mecca is saved from a pursuing avenger. The concept of "eye for an eye" (Exod. 21:24) also need not bother us, because in light of the legal conception of Jethro's day, there is no difficulty in understanding the words in their simple sense, as rendered by the *Targum*: "an eye in exchange for an eye," as in *The Code of Hammurabi*. However, once God had issued instructions regarding these things, our sages strove to interpret this concept as referring to money, in accordance with the gracious ways of our Torah. The awful concept "he is not to be avenged, since he is the other's property" (21) similarly is one that belongs strictly to the time of Jethro. God concurred only with the law, not with the rationale, and recorded the rationale in order not to absolve another person from punishment if [the victim remained alive] a day or two, as written by Rashi. Letting [a slave] go free on account of [knocking out] his tooth is an extraneous instruction, but anyone familiar with the pride that the desert dwellers and Africans take in their white teeth will understand that, for them, the loss of a tooth is an incalculable one, because they still lack experience with dentures. This, too, indicates that this belongs to what Jethro said.

"His master shall take him before *ha-elohim*" (6) in Jethro's conception similarly refers to God per se [as opposed to judges]. The piercing of the ear was a kind of covenant among the ancient nations, who made do with piercing the ear of a slave to symbolize that he belonged not to the slaveholder, but to God. However, once the Lord had issued instructions regarding these things, the sages strove to interpret the phrase as referring to judges. In the view of our sages, the fact that the Torah arranged this section without mentioning Jethro's name, but instead juxtaposed it to the revelation at Mount Sinai, shows that the Torah wished for the Israelites to accept these rules. However, the Torah intended for them to accept the rules not as Jethro intended, but according to the gracious ways and peaceful paths of the Torah, which were transmitted to the sages in the Oral Torah.

Rabbi Chaim Hirschensohn, *Seder la-Mikra* (Jerusalem: Defus ha-Ivri Y. Verker, 1932/1933), 2:133–135.[18]

The Possible Divine Source of Gentile Laws and Customs

Belief in the Torah is held by many to require that believers wholly reject the content of other faiths: not only is the Torah inherently good in all its details and particulars, but other beliefs are inherently bad. Is it really true, though, that the divinity and purity of the Torah necessitate the conviction that other religions and laws contain nothing godly? Most rabbinic authorities through the ages did not discuss this question. The fact that they were privy to the greatness of the Torah left them uninterested in whether other holy books might offer some lesser degree of spiritual sustenance, and some scholars also stressed the adverse aspects of other faiths. A few figures, however, were willing to grant that foreign laws and beliefs contained a degree of godliness and goodness. For them, the similarities between the Torah and other faiths were the simple result of their common divine source, while the differences were assigned various causes. Some attributed them to the limited nature of revelation enjoyed by gentile nations, others believed that other peoples that had corrupted the true religion over the course of time, and a third group viewed the disparities as the necessary product of the different characters and abilities of different national groups.

219

Know, my brothers, that it is not impossible for the Lord, may He be blessed and exalted, to send to His world whomever He desires whenever He desires, because the bounty of the holy world is constant and unending.... Indeed, He, may He be lauded, sent prophets to the nations even before the Torah was given, as the sages said, "Seven prophets prophesied to the nations of the world before the Torah was given"... and it is not impossible for Him to send to them whomever He desires so that the world will not be left without faith. Indeed, the prophets said that He will be worshiped by the nations from sunrise to sunset ... but He selected us and honored us more than all other nations, not because of our prior righteousness, but out of the grace shown by the Lord to our forefathers Abraham, Isaac, and Jacob. Indeed, the law of the Arabs [i.e., the Quran] discusses how He benefited us and magnified us more than all other mortals, at it states, "O Children of Israel! Call to mind the favor which I bestowed upon you, and that I preferred you over the worlds" (Surah Al-Baqarah, 47,122).[19] ... Know that the Lord, may He be exalted, commanded that every nation worship Him according to its law, permitted each nation things that He forbade others, and forbade each things that he permitted others. For He knows what benefits His creatures and what befits them ... and it is right that we be prudent in observing that which we already have in hand and with which we grew up, and not challenge any person who belongs to another religion. . .. It thus is right that each nation conduct itself according to what has been transmitted and imparted to it, and follow its own prophets, priests, and leaders, and that no one be left without a law, because all is from the single God. They all return to Him, all pray to Him and turn to Him, and every righteous soul migrates to Him, as it is stated, "And the lifebreath returns to God Who bestowed it" (Eccl. 12:7).... It is not right for any person to challenge the other nations, because their laws and punishments are in the hands of Him who is not of us, may He be lauded and exalted.... Indeed, a certain sage has spoken against religious fanaticism and religious debates. Never pursue fanaticism.

Rabbi Nathanel Beirav al-Fayyumi, *Gan ha-Sekhalim* (The garden of wisdom), ed. Joseph Kafiḥ (Jerusalem: ha-Aguda la-Hatzalat Ginzei Teman, 1953/1954), 1114–1122 (chap. 6).[20]

220

In my view, their [i.e., the Rabbis'] inclusion of judges among the commandments of the children of Noah does not mean only that they must appoint judges in every locality. Rather, He commanded them concerning the laws applying to theft, deceit, exploitation, and payment of employees, and the laws applying to guardians, rapists, seducers, the broad categories of damages, and physical injury, and the laws applying to lenders and borrowers, and the laws applying to purchases and sales, and so on, as with the laws that the Israelites were commanded to follow.

Nachmanides, Commentary on Gen. 34:13.[21]

221

There are others who believe that it is impossible for the human heart to attain wholesome, true, and proper belief in the Torah of Moses, and that instead he should consider that other faiths are vain and specious and are of no use to their adherents. However, this is untrue. To be sure, there are ideas with advocates in the Israelite nation that cause many common people to think this. Furthermore, this attitude occasionally has had the effect of strengthening the Israelite faith in the hearts of the simple, who are able to fathom the loftiness and sanctity of our holy Torah only by considering other faiths to be erroneous things of no value whatsoever. However, this unenlightened idea has many harmful consequences as well. The derision for other faiths deeply imprinted on the hearts of the common people causes sacrilegious wicked individuals to judge the pure Israelite faith as well, saying that all [faiths] are comparable in character: this is a faith and that is faith. Therefore, in order to save the youth of our generation from such dangerous traps, we must examine the nature of other faiths as viewed by the Torah. . . . True, where idolatry is concerned, we are forbidden to be tolerant in practice, and this is unique to us, the nation of the Lord . . . because the Lord established us in His world as witnesses to His glory, to the light of His divinity and providence and the knowledge of His name, blessed be He. . . . Although we should not hatefully rage at idolaters and think that they are to blame for engaging in idolatry—because for what can we blame them in light of the fact that they retain their ancestors' practice?—we must guard ourselves and the entire human race so that it comes to perceive the truth by bearing before the Lord the banner of His name and glory. We therefore must strenuously distance ourselves from all aspects of idolatry and its trappings. . . .

Not all forms of idolatry are equal. There are some nations that have developed morally to such a degree that, although they are idolaters, they exhibit an honorable level of morality, virtue, and etiquette. Their idolatrous ways are thus not so very vile and abominable as others'. Therefore, it is not right to view all idolaters nations as equivalent and comparable. Indeed, even idolatry contains a spark of morality, as they reverentially shun the most egregious things, each nation according to its conceptions, and adhere to good deeds, at least with regard to human society. Through habituated good deeds and self-restraint, even idolaters will indeed become better able to assimilate the light of truth. . . . In general, because the world works, according to divine providence, to bring humans to their happy purpose, we must contemplate and know that as long as there is idolatry in the world, it has a purpose. . . . Indeed, even amid the darkness of idolatry, there are to be found select individuals of pure heart who wish to critique and improve the ways of their nation . . . and of such individuals it is said in *Tanna de-Vei Eliyyahu*, "I call heaven and earth to witness me attest that whether man or woman, slave or maid, gentile or Israelite—the holy spirit rests on that person entirely according to his deeds."[22] It is entirely possible for there to be extraordinary individuals who play the divine role of laying down moral standards and customs that will ultimately bring those who follow them to perceive the truth and the divine light. . . . Such customs indeed have religious value that truly must be commended. Even though a great distance separates them from us, we can acknowledge them as individuals who draw themselves nearer to the light of the Lord, and we can perceive that they are acting appropriately by upholding the heritage of their ancestors and the customs instituted for them by the elders of their nation, who were people of insight—sometimes quite great insight—and dedicated themselves to the moral and material advancement of their nation. Thus it is not right to conclude that their religion is entirely erroneous, and to demean and revile them beyond the point of taking to heart the extent of the good and the sacred tradition bestowed on us; He separated us from those astray, gave us a Torah of truth, and planted eternal life in our midst. . . . Meanwhile, those religions based on the Torah and the prophets certainly are respectable, because those who adhere to them are close to the light of the Lord and the knowledge of His glory, albeit most lack a certain element that is manifest only to a few of them. . . . In any case, due to the great moral principles that they took from the light of the Torah, which also revivified pure human feeling within them, there indeed are among them individuals of pure spirit, in assemblies of whom they establish religious customs that fulfill their purpose of uplifting the soul toward virtue and toward love and reverence of the Lord. They must follow the ways of those who formulate their laws, who in their nation are regarded as holy people in accordance with their greatness and character.... It is fitting that each nation follow the counsel of its greatest leaders, who enjoy high regard and acceptance within it, because these were generally individuals who revered the Lord and conceived of ideas to improve their nation's inner life.... The lower virtues of sensitivity to justice and goodness, which are not fit to be established as a universal nexus of humankind but are fit for the particular nation to which they belong, can be found amid every nation and culture. Religious customs established by the greatest and most pious of these nations should thus be recognized in their particular circumstances as worship of the Lord, and it is entirely inappropriate for us to revile them, because "the Lord is near to all who call Him, to all who call Him with sincerity" (Ps. 145:18), and "the Lord searches all minds" (1 Chron. 28:9).... However, for the purposes of the individual, every person ought to be happy with his religion and cling to it as his stronghold, and to distance himself from any commingling resulting from a practical coupling with the customs of another religion that is not the patrimony of his ancestors. This will avoid any diminution of the power of proper morality, which will bear fruit only if it works in the way it was made to fall by fate, which is controlled by the Lord: in accordance with his origin and race.

Rabbi Abraham Isaac Kook, *Li-Nevukhei ha-Dor,* 99–105 (chap. 14a).

222

If we correctly and thoroughly understand prophecy, then we understand as well its relationship to the human intellect and all practical knowledge, and how all the particulars of knowledge, whether theoretical, practical, or prophetic, in reality are like one: a revelation of divine light in shades that appear to vary, but in reality are but a single force of unity. For that reason they influence and are influenced by one another.

It necessarily follows that many things stated in the Torah, both commandments and narratives, are predated by analogues in the works of the greatest and most pious of the ancient nations—but the divine light that is the prophecy of our master Moses, which penetrates to the end of generations, separated out and purified them from what had accreted to them out of confusion and error. Things found to be of practical or narrative value were endorsed by the desire of the Most High, which at once comprises all things. The People of Israel do not boast at all of having brought the laws of morality and rectitude to the world, or even of having conceived the principle of the oneness of the Lord, blessed be He. To the contrary, the seven commandments incumbent on the descendants of Noah were transmitted from the first man and to Noah, and then were more widely promulgated, having been forgotten by the masses and personal morality having declined, by our forefather Abraham, may he rest in peace, and the other patriarchs and the righteous of the generations. . . . . The Israelites thus may be lauded for taking constructive, practical action to accomplish what is good—a power that is not diminished in the least by their not being the initiators. On the contrary, the power of truth, which is Israel's true patrimony, is intensified and heightened by the fact that it is fundamentally the patrimony of all individuals created in the image of God. God made men upright, but then, when their situation degenerated, they [i.e., the Israelites] became the driver of the world's restoration, reestablishment, and ultimately destiny.

Certainly, many good things remain from the prophets and disciples of the earliest generations, such as Methuselah, Enoch, Shem, Eber, and so forth, concerning character, etiquette, thought, and true stories that were retained by the ancient nations and etched in their inscriptions, so that some parallels to the Torah are found in them after laborious searching. It is certain as well that there are a number of commandments toward which inner human nature causes select individuals to incline because they have comprehended some part of their rationale and value. However, the complete divine edict of which they are a part was properly legislated only by the Torah and its being given to Israel as an eternal covenant. For prophecy, in combination with the power of wisdom that had preceded it and bringing those who possessed it to the level of prophecy, selected those things fit to select as the laws and statutes of God. We thus derive honor, glory, strengthened faith, and fear of the Lord, blessed be He, from the power to inquire into history, which identifies numerous parallels to the Torah among the antiquities of ancient nations, just as we sometimes identify an intellectual basis for statements of the Torah because we know that the light of intellect is a spark of the divine light. We thus find within it some parallels, as explained in *Sefer ha-Yashar* [purportedly by Rabbi Jacob ben Meir, known as Rabbenu Tam], to divine things, just as we find that the human intellect correlates with various things in nature because it is derived from the universal divine light.

Rabbi Abraham Isaac Kook, *Li-Nevukhei ha-Dor,* 167–169 (chap. 32).

223

Similarly, when Assyriology emerged, disquieting many due to the similarities in views, morality, and practice that its groundless hypotheses identified between our holy Torah and things in cuneiform documents, did these misgivings have even a tenuous intellectual basis? Is it not well known that among the ancients there were individuals with knowledge of divine wisdom—prophets and intellectual giants, Methuselah, Enoch, Shem, Eber, and so forth? Could it be that they made no impression on their contemporaries, even if their work did not gain such renown as that of Ethan the Ezrahite, i.e., our father Abraham, may he rest in peace? How could it be that their influence made no impression on their respective generations, and did it not necessarily correspond to the content of the Torah? . . . Any thinking person first considering the matter ought to arrive at these and other such insights: there was no reason at all for that factitious heresy to appear, spread, and gain strength due to these developments.

Rabbi Abraham Isaac Kook, "Ra'yonot le-Toledot ha-Ga'on Adderet," 42–43.

224

Based on this [long, detailed comparison of *The Code of Hammurabi* and the commandments of the Written and Oral Torah], all of the laws of Hammurabi belong to the seven commandments that the descendants of Noah were commanded to observe. The use of the word "commanded" indicates that, according to the tradition of our sages, the descendants of Noah did not independently derive these rules through analysis and inquiry or by analogy. They were revealed to them through divine inspiration and already had been given to the first man, as described in Babylonian Talmud, tractate *Sanhedrin* 56a ("'Commanded'—this refers to judges") and by him to Lamech, Noah, and our father Abraham. All of these commandments were revealed to them orally. . . . Yet this inspiration was not as powerful as the manifest law that was revealed to Moses, the master of prophets, at Sinai. This idea is encompassed by their statement that decorum preceded the Torah by two thousand years: the main goal of the commandments is that everyone be able to live a civil life, with no person injuring his fellow either bodily or financially, and that the body politic be maintained by the consensus of all the men of the state according to convention.

Rabbi Mayer Lerner, *Hadar ha-Karmel*, ed. Yitzchok Dov Feld (London: S. Rabbi Lerner, 1970/1971), 1:26–27.[23]

225

We can acquaint ourselves with the culture of the ancient world not only through the admonitions and penalties with which courts were charged, but also through certain positive actions associated with that world. Everyone knows that sacrifices were the crux of idolatrous religious worship, no species of which failed to erect altars. How did such a consensus emerge between all of the idol worshipers, spread and scattered as they were to the extremities of the earth, in no way related whatsoever? We can only say that all were informed by an ancient Semitic source. Noah or the school of Shem and Eber instructed the masses concerning the sacrificial rites of Adam, Abel, and Noah, teaching them that sacrifices are pleasing to Him at whose word the world came into being, and that they are a vehicle for the worship of the Lord. Or, perhaps, this was prophetically revealed to the select of the generations, just as the friends of Job experienced the revelation, "Now take seven bulls and seven rams and go to My servant Job and sacrifice a burnt offering for yourselves" (Job 42:8), and virtuous individuals through the generations did as they had, seeking intimacy with God through sacrifice. This mode of worship became so entrenched in the life of the people that even when religious beliefs became corrupted and the precious pearl of belief in the Creator was replaced with trinkets, it was neither discarded nor displaced despite their impurity and intellectual dullness.

Rabbi Saie Reicher, *Torat ha-Rishonim*, 1:18.

Endnotes

1. See *Guide of the Perplexed*, 3:29.
2. For similar remarks in this vein, see, e.g., Maimonides, *The Guide of the Perplexed*, 3:30; 3:46; 3:47; 3:48; 3:49.
3. See also Maimonides, *Guide of the Perplexed*, 3:48; Rabbi Joseph Ibn Kaspi, *Mitzraf la-Kesef*, in *Mishneh Kesef*, ed. Isaac Last (Jerusalem: Sifriyat Mekorot, 1969/1970), 2:228 (Exod. 34:26); Rabbi Obadiah Sforno, commentary to Exod. 23:19; Rabbi Meir Leibush Wisser, commentary on Exod. 23:19. Rabbi Menachem M. Kasher, *Torah Shelemah* (New York, 1955/1956), 17:222n4 (*Mishpatim* I), calls on textual evidence in support of previous scholars' conjectures:

   > There similarly have been found ... inscriptions on tablets and tablet fragments of literary remnants written in Ugaritic, an ancient language used in Syria during the time of the Patriarchs, containing expressions and words that are helpful in understanding difficult words in the Hebrew Bible. It is interesting to note regarding ... the rationale of the prohibition of cooking meat and milk together that the Torah sought to put an end to a pagan practice associated with such a ritual. One of those tablets says, "Slaughter a kid in milk and a lamb in butter," and it is explained that such a religious ritual was intended to bring blessing to the land. For this reason, the Torah juxtaposed the prohibition as it did in the verse: "The choice first fruits of your soil you shall bring to the house of the Lord your God"—but—"you shall not boil a kid in its mother's milk."

It must be noted, however, that this reading of the tablet is very much in doubt. See, e.g., Robert Ratner and Baruch Zuckerman, "'A Kid in Milk'?: New Photographs of *KTU* 1.23, Line 14," *Hebrew Union College Annual* 57 (1986): 15–60.
4. Nachmanides, *Torat ha-Shem Temimah ha-Shelemah*, ed. Yehuda Meir Dvir (Jerusalem: Y. M. Dvir, 2005/2006), 27–31. However, compare Nachmanides' view in source 220 below.
5. For a brief explanation of Jacob's arguments against Laban here in light of *The Code of Hammurabi*, see the commentary by J. H. Hertz on Gen. 31:39 (*The Pentateuch and Haftorahs*, 116). For additional examples, see the commentary by Rabbi Abraham Maimonides to Gen. 35:2–4 (118–120) and Exod. 10:11 (260).
6. This text is excerpted from the manuscript by Kasher, *Torah Shelemah*, 17:224.
7. See also Benamozegh, commentary to Deut. 23:19 (91a–92a); notes and addenda to Lev. 10:6 (165a–b).
8. *Parashat* Yitro, 2.
9. *Parashat* Yitro, 67b.
10. Babylonian Talmud, tractate *Zevaḥim* 116a.
11. See explanation in sec. 2, 34.
12. Babylonian Talmud, tractate *Bava Batra* 15b.
13. This excerpt forms the basis of the argument made by Rabbi Avia Hacohen in his article "The Mosaic Law and the Laws of the Nations: A Study in the Teachings of Rabbi Zadok of Lublin," first published in this volume, 439–450. Many thanks to Rabbi Hacohen for providing a draft of his article.
14. Jerusalem Talmud, tractate *Nedarim* 9:4; *Bereshit Rabbah* 24:7.
15. This excerpt appears in Rabbi Abraham Isaac Kook, *Li-Nevukhei ha-Dor*, 173–175 (chap. 34). Concerning the relationship between the Bauska Journal and *Li-Nevukhei ha-Dor*, see note 5 above.
16. Concerning this passage, see also Aviner, *Yotzer Or* (note 154 above), 301–302, 323–324.
17. See also Hirschensohn, *Sefer Nimmukei Rashi*, 2:148b (§ 491) on Exod. 25:22.
18. See also source 11 above.
19. The omitted text contains numerous additional examples from the Quran.
20. Rabbi Nathanel Beirav al-Fayyumi (d. 1172) was the political leader of Yemenite Jewry. His son Rabbi Jacob al-Fayyumi was the addressee of Maimonides' *Letter to Yemen*; Maimonides extensively praises his father there.
21. For a similar approach, see Rabbi Saie Reicher, *Torat ha-Rishonim: Yesodot ha-Torah she-be-'al Peh ve-Hitpatteḥutah ha-Ḥiyyunit ba-Ḥayyim u-ba-Sefer ba-Dorot ha-Rishonim* [The Torah of the ancients: Fundamental principles of the Oral Torah and its critical development in life and in writing in the time of the *Rishonim*] (Warsaw: Yeshurun, 1935), 1:5–6; and Rabbi Menachem M. Kasher, *Torah Shelemah*, 17:222–223; see also sources 252 and 256 below.
22. *Tanna de-Vei Eliyyahu*, ed. Meir (Ish Shalom) Friedmann (Vienna: Aḥiasaf, 1901), *parashat* 10.
23. Rabbi Mayer Lerner (1857–1930) was the presiding judge of the rabbinical court of Altona and the founder of Moria, an organization that served as a counterbalance to Mizrahi and was ultimately absorbed by the younger Agudath Israel movement.

Articles

A Personal Perspective on Biblical History, the Authorship of the Torah, and Belief in its Divine Origin

Shawn Zelig Aster

I am a researcher in the fields of biblical and ancient Near Eastern studies, and, in this capacity, have held faculty positions at Yeshiva University and in Israel. I do not view the Bible solely (or even primarily) as a topic for research, but as part of Torah. This personal essay results from issues raised in the course of my teaching, primarily by students in the United States. I encountered a significant number of students who questioned basic religious principles and correlated their doubts about these principles to questions about biblical studies. It seems to me that many of their questions and doubts stem from the perception that there is a direct conflict between faith and science, a perception that is to some extent fueled by the nature of Jewish religious education in the United States. The objective of the following discussion is to argue that no such direct conflict exists in the area of biblical studies.

I do not in any way aim to create complete harmony between science and faith, two worlds based on entirely different principles. Rather, I am to define areas in which the conclusions of academic investigation overlap with principles of faith, and thereby to present, for those interested, an "intellectual space" where reason and faith can coexist. Ultimately, Torah and academic studies ought to have the same objective: truth. Academic studies seek truth by means of knowledge discovered by human intelligence. The Torah, in contrast, recognizes the existence of a level of consciousness above the human intellect, and integrates knowledge gleaned by means of human intelligence with knowledge derived from God's revelation to humankind.

This idea of revelation is central to classical Jewish belief, by which I mean the belief of Jews throughout the ages, which is grounded in classical Jewish texts. God's revelation to the prophets, and his involvement in the human sphere, have always been seen as a critical aspect of the relationship between humans and God, complemented by humans' voluntary decision to turn to God. As in any human relationship, our decision to turn to God is the product of desire and emotions that are influenced by intellectual experience, though not dependent upon it exclusively. For any relationship to exist, there must be a certain space where emotion and intellect coexist and overlap.

The most fundamental premise of the relationship between Jews and God is that God transcends human experience, meaning that His intellect, abilities, and nature are infinitely superior to those of the most capable humans. On this premise is built the belief that God reveals his will to humans, as well as a more particular expression of this belief: that God chose the People of Israel and gave them the Torah. It must be emphasized that none of these premises can be proven scientifically. Even if evidence were to be found of the gathering of millions of people at the foot of Mount Sinai in the thirteenth century BCE, that would not prove the divine revelation of the Torah. In other words, people accept or reject these premises, which undergird the relationship between Jews and God, without reference to scientific or objective criteria.

Is it possible to base a relationship on unprovable beliefs? The answer is quite simply and clearly affirmative. All relationships are based on subjective beliefs that cannot be proven. I love my wife because she is the prettiest, nicest, gentlest, and kindest of all women. No reasonable person would ask me to prove this. Similarly, the decision to maintain a relationship with the God of Israel is not based upon pure logic, but on unprovable beliefs. These beliefs often stem from personal identity, and they require a certain leap beyond logic, and are therefore called "leaps of faith." I pity the lonely person who does not make at least two such leaps in his life, into faith and love.

Conflict

If the premises at the heart of the relationship between human beings and God are neither scientifically provable nor disprovable, what then is the source of the conflict between science and faith? The conflict inheres in areas where academic research reaches conclusions which appear to differ from beliefs about the nature of the Torah. Among the most intense areas for this conflict are the authorship of the Torah and the historical authenticity of the biblical narratives.

The question of the Torah's authorship is, in my opinion, the more difficult and more pivotal of the two. However, I will first discuss the simpler question of historical authenticity, which is central to my own research. This question is fueled by the perception that the knowledge derived from archeology and epigraphy (the study of texts from the biblical world discovered in archeological excavations) contradicts the biblical narrative.

Biblical Narrative and History

The apparent conflict between the biblical narrative and archeological and epigraphical discoveries is a product of the unrealistic expectation that the events described in the biblical narrative will conform exactly to the events portrayed in archeological and epigraphic sources. The absurdity of this expectation becomes clear when we reflect on the fact that no narrative narrates every single event taking place in a particular time and space. Every narrative selects certain events, emphasizes and presents them, connects them to each other, and describes the main characters in accordance with certain literary decisions. These literary decisions usually reflect the desire for the narrative to present a moral, a message, or a particular portrayal. By means of this process of selection and connection, a narrative that reflects this desire is created. Historical narratives do not differ in this respect from any other narrative.

This point can be illustrated by an analysis of the story of the Exodus from Egypt, which many claim has no historical basis. On the one hand, we do not have a single scrap of historical evidence showing that millions of people migrated from Egypt to the Land of Israel over the course of exactly forty years. Anyone seeking such evidence will be disappointed.

On the other hand, we do have clear knowledge, based on archeological and epigraphic evidence that between the late fourteenth and the twelfth centuries BCE, Egyptian rule weakened in the region of Canaan and Sinai. During this period, many groups of Semitic nomads, some of whom were called "Shasu" in Egyptian writings, began to migrate both within Egypt and through the administrative region that the Egyptians called the "Way of Horus" in the north of the Sinai Peninsula. Egyptian officials found it difficult to control their movements, and at times battled them.[1]

During this period, starting in the late thirteenth century, small settlements, characterized by simple pottery, four-room houses, and multiple sites of terrace farming, were established in the Manasseh Hill Country.[2] Over the course of the twelfth and eleventh centuries, these settlements spread from Manasseh over the highlands of the Land of Israel. Late in the thirteenth century BCE, the Egyptian pharaoh Merneptah wrote of his battles with a Semitic-speaking group called "Israel" who appear to have been located somewhere between Gezer and Galilee. Merneptah's statement alone does not prove that these settlers were Israelites, but there are other arguments strongly suggesting this. Ethnic characteristics found in these early highland settlements also appear in settlements clearly identified with the Israelites from the tenth century onwards (Iron Age II, as it is known to archeologists).[3] While it cannot be proven conclusively that the Israelites who settled in the land originated among the "Shasu," the evidence for it is very convincing.[4]

Do these events correspond to the biblical narrative? In my opinion, the question itself is problematic. Events cannot be compared to a story. Events are the building blocks with which a narrator builds his story.[5] Therefore, the question ought to be: Are these the historical events that the Torah adapted in its presentation of the narrative of the Exodus from Egypt (Exod. 1–15)? There are many discrepancies between these events and the biblical narrative. A striking example of this is the question of the non-Israelites included among the "Shasu." The Egyptian documents refer to numerous and various groups of "Shasu" (including groups known as Shashu-Se'ir, Shasu-Laban, Shasu-Edom, and Shasu-Yahwe). As discussed above, it appears that some of the early Israelites were one group of such nomads. By means of literary techniques, the biblical story focuses on the Israelites and follows their story, yet mentions, *en passant*, the "mixed multitude [that] went up with them" (Exod. 12:38). The discrepancy between the biblical focus on the Israelites and the Egyptian documents' broader perspective on the Shasu overall is not the result of a historical discrepancy, but rather of the narrative focus of the Bible. It follows, therefore, that the story of the Exodus from Egypt is not an objective description of an historical event, but a narrative interpretation of historical events. As commentary written in a narrative style, the Torah attempts to explain to us the conceptual significance of the complicated events that took place between Egypt and Canaan between the fourteenth and twelfth centuries BCE. The Torah describes the Exodus from Egypt in Exodus 1–15 in a manner that emphasizes that both the Israelites and the Egyptians learned about the sovereignty of God. The climax of this realization is also the climax of the story, at the parting of the Red Sea in Exodus 14–15.

It is perhaps difficult to accept that events that we consider to be of the upmost importance are not emphasized in the contemporary Egyptian records. It must be pointed out, however, that emphasis is the prerogative of the narrator. Even when the narrative is constructed from historical events, it is the narrator who decides which events to emphasize. The historian E. H. Carr provided a good example of this in his book *What is History?*, in his description of a riot over the price of gingerbread sold at a fair in the English town of Stalybridge in 1850.[6] Can this act of violence be considered an historical fact? According to some historians, this event occupies an important place in nineteenth-century English history because it reflects economic power struggles in industrial cities. According to many others, however, this was a marginal and common incident of no significance whatsoever. It would therefore appear that it is neither strange nor surprising that the biblical narrator focused only on those groups that were to become the "Israelites."[7] Every narrator, including both the English historians described by Carr as well as the narrator of the Torah, chooses to emphasize certain events and ignore others; this is the nature of narrative.[8]

Because of the nature of narrative, we ought not to demand direct correspondence between the biblical narrative and long-term historical processes. Nonetheless, the events at the heart of most biblical stories of a historical nature correspond to a large degree with the events described in archeological and epigraphic sources. An example of this can be found in the book of Joshua. A cursory reading of the book leads to the impression that Joshua led the Israelites to conquer the land within a relatively short period of time. This reading contradicts archeological evidence from the period. However, in addition to contradicting the archeological evidence, this cursory reading stands in complete contrast to the first chapter of the book of Judges, which describes the conquest as slow and gradual and carried out by the tribes, with varying degrees of success.

The aim of the story in Joshua 1–11 is not to describe the process of the conquest in an exact chronological format, but rather to show that the special relationship between God and the People of Israel continued even after the death of Moses. Its purpose is to convey the message: "As I was with Moses, so I will be with you; I will not fail you or forsake you" (Josh. 1:5). Therefore, in chapters 1–5, Joshua reaches levels of achievement equal to or even greater than those of Moses. These successes reveal God's support of him and his deeds: The spies discover the Canaanites' fear of the Israelites, in contrast to the story of the spies in the Torah (Num. 13). The crossing of the Jordan River reveals Joshua's ability to perform miracles by means of the Holy Ark, just as Moses performed miracles with his staff at the parting of the Red Sea. The celebration of Passover in chapter 5 signals a turning point in the book: Under Joshua's leadership, the People of Israel had to undergo a transition from the celestial nourishment of manna to a diet based on the natural produce of the land.

At the same time, the people had to undergo a similar transition from leadership through miracles to strictly human leadership. This transition was gradual, and the wars described in Joshua chapters 1–11 are depicted in a way that illustrates this. In the battle of Jericho (Josh. 6), Joshua does not need to fight, only to implement divine strategy and tactics. In the second battle of Ai (Josh. 8) God determines the strategy (the ambush, 8:2) as well as the timing of this strategy (the tactics in 8:18). All that was left to Joshua was to implement the tactic and determine its exact location (8:3–9). In the following war, against the southern kings, God restricts himself at the beginning to general words of encouragement (10:8), and Joshua determines the battle strategy and implements it (10:9). Afterwards, God functions as a sort of "back-up unit" to Joshua by raining hailstones on the fleeing Canaanites (10:11). God also helps by extending the time available for the battle by making the sun stand still (10:12). This assistance is given in response to Joshua's request, a factor that emphasizes the increasing responsibility taken by Joshua. In the story of the battle in the north, in chapter 11, Joshua continues to receive words of encouragement from God, but develops the strategy and tactics and fights the battle on his own. The stories in Joshua 1–11 are meant to indicate that the People of Israel made a successful transition from miraculous leadership to human leadership. The desire to convey this message determined the choice of events to be included in the story, how they are described, the emphases placed on various aspects, and the order in which they are presented. The stories in Joshua 1–11 are thus not intended to be an objective presentation of the historical events in the period of the settlement.

Some of the events that underlie the narrative descriptions can be corroborated by external historical sources. For example, Hazor was destroyed (according to its excavator) in the thirteenth century BCE, sometime before Egyptian-Canaanite rule in the northern valleys of the Land of Israel collapsed. The battles described in Joshua 10:28–39 were concentrated, among other places, in Makkedah and Eglon. Both of these sites are identified in the area of the Canaanite enclave that continued in the eastern part of the Shephelah, at sites like Tel Yarmut, Tel Eton, and Tel Beit Mirsim, after most of the Canaanite cities in the coastal plain had ceased to exist.[9] Most of the battles in the book of Joshua, especially in chapters 1–11, took place in areas where there is evidence of continued Canaanite presence even after the decline of Canaanite culture in the twelfth and thirteenth centuries.

It is difficult for me to accept Israel Finkelstein's opinion that the conquest narrative might preserve "sherds of memory" but does not reflect the events of the thirteenth century BCE.[10] On the other hand, there is no doubt that Joshua 1–11 does not describe all the historical events that occurred at the time of the conquest, as is clear from a comparison of these chapters with Judges 1–3. The chapters in Joshua are a narrative that weaves together a nonrepresentative selection of specific incidents from a long, complicated, and convoluted process. This involved the selection of very specific points and their presentation with maximal emphasis on the figure of Joshua. As I mentioned earlier, the aim was to demonstrate the transition from miracles to human agency. Because they are a narrative, these chapters contain a partial selection and presentation of events. Judges 1:17–36 is the only biblical source to describe the complicated and gradual process of the penetration of the Israelites into the Land of Israel from the end of the thirteenth to the beginning of the eleventh centuries BCE, a process increasingly revealed to us by archeological discoveries.

Reading the stories in Joshua with an awareness of the historical and archeological research lends a new perspective to the question of the historical authenticity of the Bible. Not only is there no reason to see tension between archeological/epigraphical research and the study of the Bible, it is often even possible to find a great degree of correlation between the core events of these narratives and historical events. Moreover, this perspective makes it easier to identify the narrative frameworks and to discover the spiritual and moral lessons that the Bible intends to convey.

The Flood Story and the Question of the Authorship of the Torah

From the relatively simple question of the connection between historical reality and the biblical narrative, I would now like to turn to the more difficult problem: the authorship of the Torah. I will first present the "dry" literary truth: a person who studies the Torah with the aid of literary analytical tools—"according to its exoteric meaning," in the words of Naḥmanides—will realize that many of the stories, especially in Genesis, are narrated in "two voices." A classic example of this is the double creation story. Another good example is the story of the Flood. This literary assessment is irrefutable. My question is: What are the theological implications of this assessment?

If I were to approach the Torah as an objective reader, it would not be difficult for me to conclude that the different voices derive from different authors whose perspectives have been woven together for reasons unknown to me. But because I am not objective, I will take a different approach: the two voices often present different aspects of a certain idea. I will illustrate this approach, which can perhaps be called "deliberate multivocalism," by analyzing the story of the Flood.[11]

The story of the Flood is clearly comprised of two currents, or voices. In one of them (identified in scholarly research as "J") the central problem is expressed in Genesis 6:5: "The Lord saw how great was man's wickedness on earth, and how every plan devised by his mind was nothing but evil all the time." Noah is commanded to take "seven pairs, males and their mates" from every clean animal. Pursuant to this commandment, Noah offers sacrifices at the end of the Flood and upon leaving the ark. In response, God acknowledges that "the devisings of man's mind are evil from his youth," yet nonetheless promises "nor will I ever again destroy every living being, as I have done" (8:21). According to this story, the cause of the Flood was the human inclination to evil, and the solution to this problem is the institution of the sacrificial rite. This institution establishes a clear, universal, social hierarchy: one who offers sacrifices declares his superiority over the sacrificed animals, yet acknowledges God's superiority over him.[12] From a state of subjugation to God, he must control his evil impulses. Therefore, Noah offers sacrifices and forms an emotional connection with God: "The Lord smelled the pleasing odor" (8:21).

Parallel to this story of emotion and impulse there is another story, told using the name *Elohim* (a story often identified in research with the "P" source). At its core are legal principles, and the primary problem presented here is robbery and violence (*ḥamas*, "lawlessness," in the language of the Bible) (Gen. 6:11). Here there is no mention of the distinction between the number of clean and unclean animals. The problem of violence is solved by the establishment of divine law (9:1–7) and the covenant (9:8–17). The divine decree "whoever sheds the blood of man, by man shall his blood be shed" (9:6) is intended to contain the lawlessness. Just as the institution of the sacrificial rite was a response to the problem of the evil inclination, law is the answer to lawlessness. Just as after the sacrifices God took mercy on humankind and decided to never again to destroy all living things (8:21), so too after the giving of the law, God establishes a covenant in which he promises to protect the human race. A covenant, in the biblical sense, involves the promise of protection granted by the sovereign (God) to the subject (human beings), yet also determines the obligations of the subject to the sovereign. These obligations are formulated legally in Genesis 9:1–6.[13] The Flood itself did not solve either problem, but provided a pretext and an opportunity for the presentation of the solution—in fact two solutions, a solution for each problem.

This analysis raises an obvious difficulty: Why does the Torah tell the same story twice? I think it no less reasonable to explain the duality of the narrative as an intentional and purposeful feature than to argue that the two sources were combined in an arbitrary editing process simply because they were there.

The narrative structure of each of the Flood stories is comprised of five sections: (1) the presentation of the problem; (2) the divine command to Noah to enter the ark with the animals; (3) the Flood itself; (4) after the Flood, an act expressing the connection between God and mankind (the altar in 8:20 and the blessing in 9:1–7); (5) at the end of each story, the divine promise that the Flood would not be repeated (8:21–22; 9:8–17). This structure is remarkably similar to the Mesopotamian flood story, known to us from the fragments of the Sumerian story of Ziusudra, the Akkadian fragments of the story of Atrahasis, and the adaptation of the story in the eleventh tablet of the Akkadian *Epic of Gilgamesh*.[14]

In the story of Atrahasis, the problem is that the gods are unable to sleep owing to the noise made by human beings "because they began to increase upon the face of the earth." After repeated efforts to reduce the number of humans in various ways, the gods decide upon a flood. At the end of the flood, Atrahasis offers a sacrifice, and a goddess promises that she will not send another flood. In order to prevent overpopulation, the gods assign various demons to kill babies and also determine that certain women will not bear children. It is important to note that in both the Mesopotamian and biblical stories the flood is not the solution to the problem presented at the beginning of the story. The flood is merely a device that allows a transition from the problem to the solution.

In each of the stories, the selection of the problems and the solutions reflects the human experience and the relationship between God and humankind. Tikva Frymer-Kensky argued that Atrahasis is a type of etiological explanation for the phenomenon of bereavement. It would appear, however, that the story has deeper meaning. The Atrahasis story examines a fundamental social problem in society: the higher echelons need the lower echelons to serve and obey them. In contrast, the Torah posits a different fundamental problem: the main problem of human existence is human self-control. The loss of this self-control is expressed in two ways: (1) lust and unrestrained sexual libido, and (2) the desire for power and wealth, and the risk of acquiring these by means of robbery and violence. The "J" story addresses the subjugation of the sexual and animal evil inclination, while the "P" story tells of controlling lawlessness and robbery.

The biblical story of the Flood is a negative response to the Babylonian story in so far as it attacks its basic premise. But the Torah's narrative is not only a polemic. It also teaches a basic truth. Maimonides maintained that many of the laws of the Torah were polemical, directed against idolatry (*Guide of the Perplexed*, 3:26 and following), and yet have to be observed regardless of their polemical nature. So too, some stories in the Torah have polemical aims, directed against the idolatry pervasive in the ancient world, but still teach basic values, values more apparent to us when contrasted with the ancient Near Eastern stories.

The answer to the question, "Why does the Torah include two contradictory stories?" is related to the need to present the two answers to the question, "What is the basic problem of human existence and what is its solution?". In one story the Torah posits the control of sexual impulses and in the second the control of greed.

The story of the Flood is a true story because it embodies truth. However, it is not a historical story because it is unlikely that the events it relates occurred as described in the real world. Similarly, Maimonides did not classify the stories of the Patriarchs describing angelic revelation as "historical," and thus categorized large sections of the book of Genesis as "ahistorical." In *The Guide of the Perplexed* he established an important principle regarding the stories in the Torah: we must not assume that the events occurred in the real world when this assumption contradicts reason. (He interprets the appearances of angels in the stories of the Patriarchs as having occurred "in a prophetic vision.")

Thus far I have not demonstrated that the story of the Flood is necessarily of divine origin. I have merely presented an interpretation of the story that enables it to be read as an integral work of divine origin, despite the fact that it includes a double message and does not necessarily correspond to exact historical reality.

When Was the Torah Written?

The person of faith who reads the Torah and wants to believe in its divine origin faces a very difficult challenge: the question of when the Torah was written. For reasons that I will explain below, it is not easy to date the composition of the

Torah to the twelfth century BCE, the latest century in which it is possible to place the wandering in the desert and the revelation on Mount Sinai.

The uncertainty regarding the time of the Torah's composition, together with the question of its multiple voices, has led certain scholars to maintain that, while the Torah is of divine origin, it was not dictated by God to Moses in the aforementioned period of time. The following statement by the late Professor Jacob Milgrom clearly reflects this approach: "Instead of understanding the Torah's 'YHWH spoke to Moses' as a claim that the laws that follow came from the mouth of Moses, we can understand the Torah as signaling that the principles underlying the laws are Mosaic principles, emanating from Moses himself."[15]

Milgrom accepts the concept of God's revelation to Moses, but limits this revelation to the Ten Commandments, and posits that the rest of the Torah's laws and stories were written later by a scribe who drew from Moses' words. Milgrom compares the process of the composition of the Torah to the Talmudic story of Moses' visit to the *beit midrash* of Rabbi Akiva, in which Rabbi Akiva expands upon legal principles established by Moses.[16] According to Milgrom, the later writers of the Torah expanded upon the principles embodied in the Ten Commandments, principles that Moses himself formulated during the revelation.

I do not agree with Milgrom's approach because I see no reason for its constraints. As soon as we accept God's revelation to humankind, a process that can never be proven or even understood by scientific means, what is gained by limiting it to specific content such as the Ten Commandments, rather than the wider scope of "the Torah and the commandments," posited by Maimonides, that includes at the very least the laws of the Torah and their explanations? In my view, the reasons for accepting that the Torah and commandments were given by God in Moses' time, reasons related to faith, outweigh the reasons for dating its composition to a later period. This is not to make light of the reasons for dating its composition to a later period, as I discuss below. These reasons seem to provide the rationale behind Milgrom's proposed limitations on the scope of revelation.

In academic research, it is generally agreed that the Torah was composed in the second half of the First Temple period. Most sections of the Torah do not include a solid chronological anchor that could date the Torah to this time. In addition, we do not have enough linguistic evidence to distinguish between the Hebrew of the beginning of the First Temple period (the tenth century) and the

Hebrew of the twelfth century. If we accept the dating of the Exodus to the period predating the tenth century, it follows that we must date Moses to that period.

One of the few chronological anchors to a period later than the tenth century are phrases in Deuteronomy 28:49–63 reminiscent of parallels in Akkadian literature—for example, the description of the "ruthless nation" (50) and the word *ve-nisaḥtem* (63). Most of the idioms in the Bible influenced by Akkadian and describing political or state phenomena (such as foreign rule or exile) are to be found in books from the period of Assyrian rule, which began late in the eighth century. Their appearance in Deuteronomy 28 is one of the reasons for dating Moses' speech of admonishment (Deut. 28) to this period. In my opinion, this problem can be solved in one of two ways. First, it can be assumed that these idioms entered the Hebrew language in an earlier period for reasons unknown to us. This is a faith-based assumption that is very problematic from an academic perspective because it is currently unsubstantiated.[17] A second possibility is to accept the interpretation of Abraham Ibn Ezra, in the framework of his thesis known as "The Secret of the Twelve," that the Torah contains later additions. In my opinion, this possibility is also preferable to dating all of the Torah, or entire sections of it, to a later period, because it is best not to make important and exalted matters of faith and belief conditional on specific points. It is preferable to identify later additions within the text than to date the entire text to a later period.

On the other hand, there is no scientific way to prove that most sections of the Torah date to the eleventh century BCE or earlier. Nonetheless, in my opinion, it can be easily proven that many of the ideas presented in Deuteronomy, which according to many scholars is one of the latest books of the Torah, were known among the Israelites before the eighth century. It can be proven that large sections of the book of Isaiah were written in the eighth century, and were based on the ideas of absolute monotheism familiar to us from Deuteronomy. In an article on Isaiah 19, I argued, based on literary and historical evidence, that the author of this chapter lived at the end of the eighth century, and was familiar with the language attributed to "P" in Exodus 1–15.[18] It is therefore possible to narrow the gap between the latest dating of sections of the Torah that is scientifically credible and the latest dating acceptable from a faith-based perspective to a period of two hundred years, between the eleventh and ninth centuries BCE. It is clear that from a scientific point of view, the more cautious dating, before the eighth century, is preferable. However, it is difficult for me to challenge important religious principles on the basis of this preference.

Why Leap?

I have proven nothing in this article. I have not proven that the Torah is historically authentic, nor that its multiplicity of voices is intentional, nor that its legal contents do not postdate the tenth century. Neither was it my intention to prove these points. On the other hand, I have attempted to show that these points do not contradict science, and that an intellectual space exists that is wide enough to allow someone to believe that God gave the Torah to Moses and yet remain cognizant of what can be proven scientifically.[19]

Another very important question remains unanswered: Why would a person want to believe that God gave the Torah? Why does a person make this "leap of faith"? In my opinion, the answer to this question is personal and emotional, as is any other decision to enter into a relationship. Therefore, I doubt if the reasons that I find for making the leap of faith will help others. I can only say that in times of crisis I turn to the God of my fathers. I am reminded of the words of Jeremiah (2:27) who describes how the People of Israel follow other gods, but in their "hour of calamity" abandon them and turn to the God of Israel, calling out "Arise and save us!" Turning to God in the hour of need reflects the faith, embedded somewhere in the soul of every Jew, that the God of his fathers can save him. The God of our fathers has a specific identity, expressed in His revelation to humankind, His selection of the People of Israel, and His revelation of the Torah.

Endnotes

1. Evidence of this can be found in the Papyrus Anastasi VI and VII, English translation in William Hallo, ed., *Context of Scripture* (Leiden: Brill, 2002), 2:20–27 and 3:16–17; and in Raphael Giveon, *Les Bedouins Shosou des documents Egyptiens* (Leiden: Brill, 1971). A very informative summary can be found in the ninth chapter of Anson F. Rainey and Steven Notley, *The Sacred Bridge: Carta's Atlas of the Biblical World* (Jerusalem: Carta, 2006). A description of the "Way of Horus," which runs through the biblical land of the Philistines, can be found in Eliezer Oren, "The Establishment of Egyptian Imperial Administration in the 'Way of Horus': An Archeological Perspective from North Sinai," in *Timelines: Studies in Honor of Manfred Bietak*, ed. Ernst Czerny et al. (Leuven: Peeters, 2006), 2:279–292.
2. For an introduction to this subject see Adam Zertal, "Be-Eretz ha-Prizi ve-ha-Refaim: al ha-Hitnaḥalut Ha-Yisraelit be-Har Menasheh" ['To the land of the Perizzites and the Giants': On the Israelite settlement in the hill country of Manasseh], in *Me-Navdut le-Melukha* [From

nomadism to monarchy: Archaeological and historical aspects of early Israel], ed. Nadav Na'aman and Israel Finkelstein (Jerusalem: Yad Ben-Zvi, 1994), 47–69.
3. For a discussion of these phenomena, see Avraham Faust, *Israel's Ethnogenesis: Settlement, Interaction, Expansion and Resistance* (London: Equinox, 2006).
4. Anson F. Rainey, "Israel in Merneptah's Inscriptions and Reliefs," Israel Exploration Journal 51 (2001): 57–75. It is beyond dispute that a large portion of those who became Israelites were not originally Shasu. But some of those who settled in the thirteenth–twelfth-century highland settlements were certainly nomads, and the Egyptian texts make it clear that the Shasu were Semitic speakers, as were the "Israel" mentioned in Merneptah's inscription. These hints strongly suggest (even without the pictorial evidence) that some of the nomads who formed part of the thirteenth–twelfth-century settlers were those called Shasu by the Egyptians.
5. For a discussion of the stages of development from events to narrative, see Mieke Bal, *Narratology: Introduction to the Theory of Narrative* (Toronto: University of Toronto Press, 2009), chap. 2.
6. E. H. Carr, *What is History?* (Harmondsworth: Penguin, 1968).
7. It is also difficult to accept that perhaps the "mixed multitude" constituted the numerical bulk of the People of Israel, while the nucleus who were the descendants of Jacob were the minority. This possibility also does not contradict faith-based beliefs because the Torah demonstrates that familial allegiance does not necessarily indicate genealogical origins. The comparisons of the numbers in the family censuses in the book of Numbers indicates that people moved from family to family and joined families according to their own preferences. On this subject see Naḥmanides' commentary on Num. 26:52–53.
8. For a detailed discussion of the factors that turn events into a story, see Bal, *Narratology*, 75–77.
9. Avraham Faust and Hayah Katz, "Philistines, Israelites, and Canaanites in the Southern Trough Valley in Iron Age I," *Agypten und Levante/Egypt and the Levant* 21 (2011): 231–247; David A. Dorsey, "The Location of Biblical Makkedah," *Tel Aviv* 7 (1980): 185–193.
10. Israel Finkelstein, "Shechem in the Late Bronze and Iron I," in *Timelines: Studies in Honor of Manfred Bietak*, 2:351.
11. The story of the Flood in the Torah has been discussed extensively. It is worthwhile to begin with Rabbi Mordecai Breuer's discussion in *Pirkei Bereshit* [Essays on Genesis], ed. Yosef Ofer (Alon Shvut: Herzog College, 1999), 1:136–206. In the current discussion, I will not analyze the verses closely, but will rather emphasize the connection between the biblical story and the Akkadian version, a connection that, in my opinion, can explain the deliberate multivocalism of the Torah.
12. It is possible to connect the verses that raise the problem of the evil inclination (Gen. 6:5–8) with the verses that present the problem of the "divine beings" and the "daughters of men" (6:1–4), in which the effacing of the hierarchy by means of unusual mating can be seen. The sacrificial rite reestablishes the hierarchy of God, man, and beasts.
13. There is an extensive literature on the meaning of "covenant" in the ancient Near East and its parallels in the Bible. A good introduction to this subject can be found in Dennis J. McCarthy, *Treaty and Covenant: A Study in Form in the Ancient Oriental Documents and in the Old Testament* (Rome: Pontifical Bible Institute, 1963), 28–48.
14. Tikva Frymer-Kensky has demonstrated that the biblical story is based on the Babylonian story. See "The Atrahasis Epic and Its Significance for our Understanding of Genesis 1–9," *Biblical Archeologist* 40 (1977): 147–155. See also the more recent article by Jacob Klein,

"A New Look at the Theological Background of the Mesopotamian and Biblical Flood Stories," in *A Common Cultural Heritage: Studies on Mesopotamia and the Bible in Honor of Barry L. Eichler*, ed. Grant Frame et al. (Bethesda, MD: CDL Press, 2011), 151–176. For an English translation of the Atrahasis epic, see Benjamin Foster, *Before the Muses: An Anthology of Akkadian Literature* (Bethesda, MD: CDL Press, 2005), 227–280.

15. Jacob Milgrom, Leviticus, *A Book of Ritual and Ethics: A Continental Commentary* (Minneapolis: Fortress Press, 2004), 3.
16. Babylonian Talmud, tractate *Menaḥot* 29b.
17. Scientific research is based upon the findings that are at our disposal. It is therefore unwise to overturn principles of faith and belief on the basis of current evidence. Who knows what documents will be discovered in the future? Scholarly opinions on matters of dating tend to change over time.
18. "Isaiah 19: The "Burden of Egypt" and Neo-Assyrian Imperial Policy," *Journal of the American Oriental Society* 135 (2015): 453–470.
19. By "intellectual space" I am referring to a certain range of conceptual possibilities that make it feasible to accept scientifically proven principles as well as basic principles of Jewish faith as formulated by Maimonides.

The Sages as Bible Critics

Yehuda Brandes

The Critical Reading of the Bible

Devoutly religious Jews, even if they have never heard of biblical criticism or ventured outside the confines of traditional Torah study, are proficient in the critical reading of the Bible. Because strict adherence to the simple meaning of the biblical text is impossible, the reader cannot merely accept the text as it is written, and must therefore examine it critically. If under examination, the text appears to contradict reality, other verses, or reason, it must be stripped of its simple meaning and interpreted appropriately. The traditional Hebrew term for biblical criticism is "midrash"—the diametric opposite of a fundamentalist reading of the Bible that adheres to the literal meaning of the text.

The Jewish encounter with Islam in the gaonic period generated a revolutionary trend toward studying the Bible according to its plain meaning. This deviation from the traditional method of bible study, rabbinic midrash, was influenced by Muslim literal interpretation of the Quran that also inspired the Karaite Jews. Rabbinic scholars were forced to make use of contemporary intellectual and hermeneutic tools in order to defend the traditional faith and *halakhah*.[1]

Notwithstanding the opinion of early academic scholars of Judaism, the traditional midrashic method of studying the Bible developed by the sages is actually closer to modern biblical criticism than the method of the *peshat* (literal or contextual) exegetes of the Middle Ages, because it allows a wider range of possible interpretations.[2] The sages already posed all the questions later raised by biblical critics. Moreover, they enjoyed more intellectual freedom than traditional commentators of the modern period because, unlike the later, they did not have to face refutations of the sanctity of the Bible and the consequent challenges to Jewish religious belief.[3] The faith of the sages was neither based on the belief in the sanctity of each letter of the biblical text, nor on the sanctity of the books of the Bible or their historical validity. The sages themselves, in the *beit midrash,* endowed these books with authority and sanctity. They determined which books were to be left outside the canon, and forbad Jews to read them.[4]

Critical analysis is based on three parameters: text, language, and history.[5] The sages worked intensively in each of these fields. In the field of textual analysis, they counted the words and letters in the Bible,[6] compared the texts of the Torah scrolls kept in the *Azarah* of the Temple to the text of other scrolls,[7] pointed out variations between what they referred to as "our Torah" and the "Torah of Rabbi Meir,"[8] and were aware of the discrepancies between the Septuagint and the traditional text,[9] inter alia.

In the field of linguistics, the sages used words from Greece,[10] Syria,[11] Africa[12] and Arabia[13] in order to explain unclear words in the Bible.[14] They were aware of differences between biblical and mishnaic Hebrew,[15] and the difficulties inherent to every attempt to translate the Bible to other languages.[16] Above all, their sensitivity to language is expressed in the midrashic interpretations of words and verses, and the connections they made, through linguistic tools, between different subjects and places in the Bible.

The sages also discussed the historical context of the biblical texts. To this end, they attempted to construct an outline of world history from creation until their own time, based on the Bible, tradition, and the few external sources available to them.[17] They had neither significant, reliable, external historical sources nor modern historical methodology. This did not, however, prevent them from meticulously examining the information they did have, or attempting to place each source in its historical context to the best of their abilities and in their own way.

It is customary to divide biblical criticism into two categories: "lower" or "textual" criticism examines the accuracy of the text, word for word, while "higher" or "literary" criticism examines the characteristics of the books, their authors, sources, editing, and time of completion.[18] The sages engaged intensively in both these fields. They analyzed the language of the Bible to the letter: "the early sages were called *sofrim* ["scribes," but also "counters"] because they counted all of the letters in the Torah."[19] They also investigated the literary sources of the Bible and its redaction, editing, and canonization. The purpose of this article is to bring to light classical rabbinic sources which can validate and legitimatize modern biblical scholarship.

The Sages and Modern Scholarship

There is no fundamental difference between the sages and critical Bible scholars in their approach to asking questions, an approach that contrasts with the fear of heretical inquiry characteristic of the "faith-based" or *haredi* approach to Bible study.[20] The sages developed defense mechanisms against heretical questions. Sometimes the question was put in the mouth of a heretic,[21] a Roman matron,[22] or a wicked gentile.[23] Sometimes the sages used a strategy of dual interpretation: they answered the annoying questions of heretics and gentiles polemically, but responded to their students, the audience within the *beit midrash*, in a different way.[24] In general, it was the sages' policy to differentiate between what they taught in the *beit midrash* and what they taught in a public forum comprised of the less-sophisticated and less-learned general public.[25] However, they did not refrain from raising even the most difficult questions in the *beit midrash*.

Precedents can also be found in rabbinic literature that can legitimize all of the methods used by modern biblical scholarship to find answers to their questions: linguistics (including analyses of both Hebrew and other languages), textual emendations, source criticism, dating, historical identifications, the use of the sciences and external literature—all these exist in classical rabbinic literature. Although the frequency of use, the database, and the methods differ from those of modern scholarship, there are enough examples to prove that the sages authorized the use of these methods in their *beit midrash*.

The approach of the sages differs from that of modern scholarship in three major aspects. These differences do not challenge the legitimacy of modern scholarship, but demand clarification and a precise understanding of the reason for the gaps and the way of bridging them.

The first difference is methodology. The tools available to the modern Bible scholar, such as archeological, historical, linguistic, and cultural information, and methods of literary analysis, were not available to the sages. However, the absence of these tools in the past does not invalidate their use in the future.[26]

The second difference is the sanctity of the texts. The sages regarded the Bible as a divine, holy source, and its study as the fulfillment of a commandment. They looked upon it as an authoritative source for beliefs and opinion and halakhic practice. The modern critical scholar usually views the Bible, at best, with academic dispassion, and, at worst, as a means to justify his belief system, which differs from that of the sages. At its inception, biblical scholarship served the aims of Christian theology and, later, of atheism.[27] When Orthodox Jews began to confront biblical criticism they were unable to change the preexisting skepticism towards it among religious Jews. Although these are indeed valid arguments against both the scholars and their biased and misleading scholarship,[28] they do not delegitimize critical Bible study itself.[29] One has to know how to discard the peel of the pomegranate and eat its seeds, as Rabbi Meir did with the teachings of his master, the heretic Elisha ben Abuya.[30]

The third difference concerns the relationship between *peshat* (plain, contextual meaning) and *derash* (homiletic or creative interpretation). The modern scholar thinks that he must find religious answers to his critical questions by means of *peshat* exegesis. In contrast, the sages believed that answers to critical questions should be proposed by means of *derash*.[31] Like the Karaites, critical biblical exegetes since Spinoza based their faith on *peshat*, while the critical exegetes among the sages based their faith on a tradition that is not dependent on the plain meaning of the biblical texts, and interpreted the texts in accordance with their accepted beliefs and opinions.

In this respect, the contemporary naïve believer and nonbelieving biblical scholar are similar to each other, and different from the sages. Both believe that faith is founded upon the simple meaning of the biblical text. The scholar reasons that if he proves that the Red Sea did not part as the text describes, either by directly challenging the historical/scientific validity of the story or by eroding the credibility of the storyteller through literary devices, he will undermine the purity of faith. The naïve believer is likewise apprehensive that if he is confronted with difficult questions about the simple meaning of the biblical narrative of the parting of the Red Sea, his faith will be uprooted.

In contrast, the sages did not fear contradictions between the simple meaning of the text and their beliefs. For example, when faced with difficult discrepancies between the book of Ezekiel and commandments in the Torah, they considered the possibility of excluding the book from the canon. In the end it was canonized, after the contradictions were reconciled by this interpretative project.[32] This decision to retain the book of Ezekiel was faith based and entirely unrelated to the straightforward interpretation of the text. The believing Bible scholar of today should follow this path—to remain attentive to the contextual meaning of the text, as it appears, and resolve his crises of faith by means of midrash.

Peshat and Derash

Modern scholarship is interested in the *peshat*. In this respect, it follows in the footsteps of both the greatest of the medieval rabbis and the modern scholars of philology and hermeneutics, who regarded the *peshat* as the direct path to understanding the early sources.[33] For the purpose of this discussion, I will define *peshat* as reading the text in its context, as it was written by its author at the time of its composition, in an attempt to understand the meaning of the words intended by their author and understood by those who heard or read them for the first time. *Derash* attempts to infuse the text with additional meanings. It is possible that these meanings were already latent within it, though not apparent on its most basic and obvious level.[34] It is also possible that these meanings were hidden from the listeners and readers of the text and from its author, even if he was a prophet.[35]

The sages did not disapprove of *peshat*. They wanted to find the reason and purpose in the simple meaning of the text. The question, "What is the *peshat* of the text?" is repeated in several places in the Talmud where a verse is interpreted by means of *derash*.[36] They did not, however, consider the *peshat* to be the most important meaning of the text and certainly not its exclusive meaning. It would be more accurate to say that they presented the *peshat* as a secondary option in the interpretation of Scripture. In certain sources it appears that the sages regarded the *peshat* itself as a kind of *derash*. There were sages who expressed excitement over the new insights revealed to them by a *peshat* reading of the text, as opposed to the traditional midrashic reading with which they were familiar.[37]

The sages were well aware that the simple meaning of the words "eye for eye" (Exod. 21:24) is "an actual eye." However, because the accepted halakhic tradition holds that monetary compensation was sufficient, the Gemara presents nine different justifications for the deviation from the actual meaning of the words. Even the opinion of Rabbi Eliezer, "eye for actual eye," was shorn of its literal meaning and his words were interpreted to mean that he agreed that the verse refers to monetary compensation but argued that the simple meaning of the verse has implications regarding the nature of this compensation.[38]

The Purpose and Method of Midrash

The accepted understanding of the need for midrash is influenced by the perspective of *peshat* exegesis. It is naïvely assumed that the purpose of the midrash is to resolve difficulties in the text. There are midrashim that grew out of exegetical questions, such as a contradiction between verses. Other midrashim bridge the gap between the sages' worldview and the plain meaning of the text. However, in truth, *derash* interpretation is not primarily a means of solving exegetical difficulties, but a way of studying the Torah that enriches and expands. The underlying assumption of *derash* is that the Torah was given for this very purpose—so that its students will reveal the various possible perspectives within it, and even read external insights and ideas into its verses.[39] Structurally speaking, a midrash will often ostensibly open with an exegetical question, but the problem raised is merely a means to arrive at the midrashic saying. Occasionally, from a strictly exegetical perspective, it would be possible to suggest a simple and easy answer, yet the commentator prefers a convoluted explanation far removed from the *peshat*, whether in order to derive *halakhah* from the verse or to weave it into an *aggadah* (parable or homily).[40]

The sages' exegetical questions are not necessarily identical to those of *peshat* exegetes, because their underlying assumptions regarding the *peshat* differed. Sometimes the sages revealed basic, coherent, exegetical assumptions based on linguistic *peshat*.[41] There is however another type of midrash that is totally disconnected from the *peshat*, although it appears to be based upon it.[42]

To conclude, the fundamental difference between the *peshat* exegetes, scholars, and Bible critics on the one hand, and the sages on the other, is the level of "sincerity"[43] with which they relate to the *peshat*. The *peshat* exegetes regard this as the primary and fundamental way of interpreting the Bible, and ascribe enormous significance to its role in the formation of the believer's worldview and perception of reality. The *derash* exegetes, in contrast, derive their worldview and perception of reality from the Oral Law, and regard the *peshat* as an additional exegetical option that can never take precedence, either in understanding the Bible or in the formation of the believer's worldview.[44] Principles of faith and the finer points of *halakhah* are not determined by their conformity to the plain meaning of the biblical text. On the contrary, by means of *derash*, the verses are made to conform to the beliefs and opinions, and laws and customs of the Oral Law. This approach allows the sages and those following in their path to relate freely to the *peshat* and accept the possibility that it contains contradictions and difficulties, both intrinsic and theological.

The "Lower" Criticism of the Sages—Textual Criticism

Talmudic and midrashic literature reveals the sages' confrontation with textual questions—that is, "lower criticism."[45] The sages understood the differences between the Paleo-Hebrew alphabet and the Assyrian alphabet, which they brought back with them from Babylonia.[46] They were aware of their own lack of proficiency in defective and plene spellings of words,[47] knew of the existence of variations between different textual witnesses,[48] and pointed out the discrepancies between their text of the Torah and the texts of Septuagint[49] and the Samaritan Torah.[50] There are "scribal emendations" (*tikkunei soferim*) of the Torah text attributed to the Men of the Great Assembly.[51] The vocalized letters in the Torah were ascribed to Ezra the Scribe.[52] In addition to the scribal tradition, there is also an unwritten oral tradition of pronunciation that changed from place to place, and could influence exegesis and homiletics.[53] Some *derashot* are based upon variations in vocalization,[54] and some involve changes in consonants that are in effect textual variants.[55]

Even if the sages regarded one primary text as authoritative according to *halakhah* and used it to proofread Torah scrolls, they nonetheless recognized the existence of other texts and used them (or even created them) as exegetical and midrashic tools. The disturbing question of whether pointing out textual variations and corrections detracts from the sanctity of the Bible does not seem to have occurred at all to the authors of the midrash, who referred to these matters freely. It is therefore possible to adopt the "relaxed" approach of the sages in response to modern scholars' proposals for emending the biblical text. If the proposal appears reasonable and offers a cogent interpretation of a difficult verse, it can become a midrash in the style of *al tikrei* ("don't read 'a', read 'b'"),[56] and can be welcomed as an additional interpretation, though not as a potential emendation of the authoritative Masoretic text.[57]

"Higher Criticism"—Dating the Text and Identifying its Author

The sages discussed the dating of the composition, completion, and editing of the biblical books. Their considerations were similar to those of critical scholars. For example, the examination of linguistic compatibility, the method used by the sages, though not based on modern linguistics, was similar to it in many respects. One of the most important sources for the rabbinic treatment of these issues is the passage in the Babylonian Talmud that discusses the dating of the biblical books.[58] At the heart of the discussion is a *baraita* (mishnaic material external to the Mishnah) that lists the authors and editors of the books of the Bible. The Gemara discusses this *baraita*, searches for explanations for its statements, and disagrees with it, or qualifies it, after an examination of the biblical sources.

The longest section of the passage is the discussion of the dating and authorship of the book of Job.[59] The Gemara proposes a wide range of possible time periods for the book's composition, from the time of Moses until the days of the *beit midrash* in Tiberius at the end of the Second Temple period. The dating of the book was accomplished by means of various kinds of *derashot*. Some are quasi-linguistic—the discovery of a unique word common to both Job and another verse in the Bible. Some are quasi-historical—the discovery of an event common to both Job and another period in the Bible. Some are topical—the connection between the figure of Job and his actions, and another period in the Bible. Talmudic *derashot* vary with regard to the proximity of the *derash* to the *peshat*. Some linguistic and topical connections appear to be far removed from the *peshat*, while others are very similar to attempts by modern scholars to date the book of Job. A faith-based argument claiming that it is forbidden to deviate from the early tradition that Job was written by Moses is not raised at any point in the discussion.

The Gemara includes another approach, more "critical" than the others, according to which Job never existed and his story is an allegory.[60] The Gemara does not take an ideological stand with regard to this approach either, and does not argue that it is forbidden to say that Job is a work of fiction. The discussion focuses on a literary question: Do its many factual details constitute proof of the historical veracity of the story?

The principles that can be derived from this discussion are as follows:

1. The identification of a book's author, date, and place of composition are integral to the task of its interpretation.
2. The identification of a book's author and its time period are not bound by authoritative tradition but rather demand investigation and interpretation by use of various exegetical methods.
3. It is possible to date a biblical book to a later time period, even to the end of the Second Temple period.
4. One of the best ways to ascertain the timeframe and author of a book is a linguistic and topical comparison with parallel biblical texts.
5. Theological considerations are not determining factors in the identification of a book's time period or author.
6. It is possible to propose an interpretation that negates the historical reality of a biblical story and presents it as allegory and fiction. It is,

therefore, worthwhile to acquire a literary methodology with which to determine if a certain textual unit is realistic or fictitious.

7. Halakhic authority is not to be exercised in this type of discussion; the full range of possibilities remains open.

Higher Criticism—The Division of a Book according to Authors and Time Periods

The *baraita* about the order of the biblical canon opens additional possibilities for "criticism" of the biblical corpus, including the possibility of deconstructing one book into different sources. The *baraita* states that King David, along with "ten elders," wrote the book of Psalms.[61] Another *baraita* includes a selection of tannaitic attempts to ascribe the group of psalms known as "*hallel miztri*"[62] to poets from different periods, from the time of the Exodus from Egypt until the days of Mordecai and Esther.[63]

The following conclusions can be drawn from the discussion of the composition of the book of Psalms:

1. The statement that Kind David wrote the entire book of Psalms is a generalization with many exceptions.
2. It is possible to ascribe psalms to other poets, especially if they lived before the time of King David.
3. It is possible to point to groups of psalms, within the book of Psalms, not written by David but created earlier in the framework of Jewish liturgical poetry and included within the book at the time of its redaction.[64]

In the Middle Ages, the "rabbinic" approach to the integrity of the book of Psalms and its antiquity was polarized. On one extreme stood Saadya Ga'on, who argued that the entire book, including its futuristic and prophetic chapters, was the word of God to King David. On the other extreme, Rabbi Moses ha-Kohen ibn Gikatilla dated certain psalms to as late as the time of the Return to Zion.[65] It is reasonable to assume that the resolute position of Saadya Ga'on with regard to the antiquity, integrity, and divine origin of the book of Psalms is connected to his involvement in the polemic against the Karaites. Rabbi Moses ibn Gikatilla's approach, on the other hand, is compatible with the sages' tolerant and relaxed discussion of the dating and sources of the book of Psalms.[66]

Higher Criticism: The Distinction between the Composition of a Book and its Editing and Canonization

Another critical feature that clearly emerges from the discussion in the Babylonian Talmud, tractate *Bava Batra,* about the editing of the biblical books is the sages' distinction between the principal author of a book, its final editor, and other editors. The *baraita* declares that Joshua must have written the last eight verses of the Torah because it is impossible that Moses wrote the words, "So Moses the servant of the Lord died" (Deut. 34:5) and the following verses. The *baraita* expresses a similar opinion regarding other biblical books that were completed by later authors or editors. It attributes the books of Isaiah, Proverbs, the Song of Songs, and Ecclesiastes to "Hezekiah and his group" rather than to the prophet Isaiah and King Solomon, despite the fact that the books ascribe themselves to these authors. The *baraita* attributes the books of Ezekiel, the Twelve Minor Prophets, Daniel, and Esther to the Men of the Great Assembly, in other words to the period of the Second Temple, despite that fact that several of them, including the early minor prophets, were written much earlier. This *baraita* was not accepted as an authoritative source. There are those who disagreed with it and maintained that Moses wrote the concluding verses of the Torah, even though this means that he recorded his own death. They did not, however, argue that it is heretical to believe that a section of the Torah was not written by Moses, but rather explained their reasoning with exegetical arguments. When the Gemara allowed the possibility, on the one hand, of disagreeing with the *baraita* about the editing of Bible, and, on the other hand, of using rational considerations to date the book, it paved the way for all modern critical discussion about the editing of the biblical corpus.[67]

The Sanctity of the Biblical Books—Theological Difficulties

The Mishnah, in tractate *Yadayim,* records an argument among the sages on the question of which books "defile the hands."[68] It is accepted that this discussion reflects the historical process of the canonization of the Bible. Even if the discussion has conceptual rather than historical validity, it testifies to the positions of the sages discussing the question of what should and should not be included in the biblical canon.[69] The sages questioned the sanctity of Ecclesiastes, Song of Songs, and Esther. They also discussed the possibility of excluding books from the canon: Ecclesiastes, because it contains internal inconsistencies, and ostensibly heretical ideas and contradicts the Torah; Proverbs, because of its internal inconsistencies; and Ezekiel, because it contradicts the Torah.

The principle that emerges from these discussions is that there is no valid, authoritative, early rabbinic source that invests the books of the Bible with inherent and absolute sanctity. The decision that one book would enter the canon (and thus "defile the hands") while another would be excluded from it, condemned to oblivion or even banned, was determined by the sages' assessment of the general worth of the book and its educational and practical efficacy. They also took into consideration the possible use of creative interpretation to solve problems that could arise during study, in order to prepare the book for study by the general public. Because the source of the validity and sanctity of the books lies not in their authors or their manner of composition but in the halakhic ruling of the sages, there is no reason to fear that a critical examination of them will impinge upon their sanctity.[70] The critics will raise questions, and *peshat* and *derash* exegetes will answer them, in their different ways, but nonetheless, the book will retain the sanctity invested in it by the *halakhah*, as determined by the sages. If these same researchers "discovered" that the Torah scroll is made out of cowhide and written in gall ink, would its sanctity be diminished in any way?

The Documentary Hypothesis

After generations of controversy surrounding the documentary hypothesis, Alexander Rofé summarized the approach of contemporary modern research to this theory in four principles: (a) There are serious difficulties in the sequence of the biblical narrative; (b) These difficulties were created by the redaction of different sources; (c) It is possible to identify these various sources by means of comparative analysis of style and content; (d) It is possible to date approximately, and sometimes even definitely, the creation of some of the sources that have been identified.[71]

Many biblical scholars have rejected the documentary hypothesis. Some did so from "within," using the same premises and methodology as the authors of the hypothesis in its various forms.[72] For their part, many religious Jews have rejected the hypothesis from "outside" because it contradicts the basic principle of faith, that the entire Torah was given to Moses from heaven as a single unit.

The principles of the documentary hypothesis are not entirely foreign to the world of the sages. The midrash raises problems and solutions that are similar to those of the critics. First of all, the sages clearly acknowledged the existence of inconsistencies in the text and were not frightened by them. On the contrary, the hermeneutic principle "two verses that contradict each other" is a fundamental principle of midrash. Hundreds of midrashim are structured in the framework of the juxtaposition of contradictory sources: "One verse says... another verse says...."

Not infrequently, the contradiction between verses is resolved by reexamining each verse in its context: "Here, when they are doing the will of God, and there, when they are not doing the will of God";[73] "This refers to a time when the Temple is standing, and that to a time when it is not standing."[74] Distinctions along the lines of "Here, when... there, when...," which understand contradictory verses as reflecting different historical periods or spiritual states, are very common. This does not mean that the sages believed that these verses were written at different times. They were, however, clearly indicating that the verses must be read as referring to different periods and reflecting the differences between them.[75]

The concept of source criticism is also expressed in midrashim declaring that two contradictory verses were said "in a single utterance."[76] The solution, expressed by means of the verse "One thing God has spoken; two things have I heard" (Ps. 62:12),[77] does not attempt to resolve the contradiction, but rather accepts the possibility that the Torah includes contradictory verses, each of which has its own meaning in its own context.

Rabbi Mordecai Breuer accepted the documentary hypothesis as the correct way to solve difficulties in the Torah. He was not able, however, to accept its theological implications, and therefore confronted the theological problem raised by biblical criticism in the same way that the sages wrote midrash. He accepted the tools of critical analysis, and used them to explain the Torah without committing himself to any superficial conclusions regarding the sources of the sacred text. Rabbi Breuer even regarded his method as "midrash." He believed that the Torah was given by God to Moses as a single integral unit, yet it can be interpreted as if it were compiled from various sources.[78]

According to Breuer's approach, the Torah reflects "two aspects": "mercy" and "judgment." One uses the Tetragrammaton, the other *Elohim*; one describes festivals from a sacral perspective, and the other from a social/national perspective. This approach raises the possibility of including within the variations in aspects reflections of historical and cultural differences. In Genesis, the Torah uses the language of the Patriarchs; in Deuteronomy, the language of the kings; in Leviticus, the language of the priests; and in Exodus, the language of the people.[79]

History and Chronology

I will now turn to the question of the historical authenticity of the Bible.

There is a contradiction between the prohibition of erecting a stone pillar given in Deuteronomy and references to stone pillars that were erected in the days of the Patriarchs. The sages' solution to this problem is that the stone pillar, popular among the Patriarchs, became hateful to their descendants because of a change in circumstances.[80] Thus, significant contradictions between verses in the area of beliefs and opinions, or halakhic and ethical practice, can be resolved by historical distinctions. The contradiction can be explained as a change that occurred during the giving of the Torah, from the mouth of God, or as the result of changes that occurred, or were going to occur, in the cultural environment.

The traditional approach to biblical chronology gave particular weight to early rabbinic midrash at the expense of the simple meaning of the verses. The result was that even traditional *peshat* exegetes found it difficult to grasp that the chronologies developed by the sages were, in fact, *derashot*. They therefore attempted to reconcile them with the simple meaning of the text.[81] For example, midrash *Seder Olam Rabbah*, attributed to Rabbi Yose ben Halafta, became accepted as an authoritative chronology even by the *peshat* exegetes. As a result, they attempted to justify the historicity of the chronologies even when they appeared to be completely fictitious *derashot*,[82] or totally contradicted what was known from other chronological sources.[83] In truth, like any other midrashim, the sages arrived at the biblical timeline in their own way, the way of *derash*.

In the Zohar, it is made very clear that biblical stories are not to be read as historical narrative.[84] This book nullified the requirement to accept the literal historical dimension of biblical stories as necessarily true, and thus opened the door to an ahistorical exegesis that examines what can be learned from the verses conceptually without regard for their historical context. At the same time, it can be understood from the Zohar that historical exegesis is also acceptable, as long as it does not negate the compelling spiritual meanings of the verse. Just as the *peshat* did not determine the historical understanding of the sages, the *derashot* of the sages do not define history. Neither are damaged when new interpretations based on historical methodology and current historical knowledge are proposed. This has been the task of commentators throughout the generations. Their work should not be obstructed for fear of undermining the sanctity of the Torah or the importance and value of the words of the sages when they do not conform to contemporary historical perspectives.

When was the Torah Given and When was it Written?

According to the simple meaning of the biblical text, after the Ten Commandments were given to Moses on Mount Sinai, he studied the Torah for forty days on the mountain, and then taught it to the People of Israel. Over the course of their subsequent journey through the desert, Moses received additional parts of God's Torah. On the plains of Moab, he explained the contents of the Torah, and these words form the basis of the book of Deuteronomy.[85] Just before he died, Moses completed the Torah, wrote it down as a book, and gave it to the People of Israel.[86]

The question of whether the Torah was written by Moses by hand is not necessarily synonymous with the question of the divine origin of the Torah. According to the Midrash, Korah first challenged the divine origin of Moses' Torah, although he clearly did not refute that the Torah was given by Moses.[87] On the other hand, the expression *Torah min ha-shamayim* (Torah from heaven) is not limited only to the Torah of Moses. The Oral Torah, at least that part that is based upon the Written Torah, is also considered to be of divine origin, as the Talmud states: "Even if he said, 'The entire Torah is from heaven, except for this point that is deduced by extrapolation (*kal va-homer*) or analogy (*gezerah shavah*),' he is still included in the verse, 'Because he has spurned the word of the Lord and violated His commandment, that person shall be cut off—he bears his guilt'" (Num. 15:31).[88]

The definition of the concept "from heaven" (of divine origin) in the context of the Oral Law, requires a separate discussion, along theological lines.[89] The tension between "from heaven" and "it is not in the heavens" (Deut. 30:12) is reflected in the *aggadah* concerning Akhnai's oven that has occupied generations of commentators.[90] The sages believed it possible both to reject the divinity of the Torah while standing beside Moses on Mount Sinai, and to consider new ideas originating in the *beit midrash* of the sages, even if they are controversial, as "Torah from heaven": "both are the words of the living God."[91] The saying, "Anything that an advanced student will teach in the presence of his master was already said to Moses on Sinai,"[92] is not a paradox or a contradiction in terms if the words "will teach" and "to Moses on Sinai" are not understood literally.

Religious people confronted by critical research are deeply disturbed by the chronological and historical timeline of the giving of the Written Torah. This seems to be the most difficult challenge to religious faith posed by academic biblical scholarship. However, the sages would, it seems, not have condemned someone as a heretic for believing that the book known as "the Torah of Moses" originated on Mount Sinai, developed over the generations, and was completed only at the beginning of the Second Temple period, as long as that person believed it to be "Torah from heaven"—meaning sacred, divine, and binding on belief and practice.

This subject can be compared to Maimonides' negation of God's corporality. Maimonides argued that all the verses that contain a reference to the corporality of God should be interpreted otherwise. He devoted a significant part of *The Guide of the Perplexed* to validating his approach on principle, and using it to reinterpret the Bible. On the basis of this approach, Maimonides declared that the angels revealed to the Patriarchs in Genesis were prophetic visions rather than real entities, and he was severely attacked for it.[93] Maimonides survived the bitter attacks against his philosophical and exegetical approach, and remains one of the greatest authorities of all times, not only in *halakhah* but also in Jewish thought. Maimonides also stated (and he was not alone in doing so) that if, by means of the rational and scientific tools of his time, he had arrived at the conclusion that the world is eternal, he could have reinterpreted the Torah by means of *derash*, and explained the verses describing creation in accordance with this belief.[94] Applying Maimonides' approach to the composition of the Torah, it can be assumed that it is possible to interpret the verses that describe Moses writing the Torah in such a way as to separate them from their plain meaning, although they would nonetheless continue to be the cornerstone of the belief in the divine origin of the Torah.

Conclusion

In this article I have argued that modern academic biblical criticism should be treated as an additional branch of biblical exegesis. Though a product of the relatively recent past, it is an extension of the broad and well-established genre of rabbinic midrash. While the early academic scholars of Judaism attempted to find a source for their analytical approach in the methodology of the medieval *peshat* exegetes, I have suggested that biblical scholarship should be seen as an approach based on the traditional midrashic methodology of the sages, as it has been continued in *derash*-based literature throughout the subsequent generations.

The approach that declares biblical scholarship to be the continuation of medieval *peshat* exegesis creates tension. It claims to represent the fundamental exegetical truth, and creates a direct correlation between the "correct" understanding of the *pesaht* and the foundation of beliefs and opinions on the Bible, revelation and prophecy. This is not the case if we approach biblical scholarship from the liberal spirit of rabbinic midrash. Beliefs and opinions, as well as ethical principles and *halakhah*, are grounded in variety of sources in *halakhah* and *aggadah*, authenticated by the sages of the Oral law, while the field of Bible study, including the academic and critical approach, is left open to the "interpretations that are being discovered every day."[95]

Endnotes

1. J. M. Grintz, *Mevo'ay Mikra* [Introductions to the Bible] (Tel Aviv: Yavneh, 1972), 158–181; Hava Lazarus-Yafeh, *Intertwined Worlds: Medieval Islam and Bible Criticism* (Princeton: Princeton University Press, 1992). On Muslim influence on the Karaites, see Yoram Erder, *Avlei Tzion ha-Kara'im u-Megilot Kumran: Le-Toldot Ḥalufa le-Yahadut ha-Rabanit* [The Karaite mourners of Zion and the Qumran scrolls: The history of an alternative to rabbinic Judaism] (Ra'anana: Hakibbutz Hameuchad, 2004), 355–364; Mordechai Cohen, "Mekor Sefaradi Efshari le-Tefisat 'Peshuto shel Mikra' etzel Rashi" [A possible Sephardic source for Rashi's understanding of "peshuto shel mikra"], in *Rashi: Demuto ve-Yetzirato: Mekorotav shel Rashi ve-Haspha'ato* [Rashi: His image and works: Rashi's sources and his influence], ed. Sara Japhet and Avraham Grossman (Jerusalem: Zalman Shazar, 2009), 2:353–379. On the Christian influence on *peshat* exegesis, see Joseph Dan, "Midrash: Me-Parshanut le-Anarkhia" [Midrash: From exegesis to anarchy], in *Devarim u-Shivrei Devarim* [The Jewishness of Israel], ed. Aviezer Ravitzky and Yedidia Z. Stern (Jerusalem: Israel Democracy Institute, 2007), 237–279. On the essential difference between the classical rabbinic pattern of thought and Greek patterns of thought that were absorbed into Jewish thought from the beginning of the gaonic period, see also Yitzhak Ezuz, *Meharsai'ikh u-Meharivai'ikh me-Ohavai'ikh Yetzu* [Thy destroyers and they that made thee waste shall come from amongst your lovers: On the process of the dissolution of the Jewish in the Western (from paradigm to "reasonable possibility")] (Tel Aviv: Mofet Institute, 2012).
2. This article refers to the sages as a single unit only for the purposes of the discussion. Although the sages differed in their approaches to Bible and midrash, in order to argue that a particular approach enjoyed official rabbinic legitimacy it is sufficient to show it was accepted by some of the *tannaim* and *amoraim*, and preserved in the Talmuds and the classical midrash.
3. Judah Rosenthal, "She'elot Atikot be-Tanakh" [Ancient questions about the Bible], *Hebrew Union College Annual* 21 (1948): 29–91.
4. Grintz, *Mevo'ay Mikra*, 38–48; Menahem Haran, *Ha-Asufa ha-Mikrait* [The biblical collection] (Jerusalem: Mosad Bialik, 1996), pt. 1A; Abraham Kahana, *Ha-Sefarim ha-Hizoni'im* [The Apocrypha], vol. 1, *Mavo Klalli le-Sefarim ha-Hitzoni'im* [General introduction to the Apocrypha] (Jerusalem: Makor, 1970), 7–10.
5. Eliezer Rosenthal, "Ha-Moreh" [The Teacher], *Proceedings of the American Academy for Jewish Research* 31 (1963): i–vxxi.

6. Moshe Katz, "Yesh Shishim Ribo Otiot le-Torah, ha-Amnam?" [Are there really six hundred thousand letters in the Torah?], *Tehumin* 21) 2001): 555ff.
7. Jerusalem Talmud, tractate *Ta'anit* 4:2, 68a.
8. *Bereshit Rabbah* 20:12.
9. Babylonian Talmud, tractate *Megillah* 9a-b
10. Babylonian Talmud, tractate *Sukkah* 35a, inter alia.
11. Babylonian Talmud, tractate *Pesahim* 61a; Jerusalem Talmud, tractate *Sotah* 7:2, 21c.
12. Babylonian Talmud, tractate *Sanhedrin* 4b.
13. Babylonian Talmud, tractate *Rosh Hashanah* 26a. It would appear that this is an exegetical method typical of Rabbi Akiva, who used foreign words that he learned on his travels to "Arabia," "Gaul," and "Africa."
14. The Torah was given on Sinai in four languages. *Sifrei Devarim*, piska 343.
15. Babylonian Talmud, tractate *Avodah Zarah* 58b, inter alia.
16. Babylonian Talmud, tractate *Shabbat* 115a-b, inter alia.
17. Primarily in *Seder Olam Rabbah*. See Anat Reizel, *Mavo le-Midrashim* [Introduction to the midrashic literature] (Alon Shvut: Herzog College, 2011), 305–314.
18. Emanuel Tov, *Bikoret Nusah ha-Mikra* [The textual criticism of the Bible: An introduction] (Jerusalem: Mosad Bialik, 1989), 11–12.
19. Babylonian Talmud, tractate *Kiddushin* 30a.
20. Eliezer Schweid, *Toldot Pilosofiat ha-Dat ha-Yehudit be-Zeman he-Hadash* [A history of modern Jewish religious philosophy] (Ra'anana: Am Oved, 2002), pt. 2, 95–143.
21. Moshe David Herr, "The Historical Significance of the Dialogues between Jewish Sages and Roman Dignitaries," *Scripta Hierosalymitana* 22 (1971): 123–150.
22. Chayuta Deutsch, "Ha-Matrona Rabat ha-Panim" [Encounters between sages and matrons: Fixed patterns and variations], PhD diss., Bar Ilan University, 2011.
23. E.g., Turnus Rufus (*Bereshit Rabbah* 11:5) and Adrianus (*Bereshit Rabbah* 28:6). See Ido Hevroni, "Brit Milah ke-Mered" (Brit Milah as rebellion), *Tekhelet* 28 (2007): 61–73.
24. Jerusalem Talmud, tractate *Shabbat* 3:3, inter alia.
25. Mishnah, tractate *Hagigah* 2:1. Tosefta, *Megillah* 3:31–35. See Yehuda Brandes "Bemai Kamipalgi: le-Mahloket Ha-Aharonim be-Parshanut Heto shel David" [What is this argument about?: The controversy among contemporary scholars over the interpretation of the sin of David], *Megadim* 26 (1996): 107–127.
26. Rabbi Aharon Lichtenstein, "U-be-Yad ha-Nevi'im Adameh: Nituah Sifruti ve-Kitvei ha-Kodesh" ["And spoke parables through the prophets": Literary analysis and the Bible], in *Hi Sihati: Al Derekh Limmud ha-Tanakh* [It is my study], ed. Yehoshua Rice (Alon Shevut-Jerusalem: Yeshivat Har Etzion and Sifrei Maggid, 2013), 73–82.
27. "The story of modern bible scholarship is thus essentially a Protestant story. . . . It can be said that the order is reversed, atheist biblical criticism began as it were with Spinoza." James Kugel, "Heker ha-Mikra le-Toldotav" [The history of biblical scholarship], in *Sifrut ha-Mikra: Mevo'ot u-Mehkarim* [The literature of the Hebrew Bible: introductions and studies], ed. Zipora Talshir (Jerusalem: Yad Ben-Zvi, 2011), 1:18, n. 22.
28. "We have to reject deliberate tendentiousness and at least attempt to overcome our biases when we examine historical questions." Alexander Rofé, *Mavo le-Sifrut ha-Mikra* [Introduction to the literature of Hebrew Bible] (Jerusalem: Carmel, 2006), 16.
29. Evidence of this can be found in the success of the *peshat* "revolution" in the period of the Rishonim (the Middle Ages). Rashbam (Samuel ben Meir), for example, lived in two worlds, and did not see a contradiction between them. He was a commentator on the Talmud, a scholar of *halakhah* and a Tosafist. As a biblical exegete, he was firmly entrenched in the

world of the Sephardic *peshat* exegetes and created many of the new *peshat* interpretations (that were, in his words, appearing daily) without committing himself to the interpretation of the sages or that of his grandfather, Rashi.
30. Babylonian Talmud, tractate *Ḥagigah* 15b.
31. The tendency to base the principles of faith on the *peshat* exegesis of the Bible, while distancing them from the sages' method of midrash, is closely connected to the influence of Greek-Arabic philosophy on the Ge'onim. See Robert Brody, *Rav Se'adya Gaon* (Jerusalem: Zalman Shazar, 2006), 70–90.
32. Babylonian Talmud, tractate *Shabbat* 13b.
33. Ze'ev Levy, *Hermeneutica be-Maḥshevet ha-Yehudit be-Et ha-Ḥadasha* [Hermeneutics in Jewish modern thought] (Haifa: University of Haifa, 2006), 25–34 and 67–86.
34. Sara Japhet, *Dor Dor u-Parshanav: Asufat Meḥkarim be-Parshnut ha-Mikra* [Collected studies in biblical exegesis] (Jerusalem: Mosad Bialik, 2008), 35–54; Shalom Rosenberg, "Ben Peshat le-Derash" [Between *peshat* and *derash*], *De'ot* 37 (1969): 91–99; Rabbi Mordechai Breuer, "Limud Peshuto shel Mikra: Sakanot ve-Siku'im" [Studying the *peshat* of the Bible: Risks and chances], *Ha-Ma'ayan* 18 (1978): 1.
35. This is the meaning of the *aggadah* that describes the astonishment of Moses at the insights that Rabbi Akiva derived from his Torah (Babylonian Talmud, tractate *Menaḥot* 29b).
36. Babylonian Talmud, tractate *Eruvin* 23b and parallels. The sages differ in this respect from the *derash* and faith-based approaches that ascribe no value to the *peshat*, but rather regard the entire Torah as a type of code to reveal hidden secrets.
37. Babylonian Talmud, tractate *Shabbat* 63a.
38. Babylonian Talmud, tractate *Bava Kamma* 83b-84a. Rabbi Solomon Luria (Maharshal) in his commentary on these passages discussed the question of whether the sages interpreted the verses according to their own halakhic preconceptions, or whether their *derashot* shaped the development of the *halakhah*. See his commentary *Yam shel Shlomo, Bava Kamma*, chapter 8, *siman* 1. See also Shalom Rosenberg, *Lo ba-Shamayim Hi: Torah She-be-al peh: Masoret ve-Ḥidushim* [It is not in heaven: Oral Law: Tradition and reinterpretation] (Alon Shvut: Tevunot, 1997), 9–53.
39. Rabbi Abraham Isaac Kook distinguished between these two types of *derashah* by means of a theoretical distinction between explanation and exegesis. See his introduction to *Ein Ayah: Al Aggadot Ḥazal she-ba-Ein Yaakov* (Jerusalem: Ha-Makhon al shem ha-Ratziyah Kook, 1986), tractate *Berakhot*. See also Hananel Mack, *Ha-Parshanut ha-Keduma le-Mikra* [The early commentary to the Bible] (Jerusalem, Ministry of Defense, 1993), 11–16.
40. Isaac Heinemann, *Darkhei Ha-Aggadah* (Jerusalem: Magnes, 1950), 1–13 and 153–157.
41. This is the fundamental approach of Rabbi Akiva. Shmuel Safrai, *Rabbi Akiva ben Yosef, Ḥayyav u-Mishanto* [Rabbi Akiva ben Yosef: His life and teachings] (Jerusalem: Mosad Bialik, 1970), 50–55.
42. Tosafot commentary on Babylonian Talmud, tractate *Kiddushin* 2b, s.v. *kashu k'ra'i*: "Nevertheless, wherever it is possible to explain this, the Gemara does so."
43. In the words of Isaac Heinemann, *Darkhei Ha-Aggadah*, 186–195.
44. Umberto Cassuto is attributed with the insight of understanding biblical criticism as one of the seventy facets (or faces) by which the Torah is interpreted.
45. Yeshayahu Maori, "Midrashei Ḥazal ke-Edut le-Ḥilufei Nusaḥ ha-Mikra" [rabbinic midrash as evidence of textual variations in the Bible], in *Iyunei Mikra u-Parshanut* [Studies in Bible and exegesis], ed. Moshe Bar-Asher et al. (Ramat Gan: Bar Ilan University, 1993), 3:267–286; David Rosenthal, "Al Derekh Tipulam shel Ḥazal be-Ḥilufei Nusaḥ be-Mikra" [The sages' treatment of textual variations in the Bible], in *Sefer Yitzhak Aryeh Zeligman: Ma'amarim be-mikra u-va-Olam he-Atik* [Isaac Leo Seeligman Anniversary Volume: Essays in Bible and

the ancient world], ed. Yair Zakovitch and Alexanader Rofé (Jerusalem: Rubenstein, 1983), 2:395–417; Zipora Talshir, "Le-Toldot Nusaḥ Ha-Mikra" [The history of the biblical text], in *Sifrut ha-Mikra: Mevo'ot u-Meḥkarim*, 1:38–48.
46. Babylonian Talmud, tractate *Sanhedrin* 21b-22a; Rosenberg, "Ben Peshat le-Drash," 28–36.
47. Babylonian Talmud, tractate *Kiddushin* 30a.
48. Daniel Sperber, *Netivot Pesika* [Paths of pesika: methods and approaches for proper halakhic decision making] (Jerusalem: Reuven Mas, 2008), 72 and n. 120 there.
49. *Masekhet Soferim* 1,7.
50. The sages explained the discrepancies between their Torah and the Samaritan Torah as the result of forgery. Babylonian Talmud, tractate *Sotah* 33b, and parallels.
51. In the midrash, the corrections are attributed to the Men of the Great Assembly. *Tanḥuma Shemot*, 16.
52. *Avot de-Rabbi Natan*, *nusaḥ* B, chap. 37. *Ba-midbar Rabbah* 3, 13, indicates that Ezra wrote the text of the Bible and in doing so also added the vowel signs.
53. The interchange of alef and ayin (Babylonian Talmud, tractate *Berakhot* 32a); hey and ḥet (ibid., 30b). See Jerusalem Talmud, tractate *Shabbat* 7:2, 9b on the legitimacy of interchanging *hin* and *ḥitin*.
54. For example, *ḥarut* (engraved) and *ḥerut* (freedom). *Avot de-Rabbi Natan*, *nusaḥ* A, chap. 2.
55. For example, *shibbarta* (you broke)–*shirbabta* (you stretched out), Babylonian Talmud, tractate *Berakhot* 54b; *ain biltekha* ("there is none beside You" [1 Sam. 2:2])–*ain lebalotekha* ("you cannot be consumed"). Ibid., 10a, inter alia.
56. Naftali Herz Tur-Sinai, "Al Tikrei," *Entzeklopedia Mikrait* [Encyclopaedia biblica] (Jerusalem: Mosad Bialik, 1950–1988) 1:420–422; Henoch Yalon, *Pirkei Lashon* [Essays on linguistics] (Jerusalem: Mosad Bialik, 1971), 123–125.
57. On Levinas' opinion of the role of midrash, see Elizabeth Goldwyn, *Revaḥ ben ha-Otiot: Shiurav ha-Talmudi'im shel Levinas: Hatama ben Tokhen ve-Tzura* [Space between the letters: Emmanuel Levinas' talmudic readings between form and content], ed. Yoram Vereté (Bnei Brak: Amutat Hillel ben Hayyim, 2011).
58. Tractate *Bava Batra* 15a.
59. Hananel Mack, *Ele Mashal Haya: Iyov beinei Ḥazal* [It was a metaphor: Job in the eyes of the sages] (Ramat Gan: Bar Ilan University, 2004).
60. There are modern scholars who interpret other books, such as Jonah and Esther, in this manner.
61. Babylonian Talmud, tractate *Bava Batra* 14b-15a.
62. Ps. 113–118.
63. Babylonian Talmud, tractate *Pesaḥim* 117a
64. According to the methodology of Hermann Gunkel, who identified sections of the Bible according to their genre, and Umberto Cassuto, who revealed ancient poetry integrated within the later biblical books.
65. Ps. 137 ("By the rivers of Babylon . . .") is described in the Gemara as a prophetical psalm by King David (Babylonian Talmud, tractate *Gittin* 57b). However, the midrashim on Lamentations indicate that Jeremiah and the exiles to Babylon wrote the psalm (*Midrash Zuta*, ed. Shlomo Buber [Vilna: Rem, 1925] *parasha* 1, *piska* 19).
66. Uriel Simon, *Arbah Gishot le-Sefer Tehillim* [Four approaches to the book of Psalms] (Ramat Gan: Bar Ilan University, 1982).
67. It is important to distinguish between discussion of the books of the Prophets and the Writings, and discussion of the five books of the Torah of Moses. The dating of the Torah to the time and place of Moses is the cornerstone of the belief in its divine origin. I will return to this point below.

68. Mishnah, tractate *Yadayim* 3:8. Paradoxically, the sages ordained that it was holy books that render one ritually unclean, in order to prevent people from putting *terumah* (a food offering) next to the books and damaging them thereby.
69. Haran, *Ha-Asufa ha-Mikrait*, pt. 1, 201–303.
70. Grintz, *Mevo'ay Mikra*, 30–48.
71. Rofé, *Mavo le-Sifrut ha-Mikra*, 112.
72. See, e.g., M. H. Segal, *Mavo ha-Mikra* [Introduction to the Bible] (Jerusalem: Kiryat Sefer), 127–147.
73. Babylonian Talmud, tractate *Yoma* 3b.
74. Babylonian Talmud, tractate *Ḥagigah* 13b.
75. There are those who see in the idea that "the Torah was given in sections" (Babylonian Talmud, tractate *Gittin* 60a-b) the initial nucleus of the concept of identifying various documents within the Torah.
76. Jerusalem Talmud, tractate *Nedarim* 3:2.
77. Babylonian Talmud, tractate *Sanhedrin* 34a.
78. Yosef Ofer, ed, *'Shitat ha-Beḥinot' shel ha-Rav Mordekhai Breuer* [The aspects theory of Rabbi Mordechai Breuer] (Alon Shvut: Tevunot, 2005).
79. David Zohar, *Mehuyavut Yehudit ba-Olam Moderni: ha-Rav Hayyim Hirschensohn ve-Yaḥaso el ha-Moderna* [Jewish responsibility in the modern world: Rav Hayyim Hirschensohn and his approach to modernity] (Jerusalem: Shalom Hartman Institute, 2003), 277–283.
80. Deut. 16:22. In contrast to Gen. 28:18, inter alia. *Igrot ha-Ra'aya* [The letters of Rabbi Abraham Isaac Ha-Kohen Kook] (Jerusalem: Mosad Harav Kook, 1961–1965) 3:746.
81. Rabbi Hayyim Hirschensohn argued that the chronology of the sages is binding according to the *halakhah*, despite the fact that it is based on derash and serves theological objectives. However, the halakhic requirement applies to dating a *get* (certificate of divorce) or calculating sabbatical and Jubilee years. It is not relevant to a historian writing the history of the world. See Zohar, *Mehuyavut Yehudit*, 236.
82. For example, the midrash that Isaac married Rebekah when she was three years old (see Rashi's commentary to Gen. 25:20). While Rabbi Eliyahu Mizraḥi attempted to explain the feasibility of this midrash, Isaac Abravanel rejected it because of its improbability. The Tosafot expressed the opinion that she was fourteen at the time of her marriage. It is possible that they had a variant text of *Seder Olam Rabbah* (chap. 1).
83. In *Seder Olam Rabbah* the length of the Persian period of the era of the return to Zion is much shorter than the chronology accepted by historians. See Hayyim Hafetz, "Malkhut Paras u-Madai ba-Tekufat Bayit Sheni u-lefaneha: Iyun Meḥudash" [The Persian and Median kingdom in the Second Temple period and before: A new examination], *Megadim* 14 (1990): 78–147. See also the comments of Rabbi Yaakov Medan "Mavo le-Ma'amro shel H. Ḥafetz al Malkhut Paras u-Madai" [Introduction to H. Ḥafetz's article on the Persian and Median kingdom], *Megadim* 14 (1990): 47–77.
84. *Zohar*, part 3, *parashat* Be-ha'alotekha, 149a-b.
85. Deut. 1:1, and the *Sifrei* there.
86. In Exodus 24:4, Moses writes down the commandments. In Numbers 33:2, he records the journeys in the desert. In Deuteronomy 31:9, he writes down the Torah and gives it to the priests. In Deuteronomy 31:22, he writes his poem.
87. Jerusalem Talmud, tractate *Sanhedrin* 10:1, 27d.
88. Babylonian Talmud, tractate *Sanhedrin* 99a.
89. Maimonides included belief in the divine origin of the Torah in his thirteen principles of faith. The meaning of the concept as it appears in various places in his own writings requires

close examination. Mark B. Shapiro, *The Limits of Orthodox Theology: Maimonides' Thirteen Principles Reappraised* (Oxford: Litman, 2004), 91–121. See also Shlomo Kassierer and Shlomo Glicksberg, *Mi-Sinai le-Lishkat ha-Gazit: Torah she-be-al peh be-mishnatam shel ha-Rambam ve-ha-Ramban* [From Sinai to Sanhedrin: The Oral Law in the thought of Maimonides and Nachmanides] (Ramat Gan: Bar Ilan University, 2007).

90. See Izhak Englard, "'Tanuro shel Akhnai': Perusheiha shel Aggadah" [The oven of Akhnai: Interpretations of the *aggadah*] *Shnaton ha-Mishpat ha-Ivri* 1 (1974): 45–50.
91. Babylonian Talmud, tractate *Eruvin* 13b.
92. Jerusalem Talmud, tractate *Pe'ah* 2:4, 17a, inter alia.
93. For example, Nachmanides' commentary to Gen. 18:1.
94. *The Guide of the Perplexed*, 2:25. Rabbi Abraham Isaac Ha-Kohen Kook wrote in a similar vein with regard to the idea of evolution. See his *Orot ha-Kodesh* (Jererusalem: Mosad Harav Kook, 1964), 2:542. See also Rabbi Amit Kula, *Havaya o lo haya* [Existential or nonessential: History and literature, religious language and the nature of deity] (Jerusalem: Ha-Kibbutz ha-Dati, 2011), 68–74. Rabbi Kula's book in its entirety addresses the question of the historicity of the Torah. Exegetes from Rabbi Isaac the Blind to modern thinkers perceived the Written Torah as a type of Oral Torah. See Alexander Even Chen, *Akedat Yitzhak: Be-Parshanut ha-Mistit ve-ha-Pilosofit shel ha-Mikra* [The Binding of Isaac: Mystical and philosophical interpretation of the Bible] (Tel Aviv: Mishkal, 2006), 11–13; and Tamar Ross, *Expanding the Palace of Torah: Orthodoxy and Feminism* (Hanover, NH: Brandeis University Press, 2004), 163–224.
95. See the comment by Rabbi Samuel ben Meir (Rashbam) on Gen. 37:2.

The Tanakh as History

Marc Zvi Brettler

As a scholar of the Hebrew Bible, one of the most difficult questions that I regularly face is determining the genre of different biblical texts.[1] Interpretation of any literary text, including the Bible, involves much more than understanding its grammar and lexicon—it must take into consideration genre as well, since the very same words take on different meanings depending on the genre to which they belong. To take a contemporary example: the same words appearing in a newspaper headline and in a comic strip or in a satire may convey or mean something different.[2]

The Bible, like other ancient Near Eastern texts, does not include genre labels that help us understand how particular texts should be "genrified." To stay within the Torah: Are the initial chapters of Genesis to be understood as science or as natural history? Are the ancestral stories meant to be "real" history, narrating the true events of real people in real places at real times—in other words, "history" in its most common contemporary usage? Or do these stories have a different purpose, and are we misreading them if we take them as intending to convey real history, just as we would be misreading a mystery novel set in the past if we read it as history?

This problem is severe and difficult to solve. It is even difficult to know what our presumptions as readers of this material should be, since, after all, the Torah does not open with the words "read me as science (or natural history)," nor does *parashat* Lekh Lekha (Gen. 12:1 and following) begin by saying, "The following should be read as an account of what actually happened in the x-th century BCE." This last point is not trivial, and suggests that as we approach each text, we must ask: What is its genre? Why was it written? What was it trying to convey?

Unlike most of the contributors to this volume, I am American, and thus I am especially sensitive to how issues concerning the Bible as history resonate in the U.S., in both the Jewish and general community. In the non-Jewish,

Protestant world, many conservative believers take as a matter of faith the literal truth of the Bible and its inerrancy. An important evangelical document from 1978 includes a declaration of the wholeness of the Bible and its inerrancy. Its fifteenth article states:

> WE AFFIRM the necessity of interpreting the Bible according to its literal, or normal, sense. The literal sense is the grammatical-historical sense, that is, the meaning which the writer expressed. Interpretation according to the literal sense will take account of all figures of speech and literary forms found in the text.
> WE DENY the legitimacy of any approach to Scripture that attributes to it meaning which the literal sense does not support.[3]

I believe that especially in America, this Protestant view, which was developed late in the nineteenth century and early in the twentieth, has influenced Judaism, and as a result some Jews, trying to show that they are at least as "frum" as their Protestant counterparts, have taken over as doctrine some of these fundamentalist principles. For different reasons, often connected to politics, the history of Israel as recounted in the Bible is often taken at face value among various groups of the contemporary Israeli population as well, just as some anti-Zionist biblical scholars have been quick to overemphasize the problems of using the Bible as a historical source.[4] Yet a close look at the historical record of Jewish interpretation indicates that material such as the primeval story in Genesis 1–11 and the ancestral narratives in 12–50 have often not been understood as literal—or as primarily literal—within Jewish tradition. I will address this later, when I explore precedents for this position. I am happy for these precedents—it is important that each generation not recreate the wheel. Yet for me, such precedents are not crucial. It is clear that Judaism, even (!) traditional Judaism, innovates, and thus I do not want to exaggerate the importance of precedents, or to buy into the position that *ḥadash asur min ha-Torah*, that we are enjoined by the Torah from innovating.[5]

As I have indicated elsewhere, I do not believe that the ancients understood the writing of history as we now do.[6] There was little, if any, interest in narrating the past for its own sake. Stories were set in the past for a variety of reasons, but antiquarian interest was not one of them.[7] Though sparks of such interest developed in the Renaissance, it came to fruition only in the nineteenth century, and it would be a grave mistake to read the biblical books as the products of those German universities with an interest in recreating history "*wie es eigentlich gewesen*,"[8] namely, how it really was. Instead, the "historical" traditions of the Bible should be understood broadly within their ancient context, and more narrowly within their ancient Near Eastern context. In that world, what were the purposes of narratives depicting a past?

One of the most clear, provocative, and convincing discussions of this issue is reflected already in the title of ancient historian Paul Veyne's *Did the Greeks Believe in Their Myths? An Essay in Constitutive Imagination*.[9] Although his answer to this question is subtle and multifaceted—for after all, there is no single Greek conception just as there is no single Jewish conception—his main contention (and here he is far from alone) is that the ancient classical historians were not primarily interested in presenting the past accurately from a historical perspective, but in producing useful narratives about the past.[10] Veyne suggests that, in general, the ancients did not understand their myths and their historical accounts (and there is good reason to combine these two types of stories and to treat them together) as true in the same sense as simple declarative sentences such as, "This amphora is made of clay." The ancient Greek myths were understood to be true in a different, nonliteral sense.

Coming closer to the biblical world, the same conception is well attested in the Mesopotamian historiographical tradition. Concerning one Mesopotamian chronicle, the modern Assyriologist Jean-Jacques Glassner notes: "The author was not interested in producing a chronicle of past centuries . . . his aim was to make a theology of them. . . . He wished to propose an explanation of them on the religious level."[11] He also notes the use of figurative, metaphorical, and nonliteral use of language in some of these texts.[12] Several scholars call these texts propaganda, using this term not in its contemporary pejorative sense, but in its more neutral, earlier sense of a text that is attempting to establish and propagate a particular viewpoint.[13] Others note similarly the ideological cast of these texts,[14] and their "outright political polemic."[15] Many of these points can be seen most clearly in texts such as the Weidner Chronicle, which contains many historical fabrications, and uses the past to show that the king must properly honor the Babylonian high god Marduk.[16] By highlighting such texts in reference to biblical historical texts, I am simply saying that these ancient Jewish texts should be understood in their broader context, taking into consideration that "disinterested research into the past or objective reporting of current events was virtually nonexistent in antiquity."[17]

This idea that the past is not important for its own sake is also amply illustrated in rabbinic texts, as noted by Isaiah Gafni, who observes that "the events of the Bible were known to all, and it was their meaning and moral implications that would be taken up by the rabbis."[18] I would go a step further—the rabbis take up "their meaning and moral implications" precisely because that is what these texts were originally about. Gafni notes astutely that the biblical injunction, "You have to inquire about bygone ages that came before you, ever since God created man on earth, from one end of heaven to the other: has anything as grand as this ever happened, or has its like ever been known?" (Deut. 4:32) was *not* used by the rabbis to encourage study of the past for its own sake. I would add that in this case the rabbis were simply following biblical precedent, according to which the past also was not important for its own sake. Gafni also studies the expression *mai de-hava hava*, which appears fourteen times in the Babylonian Talmud. He notes that the expression does not suggest that history in the sense of recreating the real past is irrelevant, but that it is a distraction.[19] I believe that the same is true of biblical texts as well; they were interested in what stories might teach, rather than in the real, actual past.

Had the Bible shown a strong interest in the actual past, it would look very different. It would not state in its first chapter that land animals were created, and then man and woman, and then one chapter later claim that man was created first, then land animals, and then woman. Works that are historical, in the sense of recapitulating the actual past, clean up such basic inconsistences. Nor do books interested in the real past tell the same story twice—as is the case in Samuel-Kings and Chronicles. Not only would a real historian in the modern sense have included only one of these texts, but he or she would have also decided such basic issues as whether David or Elhanan killed Goliath (1 Sam. 17; 2 Sam 21:19), or if Elhanan killed Goliath's brother (1 Chron. 20:5), to say nothing of whether or not David sinned with Bathsheba (2 Sam. 11–12; 1 Chron. 20:1–3). A work interested in "real" history would know the number and order of the plagues in Egypt (Ps. 78; 105), and would have been clear about whether the plague of blood, for example, only affected the Nile or all Egyptian bodies of water (Exod. 7:20–21). The conclusion to my mind is clear: the Bible as a whole—as well as individual biblical compositions that discuss ancient events—is not interested in the real history of the past.

Though I wish I could find a better term, I contend that the biblical stories about the past are best understood as "myth." I am not using "myth" in the sense of a primitive story, a story that is wrong, or a story about the gods, but rather in the more technical sense, as the word is used by anthropologists and others. I find most useful, and am most sympathetic to, a modified version of the definition offered by the classicist Walter Burkert: a myth should be understood as a traditional tale dealing with issues of collective importance, and is an extended metaphor.[20] For him, as for me, "myth" is a descriptive term, with no negative value judgment whatsoever.

As such, I do not accept the frequent scholarly distinction that classifies the introductory stories of Genesis as myth, while considering those beginning with Abraham as history. Both groups of stories are traditional tales dealing with issues of collective importance. The late biblical scholar Matitiahu Tsevat expressed this notion brilliantly in observing that from the biblical perspective "the waters of Noah are no less real than the waters of Shiloah."[21] In other words, the stories in Genesis are not presented differently than other accounts, suggesting that they belong to the same genre as the stories in Kings (e.g., 2 Kings 20:20), including those that have archeological corroboration. His observation is supported by the structure of Genesis, which does not indicate a clear break between what many scholars consider myth and what they consider to be history; indeed, Abraham is introduced in the genealogy in Genesis 11:26, and that genealogy in its first verse (11:10) dates the birth of Shem to "two years after the flood." It is also supported by the structure of so-called "historical psalms," such as Psalm 136, which notes both "who made the heavens with wisdom, His steadfast love is eternal" (5) and "who led His people through the wilderness, His steadfast love is eternal" (16). In sum, my inclination is to treat all biblical narratives that depict a past as myths in Burkert's sense.[22]

These traditional tales may, of course, contain "kernels," to use a word fashionable last century, of historical veracity. In some cases they may even be used to reconstruct the real history of Israel, a real people in the Iron Age Levant. But that was not their main purpose. To return to Burkert, as myths they are metaphors on the story level. It is a fundamental mistake of mis-genrification to read them as if they intended to retell the story of ancient Israel in the same way that, for instance, a modern historian of the 1948 War of Independence is judged by how well he or she fulfilled the goal of approaching the real truth of what happened.

As such, I find myself in basic disagreement with Saadya, the first Jewish biblical commentator, who has been unduly influential in the world of Jewish commentary. In his *Book of Beliefs and Opinions* he notes that a literal sense of the biblical text should be upheld unless it contradicts the senses, reason, another biblical passage, or rabbinic tradition:

> Now that I have finished explaining the three types of knowledge [i.e., rational, scriptural, and traditional] which are necessary for the commentator on the Torah, I see fit to preface [a description of] the [proper]

method of expounding the Torah and the other books of the Prophets. I say: since these three types of knowledge are the very foundations of Scripture, and since every speech includes perforce both unambiguous and ambiguous [expressions; in Arabic, *muhkam* and *mutashabih*] ... the exegete should consider all words that accord with the prior dictates of reason and the later dictates of tradition as unambiguous, and words that are inconsistent with one or the other as ambiguous.

To explain further: a reasonable person should always understand the Torah according to the external meaning of its words, that is, the meaning generally recognized among speakers of the language—because the purpose of any book is to convey its meaning perfectly in the reader's heart—except where perception or reason contradict the usual meaning of a particular expression or where the usual meaning of an expression contradicts an unequivocal verse found elsewhere in Scripture or tradition. However, if retaining the simple meaning of an expression leads the exegete to profess one of these four things [discussed below] he must know that this expression is not to be understood according to its simple meaning, but that it carries one or more nonliteral meanings [*majaz*]; and once he knows the type of *majaz* involved ... in order to bring [the expression under consideration into agreement with] its unambiguous equivalent [*muhkam*], the verse will be reconciled with the senses, with reason, with other scriptures and with tradition.[23]

This position, which has its contemporary advocates,[24] assumes a clear bias toward the literal, and has been extremely influential within Judaism. Yet it is far from determinative, and Maimonides, considered by many to be the greatest of the medieval theologians, did not support his predecessor's view. Maimonides argues quite differently in his introduction to *The Guide of the Perplexed* that the true and important words of Scripture are like a hidden pearl, and external meanings do not suffice; rather "their internal meaning, on the other hand, contains wisdom that is useful for beliefs concerned with the truth as it is."[25] Throughout the *Guide* he develops this principle, offering, as is well-known, many allegorical interpretations of biblical passages; in fact, Mordechai Cohen has claimed that he "made metaphor the exegetical focus of his *Guide for the Perplexed*."[26]

In his exposition about the importance of inner meaning, Maimonides cites Proverbs 25:11: "Like golden apples in silver showpieces is a phrase well turned." The late great medievalist Frank Talmage used this citation as the basis for his brilliant essay "Apples of Gold: The Inner Meaning of Sacred Texts in Medieval Jewry."[27] Talmage shows that this idea that biblical texts possess an *inner* meaning is key in much medieval interpretation. For example, Joseph Kimhi in *The Book of the Covenant* noted that Jews understand the Bible figuratively in a way that is comparable to eating the marrow of the bone and wheat rather than the chaff.[28] This is, of course, especially remarkable since that book was written in the context of Jewish-Christian polemics, and Christianity typically understood the Hebrew Bible allegorically. Nevertheless, Kimhi did not draw a clear contrast between Jewish literal and Christian allegorical interpretation, although he did suggest a difference of extent concerning the allegorical interpretation of the Bible.[29] Talmage sees the Zohar as epitomizing this attitude in its claim:

> Rabbi Simeon said: Alas for the man who regards the Torah as a book of mere tales and profane matters. If this were so, we might even today write a Torah dealing in such matters and still more excellent. In regard to earthly things, the kings and princes of the world possess more valuable materials. We could use them as a model for composing a Torah of this kind. But, in reality, the words of the Torah are higher and higher mysteries. When even the angels come down into the world [to fulfill a mission], they don the garments of this world, and if they did not, they could not survive in this world and the world could not endure them. And if this is true even of the angels, how much more true is it of the Torah, with which he created them and all the worlds and through which they all subsist. When she descends into the world, how could the world endure it if she did not don earthly garments? If anyone should suppose that the Torah herself is this garment and nothing else, let him give up the ghost. Such a man will have no share in the world to come. That is why David (Ps. 119:18) said: "Open thou mine eyes, that I may behold wondrous things out of thy Torah," namely, that which is beneath the garment of the Torah. Come and behold: there are garments that everyone sees, and when fools see a man in a garment that seems beautiful to them, they do not look more closely. But more important than the garment is the body, and more important than the body is the soul. So likewise the Torah has a body, which consists of the commandments and ordinances of the Torah, which are called *gufei torah*, "bodies of the Torah." This body is cloaked in garments, which consist of worldly stories. Fools see only the garment, which is the narrative part of the Torah; they know no more and fail to see what is under the garment.

Those who know more see not only the garment but also the body that is under the garment. But the truly wise, the servants of the Supreme King, those who stood at the foot of Mount Sinai, look only upon the soul, which is the true foundation of the entire Torah, and one day indeed it will be given them to behold the innermost soul of the Torah.[30]

Talmage adduces much more evidence from a variety of periods. He observes that the beginning of Genesis was considered esoteric, and thus non-literal, by the sages in Babylonian Talmud tractate Ḥagigah 11b.[31] He notes, for example, that Isaac Arama understood Abraham's saddling his ass in Genesis 22:3 as a symbol for subduing the material aspects of life,[32] as well as referring to Bahya ben Asher's[33] more general pronouncement that "the superiority of the esoteric over the exoteric is as the superiority of gold over silver."[34] Talmage concludes the essay with an afterword where he observes that from the study of medieval interpretation we might glean the very principle of freedom of interpretation itself, that the scriptures, biblical or postbiblical, bear more than one meaning, that a modernist approach to a text need not rule out a commitment to belief in tradition. Thus, one retains one's foundation without fundamentalism, one's faith in the Creator without creationism.[35]

The position that biblical texts that depict the past should not be read as depicting the actual past is especially pronounced in the interpretive traditions surrounding the book of Job. As is well-known, among the various opinions cited concerning Job in the long Talmudic discussion in Babylonian Talmud tractate *Bava Batra* 15a-b is the opinion that Job never existed, but was written as a parable.[36] This position was sometimes reasserted in medieval Jewish interpretation—for example, in the work of the late thirteenth-century scholar Zerahiah of Barcelona.[37] Maimonides understood Job as a parable, and suggested that readers of the book should "meditate and reflect on this parable, grasp its meaning, and see what the true opinion is [concerning divine retribution]."[38]

The case of reading Job as a parable is especially important. Job does not open with the words "do not read me literally." Its initial chapter seems to describe real people, real sheep, and even three real friends who travel from real countries, and, who upon seeing Job, perform real mourning rituals. The book begins: "There was a man (*ish haya*) in the land of Uz named Job. That man was blameless and upright; he feared God and shunned evil. Seven sons and three daughters were born to him; his possessions were seven thousand sheep, three thousand camels, five hundred yoke of oxen and five hundred she-asses, and a very large household. That man was wealthier than anyone in the East" (Job 1:1–3).

As Avi Hurvitz has shown, the construction *ish haya* is the Late Biblical Hebrew equivalent of *vayehi ish eḥad*.[39] In that sense, the book's opening is nearly identical to that of the book of Samuel: "There was a man (*vayehi ish eḥad*) from Ramathaim of the Zuphites, in the hill country of Ephraim, whose name was Elkanah son of Jeroham son of Elihu son of Tohu son of Zuph, an Ephramite. He had two wives, one named Hannah and the other Peninah; Peninah had children, but Hannah was childless" (1 Sam. 1:1–2).

To my mind, this raises an obvious question: Should we read Samuel as a parable, and not as a literal, factual narration of the beginning of the monarchy in ancient Israel? And what of other stories that seem to begin with the factual words *vayehi ish eḥad*, such as the Samson narrative in Judges 13? And what of similar stories about the past that happen not be begin with those same words? I would answer yes to all of these questions. Given what we know about how and why stories set in the past were written and used in ancient Israel, there should be no bias toward reading these stories as accounts of real historical events. To borrow the image of Joseph Kimhi, that type of reading would involve silver and chaff rather than gold and wheat.

The position that sections of the Bible should not be read literally has found much resonance in Jewish discussions of the beginning of Genesis in the recent century and a half. This resonance is related to the Jewish acceptance of many (though not all) aspects of Darwin's theory of evolution, which certainly contradicts a literal reading of the beginning of Genesis; the Bible nowhere suggests that life on earth evolved from a common, original life-form. To return to my earlier discussion concerning biblical language and myth, this reading involves understanding these biblical texts nonliterally, and suggests that science and religion speak different languages.[40] Abraham Isaac Kook, the first Ashkenazi chief rabbi of Mandatory Palestine (1865–1935), was especially well-known for his attraction to aspects of evolution, which he believed conformed to certain kabbalistic notions. In a letter to his friend, the traditional biblical scholar Moshe Seidel, he noted: "The Torah obviously obscures the account of creations and speaks in allusions and parables."[41] Yeshayahu Leibowitz, a scientist by training, also believed that the Bible cannot be taken literally, and claimed that "religion is not about facts; it is a decision to worship God."[42]

Perhaps the best articulation of this position was in a letter written by the young S. R. Hirsch, considered the founder of Neo-Orthodoxy (1808–1888): "As Jews we will read this book, as a book tendered to us by God in order that we learn from it about ourselves, what we are and what we should be during our earthy existence. We will read it as Torah—literally, 'instruction'—directing and guiding us within God's world and among humanity, making our inner self come alive."[43] He also noted that "Jewish scholarship has never regarded the Bible as a textbook of physical or even abstract doctrines," and he was thus open to many facets of the theory of evolution.[44]

Throughout history, many Jewish rabbis and scholars accepted scientific theories produced by any scientist, regardless of his or her religious commitment. In medieval times, Judaism appropriated Greek and Arab science[45]; later Rabbi Moshe Isserles (Rama) even wrote a commentary on Georg Peurbach's 1456 *New Theory of the Planets*.[46] The medieval Jewish reception of (Christian) scientific theories in the early modern period was varied, but overall open and positive.[47]

The nineteenth-century rabbinic attitude to modern science included positive responses.[48] Certainly there are significant pockets of resistance, including Chabad and others who insist on the literal interpretation of the beginning of Genesis in conjunction with the claim that science can only develop theories, as opposed to the ultimate truths of the Torah (taken literally).[49] More recently, Natan Slifkin's positions concerning the commensurability of evolution and the creation stories of Genesis received some support in the Orthodox community, until it was roundly condemned in the Haredi community.[50] The contemporary American Jewish philosopher Norbert Samuelson has also argued for commensurability by interpreting biblical texts nonliterally as "Holy Narrative," a term that he uses in a manner similar to my use of "myth."[51] I commend his honesty in noting that "in my judgment this problem of the reliability of the historical sections of the Hebrew scriptures is the single most important challenge raised by modern science to the believability of any form of rabbinic or neo-rabbinic Judaism."[52]

The position of Leibowitz and others that science and religion speak different languages should be more generally aligned with a Kantian argument that was more fully developed by the great (Jewish) Harvard University evolutionary biologist Stephen Jay Gould (1941–2002). Gould spoke of science and religion as "non-overlapping magisterial"; this phrase was so important for him that he even abbreviated it as "NOMA."[53] The American analytic philosopher Alvin Plantinga has defended a similar position in *Where the Conflict Really Lies: Science, Religion, and Naturalism*,[54] arguing that "there is superficial conflict but deep concord between science and theistic religion."[55] As a neo-Kantian, it is not surprising that Joseph B. Solovetchik was also sympathetic to this position.[56] Of course, much of this discussion depends on the precise definitions of science and religion, and it is not the case that all of the insights offered by Christian scholars concerning this issue as it relates to Christianity are appropriate to Judaism. Nevertheless, the broad distinction between scientific and religious (in this case biblical, and, in my belief, biblical mythical) language is very helpful.

There is some similarity between the position I am advocating and the use of the rabbinic phrase *dibrah torah bi/kilshon benei adam* (the Torah speaks in human language), already found in tannaitic literature.[57] The phrase was used often in medieval Jewish (Rabbanite and Karaite) literature in relation to the philosophical concept of divine accommodation, and some Modern Orthodox scholars have used it as well, even extending its purview.[58] As many scholars have shown, the meaning of that phrase has not been stable and unified throughout its history; nevertheless for those who find precedents persuasive, its use throughout postbiblical interpretation may be important. It is not, however, fully identical with the position I am suggesting. To my mind, many biblical texts should be understood as metaphors, allegories, or myths, not because of divine accommodation, but rather, as I argued above, the nonliteral understanding of such texts stems from how the ancient genre of history should be understood. To repeat my earlier contention: there was little, if any, interest in the past for its own sake in antiquity, and we are mis-genrifying the Bible and reading it anachronistically if we read biblical texts as history in our modern sense.

This exploration, which has highlighted the importance of genre for understanding the issues at hand, has not answered some of the most fundamental questions that it raises: Are we to treat all narratives about the past in the Hebrew Bible in the same way? Should we make the same presuppositions about, for instance, Genesis, Exodus, Judges, Kings, Ruth, Ezra-Nehemiah, and Chronicles? More significantly, how do we know that we have interpreted a biblical text according to its correct, original genre? I simply do not believe that this question can be answered in a clear, univocal way. A glance at almost any biblical passage suggests that it has been understood in multiple ways, and been included in multiple genres. If precedent is definitive, then we are left to our own devices in understanding the genres of these texts. And I would argue further that the Jewish biblical tradition is not entirely precedent based; it is in that sense, as I stated above, that *ḥadash* is not *asur min ha-Torah*; the innovative is not prohibited. Thus, if modern scholarship suggests new understandings or genres that were not known by the classical and medieval rabbis, these need to be considered as well.

Another question that I cannot answer is whether particular biblical stories should be seen only as didactic, or whether they should *also* be understood as using true events for didactic purposes. For example, in his gloss on the Tower of Babel story in Genesis 11:5, Rashi, basing his commentary on the *Tanchuma* (Noah 18 and parallels), says that biblical text states concerning "God came down to look at the city and tower" under construction: "He really did not need to do this [since He is omniscient], but Scripture intends to teach the judges that they should not proclaim a defendant guilty before they have seen the case and thoroughly understood the matter in question." Rashi's glosses here and elsewhere suggest that he read the text as primarily didactic—it uses stories to teach, and is not interested in the real past for its own sake. This point is equally obvious from Rashi's initial comments on Genesis 1:1, where he does not discuss natural science, but how the text teaches that the entire world belongs to God, who may apportion it to whomever He pleases, and how the world was created for the sake of Israel or for the sake of the Torah. A fundamental question that I do not know how to answer, at least from Rashi's perspective, is whether he is saying that these stories are stories, and not literal retellings of the past, and that they are told for their didactic value (a strong claim), or if he is suggesting that these stories present real events that are told in a particular way to foster particular lessons (a much weaker claim). In either case, the story is not to be studied for its antiquarian value, for appreciating the past *"wie es eigentlich gewesen."*

Many will think that *the most* fundamental question is whether or not there are any traditions or texts that are found in the Torah that must be taken as historically true. Belief in a historical Abraham, in Moses, in the Exodus, and in the revelation at Mount Sinai come to mind as obvious candidates. I will leave it to others to decide which, if any of these, must be part of a dogmatic credo, a literal *ani ma'amin* (I believe). I would conclude by noting that in many of the retellings of "history" in the Bible, one or more of these "events" is omitted; consider, for example, the absence of Sinai in Deuteronomy 26:5–9 and in the historical psalms such as Psalm 136. Furthermore, the place of *ani ma'amins*—of dogma—in Judaism remains hotly contested. A historical survey shows that Maimonides was highly innovative here as elsewhere, and many of his *ikkarim* are contradicted by the classical rabbis who preceded him and the medieval and modern authorities who followed.[59]

Professor Menachem Kellner has made a compelling argument that Judaism insists that Jews believe *in* certain things, rather than believing *that* certain creeds are true.[60] If he is correct—and I believe he is—then the fact that much (though not all!) of premodern Jewish interpretation took the Bible as science and as history is not terribly important. We should be free to understand the Bible using modern tools, and to decide based on our understanding of the Bible and the ancient Near East if the text indeed was meant as a straightforward historical document, conveying the "real" past. And based on both internal and external evidence, I believe that the answer is no. Though others may disagree with him and me, I hope they will consider Kellner's observation: "Two individuals can both be good Jews, fastidiously obeying the commandments, while disagreeing over fundamental matters of theology."[61]

I raised the question above whether certain Jewish attitudes reflect an adoption of Christian attitudes that may not be totally at home in Judaism. For that reason, I would like to conclude this essay on Jewish attitudes to the Bible as history with a quote from Mark Noll, an Evangelical Christian, and prominent professor of American Christianity: "The Christian stake in history is immense. Every aspect of lived Christianity—worship, sacraments, daily godliness, private devotion, religiously inspired benevolence, preaching—every major theme of Christian theology—the nature of God in relation of the world, the meaning of Christ, the character of salvation, the fate of the universe—directly or indirectly involves questions about how the present relates to the past."[62]

How might or should one translate this quotation into Judaism? Is the Jewish stake in history "immense"? Does the entirety of Judaism concern "how the present relates to the past"? Is the Bible's literal historical veracity a crucial issue within Judaism? As my previous remarks suggest, I think that Judaism and Christianity have parted on many of these issues, and as Jews, including observant Jews, we would do well to genrify the Bible properly, and not to read it as literal history. Reading biblical texts nonliterally has ample precedents within tradition, and, to my mind, properly contextualizes the Bible within its ancient world. More importantly for me, it allows the entire Bible to become Torah, instruction, rather than an arcane recounting of past events.

Endnotes

1. I discuss the issues that are dealt with below, and many others concerning Jewish belief and the Bible, in my contributions to Marc Zvi Brettler, Peter Enns, and Daniel Harrington, *The Bible and the Believer: How to Read the Bible Critically and Religiously* (New York: Oxford University Press, 2012). My insistence on the importance of genre continues to be informed by John Barton, *Reading the Old Testament: Method in Biblical Study*, rev. ed. (Louisville, KY: Westminster John Knox, 1996.), esp. 16–18.
2. I expand on this point in my *How to Read the Bible* (Philadelphia: Jewish Publication Society, 2005).

3. "Chicago Statement on Biblical Hermeneutics, with Commentary by Norman L. Geisler," *Bible Research*, accessed November 8, 2016, http://www.bible-researcher.com/chicago2.html.
4. On the debate over the truth, see Lee I. Levin and Amihai Mazar, eds., *Ha-Pulmus al ha-Emet ha-Historit ba-Mikra* [The debate over historical truth in the Bible] (Jerusalem: Yad Ben Zvi-Dinur Center, 2002).
5. See, e.g., the recent comment by Jonathan Grossman, "Al ha-Pashtut ha-Mithadshim be-Kol Dor ve-al Ahavat ha-Torah" [On the simplicity renewed in every generation and on the love for the Torah], in *Hi Siḥati: Al Derekh Limmud ha-Tanakh* ["It is my study"], ed. Yehoshua Rice (Alon Shevut-Jerusalem: Yeshivat Har Etzion and Sifrei Maggid, 2013), 215:

> The renewal of Bible study is also connected with the faith in Providence and reality's advance towards its revelation. It is illogical that God's word, which shone for the People of Israel, was exhaustively interpreted in a particular year, and that no room remains for new interpretations. Literary studies continue to develop and become more sophisticated, and we are more and more exposed to literary tools that can reveal the message of a story to its readers. God's Torah is eternal, and even if two measures of it were revealed in earlier generations, a new measure is revealed in every generation. We have an obligation, as dwarves standing on the shoulders of giants, to add our generation's discoveries for the sake of a complete understanding of God's word. If there is awareness today of the general structure of a certain kind of story, of the development of the plot, of literary analogies, etc., we must make use of it in order to understand the Bible—in order to understand the will of God. This is devotion in God's name, a willingness to consider the smallest details, the chiastic structures, the allusions, the key words, and the parallel passages, solely in order to understand the Torah better. The truth must be stated, and this is the sweetest devotion: the greatness of the Torah unfolds again and again for the student, and the encounter with God's word and with His manners of expression enlightens the soul and brings joy.

6. Marc Zvi Brettler, *The Creation of History in Ancient Israel* (London: Routledge, 1995).
7. See my review of Baruch Halpern, *The First Historians*, in *Journal of Religion* 70 (1990), 83–84.
8. This definition is attributed to Leopold von Ranke (1795–1886).
9. Trans. Paula Wissing (Chicago: University of Chicago Press, 1988).
10. See, e.g., the provocative title of the article by David Pipes, "Herodotus: Father of History, Father of Lies," *Loyola University New Orleans: The Student Historical Journal* 30 (1998).
11. Jean-Jacques Glassner, *Mesopotamian Chronicles* (Atlanta, GA: Society of Biblical Literature, 2004), 26.
12. Glassner, *Mesopotamian Chronicles*, 39.
13. John Van Seters, *In Search of History: Historiography in the Ancient World and the Origins of Biblical History* (New Haven: Yale University Press, 1983), 88.
14. Mario Liverani, "The Deeds of Ancient Mesopotamian Kings," in *Civilizations of the Ancient Near East*, ed. Jack M. Sasson (New York: Scribners, 1995), 4:2354.

15. Hayim Tadmor, "Propaganda, Literature, Historiography: Cracking the Code of the Assyrian Royal Inscriptions," in *Assyria 1995*, ed. S. Parpola and R. M. Whiting (Helsinki: The Neo-Assyrian Text Corpus Project, 1997), 333.
16. A. K. Grayson, *Assyrian and Babylonian Chronicles* (Locust Valley, NY: Augustin, 1975), 43–45; 145–151.
17. John Van Seters, "The Historiography of the Ancient Near East," in *Civilizations of the Ancient Near East*, 4:2433–2444.
18. Isaiah Gafni, "rabbinic Historiography and Representations of the Past," in *The Cambridge Companion to the Talmud and rabbinic Literature*, ed. Charlotte Elisheva Fonrobert and Martin S. Jaffee (Cambridge: Cambridge University Press, 2007), 295.
19. Gafni, "rabbinic Historiography," 298–300.
20. See my discussion of Burkert's *Structure and History in Greek Mythology and Ritual* (Berkeley: University of California Press, 1982) in *The Creation of History in Ancient Israel*, 173.
21. Brettler, *The Creation of History*, 22n44.
22. This is the definition of the term "history" that I discussed in my *The Creation of History*, 12.
23. Cited in Robert Brody, *Saadya Gaon*, trans. Betsy Rosenberg (Oxford: Littman Library of Jewish Civilization, 2013), 67; See also Saadya Ga'on, *Pirushei Rav Saadya Ga'on le-Bereshit* [Saadya's commentary on Genesis], trans. and ed. Moshe Zucker (New York: Jewish Theological Seminary of America, 1984), 191–192.
24. See Joshua L. Golding, "On the Limits of Non-Literal Interpretation of Scripture from an Orthodox Perspective," *Torah U-Madda Journal* 10 (2001): 3–59.
25. Book 1, "Introduction to the First Part," 6b.
26. Mordechai Z. Cohen, *Three Approaches to Biblical Metaphor: From Abraham ibn Ezra and Maimonides to David Kimhi* (Leiden: Brill, 2003), 4.
27. Frank Talmage, "Apples of Gold: The Inner Meaning of Sacred Texts in Medieval Judaism," in *Jewish Spirituality: From the Bible through the Middle Ages*, ed. Arthur Green (New York: Crossroad, 1987), 313–355. I would like to thank Professor Alan Cooper for referring me to this important essay.
28. Talmage, "Apples of Gold," 313.
29. Ibid., 314. For more on Jewish-Christian debates concerning allegorical interpretation of Scripture, see Günter Stemberger, "Elements of Biblical Interpretation in Medieval Jewish-Christian Disputation," in *Hebrew Bible/Old Testament*, ed. Magne Saebo (Gottingen: Vandehoeck & Ruprecht, 2000), 578–590.
30. Talmage, "Apples of Gold," 324–325.
31. Ibid., 325.
32. Ibid., 330.
33. A student of Nachmanides and author of a Bible commentary.
34. Ibid., 343.
35. Ibid., 344.
36. See the detailed discussion of rabbinic views in Hananel Mack, *Ela Mashal Haya: Iyov va-Sefer Iyov ba-Sifrut ha-Mikrait* [Job and the book of Job in rabbinic literature] (Ramat Gan: Bar Ilan University Press, 2004).
37. Moshe Greenberg, "Did Job Really Exist? An Issue of Medieval Exegesis," *In Shaarei Talmon: Studies in the Bible, Qumran, and the ancient Near East Presented to Shemaryahu Talmon*, ed. Michael Fishbane, Emanuel Tov, and Weston W. Fields (Winona Lake, IN: Eisenbrauns, 1992), 6–9.
38. *The Guide of the Perplexed* 3:22.

39. See Avi Hurvitz, "The Date of the Prose-Story of Job Linguistically Reconsidered," *Harvard Theological Review* 67 (1974): 17–34.
40. See the studies by Michael Shai Cherry, in particular "Three Twentieth-Century Jewish Responses to Evolutionary Theory," *Aleph* 3 (2003): 247–290.
41. Abraham Yitzhak Hacohen Kook, *Igrot ha-Ra'aya* (Jerusalem: Mosad Harav Kook, 1962), 1:105.
42. Cited in Shai Cherry, "Three Responses," 286.
43. Cited in Lawrence Kaplan, "*Tora U'Mada* in the Thought of Rabbi Samson Raphael Hirsch," *Bekhol Derakhekha Daehu: Journal of Torah and Scholarship* 5 (1997): 10.
44. Kaplan, "Tora U'Mada," 11, 22–25.
45. Noah J. Efron, *Judaism and Science; A Historical Introduction* (Westport, CT: Greenwood, 2007), 79–98. On evolution in particular, see Geoffrey Cantor and Marc Swetlitz, eds., *Jewish Tradition and the Challenge of Darwinism* (Chicago: University of Chicago Press, 1996).
46. David B. Ruderman, *Jewish Thought and Scientific Discovery in Early Modern Europe* (Detroit: Wayne State University Press, 2001), 68–76.
47. Efron, "Judaism and Science," 116; Ruderman, "Jewish Thought," 68–76.
48. Shnayer Z. Leiman, *rabbinic Responses to Modernity* (Kew Garden Hills, NY: S. Z. Leiman, 2007).
49. See, for e.g., the Lubavitcher Rebbe's 1962 letter: "I can tell you without fear of contradiction that it [the theory of evolution] has not a shred of evidence to support it." Quoted in Avraham M. Hasofer, "A Statistician Looks at Neo-Darwinism," in *Science in the Light of Torah: A B'or ha'Torah Reader*, Herman Branover and Ilana Coven Attia, eds. (Northvale, NJ: Jason Aronson, 1994), 185. This position is expressed in some of the essays collected in Aryeh Carmell and Cyril Domb, eds., *Challenge: Torah Views on Science and Its Problems* (Jerusalem: Feldheim, 1976).
50. Natan Slif kin, *The Challenge of Creation: Judaism's Encounter with Science, Cosmology, and Evolution* (Bet Shemesh: Zoo Torah/Gefen Books, 2012); Cantor and Swetlitz, *Jewish Tradition and the Challenge of Darwinism*, 16–17.
51. Norbert M. Samuelson, *Jewish Faith and Modern Science: On the Death and Rebirth of Jewish Philosophy* (Lanham: Rowman & Littlefield, 2009), 224.
52. Samuelson, *Jewish Faith*, 97.
53. Stephen Jay Gould, *Rock of Ages: Science and Religion in the Fullness of Life* (New York: Ballentine, 1999), 5.
54. Alvin Plantinga, *Where the Conflict Really Lies: Science, Religion, and Naturalism* (Oxford University Press, 2011).
55. Plantinga, *Where the Conflict*, ix. On this issue in non-Jewish circles, see, e.g., Harold W. Attridge, ed., *The Religion and Science Debate: Why Does it Continue?* (New Haven: Yale University Press, 2009); Thomas Dixon et al., eds., *Science and Religion: New Historical Perspectives* (Cambridge: Cambridge University Press, 2010); Ian G. Barbour, *When Science Meets Religion: Enemies, Strangers, or Partners?* (New York: HarperOne, 2000); Thomas Dixon, *Science and Religion: A Very Short Introduction* (Oxford: Oxford University Press, 2008); James W. Haag et al, eds., *The Routledge Companion to Religion and Science* (London: Routledge, 2012); John Hedley Brooke, *Science and Religion: Some Historical Perspectives* (Cambridge: Cambridge University Press, 1991).
56. Carl Feit, "Modern Orthodoxy and Evolution: The Models of Rabbi J. B. Solovetchik and Rabbi A. I Kook," in Cantor and Swetlitz, *Jewish Tradition and the Challenge of Darwinism*, 212.

57. For a history of this term, see, e.g., Haggai Ben Shammai, "'Dibbrah Torah ke-Lashon Benei Adam': Ad Kamah Lashon Benei Adam? Iyun Mashveh ba-Gishoteihem shel Rasag va-Karaim Benei Zemano" ["The Torah speaks in the language of human beings": How much "a language of human beings"? Comparative observations on the approaches of Saadya Ga'on and his contemporary critics], in *Le-Yashev Peshuto shel Mikra* [To settle the plain meaning of the verse: Studies in biblical exegesis] Sara Japhet and Eran Viezel, eds. (Jerusalem: Mosad Bialik, 2011), 59–69.
58. See, e.g., Joel B. Wolowelsky, "A Note on the Flood Story in the Language of Man," *Tradition: A Journal of Orthodox Jewish Thought* 42, no. 3 (Fall 2009): 41–48.
59. See Brettler, Enns, and Harrington, *The Bible and the Believer*, 32–34.
60. Menachem Kellner, *Must a Jew Believe in Anything?* (London: Littman Library, 2006), 9.
61. Kellner, *Must a Jew Believe*, 43.
62. Mark A. Noll, "History," in *Dictionary for the Theological Interpretation of the Bible*, ed. Kevin J. Vanhoozer (Grand Rapids, MI: Baker Academic, 2005), 295.

Kabbalah as a Shield against the "Scourge" of Biblical Criticism: A Comparative Analysis of the Torah Commentaries of Elia Benamozegh and Mordecai Breuer

Adiel Cohen

The belief that the Torah was given by divine revelation, as defined by Maimonides in his eighth principle of faith and accepted collectively by the Jewish people,[1] conflicts with the opinions of modern biblical scholarship.[2] As a result, biblical commentators adhering to both the *peshat* (literal or contextual) method and the belief in the divine revelation of the Torah, are unable to utilize the exegetical insights associated with the documentary hypothesis developed by Wellhausen and his school, a respected and accepted academic discipline.[3] As Moshe Greenberg has written, "orthodoxy saw biblical criticism in general as irreconcilable with the principles of Jewish faith."[4] Therefore, in the words of D. S. Sperling, "in general, Orthodox Jews in America, Israel, and elsewhere have remained on the periphery of biblical scholarship."[5] However, the documentary hypothesis is not the only obstacle to the religious *peshat* commentator. Theological complications also arise from the use of archeological discoveries from the ancient Near East, which are analogous to the Torah and can be a very rich source for its interpretation.[6] The comparison of biblical verses with ancient extra-biblical texts can raise doubts regarding the divine origin of the Torah and weaken faith in its unique sanctity.

The Orthodox *peshat* commentator who aspires to explain the plain contextual meaning of the Torah and produce a commentary open to the various branches of biblical scholarship must clarify and demonstrate how this use of modern scholarship is compatible with his or her belief in the divine origin of the Torah. To a certain extent, the commentator is required to "convert" the findings of scientific research to enable them to enter the "congregation" of traditional exegesis.

In this article, I will attempt to trace the path of two commentators who rose to this challenge: Rabbi Elia Benamozegh and Rabbi Mordechai Breuer. Both men were traditional Torah scholars who wrote commentaries on the Torah that opened doors to the world of modern biblical scholarship. Rabbi Benamozegh attempted to explain the text of the Torah in the context of various parallels from the cultures of the peoples of the ancient Near East, especially Egypt. Rabbi Breuer based his commentary on the documentary hypothesis of Wellhausen and his school. Both these scholars, each in his own way, assimilated the insights of modern scholarship into a traditional, almost mystical, commentary. Their commentaries received criticism from both academic and religious circles, and generated extensive debate.

The recourse to Kabbalah in confronting modern biblical scholarship is not self-explanatory, and could even be called surprising; the mystical-homiletical reading of the Torah and its critical-literal reading do not occupy the same plane of reference. We must, therefore, ascertain how Benamozegh and Breuer used Kabbalah in the framework of what purport to be *peshat* commentaries. What was the hermeneutic-theological mechanism that enabled them, on the one hand, to maintain connections with modern biblical scholarship and, on the other, to continue to adhere to the belief in the divine revelation of the Torah in its traditional sense? In my opinion, this analysis transcends the mere clarification of an historical point and will enrich the current, revived discussion of the question of the feasibility of "religious biblical scholarship." We will first discuss each commentator separately, and conclude by comparing and contrasting the two.

Rabbi Elia Benamozegh: His Life and Sources of Influence

Rabbi Elia Benamozegh was born in Livorno (Leghorn), Italy in 1823 to a Jewish family that had emigrated from Fez, Morocco.[7] He lived and worked in the city his entire life, until his death in 1900. In his search for harmony between academic study and the Jewish tradition, Rabbi Benamozegh saw himself as continuing the path of Maimonides, and even took upon himself the task of "removing the rust of centuries" during which there had been a separation between unfettered research and Torah study. Abraham Berliner described him as a genius "born under the wrong star," and he has also been called "the Plato of Italian Jewry."[8]

Rabbi Benamozegh left behind a diverse and varied literary *oeuvre*, including polemical writings that attempted to prove both the antiquity of the Kabbalah and the superiority and antiquity of Jewish over Christian ethics,[9] as well as a book analyzing the relationship between Israel and the nations of the world, a subject that lay at the heart of his intellectual activity.[10] He also wrote a general introduction to the books of the Oral Law,[11] and a halachic treatise about the custom of cremating the dead.[12] I would like to focus here on his commentary to the Torah, *Em la-Mikra*.

The Commentary Em la-Mikra and Its Connection to Kabbalah

The commentary *Em la-Mikra* on the Five Books of Moses was published in Leghorn at a press owned by Rabbi Benamozegh between the years 1862 and 1863. On the title page of the book the author explains its contents: "It includes comments, studies, and new elucidations on the basis of philology, critique, archeology, the history of Babylonia, Syria, Egypt, etc., and the beliefs and customs of ancient peoples; a definitive assessment of some opinions and theories of contemporary scholars and critics; as well as a thorough examination of some midrashim of the sages and their Talmudic and metaphysical traditions according to the spirit of the text."

How did Rabbi Benamozegh justify the integration of "the history of Babylon, Syria, and Egypt" and "the beliefs and customs of ancient peoples" within the framework of his unqualified belief in the divine origin of the Torah? In order to answer this question, I will demonstrate that despite this opening precis, one must not make the mistake of categorizing this book as a mere linguistic, contextual commentary. First of all, the commentary includes innumerable references to the Zohar and mystical lore not appropriate for a "normal," scholarly *peshat* commentary,[13] though these references are not always explicitly stated.[14] However, this does not exhaust the connection between the commentary and the Kabbalah. Rabbi Benamozegh understood the Kabbalah as the essential, ancient, esoteric kernel of the Jewish religion, without which it is impossible to understand the Written Torah.[15]

Aimé Pallière, Rabbi Benamozegh's devoted disciple, testified to the centrality of the Kabbalah in his thought:[16]

> It is essential, therefore, to point out at once that the Kabbalah—which Benamozegh always considered to be "the most legitimate theology in Judaism"—is in no sense a mere mass of superstitions. . . . In his opinion, Kabbalism was not even a separate, discrete branch of knowledge. Instead he readily said of it what Renan[17] said of philosophy in general: "That it is the distillation of all departments of knowledge—the sound, the light, the vibration of that divine essence within each of them." . . . Not only do Jewish doctrines thus gain an amplitude and force which anti-kabbalistic exegesis is powerless to give them, but certain religious practices as well.[18]

According to Rabbi Benaozegh, Kabbalah is ancient Jewish wisdom that was passed down from generation to generation along with the Oral Law, though there is no known written record of it until its much later appearance in the Zohar. For him the Written Law is merely an external shell into which Kabbalah breathes life and spirit:

> In all that is related to religion, in other words, internal beliefs and opinions, the Written Torah has nothing to say because it is merely a book about the external aspects of the national religion and generalities. Only the Oral Law, or Kabbalah, is internal, and the treasury of beliefs and the religion of the individual Jew, in that he is a man and spiritual being. Therefore, with regard to the degrees of spirituality and the station of a man in the levels of wisdom and holiness, [the Written Law] will not address it at great length, and sometimes will be completely silent on the subject.[19]

These viewpoints are what allowed Benamozegh to include "archeology and the history of Babylonia, Syria, and Egypt, etc., and the beliefs and customs of ancient peoples" within the context of his commentary to the Torah without any theological difficulty. The Oral Law and the Kabbalah are the primary sources of human culture in all of its varied forms of expression, and the Written Law is the partial revelation of this ancient tradition. This implies that the many parallels to the Written Torah known to us from discoveries in the Near East do not challenge the Written Torah's validity and sanctity. On the contrary, they confirm its ancillary status. According to Rabbi Benamozegh, the use of the various mythologies and literatures of ancient religions is justified because they include much of the ancient *hebraica veritas* within their legends and pagan rituals. Comparative philological analysis of that time revealed insights similar to the wisdom of the ancient Kabbalah: "The cutting edge of the latest secular research is connected to and linked with the outer limit of the very earliest metaphysical wisdom."[20]

I would now like to demonstrate Rabbi Benamozegh's methodology by way of an example taken from his commentary to Numbers 3:45.[21] I will begin with some brief background information that is necessary for understanding the commentary. The Torah teaches that Moses was commanded to take the Levites in place of the firstborn children of the other tribes, as well as "the cattle of the Levites in place of their cattle" (Num. 3:45). Rabbi Benamozegh deliberates over the meaning of this exchange of cattle.[22] Rashi explains that "the cattle of the Levites did not redeem the firstborn, clean animals of the other tribes, but rather the firstborn donkeys." Rabbi Benamozegh notes that it can be inferred from this commentary that the Torah spoke of "cattle" in the generic sense, even though the specific intention was donkeys. Likewise, in the laws of redemption given in Exodus 13:13, the Torah uses the word "ass," while in Numbers 18:15 it refers only to an "unclean animal." Rabbi Benamozegh tries to explain why the phrase "unclean animal" is used in the Torah to refer specifically to donkeys (For the sake of clarity I have divided the following passage into sections):

> [A] I would now like to add that it is very possible that Moses and the People of Israel referred to the donkey as, simply, the "unclean animal." Here the Kabbalah agrees with recent research on ancient Egypt, for we know that in their culture the donkey is the animal sacred to Typhon,[23] the god of evil, and is the generic "unclean animal."[24] It is the antithesis of the bull, sacred to Osiris, the good god who fights against Typhon.[25] The kabbalists say the exact same thing: the bull alludes to the principle from which Osiris sprung, just as man is hewn from the monkey,[26] and the donkey is from the impure side, as is known. The Torah expressed itself with language that is agreeable to both Kabbalah and the culture of ancient Egypt.
>
> [B] And this is to signify that the soul of the Torah is the wisdom of the Kabbalah, which is compatible with the beliefs current in that time and place. This alone will silence the critique that claims that the laws of the Torah were copied by us from the laws and customs of Egypt. In truth, they are similar in many ways, and not, as some thought, easily differentiated.

However, Moses did not learn from them, as the heretics believe. It is simply that the divine wisdom within him, known to the ancestors of the Patriarchs, agrees in some respects with what remained known and accepted among the important priests of Egypt, as well as the priests of India, Persia, and Greece, who had the same laws and beliefs as the Egyptians.

[C] The kabbalists demonstrated their brilliance when they said that, of all the nations, Egypt is closest to holiness. They called it the "second chariot," second in rank after the Land of Israel, the kingdom that is the first chariot. If they had been familiar with the culture of ancient Egypt as we know it now, we would have suspected that they said this because of their knowledge of the similarity between Egypt and Israel. The truth is that they knew nothing about it. Nonetheless, they came to a conclusion that proved correct with startling accuracy. Moreover, they prepared in advance a means of silencing those who deny the divinity of our Torah. Is the fact that this wisdom was hewn from the gut of Israel and the bedrock of the forefathers not an open rebuke to them?

[D] Perhaps this is the reason why the bull and the donkey are always mentioned together in the laws of work on the Sabbath, in the prohibition on plowing with an ox and an ass together, and in other places.

The catalyst for this commentary, as we have seen, was a stylistic-linguistic clarification of the biblical text: Why does the phrase "unclean animal" refer specifically to the donkey, and not to the many other unclean animals? In order to answer this question, Rabbi Benamozegh turns both to Egyptian mythology and to Kabbalah, and points out (in the first section, with characteristic brevity) that in both these corpora the donkey is described as the embodiment of evil and anarchy, and the bull as the force of creation and holiness. The terminology adopted by the Torah corresponds with this concept.

The parallels between the Torah and Egyptian mythology are liable to raise the argument that this is a case of unilateral influence: ancient Egyptian literature influenced the wording of the Torah. It is self-evident that this kind of argument undermines the belief in the divine origin of the Torah. However, according to Rabbi Benamozegh (in section B), the fact that we also find the concept of the inferiority of the donkey and the superiority of the bull in kabbalistic literature uproots this heretical, exegetical possibility. In his opinion, one cannot separate the Kabbalah from the Written Torah because the Kabbalah is the "soul" of the Written Torah. Therefore, "this alone" (i.e., only the Kabbalah) will be able to "silence the critique [biblical criticism] that claims that the laws of the Torah were copied by us from the laws and customs of Egypt." How is this so? The fact that the characteristics of the donkey also appear in kabbalistic literature demonstrates that Moses did not take this idea from the Egyptians. More specifically, the Kabbalah, despite its belated realization in literary form, is the ancient wisdom of the People of Israel passed down to Moses from generation to generation. Thus, an ancient tradition about the uncleanness and singular inferiority of the donkey, which was transmitted orally and reached Moses, is what determined the use of the phrase "unclean animal" in connection with the donkey in the Written Torah. A shred, a crumb, or an echo ("what remained known") of this ancient universal tradition remained in the hands of "the important priests of Egypt"; not only with them, but also among "the priests of India, Persia, and Greece." The seeds of the Kabbalah, the ancient divine wisdom, did not remain with Israel alone; they were dispersed and disseminated far and wide.

The Controversy Surrounding Em la-Mikra: "The Great Derision with which He Ridiculed the Wisdom of the Kabbalah"

Rabbi Samuel David Luzzatto (Shadal, 1800–1865), the well-known contemporary of Rabbi Benamozegh, did not accept the *Zohar* as a legitimate source for the interpretation of the Torah. In general, it is obvious why Rabbi Benamozegh's work did not resonate well in an enlightened intellectual atmosphere that regarded the Kabbalah as a "black stain on the fabric of pure Judaism."[27]

However, *Em la-Mikra* also received harsh criticism from conservative forces within the Jewish world. The rabbis of Aleppo placed a ban on the book and ordered it to be burnt. Led by chief rabbi, Ḥayim Mordecai Leveton, Aleppo's rabbinical leaders, in an 1865 letter to the rabbis of Jerusalem, denounced Rabbi Benamozegh as a heretic and banned his commentary on the grounds that it was based on innovative modern research involving the comparative analysis of Judaism and ancient pagan religions.

Rabbi Benamozegh responded to the ban on his works in the framework of a series of articles in the journal *Ha-Levanon*, under the title "*Zori Gilad—Iggeret Hitnatzlut le-Ḥakhmei Yerushalayim*." Among other matters, he responded at great length to the claim that he "ascribes knowledge of the Kabbalah to non-Jews, heretics, and philosophers. Furthermore, he also attempted to prove the affinity of kabbalistic terminology to terms found in Near Eastern mythologies.

Rabbi Mordechai Breuer: His Life and Sources of Influence

Rabbi Mordechai Breuer was born on 14 May, 1921 in Frankfurt, Germany and died in Jerusalem on 24 February, 2007.[28] Breuer published a new edition of the Hebrew Bible, based on extensive study of the most reliable biblical manuscripts, in particular the Aleppo Codex, that is generally considered the best and most authoritative extant edition. Rabbi Breuer also published books on the cantillation notes and translated from German part of the commentary on the Torah written by his great-grandfather, Rabbi Samson Raphael Hirsch. His first work on biblical exegesis, *Pirkei Moadot* (Essays on the Festivals) was published in 1986, followed by *Pirkei Bereshit* (Essays on Genesis) in 1998. In 1999, Rabbi Breuer was awarded the Israel Prize for his work in the field of rabbinic literature.[29] Two books, *Pirkei Mikraot* (Essays on Biblical Texts) and *Pirkei Yishayahu* (Essays on Isaiah) were published posthumously. These works reflect his exegetical methodology, known as *shitat ha-beḥinot*, the "aspects theory" or "aspects approach."

The Kabbalah in the Framework of the Aspects Theory

Rabbi Breuer explained that the scientific conclusions of biblical criticism "not only do not harm Jewish faith, they are important and necessary to every genuine student of the Bible." However, as a devout believer in the divine origin of the Torah, he acknowledged that "biblical criticism was revealed in a foul and ugly form, conceived and born in impurity, raised and nurtured in iniquity." If so, how can a believing Jew make use of its conclusions, which he himself described as "important and necessary to every genuine student"? In answering this question, Rabbi Breuer invoked the mystical tradition: "The mystical tradition is the spiritual meaning of the conclusions of scientific research, it is the inner content of all the layers that are revealed to the scholar by means of linguistic and stylistic analysis."[30]

Rabbi Breuer's attempts to reconcile contradictory passages in the Torah were based on the premise that there are various reflections of divinity.[31] He took the concept of various divine aspects, facets, or demeanors from kabbalistic theosophy, which delineates a complex and multi-faceted structure of divine emanations (*sefirot*).[32] Rabbi Breuer integrated the mystical tradition into his exegetical methodology because it provided him with the terminology he needed.[33]

Rabbi Breuer illustrated his methodology with the classic example of the two creation stories that open the book of Genesis.[34] Biblical scholarship explains the radical differences between these stories by ascribing them to different sources. Rabbi Breuer however explained that they reflect different aspects of God.

The exegetical strategy of the aspects theory, including its kabbalistic element, is not effective in resolving all of the contradictions that emerge from the biblical text. For example, in his introduction to *Pirkei Moadot*, Rabbi Breuer used the contradictions between the passages in the Torah concerning Hebrew slaves to demonstrate his methodology. However, in this example, Rabbi Breuer did not distinguish between the various passages on the basis of different divine qualities or manners but on the basis of the passages' different aims.

In conclusion, the mystical tradition served Rabbi Breuer only as a theological-conceptual vessel for the various sources identified by the school of biblical criticism. The kabbalistic element is not an inherent part of the aspects theory; when Rabbi Breuer was able to "get by" without it, he turned to an alternate, exoteric, conceptual source.

Rabbi Breuer was doubtless aware of the apparent lack of coherence in his approach, and at the beginning of *Pirkei Bereshit* he explained that the "Elohist" and "Yahwist" names of God used consistently in the many double stories in Genesis serve as strong anchor for his method. However, it is important to determine whether the categorization of these passages according to various divine attributes also helps to explain their content. Does the classification of a particular passage as reflecting the aspect of the Tetragrammaton help us to understand its meaning? The answer to this question is very complex.

In the framework of clarifying the relationship between the creation passages, Rabbi Breuer made an explicit connection between the classification of the stories according to various divine attributes (justice/mercy, nature/revelation) and the contextual meaning of the verses.[35]

For example, he explained Jacob's dream at Bethel (Gen. 28:10–22) in a similar vein: "We find that Jacob saw two visions here, each with a different content, deriving from two different divine attributes. The difference between the content of the two visions is the *direct result* of the fundamental difference between these two attributes."[36] In other cases, however, the difference in content is not the direct result of a fundamental difference between two attributes. For example, in discussing the contradictions within the narrative of the sale of Joseph into slavery, Rabbi Breuer concluded: "It can be seen that the brothers' words in each of the two attributes are not the same : in the attribute of

'YHVH,' the brothers sought only to 'kill him,' while in the attribute of '*Elohim*' they also turned their attention to his corpse: 'throw him into one of the pits.'"[37] Here it is difficult to explain how the difference between the brothers' words is connected to the different divine attributes. Why does the divine attribute of "YHVH" not relate to Joseph's corpse while, the attribute of "*Elohim*" does?

The kabbalistic element, which Rabbi Breuer used to a limited degree in the framework of the aspects theory, was developed further by Yosef Avivi in his 1977 book *Al Signonot ha-Kodesh ba-Torah* (On the Forms of Holiness in the Torah).[38] This work was described as "an attempt to unite the Kabbalah and biblical criticism," and its author saw it as an expansion of Rabbi Breuer's idea of uniting faith and science in biblical exegesis. In my opinion, this book can be characterized as an essentially kabbalistic work, as its aim is not to explain the biblical text, but rather to clarify the Bible's kabbalistic foundations. In effect, the essay refines the exegetical application of the Kabbalah, which was only put to limited use within the aspects theory as formulated by Rabbi Breuer.

We can close this section by concluding, on the basis of Rabbi Breuer's own statements about the principles of his method, that the Kabbalah is an integral part of his approach. However, in practice, an examination of his commentaries reveals that he did not always make use of the Kabbalah, and sometimes even used it in a way that could be described as "mechanical": passages are categorized according to different aspects, yet the aspects do not help close the gaps or resolve the tensions between the texts.

The Controversy Surrounding the Aspects Approach: "We Will Not Hide in the Mist of Esoteric Wisdom and Mysticism"

Despite the limited use of the Kabbalah in the aspects approach, its very inclusion within an exegetical method purporting to be academic and critical has elicited harsh criticism. Jacob Katz argued that Rabbi Breuer applied different standards to the Bible than he did to the Kabbalah.[39] While Rabbi Breuer used research, investigation, and critical analysis in the context of his commentary on the Bible, he treated the Kabbalah as an endemic Jewish tradition that must not be critically analyzed or challenged.

Professor Yosef Heinemann has likewise argued that, despite the distress inherent in the confrontation between traditional belief and biblical criticism: "If the price we have to pay to be free from this distress is the acceptance of mystical traditions, we will have to totally relinquish the rationalist approach to every question of faith and religion, and it seems to me that for all those who are troubled by the arguments of biblical criticism . . . his solution does not solve anything. On the contrary, it takes us out of the frying pan and into the fire."[40]

The renowned biblical scholar Meir Weiss has declared that Rabbi Breuer's approach is marred by dogmatism in that it calls for a rejection of all exegesis that is not kabbalistic, "even the exegesis of the sages."[41] Another argument against Rabbi Breuer, made by Rabbi Yaakov Zaidman, concerns the public revelation of the secret wisdom of the Torah. "We will not hide in the mist of esoteric wisdom and mysticism, and he who makes his theories public like Rabbi Breuer cannot hide behind claims of secrecy and hidden wisdom."[42]

Rabbi Breuer responded to his critics. A distinctly polemic tone can be detected in his second article, published in *De'ot*:

> There is more than one approach to the sanctification of the secular that is required with regard to biblical criticism. . . . Therefore, whoever thinks that he can accomplish this task by means of exoteric wisdom alone—may his strength increase and his faith grow, and may he succeed in the path he has chosen. . . .
>
> In truth, after all the spiritual upheavals of the last centuries, today it is impossible to reduce the faith of Israel to the single dimension of the exoteric tradition. Go and see if in any of the communities of the diaspora there is one group among our people that has not been influenced in one way or another by the esoteric wisdom of Kabbalah.[43]

Rabbi Breuer even pointed out which type of kabbalistic readings he thought would prove successful; not all branches of kabbalistic hermeneutics are appropriate for the task of "sanctifying the secular":

> When we talk about the exegesis of the Torah according to esoteric wisdom, our intention is not those esoteric techniques, such as letter combinations or assigning letters numerical value (*gematria*), that have nothing to do with the contextual meaning of the text. For it is the contextual meaning of the text that we are trying to ascertain, and from this goal we will neither waver nor desist.[44]

An additional, if less significant, criticism was leveled against Rabbi Breuer from the traditional side of the religious world. Predictably, these critics warned of the danger to religious belief inherent in exposure to the ideas of biblical criticism. Rabbi Moshe Lichtenstein, one of the heads of the Har Etzion Yeshiva explained: "Even if a man is himself wholehearted and God-fearing, regarding the Torah as the holy and pure word of God, whose only intention is to take from biblical criticism what is useful and reject the rest, the question of the spiritual price that he is liable to have to pay for this exposure hangs over his head nonetheless."[45] Rabbi Shlomo Aviner also opposed confronting biblical criticism because "our master, Rabbi Kook considered it to be completely false."[46]

Rabbi Benamozegh and Rabbi Breuer: A Comparison

R. J. Zwi Werblowsky has divided the different theological approaches used in the confrontation between the belief in the divine origin of the Torah and biblical criticism into four categories:[47]

1. The **fundamentalist approach** utterly rejects biblical criticism and its findings, and regards the belief in the divine origin of the Torah as a fact, completely ignoring biblical criticism. This, as we have seen, is the approach of most Orthodox Jewish commentators.

2. The **"Catholic" approach** argues that religion, the world, and reason were all given by the same benign Providence, and that, therefore, a contradiction between the findings of biblical criticism and the faith in the divine origin of the Torah is impossible. If biblical criticism leads to conclusions that undermine the belief in the divine origin of the Torah, its scientific validity must be questioned, and even denied. This is the approach of Rabbi Samuel David Luzzatto.

3. The **"Protestant" approach** does not deny the existence of contradictions between biblical criticism and faith, but rejects the attempt to reconcile them. Each is correct within its own sphere and we must live in a state of dialectic tension. This is the approach of Yeshayahu Leibowitz, who argued that, while biblical scholarship is valid and accurate, it is irrelevant to religious faith. Faith mandates the acceptance of the authority of *halakhah*, which in turn determines the nature of the correct approach to the biblical text.

Werblowsky placed Rabbi Breuer's aspects theory under the category of the **dialectic-mystical approach.** His method receives its own category because the other categories are too narrow to encompass it. Like the "fundamentalist," Rabbi Breuer accepts the traditional belief in the divine origin of the Torah as fact. However, unlike the "fundamentalist," he does not reject modern scholarship as a complete falsehood. Like the "Protestant," he separates religious faith from the physical world. However, he adds a "Catholic" layer: there is a connection between biblical criticism and faith. The findings of critical scholarship lead to the esoteric and to the realization that "the mystical tradition is the spiritual meaning of the conclusions of scientific research."[48]

In this article, I have attempted to show that it would be appropriate to include Rabbi Benamozegh among those adhering to the dialectic-mystical approach. Rabbi Breuer and Rabbi Benamozegh made use of different branches of modern biblical scholarship in their commentaries: Rabbi Breuer accepted the documentary hypothesis of biblical scholarship (although rejecting its historical conclusions), whereas Rabbi Benamozegh used Near Eastern mythology as a source for comparative exegesis (and never once referred to the documentary hypothesis). While they made use of different elements of this research, they both shared the realization that they could find their place in the framework of an exegesis faithful to the principle of the divine origin of the Torah only by means of that same "mystical dialectic."

The exact nature of this mystical dialectic differs in the work of each of the two scholars. Rabbi Benamozegh's exegesis is part of his basic, comprehensive perception that the Written Torah is by nature partial and fragmented, in two ways: in its representation of ancient traditions, including esoteric lore, passed down orally from generation to generation, and in its linguistic limitations that necessitate exegesis, elaboration, and explication drawn from the wellsprings of the esoteric tradition. The surprising integration of mysticism and Near Eastern mythology in his commentary can be understood only within the context of this basic viewpoint. Rabbi Benamozegh was raised and educated in the world of the Kabbalah, considered himself a kabbalist, and conducted an extensive campaign for the recognition of the authenticity of the Kabbalah and its inclusion in the canon of Jewish literature. Thus, in his opinion, the Written Torah must not be severed from the mystical tradition. The Kabbalah is the soul of the Written Torah and an essential exegetical tool.

Unlike Rabbi Benamozegh, Rabbi Breuer did not study kabbalah systematically and was not known as a kabbalist. It is apparent that the kabbalistic element occupied a marginal role in his thinking. He made use of the Kabbalah primarily for the purpose of demonstrating his method; in his commentary on the Torah, he used it neither consistently nor continuously. The decentralization of divine power characteristic of kabbalistic theology provided him with an alternative exegetical framework in place of the heretical, historical exegesis of modern biblical scholars. The mystical tradition enabled Breuer to reject the argument that the Torah had several authors.

Werblowsky's remarks on Rabbi Breuer's method are without a doubt applicable to Rabbi Benamozegh as well:

> The literal meaning of the text [as revealed by biblical criticism] leads to the hidden meaning at least in the sense that it reveals the exterior structures, whose interior and true content is the subject of esoteric wisdom. The *peshat*, in its essence, hints at the hidden meaning, but the hidden meaning itself is not understood in its immanent inevitability, without the critical *peshat* that should be "transparent" in the eyes of the believer until the inner meaning of the biblical text is seen outside its husk.[49]

The writings of both scholars demonstrate that isolation and apologetics are not mandatory responses to the findings of modern biblical research. Their approaches reflect growth, empowerment, and a broadening of the accepted religious outlook. The intensity of both scholars' religious zeal was equaled only by their integrity, and by their willingness to take an honest look at the subject and accept the truth without prejudice—even if that truth was found on foreign ground, far from the pastures of Jewish tradition. Their attempt at synthesis compelled them to stand in the eye of a storm of criticism leveled at them from all sides, as their positions were fundamentally misunderstood. The importance of their bold enterprise lies in the very fact of its initiation and in its perspicacity. We are not called upon to venerate, or even to accept, their commentaries as they are, but we are obligated take a keen interest in their work because their ideas stimulate discussion and thought, and enhance and inspire faith.

Endnotes

1. M.B. Shapiro, *The Limits of Orthodox Theology: Maimonides' Thirteen Principles Reappraised* (Oxford: Oxford University Press, 2004), 115–121; K. P. Bland, "Moses and the Law According to Maimonides," in *Mystics, Philosophers, and Politicians: Essays in Jewish Intellectual History in Honor of Alexander Altmann*, ed. J. Reinharz and D. Swetschinski (Durham, NC: Duke University Press, 1982), 49–66.

2. For a survey of the origins of modern biblical scholarship and its achievements, see the recent work: Y. Kedourie, "Ḥeker ha-Mikra le-Toldotav" [The history of biblical scholarship], in *Sifrut ha-Mikra, Mevo'ot u-Meḥkarim* (The literature of the Hebrew Bible: Introductions and studies), ed. Zipora Talshir (Jerusalem: Yad Ben-Zvi, 2011), 1:3–36.
3. For a clear survey of the history of the documentary hypothesis, see Moshe Weinfeld, "Torah, Meḥkar ha-Torah be-Et ha-Ḥadasha" [Torah and biblical scholarship in the modern period], *Entzeklopedia Mikrait* [Encyclopaedia biblica] (1982), 8:492–507.
4. Moshe Greenberg, "Tefisot Yehudiot shel ha-Gorem ha-Enoshi be-Nevua ha-Mikrait" [Jewish perspectives on the human factor in biblical prophecy], in *Sefer ha-Yovel le-Rav Mordekhai Breuer* [Rabbi Mordechai Breuer Jubilee Volume], ed. M. Bar-Asher (Jerusalem: Akademon, 1992), 1:63.
5. D. S. Sperling, "Judaism and Modern Biblical Research," in *Biblical Studies: Meeting Ground of Jews and Christians*, ed. L. H. Boadt et al. (New York: Paulist Press, 1980), 39.
6. On this subject see, in particular, Y. Shavit and M. Eran, *Milḥemet ha-Luḥot: ha-Hagana al ha-Mikra be-Mea ha-Tsha-Esreh u-Pulmus Bavel ve-ha-Tanakh* [The war of the tablets: The defense of the Bible in the nineteenth century] (Tel Aviv, Am Oved: 2003).
7. A concise autobiography of Rabbi Benamozegh appeared in M. Halter, *Sefer Zikaron le-Sofrei Yisrael ha-Ḥayim Itanu ka-Yom* [Memorial volume for contemporary Jewish authors] (Warsaw: M. Halter, 1889), 128–131. For a comprehensive biography of Rabbi Benamozegh, accompanied by an extensive up-to-date bibliography, see Yair Yarbachty, *Rav Eliyahu ben Amozeg ve-Hagut ha-Renesans* [Rabbi Elia Benaozegh and the philosophy of the Renaissance], master's thesis, Bar Ilan University, 2008, 16–33.
8. Aimé Pallière (on whom see below), in his introduction to the first edition of Élie Benamozegh, *Israël et l'humanité: étude sur le problème de la religion universelle et sa solution* (Paris: E. Leroux, 1914). The introduction also appears as a preface to the English translation: Aimé Pallière, "Preface to the First Edition (1914)," in Elijah Benamozegh, *Israel and Humanity*, trans. Maxwell Luria (New York: Paulist Press, 1995), 31.
9. On the Kabbalah, see *Eimat Mafgia al Ari* (Livorno: Benamozegh, 1855). This work was written in response to Judah Modena's *Ari Nohem*, rev. ed. (Jerusalem: Makor, 1970); *Ta'am le-Shad* (Livorno: Benamozegh, 1863) was written in response to *Vikhuach al Ḥakhmat ha-Kabbalah* by Samuel David Luzzatto. On ethics, see E. Benamozegh, *Morale juive et morale chrétienne: Examen comparatif suivi de quelques réflexions sur les principes de l'islamisme* (Paris: Michel Lévy frères, 1867). Trans. E. Blockman as *Jewish and Christian Ethics: with a Criticism on Mahomedism* (San Francisco: E. Blochman, 1873).
10. Benamozegh, *Israel and Humanity*.
11. This was published recently in a critical edition by Mordecai Goldstein, "Mavo le-Kol Sifrei Torah she-be-al peh: Mahadurah mad'aiti" [An introduction to the *Torah she-be-al peh*: Critical edition], PhD diss., Bar Ilan University, 2000.
12. *Sefer Ya'ane be-Eish* (Livorno: Benamozegh, 1906). This work was published posthumously in memory of the author.
13. M. Agmon (*Eliyahu ben Amozeg: Kavim le-Dmuto ke-Mefaresh ha-Mikra* [Elia Benamozegh: Toward an assessment of his exegesis], master's thesis, Hebrew University, 1971, 61ff.) divides these references into two categories: polemical references—part of Rabbi Benamozegh's attempt to prove the antiquity of the Zohar and the Kabbalah—and exegetical references—in which he uses the Zohar to determine the *peshat* meaning of the biblical text.
14. Perhaps he did so in order not to obscure the *peshat* character of the commentary. This is, apparently, also the reason why he mentioned "the midrashim of the sages," and his use of them, only at the end of his declaration.

15. Moshe Idel has strongly emphasized this point. See Moshe Idel, "Appendix," in *Israel and Humanity*, 378–402. For a description of Rabbi Benamozegh's kabbalistic approach, see Moshe Idel, "Al ha-Kabbalah Ezel ha-Rav Eliyahu ben Amozeg" [On the Kabbalah in the work of Eliyahu Banamozegh], *Pe'amim* 74 (1998): 87–96; Alessandro Guettta, "Kabbalah ve-Natzrut be-Haguto shel ha-Rav Eliyahu ben Amozeg" [Kabbalah and Christianity in the thought of Rabbi Eliyahu Benamozegh], *Pe'amim* 74 (1998): 97–103.
16. Aimé Pallière (1868–1949) was born a Catholic and graduated from a Christian theological seminary. Over the years, he developed a strong affinity for Jewish beliefs, the Hebrew language, and Jewish sacred writings. He wanted to convert to Judaism but Rabbi Benamozegh, who played a decisive role in his religious development, dissuaded him.
17. Ernest Renan (1823–1892) was a French philosopher, historian, philologist, and archeologist. Rabbi Benamozegh cited his works frequently in his commentary to the Torah.
18. *Israel and Humanity*, 32–33.
19. *Em le-Mikra* on Exod. 18:21 (Livorno: Benamozegh, 1863), 53. In this context mention should be made of the question of the "absence" within the Written Torah of references to the afterlife, an important concept in Jewish faith.
20. *Em le-Mikra* on Deuteronomy (Livorno: Benamozegh, 1863), 149.
21. *Em le-Mikra* on Numbers (Livorno: Benamozegh, 1863), 11ff.
22. "Is only the redemption of the cattle of the People of Israel by the cattle of the Levites unclear to us? For we did not find that the firstborn of the cattle of Israel from now on lose their sanctity; on the contrary, the firstborn is consecrated. Nor do we find that the cattle of the Levites becomes consecrated in place of the firstborn of the cattle of Israel."
23. Typhon is a monstrous creature from Greek mythology with a hundred snake heads and multiple arms and legs. He was the younger son of Gaia, the Earth goddess, and Tartarus, the god of the Underworld. See "Typhoeus," Theoi Project, http://www.theoi.com/Gigante/Typhoeus.html.
24. Because of its connection to Set-Typhon, the Egyptians considered the donkey to be ridiculous, contemptible, and disgusting.
25. Osiris is usually described as having the form of a bull. However, in Egypt several gods take the form of a bull: Apis, the well-known god of Memphis, and Buchis, the holy bull of Heliopolis, among others. On bull deities, see E. A. W Budge, *From Fetish to God in Ancient Egypt* (New York: Dover, 1988).
26. Benamozegh is apparently alluding to the image of the bull in the vision of the divine chariot. See Ezekiel 1:10.
27. In the words of Isaiah Tishby, *The Wisdom of the Zohar*, trans. David Goldstein (Oxford: Oxford University Press, 1989), 1:43.
28. For his biography, see M. Bar-Asher, "Ha-Rav Breuer u-Mifalo ha-Mada'i" (Rabbi Breuer and his academic *oeuvre*), in *Sefer ha-Yovel le-Rav Mordekhai Breuer*, 1:1–7.
29. It is relevant to note here that Rabbi Breuer was awarded the prize in the category of "Original rabbinic Literature," not in the category of "Biblical Studies."
30. Mordechai Breuer, "Emuna u-Mada be-Parshanut ha-Mikra (aleph)" (Faith and science in biblical exegesis (a)), in *Shitat ha-Beḥinot shel ha-Rav Mordekhai Breuer* (The aspects theory of Rabbi Mordechai Breuer), ed. Yosef Ofer (Alon Shvut: Tvunot, 2005), 24.
31. "The unity of God does not preclude the plurality of His attributes; on the contrary, the plurality of the conflicting attributes of God is the ultimate test of His unity. God is one, and within this unity He contains all of the opposites and contradictions in the universe." *Pirkei Bereshit* (Alon Shvut: Tvunot, 1999), 12.

32. For a basic survey of the system of the ten sefirot and the process of their emanation, see, in particular, Tishby, *Wisdom of the Zohar*, 1:269–366.
33. "The reduction of the Jewish religion to its exoteric elements not only diminishes its richness and vitality, but also unnecessarily encumbers the exegete struggling with the task of sanctifying the secularity of the discoveries of biblical scholarship." (Breuer, "Emuna u-Mada be-Parshanut ha-Mikra (bet)" [Faith and science in biblical exegesis (b)], in *Shitat ha-Behinot*, 36.
34. See the Introduction to *Pirkei Moadot* (Jerusalem: Horev, 1986), 14–16, and also the introduction to *Pirkei Bereshit*, 11–16.
35. "The connection between nature and the name *Elohim* and the connection between revelation and the name YHVH is proved also from the literal meaning of the verses, especially in Genesis. The name *Elohim* always indicates the concealed God who pierces the veil of nature, while YHVH represents the God who is close to man, who dwells with him as he did in Eden." "Limud Pshuto shel Mikra: Sakanot ve-Sikuim" [The study of the contextual meaning of the Bible: Dangers and possibilities], in *Shitat ha-Behinot*, 60, note 3. For further discussion, see "Yezirat ha-Adam u-Maaseh Gan Eden" [The creation of man and the story of the Garden of Eden], in *Pirkei Bereshit*, 93ff.
36. *Pirkei Bereshit*, 2:513 (emphases mine).
37. *Pirkei Bereshit*, 2:613.
38. Yosef Avivi is one of the most important scholars of Kabbalah in the world and the author of many works on the kabbalistic thought of Rabbi Moses Hayim Luzzatto, the Vilna Gaon, and Rabbi Isaac Luria. His latest work on Lurianic Kabbalah has been described as "monumental." See Avi Elqayam, "Azamer be-shvahim: Al ars poetika le-ha-Ari shikur ha-elohim" [I will sing praises: On the ars poetica of Isaac Luria, drunk with God], in *Ha-Piyyut ke-Tzohar Tarbuti* [The piyyut as a cultural prism], ed. Haviva Pedaya (Jerusalem: Van Leer, 2012), 71. Surprisingly, neither the book nor the author have yet been discussed in any published work about Rabbi Breuer and his method. Avivi's book is not even mentioned in *Shitat Ha-Behinot* of Rav Breuer, an anthology of various responses to the aspects approach.
39. Professor Jacob Katz was one of the most important historians of the twentieth century in the field of Jewish history. On his scholarly legacy, see Israel Bartal and Shmuel Feiner, eds., *Historiographia ba-Mivhan: Iyun me-Hadash ba-Mishnato shel Yaakov Katz* [Historiography reappraised: New views of Jacob Katz's *oeuvre*] (Jerusalem: Zalman Shazar, 2008).
40. "Emuna u-Mada be-Parshnut ha-Mikra (Teguvot)" [Faith and science in biblical exegesis (responses)], in *Shitat ha-Behinot*, 206.
41. Ibid., 209.
42. Ibid., 212.
43. "Emuna u-Mada be-Parshanut ha-Mikra (bet)," 28–53. This point was somewhat obscured in the editing of the collection because Rabbi Breuer's words appear before the articles of his critics, even though these articles were written before he voiced his response to the question of the use of Kabbalah.
44. *Shitat ha-Behinot*, 37.
45. Moshe Lichtenstein, "Ahat Diber Elohim—Shtayim zo Sham☒ati?" [One thing God has spoken—two things have I heard?], in *Shitat ha-Behinot*, 325.
46. See Rabbi Shlomo Aviner, "U-Mah Haya Omer ha-Rav Breuer al Limud ha-Tanakh he-Hadash?" [What would Rabbi Breuer have said about the new study of Bible?], *Arutz Meir*, accessed January 30, 2014, http://www.meirtv.co.il/site/article/?id=1061:

For many years, Rabbi Breuer taught in yeshivot according to the "aspects theory." He turned sweet what was sour and out of heresy produced a new way of learning, and usually did not reveal to his students that the source of these aspects was biblical criticism. In his opinion, there was a double benefit to his method: (1) he rescued people from the belief in biblical criticism; (2) he created a new, good, and kosher commentary. However, as we have seen above, our master Rav Kook maintained that there is no reason to confront this heresy, because it is completely false.

47. R. J. Zwi Werblowsky, "Mada ha-Mikra ke-Baaya Datit: Nisayon Birur Tipologi shel Gishot u-Pitronot" [Biblical studies as a religious problem: An attempt at typological clarification of approaches and solutions], *Shitat ha-Beḥinot*, 224–237.
48. Breuer, "Emuna u-Mada be-Parshanut ha-Mikra (aleph)," 24.
49. Werblovsky, "Mada ha-Mikra ke-Baaya Datit," 233.

Orthodoxy and the Challenge of Biblical Criticism: Some Reflections on the Importance of Asking the Right Question

Tamar Ross

Modern Challenges of Biblical Criticism and Non-Orthodox Responses

As formulated by Maimonides in his eighth principle of faith, traditional Jewish belief in a divine Torah entails the notion that the biblical text in our hands today was transmitted by God to Moses, that every word of this text is equally divine and laden with meaning, and that this written text was simultaneously accompanied by an oral commentary.

Critical approaches to the biblical text that pose problems for this formulation are not a modern invention. Nevertheless, the scope and intensity of such questions have deepened considerably in the past century. Beyond the usual difficulties (erroneous or fallible content, questionable morality, and textual evidence of evolutionary historical development), the development of sophisticated methods of textual analysis (such as those generated by hermeneutic theory, computer science, and the feminist critique) has recently problematized the very notion of divine revelation as verbal communication—given that language itself now appears so pervasively rooted in a particular perspective and cultural bias.

Before discussing possible "Orthodox" solutions, it would be useful first to survey some "heterodox" suggestions that have been proffered. One such response to these difficulties—perhaps the most intuitively obvious—has been to abandon the notion of divine revelation altogether. Thus, Mordecai Kaplan, the founder of the Reconstructionist movement, rejects any appeal to metaphysics and transcendence in describing the origins of the Torah. Instead, he prefers to view revelation naturalistically, as the human "discovery" of how to live religiously (Kaplan 1967).

Other responses (as represented in the writings of Franz Rosenzweig, Abraham Joshua Heschel, and Louis Jacobs) that have been rejected by mainstream Orthodoxy, all appear to be variations on Martin Buber's attempt to promote a more nuanced understanding of revelation that does not reject biblical claims to metaphysics altogether. This more complex approach to the biblical text, similar to Protestant "dialectical theology," understands the Torah as a human effort to convey or recapture certain genuine meetings with the Divine. Because such meetings were inevitably experienced in a particular linguistic and cultural context, and no written or oral report can convey these encounters in terms that are entirely free of the influence of historical context, the argument now consists of just what and how much of the Godly was revealed. Differences of opinion range from the divine element consisting merely in the meeting itself with all resultant texts a human response, to the belief that a complete text was given but necessarily distorted because every human "hearing" involves reinterpretation, or some in-between suggestion of a more minimalistic linguistic message that was left for humans to fill in over time.[1] At any rate, what is left for us to extract is the eternal illuminations that the Torah communicates to us from those trappings that are the fruit of passing human experience.

Viewing revelation as a dialogic encounter that entails both human and divine elements appears more satisfactory than Kaplan's reductionism. Instead of understanding the religious experience as merely the product of innately human impulses, this approach acknowledges biblical claims to a supernatural source. However, such a theology does not satisfy the traditional requirement that the *entire* Torah be viewed as the word of God and that *all* its details be regarded as equally authoritative and binding. So the question remains: Can a document so thoroughly riddled with identifiably dated and partisan human perspectives truly be divine? Can traditionalists develop an approach to the Torah that acknowledges the naturalist explanations of Mordecai Kaplan without his reductionism on the one hand, while simultaneously appropriating the metaphysical claims of dialectical theology without succumbing to its selectivity, on the other?

Orthodox Solutions Thus Far

An increasing number of Orthodox Jews are recognizing that biblical criticism is not a theory that they can accept or reject at will. Contemporary scholars may disagree regarding particular versions of the documentary hypothesis, whether there was one final redactor or many, the exact dates involved, etc., but historical evidence cannot leave the traditional picture intact. Until recently, however, the traditionalist response to such conclusions has largely been to ignore or avoid them. To the extent that Orthodox thinkers have addressed the challenges of higher criticism, they have generally adopted a modernist approach[2] associated with the slogan of *Torah u-madda* (Torah and science). This regards both sources of knowledge as valuable avenues to Truth. It presents possible discrepancies as localized controversies between science and religion regarding "the facts of the matter." Under such circumstances, the validity of the Torah's rendition will always be maintained.

Proponents of this approach often enlist the tools of science itself to defend the accuracy of traditional accounts on science's own grounds.[3] Alternatively, difficulties are resolved by appeal to Maimonides' classic statement that "the gates of figurative interpretation" are never "shut in our faces" (Maimonides 1963, 327), intimating that whenever the literal meaning of the Torah can be incontrovertibly refuted, this should be taken as clear indication that the text was meant to be understood allegorically, with deeper meanings to be extracted by the more philosophically inclined. Questionable features of biblical morality are resolved in a similarly *ad hoc* manner; drawing upon various apologetic arguments to defend their underlying values and conclusions.

Rabbi Mordechai Breuer's understanding of biblical contradictions as planted deliberately by God for educational and other reasons (1996) or Professor Weiss-Halivni's suggestion of a perfect Torah that was corrupted during a long period of halakhic negligence, whose practical consequences were corrected through authoritative midrashic interpretation (1997), offer more striking and ingenuous theories as justification for what on first blush appear to be perplexing anomalies in the text.

There is no denying, however, that this battery of tactics, which still links the sanctity of Torah to the authenticity of an original revelatory event at Sinai, and to the unique status of Moses as prophet, loses its persuasiveness when the various difficulties it purports to address can be more simply and elegantly explained by reference to their historical setting and the development of human understanding.

Nevertheless, the closest that a *Torah u-madda* approach comes to a more naturalistic interpretation is in its willingness to appropriate the notion of divine accommodation—that God deliberately expressed Himself to Moses in the language of the times (Maimonides 1963, 3:32). The inadequacies of this solution when confronted by discovery of a biblical worldview bearing more pervasive biases (such as those highlighted by feminists) of a dated or parochial nature that are so implicit and subtle that the innocent reader usually remains unaware of their existence (and therefore cannot be taken as serving some accommodative purpose), are not considered.

In line with the observation of Edward de Bono, a leading authority on creative thinking, who states that "asking the right question may be the most important part of thinking,"[4] I believe that the key to Orthodox resolution of this dilemma involves a radical departure from the *Torah u-madda* approach, which relates to all truth claims of religion cognitively, as simple statements of fact. Instead of questioning whether the doctrine of "Torah from heaven" is true empirically, Orthodox believers must rather ask: What is its function in the context of their religious lives? Is its primary concern to discuss history or to fulfil other purposes?

Initial Deviations from Cognitivism in Orthodox Theology (Soloveitchik and Leibowitz)

Some initial attempts at divergence from a strictly cognitive response to the theological dilemmas of Modern Orthodoxy—relating to religious dogma as transmitting something other than empirical data—can be discerned in efforts by several Orthodox academicians problematizing overly rigid definitions of Jewish doctrine.[5] Nevertheless, the traditional belief in "Torah from heaven" bears a unique status even in this context. Despite seeking nuance in traditional understandings of Maimonides' eighth principle of faith, Orthodox thinkers have until very recently refrained from alluding to the traditional account of the giving of the Torah as anything other than a factual description. Direct questioning of its historical accuracy or even detailed scrutiny regarding what it entails is regarded within Orthodoxy as a serious breach of religious etiquette, on the presumption that such discussion involves a weakening of the Torah's binding nature. This taboo is beginning to erode.

A few theologians and scholars in the Modern Orthodox camp seem to reject empiric data as the exclusive criterion for establishing the revelatory status of the Bible.[6] A notable passage from *The Lonely Man of Faith* by Rabbi J. B. Soloveitchik, the revered leader of American Modern Orthodoxy, professing that he has "not been perplexed by the impossibility of fitting the mystery of revelation into the framework of historical empiricism" might be construed as a first step in this direction. While asserting that "we unreservedly accept the unity and integrity of the Scriptures and their divine character," Soloveitchik nevertheless declares that he is untroubled by "theories of Biblical criticism which contradict the very foundations upon which the sanctity and integrity of the Scriptures rest," on strength of a distinction he makes between factual and nonfactual biblical accounts of human existence (Soloveitchik 1992, 10). In this context, even the latter may be justified as pointers to ineffable truths that transcend verbal expression and cannot be validated empirically.

A more radical break with cognitive truth as a criterion for establishing the divinity of the Torah is exhibited in the thought of Professor Yeshayahu Leibowitz,[7] who emphasized the sharp distinction between historic or scientific statements on the one hand, and statements of value ("religious facts") on the other.[8] For Leibowitz, questions regarding the historical grounding of the biblical account of the Sinai event are meaningless in a religious context and irrelevant in establishing the sanctified status of the Torah. As opposed to Soloveitchik, Leibowitz does not see the Torah as "speaking for itself" in any manner (Leibowitz 1976, 347). Neither its timeless existential message nor the accuracy of its description of the circumstances surrounding its transmission grants the Torah its sanctity, but rather the practical role assigned to it by historical Judaism. Rather than teach us about a past event in which God spoke to Moses, or convey any current sense of His presence seeping through the text, the proposition that "God gave the Torah" is a normative statement expressing recognition of our obligation to assume the yoke of the Torah and its commandments. Thus, instead of revelation providing the basis for a particular way of life, it is this way of life, and—more specifically—the halakhic tradition of the Oral Law, which grants the Torah its revelatory status as the word of God and establishes its prescriptions as binding (Leibowitz 1976, 348–350).[9] Because God's absolute transcendence precludes any revelation of His self in the world, the ultimate authority of the Torah as God's word is grounded exclusively on the voluntary decision of the rabbinic sages to accept it as such. Undertaking performance of mitzvot for its own sake without any thought of attunement to human needs is the only way of relating to a Being who is by definition inscrutable and totally "Other."[10]

Although a scientist mistrustful of supernaturalism, Leibowitz was also deeply religious, vociferously rejecting the contention that religion lacked ontological grounding. Leibowitz's reservations regarding literal interpretations of religious propositions—unlike those of Mordecai Kaplan—do not stem from a full-fledged flight from metaphysics, but rather from a Kantian-like objection to applying human categories to an absolutely transcendent God—ascribing this view to Maimonides as well. Thus, accepting the Torah as God's word mandates engaging the Torah in an interpretive project, whose objective is to translate the ostensibly supernatural connotations of its mythological language, which speaks of God's revelation and intervention in worldly affairs, into terms that are theologically compatible with this Kantian/Maimonidian constraint—bearing a normative thrust, rather than conveying any informative content. The opening verse of Genesis stating that "in the beginning God created heaven and earth," which makes no sense theologically (as God is above time) nor empirically (because these words correspond to nothing in our natural experience), are reinterpreted to teach us a religious lesson: "What I [Leibowitz] learn from these verses is the great principle of faith, that the world is not God—the negation of atheism and pantheism" (Leibowitz 1992, 140). So too, the proposition "God gave the Torah," which is similarly unintelligible both theologically and empirically is now understood not as a "religious fact," but as "the obligation compelling the individual to worship God" (Sagi 1997b, 213). Because God's absolute transcendence precludes any revelation of His self in the world, Leibowitz grounds the ultimate status of the Torah as God's word exclusively on the formal decision of the rabbinic sages to define it as such, rather than on any objective historical occurrence.[11]

Shortcomings of Metaphysical Minimalism (James Kugel)

Aside from a small circle of intellectuals,[12] the appeal of Leibowitz's metaphysically muted approach has been limited. Beyond his terse, polemical language and propensity for stark, paradoxical aphorisms that turn conventional views on their head without cushioning the blow, this failure reflects how a theology which grounds the divinity of the Torah merely on the voluntary decision of the Rabbis leaves many religious believers cold. If Leibowitz is not prepared to allow for any revelation of God's will on theological principle, why should rabbinic fiat be granted any privilege in determining the divine nature and meaning of Torah?[13]

A sense of the inadequacy of Leibowitz's theological position can be discerned even among some contemporary Orthodox scholars who ostensibly appear close to his view of religion as man-made. A notable example is the biblical scholar James Kugel. Although unencumbered by Leibowitz's philosophical baggage regarding God's utter transcendence, Kugel's scholarship on the transformation of the Bible into Scripture similarly precludes relating to traditional accounts of revelation as strictly factual descriptions. This leads Kugel to share much of Leibowitz's "no-nonsense" approach to Torah, regarding belief in its divinity primarily as an affirmation of the rabbinic understanding that the true way to approach God is by submitting to His commands as explicated by the Oral Law. Nevertheless, in expanding upon this notion in a theological epilogue to what is essentially a scientific work of biblical scholarship, Kugel confesses that he "could not be involved in a religion that was entirely a human artifact" (Kugel 2007, 689). Some appeal to the supernatural that extends beyond human initiative is still required in order to render compelling the rabbinic understanding of Torah as a by-product of Israel's acceptance of "the supreme mission of serving God" (684–685), and their fleshing out of this perception in a myriad of legal particulars.

Another ostensible shortcoming of Leibowitz's approach is that his narrow view of the biblical message diminishes the significance of the Torah in religious life. Can the total import of the Torah be reduced to normative statements regarding the obligation to serve God through His commandments?[14] Surely generations of believers have found greater meaning in the Torah than this![15] (Ironically, this objection has been levelled even more sharply against what has been termed Kugel's "excavational" approach to the study of biblical texts. Unlike Leibowitz, Kugel is not involved in any systematic project of re-interpretation of the biblical text. This has led some of Kugel's critics to fault him for relating to its original content as outdated Iron Age fragments, devoid of intrinsic merit, which became sanctified only by virtue of their subsequent canonization and interpretation.)[16]

There is no denying that there are grave philosophical difficulties in claiming that the voice of a transcendent God erupted into the natural world. Any such claim would render the hearing of such a voice an empirical observation, independent of how it is represented in the human mind. Kugel is not oblivious to this obstacle. He acknowledges that ascribing divine origin to even the most minimal message is, in the last resort, an act of faith and not subject to proof.

As he puts it: "words are words are words" and "who are we to determine what or how God can put in His book, or how it can arrive in our hands?" (http://kavvanah.wordpress.com/2013/01/31/conversation-with-james-kugel-about-revelation/). Perhaps for this reason he places far greater importance on the rabbinic understanding that all subsequent interpretations of God's original missive are also encapsulated within it.

As for fallible aspects of this missive (elementary mistakes in physics, biology, or history), Kugel attributes these, in a fashion somewhat reminiscent of Maimonides, to disparity between the divine "handoff" and the form it takes upon reception. Likening human apprehension of divine revelation to the human faculty of sight, whereby different wavelengths of light reflected off objects are converted in our brains into different colours, he declares: "We simply don't know the beginning of the process we call prophecy—i.e., God speaking to a human being. All we know is what comes out the other end, after the intervention of a human brain" (http://kavvanah.wordpress.com/2013/02/11/conversation-with-james-kugel-a-follow-up/).

Nevertheless, reducing the scope of the problem simply by transferring the bulk of God's message to rabbinic extrapolation and relegating the rest to faith does not solve the problem in principle or abolish it. Neither does distinguishing between an amorphous "divine original" and its human depiction.

Myth, Post-Liberal Constructivism, and Narrative Theology (Norman Solomon)

Epistemological thinking (i.e., thought pertaining to the origin, nature, methods, and limits of human knowledge) has not stood still since the time of Maimonides. Kantian scepticism dismisses the possibility of speaking empirically of anything beyond the natural world. Such scepticism is based on what Kant described as his Copernican revolution in the theory of knowledge—trading the medieval notion that man's perceptions revolve around some fixed reality, for the modern notion that this reality, far from being fixed, is filtered and shaped by the mind perceiving it. This raises the question: Can ascription of intentionality or deliberate communication to something transcending human experience (even when relegated to the realm of belief) ever be classified as reference to "an objective occurrence," distinct from its representation in the human mind? Surely the very decision that *these particular* words, rather than others, stem directly from God and bear prophetic status is of necessity dependent upon human interpretation and cultural preconditioning.

A more recent version of revelatory minimalism that might overcome these difficulties is the recommendation of Jewish Studies scholar, Norman Solomon, in a book entitled *Torah from Heaven*, that the logical status of this doctrine be changed from historical truth to a foundational myth of origin (Solomon 2012, 320–321, 346). In labelling the belief in "Torah from heaven" a "myth of origin," Solomon appears, like Leibowitz, to be arguing that religious language is not intended to impart information—metaphysical or otherwise. But there is a difference in the degree of receptivity to the original text that the two views mandate. Because Leibowitz still appeals to a form of reasoning beyond religious discourse in stipulating the existence of a God whose nature transcends human understanding, and is not revealed in history, he is driven to demythologize the "religious facts" described in the Torah which purport to talk about God and His relationship with the world. Instead of taking such descriptive statements at face value, he must relate to them as value judgements and directives for behavior, thereby avoiding clashes with his preconceived theological views. Solomon's understanding, by contrast, allows him to accept the mythic formulation unconditionally, with no theological strings attached.[17]

Irrespective of questions regarding their original intent and context,[18] Solomon argues that only when biblical narratives are treated strictly as history do questions of "accuracy" become appropriate, creating the need for apologetic resolutions with contemporary sensibilities. When treated as a myth of origin, the traditional account of revelation, even if it appears today as entirely fictitious or overwhelmingly inaccurate, can still bear theological validity as *it stands*. Its rationality or "truth" is maintained not by appeal to external evidence or reinterpretation, but in its ability to discharge a mythic function, imbuing those who appropriate it with a sense of allegiance to the past and inducing them to relate to the received text of Scripture as sacrosanct.[19]

In elucidating this view of revelation as myth, Solomon alludes in passing to some measure of affinity with the concept of "narrative theology" fashionable in some Christian circles identified as "post-liberal" (Solomon 2012, 313). Indeed, the appeal to the role of myth in religious life in both cases joins forces with a broader interest on the part of various contemporary philosophers in a school of thought known as "constructivism," which highlights the place of "as if" beliefs in all aspects of our cognitive activity.[20] Contrary to what many non-scientists tend to assume, even entities such as protons and electrons, waves of light, gravity as distortions of space, are not things that anyone has seen or proven to exist. Nevertheless, as useful constructs that work currently, we employ them "as if" they were true.

In a scientific context, "as if" beliefs help us organize our everyday reality. In a religious context, the distinctive interpretations of the past which their narrative renditions promote come to foster a cultural-linguistic picture that illuminates this practical life infusing it with more profound "meaning." When enveloped in mythic trappings linking them to metaphysical forces, such beliefs generate a stock of suggestive images and associations that tacitly direct the way we experience and deal with the more spiritually challenging aspects of human existence.

At times, these beliefs preserve our sense of wonder and awareness of the mysterious boundary conditions of human experience beyond rational comprehension. At other times, they function more politically, structuring verbal or non-verbal behaviors that define the community of the faithful and establish group membership. On this view, profession of belief in "Torah from heaven" is part of a vocabulary of religious identity rather than a fully informed judgement about history or theology. It serves, among other functions, as a signal to co-religionists that the speaker is a bona fide member of the group. Indeed, as Sam Lebens (chairperson of the virtual Association for the Philosophy of Judaism) suggests, sometimes it is precisely the strangeness of the professed "belief" or the costliness of the non-verbal behaviour it engenders that renders the signal strong and hence a credible sign of allegiance.[21]

For Orthodox Judaism, another significant point of similarity between defining "Torah from heaven" as a foundational myth and post-liberal theology (beyond a loose understanding of doctrine) is the unusual combination of radical postmodernism and nearly fundamentalist traditionalism that both positions afford.[22] Despite the extreme liberty that they display in divorcing the meaning of religious statements from the manner in which they are formulated, Christian post-liberals nevertheless insist upon absolute commitment to the formal guidelines of the religious system within which they function, and submission to their internal authority. Transposing this approach to Orthodox Judaism, accepting "Torah from heaven" as a myth of origin rather than an accurate historical account, frees the religious believer to relate to each and every word of the Torah "as if" it were literally dictated by God and to embrace the written along with the Oral Torah as "a unified whole" (Solomon 2012, 316–317). As Solomon explains:

> The narrative of Torah from heaven presents the Torah as a timeless whole, revealed by God and managed by the rabbis. . . . Since myth is impervious to historical evidence, moral questioning, and the like, we do

not have to "pick and choose" which bits of tradition to regard as "Torah from heaven"; we simply tell the story (2012, 346).

Solutions to any practical or ethical difficulties of implementation that may arise are relegated to the realm of context and interpretation.

In a sense, a constructivist approach to revelation (viewing it as a type of "placeholder" necessary for sustaining routine religious behavior) represents the apologetic of all apologetics, a meta-solution broad enough to cover even the most general and all-pervasive critique regarding the "truth" of this Jewish dogma. Since the function of myths is not strictly cognitive, nurturing rather a more elusive sensibility or way of relating to the world, it is not necessary to believe that they are true in the classical sense of the term. Far more important is to live your life "as if" they are true.

Even when accepted as literally true, biblical narratives are simply a starting point, becoming a religious reality only when embodied in props and rituals that may appear more like games than serious action, but whose purpose is to work psychologically upon the community of believers, evoking in them a sense of sacred significance. The biblical insistence upon telling, retelling, commemorating, and studying accounts of the many occasions when God engaged with Israel, as well as the rabbinic injunction that individual members of each and every generation see themselves "as if" they personally had been delivered from Egypt (Babylonian Talmud, tractate *Pesahim* 116:b), thereby existentially reenacting renewal of the covenant, illustrates this point. As noted by Lebens (http:// www.philosophyofJudaism.blogspot.com, "Evidence and Exodus" symposium, comments section): "Much of the Torah itself can be construed as a 'reminiscing,' or a call to reminisce, about the many occasions when God engaged with Israel, thereby inducing a relationship of mutual love and concern between them."

Some aggadic statements qualified by the Rabbis with the caveat of *kivjakhol* ("as it were") may also have been conceived as useful fictions (rather than symbolic expressions pointing to an ontological reality beyond them), deliberately formulated for pedagogic purposes. Maimonides' distinction between "necessary beliefs" and "correct beliefs" (Maimonides 1963, 3:28), extended even further in the writings of R. Kook,[23] is another manifestation of this stance.

In an age when the abyss between the literal meaning of religious statements and the ability of the community of believers to accept them at face value steadily increases, post-liberals can justifiably view their intra-textual narrative approach as a more effective guarantee for the continued viability of such statements than any modernist attempts to understand them in terms of their compliance with an external standard. Indeed, one might contend that it is precisely this understanding of how biblical narrative functions that explains the continued vibrancy of Judaism, despite its core theological claim now appearing scientifically weak and its commandment-centered approach to religion at odds with current notions of human autonomy. Whatever vitality Judaism has stems from the form of life that these myths engender and the grasp that it has upon its adherents. A narrative account which is inaccurate in some of its details or even a total fiction can still be adopted by a community and revealed as the word of God from within the form of life that it supports.

The Limits of "As If" Constructivism

Post-liberals do not have a monopoly on constructivism. Indeed, it would be fair to say that most believers in the past assumed such an attitude unreflectively, simply allowing the concrete experience of their everyday lives to be shaped by this traditional religious claim, without dwelling on its precise doctrinal content. Nevertheless, it must be admitted that when this approach is adopted consciously as a blanket response to newfound awareness that the doctrine of "Torah from heaven" may not be literally "real" or "true," conducting one's day-to-day living in accordance with its guidelines could be more problematic.

Applying an "as if" approach in order to speak descriptively and after-the-fact regarding the function of particular aspects of our religious language is one thing. Appropriating this approach as a general panacea is quite another—so that the grip of its picture upon us can no longer be complete.

This difficulty has been portrayed inimitably on the Internet, by a Modern Orthodox blogger tormented by his crisis of faith in the notion of a divinely revealed Torah. In his search for a solution over several years, he covered many of the positions described above, aided by the considerable virtual community he drew around him. When finally arriving at appreciation of the "as if" position, he vividly portrays the dilemma that such self-awareness raises:

> Someone once commented on one of my many former blogs that religion is a form of *kabuki* (Japanese theatre). And this time of year, the theater is in full swing. Right now it's *Tisha B'av*. We feel sad and mournful. We act sad, we do sad rituals.... But deep down, we kinda enjoy it I think. I could

have just skipped *Tisha B'av* this year completely. I mean, why bother? What's the point? But as soon as I heard the first words of *Eichah*, I was glad I didn't skip it. It's a powerful piece of theater. Just like we enjoy going to sad or scary movies, we enjoy *Tisha B'av*. It feels good to feel bad. Then of course we have *Shabbos Nachamu*, and then *Ellul*. Ever spent *Ellul* in a REAL Yeshiva? I have. And I can still remember how powerful it was, and probably always will.

Rosh Hashanah, Yom Kippur Succos—all elaborate theater. Complete with costumes, props, drama, comedy, scary parts, happy parts—it's all there. Where do you get such thrills, such feelings in everyday life? From the movies? From going to the bar every night? Maybe you can, or maybe life feels somehow emptier and more vacuous.

And it's not just the *Yomim Noroim* where the performances are stellar. Every *Shabbos,* every Friday night, every *Seuda Shelishis,* in a decent *shul* (and not some *kalte* MO intellectual place) is elaborate theater. And even every day has a little bit of theater—*shacharis, mincha, maariv*. Even a humble *bracha*—you're talking to THE SUPREME BEING for goodness sake! And not only that, HE'S FREAKING LISTENING TO YOU! The drama is overwhelming.

True, sometimes you need a break. Too much of a good thing and all that. Plus, if you keep reminding yourself that it's only a show, it can get annoying, especially when too much audience participation is required. But who goes to a great movie and sits there during the scary bits saying out loud: "They're just actors, the cameraman is right there!"? . . . We enjoy the performance; we want it to be as real as possible. . . . And maybe there's something to that. If only I could just forget about that damn camera-man.[24]

Surely the fact that religious myths of origin generally present themselves as historical accounts, imposing an aura of objectivity, has something to do with their staying power. It also has something to teach us regarding a universal human need to ground our religious commitments on firmer territory than the product of a camera man, no matter how powerful the show. Conveying reasonable import may not be the main function of religious truth claims, but a strong sense that their ultimate referent is *un*reasonable (that is to say, ungrounded in reality) might well render them ineffective in accomplishing the regulative function for which they *are* meant: composing the "picture" that stands behind the religious form of life.

The inherent inability of a constructivist approach to provide a patent "objectivity" inevitably leads all who struggle with this psychological problem to a more philosophical one: given the assumption that ultimate commitment to a revelation-based religion must be tied to *some* sense of divine transcendence, can we know or experience a God that is by definition beyond definition and beyond our grasp? If we accept the premise that even the "truth" of divine revelation can only be justified from within the specific vocabulary of a particular religious tradition, do we have *any* recourse to a transcendent vantage point that extends beyond the human desires, values, and visions that this tradition expresses? In other words, can we speak, from within an "as if" context, of a reality that is free of "as if"? And if not, what justification might there be for reference to overarching metaphysical claims that can only be judged from within? Does this leave us with anything more than a feeble motive for ultimate religious commitment?

Pragmatist philosopher Jeffrey Stout's wry characterization of the position he identifies as "skeptical realism" (questioning whether words refer to any predefined objective reality) illustrates the dilemma of a die-hard constructivist at this stage of religious belief:

> The skeptical realist is more like someone who wants to be his own father and then has the nature of that desire brought to light in therapy. He might be unhappy, perhaps even hard to console, upon realizing that he will never be his own father, but it's hard to see how he could have good reason for wallowing in the disappointment of such an incoherent desire. What fuels the unhappiness, it seems safe to suppose, is still half-thinking that maybe the desire does make sense (Stout 1988, 254).

The Need for a Mediating First-Order (Internal) Theology[25]

In recent years, a new stream of pragmatist philosophers (including Stout)[26] has struggled to rehabilitate some version of truth and objectivity whose authority extends beyond social consensus, communal solidarity, and pragmatics. In the concluding paragraphs of his book, Solomon may be alluding to the need to address this issue more specifically within a religious framework when he admits that classifying the doctrine of "Torah from heaven" as myth is "only one part of a bigger story" (Solomon 2012, 346).

Changing the status of the doctrine of "Torah from heaven" from historical truth to foundational myth may bypass many specific questions arising out of the clash between scientific and religious worldviews, thereby counteracting the dialectical theologians' basis for selectivity. But due to its anomalous juxtaposition of insider and outsider perspectives, and the centrality of this essentially paradoxical stance to the religious way of life, its metaphysical claims are *sui generis,* a special case. Simply assuming the conceptual coherence of a God that can communicate with man, while ignoring the dubious ontological status of such talk, is insufficient when conducted within a self-aware "as if" framework. To accomplish its psychological task, constructivist assumptions about divine communication must also examine seriously what "And the Lord spoke to Moses" might possibly mean, even beyond its own self-certifying justification as the linchpin for a spiritually meaningful way of life.

I believe that the solution to constructivist awareness in a religious context lies in developing a concept of God that blurs the sharp distinction between the natural and the supernatural, and between God's existence and human initiative. A few years ago, I undertook an interpretive project that might be regarded as a first step in this direction. On the surface, my book (Ross 2004a) was devoted to the challenge of feminism to belief in the divinity of the Torah. For me, however, feminism was merely an excuse and extreme case in point for addressing the larger issue of divine revelation altogether.

Ultimately, my suggestion was that it is possible to maintain belief in the divinity of the Torah despite the feminist critique and other marks of human imprint, by breaking down the strict dichotomy between divine speech and natural historic processes. This task was facilitated by reappropriating three assumptions that already have their basis in tradition.

The first assumption I drew upon was that if the Torah bears a message for all generations, its revelation must be a cumulative process: a dynamic unfolding that reveals its ultimate significance only through time.

The second assumption was that God's message is not expressed through the reverberation of vocal chords (not His, nor those of a "created voice" as some medieval commentators suggested in order to avoid the problem of anthropomorphic visions of God), but rather through the rabbinical interpretation of the texts, which may or may not be accompanied by an evolution in human understanding, and through the mouthpiece of history. History, and particularly what happens to the Jewish people—the ideas and forms they accept as well as the process of determining those they reject—are essentially another form of ongoing revelation, a surrogate prophecy.

The third assumption (supported by contemporary hermeneutic theory) was that although successive hearings of God's Torah sometimes *appear* to contradict His original message, that message is never totally replaced. On a formal level Sinaitic revelation always remains the primary cultural-linguistic filter through which new deviations are received and understood. By blurring distinctions between the natural and the supernatural, the finite and the infinite, I contended that it is possible to relate to the Torah as a divine document without being bound to untenable notions regarding the nature of God and God's methods of communication, or denying the role of human involvement and of historical process in the Torah's formulation. Such a view allows the religiously committed to understand that the Torah can be totally human and totally divine at one and the same time.

In my book, I applied the concept of cumulative revelation to the issue in question, suggesting that even the phenomenon of feminism—to the extent that it takes hold, and informs the life, of the halakhically committed, and that the community's authoritative bodies manage to find what they believe to be genuine support for this emerging worldview in a new reading of Torah—might be regarded by traditionalists as another vehicle for the transmission of God's word. Despite the new interpretation, the formal status of the original patriarchal model as an immutable element of the foundational Jewish canon is not supplanted or devalued, and its residual effects continue to function as a necessary prism for the achievement of greater moral sensibilities. Similarly, our current brush with the profound challenges of biblical criticism might also be regarded as expression of the divine will, perhaps indicating that we have outgrown more primitive forms of spirituality and are ready for a more sublime stage.

Not unexpectedly, my attempt to resolve the theological challenge of human imprints to a purportedly divine text got mixed reviews. I have already responded to these in other forums.[27] The question that I would like to refer to now is how far the amalgam of inside and outside perspectives that I proposed can be stretched even by a constructivist without reaching a dead end.

In endeavouring to formulate an understanding of divine revelation that cannot be rejected on rational grounds, I continue to engage with the internal language of tradition and its appeal to metaphysics. This led some critics, who did not take sufficient note of my post-liberal orientation, to critique me for retaining some residually fundamentalist understanding of the traditional account of revelation at Sinai (Schimmel 2008, 202), or of being bound to some literal notion of divine intervention in directing its interpretation

(Solomon 2012, 270). Others understood that even when asserting that God speaks cumulatively through history and the development of human understanding, I recognize, on a second-order level, that the basis for this mythic talk stems from internal rather than objective considerations.

While my theology is deliberately fashioned in a manner that can coexist with universal naturalistic understandings, it certainly is not mandated by them. For this reason, I offer my theology tentatively as a plausible, rather than a necessary or exclusive model for explaining the anomalies of belief in divine authorship of the Torah. Even when identifying strongly with this model, I realize that it can coexist with other models, and may eventually be replaced by another more illuminating picture.

Because my proposal views the appeal to a hypothetical metaphysical entity as a reality-producing construct open to revision, it is more capable of tolerating the fragility of theological explanations, recognizing them for the temporary stopgaps that they are. This arguably renders adherents of this approach better equipped for preserving their religious commitment than a less reflective believer still operating with naive ontological pretensions.

Nevertheless, given the self-awareness such a theoretical system affords, can the continued use of a mythic vocabulary—albeit of a softer sort that muddies the distinction between divine speech and natural historical process—still be taken as reference to anything more than the binding nature of the form of life that such talk supports? In the end, a narrative approach to Scripture as myth may satisfy the Orthodox requirement to relate to every word of the Torah as equally divine and laden with meaning. Nevertheless, does offering a theory of cumulative revelation within a constructivist framework amount to anything more than Kaplan's naturalism or Leibowitz's concept of religion as an exclusively man-made choice?

So long as a self-aware constructivist speaks of a totally transcendent God, the paradox of talking about this outside reality from within remains. Defending belief in the very possibility of divine speech with more naturalistic contentions regarding the method of its transmission is not enough to break out of the hermeneutic circle. If there is no real sense to speaking of something transcending the universe communicating a message to those who are within (remembering that even communication is a decidedly human concept), all talk of blurring between the natural and the supernatural in the mechanics of revelation (i.e., God speaking via history and the development of human understanding) does not really help us. To support metaphysical claims, we must also contend with the concept of God.

The very distinction between God's existence and our self-certifying perceptions needs to be overcome.

Christian theologians affected by constructivist views of truth have already produced a considerable literature devoted to this project.[28] Developing a concept of God that responds to this requirement in Jewish terms is an important item on the theological agenda of Modern Orthodoxy. I believe that this need is already being addressed intuitively on the ground, where the true destiny of any theology is really determined—in an increased interest in mysticism, in the interconnected nature of all that exists, and in a form of spirituality unmediated by reason and formal institutional structures. This is an issue, however, which deserves further treatment on a more philosophically rigorous theoretical plane, exploiting whatever paradigms Jewish tradition already provides for overcoming the paradoxical outsider–insider hurdle.[29] No doubt there will be much call for fine-tuning and revision once the implications of these paradigms spell themselves out. Nevertheless, it is to these theological vistas, rather than the inevitably doomed attempt to defeat the academic world on its own turf by debating "the facts of the matter," that the future of Orthodox responses to the challenge of biblical criticism beckons. Under such circumstances, the bounds of Orthodoxy will be determined not by any stable, precise, and definitive understanding of the metaphysical basis for the doctrines it assumes, but rather by the role that this understanding plays in the life of its adherents.

Disclosure Statement

No potential conflict of interest was reported by the author.

Endnotes

1. For a summary of the distinctions between Heschel's Torah as midrash (i.e., a human interpretation of some primal content revealed by God), Buber's understanding of Torah as response merely to the revelation of God Himself, and Rosenzweig's understanding that this silent theophany nevertheless also conveys a sense of commandedness, see Gillman (1990, 22–25). For various formulations of Jacobs regarding biblical reflections of both the human and the divine, see Jacobs (1957, 89–90; 1995, epilogue, 139; 1990, 50; 1973, 204–205, 225; 1964, 219, 270–311; 1999, 50–51).
2. http://questioningteachers.wordpress.com/discussion-reflection-and- resources/quotes-about-questions/general-quotes/.
3. By "modernist" I refer to a worldview based on the assumption of rigid and stable notions of truth, supported by a universal, neutral, and objective rationality that serves as their justification.
4. The Hungarian-born rabbi and Torah scholar, David Zvi Hoffman, was a prominent initiator of this approachap. For more recent examples, see Shavit and Eran (2007, 423–434).

Many of these responses rely on the findings of various Jewish biblical scholars such as Moshe Zvi Segal, Naftali Herz Tur-Sinai, Umberto Cassuto, and Yehezkel Kaufman who objected to Wellhausen's documentary hypothesis, despite their conclusions not necessarily confirming the notion of a onetime revelation to Moses (389–395). See also Schwartz (2012b, 203–229), Yedida (2013), and Bazak (2013).
5. See, e.g., Shapiro (2004), Kellner (2006), and Wettstein (1997, 423–443).
6. Such rejection is distinct from the recent willingness of some Orthodox thinkers to cite various Talmudic and medieval sources that already allowed for the possibility of later interpolations to the original Torah text, while generally acknowledging a qualitative difference between such isolated cases and the conclusions of more radical source theory. See, e.g., http://seforim.blogspot.co.il/2013/03/torah-mi-sinai-and- more.html and http://www.daat.ac.il/daat/kitveyet/deot/kanohel.htm. These concede the dispensability of Mosaic authorship on the basis of precedent, provided that more extended interpolations are also regarded as prophetically inspired. The reference here, by contrast, is not to rational claims, but rather to a variety of religious existentialism, which distinguishes between cognitive and non-cognitive statements, allocating a unique role to the latter in the religious sphere.
7. For broader discussion of similarities and differences between Soloveitchik's and Leibowitz's approach to Scripture, see Sagi (1997a).
8. See, e.g., Leibowitz (1976, 346–347).
9. See Sagi (1997b, 203–216) and Bareli (2007, 275–276):

> On the one hand, the religious Jew accepts the *mitzvot* as the *mitzvot* of God and accepts the yoke of the Torah as the word of God. On the other hand, he knows that these *mitzvot* and this word are human creations set down at a certain place and time. Is this not a contradiction? . . . No. The "word of God" does not point to a fact; it point to a special category of awareness on the part of the believer. To see a certain matter as the word of god is to maintain that it possesses a special status in the consciousness of the believer . . . in terms of his attitude to the word and to humanity and to fashioning his mode of life [as translated by Lawrence Kaplan; see http://kavvanah.wordpress.com/2013/02/11/conversation-with-james-kugel-a-follow-up/, comments section].

10. It is this insistence upon God's utter "Otherness" that leads to Leibowitz's radical theocentrism, since any humanistic considerations represent a form of idolatry, reducing God to the image of man by applying categories drawn from human experience.
11. The degree of reliability Leibowitz attached to biblical accounts of Sinaitic revelation, beyond their theocentric import, is unclear. According to Yaakov Levinger's testimony (Sagi 1995, 9), Leibowitz's somewhat circumspect response was that if the significance of the Sinai revelation lay in the event itself, it failed because, as biblical history teaches, there is no correlation between God's revelation and intervention in Jewish affairs and the Jewish people's willingness to believe in and worship Him. Shavit and Eran (2007, 433) nevertheless suggest that

> it would be a mistake to think that Leibowitz ascribed no value to the veracity of the historical description in the Bible . . . in particular formative events such as the Exodus from Egypt and the theophany on Mount Sinai. . . . His writings show that he also considered these as historical events not only because the Oral Law views them as such, but also because their veracity is self-evident.

This suggestion appears to be corroborated by Leibowitz's ahistorical attitude regarding some laws of biblical origin (see Ross 1995, 151), as well as his dismissive remarks regarding "heretical scientific and pseudo-scientific biblical research, better known as 'biblical criticism', when considering suggestions of post-Mosaic authorship of Deuteronomy" (Leibowitz 2004, 827–828). These examples, as others, indicate that Leibowitz's naturalistic view of revelation is more accurately attributed to his affinity with Maimonidean theology (Maimonides 1963, 2:32), according to which prophecy reflects some genuine, man-initiated absorption of the eternal divine effluence, than to the influence of modern biblical scholarship and its critical methods.

12. Such as philosopher Eliezer Goldman (see 2009). His aversion to metaphysical claims echoes Leibowitz's views and replicates the latter's resistance to grounding religious obligation on claims that draw upon empiric evidence or anthropological interests (albeit in somewhat milder form). Biblical scholar Schwartz (2012a, 30–31) contends that belief in Sinaitic revelation is a by-product rather than basis for commitment to the halakhic way of life; a similar argument, made by law professor Perry Dane (1994)—that belief or disbelief in a literal revelation at Sinai is neither necessary nor sufficient to either accepting or rejecting traditional halakhic commitment—might be regarded as another example of interest in divorcing the authority of halakhic demands from claims for supernatural intervention in human affairs.
13. For one pungent version of this critique, see Statman (2005, 64–66).
14. For application of this criticism to both Leibowitz and Soloveitchik, viewing each as limited in their attempt to understand the entire meaning of Scripture in accordance with one exclusive (normative or existential, respectively) hermeneutic principle, see Sagi (1997a, 437–440).
15. This aspect of Leibowitz's thought might be viewed as philosophic expression of contemporary Jewish Orthodoxy's need to define its religious world in terms of accepting the yoke of mitzvot as compensation for its loss of the sense of God's immediate presence, which typified premodern generations of believers. See Statman (2005).
16. See Alan Brill's blog-post (http://kavvanah.wordpress.com/2010/04/01/critique-of-kugel-1) and comment: "Acceptance of revelation is not pixie dust to magically wave over a human document. One cannot treat the Bible simply as primitive and then call it revelation." See also Sommers' critique (2010). With regard to Kugel, I believe this criticism is somewhat misplaced.

(1) The major theological thrust of Kugel's scholarly endeavours is that in Judaism the sanctity of the Torah was not determined by a Protestant-like faith in *Sola Scriptura* but on the ongoing internal interpretive tradition that it evoked. It is this understanding that leads Kugel to reject an "excavationalist" approach, irrespective of its academic merits, as totally irrelevant in a religious setting.

(2) Despite emphasising the critical role of subsequent interpretive layers in hallowing earlier biblical fragments, Kugel's reverence for such core texts does not rely solely on these later developments. Alongside traces of pagan influence and a primitive mindset, he finds elements of biblical narrative (such as depictions of Abraham's and Jacob's confusion between men and angels), and other testimonies to fleeting experiences of the sublime even before the "great Interpretive Revolution" (as he terms it), which he attributes to the closing centuries BCE. In his opinion, these can offer religious inspiration for our day, even when taken on their own.

Nevertheless, Kugel's religious privileging of the text as viewed through the lens of tradition does lead him to dismiss more contemporary methods of analysis originating from non-Orthodox sources, but increasingly embraced by Orthodox defenders of the faith as tools for demonstrating the spiritual superiority of the biblical text as it stands. Literary approaches relating to the final unified version of the Torah as their object of study, are increasingly invoked by religious advocates, suggesting that focus on the text itself leads to richer appreciation of the Torah's content. In this view, even without drawing any conclusions regarding its divine nature, this approach does facilitate an interpretative framework that draws attention to certain suggestive patterns lurking behind its "face value" which offer important spiritual and psychological insights. Given such considerations, Kugel's prejudice against the notion of a final redactor in his reconstruction of the process whereby the Bible was transformed into Scripture, contra Rosenzweig, may indeed be causing him to overlook important intra-textual nuances, and the lofty messages that can be derived from these.

Kugel's dichotomous approach to text-based scholarship versus traditional learning leads him to be even more critical of recent work conducted under the rubric of biblical theology. Unlike literary approaches, such efforts do not reject "excavational" assumptions regarding the text's multiple layers and the varying political/historical circumstances and interests that these reflect, but purport to extract redeeming moral and spiritual lessons even from these—an effort that amounts, as Kugel quips, to "having your Bible and criticizing it too." Kugel regards both methods as questionable samples of Western eisegesis, often made possible only through selective use of the evidence, however sophisticatedly masked (see "Kugel in JQR," http://www.jameskugel.com/kugel-jqr.pdf). From this perspective, ongoing attempts to discover spiritual significance in the Torah beyond the interpretive tradition laid down by the Rabbis might be taken as greater testimony to the continuing ingenuity and creativity of the human spirit than to any biblical (or divine) message of genuine religious import, despite the apologetic "feel good" use to which they are put.

17. This difference may be attributed to their differing philosophical orientations. Despite the striking resemblance that some scholars find between the role that Leibowitz accords *halakhah* in establishing the status of the Torah as the foundational text of Judaism and the approach developed by Ludwig Wittgenstein in his later writings, according to which religious beliefs do not stand independently of their function in the form of life in which they are embedded (see Sagi 1997b, 210–213, Bareli 2007), Leibowitz's dismissal of metaphysical truth claims as "nonsense" appears closely aligned to the logical positivist distinction between cognitive and non-cognitive statements established in Wittgenstein's earlier writings. Solomon's approach, by contrast (as intimated by his biographical account; see Solomon 2012, 7–8), is more likely attributable to indirect influence of Wittgenstein's later writings, according to which such claims are not nonsensical, but can only be judged from within the parameters of the language game itself, and not by appeal to objective referents "out there" that simply force such doctrines upon us. Moreover, as Sagi (1997b, 203–204) notes, although Leibowitz admired Wittgenstein, most of his ideas were framed long before publication of the latter's writings.

18. Whether biblical narratives were originally written for mythic purposes remains a moot point. Some of the Torah's genealogies or chronologies, which bear no moral or theological message, do not lend themselves to this assumption and are better understood as bona fide attempts at reporting history, whose inaccuracies simply reflect mistaken beliefs of the time. However, the fact that other aspects of the text, such as repeated barrenness of the matriarchs or even the sacrificial binding of Isaac, have striking parallels in other religions and cultures of the time (with regard to the latter and its Christian and Islamic adaptations, see Spiegel 1967), strongly suggests the influence of prevailing conventions on how tales of origin should be written, and perhaps the lack of a clear distinction between myth and systematic history in ancient times.

19. While professing personal faith that such an event did take place, Kula (2011) similarly distinguishes between the facticity of the biblical account of Sinaitic revelation and its mythic function. Kula's stance resonates with the position adopted by Rabbi A. I. Kook, who undoubtedly granted great credence to biblical accounts of early Jewish history, yet was

prepared in principle to accept Torah for its beneficial mythic influence, rather than on faith in its accuracy (Kook 1985a, 48–49).

20. For two notable precursors of this constructivist trend, see Bentham (1932) and Vaihinger (1924). More radical and contemporary extensions of this view, as represented by Continental postmodern philosophers such as Jean Boudrillard (1929–2007), reject all distinction between reality and its representation, contending that there is no truth beyond language and the depictions that we construct. Common to both is their opposition to a philosophy of objectivism, which embraces the belief that humans can come to know the natural world with varying degrees of accuracy in a form of truth that is not mediated by any interpretive approximations. Although a constructivist might, in principle, adhere to either of these positions, it would be a mistake to equate even the latter version with wholesale dismissal of truth or a denial that there is a particular state of affairs or "way things are." Rather, one must move beyond the reduction of truth in cognitive-propositional terms to a more relational, pragmatic, or communal understanding of its nature. Instead of viewing knowledge as the discovery of a fixed ontological reality, it is now understood as the product of an active ordering and organization of a world constituted by our experience.

21. For formulation and lively discussion of this and related topics, visit the Association's website (www.philosophy of Judaism.blogspot.com), particularly the symposia entitled Wettstein's "Doctrine"/"Theological Impressionism"; "Religious Belief, Make-Believe, and Science"; "Foundational Questions for the Study of Judaism"; and "Evidence and Exodus."

22. For further amplification, see Ross (2013).

23. See, e.g., Kook (1985b, 48). For further sources, and elaboration upon the precise nature of R. Kook's extension of the Maimonidean conception, see Ross (1997, 491–492). For a possible medieval precedent for this type of extension, see Twersky (1979).

24. Copied from the blog of Modern Orthoprax, 30 July, 2009, which has since been deleted from the Internet.

25. "First order" in this context designates theological understandings that are primary to any belief system, functioning in accordance with that system's own internal concepts and guidelines. "Second-order" understandings, by contrast, function less immediately, as a type of meta-view which comes to reflect, in terms that are external to the tradition, upon the talk and practice of theology from within.

26. See Levine (2010) and Misak (2007), including Stout's own contribution: "On our Interest in Getting it Right: Pragmatism without Narcissism," 7–31.

27. See, e.g., Ross (2004b, 2008). See also (2004a, chap. 11).

28. See, e.g., Cathey (2009), Griffin (1989), and Lehtonen (2012), several relevant chapters in Vanhoozer (2009) and in Hart, Kuipers, and Nielsen (1999), and the many works of Don Cupitt and John D. Caputo struggling with this issue.

29. See http://thetorah.com/the-challenge-of-biblical-criticism/ and a forthcoming Hebrew version of this paper for one paradigm I find particularly promising here, because of its ability to suggest a layered view of reality in bridging the gap between inside and outside perspectives. This paradigm, which was developed in kabbalistic writings in the modern period and has come to be known as "the allegorical interpretation to the doctrine of Tzimtzum" promoted by the sixteenth-century mystic, R. Isaac Luria, has produced several models that are fruitful for our discussion. Common to all of them is a unique mix of realism and non-realism that transfers the question of God's relationship to the world from the realm of ontology to that of epistemology. In their struggle to acknowledge the mediating role of human perception while simultaneously defending a view that makes claims upon how "faith in God" should be conducted in actual practice, I believe these models have much to offer in resolving the self-aware constructivist's theological dilemma.

Bibliography

Bareli, Gilad. 2007. "Faith and Mitzvot: 'The Content Contains No More Than What Is Embodied in Its Shell': Leibowitz's and Witgenstein's Content-laden Shells (Hebrew)." In *Y. Leibowitz: Bein shamranut leradicaliyyut-diyunim bemishnato,* ed. Aviezer Ravitzky, 267–279. Jerusalem: Van Leer/Hakibbutz ha-Meuhad.

Bazak, Amnon. 2013. *Ad hayom hazeh.* Tel Aviv: Yediot Aharonot.

Bentham, Jeremy. 1932. *Bentham's Theory of Fictions,* comp. and ed. C. K. Ogden. London: K. Paul, Trench, Trubner & Co.

Breuer, Mordechai. 1996. "The Study of Bible and the Primacy of the Fear of Heaven: Compatibility or Contradiction?" In *Modern Scholarship in the Study of Torah: Contributions and Limitations,* ed. Shalom Carmy, 159–180. Northvale, NJ: L Jason Aronson.

Cathey, Robert Andrew. 2009. *God in Postliberal Perspective: Between Realism and Non-Realism.* Surrey: Ashgate.

Dane, Perry. 1994. "The Yoke of Heaven, the Question of Sinai, and the Life of Law." *University of Toronto Law Journal* 44: 353–400.

Gillman, Neil. 1990. *Sacred Fragments: Recovering Theology for the Modern Jew.* Philadelphia, PA: Jewish Publication Society.

Goldman, Eliezer. 2009. *Yahadut lelo ashlaya,* ed. Daniel Statman and Avi Sagi. Jerusalem: Machon Hartman/Keter.

Griffin, David Ray. 1989. *God and Religion in the Postmodern World.* Albany: State University of New York Press.

Hart, Hendrik, Ronald A. Kuipers, and Kai Nielsen, eds. 1999. *Walking the Tightrope of Faith: Philosophical Conversations about Reason and Religion.* Amsterdam: Rodopi.

Jacobs, Louis. 1957. *We Have Reason to Believe.* London: Vallentine-Mitchell.

Jacobs, Louis. 1964. *The Principles of Jewish Faith: An Analytical Study.* London: Vallentine- Mitchell.

———. 1973. *A Jewish Theology.* London: Behrman House.

———. 1990. *God, Torah and Israel.* Cincinnati: Hebrew Union College Press.

———.1995. *We Have Reason to Believe: Some Aspects of Jewish Theology Examined in the Light of Modern Thought.* London: Vallentine, Mitchell.

———. 1999. *Beyond Reasonable Doubt.* London: Littman Library of Jewish Civilization.

Kaplan, Mordecai. 1967. *The Future of the American Jew.* Philadelphia, PA: Reconstructionist Press.

Kellner, Menachem. 2006. *Must a Jew Believe Anything.* Oxford: Littman.

Kook, Abraham Isaac. 1985a. *Iggrot hare'ayah.* Jerusalem: Mosad Harav Kook.

———. 1985b. *Orot ha'emunah,* ed. R. Moshe Gurevitz. Brooklyn: Langsam Associates.

Kugel, James. 2007. *How to Read the Bible: A Guide to Scripture Then and Now.* New York: Free Press.

Kula, Amit. 2011. *Havaya o lo haya: historia vesifrut safa datit, ud'mut ha'el*. Ein Tzurim: Amutat Bogrei Ha-kibbutz Ha-dati.

Lehtonen, Tommi. *2012. After Secularization: A Philosophical Study of the Preconditions of Religion.* Elon: Magnus *Publications.*

Leibowitz, Yeshayahu. 1976. "The Sanctity of Scripture" (Hebrew). In *Yahadut, Am Yehudi, uMedinat Yisrael*, 346–350. Jerusalem: Schocken.

———. 1992. "Religion and Science." In *Judaism, Human Values, and the State of Israel*, trans. and ed. Eliezer Goldman, 132–141. Cambridge: Harvard University Press.

———. 2004. *Sheva shanim shel sikhot al parshat hashavua*. Jerusalem: Dfus Hemed.

Levine, Steven. 2010. "Rehabilitating Objectivity: Rorty, Brandom, and the New Pragmatism." *Canadian Journal of Philosophy* 40 (4): 567–589.

Maimonides. 1963. *Guide for the Perplexed*. Trans. Shlomo Pines. Chicago, IL: University of Chicago Press.

Misak, Cheryl, ed. 2007. *New Pragmatism*. New York: Oxford University Press.

Ross, Tamar. 1995. "The Status of Woman in Judaism: Several Reservations Regarding the Stance of Leibowitz" [in Hebrew]. In *Yeshayahu Leibowitz: Olamo vehaguto*, ed. Avi Sagi, 148–162. Jerusalem: Keter.

———. 1997. "The Cognitive Value of Religious Truth Statements: Rabbi A.I. Kook and Postmodernism." In *Hazon Nahum: Studies in Jewish Law, Thought and History*, ed. Yaakov Elman and Jeffrey S. Gurock, 479–527. New York: Yeshiva University Press.

———. 2004a. *Expanding the Palace of Torah: Orthodoxy and Feminism*. Hanover: New England University Press.

———. 2004b. "Response to Yoel Finkelman's Review of Expanding the Palace of Torah." *Edah Journal* 4 (2): 11–25.

———. 2008. "Guarding the Treasure and Guarding the Tongue *(Shemirat ha-lashon)* Response to Aryeh Frimer's." *Review of Expanding the Palace of Torah: Orthodoxy and Feminism, Badad* 19: 93–123.

———. 2013. "Religious Belief in a Postmodern Age." In *Faith: Jewish Perspectives*, ed. Avi Sagi and Dov Schwartz, 188–240. Boston, MA: Academic Studies Press.

Sagi, Avi. 1995. "Religion without Metaphysics? Between Leibowitz and Wittgenstein" [in Hebrew]. *Mahshavot* 67: 6–17.

———. 1997a. "Contending with Modernity: Scripture in the Thought of Yeshayahu Leibowitz and Joseph Soloveitchik." *The Journal of Religion* 77 (3): 421–441.

———. 1997b. "Yeshayahu Leibowitz—A Breakthrough in Jewish Philosophy: Religion without Metaphysics." *Religious Studies* 33 (2): 203–216.

Schimmel, Solomon. *2008. The Tenacity of Unreasonable Beliefs: Fundamentalism and the Fear of Truth.* Oxford: Oxford University Press.

Schwartz, Barukh J. 2012a. *"Matan Torah:* Biblical Scholarship's Contribution to Past and Present Understanding of this Concept" [in Hebrew]. In *Mahshevet yisrael ve"emunat yisrael*, ed. Daniel Lasker, 21–32. Beersheva: Ben Gurion University Press.

_____. 2012b. "The Pentateuch as Scripture and the Challenge of Biblical Criticism: Responses among Modern Jewish Thinkers and Scholars." In *Jewish Concepts of Scripture: A Comparative Introduction,* ed. Bemjamin D. Sommer, 203–229. New York: NYU Press.

Shapiro, Marc B. 2004. *The Limits of Orthodox Theology: Maimonides's Thirteen Principles Reappraised.* Oxford: Littman.

Shavit, Yaacov, and Eran, Mordechai. 2007. *The Hebrew Bible Reborn—From Holy Scripture to the Book of Books: A History of Biblical Culture and the Battles over the Bible in Modern Judaism.* Trans. Chaya Naor. Berlin: Walter de Gruyter.

Solomon, Norman. 2012. *Torah from Heaven: The Reconstruction of Faith.* Oxford: Littman.

Soloveitchik, Joseph.B. 1992. *The Lonely Man of Faith.* Ed. David Shatz. New York: Doubleday.

Sommers, Benjamin. 2010. "Two Introductions to Scripture: James Kugel and the Possibility of Biblical Theology." *The Jewish Quarterly Review* 100 (1): 153–182.

Spiegel, Shalom. 1967. *The Last Trial—On the Legends and Lore of the Command to Abraham to offer Isaac as a Sacrifice: The Akedah. Translated and Introduction by Judah Goldin.* New York: Pantheon Books.

Statman, Daniel. 2005. "Negative Theology and the Meaning of the Commandments in Modern Orthodoxy." *Tradition* 39 (1): 55–68.

Stout, Jeffrey. 1988. *Ethics after Babel: The Languages of Morals and Their Discontents.* Boston, MA: Beacon Press.

Twersky, Isadore. 1979. "Joseph ibn Kaspi: Portrait of a Medieval Jewish Intellectual." In *Studies in Medieval Jewish History and Literature,* vol. 1, ed. Isadore Twersky, 239–242. Cambridge: Harvard University Press.

Vaihinger, Hans. 1924. *The Philosophy of As-If: A System of the Theoretical, Practical and Religious Fictions of Mankind.* Trans. C. K. Ogden. London: K. Paul, Trench & Co.

Vanhoozer, Kevin J., ed. 2009. *Postmodern Theology.* Cambridge: Cambridge University Press.

Weiss-Halivni, David. 1997. *Revelation Restored: Divine Writ and Critical Responses.* Boulder, CO: Westview.

Wettstein, Howard. 1997. "Doctrine." *Faith and Philosophy* 14 (4): 423–443.

Yedida, Asaf. 2013. *Bikoret mevukeret: Alternativot ortodoxiyot le "mada hayahdut" 1873–1956.* Tel Aviv: Mosad Bialik.

Ask the Rabbi: "Biblical Criticism is Destroying my Religious Faith!"

Yuval Cherlow

Dear Rabbi Cherlow, *shlita,*

I am writing to you in a state of profound crisis, searching for help.

To my discredit, I rejected the instruction of my rabbis and went to university. During my studies there I encountered the theory of biblical criticism for the first time. At first I rejected it absolutely, without even taking it seriously. However, over time, the arguments of biblical criticism began to appear very rational and even correct to me. I feel as though I am approaching a total collapse of my religious faith. My trust in my rabbis has also weakened considerably because they apparently know nothing about biblical criticism, and, if so, how can they be my rabbis?

I am turning to you and asking for guidance that will help me to confront all these critical arguments and still remain a believing Jew. (I am married to a very religious woman and we have children—if this is relevant.)

Please respond quickly!

Rabbi Cherlow replied:

Are you prepared to undergo a real transformation that will lead you to new spiritual heights, deep faith, and a profound connection to the Torah and its meaning? If so, the appropriate blessing for your current situation is "*pokeaḥ ivrim*" (he who gives sight to the blind) rather than "*dayyan ha-emet*" ("the true Judge," said upon hearing of a death). Both blessings express deep gratitude to God. In the first blessing, as descendants of Adam whose eyes were opened when he ate the fruit of the tree of knowledge, we give thanks out of gratitude that our eyes have been opened to new spiritual sources to satisfy our deepest yearning for the divine. In the second blessing, on the other hand, we bless God, out of pain, when a tragedy has occurred. The decision is essentially yours. Your eyes have been opened to see things that you had not been exposed to before. This experience can blind the eyes of the wise and distort the opinions of the righteous. However, it can also deepen your faith, your understanding of the Bible, your fear of God, and your observance of the commandments. It all depends on what you choose to do, and how you choose to make use of the new world that has been revealed to you. Two paths lie in front of you: light and darkness. Choose life. Not out of fear or anxiety, not by closing your eyes, but by opening them wide, by "changing the ending of the story," by transforming the darkness of criticism into the light of Torah.

Biblical criticism, as its name implies, is a method of critically reading the Bible. However, the word "criticism" can sometimes be misleading. We naturally associate the word "criticism" with the feelings of the critic, who, detached from the written text, evaluates its quality, authenticity, coherency, and morality. Moreover, the word "criticism" has a negative connotation; the critic reacts negatively to what is critiqued. When that is truly the case, one must keep a distance from the conceit of criticism that considers itself competent to stand in judgment of the holy Torah. We are committed to the Torah and this commitment is not conditioned upon the Torah's ability to pass the test of our critique.

In reality, however, and in keeping with the fundamental meaning of the word "criticism," biblical critics do not discuss whether the Bible is good or bad, or evaluate it according to predetermined criteria. The biblical critic reads the Bible with a critical eye, examining it from the outside, attempting to answer basic questions asked by the Torah itself, through the eyes of an external observer. The critic's fundamental task is to attempt to derive from within the Torah what the Torah itself says about itself. He attempts to read the Torah without preconceived ideas (as far as it is possible) or ulterior purposes, with honesty and integrity, and to examine what is in fact written in the Torah. He asks if the Torah itself indicates the date of its composition, the identity of its author, or the way in which it was given or passed down, among other questions that can be answered from within the Torah itself. It would seem therefore that biblical criticism can be approached as an aide to better understanding the Torah.

However, this is a very naïve, simplistic, and perhaps even deceptive presentation of biblical criticism. There is no doubt that many of the founders of biblical criticism deliberately intended to undermine the sanctity of the

Bible by proving that what the Torah says about itself—and certainly what the tradition says about it—is wrong, impossible, and misleading. They aimed to prove that the Torah did not emanate from one source, that its many authors lived long after its purported date, that the events recorded in it could not have occurred in the biblical period, and—above all—that it was the product of human creativity, not divine revelation. Some of the biggest supporters of biblical criticism had a very clear agenda: to destroy belief in the Bible, and thereby destroy faith that God is the source of the Bible. Some followers of biblical criticism did not share these motives. However, they presented their readings of the Bible as unprejudiced (which is, of course, impossible) and thereby undermined principles of faith and tradition. Biblical criticism joined the list of other opponents of faith—philosophers and Darwinists, archeologists and philologists, Assyriologists and physical scientists—and led to heresy and loss of faith in the Torah. For this reason, biblical criticism was regarded by religious Jews as the most heinous of spiritual outlooks and scholarly methods. It hit at the heart of the most sacred aspect of Judaism: the book of books, the holy of holies, the root of faith, and the lasting impression of divine revelation to humanity. The image of biblical criticism is so tarnished that it is not considered worth learning. In the vast majority of yeshivas, of every type and every denomination, biblical criticism is completely ignored. I would estimate that the overwhelming majority of yeshiva students are unaware of its existence even on the most basic level. They have never heard of the questions it raises or the proofs that it supplies; they do not analyze the simple meaning of the Bible with the precision demanded by the critics. They simply do not regard it as something worthy of being taken seriously. Those who do refer to biblical criticism usually deride it or caricature it, to ease their minds and justify its total neglect.

This is one possible approach. From the approach to idolatry found in the Written Torah, the Talmud, and the practical *halakhah*, we find that one method of confronting alternatives to the sacred tradition is to simply ignore them. The logic of this approach is that the very act of confronting a certain idea implies that it is worthy of confrontation, whereas ignoring it completely conveys the message that it has no standing whatsoever and is totally unworthy of attention. However, evasion also has repercussions; in this particular case, it has two. The first repercussion is internal: It is impossible to completely block out information. Many former students of yeshivas and women's seminaries are exposed to biblical criticism at a later period in their lives. Convinced by its arguments and unable to respond to its claims, they feel their faith crumble. Some even harbor resentment toward their rabbis and teachers for having deceived them by withholding this information from them. I cannot count the number of people who, having reached this state, have turned to me, begging: "Please save me from losing my faith!" Yeshivas do not even teach their students how to respond to the claims of biblical criticism. This is also the case in the yeshiva in which I teach, although my students do know of the existence of biblical criticism and are familiar with some of its questions, which I use in teaching, as I will explain below. Note that this repercussion has two aspects. First, when the student does ultimately confront the claims of biblical criticism he is unprepared, vulnerable, and defenseless. Second, the student accuses his Torah teachers of having hidden criticism's claims from him, and a feeling of having been systematically deceived grows within him.

The second repercussion is on a higher level. Our revered rabbi and teacher, Rabbi Mordechai Breuer, may his memory be for a blessing, taught us that heretical worldviews were not merely the tools of the devil. Medieval scholars, for example, did not simply dismiss Aristotle as the "dark side" or "Satan," but "converted" him and thereby turned a source of heresy into a source of faith. "Cursed philosophy" turned into a wellspring for some of the most significant creativity in Torah literature. Rabbi Breuer taught that the most profound and important principle in the worldview of an open-minded person of faith is to "produce what is noble out of the worthless" (Jer. 15:19). Biblical criticism presents a certain way of reading the Torah. One cannot close his eyes to this reading, for several reasons. First, it is impossible to close one's eyes. Even if one constructs multiple barriers, these ideas will penetrate them all—as you well know. Second, our fundamental religious outlook must be that of seeking faith not by concealment, but by openness; not by closing our eyes, but by opening them wide; not out of fear, but through searching for truth at its highest level and choosing it wholeheartedly. One also discovers that most of the central topics of biblical criticism were discussed by the sages, and their approach indicates how we should respond to the various claims of the critics. The sages also read the last eight verses of the Torah and asked how Moses could have written them. They also asked whether the Torah was given in its entirety at Sinai or in sections throughout the years of wandering in the desert. The sages understood the differences between Deuteronomy and the other four books of the Torah, and especially between the blessings and curses mentioned by Moses in Deuteronomy and those appearing at the end of Leviticus. All these matters were explored by the sages. Medieval scholars, most notably Abraham Ibn Ezra in Spain and Rabbi Judah the Pious and his students in

Germany, also discussed these issues extensively, with an open mind and motivated by a genuine search for the truth. The following example from rabbinic literature is illustrative:

> Rabbi Ḥaninah said: When God decided to create the world, he saw the future acts of the wicked—the generation of Enosh, the generation of the Flood, the Tower of Babel, and the behavior of the Sodomites—and decided not to create the world. Then he looked again and saw the deeds of the righteous—Abraham, Isaac, and Jacob—and he looked again and said: "Because of the wicked, I won't create the world?! I will create the world, and if someones sins it will not be difficult to subdue him!" He therefore decided to create the world by using the attribute of justice, but could not do so because of the deeds of the righteous. He then decided to create it using the attribute of mercy, but could not do so because of the deeds of the wicked. What did he do? He combined both of them, the attributes of justice and mercy, and created the world, as it is written, "When the Lord God made earth and heaven" (Gen. 2:4).[1]

What is the basis of this midrash? Without doubt this and other similar midrashim refer to the differences between the divine names that appear in the first and second chapters of Genesis. In chapter 1 the divinity is systematically and consistently referred to as *Elohim* (God), thereby expressing the attribute of justice. In chapter 2, however, the attribute of mercy is added, and therefore the Holy One is referred to as *YHVH Elohim* (the Lord God). This analysis also forms part of the documentary hypothesis of biblical criticism!

It would appear, then, that precisely this type of textual analysis can lead us directly to a deeper understanding of the Torah. This is only one example of many. There are countless similar topics and issues that commentators throughout the generations have addressed. However, the crucial significance of "producing the noble out of the worthless" lies in the ability to use the analytical tools of biblical criticism to understand the Torah more clearly and to discover its inner meanings.

Let me explain this another way: biblical criticism is here to stay. We cannot deny its existence, nor is there any reason to do so. It makes its claims. One who searches for the truth within *torat emet* (the Torah of truth) does not close his mind to these claims, but identifies in them textual analyses reflecting the most profound questions about the Bible. At the same time, biblical criticism makes conclusions. One who searches for the truth of the Torah does not, heaven forbid, accept these conclusions. He uses the tools that have been given him to discover his own conclusions based on the questions raised by biblical criticism and answers inspired by faith. When one takes this approach, one realizes that, in fact, the overwhelming majority of biblical commentators have also taken this path. Rather than avoiding questions they confronted them directly. We reap the fruits of their labors, and therefore it is not at all clear why we are so paralyzed by fear.

Biblical critics ask, "Is that true?" and "Is that so?" and attempt to undermine what is written in the Torah. I do not ask those kinds of questions about the Torah. I believe with perfect faith in the truth of the Torah and the halakhic obligations that derive from this truth. I, along with others who take a similar approach, ask a completely different question: What is written in the Torah? We use the tools of biblical criticism to better understand what the Torah says. As I have said, this is the path followed by all the medieval scholars both in biblical exegesis and many other fields. "Producing the noble out of the worthless" is the best way of confronting biblical criticism. In their meticulous questions about the Bible, Bible critics have helped us to clarify what the Torah itself says concerning the belief that Moses wrote the entire Torah. (Although, as I have said, the sages themselves discussed the question of the final eight verses of the Torah; Abraham Ibn Ezra discussed the "secret of twelve," the twelve verses in Deuteronomy that might indicate that Moses did not write the Torah; and Rabbi Judah the Pious discussed a wide variety of issues.) Biblical criticism has taught us to clarify what the Torah itself says regarding the concept that it was revealed in its entirety by God directly to Moses. Biblical criticism requires us to take notice of the fact that the Torah contains different writing styles.

This idea inspired Rabbi Mordechai Breuer's aspects theory. Biblical criticism raises many questions about the contradictions in the Bible. Although these questions were addressed in almost every rabbinic midrash, biblical criticism demands a comprehensive and coherent explanation for the contradictions, rather than point by point answers to specific questions.

These are all excellent ways to delve deeper into the study of the Torah. It cannot be denied that they can also lead to heresy, heaven forbid. Every light casts a shadow. Every careful analysis of the language of the Torah can lead to doubt. God also included elements in his Torah that are liable to lead to total heresy, as noted in several midrashim. However, biblical criticism's openness and linguistic analysis can lead us to a deeper and clearer understanding of the Torah. This is the path followed by the important rabbinic scholars throughout the ages in their study of the Bible. Careful analysis of the Torah and attention to its linguistic details, as well as repeatedly asking what the Torah itself says on the subject, can reveal new aspects of the Bible.

I would like to illustrate several of the new directions that knowledge of biblical criticism can open to you. I have compiled this list from questions that I have been asked on the various "Ask the Rabbi" websites. Though the list does not comprise a cohesive viewpoint, it is not an eclectic compilation. It reflects the crucial issues that engage many people who derive spiritual nourishment from the same sources that you do, and identifies the possibilities latent in interaction with the field of biblical criticism.

The first example, already mentioned above, is that the Torah itself indicates that it was not revealed in a single onetime event, but over time in a continuing process. The Ten Commandments were given at Sinai along with the "record of the covenant" (Ex. 24:7); Leviticus was given in the Tent of Meeting as explained in the first verse of the book. Numbers was revealed over the course of many years and Deuteronomy in the fortieth year. There is a fundamental difference between Deuteronomy, Moses' speech to the People of Israel that received the status of Torah, and the first four books of the Torah. The list continues. Moreover, important rabbinic scholars throughout the ages have noted that there are verses in the Torah that were said after Moses' death. The compilation of these aspects of the revelation of the Torah is not intended as an attempt to reconstruct its historical process. That, I think, would be presumptuous. Furthermore, history, as history, is not, in my opinion, one of the essential foundations of faith. However, addressing this question is a necessary condition for understanding the essence of the Torah. Does believing in the Torah mean believing that God dictated the entire Torah word for word? Or should we take a deeper look at this question, as the sages and many of the medieval rabbis did? What is the nature of divine revelation on a level inferior to that of the Torah, such as that of the prophets or divine inspiration? What is the connection between the personality of a prophet and the content of the prophecy revealed to him? These questions and others have emerged from discussion of the issues raised by biblical criticism.

Furthermore, the recognition that the Torah includes a variety of literary styles opens startling new intellectual horizons. The differences are not only linguistic. There is a long list of conceptual inconsistencies. The sabbatical year, for example, is presented in Exodus as a socio-economic measure similar to the commandments of *pe'ah* and *leket* (leaving the corner of the field and the gleanings for the poor). In Leviticus, however, the sabbatical year is presented as a *mitzvah bein adam le-makom*, a commandment relating to the relationship between man and God, whose purpose is to ensure that the land rests. The contradictions between the two passages relate even to the practical *halakhah*, specifically what should be done with the produce: "But in the seventh [year] you shall let it rest and lie fallow. Let the needy among your people eat of it" (Ex. 23:11), or "but you may eat whatever the land during its sabbath will produce" (Lev. 25:6). (The second verse does not mention the poor.) The linguistic style of the two passages also differs. This is one example of countless discrepancies between different versions of a single commandment. It can even be said that any commandment mentioned more than once in the Torah appears each time in a radically different form (with the exception of one commandment: "You shall not boil a kid in its mother's milk" [Deut. 14:21]). The sages were very aware of this fact, as evidenced by the many midrashim following the pattern of, "One verse says . . . another verse says. . . ." One of the rules by which the Torah is interpreted begins, "Two verses that contradict each other."

Moreover, the sages themselves observed that "words of Torah are poor in one place and rich in another,"[2] meaning that the same idea or commandment is expressed differently in different places. This statement raises the question: Why is the Torah written in this way? Why are the commandments not written in a uniform manner, centralized in one place, and in the same language? The answers to these questions can help us understand Rabbi Breuer's aspects theory, as well as other explanations for the contradictions and discrepancies within the Torah. This leads us to esoteric traditions that claim that God is revealed in this world in different forms and in various *sefirot* that descend to the human level, as well as to the understanding that "the Torah is written in human language." All of this enables us to understand the contradictions in the Torah, the coherence in dichotomy, controversies, how to reconcile differing perspectives, and so forth. (I devoted two chapters of my book, *Halakhah ke-Beit Hillel* [The *halakhah* follows the school of Hillel] to this subject.)

Comparisons to extra-biblical sources can aid Torah study and lead to important conclusions. Many passages in the Torah can be understood more clearly in the context of ancient Near Eastern literature. In general, it is often easier to understand a text when one has an alternative version, in the sense of "to begin with disgrace and conclude with praise."[3] This comparison not only accentuates the illumination revealed in the Torah, but also explains references within the Torah to the surrounding culture. How is it possible to understand the commandment "he must still weigh out silver in accordance with the bride-price for virgins" (Ex. 22:16) without understanding the custom of the "bride-price for virgins" in that society? How is it possible to understand the verse "I will set a king over me, as do all the nations about me" without thoroughly understanding the nature of monarchy and the image of the king in the ancient Near East? How can one understand the story of Judah and Tamar (Gen. 38) without a familiarity with the laws and customs of the surrounding society?

A good illustration of these possibilities can be found in Maimonides' discussion of the story of Judah and Tamar:

> As for the reason for the *levirate*, it is literally stated [in Scripture] that this was an ancient custom that obtained before the *giving of the Torah* and that was perpetuated by the Law. As for the ceremony of *taking off the shoe*, the reason for it is to be found in the fact that the actions of which it is composed were considered shameful, according to the customs of those times, and that on account of this the brother-in-law might perhaps wish to avoid this shame and consequently to *marry his brother's widow*. This is made manifest in the text of the *Torah: so it shall be done unto the man and so on. And his name shall be called in Israel and so on.*
>
> From the story of *Judah* a noble moral habit and equity in conduct may be learnt; this appears from [Judah's] words: *Let her take it, lest we be put to shame; behold, I sent this kid.* The interpretation of this is as follows: Before the *giving of the Torah* sexual intercourse with a harlot was regarded in the same way as sexual intercourse with one's wife is regarded after the *giving of the Torah*. I mean to say that it was a permitted act that did not by any means arouse repugnance. The payment of the hire that was agreed upon to a harlot was in that time something similar to the payment now of a *wife's dowry* when she is divorced, I mean that it was one of the rights of the woman with regard to which the man had to discharge his obligation.[4]

Maimonides distinguishes here between local customs that the Torah retained because it accepted the idea behind them, and customs that the Torah changed or forbade altogether after Sinai, such as having intercourse with a prostitute. These conclusions correspond easily to our belief that the entire Torah is of divine origin and, as I have said, open new possibilities for interpretation.

But I would like to go even further. For thousands of years we have been studying the story of the Flood, its uniqueness and the divine promise it contains, without the need to consult external sources. Yet I recommend learning the story of the Flood against the backdrop of the *Epic of Gilgamesh*. You will find that the realization that the Flood story is not unique to the Bible, but adopted by other cultures as well, a discovery that could destroy a person's faith, can also strengthen his faith, precisely because it reveals the uniqueness of the biblical narrative in comparison with other versions. These portals to new depths of meaning have opened in our generation because of biblical criticism. We are capable of following this same unique path, to "produce what is noble out of the worthless," by turning the critical approach (contrary to its intended purpose) into an aid to Torah study.

Historical narratives are not the only parallels between the Torah and external literature. I recommend undertaking a comparative analysis of the Torah and ancient legal codes. The most famous of these is *The Code of Hammurabi*, which bears a certain similarity to Exodus 21–24:18. After this comparison, obtuse readers feel compelled to admit that the Torah is not unique. Astute readers, however, perceive two things. First, they realize the similarity between the legal codes and the profound spiritual significance of this similarity. Rav Kook's thoughts on this subject are illuminating:

> When Assyriology made known its findings, many were troubled because of some similarities that were found, according to their baseless suppositions, between the teachings of the Torah and some cuneiform texts, in certain ideas, ethics, and customs. Is there any basis whatsoever for this unease? It is well known that among the ancients there were those who knew of God, prophets, and spiritual giants such as Methuselah, Enoch, Shem, Eber, and others. They must have influenced the people around them, even if they did not reach the level of influence of "Ethan the Ezrahite," that is Abraham, our father. If so, this influence must have left some impressions on their culture, and these impressions would be very similar to the Torah. Regarding the similarity in practices, both Maimonides and the sages before him understood that prophecy functions in accordance with human nature, because this nature and human inclinations must be elevated by divine guidance, as "the commandments were only given to purify humanity." Therefore, the holy Torah included within itself existing practices from before the revelation of the Torah that had ethical foundations and could be elevated to a more advanced, enduring, moral state. From a clearer perspective, this is the true foundation for the positive cultural awareness deep in the nature of man. Therefore the verse "This is the book of Adam's descendants. When God created man, He created him in God's image" (Gen. 5:1,2), is the basic principle of the entire Torah and is more important than the verse "You shall

love your neighbor as yourself" (Lev. 19:18), considered by Rabbi Akiva to be the basic principle. These and other similar matters should concern any knowledgeable person, upon his initial consideration of the issues. However, there is no basis whatsoever for the fraudulent heresy that is spreading throughout the world and being strengthened by these discoveries.[5]

When you free yourself from needless fears, you will be able to learn even more from the profound differences between the Torah and the other legal codes. Then you will understand that the Torah is deeply connected to the realities of the world. Although it was written before the creation of the world, the Torah reflects a deep understanding of the world that it creates and is created within. In certain cases, the Torah adopted Near Eastern laws; in other cases, it rejected or amended them. It had many ways of accomplishing this. All of this will open new perspectives for you. This is not merely a matter of knowing how to answer nonbelievers, or confronting claims that challenge our faith in the sanctity of the Torah or its divine origin. This study will introduce you to new ideas. What is in fact the relationship between the "ways of the world" (*derekh eretz*) that preceded the Torah and the Torah itself? I have found a wealth of material on this subject. What are the possible meanings of the saying "God looked in the Torah and created the world?" New dimensions can be added to the discussion of the relationship between the Oral and Written Torahs. Is there an innate ethical code incumbent on all human beings, or is morality contingent upon the revelation of the Torah? These, and others, are fascinating questions.

Comparing the Torah with other scientific fields opens new horizons. When we discover apparent contradictions between geological findings and the story of the creation or between historical and archeological findings and the contents of the Torah, we should not become defensive, but rather look forward enthusiastically to what we will discover. It is understood that, first of all, we have to ask ourselves if the findings in question are scientific conclusions or merely currently popular theories that will be ultimately rejected, and thus do not warrant our attention. Not everything that purports to be scientific really is science. We must distinguish between scientific theory and proven facts. Those claims that have been substantiated heighten our awareness that the purpose of the Torah is, as its name implies, to teach us how to live, not to record history. Nonetheless, we do try to reconcile the two because there should be some connection between a historical narrative and what "really" happened (if such a term can even be used now). It is however clear that, fundamentally, the Torah is not attempting to tell us what happened, but to show us what we are supposed to create within ourselves in response to what happened—active memory rather than history for its own sake. I would like to draw your attention again to the well-known words of Rav Kook:

> In reality, all of this is unnecessary. Even if it became clear that the world was created according to the theory of evolution, there would be no contradiction because we reckon according to the simple meaning of the verses, which is more relevant to us than all the preconceived ideas that we do not highly value.... The essential message is to know God, to lead a truly moral life. God even carefully allotted the spirit of prophecy. He restricted it so that when the important matters in these subjects would take shape and form, people could draw from them, with great effort, that which is most useful and lofty.[6]

I therefore advise you to listen carefully to the questions raised by the critics, and remember that many deeply religious people who understand very well the claims of biblical criticism are able to extract positive things from it. Rather than negating it and waging total war against it, they differentiate between those aspects that can actually increase our understanding of God's Torah, those that can be easily dismissed, the difficult questions that require great effort to answer, and those about which we have to pray to God for insight. I will be happy to answer all the questions I can, and if there are questions that I cannot answer, we will search together for a Torah scholar who will be able to provide us with adequate answers. If we accept these answers, all the better. If not "we will put a knife to our throats" and search for a wiser rabbi,[7] until we find the right answers. Do you feel comfortable with this approach?

Sincerely Yours,
Rabbi Yuval Cherlow

Endnotes

1. Pesikta Rabati, 40.
2. Palestinian Talmud, tractate *Rosh Hashanah*.
3. Mishnah, tractate *Pesaḥim* 10:4.
4. *The Guide of the Perplexed*, 3:49.
5. *Eder ha-Yakar* (Jerusalem: Mosad Harav Kook, 1967), 42–43.
6. Letter 91.
7. See Babylonian Talmud, tractate *H.ullin* 6a and Rashi there.

"I Shall Fear God Alone and Not Show Favor in Torah": A Conceptual Foundation for Wrestling with Biblical Scholarship

David Bigman

The thoughts that I will present in this article began to develop during my studies as a high school student at the Skokie Yeshiva. It was then that I became aware that the doctrine that the entire Torah was dictated by God to Moses seemed in conflict with the plain meaning of the biblical text. I did not dispute the exalted and binding status of the Written Torah, but I did not understand why this belief should require accepting this particular model of its composition. Though many important authorities, including Maimonides, supported contrary opinions, I clung to the understanding that I had reached from a plain reading of the sources.

I was told that questioning the story that the Torah was dictated undercut the foundation of our faith and our ability to prove its truth. On the contrary, I believed that a more complex notion of belief would be more compelling than this simplistic doctrine. Years later, I discovered biblical scholarship in its various forms, and I was astonished at the extent to which it challenged my friends' and students' worldview. In light of my personal experience, I have reformulated the ideas that occurred to me when I was young, and hope that they will help reduce the confusion that biblical scholarship causes many observant Jews.

The "Dictation" Model of Torah Revelation: "Dictation" according to Maimonides

The idea that the Torah was dictated to Moses in a single act of revelation, and, therefore, that every word and every verse of the Torah is equal to all others in importance, has become one of the foundational principles of contemporary religious education. This doctrinarian stance needlessly leads to a difficult struggle with biblical criticism.[1]

When did this become a common belief, and what are its roots in rabbinic literature and the writings of the *Rishonim*? This position was first expressed by Maimonides in his eighth principle of faith. These principles are enumerated in his introduction to Mishnah *Sanhedrin* 10:

> The eighth fundamental principle is that the Torah is from Heaven, that is to say that we believe that this entire Torah which is found in our hands today is the Torah which was given through Moses, and that it is all of divine origin. This means that it all reached him from God in a manner that we metaphorically call "speech." The exact quality of that communication is only known to Moses, may he rest in peace, to whom it came, and that he acted as scribe to whom one dictates and who writes all of it including its chronicles, its narratives, and its commandments. For this reason, he is called "the inscriber."[2] And there is no difference between: "The descendants of Ham: Cush, Mizraim, Put, and Canaan" (Gen. 10:6), or "his wife's name was Mehetabel daughter of Matred" (Gen. 36:39), or "I am the Lord your God" (Deut. 5:6), or "Hear, O Israel! The Lord is our God, the Lord is alone" (Deut. 6:4). For all are of divine origin[3] and all belong to the Law of God which is perfect, pure, holy, and true. For this reason, in the eyes of the sages, there was no greater unbeliever and heretic than Manasseh because he thought that in the Torah there are grain and chaff and that these chronicles and narratives have no value at all, and that Moses said them on his own.[4]

Following the Rabbis' statement in tractate *Bava Batra* that the entire Torah was dictated to Moses, which will be examined below, Maimonides created the principle of the uniformity and equality of all the words and verses in the Torah. According to this principle, it is considered heresy to distinguish between narrative frame and content, as well to attribute greater importance to certain parts of the Torah over others.

The Development of Maimonides' Principle of "Torah from Heaven"

We must now examine the two assumptions underlying Maimonides' words: First of all, is Maimonides' claim that Moses merely recorded God's words the only view of Moses' role in the giving of the Torah that appears in rabbinic literature? Secondly, was the idea that all the words of the Torah are equally accepted throughout the rabbinic period?

Rather than supporting Maimonides' view, a close study of the rabbinic sources reveals a more complex picture. The Mishnah, in tractate *Sanhedrin*, chapter 10, enumerates a list of people who have no portion in the world to come: "These are they who have no share in the world to come: he who says that the doctrine of resurrection is not from the Torah and [he that says says] that the Torah is not from heaven."[5]

The Babylonian Talmud takes a firm stand on the nature of the revelation of the Torah. It states that the Torah in its entirety was revealed from heaven, and that all who say otherwise are counted among those described by the verse "because he has spurned the word of the Lord" (Num. 15:31):

> Another [*baraita*[6]] taught: "Because he has spurned the word of the Lord"—This refers to one who maintains that the Torah is not from heaven. And even if he asserts that the whole Torah is from heaven, excepting a particular verse, which [he maintains] was not uttered by God but by Moses himself, he is included in "because he has spurned the word of the Lord." And even if he admits that the whole Torah is from heaven, excepting a single point, a particular *ad majus* deduction [*kal va-ḥomer*], or a certain analogy [*gezerah shavah*], he is still included in "because he has spurned the word of the Lord."[7]

A simple reading of the Mishnah indicates that the expression "Torah from heaven" at the start of this *baraita* refers to the Torah's heavenly validity. However, the continuation of the *baraita* hints that the meaning of the expression changed, and it came to be a description of the method of the transmission of the Torah. The moderate heresy described in the *baraita*—the statement that a certain verse was not said by God, but rather by Moses—is based on the assumption that all the other verses were spoken by God to Moses. If this statement is so objectionable and so grave, one must conclude that the acceptable and proper statement is that the entire Torah, with no exception, was spoken by God to Moses. This stance is also reflected in the debate over the final verses in the book of Deuteronomy that narrate Moses' death. These verses pose a problem for the model that God dictated the entire Torah to Moses, but the Talmud suggests the following resolution:

> Joshua wrote the book that bears his name and eight verses of the Torah. This statement is in agreement with the authority who says that eight verses in the Torah were written by Joshua, as it has been taught: "So Moses, the servant of the Lord died there" (Deut. 34:5). Now, is it possible that Moses was alive and wrote "Moses died there"? The truth is, however, Moses wrote up to that point, and Joshua wrote from this point onward. This is the opinion of Rabbi Judah, or, according to others, of Rabbi Nehemiah. Rabbi Simeon said to him: Is it possible that the Torah was missing one letter? And is it not written, "Take this book of Teaching" (Deut. 31:26)! No; what we must say is that up to this point the Holy One, blessed be He, dictated and Moses repeated and wrote, and from this point God dictated and Moses wrote in tears.[8]

Maimonides combines our two sources. The passage in tractate *Sanhedrin* declares that one who denies that the entire Torah is from heaven despises the word of God. However, the text does not explain what "Torah from heaven" means, even though it is the source of Maimonides' "dictation" model. The passage from tractate *Bava Batra* deals explicitly with the transmission of the Torah, but it does not address the fundamental question of "Torah from heaven." Taken together, these statements yield the view that the entire Torah was dictated to Moses by God according to the theological principle of "Torah from heaven"; those who reject this principle are indicated by the verse "because he has spurned the word of the Lord." That is to say, in his commentary on the Mishnah cited above, Maimonides created a new idea: that all parts of the Torah are unified and equal.

The Halakhic Attitude toward the Decalogue

The primary litmus test of the view that all parts of the Torah are equal is the halakhic attitude toward the biblical passages containing the revelation at Sinai and the Decalogue. With regard to this section of the Torah in particular, some *posekim* expressed concern about customs that convey a special attitude toward these chapters. When Maimonides was asked about the practice of standing when the Decalogue is read, he issued the following responsum:

> Wherever there is a custom to stand [during the reading of the Decalogue], one should stop people from doing this, *lest there result a loss of faith, when they come to believe that parts of the Torah are greater than others, and this is very grave, and one should close off any possible opening to this bad belief.* . . . And the sectarians are those for whom the fundamentals of our holy Torah are confused, and among them is one who says that the Torah is not from heaven. [The Rabbis] already explained that there is no difference between one who repudiates the entire Torah and one who repudiates one verse, saying that Moses said it himself. There are sectarians who believe that none of the Torah is from heaven except the Decalogue and that the rest of the Torah was spoken by Moses himself, and it is because of this that the daily recitation [of the Decalogue] was abolished. *And one should not under any circumstances assign greater status to one part of the Torah over others. You may investigate our words on this subject in the commentary on the Mishnah in perek Ḥelek.*—This is the writing of Moses [Maimonides].[9]

Maimonides adopted the position that it is impermissible to stand during the reading of the Decalogue in opposition to those sectarians who rejected the heavenly origin of the rest of the Torah. While Maimonides' position is based on the talmudic passage that we will consider below, it goes beyond the passage's plain meaning by stating that all the verses of the Torah are entirely equal. Since this reading is forced, it is likely that Maimonides intended this strong statement as a polemic against heretical sects, and that it does not reflect his true opinion. His source is Babylonian Talmud tractate *Berakhot* 12a:

> They recited the Decalogue, the *Shema*, the sections "Now, if you obey the Lord your God" (Deut. 11:13–21), and "And the Lord said" (Num. 15:37–41), "True and firm," the *Avodah*, and the priestly blessing. Rabbi Judah said in the name of Samuel: Outside the Temple people wanted to do the same, but [the recitation of the Decalogue] had already been abolished on account of the contentions of the sectarians. . . . Rabba b. bar Ḥanah thought to institute it in Sura, but Rav Ḥisda said to him: It has already been abolished on account of the contentions of the sectarians. Amemar thought to institute it in Nehardea, but Rav Ashi said

to him: They already abolished it on account of the contentions of the sectarians.

The Jerusalem Talmud has a parallel passage:

> Rabbi Matana and Rabbi Samuel b. Nachman both say: By law one should read the Decalogue every day. Why is it not read? On account of the claims of the sectarians, lest they say: These alone were given to Moses at Sinai.[10]

The difference between these two passages is that the Babylonian Talmud tells the story of attempts to establish the recitation of the Decalogue outside the Temple as part of the *Shema* service, following the customary practice when the Temple was standing, while the Jerusalem Talmud adheres to a basic presumption that one should recite the Decalogue every day. In any case, many commentators equated these passages and understood, rightly, that, if not for the sectarians' claims, the Rabbis mentioned in the Babylonian Talmud would have established the recitation of the Decalogue and afforded it its rightful, meaningful place.[11] Both passages recognize the Decalogue's elevated standing, but are wary of the sectarians who want to entirely invalidate the status of the other commandments.

The debate concerning the proper place of the Decalogue was reopened after the Talmudic period. Jews in later generations sought to reaffirm the special status of the Decalogue. In response to this desire, Rabbi Shlomo b. Aderet (Rashbah, 1235–1310) entirely prohibited the communal recitation of the Decalogue, relying on Shmuel's statement in tractate *Berakhot*, even though the original statement relates only to the *Shema* service.[12] Rabbi Joseph Karo (1488–1575), in the *Shulḥan Arukh*, recognized the unique status of the Decalogue and other portions of the Torah, and he recommended reciting them every day. Rabbi Moses Isserles (Ramah, 1520–1572) also recognized their uniqueness, but, in accordance with Rashbah's responsum, he noted that it is prohibited to recite the Decalogue in public. Similarly, Rabbi David Ha-Levi Segal (Taz, 1586–1667) and Rabbi Abraham Gombiner (Magen Avraham, 1635–1682) ruled that reciting the Decalogue is only permitted in private.

The Unique Status of the Decalogue

All the *posekim* agree that the Decalogue has a superior status, whether because of its content or because it was given in a special revelation. In fact, this special status is the reason why people might risk thinking that only the Decalogue is true. This position is quite far from the spirit of Maimonides' approach in his commentary on tractate *Sanhedrin* and in the responsum cited above, where he is unwilling to acknowledge any difference in status among the verses of the Torah.

The view of the *posekim* that the revelation at Sinai and the Decalogue have privileged status is supported by countless sources that discuss their uniqueness. For example, the *Mekhilta de-Rabbi Yishmael* distinguishes between divine speech at Sinai and statements in the rest of the Torah:

> "All these words" (Exod. 20:1): Scripture hereby teaches that God spoke the Decalogue with one utterance—something impossible for creatures of flesh and blood—for it says: "And God spoke all these words, saying." If so, why then is it said: "I am the Lord your God.... You shall have no other gods besides Me" (20:2–3)? Rather, it teaches that the Holy One, blessed be He, after having said all the Decalogue in one utterance, repeated them, saying each commandment separately. One might think that the other commandments of the Torah were also spoken all with one utterance. Therefore it says "these." *These words only were spoken in one utterance, but all the rest of the commandments of the Torah were spoken separately, each one by itself.*[13]

An additional example of the recognition of the importance and gravity of the Decalogue is found in *Eikhah Rabbah*. This passage interprets the first verse of Lamentations, and explains the background of the book in the abandonment of the Decalogue: "'Alas! Lonely sits' (Lam. 1:1)—Alone from those who abide by the Decalogue, which you abandoned. [This is derived from the fact that] the numerical value of *badad*, "alone," is ten.[14]

Similarly, *Pesikta de-Rav Kahana* explains the payment of the half shekel (equivalent to ten gerahs) that saved the Israelites from the plague as a ransom for abandoning the Decalogue: 'This is what everyone who is entered in the records shall pay' (Exod. 30:13)—Rabbi Joshua b. Rabbi Nehemiah said in the name of Rabbi Yohanan b. Zakai: Because the Israelites transgressed the Decalogue, each of them must give ten gerahs.[15]

It is significant that the rabbinic approach, which was completely accepted by the *posekim*, views the Sinaitic revelation as a special, onetime event, and the Decalogue as a supremely important divine utterance. Of course, they believed that the rest of the Torah was also divine truth, but it did not occur to them that a verse such as "The descendants of Ham: Cush, Mizraim, Put, and Canaan" (Gen. 10:5) was equivalent to "I am the Lord" (Exod. 20:2). Moreover, it seems that the question of how the rest of the Torah was transmitted did not trouble them. They were not compelled to depict the dictation of the entire Torah at Sinai as Maimonides did.

Unlike the view professed today, the importance that tradition ascribes to the Sinai revelation and the Decalogue points to a recognition that there are different levels of revelation, and that certain verses are relatively more important than others.[16]

Uncovering Different Kinds of Torah Passages: Sections of the Torah that have Special Status in Rabbinic Literature

Rabbinic literature exhibits several approaches to the status of the revelation of different parts of the Torah—approaches that differ substantially from that of Maimonides. I have chosen several examples from among the many sources in which this phenomenon is particularly significant.

We will begin with the approach found in the Jerusalem Talmud, in which the singularity of particular parts of the Torah is expressed in the obligation to recite blessings before and after reading them:

> Rabbi Jonathan the Scribe came here from Gufta. He saw Bar Avuna the Scribe reading the Song of the Well and reciting blessings before and after it. He said to him: Is this done? He responded: Do you still not know this? All [biblical] songs require blessings before and after them. It was asked of Rabbi Simon. Rabbi Simon said in the name of Rabbi Joshua b. Levi: The only passages that require blessings before and after them are the Song of the Sea, the Decalogue, the curses in Leviticus, and the curses in Deuteronomy. Rabbi Abahu said: I had not heard this, but these words make sense in connection with the Decalogue. Rabbi Jose said in the name of Rabbi Bon: The last eight verses of Deuteronomy require blessings before and after them.[17]

In the parallel passage in the Babylonian Talmud, there is a narrower reference to the topic with a different halakhic implication:

> A *tanna* taught: He commences his reading [of the blessings and curses that are read on fast days] with the verse before them and concludes it

with the verse after them. Abaye said: This is taught only with respect to the curses in Leviticus, but a break may be made with respect to the curses in Deuteronomy. What is the reason? In the former Israel are addressed in the plural, and Moses spoke what God said. But the latter address Israel in the singular, *and Moses said them in his own name.*[18]

This source notes that there are verses in the Torah that were spoken by Moses and not by God. This fits the plain meaning of the biblical texts, but it is the very statement that the Gemara in tractate *Sanhedrin* defines as despising the word of the Lord: And even if he asserts that the whole Torah is from heaven, excepting a particular verse that [he maintains] was not uttered by God but by Moses himself, he is included in "because he has spurned the word of the Lord."[19]

The commentators sensed the contradiction between the plain meaning of the biblical texts and the Gemara in tractate *Sanhedrin*, or else just the contradiction between the Talmudic passages. Nachmanides (1194–1270) and others claimed that although Moses spoke the words himself, at some stage God had them written down and they thus became words of the living God.[20] Rabbi Nissim of Gerona (Ran, 1320–1376) followed a similar approach. However, in light of Abaye's ruling, which argues that there is a difference between these verses and the rest of the Torah, he claims that at the end of the process a difference in status remained.[21]

"Torah from Heaven" or "The Law of Moses from Sinai"

The expressions "Torah from heaven" and "the law of Moses from Sinai" appear in rabbinic literature with various meanings that do not fit the image of the "dictation" model of the Torah. In some instances, the word "Torah" describes only parts of the Pentateuch. The expression "the law of Moses from Sinai" is applied, at times, to laws that were not revealed at Mount Sinai.

The passages that discuss Moses' rebuke of the people in the book of Deuteronomy are not the only ones that attribute different degrees of revelation to different verses. The following midrash from *Va-yikra Rabbah* describes the reception of the Torah in several stages and through different types of revelation:

A different interpretation: "The Lord called to Moses and spoke to him" (Lev. 1:1)—From here they said that a boor is better than any scholar who does not have sense. Know that this is true: Come and learn from Moses, the father of wisdom, father of the prophets, who brought Israel out of Egypt and by whose hand several miracles were performed in Egypt, "wondrous deeds in the land of Ham, awesome deeds at the Sea of Reeds" (Ps. 106:22). *He went to the highest heavens and brought the Torah from heaven*, and he was involved in the building of the Tabernacle. Yet even he did not go in to the Holy of Holies until He called him, as it says: "The Lord called to Moses and spoke to him."[22]

Va-yikra Rabbah tells the story of the formation of the Torah in a completely different way than the Babylonian Talmud in tractate *Megillah*. According to the authors of this midrash, the Torah given at Sinai is either the Book of the Covenant and the commandments relating to the Tabernacle, or Genesis and the events preceding the revelation at Sinai. This midrash argues that the "Torah" that was given from heaven at Sinai does not include the divine revelation to Moses described in the book of Leviticus, or any later, post-revelation narratives.

The difference between these views is reminiscent of the debate mentioned in the Babylonian Talmud: "Rabbi Ishmael said: The general principles were given at Sinai, and the details at the Tent of Meeting. But Rabbi Akiva said: The general principles and the details were given at Sinai, repeated in the Tent of Meeting, and repeated a third time in the plains of Moab."[23]

"The Torah" as a Term Referring to Particular Revelations or Sections

The rabbinic sources that we have seen so far suggest that the Torah was given in various revelations, as the plain sense of the verses indicates. In different places, the Rabbis used the expression "Torah from Sinai" and "Torah from heaven" in order to comment on a particular revelation, or, alternatively, on the truth of certain sections of the Torah, and not as a precise description of the means of their transmission. We have seen this usage in the *posekim*, the *Rishonim*, and the *Aḥaronim* with respect to the status of the Decalogue. In *Sifrei Devarim* it is clear that the Rabbis call only the revelation at Sinai "Torah from heaven": "A different interpretation: 'Give ear, O heavens, let me speak' (Deut. 32:1)— This refers to the fact that the Torah was given from heaven, as it says: 'You yourselves saw that I spoke to you from the very heavens' (Exod. 20:19). 'Let the earth hear the words I utter' (Deut. 32:1)—on which the Israelites stood and said, 'All that the Lord has spoken we will faithfully do' (Exod. 24:7)."[24]

Similarly, Rabbi Joshua b. Levi, refers to *parsahat* Mishpatim alone as "Torah." Another source, Babylonian Talmud tractate *Gittin* 70a, argues that the Torah was given in individual, unsealed scrolls, and that the whole Torah was therefore not given at Sinai.

The Babylonian Talmud in tractate *Sanhedrin* interpreted the idea of "Torah from heaven" that appears in the Mishnah as a description of the means of transmission of the Torah. However, as is generally the case in rabbinic literature, this is not always what the expressions "from Heaven" and "from Sinai" indicate. In *Kohelet Rabbah*, Rabbi Nehemiah includes the additional writings (the Tosafot) of the house of Rabbi and Rabbi Nathan, and "even what a senior student will say to his teacher in the future," within the rubric of the "law of Moses from Sinai":

> Rabbi Nehemiah says: "Thus the greatest advantage (*yitron*) in all the land is his" (Eccles. 5:8)—Things that seem extra (*meyutarin*) in the Torah, such as the additional writings of the house of Rabbi and the additional writings of Rabbi Nathan, and the laws of sojourners and slaves—even these were given to Moses at Sinai. And, for example, the laws of *tzitzit*, tefillin, and *mezuzot* are included in "Torah," as is written, "And the Lord gave me the two tablets of stone inscribed by the finger of God, with the exact words" (Deut. 9:10); and it says there "all the instructions that I enjoin upon you" (Deut. 8:1). Not only "all" but "according to all"; not only "words" but "the words"; not only "commandments" but "the commandments." This means that Scripture, the Mishnah, the law, the Talmud, additional writings, legends, and even what a senior student will say to his teacher in the future were all given to Moses at Sinai.[25]

Likewise, the Jerusalem Talmud also implies that there are legal rulings that are considered "law of Moses from Sinai": Rabbi Lazer said: "Everywhere where they learned truth (*be-emet*), it is the law of Moses from Sinai."[26]

The problem is that the phrase "they spoke in truth (*be-emet*)" is also applied to things that are clearly rabbinic in origin. Thus, Rabbi Asher b. Yehiel (Rosh, ca. 1259–1327), referencing Rabbi Isaac b. Samuel of Dampierre (Ri the Elder, 1115–1184), writes:

> Ri says that we do not find anywhere that the rules of what invalidates a ritual bath are the "law of Moses from Sinai." And if we do find a source that states this, we should interpret it in accordance with the meaning of

this phrase in the *baraita* in tractate *Ḥagigah:* "There is a law of Moses from Sinai that the lands of Ammon and Moab are subject to the laws of the poor tithe in the sabbatical year,"[27] which means only: *This is a clear ruling, as if it were a law given to Moses at Sinai.* Moreover, any time the term "in truth" (*be-emet*) is used, it is a law [of Moses from Sinai, so to speak], as it says throughout the Talmud regarding matters of rabbinic origin.[28]

Echoes of Maimonides' View in Medieval Biblical Interpretation: Nachmanides

The two sections of the Babylonian Talmud that describe the writing of the Torah as dictation by God profoundly influenced later commentators. Nachmanides, for example, wrote in an introduction to his commentary on the book of Genesis:

> But Moses wrote the history of all former generations and his own genealogy, history, and experiences in the third person. Therefore he says, "The Lord spoke to Moses, saying" (Exod. 6:10, etc.) as if he were speaking about another person. And because it is so, Moses is not mentioned in the Torah until his birth, and even at that time he is mentioned as if someone else was speaking about him. Now do not find a difficulty in the matter of Deuteronomy, wherein he does speak about himself—"I pleaded" (Deut. 3:23), "I prayed to the Lord" (9:26), "I said" (1:9, etc.)—for the beginning of that book reads, "These are the words that Moses addressed to all Israel" (1:1). Thus throughout Deuteronomy he is like one who narrates things in the exact language in which they were spoken. The reason for the Torah being written in this form is that it preceded the creation of the world, and, needless to say, the birth of Moses, in keeping with the Kabbalah's statement that it was written in black fire on white fire. Thus Moses was like a scribe who copies from an ancient book, and therefore he wrote anonymously. *However, it is true and clear that the entire Torah—from the beginning of the book of Genesis to [the last verse in Deuteronomy,] "before all Israel" (34:12)—reached the ear of Moses from the mouth of the Holy One, blessed by He*, ***just*** as it is said elsewhere [where Baruch the scribe describes his writing the words of Jeremiah]: "He himself recited all those words to me, and I would write them in the scroll in ink" (Jer. 36:18).[29]

In this passage, Nachmanides struggles with one of the obvious problems that the plain meaning of the biblical texts creates for the "dictation" model. If Moses wrote the Torah, why is the book of Genesis narrated by an omniscient third person narrator, while the book of Deuteronomy is narrated by Moses in the first person? Nachmanides explains that the earlier parts of the Torah are related by an omniscient narrator because Moses is not mentioned in the Torah until the moment of his birth, "his entry into the story." He also explains why there is no gap between Moses' knowledge and the contents of the Torah: the entire Torah preceded the creation of the world, and was dictated to Moses by God. It is important to note that Nachmanides elaborates considerably on the quoted passage. While the text merely states "Moses wrote," Nachmanides argues that the entire Torah preceded the world, and that Moses wrote exactly what God said, just as Baruch the Scribe wrote exactly what Jeremiah said. The solution that Nachmanides proposes explains the changes in genre within the Torah in accordance with the Babylonian Talmud's model of dictation. It creates a harmonized picture that obscures the contradictions between this model and the plain meaning of the biblical texts. However, Nachmanides does not claim that all the verses of the Torah are equal.[30]

Abarbanel

Don Isaac Abarbanel (1437–1508), following Nachmanides, explains more broadly that the prophets themselves composed all the poetic passages in the prophetic books:

> From this you should know and understand that every poem found in the words of the prophets is something they composed themselves with divine inspiration and not something they saw in prophecy.... Poetry is the prophet's work, composed according to the holy spirit within him, not a vision shown to him in prophecy. Therefore, Scripture always attributes [the poem] to the prophet who composed it, as it says in the Song of the Well, "Then Israel sang" (Num. 21:17); [and likewise:] "Deborah and Barak son of Abinoam sang" (Judg. 5:1); "The Song of Songs, by Solomon" (Songs 1:1); and Isaiah says, "Let me sing for my beloved" (Isa. 5:1)—the song is attributed to him as the one who composed it. So, too, in the case of the Song of the Sea it says "Then Moses and the Israelites sang this song.... They said: I will

sing to the Lord" (Exod. 15:1), which is to say that they themselves composed it and sang it. Thus, at the end they prayed for their success: "Terror and dread descend upon them" (15:16), "You will bring them and plant them" (15:17). . . . It was thus with the Song of the Sea, which Moses composed to praise and laud the God who answered him in the time of his distress, and for this Miriam his sister also composed a song with tambourines and dance, as explained further on. Indeed, these songs were written in the Torah and in the words of the prophets because God received them and favored them and commanded that they be written there. *If so, the composition of this song was by Moses, and its inclusion in the Torah was from God.*[31]

Abarbanel explains that the poetic texts in the Torah were divinely inspired; they were composed and sung by the prophets. Nonetheless, their inclusion in the Torah and the prophetic books was by divine command.

Distinguishing between Different Types of Biblical Texts

At this stage, it is worth noticing that the *Rishonim* identified and distinguished between different genres and the different content that they communicate. For example, the opening phrase "The Lord spoke to Moses, saying" is always understood as the narrator's introduction to the binding legal content spoken by God, while the narrative portions of the Bible begin with "When God began to create" (Gen. 1:1) expressed from the viewpoint of the narrator. Each style has a different role and status.

The poetic texts and the book of Deuteronomy attracted great attention because the sages sensed that the Torah did not present them as words that were spoken in the course of prophetic revelation. They discerned the singularity of the revelation at Sinai and similar revelations relative to the "regular" prophecy of Moses. Nachmanides and Abarbanel, whose words we have read above, faced a difficult contradiction: a narrow reading of the Torah creates the impression that it includes various genres from different times and revealed in different ways, in contrast to the model of "dictation" and equality. The solution they proposed was to distinguish between the creation process of the different parts of the Torah, and the process by which they were written. The different parts were revealed and took shape in a lengthy process and in various ways. It was only afterward that God commanded Moses to record these words in the Torah.

Or ha-Ḥaim—Chaim ibn Attar

At the beginning of his commentary on Deuteronomy, Rabbi Chaim ibn Attar (1696–1743) went far beyond Nachmanides and Abarbanel in his distinction between the words that Moses wrote himself and the words he heard from God:

> "These are the words" (Deut. 1:1)—These exclude the preceding, which is to be interpreted as follows: Because it says "that Moses spoke," meaning that they are his own words, the entire book of rebuke is Moses' reproof of those who transgressed the word of God. Our sages said that the curses in Deuteronomy were spoken by Moses himself, and even where he repeated and interpreted the Lord's earlier statements *he was not commanded to do so; rather, he himself repeated the words.*[32] Scripture took pains to say this because [one might think] that just as Moses spoke such words himself, so too in earlier speeches Moses said some things himself. Rather, he did not say even one letter himself of everything in the preceding four books of the Torah, only the words that came from mouth of the Commander in their original form, without any alteration, even adding or removing one letter.[33]

Ibn Attar's views contradict the "dictation" model. He states simply that the entire book of Deuteronomy is Moses' book; he was not commanded to reveal it, but rather spoke on his own accord. In spite of his strong words about the other books of the Torah, which Moses did not compose "even one letter himself," Ibn Attar recognizes the uniqueness of poetry, and claims that, after an appropriate preparation, Moses himself recited the Song of the Sea: "'Then [Moses] sang' (Exod. 15:1)—It did not have to say 'then,' only 'Moses sang,' and it would be understood that [Moses and the Israelites] sang then. However, Scripture means to inform us of the preparation of the idea. For when the awe of [God's] majesty and full faith entered their hearts, then they merited to utter the song with divine inspiration."[34]

Beyond the "Dictation" Model

All the commentators presented thus far agree with the "dictation" model, even though they sensed the Torah's different genres and the difficulties that their presence poses for this position. But the assumption that the entire Torah was dictated by God to Moses was a matter of dispute among the *Rishonim*. Rabbi Abraham Ibn Ezra (1092–1167) often alludes to this dispute, and Rabbi Judah Ha-Chasid (1140–1217) says so explicitly in his commentary. Rabbi Joseph ben Eliezer Bonfils (Tov Elem, 14th cent.), author of the *Tzofnat Paneaḥ*, a supercommentary on Ibn Ezra, went so far as to differentiate among the genres in the Torah (Gen. 12:6), claiming that although the sections containing commandments were composed by God, prophets were allowed to add their own words to texts of other genres in order to explain and interpret them.[35]

Reclaiming the Multi-Genre Perspective: Time to Reevaluate "Necessary Belief"

In presenting the Torah as uniform and equal, Maimonides made an important contribution to Jewish belief. His view affirms the exalted and binding status of the Torah—a status that I would certainly never contest. In light of what we have seen, however, it seems to me that the time has come to revive the predominant view of the Rabbis, the *posekim,* and the commentators. This view identifies different genres in our Torah that testify to diverse facets of revelation and different levels of importance. In a passage that appears in *Orot ha-Emunah* and in *Shemonah Kevatzim,* Rav Kook distinguishes between two types of beliefs: "All beliefs can be divided into the two systems that Maimonides identified: true beliefs and necessary beliefs. The true beliefs are the foundation that sustains the principles of faith, and the necessary beliefs are like a peel protecting the fruit."[36]

At times, one of the "necessary" beliefs becomes extraneous, and it may even harm true belief:

> Sometimes it becomes imperative to banish one of the "necessary" beliefs from the sphere of faith, because the collective has already arrived at a level at which it no longer needs to be supported by this "necessary" part of the belief system. Then a kind of turbulence begins: from one angle, it looks like a breach of the foundation of the faith, while from the other it looks like a light appearing on the horizon of faith and a reinforcement of its foundations. And in fact, there is truth to both perspectives.[37]

My prayer is that the publication of these ideas will strengthen the foundations of faith, discarding beliefs that, while once necessary to protect true belief, now merely cause confusion.

Maharal: Two Views of the Torah

The perspective of Rabbi Judah Loew of Prague (Maharal, 1520–1609) can serve as an opening to a broader view of the arc of literary genres found in the Torah, based on a complex picture of divine revelation.

> The intention of this is not, God forbid, to say that Moses said something himself, even one letter. Only [to observe] the distinction between Deuteronomy and the rest of the Torah. For the Torah that blessed God gave to Israel contains two points of view: One point of view is that of God, who gave the Torah. The other point of view is that of Israel, which received the Torah. If one person gives something to his fellow and they are of equal standing, there is only one point of view, since both are at the same level. But when blessed God, who is above everything, gave the Torah to Israel, and they were on earth, it was impossible for there not to be a special point of view from the perspective of the giver and a different point of view from the perspective of the receiver. Therefore, the entire Torah, except Deuteronomy, which is the last book, is told from the point of view of the giver. Because the receiver receives at the end, after the giver has finished his decree; only then does the receiver receive. This is why Deuteronomy is called *mishneh Torah* [the reiteration of the Torah], as if it were a distinct thing, which is from the perspective of the receiver. And there is a particular point of view on the receiver's end, as it says in Deuteronomy: "Moses undertook to expound this Torah" (1:5), for the receiver needs more interpretation and explanation. And this is the distinction between the "Torah" [the first four books] and the *mishneh Torah* [Deuteronomy].[38]

In prophecy, and even in Moses' prophecy, the Maharal sees an encounter between God and humanity. Prophecy is a phenomenon that will always have a divine facet and a human facet. On the basis of these words, albeit not necessarily in their original meaning, I would like to propose the following perspective, which allows us to read the Torah and be impressed by the full variety found in it.

The entire Torah is situated between the point of view of the giver and the point of view of the receiver, and the various genres that we identify in the Torah express particular points along the continuum of communication between the infinite and human beings. This observation enables a "close reading" of the

Torah, free of apologetics, but guided by the fear of heaven. All reality stands between that which is given from heaven and human observation. Therefore, a human being can experience various points of contact between these two poles. I do not claim that these encounters, even sublime experiences of self-nullification or inclusion, are true prophecy. Prophecy is a special phenomenon. The prophet succeeds in expressing the will of God in an edict designed to shape and direct the behavior of all people. In contrast, other inspirational experiences are expressed morally, poetically, or artistically, but not normatively. In biblical prophecy, the prophet receives verbal messages that can be translated into practical guidelines. A plain reading of the Torah, without prior assumptions, inevitably leads to the conclusion that the Torah does not present itself as uniform, but rather the opposite: its various parts take the form of diverse literary genres that embody different facets of revelation.

This reading accords with the care that the Torah takes to note the context of a given revelation, such as, "The Lord called to Moses and spoke to him from the Tent of Meeting, saying" (Lev. 1:1), or the context of a prophetic speech, such as, "These are the words that Moses addressed to all of Israel" (Deut. 1:1). The care the Torah takes to distinguish genres reveals the significance of their different revelatory characters.

Conclusion: The Value of Modern Biblical Scholarship

It is critical to recognize the methods of biblical scholarship as *interpretive tools* in the toolbox of the Torah student, tools that can shed light on the Torah's composition and formation. Biblical scholarship can help us understand difficult passages that we otherwise would not have been able to interpret. On the other hand, we must not forget that these tools cannot judge the revelation of our holy Torah. Science is a technical tool; it does not have the capacity to determine the value and meaning of the things it investigates.

An analysis of the historical formation of our Torah can never touch the secret of the encounter between humanity and God. Even after many years in which cultures changed and new scientific tools were developed, the individual who ties his soul to the Torah is able to experience something of this encounter. Biblical scholarship does not impinge on the exalted stature of the Torah, just as the study of art is not able to expose the inspiration behind painting, musical composition, literature, and poetry.

What theology, then, is relevant in our generation, and how can we direct our students toward it? It seems to me that there is no other option but to let go of the "dictation" model, which does not accord with the simple meaning of the biblical texts or modern biblical scholarship. Prophecy is communication between God and humanity, so it is inevitable that our Torah should contain echoes of the language and culture of the time when it was revealed.[39] Even the Torah, which was given as a foundational and binding document, is not an exception to this rule. Rabbinic literature offers a key to an appropriate view of revelation: "The Torah speaks in the language of human beings."[40] This indicates that communication between the infinite and humanity is tied up in human language and constrained by human limitations, especially the limitations of time and place.[41] But when there is a notion of absolute difference between God and humanity, this view only causes surprise.

This notion, which is pervasive in many circles of Western philosophy in our time, need not discourage us from expressing the view that there can be encounters with the sublime, the mysterious, and the wondrous. There is no reason to renounce the traditional view that our Torah is a prophetic document with no peer in human history. Our Torah is a faithful expression of God's will, translated into human language, with all that it entails. The process of its creation is complex, and includes different prophetic moments that occur in the wondrous course of communication between God and the human beings created in His image and likenes

Endnotes

The author would like to thank Ilan Wolff for helping prepare the English version.
1. For some other approaches to the "dictation" problem, see Samuel Fleischacker, "Making Sense of the Revelation at Sinai," *TheTorah.com*, accessed September 12, 2016, http://thetorah.com/making-sense-of-the-revelation-at-sinai/; and Baruch Schwartz, "'The Lord Spoke to Moses'—Does God Speak?," *TheTorah.com*, accessed September 12, 2016, http://thetorah.com/does-god-speak/.
2. The original Hebrew is *meḥokek*; the term also means "lawgiver."
3. Moshe Feinstein, *Sefer Iggerot Moshe* (New York: M. Feinstein, 1985), 6:358–359 (*Yoreh Deah*, pt. 3, §114, s.v. *she-kibalti me-aḥer*).
4. The translation is adapted from Maimonides, *Commentary on the Mishnah*: Tractate *Sanhedrin*, trans. Fred Rosner (New York: Sepher-Hermon Press, 1981), 155.
5. Mishnah, tractate *Sanhedrin* 10:1. The translation is adapted from Herbert Danby, trans., *The Mishnah* (Oxford: Oxford University Press, 1933), 397.
6. A *baraita* is a traditional interpretation or statement of biblical law from the mishnaic period not incorporated in the Mishnah.
7. Babylonian Talmud, tractate *Sanhedrin* 99a.
8. Babylonian Talmud, tractate *Bava Batra* 15a.
9. Maimonides, *Teshuvot ha-Rambam*, ed. Joshua Blau (Jerusalem: Reuven Mass, 1989), 498 ("Laws of Prayer and the Priestly Blessing," 12:263).

10. Jerusalem Talmud, tractate *Berakhot* 1:5.
11. See the commentary of Rabbi Nissim Gaon and Rashi on Babylonian Talmud, tractate *Berakhot* 12a; *Sefer Abudirham*, "Laws of Recitation of Shema," in *Abarbanel ha-Shalem* (Jerusalem: Usha, 1963), 84–85. See also Yechezkel ben Yehuda Landau, *Tselaḥ ha-Shalem* (Jerusalem: Vagshal, n.d.), 48, on Babylonian Talmud, tractate *Berakhot* 12a, s.v. *sham le-mikba'inhu be-Nehardea vekhuleh*.
12. Rashbah, *Sefer Sheilot va-Teshuvot* (Jerusalem: Mechon Tiferet ha-Torah, 1990), 86 (1:184), 123 (1:289).
13. *Mekhilta de-Rabbi Yshmael*, Yitro, de-be-ḥodesh, *parashah* 4.
14. *Midrash Eikhah Rabbah*, ed. Salomon Buber, *parashah* 1.
15. *Pesikta de-Rav Kahana*, ed. Bernard Mandelbaum, *parashah* 2 (Ki Tetse').
16. In modern scholarship, there is also a debate over the status of the Decalogue. Moshe Weinfeld claims that "among all the laws, only the list of commandments in the Decalogue is perceived as foundational and primary in the establishment of a connection between God and Israel. It was only the Decalogue that the Israelites merited hearing straight from the Deity's mouth." See his "Uniqueness of the Decalogue and its Place in Jewish Tradition," in *The Decalogue in History and Tradition*, ed. B. Z. Segal (Jerusalem: Magnes, 1990), 1–34. Yair Hoffman claims to the contrary that there are no explicit references to the Decalogue in the Bible except in three places, and that the supposed echoes of them are not conclusive. See his "The Status of the Decalogue in the Hebrew Bible," in *The Decalogue in Jewish and Christian Tradition*, eds. H. G. Reventlow and Y. Hoffman (New York: T&T Clark, 2011), 32–49.
17. Jerusalem Talmud, tractate *Megillah* 3:7.
18. Babylonian Talmud, tractate *Megillah* 31b.
19. Babylonian Talmud, tractate *Sanhedrin* 99a.
20. Nachmanides discussed this in his introduction to Genesis (*Torat Ḥayim: Ḥamiseh Ḥumshei Torah*, ed. Mordechai Katzenelenbogen [Mosad Harav Kook, 1986], 15–19), and Don Isaac Abarbanel also discussed it extensively at the beginning of his commentary on the book of Deuteronomy. See, e.g., his comments on the opening words of Deuteronomy (*Perush al ha-Torah* [Jerusalem: Benei Abarbanel, 1963], 8). His contemporary, Rabbi Isaac b. Rabbi Joseph Karo, uncle of Rabbi Joseph Karo, discussed it repeatedly in his book *Toldot Yitzḥak* (Jerusalem and Bnei Brak: Siaḥ Yisrael, 1981). See, e.g., his discussions of Deuteronomy, beginning on p. 138, and elsewhere.
21. See Ran's comment on the Rif to Babylonian Talmud, tractate *Megillah* 11a, s.v. *Hallalu Moshe mi-pi atsmo amran*.
22. *Midrash Va-yikra Rabbah*, ed. Mordechai Margoliot, *parashat* Va-yikra', 1. See also *Eliyahu Rabbah*, ed. Meir Ish-Shalom, *parashah* 7. And *Avot de-Rabbi Natan*, A, 1: "The Torah was given by Moses at Sinai, as it says: 'He inscribed them on two tablets of stone, which He gave to me' (Deut. 5:19). And further on it says: 'These are the laws, rules, and instructions that the Lord established, through Moses on Mount Sinai, between Him and the Israelite people' (Lev. 26:46).''
23. Babylonian Talmud, tractate *Ḥagigah* 6a; Babylonian Talmud, tractate *Sotah* 37b.
24. *Sifrei Devarim*, *parashat* Ha'azinu, 306.
25. *Kohelet Rabbah* 5:2, 27; likewise, *Shemot Rabbah*, ed. Avigdor Shinan, *parasahat* Va-'era', 10. And it would be impossible not to cite the Babylonian Talmud, tractate *Menaḥot* 29b, which describes Moses' visit to Rabbi Akiva's house of learning; the latter refers to a law that he is teaching, which Moses does not recognize or understand, as "law of Moses from Sinai," and it is clear that this is not a historical description. See Shmuel Safrai, "Halakhah le-Moshe

me-Sinai: Historiah o Teologiah?" (The law of Moses from Sinai: History or Theology?), in *Meḥqerei Talmud* 1, ed. Yaacov Sussman and David Rosenthal (Jerusalem: The Magnes Press, 1990), 11–38. In his treatment of the Gemara in *Menaḥot*, Safrai writes: "Moses does not understand even the very law that Rabbi Akiva calls a 'law of Moses from Sinai' because Rabbi Akiva innovated in the law, and because they refer to words of Torah as the 'law of Moses from Sinai.' This means that everything that is created and erected as a Jewish law has its origin in the law of Moses, and it is a continuation of the course of the Torah and law that was given to Moses at Sinai and spoken at Horeb."

26. Jerusalem Talmud, tractate *Kilayim* 2:27; see also Jerusalem Talmud, tractate *Terumot* 2:41; Jerusalem Talmud, tractate *Shabbat* 1:3 and 10:12; Jerusalem Talmud, tractate *Nazir* 7:56.
27. Babylonian Talmud, tractate *Ḥagigah* 3b.
28. Rosh, *Piskei ha-Rosh*, tractate *Niddah*, "Laws of Ritual Baths," 1, and following.
29. The translation is adapted from Nachmanides, *Commentary on the Torah*, trans. Charles B. Chavel (New York: Shilo Publishing House, 1971).
30. My general impression from reading his commentary is that Nachmanides recognizes the uniqueness and special significance of different parts of the Torah. I hope to return to this subject in the future.
31. Abarbanel on Exod. 15. He offers a similar explanation of *parashat* Ha'azinu (Deut. 32, ad loc.)
32. See Babylonian Talmud, tractate *Megillah* 31b.
33. Chaim ibn Attar, *Sefer Or ha-Ḥaim* (Jerusalem: A. Blum, 1990), 1 (Deut. 1:1).
34. Chaim ibn Attar, *Sefer Or ha-Ḥaim*, 89 (Exod. 15:1).
35. This is also the way Rabbi Bonfils understands the passage in tractate *Sanhedrin*. See Zev Farber, "The Significance of Ibn Ezra's Position that Verses were Added to the Torah," TheTorah.com, accessed September 26, 2016, http://thetorah.com/the-significance-of-ibn-ezras-position/; and "Seven Torah Passages of Non-Mosaic Origin according to Ibn Ezra and R. Joseph Bonfils," TheTorah.com, accessed September 26, 2016, http://thetorah.com/non-mosaic-torah-passages-ibn-ezra-and-bonfils/.
36. See Maimonides, *The Guide of the Perplexed*, 3:28. See also Rav Avraham Yitzhak Hacohen Kook, *Orot ha-Emunah* (Jerusalem: Me-alef ve-ad Tav, 1998), 48.
37. Kook, *Orot ha-Emunah*, 48.
38. Maharal, *Sefer Tiferet Yisrael*, chap. 43.
39. See the chapters on prophecy in Maimonides, *The Guide of the Perplexed*, 2:32–39. See also Rabbi Joseph Albo, *Sefer ha-Ikarim* (Jerusalem: Feldheim, 2011), 290–294, 328–332 (*ma'amar* 3, chaps. 9 and 17).
40. This quote appears frequently, beginning with texts from tannaitic times. See, for instance, Babylonian Talmud, tractate *Nedarim* 3a.
41. See the article of my student Dr. Chezi Cohen in this volume. My position is similar to his.

Revelation and Religious Authority in the Sinai Traditions

Benjamin Sommer

What, exactly, did the Israelite nation see and hear at Sinai?

This is no merely academic query. The event that transpired at Mount Sinai some three months after the Exodus belongs to the threefold cord that is fundamental to all Jewish existence. Along with the redemption from slavery and the gift of the Land of Israel, the experience at Sinai created the amalgam of religion and ethnicity known as Judaism.

Everyday religious Jews recite the blessing, "Blessed are you, Hashem our God, King of the Universe, who chose us from among all the peoples and gave us his Torah." In *Pirkei Avot* we learn that "Moses received Torah from Sinai." But what do the verbs "give" and "receive" mean in these contexts? As the authority of the *halakhah* and the sanctity of the Bible rest upon these words, a thorough analysis of their meanings is in order.[1] This inquiry is particularly important in our time, as the conclusions of biblical criticism and rational-philosophical skepticism have made it difficult for modern Jews to believe in the revelation at Sinai, at least in its pure, straightforward, simplistic formulation. Many Jews, including those who are observant, find it difficult to believe that God dictated all the words of the Torah to Moses, who then wrote them down "like a scribe taking dictation."[2]

Moreover, the Pentateuch contains internal inconsistencies and intellectual and ethical difficulties. There are verses in the Torah that command us to kill innocent people from the seven nations and Amalek, including children and babies. It is difficult to believe that these verses express the will of a merciful and just God. The identification of human elements in the Bible solves some of these problems but raises others: How is it possible to remain faithful to the Torah yet at the same time analyze it with intellectual objectivity? How can we both love a tradition and emend it? If some of the laws and commandments in the Torah were not written by Moses as dictated directly by God, but are instead the work of human scribes and lawmakers, what authority do they have?

One twentieth-century solution to this problem was to understand revelation as an interactive dialogical process. Proponents of this school of thought include Franz Rosenzweig and Abraham Joshua Heschel, as well as Nahum Glatzer and Louis Jacobs. According to these thinkers, revelation was a reciprocal process to which God and the Jewish people both contributed. To be more precise, the people received a divine message and reacted to it. The Bible is the product of those reactions. This well-known opinion was expressed by Rosenzweig in a letter to Martin Buber: "The primary content of revelation is revelation itself. 'He came down'—this already concludes the revelation; 'He spoke' is the beginning of interpretation, and certainly 'I am.'"[3]

In his book *God in Search of Man*, Rabbi Heschel explained:

> As a report about revelation the Bible itself is a midrash. . . . Judaism is based upon a minimum of revelation and a maximum of interpretation, upon the will of God and upon the understanding of Israel. . . . There is a partnership of God and Israel in regard to both the world and the Torah: He created the earth and we till the soil; He gave us the text and we refine and complete it. "The Holy One, blessed be He, gave the Torah unto Israel like wheat from which to derive fine flour, or like flax from which to make a garment."[4]

Both these thinkers viewed revelation as an actual event and rejected the idea that the revelation at Sinai was a metaphor or a mythological prototype. Moreover, Heschel, and in my opinion also Rosenzweig, understood this event as authoritative—in other words, as an event in which God gave authoritative instructions to the People of Israel.[5] Nonetheless, both also raised doubts about the precise nature of the event and argued that it is impossible to know exactly what happened there, or to what extent the specific commandments in the Torah are of divine origin. In their opinion, the text of the Torah is a human reaction to, or interpretation of, an event in which the divine will was expressed by supralinguistic means. Thus, Rosezweig and Heschel encourage us both to accept the Torah as authoritative in the halakhic sense and to question it.

They challenge us to wonder to what extent are its laws of divine origin? Their writings leave the reader to ponder the nature of the Torah: is it perfect and divine, or human and always tending towards perfection?[6]

Revelation in the Book of Exodus

These questions are not new. A careful reading of the biblical narrative of the revelation of the Torah at Sinai uncovers hints of these questions in the biblical text itself. These hints raise the possibility that the connection between the divine voice and the text ascribed to Moses is not simple. In this article, I would like to discuss several such textual phenomena in Exodus and Deuteronomy.

Several textual ambiguities in Exodus 19–24 raise the question: Did the people hear the Ten Commandments directly from God or only through Moses, acting as an intermediary? Did the people hear certain words and commandments directly from heaven, or did they hear all of them through an intermediary human voice? To answer this question, I will examine four textual phenomena:

The **first phenomenon** is the meaning of the word *qol* (which can be translated as "sound," "voice," or "thunder"). This word appears seven times in the story of the revelation of the Torah in Exodus as an important *Leitwort* (leading word). The repetition of this word raises the question of its meaning in this context: thunder or voice? This question is especially relevant regarding Exodus 19:19: "Moses would speak, and God would answer him with a *qol*." In order to understand the meaning of the word *qol* in verse 19, we must examine a previous verse in the story, verse 16: "there was thunder [*qolot*], and lightning, and a dense cloud upon the mountain, and a very loud sound [*qol*] of the horn; and all the people who were in the camp trembled." There is no question that the meaning of the first *qol* in verse 16, next to the word "lightning," is "thunder." Because the word is used to mean thunder in a verse closely preceding it, the reader can be expected to attach this meaning to the word in verse 19 as well. Moreover, the references throughout the story to clouds and lightning reinforce this understanding. However, verse 19 itself mentions speech that elicits a response, and it could therefore be assumed that *qol* in this verse refers to a human voice, a speaking voice. The wider context of the chapter points the reader in one direction, while the immediate context of the verse leads in another. The narrator raises both possibilities but does not allow the reader to decide between them. This uncertainty is important because the understanding of the word has far-reaching theological implications about the nature of the revelation: Was revelation an overwhelming nonverbal event, or one that involved language? The first possibility leads us to one trend within Jewish thought that distinguishes between the concept of "command" (termed *Gebot* by Rosenzweig), which is of divine origin, and the details of the *halakhah* (Rosenzweig's *Gesetz*), which are not necessarily of divine origin.

The second possibility, that *qol* refers to speech, leads us to a different school of thought that holds that both the concept of command and the details of the commandments are of divine, not human, origin.

The **second phenomenon** is the ambiguous syntax found in the passage immediately following the Ten Commandments: "All the people saw the thunder and lightning, the sound of the horn and the mountain smoking. The people saw it and fell back and stood at a distance and said to Moses, 'You speak to us, so that we will hear; but let not God speak to us, lest we die'" (Exod. 20:15–16).[7] When did this conversation take place? One might think: after God uttered the Ten Commandments, because the verses appear immediately after the conclusion of the last commandment. This, however, is a false impression. In biblical Hebrew, the *vav ha-hipukh* (vav consecutive) is used to express a sequence of events in which "x" occurred, and afterwards "y", and then "z". However, the beginning of verse 15 does not use the vav consecutive (that is, it does not read "**va-yar'** kol ha'am"). Instead, it reads "*ve-kol ha'am* **ro'im**." This construction (vav+ noun+participle) is used in biblical Hebrew to describe an event that occurs at the same time as an event previously mentioned.[8] In other words, it is how biblical Hebrew expresses a past perfect, or the idea conveyed in English with the adverb "meanwhile." If so, it is possible that this conversation between Moses and the people took place while God was uttering the Decalogue, in which case the people heard only some of the commandments directly from divine speech. It is also possible that this conversation took place before the declaration of the Decalogue, in which case the people did not hear any of the commandments. Moreover, Nachmanides points out that the people do not say "let not God speak to us, **anymore**" but merely "let not God speak to us." This wording would indicate that God had not yet spoken at all when the people asked Moses to act as intermediary! If so, all the laws—all of what Rosenzweig called the *Gesetz*—were given through an intermediary. What then is the relationship between the commandments in the Torah, God, and the people? Exodus raises this question but does not allow us to answer it decisively because the syntax and location of the verses in the narrative sequence can be read in multiple ways, enabling us to imagine several possibilities without imposing one definite answer.

The **third phenomenon** is the relationship between the verb *ro'im* ("saw"; past form of "see") and its objects. One usually hears thunder but here, "All the people saw [*ro'im*] the thunder and lightning, the blare of the horn and the mountain smoking" (20:15). Commentators have long debated whether this wording should be considered problematic or, even, paradoxical. Rabbi Akiva in the *Mekhilta de-Rabbi Yishmael*,[9] Rashi, and, following him, Nahum Sarna argue that the wording is deliberately paradoxical in speaking of a visual apprehension of an aural phenomenon. On the other hand, Rabbi Ishmael (in the same section of the *Mekhilta*) claims that the verse means to say that the Israelites saw the visible, but heard the aural. In a similar vein, Moshe David Cassuto maintains that this is a zeugma, an expression that includes partial incompatibility; in this case, we have a transitive verb ("see") that is compatible with some of its objects (the lightning and the smoking mountain) and incompatible with others (the thunder and the blare of the horn). Ibn Ezra also rejected the idea of paradoxical wording and argued that the semantic range of the verb *r-'-h* sometimes includes "perceive" in a general sense, not just "perceive through the eyes." In my opinion, even according to the opinion of Rabbi Ishmael and Cassuto, or Ibn Ezra, in this verse the least compatible object has been deliberately placed next to the verb in order to disturb the reader, and thereby to turn his attention to the nature of the revelation and the sensory experience involved in receiving the Torah. Was this a unique experience, inherently different from all other forms of communication? The wording of the verse is not necessarily paradoxical, but it is certainly problematic and liable to slow the readers down so that they can ponder how, precisely, the perceived matter came into the people's mind.

The **fourth phenomenon** is the absence of the indirect object in verse 20:1: "God spoke all these words, saying."[10] This wording—namely, "God/Hashem" coupled with "said/spoke" or "saying"—is very common in the Bible, appearing 339 times. In every other instance, the verse tells us who received the word of God. Here, the indirect object of his speech, prefaced by the preposition "to" (*el*, or the prefixed *lamed*) is conspicuously absent. It is extraordinary to find this ambiguity, of all places, in the story of the most crucial and significant revelation in history. God said something, but we do not know to whom he spoke. This verse raises the question: From whom did the People of Israel receive the exact wording of the Ten Commandments, from God or from Moses?

The book of Exodus, then, utilizes four phenomena of textual ambiguity to lead us to one crucial question: To what extent, and in what way, were the

People of Israel connected to God at Sinai? We may rephrase this question several ways: Was there any direct contact between God and the People of Israel at Sinai? Did the people hear all Ten Commandments from the voice of God, or only some of them? Perhaps they did not hear the speech of God at all? Did God relate specific content directly to the people through the use of language, or was the revelation an experiential event, without verbal content? The number of such phenomena in one text indicates that the book of Exodus does not want us to know exactly what happened at Horeb. Quite the opposite—it wants us to wonder, to ponder, to discuss, and to ask questions, such as those asked by Rosenzweig and Heschel. If the People of Israel did not hear even one word from God, and the entire Torah was given to them exclusively through human mediation, they cannot know for certain if God actually said the words written in the Torah. It is possible that divine speech is not speech at all in the usual sense, as Maimonides argued. If so, Moses then needed to translate the supralinguistic message into human language.

The Dawn of Jewish Exegesis: The Revelation of the Torah in the Book of Deuteronomy

However, alongside these verses in Exodus, there are other voices in the Pentateuch that must be examined. I would like to discuss several aspects of the story of the revelation in Deuteronomy that respond to, and even challenge, the narrative in Exodus. The history of Jewish thought, by and large the history of arguments for the sake of heaven, begins when Deuteronomy confronts Exodus.

In Deuteronomy 4, Moses reminds the assembled people that "The day you stood before Hashem your God at Horeb . . . Hashem spoke to you out of the fire; you heard the sound of words but perceived no shape—nothing but a voice" (4:10, 12). These verses are interesting in light of the ambiguity that we saw in Exodus. According to Deuteronomy, the *qol* was *qol devarim*, "the sound of words"—that is to say: a voice, not just thunder. At Horeb, God uttered verbal content. The chapter continues with verse 13: "He declared to you the covenant that He commanded you to observe, the Ten Commandments." According to this verse, God addressed the people, not only Moses, when he uttered the Decalogue; "He declared to you." The second person plural form of the Hebrew word for "you" indicates that the people heard. This point is accentuated by the repetition of the second person plural in verses 11 and following (where each case in bold in the following is a plural form): "**You** came forward and stood . . . Hashem spoke to **you** . . . **you** heard . . . but **saw no shape**. . . . related to **you** the covenant that He commanded **you**. . . . For **your** own sake, **be careful**—for **you** saw no shape when Hashem your God spoke to **you**" (11–15). Deuteronomy appears to clarify the ambiguity on this matter found in the narrative in Exodus. Deuteronomy also challenges several verses in Exodus 19–24 that emphasize the visual aspect of the revelation at Sinai; Deuteronomy strongly insists that the people heard God but did not see Him (see verses 12 and 15).

All these motifs are accentuated in chapter 5: "Hashem **our** God formed a covenant with **us at** Horeb. It was not with **our** fathers that Hashem made this covenant, but with us, the living, every one of **us** who is here today. It was directly that Hashem spoke with **you** at the mountain from within the fire" (2–4). The repetition of the plural forms (in bold in the translation immediately preceding) clarifies, in contrast to the verses that we examined in Exodus, that God spoke to all of the people. The direct connection between God and the people is also indicated by the phrase "face to face." These verses emphasize the auditory contact between God and the people while God uttered the Ten Commandments. This motif appears also in the passage immediately following the Ten Commandments:

> It was these words that Hashem spoke to your whole congregation on the mountain from within the fire, the cloud, and the fog—a great voice (*qol*), which did not continue. . . . When you all heard the voice (*qol*) from within the darkness—and the mountain was on fire—that the leaders of your tribes and the elders drew near to me, and you said, "Look, Hashem has shown us His glory and His greatness; it was His voice (*qol*) that we heard from the midst of the fire; today we saw that God can speak with a human, and the human lives. So now, why should we die? For this huge fire will devour us! If we continue to hear the voice (*qol*) of Hashem our God any more, we will die! For who among all flesh has heard the voice of the living God speaking from the midst of the fire like us, and then lived? You go, and hear whatever Hashem our God may say; you can tell us all that Hashem our God tells you, and we will listen, and we will carry it out." (5:19–23).

These verses are a response to the ambiguities in Exodus 19 and 20. God spoke to all the people, not only to Moses. As we have seen, the syntax in Exodus 20 indicates that over the course of a dialogue that took place during the revelation of the Decalogue, or possibly even before God began to speak, it was decided that Moses would act as an intermediary. In contrast, when the author of Deuteronomy describes this dialogue, he uses the *vav ha-hipukh* in verse 20: "When (*va-yehi*) you all heard the voice." Therefore, Deuteronomy makes it clear that this dialogue took place after receiving the Ten Commandments; the people heard the entire passage and only afterwards approached Moses. Moreover, a comparison between the people's petition in each of the two books is revealing: Exodus 20:16 reads: "let not God speak to us, lest we die," whereas Deuteronomy 5:22 reads, "If we continue to hear the voice (*qol*) of Hashem our God any more, we shall die!"

Deuteronomy addresses each of the four ambiguities from Exodus that I pointed out earlier; in each case, Deuteronomy's purpose is to reject the possibility that the people did not receive the Ten Commandments directly from God. The revelation was public, not mediated; on this point Deuteronomy is both insistent and clear. Clear—yet equivocal. Deuteronomy 5:5 contradicts the verse that comes before it (as well 4:12–13 and 5:19–20). Immediately after the vivid description of the unmediated meeting of God and Israel in Deuteronomy 5:4, there follows a comment announcing that Moses acted as intercessor: "It was directly that Hashem spoke with you at the mountain from within the fire—I was standing between Hashem and all of you at that time, so as to tell you God's word, for you were afraid of the fire, and you did not go up the mountain—saying: 'I am Hashem your God'" (4–6).

The medieval commentators—Rashi, Rashbam, and Ibn Ezra—point out that the word *lemor* (saying) in verse 5 belongs to the sentence found in verse 4, since it completes the phrase in verse 4, which begins with the words "Hashem spoke." This renders the remainder of verse 5 parenthetical. We can go a step further than these commentators: Verse 5 (other than the word "saying") is a later addition to the text. It includes the formula "at that time," which (as Samuel Loewenstamm has demonstrated) consistently serves in Deuteronomy to indicate scribal interpolations.[11] This interpolation reintroduces the idea of mediated revelation, which Deuteronomy specifically rejects.

While the unequivocal, straightforward narrative in Deuteronomy resolves the ambiguity in Exodus, this interpolation revives the possible reading originally rejected by Deuteronomy, destroys the continuity of the text, and turns the ambiguity of Exodus into a debate taking place within the final text of Deuteronomy. Because of this interpolation, the canonical text of Deuteronomy lacks the very clarity that its author had intended to achieve.

This phenomenon is not unusual, and even illustrates a developmental pattern that appears repeatedly in later Jewish literature. The initial stage of this pattern is characterized by ambiguity or disagreement; in the second stage, an unequivocal, well-organized text resolves the previous ambiguity or disorder; the third stage is a reaction to that organized text and a return to the original positions. For example, the editors of the Mishnah created a well-structured and organized text to which the Gemara added complex argumentation and interpretation. In the *Mishneh Torah*, Maimonides attempted to compile complex and unstructured traditions into an accessible and well-organized framework. However, the work was accepted into the Jewish literary canon only after commentaries were appended to it that identified the contradictory opinions and reasoning that Maimonides had rejected! For example, in *Hasagot ha-Ravad*, included in almost every edition of the *Mishneh Torah*, the commentator Rabbi Abraham ben David of Posquières (known as the Ravad) repeatedly disagrees with Maimonides and refers to the opinions that he did not include. It appears that Ravad's commentary was not the first critical commentary, or gloss, in Jewish literature. The original book to bear the title *Mishneh Torah*, the book of Deuteronomy, also received a critical commentary in the form of a later interpolation added by someone to whom we can dub "proto-Ravad" (Deut. 5:5).

This comparison between the two *Mishneh Torah*s is significant. I would even be so bold as to suggest that Deuteronomy is the first Jewish text, or, more specifically, the first text with rabbinic characteristics, not only because it explains or responds to earlier texts, but also because it has reached our hands with appended commentaries, comments, and critiques.

In these chapters, Deuteronomy expresses an opinion in another matter that is also a subject of controversy in the earlier books of the Torah. In Exodus 19–24 the revelation of the Torah is presented as an event, while in Leviticus and Numbers it is presented as a process. According to Exodus, God gave the Ten Commandments at Horeb and, almost immediately afterward, the laws in chapters 21–23. Moses then read out the laws to the people, and the people took it upon themselves to observe them. However, in Leviticus and Numbers the revelation of the Torah continues for years. At Sinai, God showed Moses the plan for the Tabernacle. After its construction, on the first day of the first month of the second year in the desert, God entered the Holy of Holies, and from there, on that very day, he first began to reveal the law to Moses, starting with the laws of sacrifices in Leviticus 1–7.

However, the revelation of the Torah did not end there. After the ceremonies of the dedication of the Tabernacle, the revelation continued. From the conclusion of the ceremonies on the eighth day of the month until the end of that month, Moses received the laws in Leviticus 11–23. In the following month, in the Tent of Meeting at Sinai, Moses received additional laws (Num. 5:6), and on the twentieth day of the month the people left Sinai. Throughout the years of wandering in the desert and when they encamped in the steppes of Moab, Moses received additional laws that are found in other chapters in Numbers. From this it can be concluded that, according to Leviticus and Numbers, the revelation continued for many years. Moreover, certain stories in Leviticus and Numbers, such as that of the man gathering wood on the Sabbath (Num. 15:32–36) and the daughters of Zelophehad (Num. 27 and 36), convey the impression that the revelation is a process conducted through dialogue: Moses turns to God with halakhic questions and receives new laws or modifications of existing laws in response.

In this matter Deuteronomy agrees with Exodus, as can be seen clearly in verse 5:19: "It was these words that Hashem spoke to your whole congregation on the mountain from within the fire, the cloud, and the fog—a great voice, which did not continue [*lo yasaf*]." The *Targumim*, or standard rabbinic Aramaic translations, understand the last words of the verse very differently from my translation; for a *Targum*, the verse expresses the idea of continuous revelation: "a great voice that did not end." However, it is clear from other verses in which the verb *yasaf* is used that the meaning of this verse is that God's voice ceased and did not continue. Moreover, in contrast to Leviticus and Numbers, Deuteronomy does not include numerous instances of revelation of commandments and laws beginning with "Hashem spoke to Moses saying," and other similar formulas.

This debate over whether revelation was an event or a process did not end with the Bible. Profesor Yochanan Silman delineates various perceptions of the nature of the Torah in classical rabbinic literature and medieval Jewish thought.[12] He defines one perspective as the "Perfection Position," according to which the Torah that the People of Israel received was fundamentally whole and unchangeable. Thinkers and treatises adhering to this approach understand Deuteronomy 5:19 according to its simple meaning: the voice of God at Sinai "went on no more." However, according to the opinion that Silman describes as the "Being-Ever-Perfected Position," the revelation of the Torah to the Jewish people is a process that continues throughout the generations, in which the Torah itself develops and reaches a higher level of perfection. Thinkers and treatises adhering to this approach understand Deuteronomy 5:19 according to the Aramaic translations to mean that the voice of God on Sinai did not cease. They understand the word *yasaf* ("yod-samech-peh") as derived from the root *s-v-p* meaning "end" (*sof*), thus indicating that the voice of God did not come to an end. A similar idea, that all the People of Israel, including generations not yet born, were present at Sinai and heard exactly what the generation of the Exodus heard, can be found in classical rabbinic literature.[13] A similar opinion is reflected in the *aggadah* describing God's revelation to Moses of future rabbinic interpretations and questions.[14] Rosenzweig and Heschel emphatically articulate this approach by arguing, in keeping with many Hasidic and kabbalistic sources, that the revelation of the Torah is happening *now*, whenever there is someone prepared to receive it. According to Heschel, in the third volume of his masterwork *Heavenly Torah: As Refracted through the Generations*, this opinion has important ramifications. Because all generations were present at Sinai, we can infer that the congregation of Israel in each generation has the right to hear through its own ears, to understand the divine imperative, and to translate it into practical *halakhah*. If so, it is possible that later authorities sometimes have the right to change the *halakhah*, to mold and to adapt certain commandments of human origin (*Gesetz* in Rosenzweig's terminology) so long as the authority of the divine command (*Gebot*) is not infringed.

On the one hand, Deuteronomy clearly belongs to the Perfection Position (in Silman's terminology) because it portrays the revelation as an event rather than a process. Moreover, Deuteronomy twice warns that it is forbidden to change its laws (4:2 and 13:1). Yet, surprisingly, in several places the book reveals an affinity to the developmental approach. At least in its current form, the passage informing us that the generation that stood at Horeb died in the wilderness (1:33–39) contradicts the verses that say that Moses' audience on the steppes of Moab witnessed the revelation at Horeb: "Hashem our God made a covenant with us at Horeb. It was not with our fathers that Hashem made this covenant, but with us, the living, every one of us who is here today" (5:2–3). The tension between these two passages is significant. Moses pointed out that the covenant he was describing happened at Horeb, because he was speaking in Moab forty years after the revelation and reminding his audience what had happened there. If he were still at Horeb, he would not have added this geographical detail. In truth, God made the covenant at Horeb with the parents of those whom Moses addressed in Moab in Deuteronomy 5. Deuteronomy mentions two covenants: one made at Horeb and the other a generation later in Moab. The verse that begins the narrative of the covenant in Moab acknowledges this: "These are the terms of the covenant which Hashem commanded Moses to conclude with the Israelites in the land of Moab, in addition to the covenant which He had made with them at Horeb" (Deut. 28:69). The words "in addition" challenge the book's portrayal of the revelation as a onetime event and present the formation of the covenant as a repeating occurrence. The people enter the covenant "today" in chapter 29, despite the fact that the covenant had already existed for forty years.

Similarly, we read: "You—all of you—are standing here today in the presence of Hashem your God. . . . It is not only with you that I am making this covenant, with its sanctions, but with everyone who is here with us, standing in the presence of Hashem our God today, and with everyone who is not here with us today" (29:9, 13–14). Chapter 5 asserts that those who were born or grew up after the revelation were present at Horeb. Chapter 29 declares that those not present in Moab nevertheless also entered the covenant made there. We can conclude from these verses that the covenantal events both at Horeb and Moab were not limited to those specific points in time. It can be said that God made a covenant with those not yet born at the time of the revelation of the Torah; Moses' speech in Moab was directed also to those born generations after the speech was given. The events at Horeb and Moab were not onetime occurrences. In an important way, they continue so that those born later can participate in them. These passages therefore challenge the claim that the revelation was a onetime event, and bring Deuteronomy closer to the developmental approach.

The word "today" (*ha-yom*), which appears frequently in Deuteronomy, is very important in this context. It appears six times in chapter 4 and three times in chapter 5. In the remainder of the book the expression "that I command you this day" appears twenty-four times. This word, so strongly emphasized in Deuteronomy, has multiple meanings. It usually refers to the day of the speech in Moab, but a few times it means the day of the revelation at Horeb (Deut. 5:21). However, the repeated use of this *Leitwort* hints that the reference is actually to the day in which the book is being read. In other words, "today" could be any day, any given time, the today of whoever reads or chants Deuteronomy. If so, the voice on Horeb continues to be heard, and the Aramaic translators Onkelos and Yonatan were to a large extent correct when they translated "a great voice that did not end." The fundamental position of Deuteronomy is that the covenant is continual; God commands the people in every generation. We can conclude that the book is an important precedent for the Being-Ever-Perfected Position. There is also a profound affinity between Deuteronomy and the perspectives of Rosenzweig and Heschel inasmuch as they emphasize the timelessness of the divine imperative with references to verses from Deuteronomy that contain the word "today."

This duality in Deuteronomy—its adherence to both of the positions described by Silman—is also reflected in the verses that warn us not to change its laws. While in principle Deuteronomy opposed emending the law, in practice its author does not obey his own rule. It is well known that, according to the straightforward meaning of the text, Deuteronomy 12–26 contains numerous adaptations of the Book of the Covenant in Exodus 21–23. The very same book that admonishes its reader, "You shall not add anything to what I command you or take anything away from it" (Deut. 4:2), changed the status of the Hebrew maidservant mentioned in Exodus 21 so that she received the same rights that Exodus gave only to the male Hebrew slave. The very book that forbids innovation and expansion itself innovates and expands earlier laws in almost all its chapters. Though the book forbids us to add to its laws, these laws must be supplemented if they are to be observed. Like all biblical and ancient Near Eastern legal codes, the set of laws presented in Deuteronomy does not constitute a comprehensive legal system. Rather, it includes a representative sample of the legal practices of the People of Israel.[15] Without additions from the tradition from which the book was derived, it is simply impossible to implement its laws. One wonders, therefore, to what extent the author of Deuteronomy expected us to take at face value the prohibition of adding to or subtracting from the laws.

The Centrality of Obligation

According to the concept of revelation propounded by Rosenzweig and Heschel, the Torah, in the sense of law and commandment, is a response to divine revelation. In other words, the People of Israel wrote the Torah in response to divine instruction. Is a response that does not express itself in legal form also legitimate? According to Martin Buber, revelation entails the creation, not of *halakhah*, but of a connection between man and God.[16] Revelation can be interpreted as theology or emotional fervor, and not necessarily as law.

For the first three thousand years, until the nineteenth century, the quintessential and universal Jewish response to revelation was the formulation of laws and obedience to them. The consistency of this response indicates that, at Sinai, the Jewish people perceived God specifically as an entity who issued a command. The fact that the Jewish people interpreted the divine imperative as law indicates that revelation was not limited to God's appearance and the establishment of a connection with him, but also included the demand for halakhic obedience, although it was left to the people to formulate the *halakhah*. According to Rosenzweig, God gave a general command, and the details of the *halakhah* were created by the Jewish people. At the revelation at Sinai, God declared "I command you to . . ."; throughout the generations the People of Israel have been completing that sentence. While the Jewish people fill in the object of the verb, God remains its subject and the verb never loses it basic meaning of demanding obedience.

The sources within the Torah itself make it clear that Israel's response to the event at Sinai has always been expressed in the form of commitment. In all the sources, we find laws that are justified by means of a story.[17] All the sources concur about the nature of the Torah, and all agree with the first commentary of Rashi to Genesis—that the Torah is a combination of legislation and narrative. Specifically, the Torah is comprised of laws that derive their justification from the narrative context in which they appear. The sources disagree on the important questions such as how, when, and where revelation occurred, and, above all, which laws specifically have to be obeyed. However, all agree unanimously that the People of Israel's response to the event of revelation must be legal or halakhic.

In the Pentateuch itself, the meaning of revelation is the giving of the law (*mattan torah*). This is true not only of the Pentateuch as it appears now, but also of all the sources that modern research identifies as comprising the Torah. The concept of revelation as the giving of the Torah or divine imperative is thus older than the Pentateuch itself, and is accepted by groups as disparate as the Karaites, Saducees, the Qumran cult, the Samaritans, and, of course, the sages. The antinomian approach cannot look for substantiation or support either in biblical criticism or the sources that it has revealed. J, E, P, and D—all affirm the centrality of the *halakhah*.

The Bible: Written Torah or Oral Law?

I must acknowledge that my argument has a far-reaching implication: the entire Bible, from the first words "In the beginning God created," is oral law. The Bible itself, including the Ten Commandments, is comprised of human language that develops and interprets the divine command. In my opinion, this characterization of the Bible as oral law is a necessary corollary of Rosenzweig and Heschel's approach, although they did not explicitly say as much in their writings, and might very well have recoiled from it.

On its face, this is a radical and problematic argument. However, on closer examination it becomes clear that, on a practical level, it does not conflict with halakhic observance or belief in the sanctity of the Torah. Texts that are clearly regarded as the Oral Law are comprised of both human and divine elements. For example, traditional belief holds that the text of the Mishnah was composed by Rabbi Judah the Prince and his colleagues, but that its content is from Sinai. In this case, it is difficult to draw the line between human content and divine imperative. Although this lack of clarity is present from the incipient stages of the Oral Law, it is not perceived as a challenge to its authority, or as problematic in any way. I would like to argue that the same is true regarding the Written Torah. For example, I know that the details of the laws of tefillin originate in the Oral Law and were formulated by human beings. This knowledge does not prevent me from putting on tefillin every morning out of a sense of obligation to fulfill a divine command, even though the details of the commandment are the inventions of human sages. I believe that the verses in Exodus and Deuteronomy that were the basis for this specific *halakhah* were written by human beings. This belief, however, does not prevent me from observing the commandant according to the *halakhah*. I believe that the verses in the Torah, like the specifics of the *halakhah* in the Mishnah, the Talmud, and the legal codes and responsa, are all human responses to divine command.

Moreover, my claim that the Bible, in a certain sense, can be regarded as oral law is less audacious than appears at first glance. Already in classical rabbinic literature there is a tendency to blur the border between the two "Torahs"— written and oral—or to eliminate it entirely.[18] Here I will limit myself to three examples. The first example is from the midrash: "The words of Torah are all one and they include Bible, Mishnah, *halakhah*, and *aggadah*."[19] The second example is from the Babylonian Talmud:

> Rabbi Levi bar Hama said in the name of Reish Lakish: It is written, "and I will give you the stone tablets, and the Torah, and the commandments which I have written, to teach them" (Exod. 24:12)—"Stone tablets'"— these are the Ten Commandments; "Torah"—this is the Bible[20]; "commandments"—this is the Mishnah; "which I have written"—these are the books of the Prophets and Writings; "to teach them"—this is the Gemara. This teaches us that all were given to Moses at Sinai.[21]

In this *aggadah* the components of the Oral and Written Torahs are mixed together. The order is not, as we would expect, "Pentateuch, Prophets and Writings, Mishnah, and Gemara." Instead, it is "Pentateuch, Mishnah, Prophets and Writings, Gemara." All of them are Torah, without any differentiation between the Oral and Written Torahs. The order might even lead us to conclude that the Mishnah is more important than the Prophets and Writings, as some traditional commentators have argued.[22]

The final example is from a midrash:

> When God appeared at Sinai to give the Torah to Israel, he presented it to Moses in the correct order: Bible, Mishnah, Talmud, and *aggadah*, as it is said, "God spoke all these words, saying" (Exod. 20:1). Every question that a student asks his teacher was revealed to Moses at that time. After God taught Moses the Torah, He asked him to teach it to the People of Israel. Moses said to him, "Master of the World, I will write it down for them." God said to him, "I do not want you to write it down for them, because I know that in the future idol worshippers will rule over them and will take it from them. Rather, I will give them the Bible in writing, and the Mishnah, Talmud, and *aggadah* I will give orally. This way, even when they are subjugated to the idolaters, they will remain distinct from them."[23]

According to this midrash, the entire Torah was originally oral, and there is no substantive difference between the material that ended up in the Written Torah and the material that remained oral. For practical reasons God decided to turn some of the material into the Written Torah. The default position, God's first choice, the original form of the Written Torah, was oral. Here the borders between the Written and Oral Law are not blurred; they are erased.

Practical Implications

There are two practical ramifications of this position. The first is that a Jew who understands the revelation of the Torah, as I have described it here, will continue to observe the commandments, but without complete certainty that all his or her actions reflect the will of God. If the Torah in our possession is a human translation of the divine command that we all heard at Sinai, we must recognize that no translation is perfect. A human translation of the divine may be especially prone to contain some errors. Therefore, when we observe the commandments we should act with humility rather than exaggerated self-confidence. This is a danger inherent to all religions: a person who is confident that he or she understands exactly what God wants will lack the humility befitting a religious person. Alas, empirical evidence abounds demonstrating the correlation between certainty regarding God's will, on the one hand, and arrogance, inflexibility, and intolerance, on the other. Moreover, people who understand that they are reading a translation of the divine will should constantly doubt their own behavior. This doubt, rather than impairing religious practice, enriches and deepens it.

The second ramification is that if the particulars of the *halakhah* are of human origin, specifically of Jewish communal origin, the possibility exists that, under certain conditions, Jewish communities can participate in the ongoing process of creating the Oral Law; that is, they can change the *halakhah*. The important and difficult questions of how, when, and under whose authority such changes can be made are outside the scope of this article. Others with greater expertise in Jewish law can address them. I will limit myself to two comments. First, God gave the Torah to the Jewish people. If the Jewish people are the "owners" of the *halakhah*, they have the right to change it. Second, not all Jewish communities have the right to change the *halakhah*. God gave the Torah to the whole Jewish nation, but not all Jews accepted it. "Ownership" of the Torah as well as the right to contribute to its development by amending it belongs only to those communities that received the Torah—in other words, those who are committed to observing it and demonstrate this commitment on a daily basis.

In light of my position that the Written Torah is an early form or example of the Oral Law, and that the Oral Law is a continuing developmental process, it can be asked: Can we conceive of the possibility of changing the text of the Written Torah? Can we eliminate verses from the Torah, such as those commanding genocide, on a moral basis? Can we rewrite the text of the Bible from a feminist perspective? The answer is no. The idea that the Oral Law is capable of development and expansion does not mean that existing texts should be rewritten. The *amoraim* did not rewrite the Mishnah but added to it. (The fact that scholars of the text of the Mishnah can point to occasional exceptions to this rule does not invalid my basic argument). The *Rishonim* did not rewrite the Talmud; they wrote new works intended to complete, not replace it. In our day, it is neither possible nor desirable to change existing texts. It is both possible and desirable, however, to add additional volumes to the corpus of Torah that interpret earlier works, respond to them, and complete them. It is my hope that these new works will help the Jews of today and future generations to come closer to the God who commands us to "expand Torah and glorify it" (Isa. 42:21).

Endnotes

1. This article outlines a specific way of understanding the revelation of the Torah. Detailed exegetical explanations, references to further primary and secondary sources, and responses to potential criticism can be found in my book *Revelation and Authority: Sinai in Jewish Scripture and Tradition* (New Haven: Yale University Press, 2015).
2. I have borrowed this expression from Maimonides' eighth principle of faith in his introduction to the commentary to *perek Ḥelek* of Mishnah tractate *Sanhedrin*. It is important to remember that immediately before these words, Maimonides warns that the expression "like a scribe taking dictation" is a metaphor, and that in fact no one really knows how Moses received the Torah. Both in *The Guide of the Perplexed* and in this passage, Maimonides clarifies that the "divine" speech at Horeb was not really speech at all.
3. Franz Rosenzweig, *On Jewish Learning*, ed. Nahum Glatzer (New York: Schocken Books, 1965), 118. Rosenzweig quotes Exod. 19:23 and 20:1.
4. Abraham Joshua Heschel, *God in Search of Man: A Philosophy of Judaism* (New York: Farrar, Straus and Giroux, 1955), 185, 274. Heschel quotes from *Tanna de-Vei Eliyyahu Zuta* 2:1.
5. On Rosenzweig as an advocate of the view that the *halakhah* is obligatory and authoritative, see Isaac Heinemann, *Ta'amei ha-Mitzvot be-Sifrut Ḥazal* [The reasons for the commandments in Jewish thought] (Jerusalem: Horev, 1993), 2:195–237; *Revelation and Authority*, 128–135.
6. A study of the discussion of these questions in classical and medieval rabbinic literature and their implications can be found in Abraham Joshua Heschel, *Heavenly Torah: As Refracted through the Generations*, ed. and trans. Gordon Tucker (New York: Continuum, 2006); and Yochanan Silman, *Kol Gadol ve-lo Yasaf: Torat Yisrael bein Shlemut le-Hishtalmut* [The voice heard at Sinai] (Jerusalem: Magnes, 1999).
7. Verses 18–19 in other editions of the Bible. On differences in the division into verses see Mordecai Breuer, "Dividing the Decalogue into Verses and Commandments," in *The Ten Commandments in History and Tradition*, ed. Ben-Zion Segal; English version ed. Gershon Levi (Jerusalem: Magnes, 1990), 291–330.
8. See Gotthelf Bergsträsser, *Dikduk ha-Lashon ha-Ivrit* [Hebrew grammar], trans. Mordechai Ben-Asher (Jerusalem: Magnes, 1982), 428–429 (pt. 2, sec. 13, d–e); and Jan Joosten, *The Verbal System of Biblical Hebrew* (Jerusalem: Simor, 2012), 125–130.
9. *Parashat Debeḥodesh*, 9.
10. This phenomenon was first pointed out by Aryeh Toeg, *Matan Torah Be-Sinai* [Lawgiving at Sinai] (Jerusalem: Magnes, 1977).
11. Samuel Loewenstamm, "Ha Nusḥa 'ba-Et ha-Hi' be-Ne'umei ha-Petiḥa shel Sefer Devarim" [The wording of the phrase "at this time" in the introductory speeches of Deuteronomy], *Tarbiz* 38 (1969): 99–104.
12. *Kol Gadol ve-lo Yasaf*.
13. Midrash *Tanḥuma*, Nitsavim; Babylonian Talmud, tractate *Shavuot* 39a, tractate *Shabbat* 146a.

14. Jerusalem Talmud, tractate *Pe'ah* 13a; several instances in *Midrash Rabbah*.
15. On this point see Samson Raphael Hirsch, who understood on a profound level the nature of the Written Torah as it contrasts to the Oral Law. On this aspect of Hirsch's work, see the discussions by Alan Levenson, *The Making of the Modern Jewish Bible: How Scholars in Germany, Israel and America Transformed an Ancient Text* (Lanham, MD: Rowman and Littlefield, 2011), 50; Jay Harris, *How Do We Know This? Midrash and the Fragmentation of Modern Judaism* (Albany: SUNY Press, 1995), 226–227.
16. For Buber's approach to *halakhah* and its connection to revelation, see in particular his correspondence with Rosenzweig in *On Jewish Learning*, 72–92.
17. I am referring to the four textual sources, J, E, P, and D, identified by biblical critics.
18. See the many examples provided in *Revelation and Authority*, chap. 4.
19. *Sifrei Devarim*, Ha'azinu.
20. Rashi comments here that this is the Pentateuch, because there is a commandment to read the Torah.
21. Babylonian Talmud, tractate *Berakhot* 5a.
22. See, e.g., *Ein Ya'akov* and its commentaries on this passage, *Ahavat Eitan* and *Iyyun Yaakov*.
23. *Shemot Rabbah* 47:1 (and parallel texts).

The Torah Speaks to People

Chezi Cohen

Introduction

The belief that the Torah was revealed by God is one of the cornerstones of Jewish faith. The Bible contains so many accounts of revelation that the event does not elicit astonishment from either the narrator, the listener, or the recipient of the revelation.[1] God's revelation to humankind is comprised of two elements: God the revealer and the human recipient to whom this revelation is directed.[2] The concept that God is beyond human comprehension could theoretically, although not necessarily, extend to divine discourse, the Torah. Jewish tradition includes various models for understanding the nature of the Torah. The belief that the Torah can be understood only by deciphering the secrets encrypted within it occupies one end of the spectrum. On the other end lies the position that the Torah can be understood only by means of human capabilities. Between these two extremes there stretches a wide spectrum of possibilities.

On one extreme, there is an approach that identifies God with his Torah, as can be seen in the following midrash: "'I the Lord am your God' (Exod. 20:2)—What does 'I' mean? Rav said: 'You will not mock the Torah that I gave you. "I" (*anochi*) is an acronym for "I, myself, wrote it and gave it" (*ana nafsi kitveit yahaveit*)."[3]

Identifying God with his Torah leads to the understanding that every detail, even the smallest, in the Torah has meaning and significance, even the shapes of the letters. This approach can be attributed to Rabbi Akiva, who drew meaning from every letter in the Torah, including from their shapes. His underlying assumption was that the Torah speaks in an encrypted divine language that can be deciphered and understood by means of the rabbinic hermeneutical rules. An example of Rabbi Akiva's method can be found in the Babylonian Talmud, tractate *Sanhedrin* 51b, where he deduces from the addition of a conjunctive letter vav the method of execution appropriate for a *Kohen*'s adulterous daughter: "Rabbi Akiva said: '[A priest's daughter], whether betrothed or married is executed by burning [rather than the lighter punishment of strangulation].' ... Rabbi Akiva replied: 'Ishmael, my brother, I deduce this from the addition of the letter vav to the word "daughter"' (Lev. 21:9). Rabbi Ishmael said to him: 'Because you make this fine distinction, should we execute this woman by burning rather than strangulation?'"

According to Rabbi Akiva, the Torah is a closed system with its own unique language that cannot be deciphered by human intelligence. The Torah scholar must therefore make use of the system of divine hermeneutical rules for the interpretation of the Torah. Many have followed this path, including Jacob ben Asher and the author of *Sefer Yetzirah*.

An opposite approach posits that the Torah is the word of God given to man, and is thus limited in its language and contents. This idea is expressed in rabbinic literature by the phrase "the Torah uses human language." According to this approach, meaning cannot be extracted from every superfluous word in the biblical text because the Torah is written according to human forms of expression. As we have seen, Rabbi Ishmael advanced this argument against Rabbi Akiva in the case of the adulterous daughter of the *Kohen*. Another example can be found in tractate *Sanhedrin* 56a, where the sages rejected Rabbi Meir's deduction on the basis of the repetition in the verse "Anyone (*ish ish*) who blasphemes his God" (Lev. 24:15), and explained the verse as conforming to patterns of human speech: "What of it? The Torah uses human language."

This phrase is repeated often in the Talmud regarding verses that contain either a repetition of words, or use the verb both in the infinitive and inflected forms. An additional example can be found in the rabbinic dispute over whether a freed slave should be given a severance payment in all cases. The dispute concerns the meaning of Deuteronomy 15:13: "When you set him free, do not let him go empty-handed: Furnish him out of the flock, threshing floor, and vat." Some deduced from the repetition of the verbal root in the phrase "furnish him" (*ha'aneik ta'anik*) that there is always an obligation to grant the slave the payment. Rabbi Elazar ben Azariah, however, limited the payment to slaves who had brought prosperity to the master's household, and thus explained the redundancy as a figure of human speech:

> Our Rabbis taught: "With which the Lord your God has blessed you" (Deut. 15:14)—One might think that this means that if the household was blessed on his account, the master must give him the payment, but if the household was not blessed on his account, he does not have to pay

him. Therefore, the Torah says "furnish him" (15:14)—in any case. If so, what is the meaning of the words "with which the Lord your God has blessed you"? [It means] give him according to the blessing that you have received. Rabbi Elazar ben Azariah said: "The matter is as it is written: if the house was blessed on his account, a gift is made to him; if the house was not blessed on his account, no gift is made to him." If so, what is meant by "thou shalt surely furnish him"? The Torah uses human language.[4]

This approach is based on the understanding that it is impossible to construct a theology that ignores the human nature of the Torah's recipients. Another midrash expresses the same idea in different words: "The Torah uses language that its audience can comprehend" (literally, "that the ear can hear").[5] Many thinkers and exegetes, in particular Maimonides, expanded on this idea.[6]

The principle underlying this approach is that, while God is infinite, the Torah is finite because it was given to human beings in a limited physical world. The transmission of the Torah to the People of Israel, as well as its temporal subject matter, makes this conclusion axiomatic. Thus, although God's power and might fill the world, in His encounter with limited mortals God constricts Himself and accepts the rules of this world. Therefore, biblical exegesis mandates consideration of the human nature of the Torah's recipients. This exegetical method is called *peshat*, an obscure term with many definitions. Abraham Ibn Ezra, in the introduction to his commentary on the Torah, defined *peshat* as an exegetical approach "bound by the rules of grammar and acceptable to reason"; in other words, the interpretation must be linguistically correct and seem logical to the reader. The exegete Samuel ben Meir (Rashbam) explained it differently: "If the reader has seen previous commentaries that lean toward a different meaning regarding other matters, he should take note that these are not based on social mores, according to human wisdom, or that this is not the meaning of the verse ... whereas I have explained them well according to both the text of the verses and social mores."[7]

These definitions express the central idea of this article—that exegesis must be clear to the reader using his common sense.[8] I will explain below that this applies specifically to the reader at the time of the revelation. It must be noted here that it is possible to propose other models for understanding *peshat*. In contrast to a radical approach that claims that there is only the *peshat*, Samuel ben Meir suggested that the Torah contains various additional layers, including esoteric meanings. However, even according to this approach, in the end, "the biblical text never loses its *peshat* meaning."[9]

Distinguishing between God and his Torah

In contrast to the identification of God with his Torah seen in the midrash cited above (*pesikta* 12), the following midrash makes a clear distinction between the two:

> They asked Wisdom: "How should a sinner be punished?" Wisdom answered: "Misfortune pursues sinners" (Prov. 13:21). They asked Prophecy: "How should a sinner be punished?" Prophecy answered: "The person who sins, only he shall die" (Ezek. 18:4). They asked the Torah: "How should a sinner be punished?" The Torah answered: "He should bring a sin offering and he will be forgiven." They asked God: "How should a sinner be punished?" God answered: "He should repent and he will be forgiven, as it is written: 'Good and upright is the Lord; therefore He shows sinners the way'" (Ps. 25:8).[10]

According to this midrash, the Torah and God are two separate entities who give different answers to the question of the appropriate punishment for sin! Although the Torah is on a higher level than wisdom and prophecy, there is an even higher level: the answer of God Himself, as it were.[11] In the Torah, offering a sacrifice brings atonement. God, however, wants repentance. Are prophecy and Torah not the will of God? They certainly are, but they express only a certain aspect of the divine will; his deeper will (if this is the right word for it) has a different answer to the question. The most astounding aspect of this midrash is that God cites his answer from the book of Psalms—written by a man! God's answer is encrypted in man's prayer.[12]

We must also differentiate between God and his Torah on a conceptual level. While God is infinite, the Torah is limited. Although it is on a higher plane than other forms of divine expression (wisdom and prophecy), it is not God Himself. In order to clarify this point, I will make use of a well-known parable—a person speaking with a small child must limit himself to the child's vocabulary. So too God constricts himself when he speaks to us in the Torah:

> A parable of a man who has a very beloved young son ... the father will not speak with him according to his own sophisticated and extensive intellect, because the son will not be able to comprehend or understand him. Because of the intensity and the strength of his love for his beloved son, he

constricts his great and vast intellect immeasurably and speaks to his son according to the child's undeveloped and immature intellect.[13]

A similar, although not identical, differentiation appears in kabbalistic literature that distinguishes between the primordial Torah and the Written Torah. This idea was adopted by Tamar Ross,[14] who argues that the primordial Torah is the reflection of God in His essence. It is a clear reflection of the secrets of His infinite wisdom, free from the finiteness of human understanding, a spiritual entity beyond this world. In contrast, the Written Torah is a reflection or shadow of this primordial infinite form. It embodies the celestial Torah, but inevitably does so in a more restricted context, anchored in the temporal dimension.

Despite differences in terminology (primordial Torah/God), the distinction between the sublime God and our Torah is common to both approaches. From this distinction, it can be concluded that any *peshat* interpretation must take into account human capacity.[15] My teacher Rabbi David Bigman has noted that the Torah, though eternal, was originally given to the first generation. In other words, along with the infinite meaning of the Torah, there is also a particular meaning for the time in which it was given. From this it may be concluded that we are compelled to search for the most reasonable *peshat* explanation by taking into account the human aspect in the process of transmission.

In this context it is important to distinguish between two hermeneutic concepts: rational interpretation as opposed to logical interpretation. The first includes any possible interpretation from within the range of options, even if its likelihood is very remote. In contrast, logical interpretation is very likely, perhaps even most likely, to be correct. For example, the sages identified Agag, the king of Amalek, who fought against Saul, with Haman the Agagite. According to a midrash, Agag had relations with a servant girl before he was executed by the prophet Samuel, and in due course Haman the Agagite was born from this union.[16] This interpretation is theoretically possible, although the likelihood is remote and the identification is tenuous. If there is a connection between Haman and the Amalekites, it is more likely that Haman is the descendent of other Amalekites (see, e.g., 1 Sam. 30:17). Neither of these terms is absolute; their meanings change constantly. Their likelihood is determined by an understanding of the cultural, linguistic, and historical context of the text and its author. Nevertheless, the *peshat* exegete must aspire to present the most logical interpretation.

Receiving the Torah: Including the Recipient in the Development of Theology

The Torah's use of human language is reflected in several areas:

The Torah's Areas of Interest

The Torah contains many references to idolatry, a common practice in the ancient world. It does not mention atheism, a concept that did not exist at the time in which the Torah was given, and would not have been understood by its original readers. Similarly, the Torah refers extensively to sacred prostitution because it was endemic to ancient Near Eastern culture; today, however, this practice is virtually unknown.[17] Likewise, the tribal division of the Children of Israel weakened and disappeared over the course of time, and as a result the laws of inheritance of land lost their significance.

Linguistics

God is limited when speaking to people; he had to address the People of Israel in a language that they understood. The Torah is therefore written in ancient Hebrew, including forms of speech not in use in modern Hebrew. For example, the use of the infinite with the inflected verb as in *hakem takim*; the addition of a vav to a verb in the future tense to create a past tense verb, as in *va-yidaber*. God constricts himself and uses a very limited vocabulary. In addressing the original recipients of the Torah, he did not use words from modern Hebrew or from foreign languages with which they were unfamiliar, though he was capable of doing so.

Peshat interpretation must reflect an understanding of the syntax and vocabulary of the Hebrew language as it would have been intelligible to the generation that received the Torah. Thus Rabbi Akiva's explanation of the word *totafot* (Deut. 6:8; understood to mean "tefillin") that "*tot* means two in Coptic and *fot* means two in African" is a midrash.[18] God is, of course, capable of speaking different languages. It cannot, however, be argued that the Torah, which was given to the People of Israel, includes a word combining elements from two languages not current in the ancient Near East, a word that the People of Israel could not have understood. In this case, I prefer the explanation of Menaḥem ibn Saruq that *totafot* derives from the word *hatafa* (exhortation), meaning that "one who sees them [the tefillin] between the eyes will remember the miracle and speak of it."[19] The suggestion, made by other commentators on the basis of the context and parallel structure, that the word refers to a type of jewelry is also plausible.[20]

Similarly, the sentence structure in the Torah follows syntax familiar to the People of Israel at the time that they received the Torah—usually the predicate followed by the subject as in *vayidaber Hashem el*... (literally, "and spoke God to...")—in contrast to current syntax—the subject followed by the predicate, as in "God spoke to." Thus, a sentence structured in a different syntactic form (subject-predicate) is irregular, and this irregularity must be explained according to exegetical principles. For example, the verse "Now the man knew his wife Eve" (Gen. 4:1) is explained by Rashi as the distant past "previous to the matter related above, before he had sinned and was banished from the Garden of Eden, as well as the pregnancy and the birth, because if it had been written *vayeda adam* (literally, "knew, the man"), it would mean that the children were born after the expulsion."[21] God had to speak to the People of Israel in the form current at the time of the giving of the Torah. Examples of this can be found in biblical literature in the parallel structure of poetry; the chiastic structure, characteristic of Near Eastern literature, found in many biblical stories;[22] and the frequent use of typological (formulaic) numbers.[23]

Language

These conclusions apply also to the concept of "language" in the wider sense of the term. The images that God used in the Torah are taken from the world familiar to people in the time of the Bible. Reward and punishment revolve around rain and agricultural produce (see, e.g., Deut. 11) that people at that time depended on for sustenance. This reality is foreign to the modern, urban lifestyle.

The personification of God was a response to the difficulty of discussing an abstract deity, as can be seen in the midrash cited above: "The vision of the glory of God is like a consuming fire at the summit of the mountain. The Torah spoke in a language that its audience could comprehend... and there are many examples of this... to draw them closer to his uniqueness."[24]

Reference to God in masculine grammatical forms is also an example of the use of human language. In a male-dominated, patriarchal society, this would have been the natural form of reference.

Conceptions of Nature and the Universe

The cosmology presented in the Torah is radically different from modern cosmology. The Torah describes the heavens as a *rakia* (expanse), meaning a physical partition separating the upper waters from the lower waters

(Gen. 1:6). Rain falls through floodgates in the sky ("And the floodgates of the sky broke open" (Gen. 7:11). The earth rests on pillars—"For the pillars of the earth are the Lord's; He has set the world upon them" (1 Sam. 2:8)—and underneath it lies Sheol, the underworld: "Sheol below was astir" (Isa. 14:9). The central aspects of this cosmology have parallels in Near Eastern literature.[25] How should we understand this in light of the very different cosmology presented by modern science? Is the Torah wrong? The Torah was given to people and it communicated with them according to their worldview. This was the scientific knowledge current at the time when the Torah was given, and the Torah does not contradict what is known to man. If so, we can conclude that the entire description of the creation of the world is couched in human language, and expresses important principles: the world was created by God; it is harmonic; man was created in the image of God. Modern man is required to act in accordance with these principles and, at the same time, can accept without hesitation modern theories about the creation of the universe.[26]

The Laws of the Torah

Do the laws of the Torah reflect a divine ideal? Many sources indicate that the Torah took into consideration the inclinations of man in its legislation, and is adapted in detail to the time in which it was given.

A prime example of this is the law of the "beautiful captive" (Deut. 21:11). The sages declared that this law was not ideal: "The Torah only decreed this in order to protect against man's evil inclination" (Babylonian Talmud, tractate *Kiddushin* 21b). In other words, the Torah established its laws out of familiarity with the human, instinctive, nature of man, and this implies a certain degree of relativity. In a world in which the rape of female captives was accepted practice, and even considered a kind of legitimate payment for the soldier (see Judg. 5:30), the commandment concerning the beautiful captive is understandable and crucial. The Torah allowed her to be taken, but demanded that relations with her be consecrated, and thus required the soldier to marry her: "The Torah only made considerations for the evil inclination; it is better for Israel to eat the flesh of dying animals, ritually slaughtered, than flesh of animals who died of natural causes."[27]

Rashi commented on this passage: "'A beautiful woman'—because he lusts for her on account of her beauty, she is permitted to him, but only just; it is preferable for the People of Israel to eat the flesh of dying animals that have been ritually slaughtered, or unhealthy meat that has been slaughtered, even if it is disgusting."

It is obvious that the central message of the commandment concerning the beautiful captive, revolutionary in its time, is eternal. The intention to minimize vulgarity and violent, unchecked sexual desire, even during war, is a basic principle that remains relevant today. Ironically, because this principle has been accepted and the modern world condemns rape and pillage, the particular details of this commandment are no longer relevant.

A classic example of exegesis based on the concept that law reflects its historical context is Maimonides' position that God commanded sacrifices because this was the universal form of ritual at the time when the Torah was given. The People of Israel were unable to accept a Torah that did not include sacrificial rites. The purpose of the commandments was to divert the sacrificial service performed by the People of Israel from idolatry to the worship of God:

> And therefore man, according to his nature, is not capable of abandoning suddenly all to which he was accustomed ... and, as at that time the way of life generally accepted and customary in the whole world and the universal service upon which we were brought up consisted in offering various species of living beings in the temples in which images were set up ... His wisdom, may He be exalted, and his gracious ruse, which is manifest in regard to all his creatures, did not require that He give us a Law prescribing the rejection, abandonment, and abolition of all these kinds of worship. For one could not then conceive the acceptance of [such a Law], considering the nature of man, which always likes that to which it is accustomed. At that time this would have been similar to the appearance of a prophet in these times who calling upon the people to worship God, would say: "God has given you a Law forbidding you to pray to Him, to fast, to call upon Him for help in misfortune. Your worship should consist solely in meditation without any works at all."[28]

Maimonides regarded the sacrificial rite as the prototype of all the commandments, designed to perfect multiple aspects of the human personality, and thus deemed it necessary to understand these commandments in the historical context in which they were given.

Another example can be found in the laws of blood vengeance (Num. 35:9–34). The Torah allows the family of a victim of manslaughter to kill the perpetrator as long as he has not entered a city of refuge. Is this an ideal situation? It is clear that the Torah intended to reduce the existing widespread practice of blood vengeance, not to institutionalize it.

According to the prevailing custom, the victim's family attempted to take revenge upon the killer (whether he acted intentionally or accidentally) and his family. Near Eastern law codes allowed the accidental murderer to pay a ransom.[29] In practice, many blood feuds continued over many years (see, e.g., 2 Sam. 3:27).[30]

In contrast, the Torah decreed that intentional killers would be put to death only after due legal process, and limited the opportunity for exacting vengeance on accidental killers to the time preceding arrival at the city of refuge, or in the event of premature departure from it. In addition, a killer's stay in the city of refuge would end upon the death of the High Priest. These changes herald an important legal development and social progress. The accidental killer does not have to pay a ransom and, more importantly, the period of time in which he may be killed in revenge is very brief. When humanity reached a state of further progress, blood vengeance ceased to exist within Jewish society as in most other societies.

The approach presented here, namely that the Torah is adapted to the time it was given, and, thus, to a reality different from the one in which we live, immediately raises the question of the Torah's eternal validity. If the Torah is subject to the influence of time and place, is it possible that it will change in the future?

Maimonides, who argued that the Torah responded to the religious and ritualistic contexts at the time it was given, affirmed that the Torah is eternal and will remain immutable even in messianic times. He even included this concept as one of his articles of faith, as if it were a universally accepted principle.[31] However, throughout rabbinic literature, from the time of the sages until the modern period, there is another, more dynamic approach that addresses changes to the commandments in the time of the Messiah. In the words of Rabbi Yoseph: "This refers to commandments that will be annulled at the end of days."[32]

This view is expressed in several midrashim. For example, in a discussion of the consumption of Leviathan and Behemoth at the end of days, it is written that God will kill them rather than ritually slaughtering them. Regarding the halakhic difficulty in this statement, Rabbi Avin bar Kahana commented: "God says: 'The Torah comes from me; innovations in the Torah also come from me.'"[33] A similar discussion takes place concerning forbidden foods and the laws of family purity: "'God releases the imprisoned'—What does this mean?

There are those who say that every animal that is considered impure in this world, God will make pure in the time of the Messiah. . . . What does 'release the imprisoned' mean? There is no greater prisoner (*asur*) than the *menstruant* woman, because when a woman sees blood she is forbidden (*asura*) to her husband, and in the time of the Messiah he will release (permit) her."[34]

This position was taken by commentators and thinkers throughout the generations. According to Rabbi Zaddok ha-Kohen, Korah's demand for equality among all the People of Israel was not a specious argument, but rather an idea before its time. His idea that "all the community are holy, all of them" (Num. 16:3) contains truth, but its implementation must be put off until the Messianic Era.[35] From this it may be concluded that the biblical hierarchy distinguishing between *Kohen*, *Levi*, and *Israel* is temporary.

The same is true regarding the sacrifices in the Third Temple. Many believe that it will be built and function according to the format of the Second Temple, while others disagree. Rabbi Chaim Hirschensohn believed that no sacrifices will be offered in the Third Temple.[36] Rav Kook maintained that at the beginning of the era of the Third Temple animal sacrifices will be offered, as stipulated in the Torah, but at a later stage in the distant future the moral state of the world would improve and the nature of animals would change until, as a result, animal sacrifices would stop.[37] Rabbi Joseph Messas argued that sacrifices will be offered at the dedication of the Third Temple (as described in the book of Ezekiel) and afterwards abolished.[38] Rabbi Messas also believed that in the Third Temple the menorah (candelabra) will run on electricity, not olive oil as in the Tabernacle and the first two Temples.[39] From the above discussion it may be concluded that the Torah is the correct path to take in this world, but, as the world changes, a change will also take place in the Torah.

According to Rav Kook, the authority to change the *halakhah* in light of a change in morality rests with the supreme *beit din* in messianic times:

> If a question arises concerning a law in the Torah, because, according to ethical values it would seem that it should be understood differently, if the supreme *beit din* decides that this law was only written in accordance with conditions that no longer exist, a source for this can certainly be found in the Torah. Concurrence between the authority of the *beit din* and the interpretation of the Torah are not a random coincidence. These are all words of wisdom emanating from the light of Torah and the truth of the Oral Law. We are obligated to obey the judge that will be officiating at that time. This is not a question of "development" or abbreviation.[40]

It appears that the divine origin of the Torah does not negate the fact that it was given at a specific time. The belief in the divine origin of the Torah implies the recognition that its principles are eternal, materializing in changing contexts. One who wishes to heed the central message in the laws concerning slaves—not to buy slaves, and even to fight for the abolition of slavery. One who pays close attention to the commandment regarding the beautiful captive will work to abolish sex trafficking and to promote sexual sublimation.

Anachronism

The phenomenon of anachronism, the existence of terms and verses that appear to be later in origin than the time in which the document was written, is widespread in the Bible in general and in the Torah in particular. In an interview, Rabbi Mordechai Breuer related a conversation with Rabbi Yehuda Amital about the appearance of the name "Dan" in the story of the war of the four kings in Genesis.[41] ("When Abram heard that his kinsman had been taken captive, he mustered his retainers, born into his household, numbering three hundred and eighteen, and went in pursuit as far as Dan" [Gen. 14:14]). This reference to the territory of the tribe of Dan appears anachronistic because, at the time of the story, Dan had not yet been born, and, consequently, the tribe of Dan had not yet conquered territory in the north of the Land of Israel (see Judg. 18). Rabbi David Kimchi commented on this verse that the name "Dan" was either mentioned prophetically, meaning that the place was described as it would later be called, or that a different place was intended. Rabbi Breuer related that he had asked Rabbi Amital how to understand the reference to Dan, and Rabbi Amital answered him: "Was God incapable of knowing the location of the tribe of Dan even before it was established?" Rabbi Breuer recounted that this answer amazed him, revolutionized his way of thinking, and led him to develop his aspects theory. In light of the arguments presented here, I cannot accept this solution because it is completely illogical. The recipients of the Torah had to understand, in some way, what was written; it is not possible that for hundreds of years a verse in the Torah was completely unintelligible.

Rabbi Amital's answer is supported by many commentaries throughout the generations, and perhaps there are those who will see in it an indication of the uniqueness of the Torah. However, the opposite approach of searching for a logical solution that includes the human factor in the Torah leads to a different path, also mentioned in early and medieval rabbinic literature. The sages themselves argued about the last eight verses in the Torah:

> Eight verses in the Torah were written by Joshua, as it is written: "So Moses the servant of the Lord died there" (Deut. 34:5). Now is it possible that Moses, while alive, could have written the words: "Moses died there"? Rather, up to this point Moses wrote, from this point on, Joshua wrote. This is the opinion of Rabbi Yehudah, or, according to others, of Rabbi Neḥemiah. Rabbi Shimon said to him: "Can a *sefer Torah* be missing even one letter? And yet it is written: "Take this book of Teaching" (Deut. 31: 26). Rather, up to this point, the Holy One, blessed be He, dictated and Moses repeated and recorded, and from this point God dictated and Moses, in tears, recorded.[42]

This is the approach taken by Abraham Ibn Ezra who added other verses to the list of anachronisms, and alluded cryptically to the concept with the phrase "the secret of the twelve."[43] His obscure references were explained by Rabbi Joseph Bonfils, in his super-commentary *Zafenat Pa'aneah*, on the verse "The Canaanites were then in the land" (Gen. 12:6): "It would appear that Moses did not write this word here. Joshua or one of the other prophets wrote it . . . since they were not concerned about this matter it is clear that they had the authority to add words in order to clarify, all the more so, that a prophet has the authority to add words to the prophecy of another prophet in order to explain them, especially regarding a non-legal, narrative passage. It therefore cannot be considered an interpolation."

Nachmanides also followed this approach in several places—for example, in his comment on Numbers 21:1:

> Scripture continued by relating here that Israel also laid their cities waste when they came into the land of Canaan, after the death of Joshua. . . . It is with reference to this that it is stated in the book of Judges. . . . It was then that this vow [recorded here] was fulfilled but Scripture however completed the account of the matter here, just as it did in the section speaking of the descending of the manna (Exod. 16:34–35) . . . [an event which occurred] after the death of Moses until "the morrow after the Passover" (Josh. 5:12). Similarly: "These are the names of the men that shall take possession of the Land for you, etc." (34:17). He should

rather have commanded Joshua [about them] at the time of the division of the Land.[44]

Isaac Abravanel opposed Nachmanides' position with the argument that God has the power to dictate to Moses statements about things that will take place after his death: "Moses wrote the Torah as God commanded him, word for word. Therefore, it is not impossible that he, may he rest in peace, wrote things that would take place after his death."[45]

The German Pietists also believed that the Torah contains verses added later. According to Gershon Brin, Rabbi Judah the Pious, in his commentary to Genesis 48, distinguished between three stylistic levels in the Bible.[46] He identified the third level with Joshua or the men of the Great Assembly.[47] Rabbi Judah the Pious also identified an interpolation from the time of the men of the Great Assembly in Deuteronomy 2:8. Israel Ta-Shma cited the from commentary of Rabbi Solomon bar Samuel Ha-Zarfati, a student of Rabbi Samuel the Pious, and his son Rabbi Judah the Pious that the name "Azazel" (Lev. 16:8) is Aramaic—a language later than the time of Moses: "Moses did not write this verse, rather someone else wrote it. Do not be shocked by my statement that someone else wrote it, because there are other such verses; that is, there are many verses not written by Moses."[48] The search for logical interpretation led commentators to add verses to this list and delete others. Sometimes there is a debate regarding a verse that some view as anachronistic, while others resolve its difficulty in another way.[49] Anachronism also occurs in the Prophets and Writings, and there as well commentators have used a variety of approaches.[50]

Approaches to Contradictions in Torah Law

The following discussion touches on a very raw nerve. Biblical criticism claims that the Torah is compiled from several sources or traditions that were incorporated in the Torah that we have today.[51] The fact that there are many contradictions, repetitions, stylistic differences, and various versions of the name of God within the Torah has led scholars to argue that the Torah is not harmonic or integrated. In addition, they argue that there is occasional unevenness in the text that can be resolved by skipping over or omitting verses to reveal an original harmonic text. Critical scholarship claims that the Bible underwent editing processes including interpolation, omission, and even adaptation of the verses.

Rabbi Mordechai Breuer was *sui generis* in that he accepted the arguments of critical scholarship and "translated" them into Jewish terminology. According to his approach, there are contradictions in the Bible, but they express the word of God in the most effective way possible. According to Breuer, God gave a Torah with internal contradictions because only by means of such tension it is possible to convey the divine truth in its entirety. The repetitions, contradictions, and changes in style are essential elements of the text. Nonetheless, he rejected the underlying assumptions of scholars who do not accept the concept of revelation and "believe" that the Torah is a human creation; he considered this belief a false axiom and an unproven opinion with no advantage over belief in the divine origin of the Torah. Acceptance of the contradictions from a position of belief in God's revelation to His people on Sinai led Rabbi Breuer to explain them as differing aspects—in other words, different points of view on the same story or law.

This is not the appropriate forum to discuss the aspects theory in all its details, but I will comment on its theological underpinnings. The difficulty here lies with pointing out God's ability to speak in a contradictory manner, while ignoring the human recipient who receives such a Torah. Is it reasonable to suggest that the recipient of the Torah, in the course of reading a legal passage, is aware that in another passage there is a contradictory position that complements it?

This point is especially valid regarding the instances in which one aspect of a law was revealed at Sinai and another forty years later on the plains of Moab. Sometimes Breuer's exegetical model is too sophisticated, and the Torah seems to be a convoluted riddle. Is the aspects theory viable? The answer is affirmative if the focus is on God's infinitude; however, the theory is not compatible with the approach that focuses on the People of Israel who received the Torah. God is able to make two contradictory statements simultaneously, but man is not capable of grasping both messages at the same time. The midrash says that *shamor* ("observe," Deut. 5:12) and *zakhor*)"remember," Ex. 20:8) were said in a single utterance, but Abraham Ibn Ezra, one of the greatest of the *peshat* exegetes, rejected the idea: "Even if we say that the speech of God is different from human speech, how did the People of Israel understand God's utterance? Because if a person were to hear *shamor* and *zakhor* at the same time, he would understand neither."[52] Ibn Ezra therefore preferred to resolve the contradiction by arguing that, in Deuteronomy, Moses changed the language of the Ten Commandments yet retained the essence of the words, because observing and remembering have the same meaning.

In light of this argument, I will present a simpler model that takes into consideration the human beings receiving the divine laws. According to this model, Torah legislation underwent changes: the original law was replaced by a new one according to changing realities, the need of the hour, and the ethical and spiritual level of the world at that time.[53] This model can be seen explicitly in the law of *basar ta'avah* (meat of lust). Initially, God commanded that all meat must be slaughtered on the altar (Lev. 17). During the preparations before entering the Land of Israel and the transition to a centralized ritual, this early law was annulled, and meat was allowed to be slaughtered for consumption alone (Deut. 12:15).

This model is also clearly seen in the story of the daughters of Zelophehad. Initially only sons were to inherit from their fathers. However, the daughters of Zelophehad, who died without sons, appealed to Moses, and God decreed a change in the law: if there are no sons, the daughters will inherit from their father (Num. 27). In response, the elders of the tribe of Manasseh, who feared that the daughters of Zelophehad would marry members of other tribes and their inheritance would be lost to the tribe, appealed to Moses. God responded by making the new law conditional upon the daughters' marriage to members of their own tribe (Num. 36).

This dynamic process, presented explicitly in the Torah, is the key to understanding the entire biblical legal system. Although this model is mentioned overtly by the sages only in reference to specific commandments (the transition in methods of slaughtering, daughters' inheritance, the consumption of meat for pleasure, and the centralization of ritual) it is latent in other sources.

According to this model, the Torah's eternity lies in the ethical messages embedded in every law, and the higher purpose revealed in the changes to laws. For example, my teacher Rabbi Avia Hacohen argues that in the law of the Hebrew maidservant, as it appears in Exodus 21:7–11, the Torah permits concubinage while protecting the rights of the maidservant, and thereby establishes an ethical basis for behavior towards her.[54] However, in Deuteronomy 15:12–18 the Torah forbids concubinage and permits only short-term slavery in order to prevent involuntary sexual relations. The eternal message is embedded also in the relationship between the passages. The Torah aims to increasingly better the condition of the vulnerable maidservant, and this inspired the sages to continue the trend by mandating that the master marry the maidservant when she reaches maturity. As part of this trend, they even substituted the payment given to the father in exchange for his daughter with a *ketubah* (marriage contract) given to the woman herself.

From the point of view of the recipient of the Torah, this solution is more logical than others. The Torah's recipients were expected to keep a new commandment. In every generation, the recipients of the Torah kept the Written Law that lay in front of them and was adapted to them. Whenever a new law was given, they would commit themselves to obeying it, and were not expected to perceive within it a new perspective that complements another point of view.

It must be admitted that this solution, too, is not without its difficulties. It does not explain the interweaving of verses, as in the story of the Flood. Furthermore, in order for a change in the law to be understood fully, its causes must be clarified. From a theological perspective, the question of the dating of the Torah's composition remains and must be clarified. It must be admitted that it will be difficult to explain why there were numerous changes in such a short timespan of forty years. Nonetheless, the strength of the exegetical model lies in its simplicity and its ability to provide logical interpretation based on an awareness of both sides of the prophetic nature of the Torah: God the giver and man the recipient.

This model is similar to the position of biblical scholarship in breaking the text into separate passages and then ascribing them to different times and places. It is however, the polar opposite of the secular perspective usually associated with this approach. In contrast to secular, academic exegesis from which God is absent, this model affirms revelation and the belief in a God who speaks to his people through the Torah.

Endnotes

I would like to thank Dr. Yoshi Fargeon for his helpful comments and criticisms. Special thanks to my student Aviad Avron for his great efforts in editing this article.

1. Rimon Kasher, "Ha-Nissim ba-Mikra: Yiḥudam ha-Fenomenologi, Ma'amadam ha-Te'ori, u-Mashma'utam ha-Teologit" [Miracles in the Bible: their phenomenological uniqueness, narrative status, and theological meaning], *Beit ha-Mikra* 31a (1986): 50.
2. While in the framework of this article, I will distinguish between divine speech and human comprehension, I am aware of the existence of more complex models of the process of revelation. See Tamar Ross, *Expanding the Palace of Torah: Orthodoxy and Feminism* (Hanover, NH: Brandeis University Press), 201.
3. *Pesikta de-Rav Kahana*, ed. Bernard Mandelboim (New York: Jewish Theological Seminary of America, 1962), 222 (*piska 24, behodesh ha-shlishi*).
4. Babylonian Talmud, tractate *Kiddushin* 17b.
5. *Pesikta Zutarta* (*Lekaḥ Tov*), Ex. 24:17, s.v. *u-mareh kavod*.
6. On the need to express deep philosophical ideas by means of metaphor in the Torah and Prophets, see the introduction to the first part of *The Guide of the Perplexed* (pages 8–14 in the Pines translation). Maimonides likened the relationship between ideas and their manner of expression to "golden apples in silver showpieces" (Prov. 25:11). On the limitations of human intelligence and the Torah's use of human language, see *The Guide of the Perplexed*

1:33. The relationship between the manner of divine speech and the human ability to comprehend it was discussed by Rav Kook in several places. For example, *Eder ha-Yakar* (Jerusalem: Mosad Harav Kook, 1967), 42; *Iggrot Ha-Ra'aya* (Jerusalem: Mosad Harav Kook, 1985), 102–103 (1:90, sec. 2 and 6).
7. This passage was discovered by Moshe Sokolow in a manuscript and cited by Elazar Touitou in *Ha-Pashtut ha-Mithadshim be-Kol Yom* [Peshat interpretations emerging daily] (Ramat Gan: Bar Ilan University, 2003), 75. In *Mikra'ot Gedolot ha-Keter* this passage is included at the end of Samuel ben Meir's commentary to Deuteronomy. Samuel ben Meir used similar language in his introduction to the Torah portion Mishpatim: "I will interpret the laws and the statutes according to social mores."
8. For an extensive discussion on this subject see Uriel Simon, "Mashma'uta ha-Datit shel ha-Pashtut ha-Mithadshim" [The religious meaning of the renewing peshat exegesis], in *Ha-Mikra ve-Anachnu* [The Bible and us], ed. Uriel Simon)Ramat Gan: Devir, 1988), 133–152.
9. Babylonian Talmud, tractate *Shabbat* 63a.
10. *Pesikta de-Rav Kahana* (Mandelboim), 355 (*piska* 24, *Shuva*). The parallel version in the Jerusalem Talmud, tractate *Makot* 2:6 is incomplete, as noted by Mandelboim in his edition of the *Peskita de-Rav Kahana* (355): "The parallel passage in the Jerusalem Talmud contains lacunae. However, the passage appears in sources from the Geniza and medieval literature. See Maimonides, *Hilkhot ha-Yerushalmi le-Rambam* [The laws of the Palestinian Talmud], ed. Saul Lieberman (New York: Jewish Theological Seminary of America, 1947), 67n7."
11. The distinction between God and his Torah appears in another midrash: "The Lord replied: 'Because they forsook the Teaching I had set before them' (Jer. 9:12). Rabbi Ḥiyya bar Ba said: 'They deserted Me' (Jer. 16:11)—I will overlook this for perchance they kept My Torah, because if they forsook Me and kept my Torah, the leaven [i.e., the enzyme or catalyst] within it would bring them back to me." (Jerusalem Talmud, tractate Ḥagigah, 1:7). The midrash raises a possible scenario in which the Jewish people are alienated from God, but at the same time connected to the Torah.
12. This is not the appropriate forum in which to discuss the midrash's approach to repentance. I will confine myself to one aspect of the issue. The answers given by Wisdom and Prophecy, and even the Torah, are correct but incomplete, because they are part of the system of law and order that are also the will of God. However, God's answer teaches us that repentance has the power to override the legal system, and allow the return of the repentant sinner.
13. Rabbi Dov Baer ben Avraham of Mezeritch, *Magid Devarav le-Ya'akov*, 297 (*piska* 191).
14. Ross, *Expanding the Palace of Torah*, 201–202. See also Yosef Chaim, *Od Yosef Chai* (Jerusalem: Htorev, 1950), 237, Emor, s.v. *ve-lakaḥat*.
15. Ross does not make room for *peshat* interpretation. See below, note 53.
16. Babylonian Talmud, tractate *Megillah* 13a.
17. On the phenomenon of ritual marriages, that is, a ritual performance of a sexual act to celebrate the marriage of gods, see the collected volume: M. Nissinen and U. Risto, eds., *Sacred Marriages: The Divine-Human Sexual Metaphor from Sumer to Early Christianity* (Winona Lake, IN: Eisenbrauns, 2008).
18. Babylonian Talmud, tractate *Sanhedrin* 4b.
19. Rashi on Exod. 13:16.
20. See Menahem Zevi Kaddari, *Milon ha-Ivrit ha-Mikra'it* [A dictionary of biblical Hebrew] (Ramat Gan: Bar Ilan University, 2006), 377, s.v. *totafot*.
21. Rashi on Gen. 4:1.

22. A chiastic structure (in which words or sentences are arranged transversely) is also found in Near Eastern literature. On this subject in general see John W. Welch, ed., *Chiasmus in Antiquity* (Hildesheim: Gerstenberg, 1981).
23. A typological (formulaic) number is a number with a special meaning that expresses a particular idea when it appears in writing. This is an accepted literary device in poetry and prose. According to Samuel ben Meir and Abraham Ibn Ezra (as opposed to Rashi), God also expresses himself with typological numbers. See their commentaries on Lev. 26:18.
24. *Pesikta Zutarta* (*Lekaḥ Tov*), Ex. 24:17, s.v. *u-mareh kavod*. This statement is also true regarding prophecy. Understanding the diversions of rivers in the Messianic Era described in Isa. 11:15 requires a familiarity with the rivers' original courses. In the modern world, in which we can travel by air it is hard to accept that the future redemption will involve changes to water transport. In a previous article, I argued that the diversion of seas and rivers is an act of divine revelation, and, in this sense, the prophecy is eternal. See Chezi Cohen, "Kriyat Yam Suf ve-Ḥiashivuta ha-Teologit" [The Parting of the Red Sea and its theological significance], *Ma'agalim* 1 (1998): 23–31.
25. See, e.g., Shemuel Efraim Levinstam, "Sha'ul," in *Entzeklopedia Mikrait* [Encyclopaedia biblica] Jerusalem: Mosad Bialik, 1988), 7:456–457.
26. Uriel Simon, "Parashat Bereshit: Parashat ha-Bria be-Heibet Sifruti" [*Parashat Bereshit*: The story of creation from a literary perspective], *Likrat Shabbat* (2006): 11–22.
27. Babylonian Talmud, tractate *Kiddushin* 21b-22a.
28. *The Guide of the Perplexed*, 3:32.
29. Chaim Noy, *Hukkim min ha-Mizraḥ ha-Kadum Arukhim be-makbil le-Ḥukkim min ha-Torah* [Laws from the ancient Near East concurrent to the laws of the Torah] (Kiryat Tivon: Ḥayyim Noi, 1989), 23–24.
30. For a detailed study, see Haim Zeev Hirschberg, "Ge'ulat Dam," in *Enzeklopedia Mikrait* 2:392–394.
31. Maimonides affirmed this idea in his introduction to *perek Ḥelek*, the ninth principle: "The Ninth Fundamental Principle is the authenticity of the Torah, i.e., that this Torah was precisely transcribed from God and no one else. To the Torah, Oral and Written, nothing must be added nor anything taken from it, as it is said, 'You must neither add nor detract' (Deut. 13:1)." Maimonides, *A Maimonides Reader*, ed. Isadore Twersky (New York: Behrman House, 1972), 421.
32. Babylonian Talmud, tractate *Niddah* 61b.
33. *Va-yikra Rabbah*, Shemini, 13:3. For a survey of the midrashim, see http://www.aharit.com/A-12html.
34. *Midrash Shoḥer Tov*, Psalms, *piska* 146, 4.
35. See Avia Hacohen, "Parashat Koraḥ: Al Sovlanut be-De'ot ve-Shivyon" [The story of Korah: On intellectual tolerance and equality], *Mishlav* 15) 1990): 57–71.
36. Rabbi Chaim Hirschensohn, *Malki ba-Kodesh* (St. Louis, MO: Moniester, 1919), 1:8–9. On the argument between Rav Kook and Rabbi Hirschensohn, see Eyal Ben-Eliyahu, "'LeHakim Binyan Ḥadash': Ha-Rav Kook, ha-Rav Hirschensohn ve-Herzl al Binyan ha-Mikdash ve-Ḥidush ha-Korbanot" [To build a new building: Rav Kook, Rabbi Hirschensohn, and Herzl on the rebuilding of the Temple and the renewal of sacrifices], *Katedra* 128 (2008): 101–112.
37. Rav Abraham Isaac ha-Kohen Kook, *Ḥazon ha-Tzimḥonut ve-ha-Shalom* [The vision of vegetarianism and peace], ed. David Cohen)Jerusalem: Netzer David Ariel, 1983); *Siddur Olat Ra'aya* (Jerusalem: Mosad Harav Kook, 1985), 292.

38. Rabbi Joseph Messas, *Otzar Ha-Miktavim* (Husiatyn: Kolak, 1905), 2:1305, also published in *Masoret be-Aidan Moderni: Ḥakhamim Sefaradim be-Dorot ha-Aḥaronim* [Jewish heritage in modern times], ed. Rabbi Itshak Shouraqui (Tel Aviv: Miskal, 2009), 230.
39. Rabbi Joseph Messas, *Ner Mitzva* (Jerusalem: Makhon Bnei Yisakhar, 1999), 15, also published in *Masoret be-Aidan Moderni*, 229.
40. *Iggerot Ha-Ra'aya*, 1:90
41. Rabbi Mordechai Breuer, *Shitat ha-Beḥinot shel ha-Rav Mordekhai Breuer* [The aspects theory of Rabbi Mordechai Breuer], ed. Yosef Ofer (Alon Shvut: Tvunot, 2005), 341.
42. Babylonian Talmud, tractate *Bava Batra* 15a.
43. A complete list can be found in Uriel Simon, "Shenayim Oḥazim be-'Sod ha-Sheim-asar' shel Rav Avraham ibn Ezra" [Two who fight over the "secret of the twelve" of Rabbi Abraham Ibn Ezra], *Megadim* 51 (2010): 77–85.
44. Nachmanides, *Commentary on the Torah*, trans. and ed. Charles B. Chavel (New York: Shilo, 1975), 230–231.
45. Abravanel, ed. Yehuda Shaviv (Jerusalem: Horev, 2007), commentary to Num. 21.
46. Gershon Brin, "Kavim le-Perush ha-Torah shel Rabbi Yehuda he-Ḥasid" [An introduction to the commentary of Rabbi Judah the Pious], *Teudah* 3 (1983): 215–226.
47. See Baruch J. Schwartz, "Perush Rabbi Yehudah He-Ḥasid le-Bereshit 48:20–22" [The commentary of Rabbi Judah the Pious to Genesis 48:20–22], *Tarbiz* 80 (2012): 29–39.
48. Israel Ta-Shama, "Mashehu al Bikoret ha-Mikra be-Ashkenaz be-Yimmei ha-Benayim" [Notes on biblical criticism in Germany in the Middle Ages], in *Ha-Mikra be-Re'i Mefarshav* [The Bible as seen by its commentators], ed. Sara Japhet (Jerusalem: Magnes, 1994), 453–459.
49. For example, in his comment on Gen. 36:31, Abraham Ibn Ezra forcefully rejected the opinion of the "Yitzhaki" that the list of the kings of Edom was from the days of Jehoshaphat.
50. For example, biblical scholarship has revealed differences in both language and content between the first part of the book of Isaiah (1–39) and the second part (40–66). In addition, the second part refers to the Babylonian exile and the return to Zion following the declaration of Cyrus (44–45), and a call to return from captivity in Babylon and rebuild the Temple (48:20). As a result, biblical scholars argued that the second part of the book was written by another prophet in the time of the return to Zion. In keeping with the thesis outlined here, I cannot accept the position that the second part of the book is the prophecy of Isaiah merely on the basis of the argument that a prophet can speak of events that took place 150 years after his time. In fact, a prophet can describe distant events, but is it logical that he would make prophesies that his audience would be unable to understand? It seems to me that the answer to this question is negative, and that we must therefore seek other answers to the question of discrepancies between the two parts of the book. See the discussion of Amos Hakham, *Da'at Mikra, Yishayahu* (Jerusalem: Mosad ha-Rav Kook, 1984), 14–17; Avia Hacohen, "Ha-Omnam Eḥad Haya Yishayahu?" [Was there only one Isaiah?], *Derekh Efrata* 9–10 (2001): 79–88.
    Another example is the reference to Josiah by name in the prophecy of the "man of God" (1 Kings 13:2) about three hundred years before the king's birth. See Yehuda Elitzur, "Eumna u-Mada be-Parshanut ha-Mikra: Ekronot, Teḥumin u-Kavanot" [Faith and science in biblical exegesis: Principles, areas, and intentions], in *Emuna, Dat u-Mada* [Faith, religion, and science] (Jerusalem: Ministry of Education, 1966), 19.
51. For a summary of biblical criticism see (among other sources) Yair Hoffman, *Sugiot be-Bikoret ha-Mikra* [Essays on biblical criticism] (Tel Aviv: Ha'universita Hameshuderet, 1997).
52. Ibn Ezra on Exod. 20:1.

53 On this type of exegesis, see Avia Hacohen, "Be-Ikvei Beur ha-Gra le-Parasht Ama Ivria" [In the footsteps of the commentary of the Vilna Gaon to the commandment of the Hebrew maidservant], in *Sefer ha-Yovel le-Rav Mordechai Breuer* [Mordechai Breuer Jubilee Volume], ed. Moshe Bar-Asher (Jerusalem: Akademon, 1992), 1:77–87; David Bigman and Avia Hacohen, "Parashat Sotah," *Mishlav* 29 (1996): 11–21; Chezi Cohen, "Mah Bein Pesach be-Shemmot le-Pesach be-Devarim?" [What is the difference between Passover in Exodus and Passover in Deuteronomy?], *Akdamut* 26 (2011): 41–56. A collection of articles on the developmental approach is soon to be published by Yeshivat Ma'aleh Gilboa.

On this basis, it is possible to speak of the idea of the cumulative revelation discussed by Shalom Rosenberg's "Ha-Hitgalut ha-Matmedet: Shlosha Kivunim" [The continual revelation: three directions], in *Hitgalut, Emuna, Tevuna* [Revelation, faith, understanding], ed. Moshe Hallamish and Moshe Schwarcz (Ramat Gan: Bar Ilan University, 1976), 131–143; and Tamar Ross's *Expanding the Palace of Torah*, 197 and following. Nonetheless, it is important to make three distinctions between the model proposed by these two scholars of Jewish thought and the ideas presented here: First, both of these scholars relate to the Written Torah as one unit, and discuss a series of "hearings" of what was said at Sinai reverberating throughout Jewish history; the reference is to commentaries and halakhic rulings (Ross, 197–200). I, on the other hand, am referring to a continuum of revelations over many years from which the Written Torah itself was compiled. Second, Ross warmly embraces the rabbinic tradition that the meaning of the Torah is "looser and richer than a strictly literal historical understanding" (199). I argue that the Torah has a logical interpretation, which is the *peshat* that commentators have disputed, as distinct from the midrash, the *remez*, and the *sod*. Third, Ross, in her comments about the term "revelation," rejects an absolute distinction between the divine and the human (200–201). Although I agree with her on the third point, I did not deem it appropriate to discuss the idea in this article.

54. Avia Hacohen, "Be-Ikvei Beur ha-Gra le-Parashat Ama Ivria."

The Revelation Narratives: Analyses and Theological Reflections on Exodus, Deuteronomy, and Classical Midrash

Avraham Shammah

Exodus 19–24 and Deuteronomy 4–5 present different descriptions of revelation. A comparison between the two sections raises philosophical and theological questions, some of which are hinted at in classical rabbinic literature. It is not my intention in this article to present a detailed exegetical analysis of these passages, but rather to identify several significant and fundamental characteristics of their description of divine revelation.[1]

The Central Narrative in Exodus: Revelation as Vision

A fundamental characteristic of the depiction of the revelation in Exodus 19 is vision; there is a human viewer and a divine object of vision. Revelation, as the term implies, is visual, and is described in several of the central verses as a single objective vision perceived by all. Those who see it are witnesses to an event external to themselves, an event in which the image of God emerges from his celestial abode and descends to earth: "For on the third day the Lord will come down, in the sight of all the people, on Mount Sinai. . . . Moses led the people out of the camp toward God. . . . Now Mount Sinai was all in smoke, for the Lord had come down upon it" (Exod. 19:11–18).[2]

The text declares that human beings are forbidden to enter the sphere of the divine, and therefore the people must be restricted to the foot of the mountain and prevented even from touching its edge: "You shall set bounds for the people round about, saying, 'Beware of going up the mountain or touching the border of it. Whoever touches the mountain shall be put to death.' Moses led the people out of the camp toward God . . . and they took their places at the foot of the mountain" (12–17).

The assumption inherent to the biblical text is that the heavens are the abode of God while the earth was given to man: "The heavens belong to the Lord, but the earth He gave over to man" (Ps. 115:16). When God crossed this boundary and descended to the mountain, he removed the people from the mountain so that the two spheres would not mix. He also disrupted the tranquility of the earth. The descent of God upon the mountain is, therefore, accompanied by a terrifying upheaval: "There was thunder, and lightning, and a dense cloud upon the mountain, and a very loud blast of the horn; and all the people who were in the camp trembled. . . . Now Mount Sinai was all in smoke, for the Lord had come down upon it in fire; the smoke rose like the smoke of a kiln, and the whole mountain trembled violently" (16–18).

The context makes clear that the cloud and the smoke do not function here as a screen, but are part of the upheaval and, along with the thunder, the lightening, and the horn, instill fear of God.

It therefore transpires that while the connection between God and man is devoid of physical contact, it includes visual contact in the form of man observing God from across the barrier. This empirical viewing requires human preparation and the people are, therefore, commanded to sanctify themselves by laundering their garments and abstaining from marital relations: "And the Lord said to Moses, 'Go to the people and warn them to stay pure today and tomorrow. Let them wash their clothes. Let them be ready for the third day.' . . . Moses came down from the mountain to the people and warned the people to stay pure, and they washed their clothes. And he said to the people, 'Be ready for the third day: do not go near a woman'" (10–15).

What did the people see? This question leaves the reader in uncertainty because of the content's inherent tension and utter sublimity. These are boldly worded verses describing divine revelation to a select group. This can be seen especially in verses 24:9–10: "Then Moses and Aaron, Nadab and Abihu, and seventy elders of Israel ascended; **and they saw the God of Israel**: under His feet there was the likeness of a pavement of sapphire, like the very sky for purity. Yet He did not raise His hand against the leaders of the Israelites; **they beheld God.**"[3]

These verses contrast with verse 20:15: "All the people witnessed the thunder and lightning, the blare of the horn and the mountain smoking; and when the people saw it." It seems to me that the intention of this verse is to clarify that they saw these things but no more; they did not see God.

In addition to these verses, there is also a description of what will happen in the future: "The Lord will come down, in the sight of all the people" (Exod. 19:11). However, this verse also creates uncertainty; it announces and anticipates the spectacle of the descent of God, but a description of the people actually witnessing the descent itself is missing. Furthermore, the verse does not say that the people will see God with their own eyes, but that God will descend before their eyes: the object of the vision is the descent, not God.[4]

Verses 20–25 state that beholding the deity is forbidden, perhaps even impossible, and will result in God "breaking out" against those who attempt to perceive him.[5] These verses limit God's presence to the summit of the mountain, where it can be seen by the people only from afar: "The Lord came down upon Mount Sinai, on the **top of the mountain**, and the Lord called Moses to **the top of the mountain**. . . . 'Go down, warn the people **not to break through to the Lord to gaze**, lest many of them perish . . . lest the Lord break out against them . . . but let not the priests or the people **break through to come up to the Lord**, lest He break out against them.'"

These verses stand in contrast to verses 10–19 that describe God's descent upon "the mountain" and even "the whole mountain": "**The Lord will come down** . . . **on Mount Sinai** . . . a dense cloud **upon the mountain**. . . . **Now Mount Sinai was all** in smoke . . . the Lord had come down **upon it** . . . **the whole mountain** trembled violently."[6]

Foreshadowing in Exodus of the Auditory Revelation in Deuteronomy

Thus far I have emphasized the visual aspect of the narrative in Exodus. Attention must also be paid to its verbal elements, to its discourse. The outstanding feature of the verses that I have described so far would seem to be the absence of verbal communication between God and man. Discourse as a component of revelation is entirely absent from chapter 19. Moses speaks to God and hears his reply, yet these words are not part of the revelation itself, but rather ancillary to it, providing instructions relating to the revelatory event, and similar matters.

Although there is a brief conversation in verse 9 ("And the Lord said to Moses, 'I will come to you in a thick cloud, in order that the people may hear when I speak with you.'") it can be argued that this segment is not part of the narrative sequence of the story, as can be seen in verses 8 and 9:

> 8a: All the people answered as one, saying, "All that the Lord has spoken we will do!"
> 8b: And Moses brought back the people's words to the Lord.
> 9a: And the Lord said to Moses, "I will come to you in a thick cloud, in order that the people may hear when I speak with you. . . ."
> 9b: Then Moses reported the people's words to the Lord.

Verse 9b puzzled the sages because the people's words reported to God by Moses are not specified prior to this verse.[7] It would appear that according to the *peshat* (plain, contextual meaning), verse 9b is a resumptive repetition (*Weideraufnahme*, or epanalepsis) of 8b. This means that 9a is not part of the narrative sequence but a parenthetical expression,[8] a flash, a secondary voice, that serves to foreshadow a similar[9] event in Deuteronomy (as I will explain below).[10] Segment 9a, which deviates from the sequence, causes segment 9b to refer back to 8b, and thereby return to the narrative sequence.

The position of the Decalogue in Exodus requires particular attention because it is quintessentially divine discourse. However, even this famous speech is not described in Exodus as the result of the descent of God or as part of the revelation. The Decalogue surprises the reader because neither verses 10–19, announcing God's descent, nor the following verses, 20–25, indicate that God is going to speak to the people. Moreover, the opening of the Decalogue speech at the beginning of chapter 20 ("God spoke all these words, saying") is odd in that it lacks an indirect object indicating to whom God spoke these words. In other words, the text does not explicitly state that the words were heard by the audience for whom they were intended.[11]

There is no choice but to acknowledge the existence of two possible readings. According to the first reading, the Decalogue is not a continuation of the preceding verse, in which case the revelation remains purely visual; as the descriptive narrative continues in the verse immediately following the conclusion of the Decalogue (20:15): "All the people witnessed the thunder and lightning, the blare of the horn and the mountain smoking; and when the people saw it, they fell back and stood at a distance."[12] This reading rests on the verses constituting the central narrative axis. According to the other reading, the

Torah's intention is to append a long series of legal passages to the revelation narrative, continuing until chapter 23: the Decalogue, the laws (*mishpatim*) beginning in verse 21:1, sections of law, and collections of written commandments as elaborated in 24:4–12,[13] and ending with the ceremony marking the sealing of the covenant and the people's acceptance of the commandments:

> He set up an altar and they offered burnt offerings and sacrificed bulls as offerings of well-being to the Lord. Moses took one part of the blood and put it in basins, and the other part of the blood he dashed against the altar. Then he took the record of the covenant and read it aloud to the people. And they said, "All that the Lord has spoken we will faithfully do!" Moses took the blood and dashed it on the people and said, "This is the blood of the covenant that the Lord now makes with you concerning all these commands" (Exod. 24:4–8).

This second possible reading, which includes the commandments, is another foreshadowing of a similar event that will occur in the future in Deuteronomy: the giving of the law and the covenant that are signaled as early as the beginning of chapter 19, in verses 3–6: "Thus shall you say to the house of Jacob and declare to the children of Israel.... Now then, if you will obey Me faithfully and keep My covenant." These verses foreshadow what is to come in Deuteronomy as indicated by the phrase "you shall be My treasured possession among all the peoples" as well as "if you will obey Me faithfully" (19:5), which are characteristic of the style of Deuteronomy.[14]

In addition, it appears that the section immediately following the Decalogue (20:15–19) also foreshadows Deuteronomy:

> All the people witnessed the thunder and lightning, the blare of the horn and the mountain smoking; and when the people saw it, they fell back and stood at a distance. "You speak to us," they said to Moses, "and we will obey; but let not God speak to us, lest we die." Moses answered the people, "Be not afraid." . . . So the people remained at a distance, while Moses approached the thick cloud where God was. The Lord said to Moses: Thus shall you say to the Israelites: You yourselves saw that I spoke to you from the very heavens.

Verses 16 and 19 mention God's verbal communication with the people: "let not **God speak to us**"; "**I spoke to you**." However, the words at the beginning of verse 18 ("So the people remained at a distance") appear to be a resumptive repetition of the end of verse 15 ("they fell back and stood at a distance").[15] This means that the intermediary verses (16–17) can be defined as parenthetical or outside the narrative sequence.[16] Moreover, verse 15 does not mention that the people heard speech, only that they "witnessed the thunder and lightning, the blare of the horn, and the mountain smoking," and therefore, in this respect also, verses 16–17 are not a continuation of verse 15. Verse 19, which describes verbal communication from heaven, is also not part of the narrative sequence, because verbal communication from heaven is not mentioned at all in Exodus, and therefore the didactic lesson—"You yourselves saw that I spoke to you from the very heavens" (20:18)—has no basis. The inescapable conclusion is that verse 19 is nonsequential, and divine verbal communication is not a part of the central narrative axis in Exodus, but rather characteristic of the account of revelation in Deuteronomy.[17]

In conclusion, it would appear that the core of the revelation in Exodus 19 is essentially visual[18] and in fact supports the first reading.[19] This core is surrounded by legal discourse, and enveloped in laws and statements about divine speech. This outer shell foreshadows what is to come in Deuteronomy, as I will attempt to explain in the following pages.

Deuteronomy: The "Audio" Revelation

The description of the event on Mount Horeb in Deuteronomy is very complicated, although less so than that in Exodus. As thorough exegetical analysis is outside the scope of this paper, I will address only the essential points and their inherent theological significance.

The narrative in Deuteronomy takes for granted a literary conception that the permanent abode of God is in the heavens.[20] Unlike in Exodus, where God pierces the veil and descends to the mountain, in Deuteronomy He does not come down to the mountain, and the people see no image. Furthermore, the axis linking man and God is switched from "video" to "audio":

> The day you stood before the Lord your God at Horeb, when the Lord said to Me, "Gather the people to Me that **I may let them hear My words**." . . . You came forward and stood at the foot of the mountain. The mountain was ablaze with flames to the very skies, dark with densest clouds. **The Lord spoke to you** out of the fire; **you heard the sound of words but perceived no shape—nothing but a voice** . . . since **you saw no**

> shape when the Lord your God spoke to you at Horeb out of the fire (Deut. 4:10–15).
>
> Has any people **heard the voice of a god speaking** out of a fire, **as you have**, and survived? (4:33)
>
> The Lord **spoke those words**—those and no more—to your whole congregation at the mountain, with **a mighty voice** out of the fire and the dense clouds.... When **you heard the voice** out of the darkness, while the mountain was ablaze with fire ... [you] said, "The Lord our God has just shown us His majestic Presence, and **we have heard His voice** out of the fire; we have seen this day that man may live though **God has spoken to him** ... if we **hear the voice of the Lord our God** any longer, we shall die. For what mortal ever **heard the voice of the living God speak** out of the fire, as we did, and lived?" (5:19–23)

In these verses the voice is heard from within the fire, and the text ignores the question of the location of the speaker. In another verse, Deuteronomy 4:36, what was described above as the divine voice heard from the fire is explained by an intra-biblical interpretation: "From the heavens He let you hear His voice ... on earth He let you see His great fire ... and from amidst that fire you heard His words." God uttered sound from heaven and on earth revealed his fire, out of which were heard the words spoken in heaven. It is possible that the verse "the mountain was ablaze with flames to the very skies" (Deut. 4:11) means that the voice heard from heaven is the voice heard from the fire, because the mountain burns with fire that reaches to the heavens.

In contrast to Exodus, Deuteronomy is characterized by the distance between man and God. The closeness in Exodus, expressed in language connoting vision, is replaced by distance. Moreover, the visual concepts in Exodus are converted in Deuteronomy to a different kind of vision, and several verses include an intra-biblical interpretation of the matter:

> But take utmost care and watch yourselves scrupulously, so that you do not forget **the things that you saw with your own eyes** and so that they do not fade from your mind (Deut. 4:9).
>
> It has been clearly **demonstrated to you** that the Lord alone is God; ... on earth He let you see His great fire (4:35–6).
>
> And said, "**The Lord our God has just shown us His majestic Presence**, and we have heard His voice out of the fire; **we have seen this day** that man may live though God has spoken to him" (5:21).

"The things that you saw with your own eyes" is a general expression for the experience of the sublime event. It refers to cognitive realization rather than visual perception. "It has been demonstrated to you" that the Lord is God, and you have even seen his majesty (in the cognitive sense) but you did not perceive a visual image other than fire.[21]

Moreover, and most significantly, Deuteronomy does not merely shift from visual revelation to phonetic, vocal revelation—to the acoustic and the auditory. It becomes verbal, transforming into discourse and speech. The revelation in Deuteronomy is verbal and lingual. In Deuteronomy, unlike Exodus, the Decalogue is the core of the revelatory event and its purpose; and the content is directed to specific listeners: "When the Lord said to me, 'Gather the people to Me **that I may let them hear My words.**' . . . **The Lord spoke to you.** . . . **He declared to you the covenant** that He commanded you to observe, the Ten Commandments; At the same time the Lord commanded me **to impart to you** laws and rules" (Deut. 4:10–14).[22]

Unlike a vision, which is by nature fleeting, the verbal, instructional revelation in Deuteronomy establishes an ongoing, eternal experience. The speaking voice, in its strict phonetic, vocal sense, was heard only once: "The Lord spoke those words—those and no more . . . with a mighty voice." (5:19). However, the verbal logos continues to be heard and persists within human consciousness and attention to it never wanes. The eternal validity of the verbal content became fixed permanently in Deuteronomy in three ways: (1) the prohibition against forgetting, (2) the commandment to learn and to teach one's children, and (3) the graphic representation on stone tablets. All three appear only in Deuteronomy, not in Exodus.[23]

> But take utmost care and watch yourselves scrupulously, so that **you do not forget** the things that you saw with your own eyes and so that they do not **fade from your mind as long as you live. And make them known to your children and to your children's children** . . . when the Lord said to Me, "Gather the people to Me that I may let them hear My words, in order that they may learn to revere Me **as long as they live on earth, and may so teach their children.**" . . . He declared to you the covenant . . . the Ten Commandments; and **He inscribed** them on two tablets of stone (Deut. 4:9–13).
>
> He inscribed them on two tablets of stone, which He gave to me (5:19).

The Commandment of Hakhel ("Gathering the People")

The commandment to learn and to teach, and to transmit the Torah to the next generation, was reinforced in Deuteronomy in the ceremony of *hakhel*:

> Moses wrote down this Teaching ... when all Israel comes ... you shall read this Teaching aloud in the presence of all Israel. **Gather the people—men, women, children ...** that **they may hear** and so **learn to revere the Lord your God** and to observe faithfully every word of this Teaching. **Their children,** too, who have not had the experience, shall hear and **learn** to revere the Lord your God ... **as long as** they **live in the land** (Deut. 31:9–13).

The similarity between these verses and the description of the revelation on Horeb is obvious: "**Gather the people** to Me **that I may let them hear My words, in order that they may learn to revere Me as long as they live on earth,** and may **so teach their children**" (Deut. 4:10). It would appear that this gathering for hearing and learning was directed toward the goal of internalizing the revelation.[24]

Moreover, the comprehensive obligation to teach both oneself and one's children, the repeated study of the laws, and constant discussion of the commandments, "when you stay at home and when you are away, when you lie down and when you get up" (Deut. 6:7), inscribing them on doorposts and gates—all of these commandments are characteristic of Deuteronomy.[25] They are connected to the total awareness that Deuteronomy establishes, the basis of which is the eternity of its verbal content. Unlike a vision, which can become faded and blurred and cannot be passed on to the next generation, the logos is designed to be an experience of perpetual awareness, a continuing revelation grounded in internal human cognitive processes.[26] Deuteronomy emphasizes not only that the voice of God spoke, but also that the speaker directed his speech to his listeners and that the listeners comprehended; in other words, it accentuates the processes of listening and paying attention:

> That I may let them hear My words (4:10).
> You heard the sound of words (12).
> Has any people heard the voice of a god ... as you have? (33).
> He let you hear His voice ... you heard His words (36).
> When you heard the voice ... we have heard His voice ... if we hear the

> voice of the Lord our God any longer.... For what mortal ever heard the voice of the living God (5:20–23).

Even when the active voice stops, the internal listening continues, and the memory of the logos serves as an active cognitive experience.

From Vision to Speech: Theological Implications

There is potential theological significance to this discussion. Deuteronomy confronts the reader with a somewhat anomalous situation. As the divine moves farther away from the human, revelation becomes grounded in an increasingly human level of cognition and awareness. It is not my intention here to discuss cognition or the characteristics of visual versus verbal cognitive processes. In any case, in the literary symbolism used in Deuteronomy, the distancing of God is symbolized by the distancing of the vision; revelation is found in the verbal listening. Intuitively (and symbolism is based on intuition), verbal auditory processes are understood to be internal human processes, part of the human cognitive processing that is hermeneutic and dynamic. In contrast, visual cognitive processes are understood, intuitively and symbolically, to be objective and external, not requiring active hermeneutic processing. In the legal world, in the laws of evidence, when objectivity is required, nothing is better than eyewitness testimony. Moreover, it is obvious that verbal communication is quintessentially human, one of the defining human attributes, distinguishing him from other living creatures.[27]

This distinction between Exodus and Deuteronomy, between sight and sound, vision and hearing is reflected in a midrash in *Mekhilta de-Rabbi Yishamael*:

> Rabbi says: "And so, what did God tell Moses to tell the People of Israel, or what did the People of Israel ask Moses to tell God? They said: '**We want to hear from the mouth of our king**. One who hears from across a partition is not like one who hears from the king himself.' The Holy One said, 'Give them what they want'—'that the people may hear when I speak with you' (Exod. 19:9). Another interpretation: They said: '**We want to see our king; hearing is not the same as seeing**.' God said, 'Give them what they ask for' ... 'the Lord will come down, in the sight of all the people'" (19:11).[28]

Both interpretations reflect the tension indicated above. The first opinion understands the revelation as auditory, while the second understands it as visual.

The dichotomy between the descent upon the mountain as related in Exodus and the voice from heaven in Deuteronomy is reflected in another midrash in the *Baraita de-Rabbi Yishmael* in *Sifra* chapter 1:

> Two verses contradict each other while a third verse decides between them. One verse says: "The Lord came down upon Mount Sinai, on the top of the mountain" (Exod. 19:20). The other verse says: "I spoke to you from the very heavens" (Exod. 20:19).[29] The verse that decides between them: "From the heavens He let you hear His voice" (Deut. 4:36). This teaches us that he lowered ... the highest heavens to the top of the mountain and spoke to them from the heavens.[30]

This midrash from the *Sifra* reconciles the two verses.[31]

Personal Hearing and Active Hearing in Classical Midrash: Sinai as a Beit Midrash

The concept of hearing, so prominent in Deuteronomy, is intensified in classical midrash and even transforms from human hearing in general to uniquely personal hearing. For example, it is written in the *Mekhilta de-Rabbi Yishmael*: "'All the people witnessed the thunder and lightning' (Exod. 20:15)—Great thunder! Much lightening! How many claps of thunder were there? How many bolts of lightning? Each man would be allowed to hear according to his capacity, as it is said, 'The voice of the Lord is power; the voice of the Lord is majesty'" (Ps. 29:4).[32]

The author of the midrash interprets the words of the verse "the voice of the Lord is power" not as referring to the power of God, but rather to the receptive attention capacity of each individual! In another midrash, the sages describe hearing as understanding and interpreting as active attention:

> "Watched over him" (Deut. 32:10)—with the Ten Commandments. This teaches that as the commandment left the mouth of God, **the People of Israel looked at him and knew** how much midrash there was in it and how much *halakhah*, how many lenient precepts and how many strict precepts, and how many *gezerot shavot* [an interpretive rule based upon comparison].[33]

The author of the midrash understood the phrase "watched over him" to mean the endowment of wisdom which includes the ability to interpret.

Both concepts of hearing, the idea that each person hears according to his ability and the theory of interpretive hearing, have a common denominator. Both come from the world of the sages and both reflect how the *beit midrash* was brought to Horeb, and Sinai brought to the rabbinic *yeshivah*. To a large extent the sages bound together the Written and Oral Torahs. Having done so, they projected their own activities in the *beit midrash* back on the People of Israel on Mount Sinai, and the method of study of their ancestors on Mount Horeb became a paradigm for their own study. Another layer of meaning was poured into the eternal vessel of the ongoing revelation: from this point on their feet did not move from the foot of Mount Sinai; reflective attention and active listening flourished and intensified.

The *beit midrash* thus became a place of revelation, as can be seen in the Tosefta:

> "The sayings of the wise are like goads, like nails fixed in prodding sticks. They were given by one Shepherd" (Eccles. 12:11)—The words of Torah are also eternal life as it is said, "She is a tree of life" (Prov. 3:18). The verse says "fixed" [literally, "planted"]—Just as plants increase and multiply, so too do words of Torah. "Prodding sticks" [literally, "masters of assemblies"]—those who congregate and sit down in an assembly and declare what is impure to be impure, and what is pure to be pure.... Lest a man will say to himself, "The school of Shammai declares it impure and the school of Hillel declares it pure, why should I continue to study Torah?" The Torah teaches us: **"sayings" [literally, "words"]—"the words," "these are the words" (Deut. 1:1), "all these words" (Exod. 20:1)—"were given by one Shepherd." One God created them, one leader gave them, the Master of all deeds, may he be blessed, spoke** them. You also must divide your heart into different chambers and place the words of the school of Shammai and the words of the school of Hillel inside it, **the words of those who declare "impure" and those who declare "pure."**[34]

The *beit midrash*, where learning grows and multiplies through disagreements, is a place of divine revelation: "One leader gave both." The sparks of divine revelation, each of which can break apart like sparks of fire, representing the multitude of opinions, will be revealed in the *beit midrash* in the form of disagreements. This is similar to the idea, mentioned above, that each individual was made to hear according to his ability and his opinion.

The *beit midrash*, and the insights into the Torah discovered there, are part of the divine Torah:

> Rabbi Berakhiah [said]: Every day God reveals a new legal insight in the celestial *beit din*. Why? "Just listen to the noise of His rumbling, to the sound (*hegeh*) that comes out of His mouth" (Job 37:2). There is no "sound" (*hegeh*) other than the words of Torah, as it is written "Let not this Book of the Teaching cease from your lips, but recite it (*vehagita*) day and night" (Josh. 1:8).[35]

This midrash is more than just a play on the phonetic similarity of the words "*hegeh/hagita*"; the midrash is saying that the daily legal insights of God in the *beit din* on high are in fact the insights of the earthly *beit midrash* where sages study Torah day and night.[36] This is a reformulation and continuation of the idea, mentioned above, that understands the revelation on Sinai as a *beit midrash* in which the commandments were heard and interpreted by the listeners.

The Primordial Beit Midrash: God Turned Two Kidneys into Two Rabbis

In several midrashim, the sages went even further. They saw the ongoing Sinaitic revelation as able to rise above and to break free completely from the bounds of space and time until eternity. It was not enough for the sages that they perceived their study as the words of the living God (in the expression of the Babylonian Talmud, tractate *Eruvin* 13b), all given by the same shepherd.[37] They reached back to an earlier time, before Sinai, to the Torah-like revelation of God, planted in the inner core of human attention.

Regarding Abraham, Genesis 26:5 says: "Inasmuch as Abraham obeyed Me and kept My charge: My commandments, My laws, and My teachings." The sages interpreted this verse to mean: "Inasmuch as Abraham obeyed Me"—Rabbi Aḥa ... (said): "Abraham even knew the laws of enclosing courtyards."[38] The sages went even further in *Bereshit Rabbah* 61:

> "Happy is the man" (Ps. 1:1)—This is Abraham who did not follow "the counsel of the wicked" ... or take "the path of sinners" ... or join "the

company of the insolent"... "rather the teaching of the Lord is his delight" ... "and he studies that teaching day and night" (1:1–2). Rabbi Shimon ben Yoḥai said: "His father did not teach him; he did not have a teacher. How did he learn the Torah? God made his two kidneys like two rabbis and they gushed with wisdom and taught him."[39]

This midrash makes use of salient imagery, comparing Abraham's kidneys to a *beit midrash*. They deliberately chose a double, even dialectic, image for the *beit midrash*, and intentionally used the wording "two kidneys as two rabbis." In the eyes of the sages, the *beit midrash*, the *yeshivah*, and divine revelation have existed since the creation of mankind. This is also reflected in the Babylonian Talmud, tractate *Yoma* 28b:

Rabbi Ḥama bar Ḥaninah said, "Since the days of our forefathers there has always been a *yeshivah*. When they were in Egypt they had a *yeshivah*. ... When they were in the desert they had a *yeshivah*. ... Our father Abraham was an elder who studied in the *yeshivah*. ... Our father Isaac was an elder who studied in the *yeshivah*. ... Our father Jacob was an elder who studied in the *yeshivah*. ... Eliezer the servant of Abraham was an elder who studied in the *yeshivah*, drawing from the well of his master's teachings and giving others to drink. Rav said, "Abraham observed the entire Torah ... even *eruvei tavshilin* [the laws of preparing food on holidays] as it is said "my Teachings" (Gen. 26:5)—both the Torah and the words of the sages.

Not only the Patriarchs and members of their households studied Torah.[40] Shem and Eber also had study halls and taught *halakhah*, as can be seen in *Bereshit Rabbah*: "'and Jacob was a quiet man, dwelling in tents' (Gen.25:27)—two tents, the *beit midrash* of Shem and the *beit midrash* of Eber."[41] In another midrash, the sages reveal their awareness of the anachronism inherent in their words: "'She [Rebekah] went to inquire of the Lord' (Gen. 25:22)—Were there synagogues and study halls in those days? She only went to the *beit midrash* of Eber! This is to teach us that when one consults an elder, it is as if he approaches the divine presence [*shekhinah*]."[42] Despite their initial question, the sages held fast to their belief that Rebekah went to the *beit midrash* of Eber, and thus going to see an elder is comparable to approaching the divine presence.

"And God Created Man in His Image, in the Image of God He Created Him"

At this point a serious question arises with regard to the dynamic, innately human capacity to pay attention: Can it be seen as divine revelation? In this context it is worthwhile to review the creation story. When the narrative reaches the creation of man the language becomes lyrical:

> And God created man in His image
> in the image of God He created him
> male and female He created them (Gen. 1:27).

The verse contains three hemistiches, each of which is composed of four units. The verb "to create" followed by a direct object (in Hebrew *b-r-a + et*) appears in each hemistich and the hemistiches are linked: "in his image"—"in the image"; "He created him"—"He created them." I believe that a careful analysis of the verses reveals that the unique quality inherent to man, the "image of God," is the capacity to pay attention. The next verse (28) says:

> God blessed them
> and God said to them
> "Be fertile and increase, fill the earth."

It would appear the narrative is returning to the previous description of the creation of marine life and birds in verse 22:

> God blessed them
> saying
> "Be fertile and increase, fill the waters in the seas."

However, the contrast between the verses is obvious. The word "saying" in verse 22 (which complements the phrase "God blessed them") uttered on the fifth day, is replaced in verse 28, in the description of the creation of man, with the word "said" in order to add to it the indirect object "to them," meaning to those listening. This is not the same blessing; man, the image of God, has been endowed with the capacity for conscious attention.

There is an analogy between the words "be fertile and increase" uttered in the context of the creation of man and the statement in the Tosefta mentioned above that words of Torah "increase and multiply." In its physical sense, human reproduction increases and multiplies the image of God. From the day that God created man and for eternity, no person has been or will be exactly like another, as the sages said: "The Holy One, blessed be He, cast everyone in the mold of Adam and yet no one is like another."[43] It appears therefore that reproduction is not merely quantitative; each person is a unique innovation. The image of God in each person, his innate divinely revealed capacity to pay conscious attention, is a unique, single spark created only once. This capacity is compelled, and the uniqueness of the capacity of each individual is ten times as compelling. He is not free to desist from his study or his teaching. If he does so, he damages the image of God.

I would now like to expand upon the analogy between reproduction and words of Torah mentioned earlier. Genetics teaches us that each person is imprinted with a specific genetic identity, inherited from his or her parents, and they from their parents, and so forth. Therefore, although each individual is uniquely him or herself, at the same time every person is also a genetic amalgamation of his or her parents. Just as in biology, families and even nations share genetic markers passed down for generations; in the "genetics" of revelation, the divine image is inherited. The unique, dynamic personal attention capacity that is the reflection of the attention capacity of his parents and the icon of the divine image within it, is a unique emanation of the proto-icon of his nation's image. His image of the likeness of God is the glitter of the radiance of the image of the likeness of Adam, the proto-image of mankind. Active attention, discourse, has to bear the conscious, national, multigenerational inheritance as well as the continuous heritage. The deep awareness of "the Lord is One" and "all were given by the one shepherd" obligates discourse and attention flowing in a national genealogical course, in a *beit midrash*-type existence in which the individual voice is one of the many voices heard in the *beit midrash*, in an experience in which, on the one hand, there is "everyone," each and every voice, and on the other hand, "all are from the same shepherd" in a chorus of all voices from the beginning to the end of time.

I now return to the meaning of the revelation narratives. These passages lay the foundations for the national consciousness required by the covenant. If one asks how it is possible to behold God, saying "We want to see our King" (as in Exodus), we will answer him that the King is to be seen by hearing his voice (as in Deuteronomy). If one asks how it is possible to hear the voice of the King, saying "We want to hear from the King's mouth," we will answer that the King's voice may be heard by actively listening to the learning process in the *beit midrash*, which bears responsibility for the attention of the divine image. For man was also put on earth for the sake of the awareness of the compulsory national covenant.

Seeking the Torah is seeking God. Adherence to the Torah is adherence to God. As it is said in the *Sifrei* on Deuteronomy: "'and holding fast to Him' (Deut. 11:22)—How can a person go up to heaven and hold fast to God? He should hold fast to the sages and their students."[44]

Endnotes

1. I will therefore refer only to the classical rabbinic commentators, and only when necessary. I will refer to the work of Arie Tweig, *Matan Torah be-Sinai [Lawgiving at Sinai]* (Jerusalem: Magnes, 1977), which contains a considerable number of sources.
2. It would appear that this description is based on the image of heaven as the permanent abode of God, found in many other verses including Deut. 26:15; 1 Kings 8:39; Isa. 63:15; and Ps. 2:4, 14:2, 53:3, 76:9, and 123:1. These verses stand in contrast to other biblical verses declaring that God is everywhere (e.g., Ps. 139:8–10); that it is impossible to determine his place (e.g., 1 Kings 8:27); or that his location varies according to the situation (e.g., Gen. 2–3; 11:5). Compare Tweig, 47, 100.
3. I will not discuss the relationship between chapter 19 and chapter 24, which is itself very complicated. There is a break between verses 1–2, which convey the command to ascend the mountain, and verses 3–8, which describe Moses' arrival (it is not clear from where), the public reading and written recording of the words of God, and the acceptance of the covenant, with accompanying sacrifices. Verses 9–11 ostensibly describe the execution of the order given in verses 1–2, but do not conform to the order in all of its details. Verses 12–18 are rife with problems of continuity—Moses' ascent is related three times (verses 13, 15, and 18), and verse 12 conveys a command that is executed at least three time—as well as other significant problems.
4. Moses ben Naḥman (Nachmanides), *Perushei ha-Torah le-Rabenu Moshe ben Naḥman*, ed. Chaim Dov Chavel (Jerusalem: Mosad Harav Kook, 1959), 1:386.
5. These verses are not a direct continuation of what preceding verses and I will not address this issue here. I have discussed these verses and their conceptual position elsewhere: Avraham Shammah, "Va-Yered Ha-Shem al Har Sinai" [The Lord came down upon Mount Sinai], *Ḥag ha-Shavuot (Sidrat Be'er Miriam)*, ed. Yaakov Medan (Tel Aviv: Miskal, 2012), 126–130. The status of 19b is also very unclear. Compare Tweig, 38–40.
6. The *tannaim* (sages of the Mishnah) noted the discrepancies between the accounts. See *Mekhilta de-Rabbi Yishmael*, tractate *de-ba-ḥodesh, parashah* 4: "'The Lord came down upon Mount Sinai' (Exod. 19:20)—On all of the mountain? The Torah teaches: 'On the top of the mountain.'"
7. For example, *Mekhilta de-Rabbi Yishmael*, tractate *de-ba-ḥodesh, parashah* 2. See the interpretation there. Above, I followed the approach of Rashbam (Rabbi Samuel ben Meir). Compare with the commentary of Abraham Ibn Ezra.
8. See Tweig, 34.
9. No more than "similar" because the idea that the people heard God speak to Moses is not mentioned anywhere else in the Bible.

10. A detailed discussion of this fragmented type of writing is beyond the scope of this paper. My intention here is only to demonstrate the existence of a central axis of verses in this chapter and identify the verses that are not an integral part of this axis. The conceptual angle of this article is not based on the lack of uniformity or continuity in the biblical text.
11. See Tweig, 14–16 and the literature mentioned there.
12. This verse is also not the continuation of the end of the Decalogue (as Nachmanides pointed out), and this again confirms that the Decalogue is not part of the narrative sequence.
13. "Moses then wrote down all the commands of the Lord.... Then he took the record of the covenant.... I will give you the stone tablets with the teachings and commandments which I have inscribed to instruct them." The exact meaning of the terms mentioned here, as well as their integration in the general system of chapters 19 to 24, are outside the scope of this article.
14. See Deut. 7:6, 14:2, 26:18, 11:13, 15:5, and 28:1. The complicated position of 3a will not be discussed here. See the commentaries of Ibn Ezra, Rabbi Yosef Bekhor Shor, and Ḥizkuni and, in contrast, Nachmanides. Compare Tweig, 34–36.
15. A similar point is found in the commentary of Ibn Ezra.
16. Compare Tweig, 38 and 95.
17. The degree of similarity between verses 16–17 and Deut. 5:20–26 will not be discussed here. See Nachmanides on verse 15.
18. Compare Tweig, 53. See also note 16.
19. It seems to me that it is correct to say that all the statements in chapters 19–20 indicating verbal communication between God and man in the core of the revelatory event (not as instructions given in conjunction with the revelation) are not part of the narrative sequence. With regard to verses 3–6, see above and note 14; with regard to verse 9, see above and note 9; with regard to verse 19b, see above note 5; with regard to the Decalogue and its introduction, see above and note 11; with regard to chapter 20 verses 16–17, see above and in notes 15–17.
20. See note 2.
21. See Tweig, 134.
22. The verses themselves indicate that the people have gathered to hear the Decalogue. A thorough and proper commentary that convincingly demonstrates the integration of the Decalogue itself into Deuteronomy is beyond the scope of this paper. Deuteronomy 4:41–43 suddenly address the allocation of cities of refuge. Verses 44–45 introduce teaching, decrees, laws, and rules; their meaning is not clear. Verses 46–49 move on to the conquest of the other side of the Jordan. Deuteronomy 5:1 introduces the proclamation of laws and rules. Verses 2–5 return to the Decalogue on Horeb and are also unclear. Verses 2–3 mention the covenant. Verses 4–5 refer to the divine speech from the fire and contradict each other: verse 4 says that God spoke "face to face," while verse 5 declares that Moses stood between God and the people. The last word of verse 5 ("saying") leads into the Decalogue but is disconnected from any visible context. This is not the appropriate framework in which to elaborate on these points.
23. The stone tablets mentioned in Exod. 24:12 are devoid of any connection to the Decalogue.
24. Maimonides, *Mishneh Torah*, Ḥagigah 3:1–6: "It is a positive commandment to gather all the People of Israel... and to read to them from the Torah... that they will hear in reverence, awe and trembling joy as in the day that the Torah was given on Sinai... and each person will see himself as if he was only now commanded to keep it and has heard it from the mouth of God himself."

25. See 6:6–9; 11:18–20.
26. The concept is not new. The innovation here is its application to the account in Deuteronomy as distinct from the account in Exodus. See Shalom Rosenberg, "'Ha-Hitgalut Ha-Matmedet': Shlosha Kivunim" [The continual revelation: Three approaches], in *Hitgalut, Emuna, Tevuna* [Revelation, faith, understanding], ed. Moshe Hallamish and Moshe Schwarcz (Ramat Gan: Bar Ilan University, 1976), 131–143.
27. I have distinguished between the visual revelation of Exodus and the verbal revelation of Deuteronomy. To a large extent, these represent different meanings of revelation: the first refers to the revelation of God while the second refers to the revelation of divine attributes. See Rosenberg, "'Ha-Hitgalut Ha-Matmedet,'" esp. 131.
28. Tractate *de-ba-ḥodesh, parashah* 2, 210–211.
29. I noted above the connection of this verse to the account in Deuteronomy.
30. *Sifra on Leviticus*, ed. E. Finkelstein (New York: JTS, 1983), 9.
31. Compare to parallel texts: *Mekhilta de-Rabbi Yishmael*, tractate *de-ba-ḥodesh, parashah* 4; *Mekhilta de-Rabbi Shimon bar Yoḥai*, ed. Jacob Nahum Epstein and Ezra Zion Melamed (Jerusalem: Mekizei Nirdamim, 1956), 144–145. It is interesting that the texts cited above do not mention Nehemiah 9:13, which combines the two accounts: "You came down on Mount Sinai and spoke to them from heaven; You gave them right rules and true teachings, good laws and commandments."
32. Tractate *de-ba-ḥodesh, parashah* 9, 235
33. *Sifre Deuteronomy, piska* 313, 355. There is a parallel text in the *Mekhilta de-Rabbi Yishmael*, tractate *de-ba-ḥodesh, parashah* 9, 235: "They heard the commandment 'and interpreted it'. . . they interpreted it."
34. Tosefta, tractate *Sotah* 7:11–12. See the parallel text in the Babylonian Talmud, tractate *Ḥagigah* 3b.
35. *Bereshit Rabbah, parashah* 64. See the parallel text in *parashah* 49.
36. This bold expression is the opposite of the famous saying in the Babylonian Talmud, tractate *Bava Metzia* 59b: "'It is not in the heavens' (Deut. 30:11)—in other words, it is not in heaven but on earth." In contrast, the midrash cited here says that what is seen on earth is really in the heavens. Both are powerful statements, expressing the tension between the word of man and the word of God, and the innovations of the Oral Law that ostensibly do not reflect the Written Torah. This tension is reflected (among other places) in an *aggadah* in the Babylonian Talmud, tractate *Menaḥot* 29b. See also the Jerusalem Talmud, tractate *Pe'ah* 2:17a and in parallel texts, *Megillah* 4:74d, *Ḥagigah* 1:76d, and other parallels throughout classical rabbinic literature. See Rosenberg, 133.
37. This is similar to the Rava's midrash in the Babylonian Talmud, tractate *Avodah Zarah* 19a.
38. *Bereshit Rabbah*, 64.
39. Ibid., 657.
40. For example, Sarah was "scrupulous about the laws of menstrual purity" (Babylonian Talmud, tractate *Bava Metzia* 87a, and parallels); Isaac tithed produce (*Bereshit Rabbah, parashah* 64 and parallels); Jacob observed the entire Torah (*Sifrei Deuteronomy, piska* 336, 386). See *Bereshit Rabbah, parashah* 94; *parashah* 95, and others.
41. *Parashah* 63. See also *parashah* 84.
42. *Bereshit Rabbah*, 63.
43. Babylonian Talmud, tractate *Sanhedrin* 38a. See also Babylonian Talmud, tractate *Berakhot* 58a.
44. *Piska* 49.

The Binding of Isaac and Historical Contextuality

Chayuta Deutsch

Introduction

One of the fundamental arguments raised in the context of biblical criticism is that the mores of the Bible do not meet the ethical standards of the postbiblical world. The examples cited are numerous and well-known. The Binding of Isaac (the *Akedah*) is an extreme case, accentuated by the central place it has received in historical and cultural consciousness.

Ethical arguments against the *Akedah* were voiced audibly during the twentieth century in nonreligious frameworks, but also previously within religious environments. The questions that have been asked (and are still being asked) about the *Akedah*, can be narrowed down to two major questions that relate to the passage itself.[1] The first question regards the position of God: How could He command a father to slaughter his own son, and moreover, after the command had been retracted, how could He praise the willingness to obey it? The second question concerns the position of Abraham: How could he obey such a command without argument, especially in light of his previous negotiation with God to stop the destruction of Sodom?[2]

In fact, these questions receive initial validation from within the Bible itself, which condemns the child sacrifice prevalent in Canaanite culture. Examples of this condemnation be found in Jeremiah (7:31; 19:5), Micah (6:6–7), and elsewhere. These verses augment the fundamental problem inherent to God's commandment to sacrifice Isaac: it could be identified, speciously, with the child sacrifice of the Canaanite cult of Molech. An example of such a verse can be found in Jeremiah 7:29–31: "For the Lord has spurned and cast off the brood that provoked His wrath. For the people of Judah have done what displeases Me—declares the Lord. They have set up their abominations in the

House which is called by My name, and they have defiled it. And they have built the shrines of Topheth in the Valley of Ben-hinnom to burn their sons and daughters in fire—which I never commanded, which never came to My mind."

In an illuminating article, Daniel Vainstub analyzes the custom of child sacrifice in Canaan in its various forms (both private and public sacrifice) and provides archeological evidence for its practice. Vainstub observes that "there are few cultures in which the adulation of God in its highest form is expressed by parents sacrificing their small children. Such a practice negates not only the instinct for acquiring property inherent to every human being, but also contradicts one of the strongest and most primal natural instincts, common to humans and animals—a mother's love for her child."[3] He divides ancient sacrifice into two basic categories: sacrifice as an expression of thanksgiving or commitment, and sacrifice in the context of a public ceremony in a time of great danger to the community. He uses familiar verses to substantiate his claim that "the sacrifice of children to Molech was the most despicable of all the Canaanite abominations in the eyes of the zealous followers of God."[4]

Against this backdrop, there emerges a third, very troubling question. It does not concern the interpretation of the verses but rather the use of the *Akedah* within the Jewish historical consciousness, as first expressed in the Jerusalem Talmud: "Rabbi Bibi Abba said in the name of Rabbi Yoḥanan, 'Abraham said to God, "You know well that when you told me to sacrifice my son Isaac . . . I suppressed my feelings and did your will. May it be your will, my God, that when the children of Isaac, my son, are in trouble and have no one to plead their cause, You will plead their cause.""[5]

According to this passage, the *Akedah* is a seminal historical event. It is the paradigm, on the one hand, of a test that was passed, and whose rewards are reaped by the Jewish people throughout the generations, and, on the other hand, of a path of suffering that many Jews have travelled in the course of trials no less difficult than that of Abraham. This path begins with Hannah,[6] who at the martyrdom of her seven sons called out to Abraham, "You built one altar; I have built seven!" It continues throughout the persecutions of the Diaspora culminating with the Holocaust, and ends with the sacrifice of sons on the altar of the wars fought to build the State of Israel.

My intention in this article is to briefly survey the different approaches to answering the ethical questions raised by the *Akedah*. Critique leveled from outside the world of faith is by nature subversive, rejecting the story and its images. Critique from within the religious world raises objections that usually culminate in resolution or apologetics rather than rejection. I will review some of the convoluted interpretations of the verses praising the deed proposed by almost every commentator who has addressed these questions. Above all, I will attempt to demonstrate that approaches to the *Akedah* in almost every case reflect the contemporary values and culture of the commentator. In the final section of the article I will apply the perspective of historical context to the story of the *Akedah* itself. This approach, despite the theological difficulties that it raises and its use in critical and antireligious forums that reject the sanctity of the Bible, has not, in my opinion, received the attention it deserves within the religious world.

"External" Criticism: The Akedah as a "Black Bird"

> A deity who is prepared to put man to such a test is a very dubious deity. . . . What is the meaning of this unconditional loyalty of Abraham? Blind loyalties of this kind are what brought upon humanity the most horrific atrocities. (A. B. Yehoshua)[7]

The writer A.B. Yehoshua is one of the most prominent of those who have spoken out vociferously against the *Akedah* in recent years. "The *Akedah* hovers over our history like a black bird," he wrote in an anthology on the subject of his novel *Mr. Mani*. "From my early childhood I have had a problem with this story, one of the seminal legends of the Jewish people. On the second day of Rosh Hashanah the story of the *Akedah* is read from the Torah and all the sounds of the Shofar and the many liturgical poems allude to it. The *Akedah* is the foundation of the religious covenant; it is the merit of the forefathers."[8] Yehoshua attempted to negate the charm and power of the act of the *Akedah* by means of a literary act. His novel *Mr. Mani* tells the story of a familial dynasty in whose past lies a terrible sin—the murder of a son by his father, described by the author as "an actualized *Akedah*." Yehoshua shaped the plot so that the murder is committed in the same place as the *Akedah* itself, on Mount Moriah, the site of the Temple in Jerusalem. The author has explained that his motivation in writing the story was to fight (!) against the myth of the *Akedah* and, in his words, "to negate the *Akedah* by realizing it."[9] Yehoshua rejects the various exegetical solutions that follow the approach of Kierkegaard,[10] and instead stresses that Christianity corrected the myth of the *Akedah* by replacing it with the ethically coherent myth of the crucifixion, in which the man-god sacrifices himself, not another, as an offering of atonement for human sin and to end human suffering. He argues that there are no subsequent references in the Bible to the story of the *Akedah* because "already then they were aware of the profound difficulties concerning this myth." Yehoshua's questions are better than his answers.[11] His interpretation of the biblical narrative, though influenced by Kierkegaard, is based on what he defines as a "secular" reading of the story.

Many others have written in the vein of this type of critique that does not hesitate to invalidate the biblical text. Hugo Bergmann, for example, believed moral qualms over the act of the *Akedah* to be ethically superior to the commandment itself.[12] Following in his footsteps, Asa Kasher[13] expressed preference for the model of the father-son relationship exemplified by David and Absalom over that of Abraham and Isaac.[14] Other examples of this approach include the comment that the late Meretz MK, Yossi Sarid made from the podium of the Knesset, and subsequently wrote in a newspaper: "The *Akedah* was a crude prank; I don't like these kind of jokes. If God wanted to test Abraham, it would have been better not to involve children. . . . I am unable and unwilling to criticize Abraham as a father, but I refuse to recognize him as a symbol and role model."[15]

"Internal" Criticism: Midrash and Liturgical Poetry

Criticism of the *Akedah* did not begin in the twentieth century. One example of an early critique can be found in the introduction to the chapter on the *Akedah* in *Bereshit Rabbah* (55:3). The section beginning with the verse from Ecclesiastes (8:4), "inasmuch as a king's command is authoritative, and none can say to him, 'What are you doing?'" contains more than a hint of censure.

Objections to both the command and the deed itself can also be found in early liturgical poetry from the Land of Israel. In her article, "Did Abraham Sin by Binding Isaac?" ("He-ḥata Avraham Avinu be-Akdo et Yitzhak?"), Shulamit Elizur presents examples of liturgical poetry from the fifth century CE that rebuke God for commanding Abraham to sacrifice his son.[16] The most striking of these is the poem "Kedushta Le-Shavuot" by Rabbi Eleazar Kallir, in which the Torah itself criticizes Abraham: "He forgot that God is like a father who has pity on His children/He should have pleaded for mercy!"

About two hundred years after Kallir, and apparently in his footsteps, Yoḥanan HaKohen, a Palestinian Jewish poet wrote, "But he should have pleaded before Him and begged for mercy/ in order to save his only son from the coals of the fire." Abraham should have pleaded for mercy on behalf of his son, but he did not.[17]

Maimonides, Kierkegaard, and Rav Kook

The story of the *Akedah* both troubled and fascinated the Danish philosopher Søren Kierkegaard all his life.[18] This passion inspired him to write a fictional description of the critical moment at which Abraham turns to slaughter his son: "Then for an instant he turned away from him, and when Isaac again saw Abraham's face it was changed, his glance was wild, his form was horror. He seized Isaac by the throat, threw him to the ground, and said, 'Stupid boy, dost thou then suppose that I am thy father? I am an idolater. Dost thou suppose that this is God's bidding? No, it is my desire.'"[19]

According to this imaginary reenactment by Kierkegaard, Isaac, terrified, turns to God and begs for mercy: "If I have no father upon earth, be Thou my father!" Abraham says silently to himself, "O Lord in heaven, I thank Thee. After all it is better for him to believe that I am a monster, rather than that he should lose faith in Thee." In this incredible narrative, Kierkegaard brings to life the full horror that lies at the heart of the *Akedah*.[20]

Kierkegaard offers two answers to the ethical question: (1) During the *Akedah* a temporary, *ad hoc* suspension of morality occurred (the "teleological suspension of the ethical"); (2) God never intended for there to be a sacrifice and Abraham was also certain that this was not his intention. Kierkegaard's first answer in effect follows the line of thought of Maimonides, Nachmanides, and Rashi. His second answer, shared by other modern thinkers, deviates from the straightforward meaning of the verses that praise Abraham for his willingness to sacrifice that which was most precious to him.

In *The Guide of the Perplexed*, Maimonides reveals his awareness of the ethical difficulty and aberration from nature inherent to the *Akedah*, and uses this issue to argue that this was an exceptional case.[21] Future generations must absorb its underlying principle but not imitate the practice. It is worthwhile to note his definition of the act as something that "one would not imagine that human nature was capable of it . . . that which is repugnant to nature." In other words, this act is contrary to the ways of nature. The crux of the ethical difficulty lies not in the harm caused by a father to his son but in Abraham's unique situation: the fact that he was childless, that the child arrived after a period of despair, and that in performing the deed he was destroying all he had hoped for—that his descendants would become a nation serving God. Maimonides, in his time and place, was prepared to make peace with this singular aberration for the sake of a worthy goal.

While Maimonides praised the *Akedah* as a singular occurrence constituting an example that must be emulated and followed, Yeshayahu Leibowitz went to the other extreme and argued that the *Akedah* represents the negation of human values.[22] According to Leibowitz, the essence of the service of God in its entirety is "Akedatic." Every performance of a commandment done for its own sake without ulterior motives "represents the motivation animating the *Akedah*." Leibowitz distinguishes between a "religion of values" and a "religion of commandments":

> The religion of values and beliefs is an endowing religion—a means of satisfying man's spiritual needs and of assuaging his mental conflicts. Its end is man, and God offers his services to man. A person committed to such a religion is redeemed man. A religion of Mitzvoth is a demanding religion. It imposes obligations and tasks and makes of man an instrument for the realization of an end which transcends man.[23]

In contrast to Leibowitz, Rav Abraham Isaac ha-Kohen Kook refused to negate human values and argued in several places that it is impossible for faith to contradict natural ethics.[24] Rav Kook discussed the *Akedah* in several places. In a letter to Moshe Zeidel, he explained that the *Akedah* provides a necessary distinction between vibrant religious fervor that allows and even compels child sacrifice, and the purification of the religious sensibility in preparation for the prohibition of child sacrifice ("a deep-seated addiction to idolatry . . . that overcame even the mercy of the parents and made cruelty to their sons and daughters into a permanent fixture of the worship of Molech"). It was necessary to put Abraham to this test in order to persuade the surrounding society that in its purification and cleansing, the religious sentiment that now recoils from child sacrifice has not lost its fervor; it continues to burn and is profoundly ready for sacrifice.[25]

In his commentary on the *Akedah* in his prayer book, *Olat Ra'aya*, Rav Kook explains that Abraham journeyed to the *Akedah* in a spirit of enthusiasm and personal commitment: "This holy old man did not walk with stooped shoulders or failing strength toward this incredible act of worship that lies in contrast to all the behaviors inherent to man's inner nature. He walked upright, at full height and at full strength." This description reflects Kierkegaard's words, "for thou didst gain all and didst retain Isaac. Was it not so? Never again did the Lord take him from thee, but thou didst sit at table joyfully with him in thy tent."[26] It appears that many thinkers have been profoundly influenced by the awe of a modern man, a non-Jew, at Abraham's stamina during his trial.

The Akedah and Contemporary Thought

In our generation, the *Akedah* has become a touchstone for philosophical and political opinions on topical subjects in Israeli society and the religious world. Rabbis Shagar, Yoel Bin Nun, Yuval Cherlow, Yehuda Brandes, Shlomo Aviner, and Yaakov Ariel, as well as professors Chana Safrai, Avi Sagi, and Binyamin Ish-Shalom are all similar in that their approaches to the *Akedah*, and their ways of resolving its difficulties correspond naturally to their general perspectives regarding matters of Torah and faith. The following survey demonstrates this succinctly.

Yoel Bin Nun and the "Double Source" Approach

Yoel Bin-Nun argues that Rav Kook never considered the possibility that "Abraham should have protested, screamed all night, asked difficult questions about the promises that had been made to him or, in particular, cried out that it was entirely impossible that God would want human sacrifice—as the Torah of Moses makes clear (Deut. 12:31)." However, Rabbi Bin-Nun acknowledges that "with all of the personal, human, and ethical difficulty in accepting this interpretation, it must be conceded that in the language of the verses describing the *Akedah* there is nothing to even hint at a fundamental opposition to the command in the opening verses, and Rav Kook's analysis does not in any way contradict the verses themselves." The solution that he offers correlates with the thesis of his book as a whole—the concept of the "double source" as a comprehensive model for understanding the thought of Rav Kook. This original solution accepts the paradox of the call to refrain from sacrificing Isaac and the call to perform it. According to Rabbi Bin-Nun's approach to understanding Rav Kook, both of these voices were heard simultaneously.[27]

Avi Sagi: Religion and Ethics

Avi Sagi's study of the *Akedah* forms a part of his larger discussion of the questions surrounding conflicts between Judaism (*halakhah*, Torah) and contemporary morality. In the introduction to his book *Judaism: Between Religion and Morality* (*Yahadut: Bein Dat u-Musar*), he presents the two fundamental questions that form the basis of his research: First, according to the philosophic and halakhic tradition, is morality determined by religion? Second, is there a normative contradiction between religious and ethical imperatives?[28] He offers three potential models for answering these questions. The first is

dependence—morality is determined by religion, and thus there is, in fact, no conflict. The second is **conflict**—dissonance is elevated to the status of a religious principle (Leibowitz). The third model is the development of **exegetical tools** that will reconcile religious and ethical imperatives. If Judaism had adopted one of the first two models, the winding exegetical and halakhic path through which the Jewish tradition has met these challenges would have been unnecessary. The existence of this exegetical path reconfirms both the existence of autonomous morality and the rejection of normative conflict as a religious ideal. This autonomy was concisely expressed by the sages in the meta-halakhic principle, "her ways are pleasant ways" (based on Prov. 3:17), understood by the rabbis as a rule dictating that all halakhic legal decisions must conform to standards of morality. In the words of the Radbaz (Rabbi David ibn Zimra), "It is written 'her ways are pleasant ways' and the statutes of our Torah must agree with reason and logic."[29] Sagi concludes by noting that "the moral of the *Akedah* appears at its conclusion—the principle that the believer is meant to derive from the *Akedah* is the harmony between religion and morality."[30]

Rabbi Shagar and the Principle of the Empty Space

Fundamental philosophical thoughts are naturally imprinted with the personality and basic positions of the thinker. Because of its depth and the intensity of the questions that it raises, the *Akedah* reflects the innermost beliefs of the many thinkers who have studied it. To paraphrase the well-known expression, it can be said, "Tell me how you understand the *Akedah*, and I will tell you your standpoint within the contemporary religious world."

Rabbi Shagar, for example, based his entire outlook on the principle of the "empty space."[31] The issues that occupied his spiritual world were questions of faith in a world that had lost its certainties. The modern world that knew the truth gave way to a postmodern world in which no truth takes precedence other another. His understanding of the *Akedah* reflects this basic position. He disagrees with Maimonides' position that the *Akedah* is proof of the truth of prophecy and emphasized instead the uncertainty of faith: "A conceited and all-knowing religious position turns the idea of a religious test, and with it all religious endeavor, into fiction. A spiritual trial in particular and religious life and genuine connection to God in general exist only within a humble personality, content not to be known."[32] From this perspective, we are all "bound on an altar" in that we live in a time of uncertainty and are asked nonetheless to believe in God and follow his ways.[33]

Rabbi Yuval Cherlow also maintains that contemporary believers are "bound." However, unlike Rabbi Shagar,[34] he does not interpret the *Akedah* as a state of comprehensive uncertainty, but rather a specific uncertainty connected to the ethical difficulty inherent in the *Akedah* itself. As Jews who do the will of God even when we do not identify with it, we sacrifice our individuality. According to Rabbi Cherlow, who deals extensively with the relationship between ethics and Judaism, we, modern believers, are the sacrifices bound for slaughter, "struggling to understand the *Akedah* but nonetheless binding our inner will to the altar of our service of God. We bind our inner worlds and sacrifice them on the altar."[35]

Safrai, Brandes, and Ish-Shalom: Educating for Freedom of Choice and Critical Thinking

Chana Safrai grappled with the question of the *Akedah* and morality by radically shifting the focal point of the story.[36] The heart of the trial does not lie in the question of whether Abraham would follow the command but "whether Abraham would object to the terrifying order as he did regarding Sodom." From this she concluded that "the believer must distinguish between the commands that he receives. . . . The call of the angel, 'Do not raise your hand against the boy' is well placed at the center of the story and serves as a clear message to refrain from all human sacrifice—of children or adults—out of pure faith." She concludes that "in this way, the story of the *Akedah* becomes a renewed asset in a thinking religious environment—a story worthy of being read on the Days of Awe, days of soul searching and examining our stance before God."[37] This commentary contains a beautiful message, in which Safrai reveals her contemporary religious outlook and her critique of a certain type of religiosity that is, among other things, uncritical. It is, however, difficult to find support for her interpretation in the simple meaning of the verses.[38]

In an article that focuses on the educational-existential aspect of the *Akedah*, Rabbi Yehuda Brandes[39] proposes three educational goals that will inculcate the legacy of the *Akedah*: (1) emulating the spiritual greatness of the Patriarchs, (2) dedication and self-sacrifice, (3) action accompanied by critical thinking and skepticism. The learner must be alerted to the positive and negative aspects of each goal. Appreciating the greatness of the Patriarchs can produce a feeling of personal insignificance, while dedication and self-sacrifice can result in moral insensitivity. Critical thinking and skepticism can weaken stamina and motivation, because it is difficult to live and function in a state of doubt. This open, enabling, and flexible approach is characteristic of the thought and educational methodology of the author.

The approach of Binyamin Ish-Shalom is fundamentally different.[40] He consciously chooses one approach over another and thus reveals his ideology and social agenda. He raises two alternative possibilities for the focal point of the story: the commandment "offer him there as a burnt offering" (Gen. 22:2) or the order "'do not raise your hand against the boy'" (22:12). According to Ish-Shalom, only the second possibility is meaningful to the contemporary reader and thus educationally viable: "Rav Kook wrote that fear of heaven must not suppress natural human morality. . . . I would like to call upon us all to come together and learn the Torah anew, from its foundations, and establish as a basic principle and starting point that human life, the existence of the Jewish people, and feelings of solidarity and mutual responsibility take precedence over any other values."

Rabbis Shagar, Cherlow, and Brandes, and Professors Ish-Shalom and Safrai—all expressed the conscious choice of a meaningful and value-based, existential-philosophical (or educational) approach to the *Akedah*, without however adhering to the *peshat* (simple) meaning of the verses.

The Akedah as Reflected in Israeli Literature: For or Against the Akedah as a Political Act

> But I am not sand on the beach
> And I do not keep the promises that God gave to Abraham
> (Hanoch Levin, "The Land that God Promised to Abraham")

Professor Hillel Weiss argues that acceptance of the *Akedah* is correlated to acceptance of Zionism, while a rejection of one involves the rejection of the other. In two important studies, he points out varying contradictory trends in the use of the *Akedah* in twentieth-century Hebrew literature.[41] Weiss claims that acceptances of the *Akedah* grants us an aspect of immortality, while its rejection endangers our uniqueness and existence as a people: "Rejection of the Jewish *Akedah* leads inevitably to the rejection of the Zionist *Akedah*."[42] In his book *Portrait of a Fighter: Studies on Heroes and Heroism in Contemporary Hebrew Narrative Fiction* (*Diukan ha-Loḥem: Iyunim al Giborim u-Gevura be-Siporet Ha-Ivrit shel ha-Dor ha-Aḥaron*), Weiss surveys how twentieth-century Jewish writers used the *Akedah*. He quotes from Agnon as an example of an author who saw belief in the *Akedah* as tantamount to belief in the unique destiny of the Jewish people: "From where do we derive this strength, that every day we are killed and slaughtered and bound on an altar and wounded, and we accept it all in love and do not consider ourselves to be superior to others?"[43] Weiss points out a paradox—death that revives: "The choice of death, as a concept, and commitment to it, revives. The acceptance of the yoke of the *Akedah* is what grants us eternity."[44] Weiss attacks contemporary secular Israeli critics of the *Akedah*—for example, Aharon Megged, who wrote the following lines: "No, he shouldn't have died. He was sacrificed on the altar. You remember the story of the Binding of Isaac: the father, Abraham, takes his son, his only son whom he loves, and offers him up on Mount Moriah. That's how it was. Exactly. But no angel."[45] Weiss uses Uri Zvi Greenberg to illustrate the shallowness of the new generation in coping with the challenges facing them.

In his article "Comments on the Binding of Isaac" ("He'arot le-Akedat Yitzhak"), Weiss condemns both contemporary education for teaching that nothing is worth dying for and contemporary literature as "protest literature that does not fight but gives in to its own self-pity and pseudo-existentialist self-expression."[46] With regard to the *Akedah* he explains that "as soon as we reject the way of the *Akedah*, we condemn ourselves to an annihilation that is the result of the recognition that life had become so shallow that it disappeared altogether."[47]

Like the rabbis and educators whose approaches I described above, Weiss overlooks the *peshat* level of the verses. However, in contrast to the others, in the heat of the political-ideological battle, he concedes too easily regarding the real ethical issues lying behind the voices rejecting the *Akedah*.

The Akedah in the Context of its Own Time: The Removal of the Ethical Onus from Abraham

Up to this point I have pointed out an obvious phenomenon: most of the interpretations of the *Akedah* are rooted in the environment of the commentator: in the place, time, and culture in which he or she lived, as well as in his basic system of beliefs. I would now like to apply this approach to Abraham himself. The interpretation that I would like to propose here—understanding Abraham's position in light of his contemporary cultural background—is not new. Atheists and Bible critics continue to use it to completely invalidate the ethical mores of the Bible as "primitive" and incompatible with the spirit of modern "enlightenment." Nonetheless, I would actually like to propose this approach from a faith-based perspective. I argue not only that it is plausible, but that, in fact, contemporary Bible readers have a moral and educational obligation to examine Abraham and his reaction to the trial of the *Akedah* against the backdrop of his historical period.

I will begin by explaining the basis of this argument. The biblical world in which Abraham heard God's call was fundamentally different from the modern world. For a member of an ancient agricultural culture that revolved around the fruit of the land, the commandment of the *Akedah* fits along the spectrum of difficult, but bearable, commandments in which man is required to offer to God the most precious fruit of his labors, as tithes and tenth-parts, first shearings, first fruits, and firstborn animals. Though child sacrifice appears on the extreme end of this spectrum, it is nonetheless on the spectrum. In the surrounding culture, the demand to sacrifice a child was a harsh demand, yet a legitimate and plausible one. This was a culture entirely devoid of the awareness of a child's inherent right to life and dignity. Simple proof of this can be found not only in the deplorable practices of the idol worshippers, such as the sacrifice of children to Molech, but also in the commandments concerning the Hebrew servant girl, a very young girl sold into slavery (Exod. 21:7), and the verse "a blessing on him who seizes your babies and dashes them against the rocks!" (Ps. 137:9). The argument that there is a significant difference between taking human life and the sacrifice of an animal, or offering the fruits of the field is disputable in a world where children were perceived as extensions of their parents rather than independent beings. In the ancient world, a child was considered to be merely a part of his father, like one of the organs of his body; if he were to be commanded to sacrifice an organ (as in the case of Bar Kokhba's soldiers), he would, with difficulty, comply. According to this perspective, the subject of the test, the one who sacrifices the most in the *Akedah*, is the father, not the son.[48]

In *The Bible according to Its Simple Meaning* (*Ha-Mikra ke-Peshuto*), Arnold Ehrlich describes the ancient custom, common in neighboring cultures, of placing a newborn immediately after birth on the knees of the head of the family, who would decide whether or not to let the infant live. Though this custom does not appear in Jewish sources, it is alluded to in several verses in the Torah that describe children as "born upon the knees of" a certain individual:

> In ancient times, the life of the newborn depended upon the will of the father. After its birth the infant was placed on the ground at the feet of

its father. If the father left him there, he would die, and if he picked him up, he would live. . . . Job refers to this practice when he says, "Why were there knees to receive me" (Job 3:12), because if his father's knees had not received him, he would have died immediately after birth. This is also the meaning of the verse, "the children of Machir son of Manasseh were likewise born upon Joseph's knees" (Gen. 50:23).[49]

God did not ask Abraham to sacrifice his wife, or his brothers, or his parents. The command to sacrifice his son, in the time period in which Abraham lived, and in light of his surrounding culture, was a harsh command, but a comprehensible one. The very request itself demonstrates that it was worthy of being heeded and that the contemporary culture allowed it to be heeded. The great innovation lay in the message: ram—yes; human sacrifice—no. Abraham could not understand the extent of this innovation as we can in our time. He was only able to comprehend it in the context of his time and place (cows and sheep—yes; people—no). The concept of the rights of all people, including women and children, to life and dignity, would, in a few thousand years, be derived from this idea. As I have said, Abraham's trial was a test of devotion and readiness to go the extra, and most difficult, mile.

The subject of the *Akedah* is not Isaac. It is Abraham who was tested, who was asked to forfeit that which was most dear to him. Critics of the *Akedah* who argue for the superiority of the crucifixion, in which the sacrifice offered himself, not his son, have missed this crucial point.[50] The potential loss of his son in the *Akedah* was infinitely more difficult and painful for Abraham than the loss of his own life.

In this type of world, God tested Abraham in order to draw a line between the sacrifice of crops and animals, and that of humans.[51] In the culture in which Abraham lived, this was a very fine line. In our culture, in part as a result of the moral outlook created by the Torah, this line is very clear, unequivocal, and easy to discern. The difference between these two lines is the crux of the argument in this paper. It is impossible to compare Abraham to a contemporary person placed in the same situation, because the attitude to offspring in the culture in which he lived was, as I have said, radically different. In other words, when God turned to him and asked him to sacrifice his beloved son, Abraham heard a difficult, although reasonable, request. Sending Ishmael to meet his fate in the desert was also not easy and can be found on the same spectrum.[52]

The Children of Sodom

It is important to note for whose lives Abraham pleaded and for whose he did not. The question of the existence or absence of righteous men in Sodom does not solve the problem of the killing of young children who had not sinned.[53] Why didn't Abraham, the fighter for justice, plead for the lives of the children of Sodom? The answer is obvious: in Abraham's world, in the reality of his time, there was no basis, either conceptual or practical, for the idea that children are beings separate from their parents. The physical and economic dependence of young children on others was a fundamental concept in the ancient world, and the basis for the way they were treated. The biblical term for young children, *taf*, is apparently derived from the word *tafel* meaning "subordinate," and connected to *tapil* meaning "parasitic"; in other words, dependent upon a primary figure for sustenance and survival.

As I argued at the beginning of this article, the *Akedah* is only an example of a larger phenomenon. We can apply the same approach to other commandments that are difficult for us to accept today, such as the biblical laws of marriage and divorce, among others.

The danger inherent in this approach is clear. The major concern is that placing Abraham in the context of his time and place makes him irrelevant as an educational role model. This would undermine the traditional Jewish approach that regards the saintly Patriarchs as timeless role models to be learned from and emulated. A number of the articles in this collection discuss these questions in depth.[54] Tamar Ross devoted a large part of her book, *Expanding the Palace of Torah: Orthodoxy and Feminism*, to similar questions related to the sanctity of the Torah and its commandments, and the transience or timelessness of the word of God.[55] In the chapter entitled "The Word of God Contextualized: Successive Hearings and the Decree of History," she attempts to answer these questions by means of the concept of "accumulating revelation," based on the theology of Rav Kook and others. According to this idea, the ethical and cultural development of the world is part of perennial divine participation in the transmission of the Torah and its changing interpretation throughout the generations.

While the dangers are great, so are the possibilities. By placing Abraham in his time and culture, the *Akedah* can once again be read, as it always was and will be, as a parable for eternal human devotion to God. The biblical *Akedah* will continue to be a metaphor for the immolation of both the human will (or consciousness, or understanding) and body, as in the Holocaust and the wars of the State of Israel, in which mothers and fathers sent their sons to defend their people and their land.

The subtle distinctions between the transience or timelessness of the Torah raised in this discussion of the *Akedah*, and their application to other difficult passages, can lead to a more complete and harmonious acceptance of the eternal message delivered to us, by means of human and historical channels, in the Torah of Moses.

Endnotes

I would like to thank the readers of the article for their helpful comments: Rabbi Yehuda Brandes, Dr. Tova Ganzel, and Dr. Yoshi Fargeon

1. An enormous amount of material has been written about the *Akedah*. I have made use of the following sources (a mere "tip of the iceberg") in writing this article: Uriel Simon and Ruth Calderon, eds., "Akedat Yitzhak be-Mikra, be-Midrash, be-Piyut, be-Shira ha-Ivrit ha-Ḥadasha u-be-Omanuyot" [The Binding of Isaac in the Bible, midrash, liturgical poetry, Hebrew poetry, and art] (Tel Aviv: Alma College, 1999); Israel Rosenson and Binyamin Lau, eds., *Akedat Yitzhak Lezaro: Mabat me-Ayin Yisra'elit* [The Binding of Isaac for the sake of his descendants: An Israeli perspective] (Tel Aviv: Yitzhak Hirschberg Memorial Foundation, 2003). Many other sources, both academic and theological, on the story of the *Akedah* can be found in Yoshiyahu Fargeon, *Lamah Tetanu ha-Shem: Meuravuto shel Elohim be-Shekarim u-be-Hatayu'ot be-Sipur ha-Mikra'i* [Why, O Lord, do you lead us astray? God's involvement in lying and deception in the Biblical narrative], PhD diss., Bar Ilan University, 2014, 108–127. For a survey of approaches to the *Akedah* over the course of time, see Alexander Even Chen, *Akedat Yitzhak be-Parshanut ha-Mistit ve-ha-Filosophit shel ha-Mikra* [The Binding of Isaac in the mystical and philosophical interpretation of the Bible] (Tel Aviv: Miskal, 2006). The website for the daily study of the Bible www.929.org has added new texts to the literature dealing with the contemporary struggle to understand the *Akedah*. These can be found on the page for Genesis chapter 22: http://www.929.org.il/chapter/22.
2. See Sara Japhet, "Nisayon ha-Akedah ve-Nisayon Iyov: Mah Beneihem?" [The trial of the *Akedah* and the trial of Job: A comparison], in *Iyov: be-Mikra be-Hagut u-be-Emunot* [Job in the Bible, in thought, and in belief], ed. Lea Mazor (Jerusalem: Magnes, 1995), 13–33. Japhet rejects the perception of Abraham as a role model and a paradigm in his willingness to perform the sacrifice. In her eyes, his decision should not be taken as an example for future generations.
3. Daniel Vainstub, "Korbonot Adam be-Cana'an ve-Yisrael" [Human sacrifice in Canaan and Israel], *Beer-Sheva* 19 (2010):117–181. Vainstub surveys the archaeological findings that testify to the existence of the practice and in an appendix to his article he brings postbiblical sources attesting to a similar practice, including Clearchus, Quintus Ennius, and others. One of his central arguments is that the practice was introduced to the Land of Israel and became pervasive there during the reign of Josiah.
4. Ibid., 180. For more on the subject of the *Akedah* and child sacrifice in the Bible see the first two chapters of Jon D. Levenson, *The Death and Resurrection of the Beloved Son: The Transformation of Child Sacrifice in Judaism and Christianity* (New Haven: Yale University Press, 1993), 3–35. Levenson argues for the existence of a biblical tradition supporting

human sacrifice alluded to in various verses including "You shall give Me the firstborn among your sons" (Exod. 22: 28), inter alia.
5. Jerusalem Talmud, tractate *Ta'anit*, 2:4.
6. In some sources, the name of the mother is not mentioned, and in midrash *Eikhah Rabbah* she is called Miriam bat Tanḥum. There is a huge difference between the story of Hannah and her Seven Sons and the *Akedah*. Hannah, like her fellow Jews who sacrificed their lives throughout the generations, had no choice, whereas Abraham did. This is the crux of the enormous ethical challenge raised by his deed.
7. A. B. Yehoshua, "Levatel et ha-Akedah al yidei Mimusha" [To negate the *Akedah* by actualizing it], in *Be-Kivun ha-Negdi: Kovetz Mekharim al Mar Mani shel Alef Beit Yehoshua* [In the opposite direction: A collection of articles about *Mr. Mani* by A. B. Yehoshua], ed. Nitza ben Dov (Tel Aviv: Hakibbutz Hameuchad, 1995), 394–398. On the profound influence of the *Akedah* on several of Yehoshua's important stories, see also: Mordechai Shalev, "Ḥotem ha-Akedah" [The impact of the *Akedah*], in *Be-Kivun ha-Negdi*, 399–447. A. B. Yehoshua recently published a long article summarizing his approach to the *Akedah* and offering an alternative reading. See A. B. Yehoshua, "Me-Mitos le-Historia" [From myth to history)], January 19, 2015, http://www.929.org.il/author/150/post/678.
8. Yehoshua, "Levatel et ha-Akedah al yidei Mimusha," 396.
9. "I wanted to create within the book a real *Akedah* story that would be actualized in the very place that the biblical story takes place, with one essential difference: what was in the biblical story only a threat would become here a horrible reality. By means of the murderous realization of the threat perhaps I would succeed in removing the magic, and even the soul, of this seminal story. I call this 'negating the *Akedah* by actualizing it.'" Ibid., 396.
10. On Kierkegaard, see further below.
11. He explains the *Akedah* as a manipulation by Abraham who founded a new religion and feared that his son would forsake it. In attempting to ensure its continuation, he staged the binding of Isaac on the altar, and at the last moment dropped the knife and said to his son, "The God that I believe in forbade me to kill you. He saved your life!"
12. Hugo Bergmann, "Ha-Shamayim ve-ha-Aretz" [Heaven and earth], *in Ha-Akedah ve-ha-Adam shel ha-Yom* (Tel Aviv: Sifre, n.d.), 21–28. "Man is able and even obligated to critically analyze even sacred texts when they conflict with his logical and, in particular, his ethical understanding" (25).
13. Asa Kasher , "She-bakol dor va-dor: shalosh akedot" [In every generation: three *Akedot*], in *Yitzhak Lezaro*, 127–133.
14. For a comparison of the model of the *Akedah* to the model of Absalom and David, see Yair Zakovitch, "Ha-Ayil be-Sevakh ve-Avshalom be-Sovekh" [The ram in the thicket and Absalom in the branches], *Tarbiz* 52 (1983): 143–144; and Marc Bregman, "Temunat ha-Ayil be-Tziur ha-Akedah be-Ritzpat ha-Pesifas me-Beit Alfa" [The picture of the ram in the depiction of the *Akedah* in the mosaic at Beit Alfa], *Tarbiz* 51 (1982): 306–309.
15. Yossi Sarid, "Yitzhak Ḥayy o Meit" [Isaac living or dead], *Yediot Aḥaronot*, 1989. Another quote: "The *Akedah* is something that riles me to no end from the depths of my soul, as does Masada." (From a debate in the Knesset, December 27, 1983.)
16. Rosenson and Lau, eds., *Akedat Yitzhak Lezaro*, 215–224.
17. Ibid. Tzadok Ha-Kohen (19th cent.) argued that Abraham should have refused, and on this he was tested. His interpretation does not conform to the *peshat* of the verses that praise Abraham.
18. The critique of Kierkegaard, a non-Jew, is "internal"; in that he was a religious man who accepted the veracity of the Bible.

19. Søren Kierkegaard, *Fear and Trembling*, trans. Walter Lowrie (Princeton: Princeton University Press, 1941), 27.
20. Kierkegaard, *Fear and Trembling*, 27. Years later A. B. Yehoshua would continue in this direction and imagine his own version of the *Akedah*, similar to Kierkegaard's in its depiction of Abraham's deceit and lies intended to preserve his son's faith, but different from it in essence. In contrast to Kierkegaard the believer, Yehoshua, who has declared himself to be a nonbeliever, is not familiar with, or does not understand, the fervor of religious faith.
21. Moses Maimonides, *The Guide of the Perplexed*, 3:24.
22. Yeshayahu Leibowitz, *Judaism, Human Values, and the Jewish State*, ed. Eliezer Goldman (Cambridge: Harvard University Press, 1992), 119, 122.
23. Leibowitz, *Judaism, Human Values*, 14.
24. For example, Rav Abraham Isaac Ha-Kohen Kook, *Shemoneh Kevatzim* [Eight collections], ed. She'ar Yashuv Cohen and Dov Schwartz (Jerusalem: n.p., 1999), *kovetz* b-102; published also in Rav Abraham Isaac Ha-Kohen Kook, *Orot* (Jerusalem: Mosad Harav Kook, 2005), 140.
25. *Igrot Ra'aya* [The letters of Rav Kook] (Jerusalem: Mosad Harav Kook, 1985), 2:43.
26. Kierkegaard, *Fear and Trembling*, 37. Rabbi Shlomo Aviner's discussion of the *Akedah* in *Akedat Yitzhak Lezaro* (135–138) is influenced by this amazing description of Abraham who succeeds in maintaining both his faith and devotion to God as well as his natural paternal feelings for his son.
27. Yoel Bin-Nun, *Ha-Makor Ha-Kaful: Hashra'a ve-Samkhut be-Mishnat ha-Rav Kook* [The double source: Human inspiration and authority in the philosophy of Rav Kook] (Bnei Brak: Hakibbitz Hameuchad, 2014), 177–187.
28. Avi Sagi, *Yahadut: Bein Dat u-Musar* [Judaism: between religion and morality] (Tel Aviv: Hakibbutz Hameuchad, 1998), 11–12. This book, which discusses the relationship between religion and morality in Judaism, is the continuation of his previous book on the subject of religion and morality in general.
29. Responsa of the Radbaz 1:52: 627. Cited in Sagi, *Yahadut*, 155–156.
30. Sagi, *Yahadut*, 266.
31. Shimon Gershon Rosenberg, "I-Vada'ut ke-Nisyon ha-Akedah" [Uncertainty as the test of the *Akedah*], in *Nehalech Be'ragesh* [We walk in fervor: Selected works of Rabbi Shimon Gershon Rosenberg-Shagar] (Alon Shvut: Institute for the Writings of HaRav Shagar, 2010), 111–124.
32. Rosenberg, "I-Vada'ut ke-Nisyon ha-Akedah," 120.
33. For further elaboration see the article by Etan Abramowitz, "Havnayat ha-Subiekt ha-Ne'ekad" [Structuring the bound subject], January 2, 2012, http://alimletrufa.blogspot.co.il/2012/01/blog-post_02.html.
34. And Yeshayahu Leibowitz (see above), who turned the observance of the commandments in general into an "*Akedah*": an act lacking reward, done only for its own sake.
35. *Akedat Yitzhak Lezaro*, 89. See also his article at the beginning of the book.
36. Ibid., 140–141.
37. Ibid., 146.
38. Compare with the statement of Sara Japhet (note 2 above). Japhet does not discuss Abraham's ethical dilemma but focuses instead on the change that God undergoes in the course of the *Akedah* as God negates once and for all the need for human sacrifice.
39. *Akedat Yitzhak Lezaro*, 91–102.
40. Ibid., 150.

41. Hillel Weiss, *Diukan ha-Lohem: Iyunim al Giborim u-Gevura be-Siporet Ha-Ivrit shel ha-Dor ha-Aharon* [Portrait of a fighter: Studies on heroes and heroism in contemporary Hebrew narrative fiction] (Ramat Gan: Bar Ilan University, 1975), 222–230; Hillel Weiss, "He'arot le-Behinat 'Akedat Yitzhak' be-Siporet ha-Ivrit Bat Zemanenu Ke-Topos, Tema u-Motiv" [Notes on the study of the Binding of Isaac in contemporary Hebrew literature as topos, theme, and motif], in *Ha-Akedah ve-ha-Tokhehah: Mitos, Temah u-Topos be-Sifrut* [The Binding of Isaac and the Rebuke: Myth, theme, and topos in literature], ed. Zvi Levy (Jerusalem: Magnes, 1991), 31–52.
42. Weiss, *Diukan ha-Lohem*, 231.
43. From his story "Lefi ha-Tza'ar ha-Sakhar" [The reward is in proportion to the effort], in *Ha-Esh ve-ha-Etzim* [The fire and the trees] (Jerusalem: Schocken, 1978), 5–19.
44. Weiss, *Diukan ha-Lohem*, 225.
45. Aharon Megged, *The Living on the Dead*, trans. Misha Louvish (London: Jonathan Cape, 1970), 247.
46. Weiss, *Diukan Ha-Lohem*, 225.
47. Ibid., 226.
48. This point was missed altogether by critics such as A. B. Yehoshua. See above.
49. Arnold B. Ehrlich, *Mikra Ki-Peshuto* [The Bible according to its literal meaning] (New York: Ktav, 1969), 84.
50. As pointed out earlier, A. B. Yehoshua prefers the Christian ethos of self-sacrifice to the biblical ethos of the *Akedah*.
51. Jephthah who sacrificed his daughter (Judg. 11) did not grasp this distinction.
52. Despite what I wrote above, it is possible that the attitude toward women in Abraham's time is also part of this phenomenon. (Abraham handed Sarah over to Abimelech and Pharaoh, and sent Hagar away.)
53. I would like to thank my friend Shulamit Kislev for calling my attention to this important point.
54. For example, the papers of Ben Sommer and Tamar Ross, especially subsections 18–19 of the article of the latter.
55. Tamar Ross, *Expanding the Palace of Torah: Orthodoxy and Feminism* (Hanover, N.H.: Brandeis University Press, 2004), 184–186, 204–207. It is important to note Uriel Simon's viewpoint in this context. In *Bakesh Shalom u-Radfehu: She'elot ha-Sha'a be-Or ha-Mikra, ha-Mikra be-Or She'elot ha-Sha'a* [Seek peace and pursue it: Topical issues in the light of the Bible, the Bible in the light of topical issues] (Tel Aviv: Miskal, 2002), he proposes the adoption of a historical-developmental approach to biblical commands that we find difficult to accept in light of our modern ethical awareness. He distinguishes between "static eternity," in which the words of God remain frozen in their place, and "dynamic eternity," meaning that "the word of God preserves its essential core while it adapts to the changing needs of each generation" (260).

Manasseh, King of Judah, in Early rabbinic Literature: An Erudite, Unfettered, and Creative Biblical Critic

Hananel Mack

1

King Manasseh of Judah is one of three kings and four commoners who have no share in the world to come. The other two kings are Jeroboam and Ahab, kings of Israel, who, according to the first mishnah in *perek Ḥelek* (tractate *Sanhedrin* 10:1),[1] join the ranks of Balaam, Doeg the Edomite, Ahitophel, and Gehazi, the servant of the prophet Elisha.

The primary sources of information about Manasseh in the Bible are concentrated in two comparable, though not identical chapters. 2 Kings 21 describes Manasseh's actions in the familiar biblical language of censure. "He did what was displeasing to the Lord, following the abhorrent practices of the nations" (21:2). However, this chapter also uses particularly harsh language, uniquely applied to the deeds of this king: Manasseh rebuilt the altars to Baal and Asherah "as King Ahab of Israel had done" (3), "bowed down to all the host of heaven" (3), "consigned his son to the fire; he practiced soothsaying and divination, and consulted ghosts and familiar spirits" (6), and, in general, "did much that was displeasing to the Lord, to vex Him" (6). He corrupted his people: "Manasseh led them astray to do greater evil than the nations that the Lord had destroyed before the Israelites" (9), and shed blood: "Moreover, Manasseh put so many innocent persons to death that he filled Jerusalem [with blood] from end to end—besides the sin he committed in causing Judah to do what was displeasing to the Lord" (16). In Chronicles 2:33 this description is repeated without significant changes, although verses 11–19 introduce a new, previously unfamiliar aspect of Manasseh's story that will be discussed later.

The "sin of Manasseh" is mentioned in several additional biblical sources. Near the end of 2 Kings,[2] the sins of Manasseh are presented as the major catalyst for the destruction of the First Temple and its accompanying horrors: "However, the Lord did not turn away from His awesome wrath which had blazed up against Judah because of all the things Manasseh did to vex Him" (2 Kings 23:26). "All this befell Judah at the command of the Lord, who banished [them] from His presence because of all the sins that Manasseh had committed" (24:3). This same idea is also expressed in the book of Jeremiah: "I will make them a horror to all the kingdoms of the earth, on account of King Manasseh son of Hezekiah of Judah, and of what he did in Jerusalem" (Jer. 15:4).

Fifty-four years elapsed between Manasseh's death and the destruction of the Temple, and to this must be added the final years of his rule when he distanced himself to a large degree from his earlier policies, as will be discussed below. For most of the period after Manasseh's reign, the righteous King Josiah ruled in Jerusalem. He made a wholehearted attempt to return Judah to the right path and to correct the Manasseh's wrongdoing: "And the altars made by Manasseh in the two courts of the House of the Lord. He removed them from there" (2 Kings 23:12). Nonetheless, the sin of Manasseh the son of Hezekiah sealed the fate of Jerusalem, and ensured that Manasseh be numbered among the three kings that have no place in the world to come.

Josephus Flavius presents a similar picture, but in one particular aspect his depiction is even more severe than that presented in the Bible: "For in his contempt for God, he hastened to kill all those who were just among the Hebrews; he did not even have mercy on the prophets, but butchered some of them every day so that Hierosolyma ran with blood."[3] Still, it must be emphasized that the biblical sources identify idolatry and its systematic proliferation, not bloodshed, as Manasseh's quintessential sin.

As I have pointed out, Chronicles adds an additional element to Manasseh's story, an element that is repeated by Josephus: Manasseh's captivity and torture at the hands of the king of Assyria.[4] As a result, "in his distress, he entreated the Lord his God and humbled himself greatly before the God of his fathers. He prayed to Him, and He granted his prayer, heard his plea, and returned him to Jerusalem to his kingdom. Then Manasseh knew that the Lord alone was God" (2 Chron. 33:12–13). This additional information led Rabbi Judah to disagree with the first opinion stated in the mishnah and declare that "Manasseh has a portion in the world to come." The other sages responded: "He was restored to his kingdom but not to the world to come."[5] This description of how Manasseh's deeds, punishment, and prayer led him to believe in God corresponds to the basic and familiar concept that Manasseh's sins were first and foremost idolatry and not murder and bloodshed.[6]

It is possible to understand the disagreement between the first opinion in the mishnah, Rabbi Judah, and the other sages as a debate over the meaning and value of the information Chronicles provides supplementing the narrative in Kings.[7] In any case, the controversy surrounds the Biblical narrative. Rabbi Akiva's discussion in *Sifrei Devarim*[8] about Manasseh and the suffering that led him to repent, and its reworking in the Babylonian Talmud are based, albeit indirectly, on the Biblical text.[9]

Rabbi Akiva presents Manasseh as an eminent rabbi who went astray, and whose knowledge of Torah was not enough to lead him back to repentance. Rabbi Akiva's conclusion that only suffering returned Manasseh to the path of righteousness is not a fanciful interpretation, but almost exactly the plain meaning of the text in Chronicles. The opinions of the Palestinian *amoraim* in the *Pesikta de-Rav Kahana* on *haftarat* Shabbat Shuva,[10] and the parallel discussion of Manasseh in the Jerusalem Talmud,[11] expand extensively on the narrative in Chronicles. They do not, however, deviate from the spirit of the biblical text regarding the nature of Manasseh's sin. In the *Pesikta*, Manasseh appears in the company of other sinners who mended their ways to a greater or lesser degree, and whose repentance was at least partially accepted. This too is based directly on the biblical text or its interpretation.[12] Rabbi Yoḥanan's opinion, found in the Babylonian Talmud, that strengthens the connection between Jeroboam, Ahab, and Manasseh is also part of this trend.[13]

However, despite what is stated explicitly in the books of Kings, Jeremiah, and Chronicles, and in the rabbinic literature cited here, there are other tannaitic and amoraic sources that emphasize another side of Manasseh's personality and the nature of his crimes. These independent amoraic sources are the products of the interpretations of Babylonian *amoraim*.

2

About ten years ago, Aharon Shemesh published an article connecting the schism between the Sadducees and the Pharisees to a *baraita* that relates a commentary in the name of Manasseh, King of Judah.[14] In the first part of the article, Shemesh cites a halakhic/legal controversy between the Boethusians and the Pharisees regarding a daughter's inheritance—one of the classic subjects of debate between the Pharisees and the Sadducees at the end of the

Second Temple period. The scholion (commentary) on *Megilat Ta'anit* relates a debate between Rabbi Yoḥanan ben Zakkai and "an elder who gossiped about him" and made false accusations against him. Rabbi Yoḥanan ben Zakkai quoted the following verse to him (or, in reference to him): "That was the Anah who discovered the hot springs in the wilderness while pasturing the asses of his father Zibeon" (Gen. 36:24). The controversy continued and, in the end, the Pharisees defeated the Sadducees "and that day was made a holiday."[15]

While Rabbi Yoḥanan's words appear to be a meaningless insult, Shemesh argues that they should be understood differently. The polemical nature of this source is indisputable. Shemesh explains that "this *baraita* is one of three *baraitot* cited in the scholion ... both they and their counterparts in an identical literary framework within the Talmud[16] are clearly polemical."[17] I will not elaborate here on the debate concerning a daughter's inheritance nor on the exegetical methods used by the Pharisees, led by Rabbi Yoḥanan, in their efforts to make a ruling on the subject. However, it is important to point out that the Pharisaic/rabbinic interpretation is not consistent with a simple reading of Genesis 36:20–30. The simple meaning of the verses is that there were two people by the name of Anah in the family of Seir the Horite, while Rabbi Yoḥanan ben Zakkai interprets the verses to mean that both "Anah"s refer to one and the same person. On this basis, genealogical conclusions are derived regarding the two women, Oholibamah and Timna, mentioned in the verses. According to Shemesh, each of these conflicting conclusions corresponds to one of the competing halakhic positions; the interpretation furthest from the simple meaning of the text corresponds to the opinion of the Pharisees. The words "and Lotan's sister was Timna" (22), therefore, have a special meaning. Shemesh argues that the identity of Timna is the basis of the Sadducee position regarding female inheritance.

Thus, in a tannaitic *derashah* (homiletic interpretation) whose source is the midrash *Sifrei* on Numbers, Manasseh, King of Judah is mentioned in the context of the discussion of Timna. This *derashah* is based on Numbers 15:30–31: "But the person ... who acts defiantly reviles the Lord; that person shall be cut off from among his people. Because he has spurned the word of the Lord and violated His commandment."

The midrash reads:

> "Who acts defiantly"—this is one who interprets the Torah inappropriately, like Manasseh son of Hezekiah. "Reviles the Lord" refers to one who makes blasphemous commentaries saying: "Did He not have anything

more important to say than 'Reuben came upon' (Gen. 30:14), or 'and Lotan's sister was Timna?'" (36: 22). To this behavior, tradition ascribes the verse: "You are busy maligning your brother" (Ps. 50:20).[18]

This *derashah* also appears with minor changes as a *baraita*, under the heading "The Rabbis Have Taught," in the Babylonian Talmud (tractate *Sanhedrin* 99b).[19]

A cursory reading of these sources reveals that Manasseh is presented as an amateur exegete who derides Moses and his Torah and claims that it contains a list of meaningless irrelevancies. Shemesh does not agree with this reading. He maintains that Manasseh is described in these sources as an exegete, and suggests the possibility that the comments cited in his name are the "opening words of commentaries, real interpretations."[20] According to this approach, behind the derision directed toward the apparently meaningless words "and Lotan's sister was Timna" lies the Sadducee interpretation mentioned above. Shemesh attempts to reconstruct the remainder of this Sadducee exegesis ascribed to Manasseh. He then analyzes the meanings of the expressions unique to the verses cited by Manasseh and to the *baraita* cited in the *Sifrei*, and the use made of these biblical expressions by the Pharisees' opponents in order to refute their rivals. Shemesh concludes that the midrash in the *Sifrei* about Manasseh was the Pharisee response to this Sadducee attack. Manasseh, King of Judah is thus presented in the *Sifrei* and in the Talmud as an educated and knowledgeable Sadducee commentator: a heretic who authors blasphemous commentaries and inappropriate interpretations. One could go even further and say that these sources present Manasseh as an ancient biblical critic, unbeholden to rabbinic opinions, commentaries, exegetical methodology, or halakhic authority, who favored the explicit, *peshat* meaning over tradition and rabbinic midrash.

Manasseh's derisive attitude toward the verse beginning "Reuben came upon" (Gen. 30:14) and the story of the mandrakes is compatible with this theory.[21] The biblical story of the mandrakes and the birth of Issachar confuses all readers. Ascribing to Manasseh the derisive question of why Moses bothered to include this episode in the Torah at all intensifies this uneasiness, and emphasizes the moral and literary difficulties inherent in the story. Moreover, Manasseh's choice of the tribe of Issachar specifically as his object of ridicule is polemical in its own right, as I will explain below.

Ridicule of the tribe of Issachar and the story of its forefather's birth is also expressed clearly in another source: the text known as *Tzavaot Bnei Yaakov* or *Tzvaot ha-Shevatim* [The wills of the sons of Jacob/the tribes]. This work is an anonymous composition from the Second Temple era whose dating, editor, and literary sources are unknown. This is not the appropriate forum for an extensive discussion of either the nature of these "wills," or the question of whether some or all of the sages were familiar with the work. It is clear, however, that if the sages were aware of these writings, they were not pleased with them. The texts include harsh criticisms of several figures in Genesis, including the Patriarchs, and many passages reveal profound Hellenistic influences. Other sections indicate Christian spiritual influences, although it can be surmised that these passages were added at a later date.

The story of the mandrakes that Reuben brought to his mother is told at length in the first part of "The Will of Issachar." On his death bed, Issachar tells his offspring the story of the mandrakes that led to his conception and birth. In a crass and popular vein, the text recounts the continued quarreling and animosity between Rachel and Leah, beginning with the unforgettable events of the first wedding night and bitter morning after. Now, Rachel grabs the mandrakes from her nephew and refuses to give them back. Leah declares: "Jacob is mine because I am his first wife!" Rachel answers: "You are not his wife! You were given to him in deceit. My father deceived me and sent me away that night ... but I will sell you one night with Jacob for these mandrakes."

In comparison, the *Book of Jubilees*, an apocryphal work, does not mention the story of the mandrakes. The author of the *Tzvaot ha-Shevatim* was far from deferent to the important figures of Genesis. He thought and wrote in a manner fundamentally different from that of the sages, and lacked their respect for the Bible and its heroes. Many rabbinic commentaries and midrashim criticize biblical figures, but not in such cheap and crude manner.

The two commentaries attributed to Manasseh complement each other in another way. His halakhic commentary on Timna favors a woman, both halakhically and financially. His aggadic commentary about the mandrakes, however, diminishes the stature of biblical women. Neither found favor with the sages because they emanated from a negative and inimical source.

Manasseh's midrash about the mandrakes and "The Will of Issachar," both reveal contempt for the tribe of Issachar. A well-known tradition from the tannaitic period regards Issachar as a tribe that studies Torah. A midrash in the *Sifrei* comments on the verse "And of Zebulun he said: Rejoice, O Zebulun, on your journeys, and Issachar, in your tents" (Deut. 33:18): "This teaches us that the tribe of Issachar excels in Torah study, as it is written: 'Of the Issacharites, men who knew how to interpret the signs of the times'" (1 Chron. 12:33). This interpretation reappears in various guises throughout rabbinic literature, and inspired the idea, developed in the time of the *amoraim*, of the partnership between the Torah scholars of Issachar and the tribe of Zebulin that supported them. A midrash in the *Sifrei* on Numbers refers to the tribe of Issachar as Torah scholars: Netanel son of Zoar, the prince of Issachar, suggested to his friends to bring the princely sacrifices to the dedication of the Tabernacle. Therefore, "he merited that wisdom be given to [from] his tribe, as it is written 'of the Issacharites,' and the Bible also praises the tribe's courts of law in Egypt."[22] There is no doubt that, in the opinion of these commentators, the Torah scholarship of the tribe of Issachar is thoroughly Pharisaic and identical with that of the *tannaim*. Ridicule of Issachar's origins implies contempt for his Torah study, and for that of the Pharisees as a group.

The complete verse from Chronicles about Issachar reads: "Of the Issacharites, men who knew how to interpret the signs of the times, to determine how Israel should act; their chiefs were 200, and all their kinsmen followed them" (1 Chron. 12:33). The phrase "to interpret the signs of the times" is understood in several places to indicate thorough knowledge of the calendar. This verse is therefore understood to mean that the members of the tribe were tasked with reckoning the calendar in all its detail and instructing the People of Israel according to their calculations and their traditions. Although this interpretation first appears in the amoraic period, it is possible that it existed earlier, and, in any case, is not far from the simple meaning of the verses. Questions relating to the calendar, such as adding a leap month, testimony about the appearance of the new moon, the timing of the holidays, and related matters, were central issues in the controversy between the Pharisees, Sadducees, and Boethusians, and are reflected clearly in both rabbinic and sectarian literature. It would appear that contempt for the tribe of Issachar and its inferior origin is connected to the heated and prolonged controversy about the calendar and the festivals. This contempt is also reminiscent of Sadducee culture, which was typically associated with the aristocracy and disdained the lower socioeconomic classes and those of low or questionable birth.

"The Will of Issachar" and the *baraita* in *Sifrei Ba-Midbar* both convey the same message: Manasseh the son of Hezekiah was an outspoken and dangerous exegete. Taken together, the two commentaries ascribed to Manasseh reveal him to be a biblical critic who adheres to the simple meaning of the text (*peshat*) and who did not accept the exegetical authority of the sages regarding either *halakhah* or *aggadah*. The figure of Manasseh that emerges from the *Sifrei* on Numbers and the parallel Talmudic passages is a prototype of the critic, educated and erudite but also crude and vulgar, who is dismissive of the sages' tradition of reading the biblical text with careful attention to its halakhic and aggadic implications.

3

The mishnah in tractate *Yevamot* cites Ben Azzai's statement that he found a secret scroll in Jerusalem.[23] A *baraita* in the Talmud elaborates on this statement and relates the three items that were found written in this scroll. The third is the terse statement that "Manasseh killed Isaiah," referring to Isaiah the prophet. From the point of view of chronology, this would appear unlikely, though not impossible.[24] It would mean that Manasseh killed a venerable person, no less than a prophet,[25] and a very elderly man.[26] Though the concept that Manasseh killed Isaiah is not grounded in the biblical text, it is essentially compatible with the verse cited above: "Moreover, Manasseh put so many innocent persons to death that he filled Jerusalem [with blood] from end to end" (2 Kings 21:16). This idea is also consistent with Josephus Flavius's description of Manasseh as a killer of many prophets, and with the descriptions found in the apocryphal work *Aliyat Yishayahu* [The rise of Isaiah] and later Christian traditions based upon it. In the Babylonian Talmud, the *amora* Raba develops his discussion of the execution of Isaiah at the hands of Manasseh into a kind of play, centered around a profound legal discussion between the prophet and the king that precedes the execution.[27] Raba declares that "he put him on trial and then killed him"; in other words, the king executed the prophet only after trying him as a criminal.

It would appear that, although obscure traditions may have preceded his discussion, it was Raba who first portrayed an open trial in which Manasseh the son of Hezekiah accused Isaiah the son of Amotz of a series of sins of heresy and rejecting the words of the Torah as written by Moses.

Here there are no blasphemous commentaries such as those found in the *Sifrei* and the *baraita*, but rather three substantial claims, all of which are based on a comparison between the Torah and the book of Isaiah.

Manasseh's first accusation is: "Your teacher Moses said: 'For man may not see Me and live' (Exod. 33:20), and yet you said: 'I beheld my Lord seated on a high and lofty throne' (Isa. 6:1)." His second claim is: "Your teacher Moses said: 'For what great nation is there that has a god so close at hand as is the Lord our God whenever we call upon Him?' (Deut. 4:7), and you said: 'Seek the Lord while He can be found, call to Him while He is near' (Isa. 55:6)." His third claim is: "Your teacher Moses said: 'I will let you enjoy the full count of your days' (Exod. 23:26), but you said: 'And I will add fifteen years to your life' (2 Kings 20:6)."[28]

These are serious arguments. The narrator of the Talmud does not elaborate or explain the contradictions. He provocatively leaves the questions open, which gives the reader the impression that there is real truth to Manasseh's accusations. Manasseh son of Hezekiah, the king of Judah, is not merely a crass and ignorant murderer and idolater, but a man well-versed in the Torah and Prophets, who reads these texts carefully, compares them, and draws conclusions. In other words, Manasseh is an intelligent and knowledgeable Bible critic. He debates the greatest Jewish spiritual figure of his generation, and his arguments are not easily refuted.

But Manasseh is not merely a biblical critic. He is also the person responsible for keeping the peace of the nation. In his role as king of Judah, he fulfills his religious duties and tries a man who dared to challenge the Torah of Moses. Isaiah's fame as a prophet and his advanced years did not merely fail to save him from death; on the contrary, they increased the severity of his sin and placed him in the category of a "rebellious elder" deserving of death. The tables have turned; Isaiah is guilty of a mortal sin and Manasseh zealously upholds the word of God, almost like Elijah the prophet in his day.

The "political" aspect of this story deviates from the framework of this article, because discussions about biblical commentary, beliefs and opinions, and doubts and certainties usually take place between a traditional believer and a sober critic and remain abstract. Usually, these kinds of discussions do not take place between a ruler and his subject, and generally speaking do not evolve into a legal or political confrontation that threatens the life of one of the disputants. Nonetheless, Raba's presentation of Manasseh's arguments sounds like debates between Bible critics and traditional, believing, Torah scholars, without the political backdrop of this talmudic story.

According to the talmudic account, Isaiah chooses not to respond to these difficult questions, and remains silent because, as he says: "I know that he will not accept any answers I give him." In other words, the scholar has convincing answers but he knows that the erudite critic will not accept them. Moreover, the conscientious scholar says to himself: "If I tell him, I will turn him into a willful sinner." On these grounds, he decides to leave his rival guilty of nothing more serious than unintentional misconduct. The prophet knows that his fate is sealed, but in the goodness of his heart he allows Manasseh to retain his self-image as one who follows *halakhah* and lawfully executed a heretic. Even in a nonpolitical debate about the Bible with no serious repercussions, a

Torah scholar, aware that his answers will not convince the critic, might choose to remain silent in order to allow the critic to remain an unintentional sinner, righteous in his own eyes.

In the talmudic account, Isaiah decides to run for his life. Using the power of the Holy Name, he causes a cedar tree to swallow him and hides inside. However, the king discovers his whereabouts and saws down the tree. When the saw reaches his mouth the fugitive dies. Does Manasseh here revert to his original biblical persona of blood-thirsty murderer? Or, does he play the role of a ruler who is ridding the world of a heretic pretending to be God's prophet? This question requires clarification in its own right, and is beyond the scope of this paper. I will, however, point out that the talmudic narrator can explain why the prophet died precisely when the saw reached his mouth. This was punishment for Isaiah's words: "I live among a people of unclean lips" (Isa. 6:5). The prophet's real mortal sin was the description of his audience as "a people of unclean lips."[29]

Up to this point, the critic's questions have been left unanswered. However, the narrator is not willing to let the matter rest. He presents detailed answers to the three questions that the wicked king asked God's prophet. I will not discuss the answers themselves, other than to point out that they answer key theological questions: What is the difference between the prophecy of Moses, who saw through "clear glass" (or "a mirror"), and the other prophets (including Isaiah)? What is the significance of Moses' special status and his unique knowledge of God? Is there a difference between the religious status of individual and communal repentance? Are there limitations, temporal or otherwise, on an individual's ability to repent? What qualities are unique to Rosh Hashanah, Yom Kippur, and the intermediate days of repentance? Is the length of a person's life allotted to him from the day of his birth or determined (also) by his way of life? Does a prophecy's fulfillment depend on the behavior of the one who prophesized?[30]

The discussion of these subjects emanates from the critic-king's questions, left unanswered by the beleaguered prophet. The talmudic narrator, not wanting to leave the questions open, answers them himself. The narrator thereby teaches us a very important lesson: even if the critic himself is an unworthy person, it is incumbent upon us nonetheless to give serious consideration to his opinions and to attempt to answer his questions. This can be seen as the fulfillment of the sound advice given by the author of Proverbs: "Answer a dullard in accord with his folly, else he will think himself wise" (26:5). Moreover, it fulfills Maimonides' adage: "Accept the truth from whatever source it proceeds"[31]—even if the speaker is a critic, a skeptic, a heretic, or a wicked king who has no portion in the world to come.

4

In conclusion, I would like to discuss the beautiful story of Rav Ashi's dream of his conversation with Manasseh, the king of Judah.[32] According to the story, the *amora* Rav Ashi concluded a daily public lecture by citing the Mishnah about the three kings who do not merit the world to come. He ended the lesson with the words: "Tomorrow we will begin with our friends." Manasseh came to him in a dream and confronted him angrily. "Do you call us your friends and the friends of your father?" Manasseh asked. Rav Ashi did not respond. Manasseh attacked him further by asking the *amora* a halakhic question in the talmudic style: "After saying the blessing on the bread, what part of the bread should one break first?" Rav Ashi answered honestly: "I don't know." Manasseh continued to badger him. "You don't even know where to break the bread, and yet you call us friends?" Rav Ashi, astounded, responded: "Teach me, and tomorrow I will teach others your opinion during my public lecture to the scholars." Manasseh responded: "One should break the bread in the place where the top of the bread is crusted."[33]

Rav Ashi did not respond directly, and it can be assumed that he fell temporarily silent because he perceived that he had been vanquished. Manasseh's justifiable anger and his words perplexed the dreaming Rav Ashi, who then asked: "If you and your royal friends are so wise, why did you worship idols?" To this Manasseh replied: "If you had been there, you would have held on to the hems of the robe [of the idol?] and run after it."[34] Manasseh's intention is that Rav Ashi would have been more devoted to idolatry than he was, or, to put it another way: "You are incapable of understanding how strong and deep the temptation to worship idols was in our day." Here Manasseh opened possibilities for further discussions of religion, philosophy, and psychology.

Rav Ashi, like the *tannaim* Rabbi Akiva and the author of the midrash in the *Sifrei*, as well as the Babylonian *amora* Raba and the talmudic narrator in tractate *Yevamot*, saw Manasseh as a Torah scholar. Here, however, in contrast to these other sources, Manasseh is depicted specifically as proficient in the Oral Law and *halakhah*.[35] Manasseh the scholar, son of Hezekiah the saint, did not succeed in repenting for his sins. Manasseh the scholar of the Written Law bested Isaiah the prophet, and the Talmud was forced to provide answers to his astute and incisive questions. Manasseh the talmudic and halakhic scholar overwhelmed one of the greatest *amoraim* in his own field.

The Rabbis of the Mishnah and the Talmud constructed an image of Manasseh far removed from the Bible's coarse and vulgar mass murderer and idolater, the king whose deeds aroused the wrath of God that did not abate for years after his death and the destruction of the First Temple! Manasseh's new friends are not Jeroboam son of Nabat or Ahab son of Omri, the kings of Israel, but anonymous Torah scholars, similar to Elisha ben Abuyah and his ilk, who reject the authority of the sages and their followers. It is worth noting the similarity between this new Manasseh and the best of the biblical critics of the recent past: erudite, intelligent, learned, and well-versed in both Written and Oral Torah; sometimes generous in spirit and pleasant, and sometimes scathing and deprecating. Consider how impressed the sages were with their opponent, and how they struggled to respond to his blasphemous commentaries, his claims of contradictions between the Torah and the Prophets, and his complaint of unfair bias toward himself and his friends. Consider also how much Manasseh's biblical criticism contributed to the bold and incisive examination of questions fundamental to Jewish belief.

Endnotes

1. As it appears in most editions of the Mishnah, and in the Mishnah within the Jerusalem Talmud. However, in the Babylonian Talmud these words are part of the preceding mishnah.
2. The well-known *baraita* in tractate *Bava Batra* 14b ascribes the authorship of the book of Kings to Jeremiah and, in fact, at least in its final chapters, the book of Kings reflects the influence of Jeremiah and the book of Jeremiah. This influence is reflected in the blame placed upon Manasseh and his sins for the destruction of the First Temple in the book of Kings.
3. Josephus, *Judean Antiquities*, ed. and trans. Christopher T. Begg and Paul Spilsbury, vol. 5 of *Josephus Flavius: Translation and Commentary*, ed. Steve Mason (Leiden: Brill, 2005), 218.
4. "And led him off to Babylon" (2 Chron. 33:11). The names Assyria and Babylon are often interchangeable in biblical passages pertaining to the end of the First Temple period. Josephus also describes the capture of Manasseh by the king of Babylon.
5. Mishnah, tractate *Sanhedrin* 10:1.
6. The apocryphal work known as *Tefilat Menashe* [The prayer of Manasseh] neither adds nor detracts from our discussion, perhaps because there is no real connection between this text and the life, sin, and repentance of Manasseh as they are described in the Bible. The author of the *Prayer* put in the supplicant's mouth words of remorse for his grievous sins and a supplication asking God to forgive him for his misdeeds. Nowhere in these passages is there an explicit reference to Manasseh. The phrases "because I am in captivity" (9) or "do not cast me out of Your presence, while I am in the depths of the earth" (13) are not enough to connect the *Prayer* to Manasseh, the king of Judah. Other factors also disprove its pseudo-epigraphic ascription to Manasseh.

7. The question of the exact connection between the opinion cited as "they responded" and the first opinion requires further examination.
8. *Sifrei Devarim*, 32.
9. Babylonian Talmud, tractate *Sanhedrin* 101a-b.
10. *Pesikta de-Rav Kahana*, ed. Dov Mandelboim (New York: Jewish Theological Seminary of America, 1987), 2:364–365.
11. Jerusalem Talmud, tractate *Sanhedrin* 10:2, 28c.
12. Manasseh's colleagues in this passage are Cain; Ahab, the king of Israel; Joachin, the king of Judah; the people of Nineveh; and the people of Anatot.
13. Babylonian Talmud, tractate *Sanhedrin* 103a.
14. Aharon Shemesh, "Mah Gilah Menashe ben Hezekiah be-Torah? Al Sridei Halakhah Zadokit-Kitatit be-Sifrut Ḥazal" [What did Manasseh ben Hezekiah discover in the Torah? Remnants of Sadducee-sectarian *halakhah* in rabbinic literature], *Meghillot* 2 (2004): 91–103.
15. *Megilat Ta'anit*, ed. Vered Noam (Jerusalem: Yad Ben-Zvi, 2004), 223–225. The quoted passage is on 223.
16. The principal passage: tractate *Bava Batra* 115b-116a
17. Shemesh, "Mah Gilah," 98.
18. The passage opens with the words: "And to the wicked, God said: 'Who are you to recite My laws ... seeing that you spurn My discipline, and brush My words aside?" (Ps. 50:16–17).
19. The version of the *derashah* in the Horowitz-Rubin edition was influenced by the version in the Talmud.
20. Shemesh, "Mah Gilah," 100.
21. A few months before the publication of Aharon Shemesh's article, I discussed the sages' image of Manasseh, the king of Judah, in rabbinic literature with my students at Bar Ilan University. I showed them the tannaitic *derashah* and its amoraic development. I suggested to my students my interpretation (presented in this article) of the derisive *derashah* ascribed to Manasseh on the verse "Reuben came upon." However, I indicated that I did not have an explanation for Manasseh's interpretation of the verse "and Lotan's sister was Timna." In response, one of my students, Aviad Hollander, told us that he had heard a lecture by Professor Shemesh on this subject not long before. Aviad explained that Professor Shemesh had shared with his students his inability to find an explanation for Manasseh's apparent deprecation of the verse beginning "Reuben came upon"; Shemesh mentions this point in his article on p. 100. That very evening I called my friend Aharon Shemesh and explained my interpretation to him, and he informed me that his article on the subject was completed and would be published within a few weeks in *Meghillot*, a journal specializing in research on the Dead Sea scrolls and Second Temple literature. I quickly contacted the journal's editors, Professors Deborah Diamant and Moshe Bar-Asher, and asked them to publish in the same issue my interpretation of the second part of the *derashah*. I committed my ideas to writing, and thus the two articles were published one after the other in the same issue: Aharon Shemesh's "Mah Gilah Menashe ben Hezekiah be-Torah?" [What did Manasseh ben Hezekiah discover in the Torah?], and my "Mah od Gilah Menashe ben Hezkiah be-Torah?" [What else did Manasseh ben Hezekiah discover in the Torah?].
22. *Sifrei Ba-Midbar* 52:140.
23. *Mishnah, Yevamot* 4:13; Babylonian Talmud, tractate *Yevamot* 49a.
24. Isaiah prophesied in the time of the Judean kings Uzziah, Jotham, Ahaz, and Hezekiah (Isa. 1:1). It is generally accepted that chapter 6 of the book is the initiation prophecy of the prophet. If we understand the opening verse "in the year of the death of King Uzziah" according to its simple meaning, it appears that the prophet was, in fact, active for one year of

Uzziah's reign, during the sixteen-year reigns of Jotham and Ahaz, and an unspecified period of time during the reign of Hezekiah (who reigned for twenty-nine years). Sennacherib's siege on Jerusalem began and ended in the fourteenth year of Hezekiah's reign (2 Kings 18:13; Isa. 36:1), and shortly afterward Hezekiah fell ill and recovered (2 Kings 20:1; Isa. 38:1). Isaiah was an active participant in all these events, and, thus, was active for forty-seven years all told. If we accept at face value the report that Manasseh murdered Isaiah, and assume that Manasseh did so after succeeding his father, it is necessary to add another fifteen years to the prophet's life and conclude that he was murdered at least sixty-two years after beginning his career. We must also assume that he began to prophesy as an adult (as opposed to Jeremiah who said of himself "for I am still a boy" [Jer. 1:6]), and, if so, at the time of his murder he was over eighty years old. A long life, but within the realm of possibility.

25. From several prophecies within the book of Isaiah, a picture emerges of a prophet connected to the people, addressing them in second person plural. See, e.g., Isa. 1.
26. In *Dikdukei Ha-Te'amim*, ascribed to Aharon Ben-Asher, the years of the prophecy of Isaiah are calculated from the beginning of the reign of Uzziah (who reigned for fifty-two years) until the first year of the reign of Manasseh, one hundred and fourteen years altogether. *Dikdukei Hate'amim le-rabbi Aharon Ben-Asher*, ed. S. Baer, H. L. Strack (Leipzig: Metzger Vetig, 1879), 57, § 70.
27. Tractate *Yevamot* 49b.
28. This is the version that appears in the book of Kings. The corresponding verse in Isaiah 38:5 reads: "I hereby add fifteen years to your life."
29. This accusation continued to haunt Isaiah for generations. For example, in *Iggeret Ha-Shemad (Ma'amar Al Kiddush Ha-Shem)* [Epistle on martyrdom], Maimonides censures Isaiah for this verse, and raises similar criticism against Moses and Elijah.
30. This question is derived from Tosafot, tractate *Yevamot* 50a (s.v., *teda*).
31. *The Eight Chapters of Maimonides of Ethics (Shemonah Perakim)*, ed. Joseph Gorfinkle (New York: Columbia University Press, 1912), 35–36.
32. Babylonian Talmud, tractate *Sanhedrin* 102b. Rav Ashi was one of the later *amoraim*, and is considered the editor of the Babylonian Talmud, or, at least, very involved in the editing process.
33. Rashi offers two explanations: The first is: "the place where the bread is crusted in the oven ... not in the middle." The second is: "the place where the bread is well baked." Rashi prefers the first explanation. See Rashi's comments to tractate *Sanhedrin* 102b.
34. Rashi: "You would have lifted up the hems of your robe from between your legs in order to run faster."
35. Manasseh's comments, revealed to Rav Ashi in a dream and not discussed elsewhere in the Talmud, entered the heart of the halakhic world as practical instructions for all time in the *Shulchan Arukh, Oraḥ Ḥaim*, section 167:1, under the section headings "Hilkhot Bitziat Ha-Pat" [The laws of breaking bread], "Seudah" [The meal], and "Birkat Ha-Mazon" [Grace after meals].

Justification, Denial, and "Terraforming": Three Theological-Exegetical Models

Amit Kula

Introduction

The disparity between human intellect and divine providence[1] has always been the basis for speculation and intense religious ferment.[2] The belief in the goodness of God, His omnipotence, and His rectitude lies at the foundation of religious consciousness.[3] This belief is challenged by the contrasting picture that emerges, as perceived by human intellect, from the realities of life and history, as well as from the Written Torah and oral traditions.

While the theological questions about how God manages the world have been explicitly discussed in the writings of Jewish thinkers, the question of the "correct" exegetical method has only recently merited specific and serious discussion. In my journey along the path of the Torah as it has unfolded over the generations, linking together human efforts to understand the word of God, I have discovered the value of comparing and contrasting the explanations of divine providence with exegetes' answers throughout the generations to the question of the correct method of interpreting the Bible. This article will attempt to delineate the principal approaches to these questions by labeling them, with emphasis on one little known approach.

* * *

He does not, or cannot, alienate himself from the reality in which he lives—its physical form, cultural foundations and ethical principles. His response comes from where he is. Sometimes he will provide a theological justification in harsh words (beginning with the words: "It is not possible that God . . .") and sometimes in soft words ("God seeks the partnership of man"), but usually he simply interprets and acts. His response comes from an unqualified belief in God. Out of dedication to this belief, he must, as one faithful to God, remove the impediments and the stains appearing occasionally on the face of the great sun.

Sometimes he wonders who filled his heart with the urge to draw near to his tempestuous surroundings and did not relieve him of this desire. He knows that God abides in the mist, but his heart tells him that he has to follow his first teacher: "Moses approached the thick cloud where God was" (Exod. 20:18).

* * *

Providence and Human Endeavor

The dilemma of the existence of evil in God's world, which ought to be the best of all possible worlds, and the collective solutions to the problem, is a central theme in the field of Jewish philosophy.[4] Nachmanides describes the crux of the problem thus: "There is something painful and worrying which in itself, in every generation, leads many to outright heresy—it is the appearance of injustice in the world, the suffering of the righteous, and the prosperity of the wicked."[5]

The traditional responses to this question fall between two extremes that can be identified with the two approaches presented in the book of Job. One approach, generally understood to be the position of Job's friends, is that human suffering is usually the result of sin and can always be justified. A person's efforts should, therefore, be directed toward revealing the righteousness in the judgments of "a faithful God, never false" (Deut. 32:4). There are various ways of justifying God's judgments. The most common way of explaining suffering is as the expiation for sin. According to this approach, the "righteous" person is not in fact righteous; either he has hidden sins, or is not entirely righteous.[6] Other explanations are that suffering purifies the soul in preparation for the world to come, or that the concepts of good and evil are different than how they appear at first sight.[7]

The esoteric nature of the conclusion of the book of Job has led some commentators to argue that the alternative approach entails denying the validity of the question.[8] This form of denial perhaps causes the repression of angst over the disparity between ideals and reality.[9] The declaration that the greatness of God precludes questioning His way of ruling the world, or that the question itself is beyond human comprehension, can be found both in commentaries on Job and in a variety of philosophical responses to this question throughout the generations.[10]

There is, however, a third option, according to which the response to suffering is not static or objective, but is rather to be found within the heart and mind of the suffering individual. It is possible to see the "happy ending" of the book of Job as the outcome of a human decision taken by those involved in this drama not to stand aloof, not to judge or complain, but, instead, to take responsibility for righting wrong. This, in turn, brought about God's blessing for the renewal of good fortune:

> Eliphaz the Temanite and Bildad the Shuhite and Zophar the Naamathite went and did as the Lord had told them, and the Lord showed favor to Job. The Lord restored Job's fortunes when he prayed on behalf of his friends, and the Lord gave Job twice what he had before. All his brothers and sisters and all his former friends came to him and had a meal with him in his house. They consoled and comforted him for all the misfortune that the Lord had brought upon him. Each gave him one *kesitah* and each one gold ring. Thus the Lord blessed the latter years of Job's life more than the former (Job 42:9–12).

Job's friends apologize to him. He does not bear a grudge and prays for them. All his relatives, who had previously rejected him, repent and commiserate with him. They take responsibility and establish a fund to help him restore his property and resume his former life.[11] God's blessing accompanies this human act, extends it, and enhances it.

There is an allusion to this approach in the closing words of *The Guide of the Perplexed*.[12] The ultimate purpose of life, according to Maimonides, is to know God and to cleave to him, "that he understandeth, and knoweth Me" (Jer. 9:23). Judaism innovated here by extending the parameters of divinity: expanding the definition of knowledge of God to include the divine attributes, deeds, and impact on earth, and the ways of His providence:

> For when explaining in this verse the noblest ends, he does not limit them only to the apprehension of Him, may He be exalted.... But he says that one should glory in the apprehension of Myself and in the knowledge of My attributes, by which he means His actions.... In this *verse* he makes

it clear to us that those actions that ought to be known and imitated are *loving-kindness, judgment,* and *righteousness.* He adds another corroborative notion through saying, *in the earth*—this being a pivot of the Law. For matters are not as the overbold opine who think that His providence, may He be exalted, terminates at the sphere of the moon and that the earth and that which is in it are neglected: *The Lord hath forsaken the earth.* Rather is it as has been made clear to us by the Master of those who know: *That the earth is the Lord's.* He means to say that His providence also extends over the earth in the way that corresponds to what the latter is, just as His providence extends over the heavens in the way that corresponds to what they are. This is what he says: *That I am the Lord who exercises loving-kindness, judgment, and righteousness, in the earth.* Then he completes the notion by saying: *For in these things I delight, saith the Lord.* He means that it is My purpose that there should come from you *loving-kindness, righteousness, and judgment in the earth* in the way we have explained with regard to the *thirteen attributes*: namely, that the purpose should be assimilation to them and that this should be our way of life.[13]

These words express the idea that divine providence, including both mercy and judgment, is actualized and applied by those who are devoted to him and follow his ways.[14] According to this approach, each individual is responsible for the welfare of the world. Each person must fight evil, do justice, and build a world of loving-kindness. When one does so, the purpose of the Creator is revealed: his thirteen attributes are revealed by human action (among other factors). In our generation, there is a growing trend to divert energy from justifying God's judgments to accepting human responsibility[15] by understanding suffering as an impetus to fix the world[16]—and, perhaps, as the reason for suffering in the first place.

I will call the first approach to human suffering (the belief in divine providence) "justification," the second approach (in its various forms) "denial" or "repression,"[17] and the third approach "terraforming."

This last term requires explanation. Terraforming can be defined as the act of altering the environment of another planet to make it compatible with the conditions of life on Earth and thus capable of supporting human life. In this article, I have borrowed the term to describe creative human activity, whether in nature, society, or biblical exegesis, intended to accommodate the inclusion of faith-based values in modern life. In this context, "terraforming" refers to taking the celestial Torah, with its infinite range of meaning, and giving it a concrete worldly meaning: bringing the Torah from heaven to earth. The term connotes a heroic act from science fiction; it is doubtful that such a project will ever be feasible. Terraforming raises ethical concerns regarding hubris: "Who are you, small, insignificant man, to interfere with the cosmic order without being able to see the whole picture—are you God?"[18] This concept is very relevant to the method of exegesis that mediates between the human and the divine.

Needless to say, these titles are not intended to indicate judgment or preference. The purpose of the labeling is to assist us in categorizing the approaches. The field of psychology, from which some of the names are derived, teaches us that every personal attribute plays a positive role in a healthy personality; personal religious awareness is also composed of many conflicting aspects. Likewise, it is understood that it is not always easy to distinguish between various solutions, and sometimes integrated approaches or interpretations develop. Nonetheless, I have found that these distinctions are instrumental in systematizing the understanding and analysis of theological questions, especially in the area of exegesis.[19]

Exegesis

In recent years, the increased awareness of the presence of the reader and his or her role in understanding the text has enhanced the importance of the study of hermeneutics. These studies have become a subject of discussion among Torah scholars, especially those involved in academic research.[20]

Faith-based scholarship has redefined old questions about the conflicts between modern science and the biblical narrative (including the more recent and quite exceptional confrontation with biblical criticism) while raising new questions related to core values of contemporary culture. We can now find studies about the Jewish approach to liberty, equality, and the value of human life. Many studies have been conducted investigating attitudes toward the other: non-Jews,[21] the disabled,[22] and, most extensively, the status of women.[23]

***

A religious man—for whom the validity of our Law has become established in his soul and has become actual in his belief—such a man being perfect in his religion and character, and having studied the sciences of the philosophers and come to know what they signify—where will he turn?

His mind is occupied with foreign cultures, and secular values and ethics have entered his heart. When he reads the Torah he finds verses that do not conform to principles of science, culture, and morality, and he begins to doubt and to become perplexed: Should he follow his reason and the values he believes in and reject the simple meaning of the verses in God's Torah? By doing so he wounds his soul, relinquishes a precious treasure, and cuts the thread of life.

Perhaps he will change his opinions in light of the verses and concede to what appears to be the opinion of the giver of the Torah? In that case he will feel as though he has betrayed his values, and he will cause himself damage and loss, and will be left with a feeling of pain and unease, and will not cease to suffer from heartache and great perplexity.[24]

* * *

Exegetical questions take on special meaning with regard to sacred texts because they are usually accompanied by rigid traditions that restrict the freedom of interpretation.[25] Nevertheless, there is an exegetical Jewish tradition that has persistently called for creativity and innovation.[26] In this exegetical tradition, this tension is reflected in the question of the transmission of the Oral Law and its sources.[27]

Classical rabbinic literature reflects a high level of awareness of ethical difficulties in the Bible in general, and in the commandments specifically. A good example of this, the subject of much scholarly analysis, is the commandment concerning "the rebellious son" (Deut. 21:18–21). The rabbinic interpretations of this verse reflect the three exegetical traditions mentioned above.[28]

The obligation of the boy's parents to have him executed for disobedience was perceived by the sages as totally unreasonable for various reasons. A midrash *halakhah* (rabbinic legal commentary) presents the question in the following way: "Is he to be stoned for eating a *tartemar* [approximately 200 grams] of meat and drinking half a *log* [approximately half a liter] of wine?"[29] There are three responses to this question. The first response considers the Torah's assumption to be that the rebellious son is destined to become a murderer.[30] This is an apologetic interpretation that assumes the simple meaning of the Torah, the demand for a severe punishment for the rebellious son, is correct. Its efforts are directed to making the profundity of divine judgment accessible to human understanding, while, at the same time, justifying the severity of the punishment by revealing the underlying argument or reasoning that is not immediately apparent.

The second approach rejects the possibility of discovering the rationale behind the law and denies the importance of human rationalization altogether.[31] According to this approach, it is both impossible and unnecessary to reconcile a divine imperative with human reason. This position advocates submission to divine authority, which is the source of the imperative to observe the commandments, traditionally perceived as the decrees of an absolute monarch.[32]

The third approach, also expressed in this context, recognizes the sanctity of the Bible and its undisputed authority, yet does not acquiesce to what appears to be an absolute decree nor adapt itself to apologetic explanations. It takes a stand and affirms the "impossible." This approach is exemplified in the Babylonian Talmud (tractate *Sanhedrin* 71a): "Rabbi Simeon said: 'Because he ate a *tartemar* of meat and drank half a *log* of Italian wine, his parents bring him to be executed? There never was such a case and there never will be. If so, why was it written? Interpret it and be rewarded.'"

The inability to accept the commandment of the rebellious son, for whatever reason, brings the commentator to a significant conclusion: this commandment will never be fulfilled, nor was there ever any intention that it should be fulfilled.[33] Why then was it written? To be interpreted: "Interpret it and be rewarded."[34] The sage, whether by means of extra-contextual interpretation or by restrictive exegesis, neutralizes the commandment and renders it palatable.[35]

There is reason to believe that one of the sources of this exegetical tradition is the school of Rabbi Akiva. He initiated an approach to religion that taught that the actions of people are greater than the actions of God. Humankind is expected to better the material world created by God, in both its physical and social aspects.[36] Similarly, in the field of Torah study, Rabbi Akiva ascribed considerable significance to the creative power and mental alacrity of the student. The breadth of his interpretation of the Torah astonished and excited his colleagues and teachers alike.[37] A good example of his exegetical approach can be seen in the following passage: "'And concerning her who is in menstrual infirmity' (Lev. 15:33)—The early sages said that when she is in a state of menstrual impurity, she should not put on makeup until she immerses in water, until Rabbi Akiva came and taught that this could cause her husband to dislike her and wish to divorce her. How then do we understand 'and concerning her who is in menstrual infirmity'?—She is in menstrual impurity until she immerses in water."[38]

Rabbi Akiva's deviation from the established interpretation was propelled by an ethical consideration (marital harmony) rather than a philological preference. He gave expression thereby to a seminal principle of his approach: the commentator has the responsibility to provide the best possible interpretation that also takes into account ethical considerations, according to his understanding and perspective—in other words, terraforming.

The following discussion provides another good example of terraforming. According to the biblical narrative, Esther was taken to Ahasuerus's palace and, after a selection process, was chosen by him to be his wife and the queen of Persia and Media. Although this chain of events led to the salvation of the Jews, traditional texts reflect dismay at the marriage of a Jewish woman to a non-Jewish king.[39] Never before had a biblical heroine been doomed to such a cruel and demeaning fate.[40] This is the background to a remarkable commentary that appears in the Zohar:

> If it seems as though Ahasuerus had marital relations with Esther, because they lived in the same house—Heaven forbid! "Esther" is derived from the word *seter* [concealment]. She hid from Ahasuerus and a demon was put in her place, and she returned to Mordechai's embrace. Similarly, God saved Sarah, and even her jewelry, from Pharaoh. For every piece of jewelry he touched, God struck him; how much more would he have received if he had touched her body, even her little finger. God did not allow him to get near her.[41]

The commentator will not leave the study hall as long as his sister, our sister, is being defiled by the Persian king. His heart, his religious perspective, and his feeling of Jewish solidarity compel him to rescue her. He uses all available means—that is, exegesis—to save Esther from impurity and disgrace.[42] It is the responsibility of senior Torah scholars to ensure that the biblical narrative contains the best possible story and that undesirable content is weeded out by exegetical means.

This example clarifies a modern aspect of the parameters of terraforming exegesis. The increasing awareness of the role of the commentator clarifies the boundary between *peshat* (contextual interpretation) and *derash* (homily). In our time, the role of *derash* as the primary means of terraforming has declined because homiletical interpretation has become difficult to accept. Today's students prefer the straightforward meaning of the text that makes no adventurous assumptions, does not offer unusual interpretations of the written word, and does not add to what is explicitly stated aside from the obvious.

In this light, we must clarify the distinction between contemporary terraforming commentary and apologetic commentary. Apologetic exegetes stretch their intellectual abilities in order to justify the simple language of the text and the content of the commandments. After the apologetics, the verses remain as if untouched by human hands.

Terraforming exegesis, however, deviates from the straightforward or accepted interpretation, and proposes an alternate meaning compatible with the values and worldview of the commentator. The terraformer is compelled to interpret in this way because he is inherently limited by his own perspective.[43] Terraforming exegesis has recently become popular once again. Thirty years ago, biblical scholars committed to Jewish tradition complained that "Judaism has not provided fertile ground for the development of a theologian cognizant of both traditional Jewish sources and contemporary critical biblical scholarship."[44] These words were a call to Jewish biblical scholars to dedicate themselves to serving the community (an approach already taken by certain Christian scholars), by producing academic research relevant to Judaism and Jewish life. It is doubtful that this call was heeded by many scholars. However, in subsequent years the development of the analytical study of the Bible has produced many articles and commentaries that meet the challenge of integrating modern knowledge and culture into a system grounded on deep-seated, traditional beliefs.[45] A significant number of these works can be defined as "terraforming."[46]

Endnotes

1. This disparity can be found in the Bible, beginning with Cain's appeal to God (Gen. 4:13–14 and Rashi's commentary there); continuing with Abraham's questions (Gen. 15:8, Babylonian Talmud, tractate *Nedarim* 32a, and the commentary of the *Kli Yakar* on this verse); Moses' desire to know the essence of God (Exod. 33:18 and Maimonides, *The Guide of the Perplexed*, 1:54); the anger of the prophets (Josh. 7:7, 1 Sam. 15:11); and ending with such straightforward questions and reflections as: "Shall not the Judge of all the earth deal justly?" (Gen. 18:25); "Why does the way of the wicked prosper?" (Jer. 12:1); and "Why do You countenance treachery, and stand by idle while the one in the wrong devours the one in the right?" (Hab. 1:13).
2. It would appear that the root of this distress was expressed in the "acute vagueness" of the Ari as "the empty void." The dichotomy between the creator and his creation is impossible according to the definitions of both and this is the origin of all the dilemmas. See *Etz Ha-Ḥayyim*, part 1, sec. 2. See also Moshe Hallamish, *An Introduction to the Kabbalah*, trans. Ruth Bar-Ilan and Ora Wiskind-Elper (Albany: State University of New York Press, 1999), 197–201.
3. This theological assumption of God's goodness and the dilemmas it creates were clarified by Rabbi Moshe Ḥayyim Luzzatto in his books. See *Kalaḥ Pitḥei Ḥoḥma (138 Openings of Wisdom)*, trans. Avraham Greenbaum (Jerusalem: Azamra, 2005), 1–15. *Derekh ha-Shem (The Way of God)*, trans. Aryeh Kaplan (Jerusalem: Feldheim, 1977), 31–87.
4. An attempt to present a comprehensive picture of the development of theodicy in Judaism can be found in Shalom Rosenberg, *Good and Evil in Jewish Thought*, trans. John Glucker (Tel Aviv: MOD Books, 1989); and Eliezer Schweid, *Le-Hagid Ki Yashar ha-Shem: Hazdakat Elohim*

be-Maḥshevet Yisrael me-Tekufat Ha-Mikra ve-ad Shpinoza ["To Declare that God is Upright": Theodicy in Jewish thought from the Bible to Spinoza] (Bat-Yam: Tag Publications, 1994). On the kabbalists' discussion of this subject, see Gershom Scholem, *Pirkei Yesod be-Havanat ha-Kabalah u-Smaleyah* [Elements of the Kabbalah and its symbolism], trans. Yosef Ben-Shlomo (Jerusalem: Mosad Bialik, 1980), 189–212; Gershom Scholem, *Kabbalah* (Jerusalem: Keter, 1974), 122–128; Isaiah Tishbi, *The Wisdom of the Zohar*, trans. David Goldstein (Oxford: Oxford University Press, 1989), 2:447–508; and Isaiah Tishby, *Torat ha-Ra ve-ha-Kelipah be-Kabalat ha-Ari* [The doctrine of evil and the *kelipah* in Lurianic kabbalism] (Jerusalem: Magnes, 1994), 13–20. A summary of the various positions in Jewish philosophy in the Middle Ages can be found in Ḥayyim Kreisel, "Tzadik ve-Ra Lo be-Pilosofia ha-Yehudit be-Yimei ha-Benayim" [The suffering of the righteous in Jewish philosophy in the Middle Ages], *Daat* 19 (1987): 17–29. Further information can be found in Ehud Ben-Or, "Modelim le-Havanat ha-Ra be-Moreh Nevuḥim" [Models for understanding evil in *The Guide of the Perplexed*], *Iyyun: The Jerusalem Philosophical Quarterly* 34 (1985): 3–33; and, also Dror Ehrlich, "Ba'ayat ha-Ra be-Sefer ha-Ikkarim le-Rabbi Yosef Albo" [The problem of evil in the *Sefer Ha-Ikkarim* of Rabbi Joseph Albo], *Pe'amim: Studies in Oriental Jewry* 116 (2008): 117–142. A discussion of this question in Jewish thought in the modern period can be found in Yehuda Gellman, "Ha-Ra ve-Tziduko be-Mishnat Ha-Rav Kook" [Evil and its justification in the thought of Rav Kook], *Daat* 19 (1987): 145–155. In addition, much thought has been devoted to the subject in connection to the Holocaust. See, for e.g., Eliezer Berkovits, *Faith after the Holocaust* (New York: KTAV, 1973); Eliezer Schweid, *Bein Ḥurban le-Yishua: Teguvot Hagut Haredit le-Shoah be-Zemana* [From destruction to redemption: Haredi responses to the Holocaust] (Tel Aviv: Hakibbutz Hameuhad, 1995). An analysis of the positions on the edge of the postmodern world can be found in Gili Zivan, "Emunah Nokhaḥ Shekhol ve-Ovdan" [Faith in the face of loss and bereavement], in ed. Moshe Halbertal et al., *Al ha-Emunah* [On faith] (Jerusalem: Keter, 2005), 490–511. A unique perspective on this subject can be found in the collection of articles in Baruch Kahana, Chayuta Deutsch, Ronny Redman, ed., *Ḥidat ha-Yisurim* [The enigma of suffering] (Tel Aviv: Miskal, 2012).
5. *Perush le-Sefer Iyov* [Commentary on the book of Job], in ed. Chaim Dov Chavel, *Kitvei Rabenu Moshe ben Naḥman* [The writings of Nachmanides] (Jerusalem: Mosad Harav Kook, 1963), 1:19.
6. See Babylonian Talmud, tractate *Berakhot* 5b ("Who can suspect the Holy One blessed be He of judging unjustly?") and the Tosafot commentary, s.v. *dina*. See also tractate *Berakhot* 7a: "The righteous man who suffers—he is not entirely righteous."
7. Saadia Gaon, *The Book of Beliefs and Opinions*, trans. Samuel Rosenblatt (New Haven: Yale University Press, 1948), 209–221. On the difficulties of this approach, see Haggai Dagan, "Kol ha-Teodikiot Miyutarot Hen: Shlomo Maimon al Teoditza" ["All theodicy is superfluous": Solomon Maimon on theodicy], *Tarbiz* 70 (2001): 587–600.
8. See, e.g., Y. M. Rosenberg, "Ha-Im Kibel Iyov Teshuva le-Ta'anotav be-Ma'aneh HaShem?" [Did Job receive divine responses to his arguments?], *Be-Sdeh Ḥemed* 2–3 (2002): 25–32: "His capitulation was the result of a deep understanding of the meaning of the human encounter with God . . . therefore there is no ground to even question why the righteous suffer and the wicked prosper." Although the article explores other angles, the author nonetheless felt it necessary to add a statement of denial.
9. Moshe Greenberg, "Hirhurim al ha-Teologia shel Iyov" [Thoughts on the theology of Job], *Hagut be-Mikra* 4 (1984): 55–62. Greenberg's argument is a kind of repression and denial of anguish through indecision, while acknowledging our inability to answer the question: "While the realistic believer does not simplistically assume the ethical causality of God

neither does he deny it completely . . . we can understand neither the peace of the wicked nor the suffering of the righteous."

10. The belief, found in classical rabbinic literature, that there is no reward in this world for fulfilling the commandments can be seen as a way of denying the validity of the question. A harsh formulation of this approach appears in Babylonian Talmud, tractate *Kiddushin* 39b: "One whose good deeds outnumber his sins is punished, and it is as if he burnt the entire Torah, not leaving even a single letter. One whose sins outnumber his good deeds is rewarded, and it is as if he observed the entire Torah, not omitting even a single letter. . . . There is no reward for the commandments in this world." The philosophical coda to this discussion declares the apparent lack of justice in the world.

11. Joseph B. Soloveitchik, *Kol Dodi Dofek—Listen My Beloved Knocks*, trans. David Z. Gordon (New York: Yeshiva University, 2006), 13–19.

12. The commentators on *The Guide* differed with regard to the explanation of the relationship between the divine attributes, providence, and devotion to God.

13. Maimonides, *The Guide of the Perplexed*, 3:54. This passage is a running commentary on Jeremiah 9:23: "But only in this should one glory: In his earnest devotion to Me. For I the Lord act with kindness, Justice, and equity in the world; For in these I delight—declares the Lord." Maimonides understands this verse to mean that the goal of attaining knowledge of God is more important than the desire for great wealth or spiritual perfection.

14. See the commentaries, including Eliezer Berkovits, "Aḥrayut ha-Adam ve-Hashgaḥa be-Historia" [The responsibility of man and Providence in history], in *Ḥevra ve-Historia* [Society and history], ed. Yeḥezkel Cohen (Jerusalem: Ministry of Education, 1980), 513–519.

15. See, e.g., Rabbi Mordechai Piron, "She'elat ha-Ra ha-Ḥevrati ve-ha-Musari ba-Yakum" [The question of social and ethical evil in the universe], in *Minḥa le-Menaḥem* [An offering to Menaḥem], ed. Hana Amit et al. (Bnei Brak: Hakibbutz Hameuchad, 2008), 19–29. The article opens with the theological question and extends its conclusions to the human responsibility to "perceive the divine essence in man."

16. See Rabbi Abraham Isaac Ha-Kohen Kook, *Orot ha-Kodesh* (Jerusalem: Mosad Harav Kook, 1963–1964), 3:70: "No redemption is truly complete unless the redeemed labored with his own hands for its arrival." The approach presented in the treatise can facilitate the development of a religious language in continuity with Jewish tradition, and give religious meaning to an idea whose revolutionary essence is capable of precipitating a break with faith and its language, and their subsequent loss. See Ze'ev Levi, "Teoditza" [Theodicy], *Moed* 17 (2007): 91–103. At the end of this article, he mentions the idea, which he ascribes to several thinkers, including Buber and Levinas, that, instead of ultimately justifying the acts of God, we should be fostering hope and productivity that will make the world a better place and eradicate evil and wickedness. Humanity must work to realize the desired good, not wait for it passively. Note the difference between the style and purpose of the two articles. It is worth reflecting on the possibility of combining these positions with the opinion currently expressed within the rabbinic world, which limits the scope of divine providence. On this point, see Rabbi Ḥayyim David HaLevy, *Aseh Lekha Rav* [Get yourself a rabbi] (Tel Aviv: The Committee for the Publication of the Works of Rabbi HaLevy, 1989), 9:278–288; and Rabbi Shemuel Ariel, "Mashmayuot Emuniot u-Ma'asiyot be-Sugiyot ha-Hashgacha" [Faith-based and practical implications of questions of providence], *Tzohar* 31 (2008): 115–130.

17. This approach involves a form of willful submission before the greatness of God and the rejection of an apologetic approach to theodicy. In certain cases, the denial stems from an inability to cope with the problem of divine providence and the subsequent desire to eradicate it.

18. On this point, see D. MacNiven, "Environmental Ethics and Planetary Engineering," *British Interplanetary Society* 48 (1995): 441–443.
19. The three exegetical voices mentioned here are paralleled by the three stages of transcendent consciousness posited by Rabbi Soloveitchik. See Joseph B. Soloveitchik, *And From There You Shall Seek*, trans. Naomi Goldblum (Jersey City: Ktav, 2008), 149–150. The first stage, escape and fear, is slightly similar to denial and repression. The second stage is similar to apologetics while the third stage has something in common with terraforming.
20. What is *peshat*? This question lies at the core of this high-level, multifaceted debate. A discussion of the legitimate boundaries of current exegesis and related issues can be found in various issues of the journal *Megadim*. The article by Rabbi Yaakov Medan, "Megilat Bat Sheva" [The scroll of Bathsheba], *Megadim* 18 (1993): 67–167, generated a chain of critical responses that analyzed the issue from multiple perspectives. See Itamar Warhaftig, "Parasht David ve-Bat Sheva" [David and Bathsheba], *Megadim* 22 (1994): 84–90, and Rabbi Medan's response in that same issue: Rabbi Yehuda Brandes, "Bemai Kamipalgi" [What is this argument about?], *Megadim* 26 (1996): 107–127; Rabbi Yaakov Medan, "Eich Lelamed Senagoria al David" [How can one defend David?], *Megadim* 26 (1996): 129–134; and Avraham Walfish, "Be-ha Kamipalgi!" [This is what the argument is about!], *Megadim* 28 (1998): 87–103; Rabbi Yaakov Medan, "Lo Rak ba-Ha" [Not only about that], *Megadim* 28 (1998): 105–106; Rabbi Yehuda Brandes, "Hakdamot Hekhraḥiot le-Kol Perush" [Essential introductions to every commentary], *Megadim* 28 (1998): 107–120; Rivka Raviv, "Be-Gvulotav shel ha-Perush ha-Legitimi" [The boundaries of legitimate interpretation], *Megadim* 31 (2000): 115–117; Avraham Walfish, "Ha-Kalut ha-Bilti Nisbelet she ha-Parshanut" [The unbearable lightness of exegesis], *Megadim* 31 (2000): 119–126.
21. See the fundamental debate between Yosef Ahituv and Rabbi Avichai Rontzki discussed, in part, in *Meimad* 16 (1999): 16–20.
22. See, e.g., Moshe Rachimi, ed., *Ve-Ḥai Aḥikha Imakh* [Enable your brother to live with you] (Elkana: Orot College, 2011), especially the article by Aviad Hacohen, "Kol Ish Asher Bo Mum lo Yikarev?" [No one who has a defect shall be qualified?], 51–77.
23. See, e.g., the articles by Tamar Ross, including "Hashlakhot ha-Feminism al Teologia Yehudit Ortodoksit" [The impact of feminism on Orthodox Jewish theology], in *Rav Tarbutiot be-Medina Demokratit ve-Yehudit* [Multiculturalism in a democratic and Jewish state], ed. Menachem Mautner et al. (Tel Aviv: Ramot, 1998), 443–464; and Amit Kula, "Hirhurim al Ma'amad ha-Isha be-Mesoret ha-Yehudit be-Re'i Zmanenu" [Reflections on the status of women in Jewish tradition from a modern perspective], in *Ha-Isha* [Woman], ed. Zeev Karov (Jerusalem: El Ami, 2000), 23–34.
24. Based on *The Guide of the Perplexed*, 5. See also Rabbi Abraham Isaac Ha-Kohen Kook, *Shmonah Kvaztim* (Jerusalem, 1999), 3:184. One can argue that being torn between two worlds is the ideal state, or at least the fate, of the believer in the postmodern world. However, it is important to distinguish between real conflict and the ideal state of latent tension. A permanent state of crisis is a form of denial without repression and perhaps even an evasion of duty and immediate responsibilities (see further below).
25. "But in the case of texts which are sacred, properly speaking, one cannot allow oneself too much license, as there is usually a religious authority and tradition that claims to hold the key to its interpretation." Umberto Eco, *Interpretation and Over-Interpretation: World, History, Texts*, ed. Stefan Collini (Cambridge: Cambridge University Press, 1992), 169. "The commentary of an exegete who interprets a verse in a way that is contrary to universally accepted *halakhah* is to be rejected because he can be considered as one who disagrees with the Oral Law that is binding upon every Jew." Moshe Arend, "Al Peshuto shel Mikra

u-Midrash Halakha" [The simple meaning of the text and midrash *halakhah*], *Iyyunei Mikra u-Parshnut* [Studies in Bible and exegesis] 8 (2008): 23. See also p. 26, and the reference to Rabbi Kasher there. This statement, which appears to be describing traditional Jewish exegesis, includes a normative declaration about the present ("binding upon every Jew"). "And furthermore, there is the fear of opening channels of critical commentary that might weaken religious belief." Eran Viezel, "Ḥibur ha-Torah ve-Hitgabshut ha-Nusaḥ shela le-Daʾat Kahane: Perek be-Demuto shel Bikoret ha-Mikra ha-Yehudit-Ortodoksit be-Mizraḥ Eropa be-Tekufat ha-Haskala" [The composition of the Torah and formation of its text according to Kahane: A study in the nature of Orthodox Jewish biblical criticism in Eastern Europe in the period of the *Haskalah*], in *"Leshev Peshuto shel Mikra": Asufat Mekharim be-Parshanut ha-Mikra* ["To settle the plain meaning of the verse": Studies in biblical exegesis], ed. Sara Japhet and Eran Viezel (Jerusalem: Mosad Bialik, 2011), 249.

26. In a story found in the Jerusalem Talmud, tractate *Sanhedrin* 4b, God declined to render judgment himself in order to leave room for future generations' commentary. See also *She'elot u-Teshuvot ha-Radbaz* 3:643 [1075]), which states that the Torah is written in a manner intended to allow a wide scope of exegetical options. See also Jerusalem Talmud, tractate *Pe'ah* 2d: "Even what an advanced student will teach in his master's presence in the future was already said to Moses on Sinai."

27. Should the nature of the Oral Torah be understood as explained by Maimonides in his introduction to his commentary on the Mishnah? (Fred Rosner, trans., *Maimonides' Introduction to his Commentary on the Mishnah*, [Northvale, NJ: Jason Aaronson, 1995], 7–12.) Or according to the explanation of Rabbi Tzadok Ha-Kohen? (*Divrei Sofrim*, 38 inter alia). On this question see Avia Hacohen, "Rabbi Tzadok ha-Kohen ve-Hitpatḥut Torah she-be-al Peh" [Rabbi Tzadok and the development of the Oral Law], *Mishlav* 35 (2000): 15–25. Or is the nature of the Oral Law as described by Rav Kook? (*Orot ha-Torah*, chapter 1:1–2). See also David Halivni, "Torah Shebe'al Peh: Hitgalut o Midrash?" [Oral Law: Revelation or commentary?], in *Yosef Da'at: Studies in Modern Jewish History in Honor of Yosef Salmon*, ed. Yossi Goldstein (Beer-Sheva: Ben Gurion University, 2010), 129–142. The impact of this debate can be seen in Louis Finkelstein, "Ha-Deah ki Yud Gimel Midot hen Halakha le-Moshe Misinai" [The belief that the thirteen rules were given to Moses on Sinai], in *Sefer ha-Zikaron le-Rabbi Shaul Lieberman* [Saul Lieberman Memorial Volume], ed. Shamma Friedman (New York: Jewish Theological Seminary of America, 1993), 79–84.

28. Moshe Halbertal, *Mahapekhot Parshaniot be-Hithavtan* [Interpretative revolutions in the making] (Jerusalem: Magnes, 1997), 43–67.

29. Louis Finkelstein, ed., *Sifrei al Sefer Devarim* (New York: Jewish Theological Seminary of America, 1969), 253. This question has been expressed in various ways. The diversity of expression is indicative of the multiplicity of difficult aspects of the commandment that did not make sense to the sages, including the disparity between the veniality of the sin and the severity of the punishment, the unlikelihood that parents would facilitate the killing of their son for over-eating, and the restrictive legal conditions (the law applies specifically to an underage boy).

30. This justification appears in two different formulations. Babylonian Talmud, tractate *Sanhedrin* 72b states: "He should die innocent rather than guilty." *Midrash Tenaim le-Devarim*, 21:21 reads "it is better that one soul is lost than that many are lost."

31. The idea that the son is judged on the basis of his future acts of burglary is meant to alleviate the difficulties discussed in the Jerusalem Talmud. See also Halbertal, *Mahapekhot*, 58.

32. Jerusalem Talmud, tractate *Sanhedrin* 8a.

33. See note 36. See also the commentary of the *Yad Ramah* to *Sanhedrin* 8a, s.v. *keman azla*. The Zohar's commentary (3:197b) is also interesting. It portrays Moses voicing the criticism to God, saying: "Leave it be! Is there a father who would do such a thing to his son?"
34. See the commentary of Rav Kook, *Iggrot Ra'aya* (Jerusalem: Mosad Harav Kook, 1961), 1:305. "It was written for the sake of 'interpret it and be rewarded.' The reward for interpretation is very great because it is the salt that preserves quality by increasing the hatred of evil in all its aspects, and because the act is accomplished through study it does not materialize at all in actuality."
35. Rabbi Yehudah uses the method of restrictive exegesis to deduce from the biblical text that the fulfillment of the commandment is contingent upon an improbable similarity between the parents in voice, appearance, and height (Babylonian Talmud, tractate *Sanhedrin* 71a). Like Rabbi Shimon, he is one of those who believe that there never was a real case of a "rebellious son." It should be noted that both sages were the students of Rabbi Akiva, while Rabbi Yonatan, the student of Rabbi Yishmael, disagrees with this position and declares: "I saw himself myself and sat on his grave." See also the position of Rabbi Akiva.
36. Babylonian Talmud, tractate *Bava Batra* 10a: "If your God loves the poor, why does he not feed them? . . . So that through them we may be saved from Hell." *Midrash Tanhuma*, Tazria' 5: "The wicked Turnus Rufus asked Rabbi Akiva: 'Whose deeds are greater, those of God or those of man?' . . . Rabbi Akiva brought him stalks of grain and cakes and said that the stalks were made by God while the cakes were made by man." It should be noted that the example of the stalks and the cakes also appears in *Midrash Eliyahu Zuta*, 2, in relation to the correct method of interpreting the Torah.
37. Mishnah, tractate *Sotah* 5:1–2: "Rabbi Yehoshua said, 'Who will remove the dirt from your eyes, Rabban Yoḥanan ben Zakkai? . . . Now Akiva your student brings a verse from the Torah to show that . . .'" Babylonian Talmud, tractate *Zevaḥim* 13a: "Akiva, whoever departs from you [i.e., your method of study] is as though he departed from life." See Shmuel Safrai, *Rabbi Akiva ben Yosef: Hayyav u-Mishnato* [Rabbi Akiva son of Yosef: His life and teachings] (Jerusalem: Mosad Bialik, 1978), 60. This book continues the approach to biblical interpretation formulated by Benjamin De Vries in *Toldot ha-Halakha ha-Talmudit* [The history of Talmudic law] (Tel Aviv: Tzioni, 1966), 14: "The congregation of Israel, an ethnic group with a high level of religious tension . . . the Torah and sacred writings are what determines its character and chart its course, and thus interpreting the Torah is the focus of spiritual life. It is an easy transition from interpretation to homily [*me-drisha le-midrash*]."
38. *Sifra*, Metsora', 9,12.
39. This event is the interpretative source for the laws pertaining to commandments for which one must die rather than transgress: "Esther was merely arable soil" (Babylonian Talmud, tractate *Sanhedrin* 74b). There is deeper bitterness in the words put into Esther's mouth as she voluntarily approaches Ahasuerus: "Until today, [I was with him] out of coercion, and today, willingly. 'And if I am to perish, I shall perish!' Just as I was lost to my father's house, so I am lost to you." (Babylonian Talmud, tractate *Megillah* 15a, based on Esther 4:16).
40. See Gen.12:17–20 and 20:3–18. In my opinion, Yair Zakovitch was incorrect when he argued that Esther's plight compares favorably with that of other biblical heroines. His commentary ignores the Jewish character of the story and its moral-religious messages: a Jewish woman should not be under the control of a non-Jewish king. Yair Zakovitch, *Mikraot be-Eretz ha-Marot* [Through the looking-glass: reflection stories in the Bible] (Tel Aviv: Hakibbutz Hameuchad, 1995).
41. *Zohar*, 3:276a. This is an approximate and partial translation.

42. I am aware of the fact that the commentator's exegetical difficulty is not related to the historical figure of Esther, the heroine of the book, but to what she represents in his system of esoteric thought—namely, the *Shekhinah*. However, on this level as well, the author of the Zohar had to construct a terraforming interpretation in order to maintain the awareness of his religious devotion. According to the position of the author/s of the Zohar, the connection between the simple meaning of the biblical story and the messages hidden within it should be self-evident. See Amit Kula, *Havaya o lo Haya* [(Existential or nonessential: History and literature, religious language, and the nature of deity] (Jerusalem: Hakibbutz Hadati, 2011), 161–164.

43. See Rabbi Aryeh Leib Heller's author's introduction to *Ketzavot ha-Hoshen* (Jerusalem: Shiloh, 1973): "The Torah was not given to the ministering angels, but to man, who has human understanding. God gave us the Torah, in his great mercy and loving-kindness, according to human understanding, even if it is not true on the level of the separate intelligences.... He gave us the Torah according to human understanding even if it is not true, and if so an original interpretation is entirely original, but it must be true according to human understanding."

44. Moshe Goshen-Gottstein, "Hakhmat Yisrael: Hekher ha-Mikra ve-Teologia Mikrait Yehudit" [The academic study of Judaism: The study of the Bible and Jewish biblical theology], *Iyyunei Mikra u-Parshnut* [Studies in Bible and exegesis] 1 (1980): 243–255. In a later article ("Teologia Mikrait Yehudit u-Mada Dat ha-Mikra" [Jewish biblical theology and the study of the religion of the Bible], *Tarbiz* 50 [1981]: 36–64), Goshen-Gottstein distinguishes between the student of religion who preserves the distance required for objectivity, and the theologian who identifies with the subject of his research and is nourished from the same sources as the thinkers of the past. In this article, he deplores the takeover of the study of biblical theology by Protestant scholar-theologians who do not include Jewish theology within the framework of their studies. See Moshe Greenberg, "Hayitakhen Mada Mikra Bikorti Ba'al Ofi Yehudi?" (Is a critical Jewish study of the Bible possible?), *Proceedings of the World Congress of Jewish Studies* 8 (1981): 95–98.

45. In this context, it is important to note in particular the new developments of the last thirty years. Firstly, the completion of the commentary *Da'at Ha-Mikra*, on which see Yehuda Keel "Al ha-Tzorekh be-Perush Mesorti-Mada'i al ha-Mikra u-Midotav" [On the need for a traditional-academic commentary on the Bible and its features], *Be-Sedeh Ḥemed* 20 (1977): 8–16. To this must be added the dissemination of Rabbi Mordechai Breuer's approach to Bible study, influenced by biblical criticism. On Rabbi Breuer see Yosef Ofer, ed., *Shitat ha-Beḥinot shel ha-Rav Mordechai Breuer* [The aspects theory of Rav Mordechai Breuer: articles and responses] (Alon Shvut: Tevunot, 1995); and Adiel Cohen, "Kabbalah as a Shield against the 'Scourge' of Biblical Criticism: A Comparative Analysis of the Torah Commentaries of Elia Benamozegh and Mordecai Breuer," in this volume. The journal of Herzog College *Megadim*, which has published hundreds of articles, reflects the strengthening of the approach anticipated by the aforementioned scholars.

46. A classic example is Rabbi Yoel Bin Nun, "Ha-Pelug ve-ha-Aḥdut: Kefel Ta'ut ve-Helem ha-Galui; Mipnei Mah lo Shalach Yosef (Shaliaḥ) el Aviv?" [The Schism and the unity: A double mistake and the shock of discovery; why didn't Joseph send a message to his father?], *Megadim* 1 (1986): 21–30. This article aims to find an alternative to understanding Joseph's deeds as an attempt to realize his dreams. The article generated responses in which the subject was reevaluated. The foundations of the new exegetical approach are embedded in the various articles. See the index to articles in *Megadim* 50 (2009): 242.

The work of Uriel Simon demands further attention. For the present, see Uriel Simon, *Bakesh Shalom u-Radfehu* [Seek peace and pursue it] (Tel Aviv: Miskal, 2004), 15. The formation of a readership with similar questions and levels of comprehension, who are the beneficiaries of the process of terraforming, is a process that involves the search for interpretations of the Bible that conform to this group's ethical outlook. For this reason, *peshat* must be defined in a certain way—in Simon's words, as "meaningful *peshat*." Uriel Simon ed., *Ha-Mikra ve-Anaḥnu* [The Bible and us] (Ramat Gan: Dvir, 1998), 149–152. See also Uriel Simon, *Reading Prophetic Narratives*, trans. Lenn J. Schramm (Bloomington: Indiana University Press, 1997), xiv-xvi. In a review article, Baruch Alster attempts to obscure the political agenda (Baruch Alster, "Arakhim be-Peshuto shel Mikra" [Values in the simple meaning of the text], *Megadim* 48 [2008]: 117–122), although without great success, as can be seen in the article of Rabbi Yaakov Medan (*Megadim*, 48 [2008]: 123–124). See also Simon's response (ibid., 125–131). Further research on this subject is necessary.

The Names of God and the Dating of the Biblical Corpus

Yoel Elitzur

Biblical Criticism and the Dating of Biblical Sources—A Brief Survey

The "documentary hypothesis," the most famous theory of critical biblical scholarship, originated in the eighteenth century from the examination of what appeared to be contradictions and repetitions in biblical stories and legislation. Scholars concluded that the Torah is comprised of four primary sources that differ from each other in language and content. Two of these sources are called after the names of God that characterize them: source "J" frequently uses the Tetragrammaton YHWH (in old scholarly literature "Jehovah" erroneously following the seemingly masoretic punctuation of this divine name), while source "E" uses often the name *Elohim*. There are two additional sources: "P," the Priestly source, which discusses sacrifices, ritual, and the priesthood, and favors numerical sums, and "D," the source of the book of Deuteronomy. Several chapters in the early prophets are also attributed to the Deuteronomic school. "D" mandates the centralization of the ritual in a location to be chosen by God, and takes special interest in the subject of exile and redemption and the fate of the Israelite people. Scholars usually date "D" to the end of the First Temple period and "P" to the Second Temple period.

There have been, and continue to be, many adherents of these theories. There have also been many opponents—primarily, but not exclusively, Jewish and Christian religious fundamentalists. The greatest of the contributors to the documentary hypothesis in the nineteenth century was Julius Wellhausen. The most famous among the early critics of the theory was Rabbi David Zvi Hoffmann who, shortly after the publication of Wellhausen's research, published in 1903 a rebuttal entitled *Decisive Evidence against the Graf-Wellhausen Theory*.[1]

In the middle of the twentieth century, it seemed as if these radical critical theories were losing support. Umberto Cassuto attacked the documentary hypothesis in general in his research, and Yehezkel Kaufmann rejected the contemporary convention of dating the sources to a very late period. The extensive research that was increasing at that time on the archeology and history of the ancient Near East did not corroborate the propensity in critical biblical scholarship to date the sources to a late period. Scholars discovered that the Babylonian flood story corresponds to the biblical story as it exists, rather than to scholarly restorations of it. None of the many biblical fragments found at Qumran revealed the division between sources presented by the documentary hypothesis. In several universities, groups of scholars formed who engaged in literary and structural analyses of biblical narrative and biblical law from within, as they appear in the text, without focusing on their sources, their order, or the estimated dates of their composition.

However, towards the end of the century, radical critical theories again gained support. Today the division into sources still dominates biblical research, and the tendency to ascribe a late date to many biblical texts and to the final editing of the Torah has gained momentum. In the last few decades even popular forums directed to the wider public outside the academic ivory tower present a viewpoint supportive of literary and historical biblical criticism in its more radical forms. Summaries of the history of the Jewish people and the Land of Israel, intended for both students and the wider public, present biblical Israel as a nation that, according to the "scientific evidence," crystalized over time in the hill country of Canaan and subsequently invented the stories of the Patriarchs, the Exodus from Egypt, the revelation at Sinai, and the conquest of Canaan.[2] The information card for the Aleppo Codex on display in the Shrine of the Book in Jerusalem informs the visitor that the five books of the Torah were created after the Babylonian exile.[3]

It is not my intention in this article to discuss the tenets of biblical criticism itself. After a brief discussion of its fundamental principles, I will propose an alternative theory.

A scientific principle is a principle that can be disproven. The first rule in any study is the clear distinction between the data and its interpretation. If no such distinction is made, the interpretation is presented as if it were the data itself, often creating a picture that is no more than wishful thinking, neither provable nor disprovable.

Interpretative suppositions, not facts, form the methodological basis of the documentary hypothesis, and for that reason it always has been, and still remains, a speculative theory. Another approach is to allow the sources to speak for themselves as they appear before us, "untouched by human hands." In this case, substantial evidence that a certain name or linguistic form is characteristic of a certain period or geographical area would constitute conclusive scientific evidence.

This type of work has been done over the last few decades in the study of the differences between standard biblical Hebrew and later biblical Hebrew. Avi Hurvitz, the most prominent scholar in the field, began his research on the subject with an investigation of one small detail,[4] and then with his seminal work, *The Transition Period in Biblical Hebrew*.[5] In his introduction, Hurvitz explains that his research is based on a comparison between biblical books that openly declare that they date from the Second Temple period, such as Esther, Ezra and Chronicles, and biblical books that describe only earlier events. Linguistic tendencies would be considered late only on the basis of accumulative and widespread evidence. These findings would be supported by comparison to other languages, in particular Aramaic and Persian, the language of Ben Sira, the Qumran Scrolls, and early rabbinic literature. On the basis of linguistic evidence culled by this method, he analyzed sources of unclear origin, such as the Psalms. For example, Hurvitz showed, on the basis of more than few occurrences, that biblical texts containing the word *ḥedva* (joy) are likely to be from the Second Temple period, and that the word *butz* (linen) in post-Exilic biblical Hebrew replaced its older synonyms *shesh* and *bad*, while *malkhut* (kingdom) replaced *mamlakha*. With these and similar findings, he examined other biblical books and proposed dates for various psalms. In another paper, on the basis of comparative analysis, he convincingly demonstrated that the cultic terminology of the "priestly" chapters in Exodus, Leviticus, and Numbers is completely different from that of parallel texts in Ezekiel, Ezra, and Chronicles, a factor that reduces the probability that these texts were written at the same time.[6]

Studying the Names of God "Untouched by Human Hands"

Both of the principal names of God, YHWH and *Elohim*, appear throughout the biblical periods in all of its literary registers and thus cannot be used as objective data with which to date biblical books, either absolutely or relatively. There are passages in which one name is favored and others in which both are used; it can be assumed that the most important considerations in choosing between the two names were literary or content-based. For example, each name expresses different aspects of God's appearance and rule on the earth. It is possible that in certain cases the decision was arbitrary or even based on a conscious desire for stylistic variety for its own sake.[7] In a similar manner, the sages sometimes used the term *ha-Kodesh* (the Holiness) which developed into *ha-Kadosh Baruch Hu* (The Holy One Blessed be He), and other times *ha-Makom* (literally, "the Place"), or *ha-Dibber* ("the Speaking One," *logos*) which later developed into *ha-Dibbur*, just as people today say or write either "God," "The Lord," *ha-Shem*, or *ha-Kadosh Baruch Hu*.

The question that I would like to pose here is: Can the usage of the names of God provide intrinsic textual evidence of chronological development? In my opinion there are four such sets of data. Two of them have been long known but their significance has not been sufficiently emphasized. Several scholars have written about the third, and the fourth is apparently my own discovery.

Shaddai

The name *Shaddai* is mentioned in the Bible, according to the Masoretic text, forty-eight times.[8] Many have attempted to explain its meaning and origin, but I am currently unaware of a cogent explanation for this name.[9] I believe that it can be demonstrated that, in the biblical text as it appears before us, the original form of the name is *El Shaddai*, and *Shaddai* is its shortened form.
The distribution of occurrences of *Shaddai* is as follows:

Genesis — six times (of which five are *El Shaddai*);

Exodus — once: "I appeared to Abraham, Isaac, and Jacob as El Shaddai" (Exod. 6:3);

Numbers — twice (Balaam prophecies 24:4 and 16). In both verses within the phrase "Who beholds visions from the Almighty (*Shaddai*)." Both verses also include the name *El* ("God" or "the Almighty") in a parallel clause. In verse 24:16, God is also referred to as the "Most High";

Later Prophets — four times: twice in the phrase, "*Ke-shod mi-Shaddai yavo*" ("It shall come like havoc from Shaddai") (Isa. 13:6; Joel 1:15), and twice in the chariot passages in Ezekiel in similar phrases, "like the sound of Shaddai" (1:24) and "like the voice of El Shaddai when He speaks" (10:5);

Ruth — once: "when the Lord has dealt harshly with me, when Shaddai has brought misfortune upon me" (1: 21);

Psalms — twice: "When Shaddai scattered the kings" (68:15); "O you who dwell in the shelter of the Most High and abide in the protection of Shaddai" (91:1);

Job — thirty-one times, fifteen in parallel construct to *El*, ten in parallel construct to *Elo^ah*, and six without a parallel.[10]

In addition to these references there are another two or three personal names containing the theophoric element *shaddai*: Ammishaddai, Zurishaddai, and apparently also Shedeur (see Num. 1).

It is very significant that only in Genesis (as well as the single occurrence in Exodus, which is a kind of summary of Genesis) does the name *Shaddai* appear in prose. Only one of the six occurrences in Genesis appears in a poem: "The God of your father who helps you, And Shaddai who blesses you" (Gen. 49:25). Throughout the rest of the Bible, the name always appears within a poetical context. The theophoric names including the morpheme *shaddai* could also attest to the prosaic rather than poetical use of the name; all three of these names are from the generation before the Exodus. In all six prose occurrences, the name appears as *El Shaddai*. In every other reference in the Bible, except one (Ezek. 10:5), the name appears as *Shaddai* without *El*, although in a large percentage of the occurrences it appears in a parallel structure to *El*, and also appears parallel to *Elyon* (the Most High), and in one instance parallel to the Tetragrammaton. Furthermore, all of the references to *El Shaddai* in Genesis are in quotations of direct speech rather than in the narrative voice.

If we let the Bible speak for itself, it reveals that from the time of the Patriarchs until the Exodus from Egypt, the name *El Shaddai* was in active use in the spoken language. In certain cases, people integrated the name *Shaddai* as a theophoric basis for names they gave their children. The Torah itself only uses this name when it quotes direct speech from an earlier period. The authors of the later books used the name primarily as a special literary device in isolated cases, sometimes for the sake of alliteration and sometimes in search of a very evocative archaic word to strengthen the power of the poetry.

The word *Shaddai* is used in the book of Job much more frequently than in any other book. The explanation for this phenomenon depends on our understanding of the origin and dating of the book of Job. If we accept the opinion that the book is ancient and of non-Jewish origin, it is possible that the language of the book reflects an ancient dialect similar to the language of the forefathers. If we accept the opinion that the book was written in a later period, it can be surmised that *Shaddai* is one of the literary devices used by the author in a deliberate effort at archaization, similar to the advanced age of Job, the camels, and the *kesita* (Job 42:11), that embellish the narrative framework of the book and set it in the world of the Patriarchs.

To summarize, a survey of the history of the use of *Shaddai* and *El Shaddai* reveals natural and logical development, including a distinction between earlier and later periods, between poetry and prose, and between the narrative voice of the text itself and quotations of direct speech. This development is reflected also in personal names. Critical scholarship maintains that the author of the priestly source put the name *El Shaddai* in the mouths of the Patriarchs and in God's speech to them, yet was careful not to use this name himself to describe the Patriarchs or their exploits. He also had the insight to include personal names containing the morpheme *shaddai* specifically in the generation before the Exodus. This explanation is plausible, but it ascribes to this author exceptional finesse and attention to detail. I have attempted here to show that the Bible, seen as a unified whole, clearly reveals how the name *Shaddai* was initially used in the spoken language, fell out of use, and was later adopted as a literary expression.

Tzva'ot (The Lord of Hosts)

The name *Tzva'ot* used as an appellation of God is one of the most striking characteristics of biblical language. It is used 285 times in the Bible, usually in the phrase *YHWH Tzava'ot* (the Lord of Hosts) and about twenty times in the phrase *YHWH Elohei Tzvaot*. *YHWH Tzva'ot* serves as an appellation of the God of Israel in Samuel, Kings, and Psalms. Most of the prophets used it frequently (except for Ezekiel, Joel, Obadiah, and Jonah) from the beginning of the period of prophecy until Malachi. The phrase *YHWH Tzva'ot* is prototypical in prophecies, prayers, and every religious saying of the heroes of the Bible as well as the narrator.

Surprisingly, *YHWH Tzva'ot*—the Lord of Hosts—does not appear before the first chapter of 1 Samuel: "This man used to go up from his town every year to worship and to offer sacrifice to the Lord of Hosts at Shiloh" (1:3), and "And she made this vow: 'O Lord of Hosts, if You will look upon the suffering of Your maidservant'" (1:11). The sages noticed this and concluded: "From the day that the world was created no one called God *Tzvaot* until Hannah."[11] Rabbi Yossi even deduced from this that *Tzva'ot* is not one of the holy names that should not be erased. In his opinion, the name is a shortened form of the construct form *ha-Shem Elohei Tziv'ot Yisrael* as it is written, "and deliver My ranks (*tziv'otai*), My people the Israelites, from the land of Egypt" (Exod. 7:4). The sages of the Talmud did not accept his opinion: "Shmuel said, 'The halakhah is not according to Rabbi Yossi.'"[12] The reason is clear: in all of the books of the prophets beginning with the book of Samuel and in the Psalms, *Tzva'ot* is a typical divine name.

Critical scholars who believe that the books of the Torah, Joshua, and Judges were written late, in the period of the monarchy, or even the beginning of the Second Temple period, need to explain how it is possible that the expression *YHWH Tzva'ot* is missing completely from all books preceding Samuel. If the author of the story of Abraham's servant's journey to Haran was writing in the period of the late prophets, why did he write, "and I will make you swear by the Lord, the God of heaven and the God of the earth" (24:3), rather than "I will make you swear by "the Lord of Hosts"? If the book of Deuteronomy was written in the time of Josiah, why did its author write "For the Lord your God is God supreme and Lord supreme, the great, the mighty, and the awesome God" (10:17), rather than "For the Lord of Hosts is God Supreme and Lord supreme..."? Why does Joshua 22:22 read "God, the Lord God! God, the Lord God! He knows," rather than "The Lord of Hosts knows"? Why does the Song of the Sea read: "The Lord, the Warrior—Lord is His name!" (Exod.15:3), rather than "The Lord of Hosts is his name," a common phrase in the books of the prophets?

The answer to all these questions is that we have before us a clear case of natural linguistic development: a concept formed at the time of the writing of the book of Samuel or just before, a phrase that did not exist in Hebrew when the five books of the Torah, Joshua, and Judges were written. Quite simply, only the order in which the Bible presents itself can explain the distribution of the name *Tzva'ot*.

Alexander Rofé presents this question in all its complexity and then follows immediately with a declaration of the axiom: "We can reject outright the traditional explanation according to which the name *Tzva'ot* entered into use at the end of the period of the Judges. The documents written about the origins of the People of Israel are far from contemporaneous with the events they describe; most were written between the tenth and fourth centuries BCE."[13] What then is the solution? Rofé reasons that later generations had theological reservations about the name *Tzva'ot*, whose original meaning was connected to the heavenly hosts and contained a syncretic element. The extant text is thus the product of an editorial purge that eradicated the name *Tzva'ot* entirely from the five books of the Torah, Joshua, and Judges. In his opinion, a clue to this can be found in the elimination of *Tzva'ot* in several instances in the passages copied from Samuel to Chronicles, as well as a significant reduction of occurrences of the expression in the versions of the book of Jeremiah in the Septuagint and the Dead Sea Scrolls (which, in the opinion of Rofé, are less authentic than the Masoretic text). However, Rofé does not convincingly explain why this resolute editing process was applied specifically to the Torah, Joshua, and Judges and not to other books of the Bible, and why other theologically problematic verses—such as "Who is like You, O Lord, among the celestials" (Exod. 15:11)—were not expunged at the same time. It is particularly difficult to explain the totality of the phenomenon: no occurrences whatsoever until Samuel, compared with 285 occurrences from the beginning of Samuel until Malachi, as Rofé himself points out.[14]

The Component YHW in Personal Names

Most of the given names in the period of the monarchy in Judea and Israel are theophoric, containing the YHWH name in a shortened form YHW, or an even more shortened form YW or YH (the latter increased especially later in the Second Temple period). This reality can be perceived both in the Bible and the epigraphic sources. However, this phenomenon developed slowly. I will illustrate this point through an analysis of the books of the early prophets. In the five books of the Torah and Joshua there are only two persons whose names contain the YHWH element: Jochebed the mother of Moses, and Joshua son of Nun. Among the names mentioned in the book of Judges, three contain a shortened form of YHWH: Joash, the father of Gideon (Judg. 18: 13); Micah (written at the beginning of the narrative as *Mikhayhu*) from the hill country of Ephraim; and the youth who was his "father and priest," Jonathan (written *Yehonathan*), the son of Gershom (Judg. 17–18).[15] In Samuel there are sixteen Israelites whose names contain YW or YH.[16] In the recounting of the life of Solomon in 1 Kings 1–11, eleven[17] out of (probably) sixty[18] Israelite names contain YHW/YH/YW. In the description of the period from the death of Solomon until the rise of Ahab (1 Kings 12–16) five out of eighteen Israelite names mentioned include YHW or its shortening.[19] From here until the end of the book of Kings we find forty-nine names that do not contain YHW/YH/YW, as compared with fifty-one that do.[20]

Out of the many names that appear in the five books of the Torah, only two contain shortening of YHWH. This corresponds well with the verse

"I appeared to Abraham, Isaac, and Jacob as El Shaddai, but I did not make Myself known to them by My name" (Exod. 6:3). The family of Levi knew the YHWH name, and in one case gave a name containing it to a girl, Jochebed.[21] The rest of the people, however, did not know the name. It was Moses who changed the name of his faithful servant Hosea son of Nun to Joshua (Num. 13:16) in a symbolic act that heralded a new age in the Israelite faith. Names containing the morpheme continued to appear infrequently until the era of the Judges; from this point onward they increased slowly, until they became the majority. No critical explanation can account for these statistics, which reflect the actual reality of the times. A later editor would not have invented a complete set of names without the YHWH element for the books of the Torah, and then afterwards sprinkled an increasing number of such names until they gradually became the majority.

There are two cases in which names without the YHWH component were changed to include it. (1) "Toi sent his son Joram [*Yoram*, containing the morpheme YW] to King David to greet him" (2 Sam. 8:10) contrasts with "he sent his son Hadoram to King David to greet him" (1 Chron. 18:10). (2) "Then Pharaoh Neco appointed Eliakim son of Josiah king in place of his father Josiah, changing his name to Jehoiakim [*Yehoyakim*, containing YHW]" (2 Kings 23:34). While the second example is difficult to explain,[22] the first is easy to understand and is of fundamental importance. It is not likely that Toi, the king of Hamat, gave his son at birth a name that refers to YHWH, the God of Israel. It would therefore appear that Hadoram was his original name, after the name of the Aramaic god Hadad, and Toi changed it to Joram in order to find favor in the eyes of his protector David.

And another surprise: it can be concluded from the data mentioned above that most people in Judah and Israel in the period of the monarchy, though accused by the prophets of forsaking YHWH and worshipping Ba'al and Astarte, chose to include the name of YHWH in their children's names.

Adonai

From the middle of the Second Temple period until today, it has been an accepted practice among Jews to pronounce the word *Adonai* (meaning "my Lord") in place of the name YHWH, and as a result readers have difficulty distinguishing between the original *Adonai* and YHWH. In fact, *Adonai* is quite rare in the written text of the Bible. In contrast to the more than 6,800 occurrences of the Tetragrammaton YHWH in the Bible, *Adonai* appears only some

440 times,[23] of which approximately three hundred are in the phrase *Adonai YHWH* (pronounced *Adonai Elohim*), five in the phrase "YHWH *Adonai*" (pronounced *Elohim Adonai*), and 134 times without YHWH. (The Masorah indicated this in the notation 134 *vaddain*).

I have discovered a major difference between the use of *Adonai* in the Torah, Joshua, Judges, and Samuel and its use in the subsequent biblical books, from Isaiah, Amos, and Kings until the end of the biblical era.[24] *Adonai* only becomes an actual name of God in the books of Isaiah, Amos, Micah, and Kings.[25] For example, in Amos, "He showed me: behold, the Lord (*Adonai*) was standing beside a wall built with a plumb line, with a plumb line in his hand" (7:7), and "I saw the Lord (*Adonai*) standing beside the altar" (9:1); in Isaiah, "In the year that King Uzziah died, I beheld the Lord (*Adonai*) seated on a high and lofty throne" (6:1); and in Kings, "For the Lord (*Adonai*) had caused the Aramean camp to hear a sound of chariots, a sound of horses" (2 Kings 7:6). Before this period, it was used only in those functions also served by the title *adoni* (my lord) when addressing human beings. In the former books of the Bible *Adonai* could be found only within a quotation of direct speech, never in the narrative voice, and always within a plea of supplication, sometimes with the suppliant expression *bi-* or the exclamation *ahah*.

On the other hand, it must be noted that nowhere in the Bible is the term *adoni* (my Lord) used in addressing God, as might be expected. From this we can conclude that the word *Adonai* was originally no different than *adoni*. Both were terms used to address someone of a higher status. From a linguistic perspective, biblical Hebrew includes both the singular form *adon* and *adonim*, a plural form used as a singular noun (the *pluralis majestatis*) as in "And I will place the Egyptians at the mercy of a harsh master (*adonim*)" (Isa. 19:4), and "And if I am a master (*adonim*), where is the reverence due Me?—said the Lord of Hosts to you" (Mal. 1:6). These forms are similar to *ba'al*/*be'alim* and *Elo^{a}h*/*Elohim*. There is an interesting differentiation in use between *adon* and *adonim*. When the word stands alone, *adon* is the common form and *adonim* is rare. However, when the word has a personal pronoun suffix, the word base becomes plural,[26] as in *adoneinu, adonekha, adonekhem, adonav*,[27] *adoneha*, and *adoneihem*. The word remains singular only in first-person singular (*adoni*). Therefore, *Adonai* is really the most natural form of address,[28] and *adoni* is actually the irregular form. It seems that at a certain time, probably quite early, a linguistic distinction was made between the term used to address a person and the same term when used to address God[29] by designating the form derived from the plural to God, and that derived from the singular to people.[30] Once there was a specific term for addressing God, it naturally developed into an actual name of God, though its previous function was not effaced. This development occurred apparently in the time of Isaiah and Amos. In biblical books from before this period, both forms of the word, *Adoni* and *Adonai*, are still only terms of addressing a superior, whether human or divine.[31] This distinction between the biblical books corresponds to the order in which they appear in the Bible, rather than that hypothesized by scholars.

Conclusion

Four facets of names of God reveal clear internal development within the classical biblical period: (1) *El Shaddai* was used in oral speech only until the Exodus from Egypt. In later periods, the name *Shaddai* existed as an archaic term used, infrequently, by prophets and poets. (2) The expression YHWH *Tzva'ot* (the Lord of Hosts) originated only in the time of the book of Samuel, and was in use from then until the composition of the books of Haggai, Zechariah, and Malachi. (3) The first two cases of the theophoric element YHW/YH/YW in personal names occurred just before and during the life of Moses. From that point, it increased gradually in frequency until the period of the late monarchy, by which time it was included in more than half of all personal names. (4) The name indicating lordship, *Adonai*, was initially a term of supplicatory address and became a name of God in the eighth century BCE.

All of these developments can be easily understood and explained according to the chronology that corresponds to the order in which the Bible presents itself, namely: the five books of the Torah followed by, in order, Joshua, Judges, Samuel, and Kings, as whole, complete books written in succession. The prevalent critical approach, which rejects this order, will have great difficulty explaining the data presented here.

Endnotes

1. D. Hoffmann, *Die wichtigsten Instanzen gegen die Graf-Wellhausensche Hypothese* (Berlin: Druck von H. Itzkowski, 1903–1916).
2. For example, Shmuel Ahituv, "Kibush Eretz Kana'an me-Beḥina historit" [The conquest of Cana'an from a historical perspective] in *Yehoshua im Mavo u-Perush* [Joshua: Introduction and commentary], vol. 6 of *Mikra le-Yisra'el* [A Bible commentary for Israel] (Tel Aviv: Am Oved, 1995), 45–53; Nadav Na'aman, "From Settlement of the Land to the Destruction of the Temple," in *Israel: People, Land, State: A Nation and its Homeland*, ed. Avigdor Shinan et al., trans. Eliyahu Green (Jerusalem: Yad Ben-Zvi, 2005), 20–37; A. F. Rainey and R. S. Notley, *The Sacred Bridge: Carta's Atlas of the Biblical World* (Jerusalem: Carta, 2006), 111–112.

3. After both Professor Yosef Ofer and I voiced our objections, Dr. Adolfo Roitman, the curator of the Shrine of the Book, agreed to add the words "according to the opinion of most scholars" to the information card. See Yoel Elitzur and Yosef Ofer, "Ha-Heichal ve-Hasefer: Rishmei Siur be-Heikhal ha-Sefer le-aḥar Petiḥato Meḥadash" [The shrine and the book: Impressions from an excursion to the Shrine of the Book after its re-opening], Appendix: "Heikhal ha-Sefer ve-Hivatzrutah shel Torat Moshe" [The Shrine of the Book and the creation of Moses' Torah], *Al-Atar* 13–14 (2006): 218–220.
4. Avi Hurvitz, "The Usage of 'Shesh' and 'Butz' in the Bible and its Implication for the Date of P," *Harvard Theological Review* 60 (1967) 117–121.
5. A. Hurvitz, *Bein Lashon le-Lashon: le-Toldot Lashon ha-Mikra be-Yimei Bayit Sheni* [The transition period in Biblical Hebrew: A study in post-Exilic Hebrew and its implications for the dating of the Psalms] (Jerusalem: Mosad Bialik, 1972). For a summary of this subject see A. Hurvitz, "Biblical Hebrew, Late," in *Encyclopedia of Hebrew Language and Linguistics*, ed. G. Khan et al. (Leiden: Brill, 2013), 1:329–338.
6. A. Hurvitz, "Dating the Priestly Source in Light of the Historical Study of Biblical Hebrew a Century after Wellhausen," *Zeitschrift für die alttestamentliche Wissenschaft* 100 Supplement (1998): 88–100.
7. See the important and well-founded opinions of Abba Bendavid on this matter: Abba Bendavid "Ta'arovet Ḥomrei ha-Lashon ba-Mikra" [The mixing of linguistic material in the Bible], in *Leshon Mikra u-Leshon Ḥakhamim* [Biblical Hebrew and Mishnaic Hebrew] (Tel Aviv: Dvir, 1967), 13–59, and especially his summary on pp. 58–59.
8. E. Knauf, "Shadday" in *Dictionary of Deities and Demons in the Bible*, eds. Karel Van Der Toorn, B. Becking, and P. W. Van der Horst (Leiden: Brill, 1999), 749–753. Knauf presented the data professionally and clearly, but hastened to date them in accordance with the conventional critical theories.
9. Ancient translators, classical commentators and modern scholars have been long perplexed by the meaning of the name *Shaddai*. Some ancient translators have transliterated rather than translated the name, perhaps assuming that it is a personal name, or perhaps due to the difficulty in translating it. Others simply bypassed it. Some understood the name to signify power and might. A widespread Jewish etymological interpretation explains the name as a compilation of the letter shin and the word *dai* (enough). This explanation is used by Aquila, Symmachus, and Theodotion, *Bereshit Rabbah*, the late Samaritan translation, Rav Sa'adia Gaon, and Rashi. Ibn Ezra quite rightly rejects this interpretation: "I do not understand the meaning of this interpretation. How can a name be called 'that which is enough'?" In modern scholarship, many etymologies and connections to Near Eastern cultures have been suggested for *Shaddai*. I have found eight different proposals in the research literature. The opinion generally accepted by scholars since it was proposed by Delitzsch is that the name is connected to the Akkadian word šadû meaning "mountain." Regarding the nature of the connection between *Shaddai* and "mountain," there are several suggestions. "Mountain" or "big mountain" is sometimes an epithet for a deity in Mesopotamian sources. Šadû can also refer to "an uninhabited land," "desert", or "plain," perhaps after the name of the arid mountains outside the lush plain of the Euphrates and Tigris Rivers. Therefore, there are those who argue that *Shaddai* is the god of the desert. Šaddā'u or šaddû'a meaning "mountain dweller" is derived from šadû (Ignace J. Gelb et al, eds., *The Assyrian Dictionary of the Oriental Institute of the University of Chicago* [Chicago: Oriental Institute, 1956–2006], Vol. 17, Š 1, 43). According to Albright, this could be the original meaning of the name *Shaddai*. Bibliography for the information in this note: Eliezer Ben Yehuda, *Milon ha-Lashon ha-Ivrit ha-Yeshanah ve-ha-Ḥadashah* [A complete dictionary of Ancient and Modern Hebrew], ed.

N. H. Tur-Sinai (Jerusalem-New York-London: Thomas Yoseloff, 1959), 7:6911–6912. L. Koehler and W. Baumgartner, *Lexicon in Veteris Testamenti Libros* (Leiden: Brill, 1985), 950; L. Koehler and W. Baumgartner, *The Hebrew and Aramaic Lexicon of the Old Testament* (Leiden: Brill, 1991), 1420–1422. See Knauf, "Shadday," note 8.

10. In Job there is also a hapax legomenon in an obscure verse that some have seen as a plural form of *Shaddai*: "Be in fear of the sword, For [your] fury is iniquity worthy of the sword; Know there is a judgment!" (Job 19:29). The last word in the verse is written *šdwn* and read as *shadoon*.
11. Babylonian Talmud, tractate *Berakhot* 31b; *Midrash Samuel* 2.
12. Babylonian Talmud, tractate *Shevu'ot* 35b.
13. Alexander Rofé, "Ha-Shem 'ha-Shem Tzva'ot' ve-ha-Mahadura ha-Ktzara shel Sefer Yirmiyahu" [The name *ha-Shem Tva'ot* and the brief edition of Jeremiah], *Mo'ed* 21 (2013): 21. I would like to thank the reader of this article in the peer review process of the Hebrew version of this volume who brought Rofé's important work to my attention.
14. "Anyone familiar with the process of editing knows well how difficult it is to do the job thoroughly. Therefore, it is no wonder that most of the editing in the Bible is incomplete." Rofé, "Ha-Shem," 30.
15. Joash the father of Gideon worshipped Ba'al, while Micah and Jonathan apparently worshipped the God of Israel, although through the intermediary devices of a sculptured image, a molten image, ephod, and teraphim!
16. It is possible that the name Zeruiah should also be included. Out of forty-nine personal names mentioned in the lists of David's warriors in 2 Samuel 23, according to the Masoretic text, six names include YHW/YH/YW: Joab, Benaiah, Jehoiada, Benaiah of Pirathon, Jonathan, and Uriah.
17. Again, it is unclear if Zeruiah was a theophoric name.
18. Perhaps we can reduce the number to fifty-seven if we assume that the two Nathans and/or three Ahiluds in these chapters were identical.
19. I did not include older names mentioned here, such as David and Solomon. I included Abijam (Aviyam) in the list of names that do not contain the YHWH component. In Chronicles the name appears as Avia, and in this form it is included in the list of names containing YH. This would appear to be connected to the increase in the names including the YHVH element. A more interesting example is the way in which Jeroboam son of Nebat revived the names of the sons of Aaron. Nadab and Abihu (Avihu) became Nadab and Abijah (Avia). The name of the second son in the Torah does not include YHVH element, while the name of the son of Jeroboam does include it. This point was noted by I. M. Grintz, *Meḥkarim be-Mikra* [Studies in the Bible] (Jerusalem: Marcus, 1979), 144.
20. This subject was addressed briefly by B. Porten, "Shem, Shemot Etzem Pratiyim be-Yisrael" [Names, proper nouns in Israel], *Entzeklopedia Mikrait* [Encyclopaedia biblica] (Jerusalem: Mosad Bialik, 1968), 8:49. In a television program presented by Dov Elbaum that aired on May 10, 2013, Professor Aaron Demsky cogently and thoroughly discussed both this subject and the divine names *Shaddai* and *El Shaddai*, as well as the personal names Shedeur, Zurishaddai, and Ammishaddai (Num. 7). His approach was similar to the approach presented here.
21. The language of the verse is precise: "but I did not make Myself known to them by My name." It means that the name already existed but was not known to the people.
22. See William Emery Barnes, *The Second Book of Kings* (The Cambridge Bible; Cambridge: The University Press, 1911), 136; James A. Montgomery, *A Critical and Exegetical Commentary of the Books of Kings*, ed. Henry Snyder Gehman (New York: Charles Scribner's Sons, 1951),

550–551; Yehuda Kiel, *Melakhim* [Kings], vol. 9 of *Torah, Nevi'im, Ketuvim im Perush Da'at Mikra* [Torah, Prophets, and Writings with the *Da'at Mirka* commentary], ed. Yehuda Kiel et al (Jerusalem: Mosad Harav Kook, 1981), 814. Mordechai Cogan and Hayim Tadmor, *II Kings*, vol. 11 of the *Anchor Bible* (New York: Doubleday, 1988), 303.

23. Biblical dictionaries, grammar books, and research literature that address this topic usually refrain from citing precise numbers. According to Otto Eissfeldt ("ʔādhôn; adhōnāi," *Theological Dictionary of the Old Testament*, ed. G. J. Botterweck and H. Ringgren, [Grand Rapids, MI: William B. Eerdmans, 1974], 62), *Adonai* appears 449 times in the Bible. Even-Shoshan (*A New Concordance of the Bible*, [Jerusalem: Kiryat Sefer, 1989], 17–18) lists 425 occurrences. I took the trouble to count the number listed in Solomon Mandelkern's concordance (*Veteris Testamenti Concordantiae Hebraicae atque Chaldaicae*, ed. F. Margolin and M. Gottstein [Jerusalem and Tel Aviv: Schocken, 1971], 16) and they total 422. In the digitalized concordance "Snopi" (http://www.snopi.com/xDic/Bible.aspx) in which the verses appear in their entirety, I counted 433 occurrences, and it is clear that the actual number is not less than this. The reckoning of "134 *vaddain*" of *Adonai* names that appear alone without YHWH, mentioned by the *masorah*, fits the data as cited in Mandelkern's Concordance.
24. I have published a detailed article on this subject. See Yoel Elitzur, "The Divine Name ADNY in the Hebrew Bible: Surprising Findings," *Liber Annuus* 65 (2015) 87–106.
25. The transition of a word from a term of address in the first person to a general noun or title is known in several languages and cultures. Examples are *Rabbi* in the language of the sages, *Mari* in various Aramaic dialects, and *Monsieur*, *Madame*, and *Madonna* in European languages, as pointed out by various scholars who have studied the subject.
26. In construct state as well, in most phrases, the basis is the plural: *Adonei Yosef* (Gen. 39:20); *adonei ha-aretz* (Gen. 42:30,33); *adonei ha-har* (1 Kings 16:24), *adonei ha-adonim* (Deut. 10:17, Ps. 136:3), all together six times. On the other hand, the phrase *adon kol ha'aretz* based on the singular form, appears also six times (Josh. 3:11,13, Mic. 4:13, Zech. 4:14, 6:5, Ps. 97:5).
27. The word *adono* appears once in the Bible in writing, but is read differently: "Do not inform on a slave to his master [*adono*]" (Prov. 30:10).
28. The word ostensibly should be written with a *pataḥ*, but when it was turned into a name, its vowel lengthened in accordance with the rules of the phonology of names, as in the cases of names such as Natan, Yitzhak, and Yigal.
29. Another example of the differentiation between sacred and secular use can be found in the traditional vocalization of the word *abir* (warrior, strong). It appears six times in the Bible vocalized as *avir* in phrases describing God, such as *avir Yaakov* or *avir Yisrael*. In contrast, in secular contexts the vocalization is *abbir*: *abbir ha-ro'im*, *abbirim*, *abbirekha*, *abbirei lev* (seventeen times). I would like to thank the reader in the peer review process who brought this example to my attention. I afterwards became aware of the article by Ezra Zion Melammed, "Shimushi Lashon ba-Mikra ha-Miuḥadim le-ha-Shem" [Linguistic uses in the Bible specific for the Lord], *Tarbiz* 18 (1948): 1–18. On the first page the author points out the distinction between *adoni* and *Adonai*, and on the second page the distinction between *abir* and *avir*, and adds many more examples (not all of which are equally convincing).
30. A similar development occurred much later with the phrase *ribono shel olam* (Master of the World) (in manuscripts of the Mishnah, *rabbuni*). In classical rabbinic literature, this is also a form of address conveying the subservience with which a person appeals to the Creator. In our time (apparently due to the influence of Yiddish), *ribono shel olam* is used also as an actual epithet of God.

31. The conclusions that I have presented here are, in my opinion, derived directly from the data. Scholars who researched the subject before me usually missed the dramatic change that occurred in the status of the word *Adonai* in the eighth century BCE. W. W. F. Baudissin commented that, in the five books of the Torah, *Adonai* is used only as a form of addressing God (*Kyrios: als Gottesname im Judentum und seine Stelle in der Religions-geschichte* [Giessen: Topelmann, 1929], 2:18; quoted by Eissfeldt, *Theological Dictionary*, 67). However, he did not realize that this situation continued until the end of the book of Samuel, and most importantly did not regard this observation as particularly important.

In the classical scholarly literature, the prevalent opinion was indeed that the word originated in the form of address meaning "My Lord!" Gustaf Dalman went so far as to suggest that the word be removed from the text in cases in which it did not conform to this interpretation, and posited that in the original sources these verses contained the YHWH morpheme, which was changed to Adonai by later scribes. See Gustaf Dalmman, *Studien zur Biblischen Theologie: Der Gottesname Adonaj und seine Geschichte* (Berlin, 1889), 33.

Others (for example, *Gesenius' Hebrew Grammar*, second ed., ed. E. Kautzsch, trans. A. E. Cowley [Oxford: Clarendon Press, 1910], 441) were less extreme and explained that the word was petrified in this form, as were other forms of address in various languages (as I pointed out in note 25 above). H. Bauer and P. Leander (*Historische Grammatik der Hebräischen Sprache des Alten Testamentes* [Halle; Max Niemeyer, 1922], 16, 253, 469, 502) proposed a clever and radical explanation: *Adonai* did not originate from *adon*, but rather the opposite: *Adonai* in the sense of "lord" is a word introduced into Hebrew from an unknown source. Over the course of time, speakers of the language came to the conclusion that the suffix of the word is the form of address in first person singular of a plural object, and in error derived from this the noun *adon* (lord).

In the last few decades, many have cited the opinion of Otto Eissfeldt, who pointed out four occurrences in Ugaritic sources in which we find an addition of the letter yod at the end of nouns. (Oswald Loretz, who followed his approach, added a fifth example.) According to Eissfeldt, the purpose of this suffix is to strengthen and emphasize the noun, and it may be assumed that it is to be pronounced "āy." He proposes that this is also the primary meaning of the suffix -ai in the Hebrew name *Adonai* (and, eventually, the form of address *Adoni* in reference to God was also adapted to this form). For discussions and references to opinions mentioned in this footnote, see Eissfeldt, 59–72; K. Spron, "Lord," in *Dictionary of Deities and Demons in the Bible*, 531–533; M. Rösel, *Adonaj –Warum Gott 'Herr' genant wird* (Tübingen: Mohr Siebeck, 2000), 17–21. I would like to thank Professor Lutz Doering of the University of Münster who brought Rösel's book to my attention.

Discrepancies between Laws in the Torah

Joshua Berman

In this essay I examine the vexing question of the seeming discrepancies between law in Deuteronomy and law as it appears in the earlier books of the Torah.

I discuss the issue here with a particular methodological assumption: that to understand how the Torah coheres as a cohesive whole we must identify and shed the anachronistic assumptions that we bring to our reading of the Torah. Moreover, we must recapture the modes of thinking and writing that were prevalent in the ancient world. Only by reading the Torah in its ancient Near Eastern context, as its first audience understood it, can we hope to grasp its message.

A Signature Example of the Problem: The Law of the Firstborn Animal—The Approaches of the Sages

To illustrate the problem at hand, I will examine the mandate to dedicate and sanctify the firstborn animal. This mitzvah appears in two places in the Torah, and is one of the clearest examples of how irreconcilable two formulations of a mitzvah can be when read on the level of *peshat*.

In Numbers 18:14–18, God addresses Aaron and issues the following promise to him and his descendants, the *Kohanim*:

> Everything that has been proscribed in Israel shall be yours. The first issue of the womb of every being, man or beast, that is offered to the Lord, shall be yours; but the firstborn of man redeemed, and you shall also have the firstling of unclean animals redeemed. Take as their redemption price, from the age of one month up, the money equivalent of five shekels by the

> sanctuary weight, which is twenty gerahs. But the firstlings of cattle, sheep, or goats, may not be redeemed; they are consecrated. You shall dash their blood against the altar, and turn their fat into smoke as an offering by fire for a pleasing odor to the Lord. But their meat shall be yours: it shall be yours like the breast of elevation offering and like the right thigh.

Note that here, the flesh of the firstborn kosher animal is expressly given over to the *Kohen*, and is considered as much his as the other priestly entitlements (*matanot kehunah*) enumerated in the opening chapters of Leviticus (18). The *Kohen* is called upon to dash the blood on the altar (17). Because these animals are considered holy, it would be expressly forbidden for a *Yisra'el* to partake of them. Compare this, however, with what the Torah says on the subject in Deuteronomy 15:19–23:

> You shall consecrate to the Lord your God all male firstlings that are born in your herd and in your flock: you must not work your firstling ox or shear your firstling sheep. You and your household shall eat it annually before the Lord your God in the place that the Lord will choose. But if it has a defect, lameness or blindness, any serious defect, you shall not sacrifice it to the Lord your God. Eat it in your settlements, the unclean among you no less than the clean, just like the gazelle and the deer. Only you must not partake of its blood; you shall pour it out on the ground like water.

Here it is clear that the firstborn animal is to be consumed by its owner, a *Yisra'el* (20). The sages were aware of the discrepancy between the two sources, and resolved it through a strategy of harmonization. Rashi, commenting on Deuteronomy 15:20, invokes the solution of the *Sifrei*. Indeed, the owner of the animal must bring it to the Temple, as is suggested by Deuteronomy 15:19. However, when 20 states "*You* . . . shall eat it," that must refer to the *Kohen*, because Numbers 18 clearly states that the *Kohanim* alone may consume these animals. This reading, however, is difficult to maintain as a *peshat* reading of Deuteronomy 15. The same addressee ("you") who consecrates the animal (19)—presumably the *Yisra'el* owner—and who must take it home to consume it if it is blemished (22) and must properly dispose of its blood (23), is the same addressee commanded, "*you* . . . shall eat it" in verse 20. In fact, verse 20 suggests the addressee here is someone who comes from afar to the Temple only periodically, and not someone who is there on a more regular basis. The implication is that this verse, too, is referring to a *Yisra'el* and not to a *Kohen*.

The Hypothesis of Competing Legal Traditions—A Critical Evaluation

Critical study of the Bible proposes a simple solution for the discrepancy: the laws of Deuteronomy and the laws of Numbers are from two separate law codes. They were not originally written to coexist in one text. The two codes are mutually exclusive. This source-critical approach maintains, in fact, that the Torah contains four distinct law codes: the Covenant Code, comprised essentially of Exodus 21–23; the Priestly Code, which includes the Torah's cultic laws; the Holiness Code, which is comprised of the laws governing life in the land, contained in Leviticus 17–26; and, finally, the Deuteronomic Code, containing the laws found in Deuteronomy. These codes, it is said, were successively composed with the intent of replacing the law found in an earlier code. Thus, for example, Deuteronomy offers its own version of the law of manumission (*eved ivri*) in chapter 15, because its author rejected the formulation of the law found in Exodus 21:1–6.

The hypothesis of four codes of law is born out of the premise that no single agent would compose a work so fraught with legal contradiction. Advocates of the hypothesis must explain, however, how these disparate law corpora came together. The proposed solution essentially kicks the ball downfield. The bringing together of these materials is not the act of an author but of an editor, or what scholars call a redactor. Scholars, however, must then explain why an editor would bring together material in a way that an author would not. The standard explanation is that the redactor did so out of duress. With the pressures of the destruction and exile, there was a need for Israel's disparate subcommunities and traditions to unite together around a compromise document, and that document is the Torah.

This hypothesis of mutually exclusive codes brought together under duress in a compromise is subject to critique from a strictly academic perspective on six accounts.

First, and foremost, it is difficult to see how the Torah in its present form could satisfactorily be termed a "compromise document." There may well have been subcommunities within Israel at the time of the destruction. And joining forces and reaching compromise may well be a wise strategy for survival. But the discrepancies within the Torah render it the antithesis of a compromise document. A document reflecting compromise between competing agendas is one where each side gives ground on its original positions, and a middle ground is found. Alternatively, one side will get its way on a given issue and the other side its way on another. Where draftsmen truly find no common ground, they may employ creative ambiguity, or skirt the issue altogether. The *sine qua non* of a compromise document, however, is that it will iron out conflict and contradiction so that the community can proceed following one, authoritative voice. What compromise is there in the competing laws of the firstborn animal? If anything, the Torah would seem to guarantee a state of anarchy, with *Kohanim* insisting that the law should follow the formulation of Numbers 18, and land-owning *Yisra'el* pointing to the formulation in Deuteronomy 15 as the right way to go.

Second, the theory that the Torah is a compromise document has no external control to validate it. There were actually a number of law codes composed in the ancient Near East, *The Code of Hammurabi* being the most famous of them. Nonetheless, nowhere else in this vast region do we see that a culture faced with catastrophe suddenly merged its competing strands of thought and law into such a so-called "compromise document." This is so even though in the annals of ancient Near Eastern history Israel hardly stood alone in experiencing dislocation and disaster. Nor is there any attestation to this process of assembling the Torah in this fashion either from extra-biblical sources, or from anywhere in the Tanakh itself. Moreover, there is no extra-biblical evidence or passage within the Tanakh itself that points to the composition of even one of these codes as an independent literary entity.

Third, the notion that the various law codes compete with one another and were not intended to be combined is challenged by evidence within the Torah itself. The book of Deuteronomy makes no claim to its own sufficiency as a source of law, and calls upon Israel to fulfill precepts "as I have instructed you" elsewhere (12:21; 18:2; 24:8; compare also 5:12; 5:16). This seemingly refers to passages contained in one of the other so-called codes.

The fourth complication for this hypothesis stems from the peculiar authority that the book of Deuteronomy ascribes to its laws. In the earlier books of the Torah, the laws are commanded to Moses by God Himself. In Deuteronomy, however, the laws seem to be *given*—not merely transmitted—by Moses himself. Abarbanel noted that nowhere in Deuteronomy does the Torah say that the laws contained in that book were dictated by God to Moses. In fact, at several junctures Moses explicitly states that these are the laws that he is giving to Israel (e.g. Deut. 4: 44–45; 5:1). This is what led Abarbanel to his theory that the laws in Deuteronomy represent corollaries (*toladot*) to the earlier laws. Moses, for Abarbanel, could not make new laws, but he could add stipulations that would buttress the earlier laws, and support their spirit. However, this theory breaks down when we come to discrepancies like the ones exhibited in the various iterations of the law of the firstborn animal. The fact that Deuteronomy maintains that its laws emanate from Moses is problematic for the hypothesis of competing sources of law. Many scholars maintain that the law in Deuteronomy comes to replace the law in the Covenant Code of Exodus 21–23. Yet those laws are revealed in God's name. Why would the later author of Deuteronomy compose laws designed to replace laws spoken by God in Exodus, and replace them with laws whose authority is only that of Moses?

Fifth, were these so-called schools truly inimical to each other, we would expect the warfare over the law to spread to many other books of the Bible. Indeed, scholarship routinely maintains that Deuteronomic, or Priestly, or Holiness editors were largely responsible for the redaction of many of the books of the Tanakh. The other books of Scripture touch upon literally dozens of areas of law. Yet nowhere in the Hebrew Bible do we find a prophet, priest, king, or narrator who argues in explicit fashion for the legitimacy of one version of a law over another. Nowhere in the Tanakh do we find a book or a prophet who can be classified as purely following Deuteronomy or the Holiness Code. In fact, quite the opposite is true. Nearly all the books of the Tanakh resonate with passages from all so-called sources of law. Often, biblical writers will weave together purportedly "competing" law sources. Nehemiah does this with the very laws we have taken as our case study—the laws of the firstborn animal in his discussion of practice in his day (Neh. 10:35–37).[1] Put succinctly, while the source critical approach sees the different law collections as mutually exclusive, all sections of the Tanakh, from the Torah and on into the other books, seem to put them together. In the Torah we find these laws all united under one cover as the Torah, and in the other books we see references to these law codes woven and cited, with no sense that affinity to one comes at the expense of the standing of the other.

Sixth, I take a page from the history of the critical study of the Torah. When we look at the early major figures of this movement, we see a curious trend. Until the mid-nineteenth century, scholars attended solely to contradictions within the narrative portion of the Torah. I'm speaking of figures like Spinoza, Astruc, Eichhorn, De Wette, and Ewald, for those familiar with the names. These figures read the *narratives* of the Torah with a keen eye, and looked for every slight indication of difference as evidence of independent sources. These are the figures that hypothesized a J source and an E source for the stories of the Torah. Yet, strangely, one finds no mention in their work of the contradictions within biblical law. That enterprise began in earnest only in the second half of the nineteenth century. Why were earlier scholars oblivious to problems in the text that would be so obviously problematic to later scholars?

All of this suggests that we should look for an alternative explanation. I conclude therefore, with a "prospectus" of what a satisfactory hypothesis would need to include to explain the discrepancies between the law in Deuteronomy and in the earlier books. This theory should explain what seems a Gordian knot: on the one hand, many laws in the Torah seem to be mutually exclusive—such as the laws of the firstborn animal. And yet, at the same time, the literature in which these laws are found—the Torah and the Tanakh generally—seems to relate to them as compatible. It should explain why Deuteronomy ascribes the laws to Moses when all the other books ascribe them to God Himself. It should explain why Deuteronomy seems to approve of prior law codes, beckoning Israel to follow certain laws "as I have instructed you," and yet, at the same time, often gives a divergent formulation of the law. Finally, our solution should explain why scholars before the mid-nineteenth century rarely if ever saw contradiction within the laws of the Bible, whereas contradiction here has been obvious to scholars working in the last century and a half.

That solution, I maintain, is available. Its root lies in identifying our anachronistic understanding of the word "law," and how legal texts are to be read. It lies in recovering how people thought about "law" and legal texts in premodern times.

The difficulties that many sense in the law collections of the Torah stem from anachronistic notions of how law functions and of what a legal text is. I will proceed by laying out the difference between modern and ancient notions of law. This will enable us to comprehend anew a host of questions concerning law in the Tanakh, and gain a greater appreciation of the relationship between *Torah she-bi-khetav* and *Torah she-be-al peh*, usually translated as "the Written Law" and "the Oral Law." I begin by laying out the assumptions we hold when we speak about law today.

Common Law vs. Statutory Law

What do we mean when we use the word "law"? Consider the following common usages of the word *law*: "uphold the law," "comply with the law," "the letter of the law," "pass a law," "against the law." These statements share a basic assumption: the "law" in question is a written formulation and is found in a law code. However, the intuitive notion that by "law" we mean written law found in a law code is itself a relative newcomer in the history of legal thought. Once upon a time, the norms of society were not written. There were no codes. This is the story of the history of the word "law," and how it came to take on the modern meaning of law written in a law code. More profoundly, this is the story of how our modern use of the term "law" has put us out of touch with the way law worked in the time of the Tanakh.

When most people today think of the word "law," they have in mind what legal theorists call *statutory law*. Law, within this conception, is contained in a *codified* text. Only what is written in the code is the law. The law code supersedes all other sources of norms that preceded the formulation of the code. No other sources of authority have validity other than the code itself. Therefore, the courts must pay great attention to the wording of the text and cite the text in their decisions. Where the code lacks explicit legislation, judges must adjudicate with the code as their primary guide. For many of us today this *statutory* approach to law is intuitive and even unremarkable. Yet as recently as the early nineteenth century, the vast majority of Germans, Englishmen, and Americans thought about law in very different terms. The prevailing view for them was a *common law* approach to jurisprudence.

For common law theorists, the law is not found in a written code which serves as the judgest point of reference and which delimits what they may decide. A judge arrives at a judgment based on the mores and spirit of the community and its customs. Norms develop gradually through the distillation and continual restatement of legal doctrine through the decisions of courts. When a judge decides a particular case, he or she is empowered to reconstruct the general thrust of these norms in consultation with previous judicial formulations. Critically, the judicial decision itself does not create binding precedent. *No particular formulation of these norms is final. There is no authoritative text called "the law" or "the law code."* As a system of legal thought, common law is consciously and inherently incomplete, fluid, and vague.

When decisions and precedents were collected and written down, these texts did not become the *source* of law, but rather a *resource* for later jurists to consult. Every decision became "a datum from which to reason," in the words of the early nineteenth-century common law theorist John Joseph Park.[2] Within this conception, judges address new needs and circumstances by reworking old norms, decisions, and ideas. Although common law attached great importance to the venerated customs of the past, the key was not the unchanging identity of its components, but a steady continuity with the past.

By the end of the nineteenth century, legal codes were being drafted across the Western world, from Germany to America. The statutory approach had won the day. But why? What was it that led sensibilities about jurisprudence to shift so dramatically in the second half of the nineteenth century from a common law approach to a statutory approach? Why do we today think of law as *statutory law*?

Common law thinking flourishes in homogeneous communities where common values and cultural touchstones are nourished and maintained by all. Where cohesion breaks down, however, it is difficult to anchor law in a collective set of mores and values. Nineteenth-century Europe witnessed large-scale urbanization and the rise of the modern nation state. Great numbers of disparate individuals were coalescing in social and political entities of ever-larger scope. A clearly formulated set of rules could unite a heterogeneous populace around a single code of behavior. The earliest known instance of codification reflects the same political logic. The first written Greek laws date to the middle of the seventh century BCE, and proliferate at just the period when Greek city-states were in a process of state formation and developing more formal political systems.

Today, we are citizens of large, polyglot political entities, far removed from the spirit that animated common law jurisprudence in the premodern period. But to appreciate the vitality of the common law system within a local, homogeneous environment, we need think no further than our own homes and the dynamics of the nuclear family. At home, we certainly do set the bar high in terms of expected behavior, but we do not typically run the house on the basis of "laws." Children may be reminded not to jump or eat on the couch, but there are no "laws of the couch" posted on the side of the refrigerator. At home, proper behavior and attitudes are modeled by parents and neighbors. Cues suggesting how a child should behave, think, and feel are all interwoven in and inculcated through the gestalt of the environment created by the home. Here parental discipline is exercised in a fluid and changing manner. Parents may address a child's misdeed one way on one day and in an entirely different way with another child at a different time. The broad set of goals and ideals remains the same. But their implementation and expression are in a constant state of flux.

This is a good model for understanding the dynamics of law in much of the premodern world. Villages were small and homogeneous. Families typically lived in the same village for generations and could assume that continuity for the future. Village members shared a common language, religion, heritage, common enemies, and common economic opportunities. There was no need for societal norms to be legislated by a formal body, let alone written. What was expected of a person in attitude and behavior was part of the warp and woof of day-to-day life, much as is the case with family life for us today. When a member of the village violated those norms, the elders convened and decided the appropriate remedy. There were no "jurists" as a professional guild. Village elders possessed the wisdom of the ages and determined on an *ad hoc* basis the best redress for the situation at hand. When the continuity and homogeneity of small community are torn asunder, however, the statutory approach to jurisprudence serves to bridge the chasm that separates the behavioral and attitudinal differences of constituent citizens.

Lessons About "Law" From Hammurabi

The dichotomy between a statutory system of law and a common law system is essential for understanding the idea of law in the ancient world. In the ancient Near East there was no "law" in the sense of a statutory code. Moreover, as I will proceed to demonstrate, there was no such "law" in the Torah either. Indeed, there was no such law *anywhere* in the ancient world. I would like to demonstrate this by laying out a series of observations that scholars have made about what some call "history's first law code"—*The Code of Hammurabi*. The "Code" of Hammurabi is an excellent place to begin our discussion of statutory law in the ancient world because the "Code" of Hammurabi, it turns out, is no code at all. Following how scholars reached this conclusion offers important context for understanding the nature of law in the Torah. A series of startling observations about this famous document speak volumes about the so-called "law codes" of the Torah.

French archeologists discovered the *Code* while digging in 1901 at Susa—ancient Shushan. They unearthed an imposing seven-foot-tall stele of black diorite inscribed with cuneiform writing on all sides, which today stands as the marquee holding of the Louvre in Paris. Scholars quickly translated the Akkadian, written ca. 1750 BCE, and saw that it contained provisions—282, to be exact—that read like this:

> [55] If a seignior, upon opening his canal for irrigation, became so lazy that he has let the water ravage a field adjoining his, he shall measure out grain on the basis of those adjoining his.[3]

Or like this:

> [229] If a builder constructed a house for a seignior, but did not make his work strong, with the result that the house which he built collapsed and so has caused the death of the owner of the house, that builder shall be put to death.[4]

As scholars sought to uncover the meaning of this text, however, the intellectual shovels at their disposal were not equal to the task. Recalling their lesson from the study of proverbial ducks, as it were, scholars concluded that if it looks like a law code, and reads like a law code, then—it must be a law code! This was, after all, the early twentieth century, and every civilized country in Europe was now incorporating jurisprudence that championed statutory law.

Scholars are always quick to identify evidence in support of their hypotheses, and, sure enough, evidence was quickly found supporting the understanding of this text as a statutory code. In time, more than fifty fragments of the "Code" of Hammurabi were found all across the Mesopotamian region. Moreover, these copies or fragments had been copied over a period that spanned more than 1500 years. Most remarkably, these fragments revealed virtually no editing of content over that time. For half a century, scholars considered it an assured result: *The Code of Hammurabi* (or CH, as scholars refer to it in shorthand) had canonical status throughout Mesopotamia and was unrivaled as the source of law.

Around mid-century, however, scholars started to identify cracks—not in the stele, but in the theory that CH was a statutory code. Scholars were puzzled: wild fluctuations of inflation and deflation were well-known throughout the ancient Near East. Nonetheless, the fines that *The Code of Hammurabi* mandates for various offenses remain unchanged across the 1500-year epigraphic record. Had CH served as a statutory code, those fines would surely have been adjusted over time. Scholars were further puzzled: Significant areas of day-to-day life receive no attention at all in CH. There are no stipulations relating to inheritance, for example. This is inexplicable if, indeed, CH was the binding law code of a culture. Puzzling even further was the evidence from the archaeological record. Archaeologists have discovered copies of *The Code of Hammurabi* in royal archives and in temples, but never at the sites of local courts, and never together with the literally thousands of court dockets that have come to light from Mesopotamia. Were CH statutory law, we would certainly expect to find it well-represented in court settings. But most puzzling to scholars was this: not one of these thousands of court dockets ever refers to or cites CH as a source of law. In fact, *not a single court docket from anywhere in the ancient Near East ever refers to any ancient law collection as a source of law.* The practice of citation is strikingly absent from the record. Think of that in modern terms. Today a judge must cite sources when he or she delivers a decision. Finally, and most crucially, many court dockets from ancient Mesopotamia record proceedings of cases whose remedy CH directly addresses. Nonetheless, in many of these, the judge rules counter to the prescription offered in the CH. If this text was the "law code" of Mesopotamia, how could a judge rule contrary to it? These complications raised two enduring and interrelated questions: if seeming "law collections" such as CH did not contain the law, where could the law be found—where was it written? And secondly, if texts like CH were not statutory codes, then what were they?

Where was the law written in Mesopotamia? The answer is: it wasn't. A judge would render a decision at the moment of adjudication by drawing on an extensive reservoir of custom and accepted norms. It would continually vary from locale to locale. One could not point to an accepted text of the law—neither CH, nor any other text, for that matter—as the final word on what the law was or prescriptively should be. Philology here speaks volumes: in ancient Greece the word for written law was *thesmos*, and later, *nomos*. But that was Greece. Nowhere in the cultures of the ancient Near East is there a word for written law. The very concept does not exist.

If CH, though, wasn't a collection of "laws," what was it? These collections, instead, are anthologies of *judgments*—snapshots of decisions rendered by judges, or perhaps even by the king himself. The domain of these texts was the ivory tower of old, the palaces and the temples, the world of the court scribe. Collections like CH were a model of justice meant to inspire; a treatise, with examples of the exercise of judicial power. They were records of *precedent*, but not of *legislation*.

Scholars have long noted that the style—if not always the content—of law in the Torah resembles the legal writings of the ancient Near East, such as the so-called "Code" of Hammurabi. In what follows, I will show how the lessons scholars learned about CH as essentially common law, as opposed to statutory law, shed great light on law in the Torah and elsewhere in the Tanakh. From there, I will show how this understanding of the nature of legal texts in the ancient Near East can bring new light to the divergent formulations of law found in the Torah.

What can the distinction between statutory law and common law tell us about the nature of law in the Tanakh generally, and in the Torah specifically? To my mind, it can tell us a whole lot, especially when we see the same law presented in highly divergent ways. The conclusions that I will draw about how law functioned in the time of the Tanakh may surprise some. Following my main presentation, therefore, I will turn to remarks by Rabbi Naftali Zvi Yehuda Berlin (the Netsiv) about the development of *halakhah* that support these conclusions.

Law in the Tanakh: Common Law, not Statutory Law

Our earlier distinction between common law and statutory law throws great light upon what we call "law" in the Torah. Intuitively, we read the legal portions of the Torah through the lens of statutory law. Yet, law in the Tanakh follows a common law conception of how law and legal writing work, as does ancient Near Eastern law generally. This explains why nowhere does the Tanakh instruct judges to consult written sources.[5] Narratives of adjudication, such as Solomon's "split the baby" trial (1 Kings 3), likewise make no reference to written sources of law. No single collection of Torah "laws," such as the Book of the Covenant in Exodus 21–23 or the "laws" of Deuteronomy (12–26), displays an attempt to provide a comprehensive set of rules to be applied in judicial cases. Here, as in *The Code of Hammurabi*, critical aspects of daily life receive no legal attention. The Torah clearly endorses and sanctifies the institution of marriage. Yet, if you want to marry a woman—just what do you have to do, ritually or contractually? The Torah nowhere says. That would be unthinkable in a work of statutory law. Biblical "law" is not "law" at all—in the sense of *statutory* law.

Let's look at two examples of how law in the Bible is negotiated through a common law mentality. Recall the parable of the poor man's ewe in 2 Samuel 12:1–4. David has slept with Bathsheba, the wife of Uriah, one of his soldiers on the battlefront. The prophet Nathan wishes to bring the errant king to an awareness of his misdoing. He brings a fictitious case to the king for adjudication in which a man blessed with large flocks steals and slaughters the ewe of his neighbor, a poor man who owned nothing but the ewe, which he loved very much. The king does not realize that the parable is a metaphor for his own lust for women. Significant for our purposes here is the punishment that David imposes upon the thief. What should be the ruling here? If Torah law is statutory law, then the answer is simple: David had no need to look farther than Exodus 21:37: "When a man steals an ox or a sheep, and slaughters it or sells it, he shall pay five oxen for the ox and four sheep for the sheep." David, however, deviates from this ostensible "statute." He indeed obligates the thief to four-fold restitution—as per the "law" in Exodus—but, also sentences him to death (2 Sam. 12:5–6)! From a statutory perspective, David's actions are out of line. A cardinal tenet of statutory law is the principle of strict construction—interpreting the law as literally as possible. If Exodus calls for four-fold restitution and no more, then no harsher sentence may be leveled.

Torah "law," however, is not statutory law; it is common law, which is to say situational and *ad hoc*. When Exodus proposes that a thief who slaughters a stolen sheep should pay four-fold restitution, that is not a prescriptive, statutory law. It is, rather, an *example* of justice. In most instances, a man steals a sheep and slaughters it because he lacks means and wishes to provide for his family. It is relatively easy to pilfer a sheep from the pasture, and so the Torah prescribes a harsh financial penalty. David, clearly aware of the proposition in Exodus 21:37, applies that teaching to the specifics of the case at hand. In the case brought to him by the prophet, the thief's actions are flagrant and contemptible in the extreme. The thief here was neither hungry nor desperate. The aggrieved—the poor man—was denied his only, beloved possession. The prescription of Exodus would simply not do here. The thief's avarice and callousness warrant his death. From the anachronistic perspective of statutory jurisprudence, the law in Exodus is plain and literal. Going beyond the letter of the ostensible "statute," David performs a miscarriage of justice, even as he cites the proposition. However, from the perspective of common law jurisprudence, David utilizes the case in Exodus as "a datum from which to reason," and applies justice to the specifics at hand in front of him.

The idea that divine law can be as malleable as human law is counterintuitive to some. It is one thing to posit that laws of human origin evolve in a common law fashion. Humans are fallible and limited in their perspective. But surely divine law is different. God's wisdom is infinite and thus His laws cannot be altered. This intuition, however, misunderstands common law thinking. The fluid nature of common law stems only partially from the limitations of the human jurist. Common law insists on fluidity because society itself is in constant flux as well. Even divine law requires adaptation to the changing needs of society.

This view of biblical law as common law is substantiated when we examine how law is approached broadly across the Tanakh. Laws in the Tanakh do not assume a single, immutable form. Rather, the basic institution undergoes restatement and receives new expression across the ages. This is seen with regard to the laws of Shabbat, Passover, *yibbum* (levirate marriage), and many other commandments. Just consider a well-known example—*yibbum* in the book of Ruth. The prescription in Deuteronomy 25:5–12 speaks solely of the obligation of a brother-in-law to his deceased brother's widow. Ruth, however, insists that Boaz has an obligation to marry her (3:9), even though Boaz was but a distant cousin of her deceased husband. Boaz, in turn, reveals that there is an obligation to redeem the land of the deceased, when a man performs *yibbum* (4:5–6). This is nowhere hinted at in the laws of land redemption in Leviticus 25, nor in the laws of *yibbum* in Deuteronomy 25. What Ruth shows us is a common law reapplication of the institutions of *yibbum* and land redemption, as they were practiced in Boaz's time. The manifestations of these mitzvot in his time were different from what the Torah had originally specified, and differed also from the *halakhah* that the sages would spell out on these matters.

The prophets of Israel censured Israel for many failings: theft, murder, idolatry. Nowhere do the prophets "throw the book" at the people with the claim that they were performing the law, but doing so in the wrong fashion, by failing to adhere to a strict reading of a passage. Modern statutory jurisprudence mandates that judges adhere to the exact words of the code because the code, by definition, is autonomous and exhaustive. As we have seen, however, the ancient Near East knew no notion of statutory law. Hence, when Boaz performed a form of *yibbum* that varies from a strict reading of Deuteronomy 25:5–10, no one thought that he was contravening that passage. That passage was an example of proper practice, reapplied anew in every generation. I have presented here a fluid notion of legal practice—certainly more fluid than we find in Talmudic writings, and much more fluid than we find in normative *halakhah* today. Yet, some of the greatest rabbinic figures envisioned that, once upon a time, law did evolve much more fluidly than it does today. I conclude with an example of one such voice—the Netziv.

The Changing Nature of Halakhah in the thought of the Netziv

In his important work *How Do We Know This?* Jay Harris reveals that the rabbinic tradition had always been of two voices concerning the continuity of the *halakhah*.[6] One voice is more familiar to most Orthodox Jews today, and claims continuity of tradition: little has changed, and much of the tradition can be traced all the way back to Sinai. A flagship source for this opinion in the tradition is the statement in the Babylonian Talmud that "*Mikra*, Mishnah, and Talmud" were all given to Moses at Sinai.[7] At the opposite end of the spectrum, Harris notes, one can cite the *aggadah* that when Moses sat and witnessed Rabbi Akiva teaching a *halakhah* to his students he was dismayed that he did not recognize the law that Rabbi Akiva was teaching, and was heartened only when Rabbi Akiva explained that this law was, in fact, *halakhah le-Moshe mi-Sinai*.[8] The suggestion is that even Moses himself might not have been familiar with the laws later granted status of *halakhah le-Moshe Mi-Sinai*. The issue here is not which approach to *halakhah* is historically correct, or even which is theologically correct. It is certainly that case that the former position has wider currency in our day. But the latter position is well represented in the sources.

In particular, I would like to bring attention to comments of the Netziv about the changing nature of *halakhah* and the Oral Law. Consider his comments on Deuteronomy 5:1:

> "Hear, O Israel, the laws (*ḥukkim*) and rules (*mishpatim*) that I proclaim to you this day"—*Ḥukkim*: these are the rules of rules of interpretation, such as the thirteen rules [of Rabbi Yishmael], through which the Torah is interpreted, down to each and every letter. *Mishpatim*: these are the actual laws derived from the rules of interpretation, thereby generating new laws. ... Moses our Teacher taught Israel several *ḥukkim* and *mishpatim* which he had derived from his powers of induction, with the intent that they, too, should do the same in each and every generation.

Elsewhere (Lev. 25:18), the Netziv underscores that the ongoing process of deducing rules of interpretation, and deriving through them actual laws throughout history. He notes that Hillel the Elder had his seven rules in his generation,[9] and later Rabbi Ishmael derived his thirteen. For the Netziv, interpretation of the Torah law changed with some degree of frequency in the pre-rabbinic period. Because the principles of interpretation—the *ḥukkim*—changed, perforce the actual practice of law changed in this time as well. Rules of interpretation in one generation likely produced a practice that was at odds with the practice determined by a different rule of interpretation in a different age. Presented with this historical development, there was no place to see in all this "contradiction." The system as a whole was meant to be fluid and changing.[10]

The Netziv nowhere uses the language of common law versus statutory law, as I have here. Yet his notion of the changing nature of the rules of interpretation suggests that the Torah, in his opinion, was not a statutory code. From here we move to address our primary question: Why do laws in the Torah seem to contradict each other?

Because my conclusions may seem radical to some, I would like to create a theological space for my analysis by opening with remarks by a seminal rabbinic thinker, Rabbi Zadok Ha-Cohen Rabinowitz of Lublin (1823–1900).

Legal Discrepancy in the Torah Within the Thought of Rabbi Zadok of Lublin

In the following passage, Rabbi Zadok takes up the age-old question of the discrepancies between the version of the Decalogue found in Exodus 20 and that found in Deuteronomy 5:

> The latter version of the Decalogue, that in Deuteronomy, was said by Moses, on his own account. Nonetheless, it is part of the Written Law. In addition to the mitzvot themselves that Moses had already received at Sinai, by the word of God, these words as well [in Deuteronomy], which were said on his own account, which are not prefaced with the statement, "And God said . . .", these, too, are part of the Written Law. For all of his (i.e., Moses') are also a complete "Torah," just like the dialogues of the Patriarchs and other similar passages are considered part of the Written Law. But the material that begins "And these are the things" (i.e., the first verse of Deuteronomy and the rest of the book that follows), material that was said on his own account, represents the root of the Oral Law, the things that the sages of Israel say of their own account.[11]

For Rabbi Zadok, the Torah contains material that is divine in origin, such as the mitzvot given to Moses at Sinai. The Torah, however, also contains material that is human in origin. This is what he refers to as "the dialogues of the Patriarchs." That is, the words spoken by the Patriarchs that are preserved in Genesis are actual, human utterances that the Torah chose to preserve. Their origin is human, and nonetheless they have the same status as God's utterances at Sinai and are on equal footing as part of the Written Law. Rabbi Zadok applies this same logic to everything found in Deuteronomy. When Deuteronomy opens with the statement, "these are the things that Moses spoke," Rabbi Zadok takes that quite literally: God may have given His imprimatur for this book, but its content originates with Moses, not God. Numerous statements throughout Deuteronomy, such as 4:44–45 and 5:1, support this understanding. Nowhere in Deuteronomy do we find the typical introduction to a mitzvah found in the earlier books of the Torah: "The Lord spoke to Moses saying: 'Speak to the Israelite people thus...'" Rabbi Zadok's position is unique because he employs this principle to explain the discrepancies between the version of the Ten Commandments found in Exodus 20 and the version found in Deuteronomy 5.

For Rabbi Zadok, God spoke only the version found in Exodus 20. The version found in Deuteronomy 5 is Moses' words. But how could this be? After all, in Deuteronomy 5:4, Moses himself says that *God* spoke the words of the Decalogue that follow (5:6–18). Here we see Rabbi Zadok's revolutionary leap. For Rabbi Zadok, the words that Moses speaks throughout Deuteronomy are an exercise in *Torah she-be-al peh*—exegesis and reinterpretation of God's law. In fact, says Rabbi Zadok, Moses' own exercise in such reinterpretation constitutes the paradigm—the "root" to use his term—for all subsequent such activity by the sages of Israel across the ages. The version of the Decalogue in Deuteronomy diverges from the version told in Exodus 20 because it is a *Torah she-be-al peh* retelling of the earlier version. For Rabbi Zadok, Moses' statement in Deuteronomy 5:4, that God spoke "these words," is not a statement that what follows is the *ipsissima verba*—a word-for-word transcript of divine speech. Rather it is a faithful interpretation and reapplication of those words. No mitzvah, then, in Deuteronomy will be identical to its precursor in the other books. The entire purpose of Deuteronomy is to present an updated version and application of God's commands on the eve of the entry into the land.

Common Law Development within The Torah Itself

Rabbi Zadok's approach to law in the Torah dovetails well with the conceptual framework developed in the previous essays of this series. For Rabbi Zadok, the mitzvot contained in Exodus, Leviticus, and Numbers cannot be read as divine statutory law. Were that the case, there would be no room to stray from a strict and close reading of the formulations of those laws. There would be no license for Moses to reinterpret those mitzvot; indeed, there would be no license for later rabbis to interpret the language of those mitzvot either. The entire enterprise of *Torah she-be-al peh* would be invalidated. We would be bound to strictly follow the literal meaning of those prescriptions.

Instead, Rabbi Zadok advocates a way of looking at those legal statements as binding, yet as fluid in their application. Put differently, Rabbi Zadok looks at those prescriptions as common law, not statutory law. For common law thinking, determination of the law is situational: the law is not found in an immutable text, but adapts with an awareness of the changing historical situation.[12] Deuteronomy presents a record of Moses' common law application of earlier teachings. God had spoken at Sinai to a people just released from bondage. With the people poised to enter the land, Moses reinterprets God's earlier words and applies the laws to an array of challenges posed by life in the Land of Israel.

This well explains the case studies of legal divergence that we examined earlier. We noted that the institution of manumission (*eved ivri*), first stated in Exodus 21, is restated in Deuteronomy 15 with the prominent addition of the mitzvah of severance pay for the released servant. This is a good example of how Deuteronomy openly reworks the mitzvot of the Covenant Code (Exod. 21–23), yet without negating it. The laws of Deuteronomy address Israel as it is poised to assume the new condition of a landed people with a central temple and a more developed government. This is why the law of manumission (*eved ivri*) in Deuteronomy 15:12–18 addresses the master and his feelings and experiences as he derives benefit from the debt-servant. This focus is far less noticeable in the Covenant Code, which appears at the beginning of the trek in the wilderness. This way of viewing Deuteronomy's revision of the Covenant Code reflects a common law approach to jurisprudence whereby changed historical circumstance leads to the evolution of the law, yet without the need of jettisoning earlier, revered texts. Revision of an earlier law did not entail a rejection of the text bearing that earlier law. We may invoke the words we cited earlier of John Joseph Park, the nineteenth-century common law theorist, who noted that texts within the common law tradition always remain "a datum from which to reason." Even as Deuteronomy interprets and reapplies the teachings of the Covenant Code, the Covenant Code remains on the books for later consultation, "as a datum from which to reason." Neither the Covenant Code nor Deuteronomy are statutory codes. They are sets of teachings. Deuteronomy borrows from the language of the Covenant Code because, in legal terms, it is a restatement and a new application of the older teaching.

This also explains the explicit contradiction between the law of the firstborn found in Numbers 18 and the version of the law found in Deuteronomy 15. When the laws of the priestly gifts are first presented (Lev. 2), firstborn animals are not listed. The law in Numbers 18 itself is an *ad hoc* exigency. The Korah rebellion necessitated legislation that would buttress the standing of the priesthood of Aaron and his descendants. One measure that God orders is that the firstborn now be consecrated for the benefit of the priests alone. The law in Deuteronomy 15:19–23 restores the status of the firstborn animal to that it had before the Korah crisis—as the property of the owner. As with many laws in Deuteronomy, the law of the firstborn seeks to ensure that cultic activity only occur at the place that God chooses (eventually, Jerusalem and the Temple), and thus he must bring it to the central sanctuary where he may consume it.

To be sure, this is not the *halakhah* as we have it today, based on the harmonization of the passages in the *Sifrei*, as we noted earlier. However, this should not provide any theological concern. As we saw, Ruth exhibits forms of levirate marriage and land redemption that are at variance both with the provisions in the Torah and with the *halakhah* as later determined by the rabbis. The comments of the Netziv that we saw, and the approach of Rabbi Zadok of Lublin discussed above provide us a theological basis with which to comprehend the fluidity of practice during the biblical period. These luminaries did not state their opinions apologetically as some sort of concession to the findings of critical study. They stated their opinions as a celebration of the evolving human process of *Torah she-be-al peh*, a process which for both of them began with Moses himself. As we saw, the tradition empowers the sages to develop the Torah and derive biblical (*de-oraita*) obligations, limitations, and conditions. The writings of Rabbi Zadok of Lublin and the Netziv suggest that Moses, too, was invested with these powers.

Endnotes

1. See *Da'at Mikra* on these verses for references to the various Torah laws woven together here.
2. John Joseph Park, *A Contre-Projet to the Humpheresian Code* (London: 1827), 21, 25 quoted in Michael Lobban, *The Common Law and English Jurisprudence 1760–1850* (Oxford: Oxford University Press, 1991), 220–21.
3. Translation by Theophile J. Meek, in James Pritchard, ed. *Ancient Near Eastern Texts* (Princeton: Princeton University Press, 1969), 168.
4. Ibid., 176.
5. Compare Exod. 18:13–26; Deut. 1:16–17; 16:19–20; 2 Chron. 19:4–7.
6. Jay Harris, *How Do We Know This? Midrash and the Fragmentation of Modern Jewry* (Albany: SUNY Press, 1995).
7. Babylonian Talmud, tractate *Berakhot* 5a.
8. Babylonian Talmud, tractate *Menaḥot* 29b.
9. Tosefta, *Sanhedrin* 7:5.
10. This, of course, raises the question of when and why the halakhic system endorsed codification, as found in Maimonides' *Mishneh Torah* or in the *Shulḥan Arukh*. I trace the history of the transition from common law to statutory law within *halakhah* in my essay, "What is This

Thing Called Law?," *Mosaic Magazine*, December 1, 2013, http://mosaicmagazine.com/essay/2013/12/what-is-this-thing-called-law/.
11. Zadok HaCohen of Lublin, *Sefer Pri Tzadik* (Jerusalem: Mesamchei Lev, 1999), 55–97.
12. This is a cardinal tenet in Rabbi Zadok's writings. See his arguments about the need for growth and change within *halakhah* in Zadok HaCohen of Lublin, *Sefer Tzidkatha-Tzaddik* (Har Berachah: Machon Har Berachah, 1997), 35 and in his *Resisei Laylah* (Har Berachah: Machon Har Berachah, 2003), 177–89.

Between the Prophet and his Prophecy: Ezekiel's Visionary Temple in its Historical Context

Tova Ganzel

We are accustomed to thinking of prophecies that address the future as timeless, and often do not ask ourselves to what extent these prophecies reflect the personal characteristics and style of the prophets or their time and place. In this article, I will examine one of many aspects of the transmission of prophecy from God to the people by means of God's prophets: the tension between the ahistorical sanctity that we customarily ascribe to prophecy, on the one hand, and the prophecy's connection to the prophet's own time, place, and personal outlook, on the other. To this end, I will examine Ezekiel's prophetic vision of the future temple (Ezek. 40–48). Despite the fact that this prophecy is God's revelation of future events, it is rooted in the conceptual world of the Neo-Babylonian period.[1]

The prophecy of Ezekiel, uniquely among the later prophets, is organized chronologically. The time and place that the prophecy was received are known and mentioned explicitly in many chapters at the beginning of the book. We are therefore able to examine the relationship between the prophet and his context more clearly with regard to Ezekiel than with any other prophet.

Words with parallels in the language spoken in Babylon during this period appear frequently in Ezekiel's prophecy. Extant Mesopotamian sources enable us to identify many words and motifs that are analogous to contemporary Mesopotamian culture and reflect the richness of the language absorbed by Ezekiel from his Babylonian surroundings. This shared semantic field is indicative of the influence of the surrounding Babylonian culture on the exiles from the Land of Israel, Ezekiel among them. This linguistic evidence is supplemented by the results of more recent research, such as archeological discoveries and Babylonian ritual texts. These texts include detailed descriptions of the structure and rituals of temples that were located in Ezekiel's Babylonian surroundings. Our discussion will focus primarily on Ezekiel chapters 40–48, which describe the prophet's vision of the future temple; for the reasons mentioned above, this subject is particularly pertinent to the examination of the interaction between the prophet and his surroundings.[2] For generations, Jews have yearned to build the future temple described in the closing chapters of Ezekiel, just as the first part of the book prophesies the First Temple's destruction. For example, the Malbim (Meir Leibush Wisser) concluded the introduction to his commentary to the book of Ezekiel by expressing his hope for the building of the prophesied temple:

> I have built in the heavens, in my mind, to you my God in heaven, a Temple for you as the prophet envisaged it, it exists in my mind rebuilt.... I have measured the plans, as I have learned from your seer, with a wick of flax and a measuring rod, and I have solved the riddle. Hear the prayer of your servant and his supplication, O Lord my God! Let your eyes be upon this house night and day, to rebuild its destruction and raise up its ruins ... and establish and build in high places your Temple, reveal it to us in your mercy, for our eyes are yearning and our souls are longing to establish it and build it, and to see it face to face.[3]

The longing throughout the ages for the building of the future temple, as described in Ezekiel's prophecy, lends an extra dimension to our search for answers to several questions: What is the nature of this temple? Is its prophetic description timeless or historically determined? Is it possible that our yearning for the building of a temple, in many ways, is reflective of the Neo-Babylonian period in which Ezekiel lived?[4]

In the following pages I will attempt to illustrate how the prophet Ezekiel's cultural context, including his familiarity with local Babylonian temples and the status of their priests, is reflected in the biblical text. The Neo-Babylonian temples offer us a meaningful context in which to situate some of the unique features of Ezekiel's description of the temple.

Ezekiel and his Babylonian Context

Ezekiel was not only familiar with the temples in his Babylonian context. He was also familiar, as he mentions, with the political events of his time. Ezekiel describes Babylonian king Nebuchadnezzar's arrival in Jerusalem and the exile of Jehoiakim the king of Judah and his officers to Babylon (Ezek. 17:12–14), and records the breach of the treaty between Nebuchadnezzar and Zedekiah (17:13).[5] Ezekiel was also familiar with the methods of divination popular in his time (21:23–29). This can be inferred from his description of how the Babylonian king's decision whether to move the Babylonian army against Jerusalem or Amman was influenced by magical rites practiced in his day: "For the king of Babylon has stood at the fork of the road, where two roads branch off, to perform divination: He has shaken arrows,[6] consulted teraphim,[7] and inspected the liver"[8] (21:26). The prophet points to these decisions as proof that God rules not only over the People of Israel, but also over all the rulers of the world. Recently, several scholars have pointed to additional connections between Ezekiel and his Babylonian surroundings.[9] This scholarly trend continues to grow as additional findings illuminating Jewish life in Babylon are discovered.[10]

Ezekiel's Visionary Temple in its Babylonian Context

Archaeological discoveries of ancient structures and numerous documents, which reveal details of daily life in the temples of Babylon in the Neo-Babylonian period, illuminate, among other things, the period of the prophecy of Ezekiel. These findings even show that many aspects of the Neo-Babylonian temples from this period are reminiscent of Ezekiel's visionary temple.[11] A comparison of the temples in Babylon with Ezekiel's visionary temple reveals a common concern: the need to preserve the sanctity of the site.

Studies of the remains of the Ezida temple of Borsippa, among other sources, have provided considerable information on the rituals performed in the temples of Babylon.[12] This temple was in active use between the years 750–484 BCE, when it was the second most important temple in Babylon.[13] The ruins of this temple were discovered in the nineteenth century at Birs Nimrud, a site located about one hundred kilometers south of modern Bagdad and twenty kilometers south of ancient Babylon. The temple was built at the end of the second millennium BCE and consecrated to the god Nabu, the servant-chronicler of Marduk, the head of the Babylonian pantheon. The temple was renovated during the time of Nebuchadnezzar II, the king who destroyed the kingdom of Judah. Then at the height of its splendor, the temple continued to flourish at least until the beginning of the Persian period (the mid-sixth century BCE)—in other words, exactly the time of Ezekiel's prophecy: "In the twenty-fifth year of our exile, the fourteenth year after the city had fallen, at the beginning of the year, the tenth day of the month—on that very day" (Ezek. 40:1).

According to the dates specifically mentioned in the book of Ezekiel, the prophet lived at least twenty-five years in Babylon, from 597 BCE, when he was exiled to Babylon with Jehoiachin and thousands of other captives, until 573, the date mentioned in the opening verse of the prophetic section in chapters 40–48. It is reasonable to assume that Ezekiel was to a large extent aware of Babylonian temple practices in general, and the Ezida temple practices in particular, both because of his long sojourn in Babylon and because of the fact that temple activities spilled out onto the roads and the city centers, especially during the Babylonian holidays. In terms of the prophet's geographic proximity to the Ezida temple, it is not known exactly where Ezekiel saw the "vision of the future temple" in the final years of his prophetic career. His location is mentioned explicitly only at the beginning of his prophetic journey: "by the Chebar Canal" (Ezek. 1:1,3). Apparently, this was the Chebar Canal that bordered the city of Nippur on the Euphrates, southeast of Babylon, adjacent to the Ezida temple in Borsippa (the distance from Nippur to Borsippa is about one hundred fifty kilometers).

Many factors limit the validity of a comparison between the temples. Most significant is the disparity between, on the one hand, Ezekiel's presentation of a utopian vision, and, on the other, the picture of the actual historical reality of a functioning temple that emerges from the Babylonian documents. Nonetheless, we must not ignore the fact that Ezekiel's visionary temple differs in many ways from the Bible's descriptions of the Tabernacle and the Temple of Solomon, as well as from the biblical descriptions of the Second Temple after the return to Zion. While neither contemporary Babylonian temples nor the Second Temple, then, can serve as direct models for the temple described in Ezekiel, the following examples do reveal an indirect connection between Ezekiel's prophecy and the physical context in which he prophesied, including surrounding Babylonian temples. The comparison of the biblical text with archaeological information about local temples in this period sharpens, highlights, and explains the unique characteristics of Ezekiel's visionary temple, as distinct from the Tabernacle and the Temple of Solomon, and clarifies how Ezekiel's prophecy was received by his local contemporaries.

Extant ancient descriptions of Babylonian temples provide details about their architectural structure and in several cases even provide their exact dimensions.[14] It is possible that some were written, as in Ezekiel, as plans for future temples, rather than as descriptions of existing temples. These texts also include lists of priests and other functionaries who served in the Babylonian temples; it can safely be assumed that the Jews of Babylon were not familiar with the extensive lists that we have today. Nonetheless, these documents illuminate how contemporary temples worked, including detailed accounts of how priestly families divided their resources over the generations and the various ritual functions performed in the hundreds of different temple chambers.[15] This information helps provide a context that brings to life the descriptions in Ezekiel's visionary temple.

The Temple Structure

Ezekiel's vision begins with the measurement of the wall surrounding the entire temple complex (Ezek. 40:5) and ends with a description of the same wall (42:20). This wall distinguishes the temple of Ezekiel from other temples described in the Bible. From this perspective, Ezekiel's temple is most similar to the Tabernacle, whose enclosure was surrounded by a wall with a simple gate (Exod. 27:9–16; 38:9–20). The wall in Ezekiel's vision, though, is wide and massive. Three gates lead to the area of the temple. The route through them is not completely clear, but it involves ascending flights of stairs and passing between recesses and a vestibule (40:6–38). The entrance area also included an additional space, unique to Ezekiel's temple, called the "vestibule of the gate" (40:39–40, 44:3, 46:2,8).[16] In contrast, the detailed description of the Temple of Solomon includes but one verse (!) describing the inner enclosure (1 Kings: 6:36). This passage refers neither to a wall or gates, nor to a description of the means of entry and exit to and from the Temple. It thereby also lacks any reference to the chambers and pavement mentioned by Ezekiel (40:17–18), as well as additional details about the structures situated there (46:21–24).

Ezekiel is also unique in its depiction of the courts and their size. The circumference of the entire consecrated area is described in the following verses:

> [A]nd he measured off the entire area. He measured the east side with the measuring rod, **500 [cubits]—in rods**, by the measuring rod. He turned [and] measured the north side: **500 [cubits]—in rods**, by the measuring rod. He turned [and] measured the south side: **500 [cubits]—in rods**, by

the measuring rod. Then he turned to the west side [and] measured it: **500 cubits—in rods**, by the measuring rod. Thus he measured it on the four sides; it had a wall completely surrounding it, **500 [cubits]** long on each side, to separate the consecrated from the unconsecrated. (42:15–20)

A unit of measure called rods (*kenim*) appears four times in these verses. This is a particularly large area, calculated, according to six cubits (*amot*) and one handbreadth (*tefaḥ*) per rod (40:5), as 3000 by 3000 cubits (approximately 1500 by 1500 meters).[17] In addition, Ezekiel's temple has two courts, an outer court (40:17), including large chambers intended for sacrifices, and a second, smaller inner (or lower) court (40:19) where the altar stands (40:47), reached by way of a network of gates and stairs (40:23–44). Structurally, the temple is divided into three parts: the portico (40:48–49), the great hall (41:1–2), and the Holy of Holies (41: 3–4).

Surprisingly, Ezekiel barely mentions the functions of these areas (in contrast to the descriptions of the Tabernacle and the Temple of Solomon), instead describing in elaborate detail the measurements of the gates and passages. One possible understanding is that this detailed description, unique to Ezekiel, of the wall and the courts speaks to their importance: **sixty-three verses are devoted to the gates, courts, and the wall surrounding the temple, while only twenty-six verses are devoted to a description of the structure of the temple itself.**

It seems that the temple plan most similar to the one described in Ezekiel is, in fact, to be found in the Mesopotamian world and in the prophet's immediate context—namely, in the descriptions we have of the Ezida temple. In addition, the detailed descriptions of temple gates found in Babylonian architectural texts include many features in common with the descriptions of the gates in Ezekiel's visionary temple. The Ezida temple in Borsippa included large courts adjacent to inner and outer rooms and a terraced entrance leading from a less holy area to the most holy area, which was also the most carefully protected. A detailed description exists of how the priests entered the temple in Borsippa: via the main gate into the court, passing through several rooms, through another gate (the gate of Nabu), to the private area of Nabu, and only from there to the innermost, holiest place.[18]

It is impossible to precisely compare the size of Babylonian temples to the temple in Ezekiel because, among other reasons, the exact purpose of the gates is unknown. In addition, scholars have not succeeded in reconciling texts describing the Borsippa temple with archeological discoveries from the site. However, it is possible to point to a similarity between the basic plan of

Ezekiel's temple and the Borsippa texts: in both, outer rooms serve as entrances to the inner room. The archeological discoveries at the Borsippa site confirm the large size of the courts. The location and purpose of the "chambers" in the courts of the temple of Ezekiel are similar to those of the temple of Ezida. There are also significant similarities between the description of the wall surrounding the entire consecrated area in Ezekiel and walls found in many temples in Babylon in this period and mentioned explicitly in Babylonian temple texts. The texts likewise demonstrate the importance of the gates and courts.[19] In Babylonian temples in general, and specifically in Ezida, the many gates and passages served to restrict access to the temple to authorized temple personnel, who are referred to extensively in the sources. It is to these individuals that we will now turn our attention.

Temple Personnel

It is well known that there are many discrepancies between the descriptions of priestly ritual in the Torah and in Ezekiel.[20] Leviticus, for instance, describes how the priests could enter the shrine and the High Priest was even commanded to enter the Holy of Holies, while the Levites and the rest of the people were only permitted as far as the court of the Tabernacle (Lev. 16). When an offering was sacrificed in the court, the animal was slaughtered by the Israelite bringing the sacrifice (with the exception of the bird offering, in which the priest severed the head), while the priests dashed the blood on the altar and placed the parts of the sacrifice there (Lev. 1–3).

Although we do not have a detailed account of priestly ritual from the time of the First Temple, which could provide the missing link between the Bible's description of sacrifice in the Tabernacle and what we find in Ezekiel, it is nonetheless clear that a significant change occurs in the latter text: all three social classes, priests, Levites, and Israelites, are described as being farther removed from the consecrated areas than in the Torah. The priests are not allowed to enter the Holy of Holies and possibly not even allowed to enter the shrine; they perform their tasks primarily in the inner court. The Levites are permitted to be in the inner court, though they cannot approach the altar at its center. Israelites are not allowed to enter the inner court at all, but only the outer court. The Israelites do not slaughter the sacrifices themselves; this task is left to the Levites (Ezek. 44:11). The group furthest removed of all are the foreigners, whose presence defiles the temple (7:21–22); they are prohibited from even entering the temple compound (Ezek. 44:6–9).[21]

The changes in the structure of the temple and the tasks of the priests and Levites outlined above have two purposes. First of all, Ezekiel denies the common people access to the inner areas of the consecrated ground, thereby maintaining its sanctity. Secondly, these changes transform the courts into the center of activity in the temple because only a few, select priests are permitted to enter the consecrated areas. According to Ezekiel's vision, when the people come to the temple on festivals, they are forbidden from entering the inner court and can only stand at the entrance to the outer court (Ezek. 44:19). Only the Zadokite priests are allowed entry to the inner court (44:15–17).

Similarly, the Babylonian temple texts state that only the worthy were permitted entry to the temple court. These texts, too, mention explicitly who is not allowed entry. The gradation of areas permitted for priests in Babylon is also very similar to the situation described in Ezekiel, according to which a priest's rank determined his degree of access.[22] The description of the personnel in the Ezida temple reveals a similar hierarchy of priests ranked according to their functions in the temple. The texts also describe how various steps were taken at Ezida to ensure that the god's place in the temple was separate and distinct.

At Ezida, the status of the priesthood in general was based on factors similar to those we find in Ezekiel and priestly literature: family origin, the priest's role in the temple, and his suitability to this role. The priests belonged to families whose priestly ancestry was traced back many generations and divided into different ranks. The members of the highest echelon held pivotal positions. By virtue of their stature, they were allowed to enter the central area of the temple where they were responsible for the performance of essential ritual functions. Those of secondary importance were only permitted to enter the court. Documents from the sixth century BCE reveal that the priests serving the idol had to meet the highest standards of lineage.[23] Babylonian priests' ancestry was scrupulously examined, with particular emphasis placed on determining that the candidate for priesthood was the legitimate biological offspring of a temple functionary. Likewise, in the prophecy of Ezekiel, the lineage of the priests of the line of Zadok distinguishes them from the other temple functionaries who are cast aside. Rules about priestly physical wholeness and marital prohibitions, however, are found already in Leviticus and are not Ezekiel's innovations.[24]

The distinction between priestly ranks is very similar to the distinction between the priests and Levites familiar to us from Ezekiel 44:11–14: "They shall be servitors in My Sanctuary, appointed over the Temple gates, and performing the chores of My Temple; they shall slaughter the burnt offerings and the sacrifices for the people. They shall attend on them and serve them. They shall not approach Me to serve Me as priests, to come near any of My sacred offerings, the most holy things. I will make them watchmen of the Temple, to perform all its chores, everything that needs to be done in it." Regarding the role of the priests, Ezekiel 44:15–16 states: "But the levitical priests descended from Zadok . . . they shall approach Me to minister to Me; they shall stand before Me to offer Me fat and blood. . . . They alone may enter My Sanctuary and they alone shall approach My table to minister to Me; and they shall keep My charge."

Overall, it is possible to enumerate other similarities as well as differences between Ezekiel's visionary temple and descriptions of the Temple in the Bible. It would appear that the purpose of all these changes is to more scrupulously safeguard the ritual sanctity of the future temple, and to ensure that the Divine Presence remains there for eternity. The principal changes in Ezekiel include the addition of a court, the enlargement of the courts surrounding the temple, the maintenance of strict surveillance over its gates, regulations concerning the suitability of priests for work in the temple, as well as restrictions on both the access of the prince (*nasi*) to specific areas of the temple compound, and on the level of involvement of the people in the sacrificial rite. All of the above were designed to prevent those considered ritually unclean from approaching the temple.

The various means employed to safeguard the sanctity of the temple can be more clearly understood through a comparison to the contemporary situation in Babylonian temples. The comparison to the Ezida temple helps us grasp how Ezekiel was understood in his day by his audience, who were living in a Babylonian context and surrounded by Babylonian temples.

Ezekiel's Visionary Temple in rabbinic Literature

The final question in our discussion is the degree of influence or correlation between Ezekiel's vision and the Second Temple, in its various stages, as well as with the description of the Temple found in the Mishnah in tractate *Middot*. The connections between Ezekiel's visionary temple, the Second Temple, and the tannaitic period, as well as the degree of Ezekiel's influence on the structure of the Second Temple, and subsequently on the description of the Temple in tractate *Middot* and Maimonides' *Mishneh Torah*, are beyond the scope of our discussion. I will therefore confine this section to the principal aspects of the question.

From the description of the Second Temple in tractate *Middot*, especially the verses from Ezekiel quoted there, it would appear that the sages were aware of the connections between Ezekiel's visionary temple and the Temple they described in the Mishnah. Although the Mishnah does not discuss the structure of the Temple as a whole, it describes in detail the measurements of its buildings, gates, chambers, and recesses. Opinions vary as to whether the discussion in the Mishnah accurately describes Herod's Temple, or whether it serves primarily ideological objectives. This is a difficult question to answer. Even an examination of the verses from Ezekiel cited in the Mishnah does not help us to form a conclusion. It appears that the Mishnah quotes verses from Ezekiel's temple vision only when specific details mentioned in those verses are required to complete or to substantiate their description of a particular aspect of the Temple. It sometimes appears that the authors of the Mishnah believed that the temple plan described in Ezekiel had already been realized in the Second Temple. For example, the Mishnah quotes Ezekiel's descriptions of the doorways, wickets, and the altar (*Middot* 4:1–2, 3:1) as referring to the past tense.

On the other hand, the Mishnah also quotes Ezekiel in reference to the visionary temple. Written at the time of the destruction of the Second Temple, these passages may reflect a yearning for the building of the temple of Ezekiel. For example, the following statement is found regarding the uncovered courts of the temple: "The court of the women **was ... and so they will be**, as it is said, 'Then he led me into the outer court' (Ezek. 46:21)" (*Middot* 2:5). In addition, in the case of the water gate, it appears that the Mishnah is describing a feature that could exist as described in Ezekiel only in the future temple because it was not included in the Second Temple. In reference to the name of this gate, the Mishnah comments: "The water gate, why was it called the 'water gate'? ... Rabbi Ekiezer ben Yaakov says, 'In it the gurgling water will in the future gush out from under the threshold of the temple'" (*Middot* 2:6; based on Ezek. 47:1). This point has been addressed by Ben-Zion Rosenfeld:

> The sage Rabbi Eliezer ben Jacob, possibly of the generation of the destruction of the Temple ... bases himself on the words of the prophet Ezekiel that are quoted, in which he says, close to the end of his prophecy, that there will be a miracle in the future temple and living waters will gush out from under the threshold of the temple and will flow past part of the temple and will rise up until they become a mighty stream and will

flow down to the Dead Sea whose waters will be sweetened and whose surroundings will bloom again. The sage identifies the threshold with the water gate, and, in his opinion, the gate is so named on the basis of future events, because the miracle will occur beneath it and water will gush out and flow under part of the temple (Ezek. 47:1–12). Rabbi Eliezer ben Jacob's identification of the water gate with the threshold mentioned in Ezekiel adds weight to the architectonic connection between the two structures as well as to the belief that there will be a future temple as described in Ezekiel and the Second Temple, which was destroyed, was built according to its plans.[25]

One possible understanding is that the descriptions in the Mishnah in tractate *Middot* refer not only to the structure built by Herod but also to the future temple.

From the reference to Rabbi Eliezer ben Jacob, who lived at the end of the Second Temple period and saw the Temple in both its glory and in its destruction (*Middot* 1:2), it can be inferred that these *mishnayot* also reflect the Temple as it appeared at the end of the Second Temple period.[26] It is possible that the references to Ezekiel in this tractate, written in the time of the destruction of the Second Temple, reflect a yearning for the building of Ezekiel's long-awaited temple. Perhaps the references to Ezekiel in tractate *Middot* should be understood as a longing to see the future Temple, which did not yet exist at the time of the sages, in all its glory.

The sages' difficulty with certain contents in the book of Ezekiel, especially the chapters describing the details and rituals of the temple, is also reflected in rabbinic literature. The Babylonian Talmud in tractate *Shabbat* (13b) quotes a statement in the name of Rav that credits Hananiah ben Hezekiah, to whom the text also attributes the authorship of *Megillat Taanit* (The Scroll of the Fasts), with rescuing the book of Ezekiel from suppression. Given the book's many contradictions, its rehabilitation necessitated a lengthy and strenuous exegetical feat by Hananiah ben Hezekiah.

Maimonides, too, at the beginning of *Hilkhot Beit ha-Beḥirah* (The Laws of the Temple) on the laws regarding the building of the future temple, assumes that it will be built according to the plan found in Ezekiel. However, he acknowledges difficulty in realizing this plan: "The Temple building erected by Solomon is clearly described in the Book of Kings. Furthermore, **the Temple that will be built, even though it is discussed in the Book of Ezekiel, is not fully described and defined therein.** Therefore, those who built the

Second Temple in the days of Ezra followed the pattern of Solomon's Temple and **adapted some of the particulars described in Ezekiel**" (*Hilkhot Beit ha-Beḥirah* 1:4).[27]

In other words, according to Maimonides, the builders of the Second Temple were unable to follow Ezekiel's model exactly, and built "in approximation" those features that are clearly described.[28] Although Maimonides does not elaborate on the details of the actual construction, it is possible to see an illustration of this idea in his description of the shapes of the altar and gates.[29] Maimonides writes that the dimensions of the altar were preserved in the tradition until it was built in the days of the Second Temple by returning exiles under the guidance of the prophet who returned to the Land of Israel with them: "They made it according to the plan for bulding altar **of the future.** It was therefore forbidden to add to, or subtract from, its prescribed dimensions." (*Hilkhot Beit ha-Beḥirah* 2:3).[30] One of the gates is also identified with the gate described in Ezekiel: "this gate is to be kept shut and is not to be opened" (*Hilkhot Beit ha-Beḥirah* 4:6, citing Ezek. 44:2).[31]

In conclusion, the difficulty in correlating Ezekiel's visionary temple with the Second Temple, as well as with the Tabernacle and the First Temple, is apparent in early rabbinic literature. It is also worth asking whether the Second Temple had features that pointed to direct or indirect Persian influence, transmitted by way of Ezekiel.[32] It is also possible that after the Second Temple was not built according to Ezekiel's vision, an alternative approach was adopted in which the temple of Ezekiel came to be considered the temple that would be built in the future.

The challenging question remains how to understand the connection between the ritual practices in the temples of Babylon and the prophecies of Ezekiel, in particular the vision of the future temple. To put the matter another way, what role should new research on the ancient Near East play in understanding this prophecy? This is but one facet of a larger question concerning the originality and uniqueness of biblical laws and beliefs; many generations of scholars have struggled with this question, most prominently Yehezkel Kaufman in *The Religion of Israel*. In the case before us it seems we can assume that Ezekiel's visionary temple is, to some extent, similar to the temples that he saw around him. Perhaps Maimonides referred to this point in the following passage from *The Guide of the Perplexed*:

> And as at that time the way of life generally accepted and customary in the whole world and the universal service upon which we were brought

up consisted in offering various species of living beings in the temples in which images were set up, in worshipping the latter, and in burning incense before them—the pious ones and the ascetics being at that time, as we have explained, the people who were devoted to the service of the temples consecrated to the stars—: His wisdom, may he be exalted, and his gracious ruse, which is manifest in regard to all His creatures, did not require that he give us a Law prescribing the rejection, abandonment, and abolition of all these kinds of worship. For one could not then conceive the acceptance of [such a Law], considering the nature of man, which always likes to that to which it is accustomed. At that time this would have been similar to the appearance of a prophet in these times who, calling upon the people to worship God, would say: "God has given you a Law forbidding you to pray to Him, to fast, to call upon Him for help in misfortune. Your worship should consist solely in meditation without any works at all."

Therefore, He, may he be exalted, suffered the above-mentioned kinds of worship to remain, but transferred them from created or imaginary and unreal things to His own name, may He be exalted, commanding us to practice them with regard to Him, may He be exalted. Thus he commanded us to build a temple for Him . . . to have an altar for His name . . . to have the sacrifice offered up to Him . . . to bow down in worship before Him; and to burn incense before Him. And He forbade the performance of any of these actions with a view to someone else . . . . And he singled out *Priests* for the service of the *Sanctuary*. . . . And because of their employment in the temple and the sacrifices in it, it was necessary to fix for them dues that would be sufficient for them; namely the dues of the *Levites* and the *Priests*.

Through this divine ruse it came about that the memory of idolatry was effaced and that the grandest and true foundation of our belief—namely, the existence and oneness of the deity—was firmly established, while at the same time the souls had no feeling of repugnance and were not repelled because of the abolition of modes of worship to which they were accustomed and than which no other mode of worship was known at that time.[33]

Maimonides believed that all temple ritual and sacrifices were nothing but a response to the need to imitate foreign practices. If so, it is no wonder that both the design of the temples and their rituals were influenced by the surrounding foreign culture.

Ezekiel is not unique in this respect. He is not the only prophet whose human characteristics, personal views, and immediate surroundings are reflected in his prophecies. The premise that prophecy was influenced by the time, place, and personality of the prophets—that the prophets of Israel did not operate in a vacuum—has been discussed by generations of traditional commentators. We can cite, to begin with, the well-known words of the sages: "The same type of communication is received by many prophets, yet no two prophets express themselves in the same manner."[34] Similarly, commentators in different eras, including Joseph Albo, Isaac Abravanel, and Malbim, discussed the question of the human dimension of divine prophecy.[35] It would seem that their words contain principles from which we can deduce that the language of prophecy is conditioned by the personal circumstances and abilities of the prophet: his history, his life experience, the surrounding intellectual climate, and his education.[36]

I cannot determine with any certainty when we are encountering the prophet as a private person, expressing his personal qualities, thoughts, and pain, and when we are encountering him as a messenger revealing the words of God. These questions are beyond the scope of the examples that I have examined here and touch on the entire book of Ezekiel. With regard to the chapters in which Ezekiel prophesies about the destruction of the Temple, we can ask whether the absence of love, compassion, and pain in these prophecies of admonition reflects Ezekiel's human qualities, or whether they demonstrate another aspect of the relationship between God and his people, substantially different from that expressed in the contemporary prophecy of Jeremiah.[37]

Ezekiel received the content of his prophetic revelations in a vision from God. His prophecy, which spans the period before and after the destruction of the Temple, describes a different temple, one suited to the circumstances of the people around him. The contents of his prophecies reveal that Ezekiel was concerned with the causes that led to the desecration of God's name, the removal of God's glory from the Temple, and its destruction—and the lessons to be learnt from them. However, his style, and how he phrased the divine messages he received, was influenced by a combination of factors, including not only associations and images familiar to him from the Temple of Solomon, but also the surrounding culture and its images, including its temples. These various facets of his experience coalesced and impacted the content of his prophecy as we know it today. If so, this prophecy is not only an expression of the sublime, the remote, and the divine. It is also an expression of an encounter between God and humankind. That is why it was expressed in forms, contents, and concepts that could be clearly understood in that time and place.

Endnotes

1. Babylon was the name of a longstanding ancient city-state. In the middle of the seventh century BCE, Babylon began to rule over extensive territories that eventually formed an empire. The period of Babylon's imperial rule, from 626 to 539 BCE (the date of the rise of the Achaemenid Persian empire) is known as the Neo-Babylonian era.
2. On the study of the Bible in light of discoveries from the Near East, see Barry L. Eichler, "Study of Bible in Light of Our Knowledge of the Ancient Near East," in *Modern Scholarship in the Study of Torah: Contributions and Limitations*, ed. Shalom Carmy (Northvale, NJ: J. Aronson, 1996), 81–100.
3. Meir Loeb ben Jehiel Michael Wisser (Malbim), *Nevi'im u Ketuvim: Im Perush Rashi u ferush nifla, nikra be-shem Mikra'e Kodesh* (Warsaw: Yitzhak Goldman, 1867), vol. 6, introduction.
4. It should be noted, however, that it is difficult to derive a blueprint of the future temple from the verses in Ezekiel, and even the classic commentators recognized this point. See, e.g., Rashi's comment on "deliberation" (42:3–4), in *Mikra'ot Gedolot ha-Keter, Yeḥezkel* [Mikra'ot Gedolot Haketer: a revised and augmented scientific edition based on the Aleppo Codex and early medieval MSS], ed. Menachem Cohen (Ramat Gan: Bar Ilan University, 2013), 321. This is in addition to the differences between the descriptions of the temple plans outlined in the commentaries of Rashi and Rabbi Eliezer Beaugency. Ibid., 322–328.
5. Agreements of this kind were common throughout the Assyrian empire (less so in the Neo-Babylonian period). See S. Parpola and K. Watanabe, eds., *Neo-Assyian Treaties and Loyalty Oaths* (Helsinki: Helsinki University Press, 1988).
6. This refers to the practice of filling a quiver with arrows, on each of which was written a different solution to the problem. The diviner would shake the arrows, and the first arrow to fall out of the quiver was believed to contain the answer of the gods. Walter Farber, "Witchcraft, Magic, and Divination in Ancient Mesopotamia," in *Civilizations of the Ancient Near East*, ed. Jack Sasson (New York: C. Scribner's Sons, 1983), 1895–1910.
7. The reference is to divination by means of statues (similar to Gen. 31:34; 2 Kings 23:24; and Zech. 10:2).
8. This is reminiscent of the archeological and textual evidence that refers to the ancient practice of "looking at the liver," in other words, divining one's fate and the future according to the state of a liver taken from an animal sacrificed as an offering (*haruspicy*). In order to teach priests the art of liver divination, the shapes of livers were copied onto clay models; sometimes handwritten explanations were etched onto them. Such clay models have been discovered in many archeological sites throughout the Near East. This practice is also mentioned in *Kohelet Rabbah* 12:8: "Rabbi Levy said 'Like those Arabs who slaughter a sheep and examine its liver.'" Realistic descriptions of haruspicy can be found in Shadal's comment on this verse, where he explains that it was an Arab practice. See Shmuel David Luzzatto (Shadal), *Pirush Shadal al Yirmiyahu, Yiḥezkel, Mishle, va-Iyov* (Lemberg: A. Isaak Menkes, 1876).
9. See A. Winitzer, "Assyriology and Jewish Studies in Tel Aviv: Ezekiel Among the Babylonian Literati," in *Encounters by the Rivers of Babylon; Scholarly Conversations between Jews, Iranians, and Babylonians in Antiquity*, ed. Uri Gabbay and Shai Secunda (Tübingen: Mohr Siebeck, 2014). These connections are not unique to Ezekiel. For an example of the connection

between the Assyrian environment and Isaiah chapter 6, see S. Z. Aster, "Images of the Palace of Ashurnasirpal II at Calah in the Throne-Room Vision of Isaiah 6," in *Marbeh Hokmah: Studies Bible and the Ancient Near East in Memory of Victor Avigdor Hurowitz*, ed. Yonah Shamir, Meyer Gruber, Shalom Paul et al. (Winona Lake, Ind.: Eisenbrauns, 2015), 13–42.

10. See S. Z. Aster, *The Unbeatable Light: Melammu and Its Biblical Parallels* (Münster: Ugarit-Verlag, 2012), 301–315.
11. See further Tova Ganzel and Shalom E. Holtz, "Ezekiel's Temple in Babylonian Context," *Vetus Testamentum* 64 (2014): 211–226.
12. The sages were familiar with a "Borsif" in Babylon. In the Babylonian Talmud, tractate *Shabbat*, Rav Ashi comments that Babylon is now called Borsif and Borsif is called Babylon (36a). In tractate *Sanhedrin*, Babylon and Borsif are described as two neighboring towns (109a). In *Bereshit Rabbah*, the student of Rabbi Yoḥanan comments that he was exiled to the Land of Israel from Borsif. (58:38,11). It would appear that all of these references concern the Babylonian town under discussion, and it is possible that its ruins were known to the sages, who believed that the Tower of Babel was built there.
13. Caroline Waerzeggers, *The Ezida Temple of Borsippa: Priesthood, Cult, Archives* (Leiden: Nederlands Instituut voor het Nabije Oosten, 2010). In her comprehensive research in the last decade, Waerzeggers has delineated the status and position of officials in the temples of Babylon in the first millennium BCE. See also M. Jursa, *Neo-Babylonian Legal and Administrative Documents: Typology, Contents and Archives* (Münster: Ugarit-Verlag, 2005).
14. On plans of temples, see A. R. George, *Babylonian Topographical Texts* (Leuven: Departement Oriëntalistiek, 1992).
15. In addition to these texts, hundreds of documents written on clay tablets in cuneiform script reveal the daily life in the temple. On Mesopotamian temples, see Michael Roaf, "Palaces and Temples in Ancient Mesopotamia," in *Civilizations of the Ancient Near East*, 423–441; and John F. Robertson, "The Social and Economic Organization of Ancient Mesopotamian Temples," in *Civilizations of the Ancient Near East*, 443–454.
16. The temple described in Ezekiel also differs in many respects from the Temple of Solomon. It is incorrect, therefore, to ascribe these differences to the fact that the structure described in Ezekiel is permanent whereas the Tabernacle is temporary.
17. The area of the entire temple, including its courts, was much greater than the area of the First or Second Temples. Indeed, the Mishnah (*Middot* 2:1) describes the area of the Second Temple in this way: "The Temple Mount was five hundred by five hundred cubits." Some have argued that the Mishnah's measurement was influenced by the measurement of five hundred cubits in Ezek. 42:20, which summarizes the preceding verses that described the area of the Temple Mount without giving precise measurements. This opinion is first found in Radak's [David Kimḥi] comment on this verse, which adds that these measurements are in cubits even though the word "rods" is repeated four times in the preceding verses. It would appear more natural to assume that verse twenty also refers to rods (see Rashi and Eliezer Beaugency). However, modern commentators have pointed out that assuming the entire consecrated area measured five hundred rods raises significant difficulties. Among other difficulties, the absence of the word "rods" in the Septuagint in verses 15–20 led them to conclude that Ezekiel referred to cubits. They also compared the circumference of the temple in Ezekiel to the description of the future temple in tractate *Middot*, which includes these same measurements. I will address these points in a future article.
18. Waerzeggers, *The Ezida Temple of Borsippa*, 13.

19. A detailed description of these findings can be found in Ganzel and Holtz, "Ezekiel's Temple in Babylonian Context."
20. The sages pointed out the severity of these discrepancies when they related that earlier sages had wanted to suppress the book of Ezekiel, "because there were in it things that contradict the words of the Torah" (Babylonian Talmud, tractate *Shabbat* 13b and parallel sources). A sage by the name of Hananiah ben Hezekiah ben Garon is remembered with honor because he "sat and interpreted"—in other words, resolved the contradictions by means of interpretation (midrash). See below.
21. A similar gradation can be found in the Mishnah (tractate *Kelim* 1:8), which only permits non-Jews to enter the *ḥayil*, the outermost and least sacred area of the Temple Mount.
22. See Tova Ganzel, "Ma'amadam shel Ba'alei ha-Tafkidim ba-Mikdash ha-Atidi be-Yeḥezkel [The status of functionaries in the future temple in Ezekiel]," *Shnaton le-Ḥeker ha-Mikra ve-ha-Mizraḥ ha-Kadum* 19 (2009): 21–23.
23. These tests based on ancestry were accompanied by punctilious examinations of physical wholeness and moral integrity, meaning the abstention from serious sins.
24. It should be noted that although distinctions of status within the priestly caste are also found later in classical rabbinic literature (Maimonides, *Mishneh Torah, Hilkhot Isurei Bi'ah*, 20), this concept does not exist in the Torah where strict attention was paid only to the preservation of the sanctity of the priestly families. (Lev. 21).
25. Ben-Zion Rosenfeld, "Yaḥas Rabbi Yehuda ha-Nasi ba-Mishnato le-Mikdash u-le-Yerushalayim," [The approach of Rabbi Judah the Prince to the Temple and to Jerusalem], *Ḥidushim le-Ḥeker Yerushalayim* 18 (2013): 267.
26. According to the Jerusalem Talmud, tractate *Yoma* 2:2, and the Babylonian Talmud, tractate *Yoma* 16a, Rabbi Eliezer ben Jacob was the tanna who taught tractate *Middot*.
27. This translation is adapted from book 8, "The Book of Temple Service," in Maimonides, *The Code of Maimonides (Mishneh Torah)*, trans. Mendell Lewittes (New Haven: Yale University Press, 1957), 5–6.
28. It is believed that the Third Temple will be built by human hands. Maimonides in his *Hakdama le-Pirush ha-Mishnah, Maseket Midot* points out that tractate *Middot* was included in the Mishnah so that the builders of the Third Temple will know how to construct it, in accordance with the commandment in Ezekiel 43:10–11. Maimonides, *Hakdama le-Pirush ha-Mishnah, Maseket Midot* [Introduction to the Commentary on the Mishnah, tractate *Middot*], in *Mishnah im Perush Rabenu Moshe ben Maimon* [The Mishnah with the commentary of Maimonides], ed. Yosef Kafaḥ (Jerusalem: Mosad Harav Kook, 1967), 17; see Rashi's comment there. See also the commentary of the *Leḥem Mishneh, Hilkhot Ma'aseh ha-Korbanot*, 2:14, who has difficulty understanding why Maimonides thought that the prophecy of Ezekiel was about the Third Temple.
29. Maimonides refers indirectly to the difficulty of reconciling the details of the sacrifices as they appear in Ezekiel with those that appear in the Torah, and determines that the verses in Ezekiel all refer to a onetime ritual marking the dedication of the Third Temple. (*Hilkhot Ma'aseh ha-Korbanot*, 2:14)
30. Maimonides, *The Code of Maimonides*, 10.
31. Ibid., 19. Yom-Tov Lipmann Heller (known as "Tosafot Yom Tov") wrote: "Even though the future building has changes and is not comparable to the Second Temple, as anyone who examines the Mishnah and the book of Ezekiel will see . . . the building of the Second Temple was only 'an approximation of some features clearly described in Ezekiel' and does not conform to everything that is written in that book." In essence he writes that one must rely upon the description of the Second Temple and adds: "When we merit to build the

future temple the Holy One Blessed be He will open our eyes and the earth will be filled with the knowledge of the lord so that we may understand the hidden meaning of the words of Ezekiel." Yom Tov Lipmann Heller, *Tzurat Beit ha-Mikdash he-Atid ha-Nirah le-Yeḥezkel* (Prague: Avraham ben Moshe, 1602). Malbim made corrections and addenda to this book in his work *Tavnit ha-Bayit*. Both works were published together at the end of Malbim, *Nevi'im u Ketuvim: im Perush Rashi u-ferush nifla, nikra be-shem Mikra'ei Kodesh*.

32. The existence of new architectural elements in the Second Temple, connected to the return of exiles from Babylon, can be inferred indirectly from the words of Maimonides in his commentary to the Mishnah: "When they returned from Susa to build the temple, as is described in Ezra, the king commanded them to draw the design of the city of Susa in the Temple so that the fear of the king would be upon them and they would remember the days when they lived there and would not rebel against the king. They therefore drew it on the most eastern gate of the Temple." This subject also warrants further study. See *Mishneh im Perush Rabbeinu Moshe ben Maimon*, 5:284.
33. Maimonides, *The Guide of the Perplexed*, 3:32.
34. Babylonian Talmud, tractate *Sanhedrin* 89a.
35. A collection of examples can be found in: Moshe Greenberg, "Tefisot Yehudiot shel ha-Gorem ha-Enoshi be-Nevua ha-Mikrait" [Jewish perceptions of the human factor in biblical prophecy], *Sefer ha-Yovel le-Rav Mordechai Breuer* [Mordechai Breuer Jubilee Volume], ed. Moshe Bar-Asher (Jerusalem: Akademon, 1992), 1:63–76.
36. Greenberg, "Tefisot Yehudiot," 76. For an example referring to Ezekiel, see Isaac Abravanel, *Perush al Nevi'im Aḥronim* [Commentary on the Later Prophets] (Jaffa: Torah ve-Da'at, 1956), 434.
37. See the dictum of the sages: "Raba said, 'Everything that Ezekiel saw, Isaiah also saw. To whom can we compare Ezekiel? To a man from the country who saw the king. To whom can we compare Isaiah? To a man from the city who saw the king.'" (Babylonian Talmud, tractate *Ḥaggigah* 13b).

The Torah of Moses and the Laws of the Nations: A Study in the Teachings of Rabbi Tzadok ha-Kohen of Lublin

Avia Hacohen

Introduction

The foundation of Jewish belief is that the holy Torah, the Five Books of Moses given by God to the Jewish people, is the word of God. But what is the Torah? The traditional belief that the Torah, as the word of God, is independent of both time and space is expressed in the well-known midrash: "As it is written, 'I was with Him as a confidant' (Prov. 8:30)—What is a 'confidant'? Rabbi Judah bar Ilai said, 'Confidant in the Torah—God would look in the Torah and create the world, as it says, 'I was with Him as a confidant.'"[1]

This midrash seems to give clear expression to the belief that the Torah, which preceded the creation of the world, is not only independent of time and space, but also eternal, beyond time and space. Maimonides, in *The Guide of the Perplexed*, forged a new path when he argued that many commandments were given in response to laws that already existed in the time of Moses. For example, the laws concerning sacrifices and the commandment to build a temple were given as a concession to contemporary forms of worship.[2] According to Maimonides, the Torah, rather than opposing accepted practices, recognized and even adopted them, while at the same time "converting" them from idolatrous purposes to the service of the God of Israel. It is clear, therefore, that Maimonides does indeed place the Torah in a temporal and spatial framework. His approach was not the dominant one in Judaism, and it may even be said that in the following centuries neither the rabbinic nor the kabbalistic schools of thought followed Maimonides' approach.

This question came to the foreground again at the end of the nineteenth and beginning of the twentieth centuries with the discovery of writings from the ancient Near East. In 1872, the eleventh tablet of the *Epic of Gilgamesh*, which recounts the story of the Babylonian flood, was discovered. The similarity between the Babylonian story and the narrative in Genesis leaves no doubt about the connection between the two accounts. In 1901, the stone stele of Hammurabi was discovered. The law code engraved upon it bears an undeniable resemblance to the laws of the Torah, notwithstanding the dissimilarities between them.[3]

The discovery of these writings shook the Christian world—and the Jewish world as well—and was discussed far beyond academic circles. In 1902, the German Assyriologist Friedrich Delitzsch, in a series of published lectures, declared that at long last humanity had succeeded in uncovering the sources of the Bible; what had once been considered an ancient spiritual wonder was revealed to be none other than a product of plagiarism, the result of literary theft.[4] With the exception of a few scattered comments, leading rabbis completely ignored the subject. One well-known example is the passage in Rav Kook's *Eder ha-Yakar*, which contains a positive, albeit brief, reference to the discovery of the texts.[5] The general response, however, was silence, and this silence requires an explanation. The question still hanging in the air is: How is it possible that the word of God was influenced by contemporary writings?

Many academic studies have been written on the relationship between the laws of the Torah and the legal codes of the Near East. The purpose of this article is not to survey the literature on this subject, but rather to shift the focus of the discussion to the theoretical plane, as reflected in Rabbi Tzadok ha-Kohen of Lublin's sermon on the Torah portion Yitro in his book *Pri Zadik*.[6] The sermon addresses the relationship between the Torah of Moses and the external sources used by Moses to write the Torah. Written in a homiletic style, the sermon can be read as a religious response to the discovery of the writings from the Near East. It is not surprising that this tension is only latent in the sermon, because in other matters as well Rabbi Tzadok adopted an allusive rather than explicit style. For example, his ongoing argument with the claims of academic scholars of Judaism affiliated with the nineteenth-century *Wissenschaft des Judentums* movement regarding the development of the Oral Law was not polemical and did not refer directly to specific scholars or their works.[7] It is reasonable to assume that Rabbi Tzadok was aware of the discovery of writings that had received so much attention in the Jewish world in his time. Even if our assumption is incorrect, and Rabbi Tzadok was entirely unaware of their discovery, his teachings nonetheless address the questions these Near Eastern texts raise; in that case, the coincidence of the discoveries and this faith-based response to the challenges they posed is truly remarkable!

Rabbi Tzadok ha-Kohen (1823–1900) was born in Lithuania to a family of *Mitnagdim* (opponents of Hasidism), and in his youth he was considered a prodigy in the study of the Talmud. He was drawn to Hasidism and became a disciple of the Izbica Rebbe, Mordekhai Joseph Leiner, the author of the work *Mei Shiloach*. At the end of his life he assumed the position of Rebbe Leibele Eiger as the Grand Rabbi of Lublin. Rabbi Tzadok was an influential scholar of Jewish law, proficient in all areas of Torah study, whose sermons reveal a pervasive tension with the intellectual world of Jewish academic scholarship.

The Sermon on Yitro

The sermon on the weekly Torah portion Yitro[8] opens with the question of why the story of Jethro immediately precedes the giving of the Torah.[9] Rabbi Tzadok's answer is that the study of gentile wisdom is a necessary condition for receiving the Torah. That is why Jethro, the priest of Midian, came before the giving of the Torah, to impart his wisdom and insights to the People of Israel. Rabbi Tzadok at this point launches into a lengthy discourse on the study of the wisdom of other nations, with specific reference to what was learned from Pharaoh, Jethro, Job, and Balaam.

Rabbi Tzadok bases his arguments on various sources, but a comparison between his own words and his sources reveals the extent of his originality: "It says in the holy Zohar that it was necessary to conquer the king and priest of the *kelipah* ("husk" or "impurity") and afterwards the Torah was given." The source of these words is the Zohar: "When this king and this priest were subdued and broken, all of the other members of the *sitra aḥra* (the forces of evil) bowed down to God and acknowledged him. Then God ruled alone in heaven and on earth as it is said, 'None but the Lord shall be exalted in that day' (Isa. 2:11)."[10] The king and priest referred to in the Zohar are Pharaoh, the king of Egypt, and Jethro, the priest of Midian. The meaning of the passage from the Zohar is that God can rule exclusively only after the forces of evil have acknowledged God and accepted divine authority. Rabbi Tzadok, on the other hand, argues that it was first necessary to encounter the forces of evil, Pharaoh and Jethro, in order to learn the truth contained within them and within their religions.

Rabbi Tzadok quotes a homily of Rabbi Isaac Luria (Ari), cited several times in *Pri Tzadik*[11]: "The essential purpose of the exile in Egypt was that they would leave with great wealth, in order to bring out the holy sparks and their souls, as it is said 'thus they stripped the Egyptians' (Exod.12:36). They made Egypt resemble a fortress without grain, the deep waters without fish,[12] which is the root of life and survival. Because of this the People of Israel merited the revelation of the Torah." The idea of the elevation of the sparks is a basic tenant of both Lurianic Kabbalah and Hasidism, but Rabbi Tzadok adds an original insight. The words of the Ari indicate that the gathering of the sparks of holiness either refers to the souls of converts who joined the Jewish people,[13] or can be understood as an abstract concept. The Ari's words have been cited often, and, in these later sources as well the verse "thus they stripped the Egyptians" (Exod. 12:36), understood as referring to the gathering of the souls that are worthy to join the Jewish people. For example, the *Orech Ḥayyim*[14] and the *Ohev Yisrael*[15] quote the Ari in the context of discussions of conversion. Rabbi Tzadok, however, changes the emphasis of the citation. He does not refer to the individual souls of converts, but rather to the concept that the Torah was composed following the study of foreign teachings and their adaptation and purification.

Rabbi Tzadok then quotes from the Zohar: "It would appear that the Torah is called the Torah of Moses because he wrote down the words of vulgar people, the words of Laban, Esau, Hagar, and so forth, and through him these became the words of the Torah,[16] and it is called his book, the 'Torah of Moses.'" The source of this idea is the Zohar:

> Even if a simple story is written in the Torah, which is the highest principle, its purpose is certainly not merely to tell that story, but to teach lofty matters and sublime secrets; not to tell about itself but to instruct about general matters. . . . For example, it is written "in the seventh month, on the seventeenth day of the month, the ark came to rest on the mountains of Ararat" (Gen. 8:4). This verse is part of the narration of a simple story. Why do we care if the ark rested on this mountain or in another place? Its purpose is to teach us a general principle . . . and anyone who says that the purpose of a story in the Torah is to teach us only the contextual narrative of the story itself deserves to die. . . . The truth of the supreme, holy Torah

is undeniable . . . for is it conceivable that he did not have sacred words with which to make a Torah?! Yet he gathered material about vulgar people, such as the words of Esau, of Hagar, the conversations of Laban and Jacob, the words of the ass and of Balaam and Balak, and the words of Zimri. He collected them all, as well as the rest of the stories that are written, and made them into the Torah. If so, why is the Torah called "the law of truth" (Mal. 2:6)? . . . And why is it called "more desirable than gold, than much fine gold" (Ps. 19:11)? . . . It is truly a sublime holy Scripture, the Torah of truth; "the teaching of the Lord is perfect" (19:8), and each and every word is intended to teach lofty ideas. The purpose of each story is not merely to relate its own particular details but to teach a general principle, as we have said. . . . (Zohar 3,149).

The Zohar declares in this passage that the meaning of the stories of the Torah does not lie in their exoteric narrative, but in their esoteric content, which is related to the mystic lore of the Torah. The author of the Torah gathered stories and turned them into Torah by virtue of the inner layer embedded within them. While Rabbi Tzadok emphasizes that Moses wrote the words, the Zohar does not refer to Moses, but to God: "for is it conceivable that the supreme and holy King, may he be blessed, did not have holy words to write down make into a Torah?! Yet he gathered the words of vulgar people." We will examine this point in greater depth below.

Rabbi Tzadok paints a comprehensive and lucid picture: The Torah was not, in a manner of speaking, written by one hand. Rather, Moses, the author of the Torah, gathered preexisting documents and, in rewriting them, made them into the Torah: "He wrote the words of vulgar people, the words of Laban, Esau, Hagar, and so forth, and through him these became the words of the Torah." There is a difference between the meaning of the phrase "the words of vulgar people" in the Zohar and the meaning given to it by Rabbi Tzadok. In the Zohar it refers to words about vulgar people that, when written in the Torah, acquired a secret and esoteric dimension. Rabbi Tzadok, however, understands the phrase to mean the words or teachings of vulgar people that Moses gathered, compiled, and wrote down in the Torah in his own words.

The continuation of the passage clearly shows that this is the correct reading. Rabbi Tzadok again emphasizes that the writing of the Torah was the result of the study and collection of earlier teachings: "Pharaoh was the oldest *kelipah*, the secret of the great crocodile, as it is written in the Zohar [2,34], and they removed from him the souls and all the words of Torah that were in exile with him. Three of the advisors and wise men of Pharaoh[17] contained within them other words of Torah and these also needed to be removed from them." In this passage from the Zohar, Pharaoh is called the great crocodile, and although the idea that the crocodile is the source of sanctity and study is not expressed here, Rabbi Tzadok emphasizes that the People of Israel learned words of Torah from Pharaoh.

To the best of my knowledge and understanding, the ideas expressed in this passage are almost entirely original.[18] Even Maimonides, who in *The Guide of the Perplexed* raised the possibility of a connection between the Torah and the beliefs of the time, did not describe the writing of the Torah as a mosaic of passages that had been edited and adapted. In explaining the reasons for the commandments, Maimonides argued that many laws were intended to uproot idolatrous practices and eradicate them from the world. Rabbi Tzadok, in contrast, describes a complex and radical process. He explains that even before the giving of the Torah the world was neither lawless nor void. The Torah was written by borrowing ideas from the world that predated it and purifying them. This by no means implies that the Torah is just another human legal code, a product of its time and place. The process of writing the Torah was an act of revelation and a manifestation of holiness. Moses collected material from which, and by means of which, he wrote the Torah. The process of writing the Torah involved not only translating from one language to another, but also infusing the material with new meaning, sanctifying it, and transforming it into "the Torah."

Rabbi Tzadok clearly implies that the Torah, though divine, was given in a specific time and place, and that its temporal and spatial context influenced its content. This description of the Torah differs from the traditional, simple, faith-based understanding of the Torah as a book written before the creation of the world, in black fire upon white fire, disconnected from time and space.

Rabbi Tzadok then proceeds to discuss the difference between the prophecy of Moses and that of Balaam:

> However, as it says in the commentary on the Torah portion Balaam in the holy Zohar (3:210b), "When you open your mouth, your tongue will not be under your control and the words will not be determined by your lips; rather, 'speak thus' (Num. 23:5, 16)." . . . His words were literally the words of God. Concerning this it is said, "Never again did there arise in Israel a prophet like Moses" (Deut. 34:10). The sages clarified: "In Israel no one arose, but among the nations of the world one did arise and that was Balaam" (*Ba-midbar Rabbah* 14:19), as it

is written in the holy Zohar (3:193; and so, too, in *Sifrei*, the end of the section Ve-zo't ha-berakhah, 16). And the meaning is that Moses' power was that when he spoke, he articulated the words of God literally. The Divine Presence spoke from within his throat, as we have seen, when it was said that "Moses exceeded them when he prophesied in this matter" (*Sifrei*, Mattot, 1). The meaning is that when he spoke, he said the actual words, rather than relating what God said to him. The latter would have been expressed by the words "thus said the Lord," as is the level of the other prophets, who did not merit that the actual words of God would be spoken by the Divine Presence from their throats. In the case of Balaam however, the Divine Presence did speak from within his mouth... but Balaam had no connection whatsoever to the word of God that was uttered from his mouth or even knowledge of it....

For this reason, it is specifically stated that Moses wrote the section about Balaam.[19] It is not included in the statement "Moses wrote his book," because in these chapters Moses our teacher, may he rest in peace, did not have to turn the words of vulgar people into the words of Torah because this section already was the word of God, as is explained in the holy Zohar [regarding the phrases] "speak thus" and "as it is said."

According to Rabbi Tzadok, Balaam was a medium who transmitted to the world the word of God without adaptation or editing, whereas Moses did not merely hear the word of God and relate what the Divine Presence told him, but said the words themselves as the Divine Presence spoke from within his throat. This explanation is not sufficiently clear. How could it be that Moses spoke the words, yet, at the same time, the Divine Presence spoke from within his throat? Rabbi Tzadok asked this very question countless times regarding the Oral Torah. On the one hand, Rabbi Tzadok describes the Oral Torah as the creation of the sages, and, on the other, as the words of the living God. This is a riddle, the solution to which is to be found in emphasizing, rather than obscuring, the role of both human and divine agency in the creation of Torah.[20]

Rabbi Tzadok's description of the prophecy of Moses, and its distinction from other prophecies, is antithetical to some traditional beliefs. The traditional explanation is that Moses prophesied through a "clear glass" or an "illuminated vision"; in other words, Moses' prophecy conveyed the pure and pristine word of God, whereas the other prophets, who did not receive an illuminated vision, interjected into their prophecies human elements that obscured their vision.[21] Rabbi Tzadok explains that as the prophet's role in the prophetic process increases, the quality of the prophecy improves, whereas the closer the prophecy is to the actual word of God, and as the influence of the prophet on its content decreases, the quality of the prophecy also declines. This approach, which grants Moses a role in the writing of the Torah, is certainly not the dominant voice within Judaism and, in fact, is very rarely heard.[22]

The tendency to blur the boundaries between written and oral law, by introducing the human voice associated with the Oral Torah into discussions about the Written Torah, recurs in many of Rabbi Tzadok's sermons.[23] This raises the question of the difference between the Written and the Oral Torah. Although Rabbi Tzadok does not answer this question, or even address it, the distinction between the expression of the divine voice in the Written Torah and the human voice in the Oral Torah is often repeated in Rabbi Tzadok's sermons. Therefore, it cannot be said that Rabbi Tzadok does not distinguish between the Oral Torah and Written Torah; his position on the issue is best described as complex.

Rabbi Tzadok places the Torah in a specific time and place, and ties it to Moses, who wrote it by adapting materials and turning them into the Torah. The concept that the Torah was given in a specific time and place, gleaned from the writings of the period and influenced by them, and the idea that Moses had an active role in writing the Torah are interconnected. Both ideas add a certain human dimension to the Torah.

What influenced Rabbi Tzadok in the formation of these ideas? Just as Rabbi Tzadok placed the Torah in a historical timeframe, he was himself a product of his own time and place. I assume that the news of the discoveries of texts from the ancient Near East, which shook the world in those years, also reached the ears of Rabbi Tzadok. I do not know the extent of his knowledge of the subject. While it is possible that Rabbi Tzadok heard of the Babylonian version of the flood story, he certainly was not aware of *The Code of Hammurabi*, which was published only after his death. It is possible that, though he was only vaguely aware of the discoveries, Rabbi Tzadok's keen insight enabled him to grasp their deeper meaning. Rather than embarking upon a pointless and hypocritical campaign of polemics and apologetics, he built a true foundation of faith. Rabbi Tzadok understood, purely and simply, that if the Torah is connected to a specific time period, an almost inevitable conclusion given its similarity to the discoveries, it must possess a certain human dimension.

The concept of the Oral Torah plays a pivotal role in Rabbi Tzadok's thought. He understood it to mean that the Torah is being developed over time by great Torah scholars in response to the spiritual needs of each generation.[24]

This conception does not begin with an analysis of the Second Temple period, but with the understanding that the Torah was revealed in a specific place and time. The idea is grounded in the belief that the Torah is not perfect but self-perfecting; its purpose is to make the world a better place. The road is long. It began with the Torah, was carried on by the sages, and continues, in different forms, in every generation.

The concept that the Torah is not perfect but self-perfecting is the basis for many sermons in *Pri Tzadik*. For example, Korah's fight for the democratization of holiness and the abolition of the priesthood was justified, but the world is not yet ready for this approach. Only in the days of the Messiah will we be worthy of observing Korah's Torah.[25] This means that the Torah does not present an ideal legal code, but one that is appropriate for the lived world. Similarly, the commandment to build a temple, according to Rabbi Tzadok, was given only after the sin of the Golden Calf; the ideal is not a physical temple, but a temple in the heart of every person, in every time and place.[26] Again, the Torah accommodated itself to the reality in which it was created—not to make peace with the current reality, but to cause the world to progress to an ideal state.

I have assumed that the discovery of the writings from the Near East prompted Rabbi Tzadok to make these statements. Nonetheless, even if he was not aware of the discoveries, his words (which would thus fall into the category of prophecy and divine inspiration) nonetheless contain a systematic philosophical methodology for addressing this issue. In contrast to Rabbi Tzadok, most of the religious world completely ignored the discoveries and continued on its way as if nothing had happened. It would seem that many chose to ignore the discoveries because they feared that confronting them would have unwelcome consequences. This period saw the breakdown of Jewish communal life, during which many people abandoned the world of Torah and faith. The Reform movement, in its various guises, claimed that the Torah and the Talmud were given in specific situations, and that, with the changing times, the old laws had lost their validity. The Reform movement and secularization prompted most of Orthodox Jewry to adopt a position of self-defense and isolation. Rabbi Tzadok, while alert to the danger to traditional Judaism posed by the Reform movement, did not refrain from broaching difficult subjects; he was by no means a secret reformer masquerading as a Hasidic rebbe. The fundamental difference between the academic scholars of Judaism of his generation and Rabbi Tzadok was his belief in the holiness of each letter in both the written and the oral Torah.

The Homilies of Rabbi Tzadok and the Contextual Meaning of the Verses

Hasidic homilies usually do not discuss the contextual (*peshat*) meaning of the biblical text. Nonetheless, despite its profoundly homiletic nature, Rabbi Tzadok's sermon on Torah portion Yitro that we have discussed in this article does, in fact, relate to the straightforward meaning of the biblical text. The question at issue, first discussed in classical rabbinic literature, is historical in nature: When did Jethro arrive? If we assume that the narrative of the Torah reflects a linear chronology, he arrived before the giving of the Torah. If we can assume however that the narrative of the Torah does not reflect a strictly linear chronology, he may have appeared after the giving of the Torah. The empirical, historical question is less relevant to our discussion than the question of the meaning of the events as they are described in the verses themselves. Why does the story of Jethro appear in the book of Exodus immediately before the story of the giving of the Torah? Rabbi Tzadok defined the question in this way: "Why does this story, which everyone agrees took place after Yom Kippur, as Rashi wrote, appear in the narrative before the giving of the Torah?" It would appear that the meaning ascribed by Rabbi Tzadok to the placement of the story of Jethro emerges from both layers of the biblical text—from the narrative itself and from the narrative in its context.

The narrative itself teaches us that we learnt how to establish a judicial system from a non-Jew, a priest of Midian. This means that it is permissible, and even advisable, to borrow beneficial laws and statutes from the outside world.

The story of Jethro appears in a certain context. The positioning of the story of Jethro and the establishment of the judicial system before the giving of the Torah is meant to teach us that *derekh eretz kadma le-torah* (the way of the world precedes the Torah). The purpose of the Torah is to improve upon the good already found in the world, not to destroy the world as it exists and build a new one.

The account of the war with the Amalekites immediately precedes the story of Jethro. Umberto Cassuto has pointed out parallels between the two narratives.[27] The Amalekites and the Midianites-Kenites appear in the Bible as tribes who wander the desert together.[28] When the People of Israel escaped from slavery and entered the terrifying desert, they were attacked by the Amalekites, who thereby incurred perpetual divine wrath ("The Lord will be at war with Amalek throughout the ages" [Exod. 17:16].) In contrast, Jethro and the Midianite and Kenite tribes received the People of Israel in friendship and the People of Israel accepted them in friendship in turn, and adopted from them laws pertaining to the judicial system. This teaches us that it is not important if a person is from Jewish or gentile ancestry, but who he is and how he behaves. Does he follow the path of Jethro or that of Amalek?

The story of Jethro is one of a series of stories preceding the giving of the Torah. These stories appear in the course of the narrative between the parting of the Red Sea and the revelation on Mount Sinai. They are similar in style to the stories in the book of Numbers, and this similarity inspired Rabbi Joseph Bekhor-Shor to argue that these are different descriptions of the same events.[29] I do not share this opinion and, in any case, the text as it appears, not the empirical-historical reality, is the focus of our discussion. A straightforward reading reveals that the Torah contains two series of desert stories, one in Exodus following the parting of the Red Sea and the second in Numbers. The similarity between the two series compels the reader to examine the differences between them. There is much to be said on this topic, but I will limit myself to a discussion of those aspects relevant to our subject.

In the story of Marah in the book of Exodus, the people complain about the water and in addition to water receive commandments:

> So he cried out to the Lord, and the Lord showed him a piece of wood; he threw it into the water and the water became sweet. There He made for them a fixed rule, and there He put them to the test. He said, "If you will heed the Lord your God diligently, doing what is upright in His sight, giving ear to His commandments and keeping all His laws, then I will not bring upon you any of the diseases that I brought upon the Egyptians, for I the Lord am your healer" (Exod. 15:25–26).

The story of the manna and the quail in Exodus also mentions the commandments: "And the Lord said to Moses, 'I will rain down bread for you from the sky, and the people shall go out and gather each day that day's portion—that I may thus test them, to see whether they will follow My instructions or not. But on the sixth day, when they apportion what they have brought in, it shall prove to be double the amount they gather each day'" (Exod. 16:4–5).

In contrast, in the story of *kibroth-hattaavah* in Numbers 11, the people are given quail but there is no reference to commandments. Both stories in Exodus, Marah and the provision of manna and quail, are preparation for receiving the commandments and the Torah at Sinai. This preparation continues with the story of Jethro and the establishment of the courts of law.[30]

The story of Jethro is also partially repeated in Numbers (Num. 10:29–31), but the subject there is not *halakhah*, but rather desert navigation. This comparison indicates that the series of narratives in Exodus constitute a preparation for receiving the Torah.[31]

Moses and his father-in-law Jethro meet twice in Exodus. The first meeting takes place at the beginning of the book (Exod. 2:15–22) and is followed by the incident of the burning bush at Horeb (Exod. 3–4). The second meeting, found in Torah portion Yitro (Exod. 18), is followed by the revelation on Mount Sinai. In both cases, the meeting with Jethro was preparation for the encounter with God on Horeb. Rabbi Tzadok's *derash* (homiletic interpretation) that the preparation for the receiving of the Torah consisted of instruction from a gentile corresponds to the *peshat* (simple, contextual meaning of the text). Rabbi Tzadok's words, which scale the heights of Hasidic thought and Kabbalah, are, at the same time, grounded in the contextual meaning of the biblical verses.

Maimonides and Rabbi Tzadok

I have already mentioned that Maimonides, in the third section of *The Guide of the Perplexed*, in his explanation of the reasons for the commandments, argues that the purpose of many laws was to contradict beliefs and opinions that were current in Moses' time. In some cases, this was accomplished by the abolition of practices associated with idol worship,[32] while in other cases the opposite approach was taken—the practices were accepted, but the Torah used them to teach faith in the one God rather than to serve idols. Maimonides explained that because in those times temples and sacrifices were the accepted forms of worship, the Torah adopted these practices but directed them to the worship of God.[33] Maimonides based his discussion of the practice of idolatry in the time of Moses on the book *The Nabatean Agriculture*, which purports to describe the Sabian cult.[34] The problem is that Maimonides mistakenly believed the book to be ancient, whereas the accepted opinion today is that it was written close to Maimonides' time and certainly does not reflect customs in the time of Moses.[35] Despite Maimonides' crucial error, his intuition was brilliant. All of the new discoveries from the Near East support the theory that the Torah engages confrontationally with the laws and customs of its time.

Maimonides' position poses challenges to the belief in the eternal validity of the commandments. Since these idolatrous practices have been abandoned and forgotten, why observe commandments that were only intended to uproot them? Our purpose here is not to examine all aspects of Maimonides' discussion, but rather to better understand the teaching of Rabbi Tzadok. Rabbi Tzadok outlines a process of gathering sparks from the ashes and the revelation of holiness. The crux of the matter is that even if the Torah was given in a specific time and place, the revelation of holiness has eternal significance.

Rabbi Tzadok, Rav Kook, and the Hasidic World

The overall similarities between the teachings of Rabbi Tzadok and the teachings of Rav Kook have been discussed elsewhere.[36] It would appear that in this matter as well there are similarities both in their responses to the specific question of the connection between the Bible and the Near Eastern legal codes and in their general approach to the subject.

In his book *Eder ha-Yakar*, Rav Kook mentions the commotion following the discovery of the writings from the ancient Near East: "When Assyriology made known its findings, our hearts were troubled because of some dubious similarities between the teachings of the Torah and some cuneiform texts."[37] Rav Kook raises several possible ways of understanding the relationship between the Torah and these cultures and concludes: "In a more enlightened outlook, this is the sure foundation for the acknowledgment of a good cultural element deep in the nature of man. This is conveyed in the statement that the most all-inclusive teaching of the Torah is the verse: 'This is the book of Adam's descendants. When God created man, He created him in God's image' (Gen. 5:1,2), and that this is even greater than the verse: 'You shall love your neighbor as yourself' (Lev. 19:18), which was cited by Rabbi Akiva." Rav Kook refers here to the dispute between Rabbi Akiva and Ben Azzai: "'Love your fellow as yourself' (Lev. 19:18)—Rabbi Akiva says, 'This is an important principle in the Torah.' Ben Azzai says, 'This is the record of Adam's line' (Gen. 5:1) is a more important principle."[38]

Rabbi Kook understood that Rabbi Akiva interpreted the word "fellow" to mean a fellow Jew, whereas Ben Azzai interpreted "Adam" to mean any human being, which teaches us that it is proper to learn laws and customs from all our fellow human beings. It follows, then, that the explanation for the parallels between the Torah and other ancient texts is that the Torah borrowed material from contemporary judicial codes. Both Rabbi Tzadok and Rav Kook accept the possibility that the Torah was influenced by neighboring cultures. It must be emphasized that most of the references to this subject in religious sources stress the originality of the Torah in relation to these cultures, whereas both of these holy men raise the simple possibility that in certain ways the Torah was influenced by contemporary culture.

Hasidism is usually focused on the inner world of the individual. This is of course a generalization, but it nonetheless contains an element of truth. A great rebbe, for example, can look into a sinner's soul and find a spark of goodness, and use it to rehabilitate him. In contrast to other Hasidic thinkers, Rabbi Tzadok and Rav Kook devoted attention not only to the private world of the individual, but also to general phenomena. Rav Kook addressed the issue of the rampant secularization in his generation and attempted to elevate sparks from the ashes. Like Rav Kook (and those before him), Rabbi Tzadok looked at his generation and found within it sparks of holiness. Rabbi Tzadok's approach to the composition of the Torah reflects his confrontation with the beliefs and opinions of his generation; his approach to the Torah itself reflects his perspective of his generation.

* * *

In closing, I would like to share my personal opinion and a prayer. Viewing the Torah in the context of its time and place often leads to regarding it from a secular perspective. I can hear the Torah crying out over its treatment in the hands of prosaic academic scholars who see in it only what is mundane and dreary. The Torah asks them, "Do you not see how beautiful and wonderful I am?!" They hear neither her question nor her sobs, nor do they see her beauty. I pray to God that the students of Torah will not be deluded by superficial charms and will respond to the Torah in joy, and that she, in turn, will delight in them, and that the sounds of rejoicing will be heard throughout the Torah world. May we also follow in the path of the great teachers and pray to God that we be worthy to graze our flocks "by the tents of the shepherds" (Song of Sol. 1:8).

Endnotes

1. Midrash Tanḥuma, ed. Shlomo Buber, Bereshit, chap. 5.
2. Moses Maimonides, *The Guide of the Perplexed*, 3:45.
3. Abraham Lebanon published a Hebrew translation of the legal codes from the ancient Near East. Abraham Lebanon, *Kivtzei Ḥukkim shel ha-Amim be-Mizrakh ha-Kadum* [Collections of laws from Mesopotamia and Asia Minor] (Haifa: University of Haifa, 1967). The poet S. Shifra has published a modern Hebrew translation of the non-legal writings. Shin Shifra and Yaakov Klein, *Ba-Yamim ha-Reḥokim ha-Hem* [In those bygone days] (Tel Aviv: Am Oved, 1996). Rabbi Umberto (Moshe David) Cassuto remains the accepted authority on these matters, especially his commentary to Genesis and to Torah portion Mishpatim in Exodus. See Umberto Cassuto, *A Commentary on the Book of Genesis*, trans. Israel Abrahams

(Jerusalem: Magnes, 1964), and *A Commentary on the Book of Exodus*, trans. Israel Abrahams (Jerusalem: Magnes, 1997).
4. See Y. Shavit and M. Eran's study of the widespread controversy generated by Delitzsch's lectures, *Milḥemet ha-Luḥot: ha-Hagana al ha-Mikra be-Me'a ha-Tsha-Esreh u-Pulmus Bavel veha-Tanakh* [The war of the tablets: The defense of the Bible in the nineteenth century] (Tel Aviv, Am Oved: 2003).
5. See Rabbi Abraham Isaac ha-Kohen Kook, *Eder ha-Yakar* (Jerusalem: Mosad Harav Kook, 1967), 42, and further below.
6. Tzadok Ha-Kohen, *Pri Tzadik* (Lublin: Schneidmesser and Hirschenhorn, 1901).
7. On Rabbi Zadok's understanding of the Oral Law and his attitude to the *Wissenschaft* movement, see my article Avia Hacohen, "Rabbi Tzadok Ha-Kohen ve-Hitpatḥut Torah She-be-al Peh" [Rabbi Tzadok and the development of the Oral Law], *Mishlav* 35 (2000): 15–25. See also Y. Elman, "R. Zadok Hacohen on the History of *Halakhah*," *Tradition* 21 (1985): 1–27.
8. *Pri Tzadik* contains Rabbi Tzadok's sermons on the weekly and holiday Torah portions. The sermon under discussion appears as sermon 4 in the portion Yitro. Tzadok Ha-Kohen, *Pri Tzadik*, 86–87.
9. On this subject see *Mekhilta de Rabbi Shimon bar Yochai, Masekhta de-amalek, dvar ha-mathil "ve-yihi memaḥarat"*; Babylonian Talmud, tractate *Zevaḥim* 116a: "My sons, Rabbi Hiyya and Rabbi Joshua ben Levi—one says Jethro comes before the giving of the Torah. . . ."; See also the commentaries of Rashi, Ibn Ezra, Nachmanides, and others on Exodus 18.
10. Zohar, Exod. 67b (Yitro).
11. See *Pri Tzadik*, Genesis, Ḥayyei Sarah, 6, "*ve-hineh*"; Genesis, Ḥanukah, 2, "*akhen pri*"; Genesis, Va-yiggash, 12, "*u-mispar esreh*"; Exodus, Yitro, 3, "*ve -amar be-Zohar ha-Kadosh*"; Exodus, Yitro, 4, "*ve-yihi memaḥarat*"; Exodus, Shekalim, 1, "*u-Moshe Rabenu*"; Leviticus, Passover, 5, "*ve-shalosh matzot*"; ibid., 39, "*torei zahav*"; Leviticus, Metzora, 6, "*u-mikol makom*"; Leviticus, Kedoshim, "*akhen yesh*"; and many more places.
12. See Babylonian Talmud, tractate *Berakhot*, 9b, inter alia: "'thus they stripped the Egyptians' (Exod.12:36)—Rabbi Ammi said, 'This teaches us that they made it resemble a fortress without grain.' Reish Lakish said, 'They made it resemble the deep waters without fish.'"
13. See Rabbi Ḥayyim Vital in *Sha'ar ha-Pesukim* at the beginning of the book of Exodus: "We need to clarify the matter of the exile in Egypt. . . the reason for the exile of the People of Israel among the nations. We have said that Adam contained all the souls and all the worlds, and when he sinned all the souls fell from him into the *kelipot*, that are divided into seventy nations, and the People of Israel have to find them there, in each and every nation, and gather together the blossoms of the holy souls scattered among the thorns." In *Sha'ar ha-Mitzvot*, Rabbi Ḥayyim Vital writes about the commandment to remember the Exodus from Egypt in the weekly Torah portion Re'eh: "The reason for remembering the exodus from Egypt more than the other exiles . . . the Divine Presence of his power (*skhinat uzo*) goes with the People of Israel into exile among the *kelipot* . . . and gathers the souls from there . . . and they were not redeemed [from Egypt] until all of the souls were selected and removed from there, as it is said 'thus they stripped the Egyptians' (Exod.12:36). They made it resemble the deep waters without fish."
14. See the commentary of the *Orach Ḥayyim* to Gen. 28:5.
15. "God did a righteous thing for the People of Israel when he dispersed them among the nations so that converts would join them. The fundamental purpose of the exile . . . is for our good, because God had mercy on the souls of Israel and the sparks of holiness scattered in the four corners of the earth. . . . All of the sparks of holiness in all the places where they lived should have been drawn to the People of Israel of their own accord, and the latter should not have needed to

make an effort to run after them, just as the branch follows the root. However, because of our many sins, they became corrupted in their behavior and no longer have that power. Nonetheless, God had mercy on them and decided not to cut any of them off, God forbid, and so it was necessary to scatter the People of Israel among the nations in order to gather all of the holy sparks which are scattered, as they were in Egypt; as our sages commented (Babylonian Talmud, tractate *Berakhot* 9b) on the verse 'thus they stripped the Egyptians' (Exod. 12:36), that they made them resemble the deep waters without fish. In other words, they collected all of the sparks of holiness that were swallowed up within [the Egyptians] and removed what they had swallowed from their mouths. That is the meaning of the verse 'for the Egyptians whom you see today you will never see again' (Exod. 14:13), as is understood by those familiar with esoteric lore. Their holy work, that is the exile, was completed because they did not leave behind a single spark of holiness. In other words, the root, the core, must leave its place and wander in exile to collect the branches, that is all its holy sparks, and gather them to the root."

16. See Zohar 3, 149b.
17. The three advisors of Pharaoh are Jethro, Balaam, and Job.
18. The only source I know of that is similar to Rabbi Tzadok's ideas is a homily in the book *Meor Einayim* by Rabbi Naḥum of Chernobyl on the weekly portion Va-yetse': "'Jacob left Beer-sheba'—Before Jacob set out for the house of Laban, there had not been a revelation of knowledge and Torah except in secret, and several roots of the Torah were scattered in the low levels because there had not been a revelation of knowledge in the world. And in the house of Laban there were several cloaked roots of Torah and this is the Torah that is written in the book of the Torah, taken from the stories of the deeds of Jacob in the house of Laban in Haran. The roots that Jacob removed were cloaked, and he selected and collected them from the depths of the kelipot of Laban, the size of which are well known." See further there.
19. Babylonian Talmud, tractate *Bava Batra* 14b.
20. Rabbi Tzadok frequently discusses the relationship between the divine and human dimensions in the Oral Torah. In his opening homily on the book of Deuteronomy, after a long discussion on the human dimension of the Oral Torah, he writes: "The verse 'He has made me dwell in darkness' (Lam. 3:6) refers to the Babylonian Talmud (Babylonian Talmud, tractate *Sanhedrin* 24a), because the Oral Torah is like the ancient dew—'My speech distill as the dew' (Deut. 32:2). Darkness symbolizes the position of man without divine assistance, and in a wondrous manner this creation is related to the word *atika* (ancient), a word that indicates the highest *sefirah*, *keter*. The connection to the *sefirah* of *keter* is through *tal* (dew). . . . Rainfall is clear and visible, whereas falling dew is not clearly apparent. Just as the dew appears wondrously, so God is revealed in the Oral Law in hidden ways."
21. "As it is taught: all the prophets saw through an unilluminated vision. Moses our teacher saw through an illuminated vision" (Babylonian Talmud, tractate *Yevamot* 49b). Maimonides in his introduction to *perek Ḥelek* distinguishes between the prophecy of Moses and the prophecy of all the other prophets, which included imagination and human impediments: "The Seventh Fundamental Principle is the prophecy of Moses our teacher. We are to believe that he was the chief of all other prophets before and after him, all of whom were his inferiors. . . . There remained . . . no deficiency, great or small, to confuse him. All his powers of sense and fantasy were repressed." Maimonides, "Commentary on the Mishnah: Introduction to *Perek Ḥelek*," in *A Maimonides Reader*, ed. Isadore Twersky (Springfield, NJ: Behrman House, 1972), 419. Rabbi Joseph Albo wrote in *Sefer ha-Ikkarim*: "God Himself made clear the difference between Moses' prophecy and that of the others. . . . From this we infer that the other prophets spoke in dark speeches which were not clear, and saw visions which were not real. . . . Moses, on the other hand, in whose prophetic inspiration the imagination

played no part at all, but reason only, as separate from all corporal powers." Joseph Albo, *Sefer ha-Ikkarim*, ed. and trans. Isaac Husik (Philadelphia: JPS, 1946), 3:17.
22. Rabbi Samuel ben Meir (Rashbam), in his introduction to the story of creation in the book of Genesis, expresses a similar idea and emphasizes Moses' role in writing the Torah: "Also this entire passage about the six days of creation was added by Moses our teacher to explain what God said at the time of the revelation of the Torah, 'Remember the Sabbath day and keep it holy. For in six days the Lord made heaven and earth and sea, and all that is in them, and He rested on the seventh day' (Exod. 20:8,11), and 'And there was evening and there was morning, the sixth day' (Gen. 1:31). At the revelation of the Torah, God spoke of the same sixth day that is the end of the six days of creation. Therefore, Moses spoke of it to Israel, to show them that God speaks the truth."
23. See, e.g., the opening sermon of *Pri Tzadik* to the book of Deuteronomy, where he defines the book as the Oral Torah and the Torah of Moses.
24. On Rabbi Tzadok's understanding of the Oral Torah and his opinion of the academic study of Judaism, see above, note 5.
25. See the homilies of Rabbi Tzadok on the Torah portion Korah in *Pri Tzadik*.
26. See Rabbi Tzadok's opening homily on the Torah portion 'Emor in *Pri Tzadik*.
27. One example is that in the narrative about Amalek it is written "But Moses' hands grew heavy" (Exod. 17:12), and in the story of Jethro it is written "For the task is too heavy for you" (Exod. 18:18). See Umberto Cassuto's discussion of the narrative of Amalek in his commentary to Exodus (see above, note 3).
28. This can be seen in Saul's speech to the Kenites before his war with Amalek: "Saul said to the Kenites, 'Come, withdraw at once from among the Amalekites, that I may not destroy you along with them; for you showed kindness to all the Israelites when they left Egypt.' So the Kenites withdrew from among the Amalekites" (1 Sam. 15:6).
29. See Rabbi Joseph Bekhor-Shor's commentary to Numbers 11, where he states that the story of the manna and the quail is an alternate version of the narrative in Exodus 16, while the story of the events at the waters of Meribah (Num. 20) is an alternate version of the narrative of the events at Massah and Meribah in Exodus 17.
30. See Babylonian Talmud, tractate *Sanhedrin* 56b on the commandments given at Marah.
31. Though, in fact, both the stories in Exodus 17, Massah and Meribah and Amalek, do not refer to the commandments.
32. See, e.g., *The Guide of the Perplexed*, 3:37, where Maimonides explains that the commandment of *sha'atnez* was instituted to counter the customs of idolatrous priests.
33. Ibid., 3:45.
34. Ibid., 3:29.
35. See the words of Rabbi Yosef Kafaḥ in his notes to his translation of *The Guide of the Perplexed* (Jerusalem; Mosad Harav Kook, 1977), 3:29, 342n59.
36. See Ḥayyim Yishayahu Hadari, "Shnei Kohanim Gedolim" [Two great Kohanim], in *Me'at Le-Zadik: Kovetz Ma'amarim al Rabi Tzadok ha-Kohen u-Mishnato* [Essays on Rabbi Tzadok Ha-Kohen and his thought], ed. Gershon Kitsis (Jerusalem, 2000), 77–95.
37. Rabbi Abraham Isaac ha-Kohen Kook, *Eder ha-Yakar* (Jerusalem: Mosad Harav Kook, 1967), 42. Translated in Ben Zion Bokser, ed. and trans., *The Essential Writings of Abraham Isaac Kook* (Amity NY: Amity House, 1988), 4.
38. *Sifra Kedoshim*, 2.

Illuminating Inscriptions

Yaakov Medan

In a series of lectures given at Yeshivat Har Hamor, the founder of the yeshiva Rabbi Tsvi Israel Tau harshly criticized religious teachers colleges for integrating academic material into their religious studies courses.[1] His remarks were summarized in a pamphlet published by a student at the yeshiva, Netanel Binyamin Elyashiv.[2] The opinions expressed in the pamphlet raised important questions about the direction of the religious colleges and their associated yeshivot (and, perhaps, primarily my yeshiva, Har Etzion).[3] In this article I will address one of the issues raised in the pamphlet, the use of non-Jewish historical sources from the biblical period to deepen and expand our understanding of the Bible.

In principle, I would like to state that I agree with Rabbi Tau that the integration of secular ideas and sources into the study of religious texts has the potential to decrease students' reverence for the sanctity of the religious sources. This clear and present danger requires us all to engage in deep soul-searching, and to place clear boundaries between the permissible and the forbidden when we begin to mix the holy with the profane. It obligates us all to ask ourselves honestly: Are we doing enough to instill a love for Torah within ourselves and our students? Are we fighting the apathy toward it found at times within the religious public in general, and among young students in particular?

However, it sometimes appears that in his justifiable anger at those who are violating what is sacred, Rabbi Tau leans toward outright negation of all assistance from the secular academic world. This attitude brings to mind the story of the rabbinical student who refused food altogether for fear that he would inadvertently eat something forbidden. Rabbi Tau's words would imply that the religious world, which by its very nature is meant to be built on the foundation of the secular world, will have to stand on its own without the secular world supporting it.[4]

For example, Rabbi Tau rejects the use of Canaanite poetry as an aid to understanding the Psalms.[5] If his intention is that the study of the psalms should not be restricted to this comparative approach, or that a comparative approach should not preclude the examination of the sacred fundamental meaning of the psalms, I support his position without reservation. However, his words could be taken to mean that he rejects the use of Canaanite literature even as an aid to understanding a difficult word or literary motif. It is difficult for me to accept this position.

Moreover, Rabbi Tau himself affirms that, in general, he does not object to secular studies, despite the considerable risk that the study of the physical sciences (especially of such subjects as evolution, the age of the universe, and human origins among others) will weaken religious faith.[6] It would appear that Rabbi Tau understands that the study of the physical sciences is necessary both for the survival of modern civilization and the integration of religious Jews within it. He relies upon the ability of the *beit midrash* to answer the challenges raised by the physical sciences. If so, why should we not make use of developments in the academic study of literature, history, and archeology in the study of our sacred texts?!

Rabbi Tau declares elsewhere: "Far be it from us to examine the Torah and the prophets by secular, historical, and literary criteria."[7] With regard to secular criteria, his words are doubtless correct. However, with regard to historical and literary criteria, his words are correct only if the word "alone" is added to them. In other words, we must not analyze the Torah and Prophets by means of historical and literary criteria *alone*, without attempting to also understand their sacred meaning. Without this correction, his words are obtuse and unintelligible, and appear to contradict the meaning of Rav Kook's letter 146, cited by Rabbi Tau in support of his opinion.

This particular point is the subject of this article: the need to rely on academic analysis of ancient non-Jewish sources in order to understand the sacred meaning of our sources. Given the scope of the current forum, I will confine my discussion to three examples (out of many), and even these will be discussed concisely, without the detailed analysis they deserve.[8] Many ancient sources assist in literary interpretation and, in particular, linguistic interpretation of difficult words and concepts in the Bible. However, this article will focus on examples of historical interpretation.

The Status of Shechem and its Environs at the Time of Joshua's Conquest of Canaan

On the plains of Moab,[9] Moses instructed the People of Israel that immediately after crossing the Jordan River they must set up large stones on Mount Ebal, inscribe upon them the words of the Torah, and build an altar.[10] As it happened, Joshua conquered Jericho, Ai, and Bethel before he was able to build the altar on Mount Ebal.[11]

Surprisingly, the biblical narrative does not mention Joshua's struggle with the enemy in the area of Mount Ebal, the inhabitants of Shechem and its vicinity, from whom, or so it would seem, the land would have to be conquered in order to perform the covenantal ceremony. From reading the biblical narrative on its own, it is not clear how Joshua and the people went from Ai to Shechem without fighting and conquering the fortified cities along the way, as well as Shechem itself. In addition, the list of the thirty-one kings conquered by Joshua (Josh. 12) does not include the king of Shechem or the known cities in its environs, even though this area is the heart of the western part of the Land of Israel.

According to the biblical narrative, after the covenantal ceremony on Mount Ebal, the Gibeonites came to make a pact with Joshua. This episode also raises questions, the most important of which is why the Gibeonites, out of all the local nations, decided to make peace with Joshua?

Archeological excavations in the last few decades near Gibeon and the foothills of Shechem have uncovered Israelite settlements that predate the Exodus from Egypt. They are apparently connected to the early immigration of the tribe of Ephraim, which began, at the latest, two generations after the arrival of the children of Jacob in Egypt. Some of the events of the pre-Exodus immigration of the descendants of Ephraim are described in Chronicles:

> The sons of Ephraim: Shuthelah, his son Bered, his son Tahath, his son Eleadah, his son Tahath, his son Zabad, his son Shuthelah, also Ezer and Elead. The men of Gath, born in the land, killed them because they had gone down to take their cattle. And Ephraim their father mourned many days, and his brothers came to comfort him. He cohabited with his wife, who conceived and bore a son; and she named him Beriah, because it occurred when there was misfortune in his house. His daughter was Sheerah, who built both Lower and Upper Beth-horon, and Uzzen-sheerah (1 Chron. 7:20–24).

Was the proximity of Gibeon to the Israelite settlements of Upper and Lower Beit Ḥoron, built by the children of Ephraim, connected to the request of the Gibeonites to make a pact with Joshua? The biblical narrative does not elucidate this point.

At the end of his life, in Shechem, Joshua renewed the covenant between God and the People of Israel. Before the sealing of the covenant he proposed to the people that they not worship the Lord, because "He is a jealous God" (Josh. 24:19), but instead choose for themselves another "god": "Or, if you are loath to serve the Lord, choose this day which ones you are going to serve—the gods that your forefathers served beyond the Euphrates, or those of the Amorites in whose land you are settled; but I and my household will serve the Lord" (24:16).

This suggestion seems incredible. After the covenants on Mount Sinai, in the plains of Moab, and Mount Ebal, and the conquest of the land, was it still possible for the People of Israel to terminate their agreement with God?! Even if it were possible, why did Joshua mention, as alternative deities, the gods their ancestors worshipped on the other side of the Jordan, rather than the Egyptian gods with whom they were now more familiar?

* * *

I will put aside for now the questions I have raised about the book of Joshua, questions hardly addressed by the classical commentators, and turn to another subject. The book of Judges relates that the "citizens of Shechem" agreed that Abimelech would rule over them, among other reasons because his father Gideon married a woman from Shechem (Judg. 9:2). However, later on a "spirit of discord" developed between Abimelech and the "citizens of Shechem" who betrayed him and planted ambushes in order to rob him (9:23).

The identity of the "citizens of Shechem" is not clear from the verses. Were they Jews or Canaanites? The temple of the people of Shechem is referred to once as the "temple of Baal-berith" (9:4) and another time as the "temple of El-berith" (9:46). Was this a temple of the Lord, who made a covenant with the People of Israel in Shechem, Gerizim, and Ebal, or a temple for the worship of Baal?

The identity of the "citizens of Shechem" is important because it indicates whether the concubine (or maidservant) of Gideon, the mother of Abimelech, was an Israelite or a gentile. Abimelech, who inherited the status and role of his father as a judge of Israel, saw himself, apparently, as a member of the People of Israel. However, the biblical narrative portrays the "citizens of Shechem" going at their harvest time to "the temple of their god" (9:27) and their leader, Gaal son of Ebed, calling to them to serve "the men of Hamor, the father of Shechem" (9:28). These are not characteristic behaviors of the People of Israel.

* * *

Analyses of the verses and the use of the accepted exegetical methods yield cogent answers to some of the questions that I have raised. For other questions, however, only partial answers, if any, can be found. This is a situation in which the philological study of ancient documents can come to the assistance of the Bible student.

Amarna is a poor village built on the ruins of the ancient city of Akhetaten, extending from Luxor along the eastern Nile. In 1887, clay tablets dating from the fourteenth century BCE were accidently discovered there. These were part of the ancillary archives of Pharaoh Akhenaten (Amenhotep IV). In 1891, the "Records Office," where many documents were discovered, was uncovered there. The documents that were retrieved and translated, referred to today as the "Amarna letters," include many letters sent to the king of Egypt from kings and various personages in Canaan.

In one series of letters, Abdi-Heba, the ruler of Jerusalem, complains to Amenhotep that many of the surrounding inhabitants are betraying him and collaborating with the Apiru tribes invading Canaan. There is no scholarly consensus on the question of whether the Apiru (or Habiru) tribes can be identified with the Hebrews, the People of Israel under the leadership of Joshua, who began the period of their conquest and settlement at this time.[12] In the context of this article, it is sufficient to note that there is a strong basis for assuming that the Apiru tribes can in fact be identified with the Israelites.[13]

In the letter catalogued as "Amarna 287," the king of Jerusalem complains about "the deed of the sons of Lab'ayu, [the king of Shechem] who have given the land of the king to the 'Apiru."[14] Similarly, in "Amarna 289" he asks: "Are we to act like Lab'ayu when he was giving the land of Šakmu to the Ḫapiru?"[15] In letter 290 he relates that "the land of the king deserted to the Ḫapiru," and in the same letter also accuses Beit Ḥoron (the city built by the daughter of Beriah the son of Ephraim) of desertion.[16]

From these documents it would seem possible to conclude that from the time that the tribes of Israel appeared in the Land of Israel there was a special relationship between them and the inhabitants of Shechem and its vicinity.

Genesis 35:5 describes Jacob's relations with the inhabitants of the land after Simeon and Levi killed the people of Shechem: "As they set out, a terror from God fell on the cities round about, so that they did not pursue the sons of Jacob." An external midrash, called *Ve-Yisu* (on the basis of its first word), discusses in depth the meaning of this verse.[17] The midrash explains that the fear of the local nations was not unreasonable; it was the result of the huge defeat suffered by the cities surrounding Shechem at the hands of Jacob and his family. According to the midrash, these cities went to war against Jacob and his sons; the latter won and conquered all of the land surrounding Shechem, including most of Samaria from Bethel until south of Mount Gilboa. The midrash goes on to explain that at the end of his life Jacob spoke to Joseph about this expansive area of land: "And now, I assign to you one portion more than to your brothers, which I wrested from the Amorites with my sword and bow" (Gen. 48:22).

With the information I have compiled so far from the Bible, the midrash, and the Amarna letters, it is possible to construct the following scenario:

As a result of the altercation between the family of Jacob and the inhabitants of Shechem over the rape of Dinah, a war broke out involving all of Samaria, Shechem, and its environs. In this war, Jacob and his family defeated the Hivites, the subjects of Hamor the Hivite, the prince of Shechem.[18] They also conquered most of Samaria and settled it with their people—their followers, and the vanquished peoples who agreed to accept the authority of Jacob's family, and perhaps even its religious faith. This sequence of events explains why even after Jacob's family moved to Hebron, his sons grazed their father's flocks in the area of Shechem as far as Dothan.

When Jacob's family went to Egypt, Canaanites and converts who had come from Haran with Jacob, and perhaps even earlier with Abraham, remained in the area of Shechem. Although these people would have maintained aspects of the Patriarchs' religious faith, it can be assumed that these beliefs became corrupted by the influence of the surrounding Canaanite culture over the course of the following two centuries.

When the children of Ephraim left Egypt and came to the Land of Israel,[19] before the "official" Exodus,[20] the natural place for them to choose to settle in was the area that had belonged to their forefathers—Shechem and the surrounding area. They returned to live with the Hivites who in the past had been the dependents of Abraham and of Jacob's family, and had intermingled with them.

After the Exodus from Egypt, the great miracles performed for the People of Israel in Egypt and in the desert were known to all the inhabitants of the land, as we learn from the words of Rahab the harlot (Josh. 2:9–11). The Hivites (and among them the descendants of Ephraim) were prepared to make peace with the Israelites and to accept their authority and their religious beliefs. Gibeon was one of the Hivite cities (Josh. 9:7), and thus its inhabitants seized the opportunity to make peace with Joshua. It can be assumed that the people of Beit Horon, the city of Beriah son of Ephraim, adjacent to Hebron, also cooperated with the Israelites, as did the king of Shechem and all the surrounding cities (whose inhabitants were Hivite, or the descendants of those who came from Haran). The king of Jerusalem was angered by this "treason," as is revealed in his letters to the king of Egypt discussed above. This is compatible with Joshua 10:1–5, which relates that the king of Jerusalem was the head of the coalition of the five kings fighting against Gibeon because it had made peace with the Israelites.

It can be assumed that, even before they crossed the Jordan, the Israelites were aware of the amity of the people of the Shechem area, and, if so, Joshua knew that he would not find it difficult to perform the covenantal ceremony on Mount Ebal even before the area was conquered. For this reason, the Israelites fought no battles in the entire region of Shechem!

At the end of the conquests under his leadership, Joshua gathered the people to make another covenant with God (Josh. 24; see above). As opposed to the covenant at Sinai and at Mount Ebal, this covenant included many non-Jews among the population of greater Shechem who had accepted the faith of the house of Abraham already in the days of the Patriarchs. Now they were asked to reaffirm this faith. Because they were not a part of the People of Israel, Joshua gave them the option of not entering the covenant. He suggested that they continue to worship the gods from beyond the river Jordan (from whence they had come with Abraham), or the gods of the Amorites (near their current place of residence) and thus to be considered Canaanites (with all the implications regarding their continued residence in the land). Joshua did not suggest that they worship Egyptian gods, because he knew that they were not familiar with them. If the inhabitants of the Shechem region were to return to the Amorite gods, the Israelites in the area who so chose, would be able (illicitly, of course!) to join them. In the end the people of the Shechem region refused Joshua's offer, and joined the chorus of the entire People of Israel pledging their allegiance to the Lord.

In the days of Abimelech, after the worship of God weakened over the course of many generations during the period of the Judges, the temple of the Hivites residing in Shechem transformed from "Beit El-berith" to "Beit Baal-berith." The situation reached the point that Gaal the son of Eved and his people no longer saw themselves as converts, but as the people of Hamor the father of Shechem.

The sequence of events that I have proposed requires additional clarifications and proofs. In general, there is no certain evidence connecting the Amarna letters of the king of Jerusalem to Joshua's conquests. Nonetheless, I have proposed a plausible scenario that resolves the difficulties raised by the simple meaning of the biblical text. This scenario is based in part on non-Jewish sources from the biblical period.

The Power of Ahab's Army

The sages describe Ahab as the ruler of the world:

> Rabbi Elazar said in the name of Rabbi Ḥaninah: There are two hundred and fifty-two regions in the world and David ruled all of them, as it is written, "David became famous throughout the lands" (1 Chron. 14:17); Solomon ruled all of them, as it is written, "Solomon's rule extended over all the kingdoms" (1 Kings 5:1); Ahab ruled all of them as it is written, "As the Lord your God lives, there is no nation or kingdom to which my lord has not sent to look for you and when they said, 'He is not here,' he made that kingdom or nation swear that you could not be found" (1 Kings 18:10). Can a man force people to swear an oath in a place that he does not rule?[21]

The verses cited by the sages as proof of the size of Ahab's kingdom are corroborated by another verse that mentions the many captives at Ahab's court: "So he mustered the aides of the provincial governors, 232 strong" (1 Kings 20:15). It was a diplomatic practice for a vassal kingdom to send young men to the court of the sovereign kingdom as a pledge of its loyalty. The more than 200 diplomatic aides held as security pledges testify to the ascendency of Ahab's kingdom in the period described in this chapter.

However, this political power does not correlate with the small size and weakness of Ahab's army during the war described there, the first war with Ben-hadad, the king of Aram: "So he mustered the aides of the provincial governors, 232 strong, and then he mustered all the troops—all the Israelites—seven thousand strong" (20:15). The same situation prevailed in the second war: "Now the Israelites had been mustered and provisioned, and they went out against them; but when the Israelites encamped against them, they looked like two flocks of goats, while the Arameans covered the land" (20:27).

The midrash cited above suggests two possible ways of reconciling the contradiction: "Rabbi Levi and the Rabbis: Rabbi Levi said that they died in a famine in the time of Elijah and the Rabbis said that Ben-hadad came and took them." On first sight, both opinions cited in the midrash require explanation. Rabbi Levi explains that a great multitude died in a famine. However, a simple reading of the text indicates that the prophecy relating to the weakening of Ahab's military power was given later, after rain had fallen at the end of the great famine: "Whoever escapes the sword of Hazael shall be slain by Jehu, and whoever escapes the sword of Jehu shall be slain by Elisha. I will leave in Israel only seven thousand—every knee that has not knelt to Baal and every mouth that has not kissed him" (19:17–18).[22] The explanation of the Rabbis that Ben-hadad had taken Ahab's army is also not clear. If Ahab was strong, how was Ben-hadad able to strike him?! I have not found an answer to these questions in the literature found in the *beit midrash*.

***

In the nineteenth century, the annals of the Assyrian kings (the records of royal journeys) were discovered in the ruins of temples and royal palaces in the Assyrian capital cities. Many of these annals were inscribed on huge statues in the form of winged bulls, some in reliefs or engravings on large stones, and others on clay cylinders or prisms.[23] The inscriptions were written in cuneiform, and it took roughly a century to decipher them.[24] Despite their limited reliability, these writings shed light on the wars described in the Bible.

The annals relate that Shalmaneser III, the king of Assyria (reigned 858–824 BCE), as part of his attempts to expand the borders of the Assyrian empire, fought the southern coalition of the twelve kings of the coast in battle at Karkar next to Hamath (Hama). The leader of the coalition was Hadadezer, the king of Aram, with an army of 1,200 chariots, 1,200 riders and horsemen, and 20,000 foot soldiers. He was joined by Irhuleni the king of Hamath with seven hundred chariots and "Aḥabu ha-Yisraeli" (Ahab, the king of Israel) with two thousand chariots and ten thousand infantrymen. The coalition armies apparently succeeded in deterring Shalmaneser, and the Assyrian invasion was halted for many years, until the time of Menahem son of Gadi, the king of Samaria.[25] The annals relate that despite their ultimate victory, the armies of the coalition sustained serious causalities at the hands of the Assyrians.

It can be assumed that Ahab's army, because it provided most of the chariots in the coalition army (as described in the annals), entered the battle first, and thus bore the brunt of the Assyrian onslaught and, in effect, repelled it. Ahab's primary ally, Hadadezer (Ben-hadad), the king of Aram, was a double winner: the king of Assyria retreated north, and Ahab, a temporary ally but permanent rival for regional hegemony, suffered the greatest loses and his army was diminished. In the war described in 1 Kings 20, Ben-hadad took advantage of this situation and demanded the now weakened Ahab to submit to a demeaning state of vassalage to Aram.

The prophecy received by Elijah at Horeb hints at this punishment at the hands of the Assyrian king: "I will leave in Israel only seven thousand" (1 Kings 19:18). In fact, Ahab only recruited 7,000 soldiers for the war against Aramean servitude (20:15). Nonetheless, in the end, he twice defeated the king of Aram by miraculous means.

The reader is probably wondering why an event as important to the history of the kingdom of Ahab as a war against Assyria and a victory achieved at a heavy price would be omitted from the biblical narrative. One possible answer is that the war was intentionally omitted because the victory was attained by means of an alliance between Ahab and Ben-hadad, the king of Aram, against whom the prophet rails (20:34–43).[26]

Once again, I have used ancient writings to understand the biblical text. In this case, to explain how Ahab was transformed from a powerful monarch with regional supremacy to a king unable to recruit an army adequate to defend himself and his kingdom!

The War of Jehoshaphat and Jehoram against Mesha, King of Moab

> Now King Mesha of Moab was a sheep breeder; and he used to pay as tribute to the king of Israel a hundred thousand lambs and the wool of a hundred thousand rams. But when Ahab died, the king of Moab rebelled against the king of Israel. So King Jehoram promptly set out from Samaria and mustered all Israel. At the same time, he sent this message to King Jehoshaphat of Judah: "The king of Moab has rebelled against me; will you come with me to make war on Moab?" He replied, "I will go. I will do what you do: my troops shall be your troops, my horses shall be your horses" (2 Kings 3:4–7).
>
> And he said, "Thus said the Lord: This wadi shall be full of pools. For thus said the Lord: You shall see no wind, you shall see no rain, and yet the wadi shall be filled with water; and you and your cattle and your pack animals shall drink. And this is but a slight thing in the sight of the Lord, for He will also deliver Moab into your hands. You shall conquer every fortified town and every splendid city; you shall fell every good tree and stop up all wells of water; and every fertile field you shall ruin with stones." And in the morning, when it was time to present the meal offering, water suddenly came from the direction of Edom and the land was covered by the water (16–20).

According to these verses, the war of Moab against Israel and Judah began when Mesha, the king of Moab, rebelled against the king of Israel and stopped paying the wool tax to which he had agreed already in the time of Ahab.[27] At this point the reader may wonder: Why was this "war of the wool tax" so important that Elisha prophesized about the revealed miracles that would be performed for Israel during the war, despite their sin of idolatry?

Furthermore, according to the simple meaning of the text, in these verses the prophet declares a temporary suspension of a prohibition in the Torah, and commands the destruction of the fruit-bearing trees of Moab during the war.[28] Is the failure to pay taxes to the king of Israel really a sufficient cause for overriding this prohibition?

**

In 1868 the "Mesha Stele" or "Moabite stone" was discovered in Dibon (Dhiban), north of the Arnon River located today in Jordan. It was almost destroyed by Bedouin in the course of an argument, but with the assistance of the French researcher Charles Simon Clermont-Ganneau, then a member of the staff of the French Consulate in Jerusalem, it was reconstructed and is now in the Louvre Museum in Paris. A replica is in the collection of the Rockefeller Museum in Jerusalem. An examination of the inscription on the stone reveals that the words "the king of Moab rebelled against the king of Israel" (2 Kings 3:5) do not refer to the non-payment of the tax alone, but to a much more serious matter.

The first line of the inscription reads: "I am Mesha, son of Chemosh [. . .], king of Moab, the Dibonite." In line 14, Mesha describes how he went as an emissary of Chemosh his god to fight Israel ("And Chemosh said to me, Go, take Nebo from Israel!"). In lines 16–17, he describes how in one battle he killed 7,000 men, women, and children for the glory of his god, Ashtar-Chemosh, and took the vessels of the temple of the Lord: "And slaying all, 7,000 men, boys, women, girls and maid-servants, for I had devoted them to destruction for (the god) Ashtar-Chemosh. And I took from there the [. . .] of Yahweh, dragging them before Chemosh." (In the inscription, the YHVH name of God is used.) In lines 25–26, Mesha describes how he used the Jewish war captives as slave labor in his land.[29]

The perceived desecration of the Lord's name in Chemosh's victory over the Lord, and Mesha's extreme cruelty toward he people of Gad, prompted Elisha to go to war against the army of Jehoram. It also led to his prophecy about the revealed miracle that was supposed to bring military victory and the complete destruction of Moab. These factors also led to the emergency ruling temporarily suspending the Torah's prohibition of the destruction of fruit trees, as an expression of God's vengeance against Mesha (and Chemosh, his god) for his deeds. Again, an ancient inscription from biblical times has helped to explain a perplexing passage in the Bible.

It is possible that information derived from the Mesha Stele can also help us understand an unclear passage in Isaiah:

> The "Moab" Pronouncement.
> Ah, in the night Ar was sacked,
> Moab was ruined;
> Ah, in the night Kir was sacked,
> Moab was ruined.
>
> He went up to the temple to weep,
> Dibon [went] to the outdoor shrines.
> Over Nebo and Medeba
> Moab is wailing;
> On every head is baldness,
> Every beard is shorn.
>
> In its streets, they are girt with sackcloth;
> On its roofs, in its squares,
> Everyone is wailing,
> Streaming with tears.
>
> Heshbon and Elealeh cry out,
> Their voice carries to Jahaz
> Therefore,
> The shock troops of Moab shout,
> His body is convulsed.
>
> My heart cries out for Moab—
> His fugitives flee down to Zoar,
> To Eglath-shelishiyah.
> For the ascent of Luhith
> They ascend with weeping;
> On the road to Horonaim
> They raise a cry of anguish.

Ah, the waters of Nimrim
Are become a desolation;
The grass is sear, the herbage is gone,
Vegetation is vanished.

Therefore,
The gains they have made, and their stores,
They carry to the Wadi of Willows.

Ah, the cry has compassed
The country of Moab:
All the way to Eglaim her wailing,
Even at Beer-elim her wailing!

Ah, the waters of Dimon are full of blood
For I pour added [water] on Dimon;
I drench it—for Moab's refugees—With soil for its remnant

(Isa. 15)

We have heard of Moab's pride—
Most haughty is he—
Of his pride and haughtiness and arrogance,
And of the iniquity in him."

Ah, let Moab howl;
Let all in Moab howl!
For the raisin-cakes of Kir-hareseth
You shall moan most pitifully.

The vineyards of Heshbon are withered,
And the vines of Sibmah;
Their tendrils spread
To Baale-goiim,
And reached to Jazer,
And strayed to the desert;
Their shoots spread out
And crossed the sea.

Therefore,
As I weep for Jazer,
So I weep for Sibmah's vines;
O Heshbon and Elealeh,
I drench you with my tears.
Ended are the shouts
Over your fig and grain harvests.

Rejoicing and gladness
Are gone from the farm land;
In the vineyards no shouting
Or cheering is heard.
No more does the treader
Tread wine in the presses—
The shouts have been silenced.

Therefore,
Like a lyre my heart moans for Moab,
And my very soul for Kir-heres. And when it has become apparent that Moab has gained nothing in the outdoor shrine, he shall come to pray in his temple—but to no avail.

That is the word that the Lord spoke concerning Moab long ago. And now the Lord has spoken: In three years, fixed like the years of a hired laborer, Moab's population, with all its huge multitude, shall shrink. Only a remnant shall be left, of no consequence. (16: 6–14)

This prophecy appears to contain allusions to the narrative of the Mesha Stele—in particular, to place names such as Dibon, Nebo, Medeba, Jahaz, Horonaim, Kir Moab (which perhaps means *Ir Moab*, "the city of Moab") Kir-heres or Kir-hareseth—and it is possible that the prophet was familiar with the stele.

Moreover, the prophecy is filled with allusions to the pride of Moab, so blatantly expressed in the Mesha Steele by the continued repetition of the word "I." In addition, the inscription alludes to the victory banquets that Mesha held to celebrate his cruel subjugation of the Israelites living east of the Jordan. We may assume that at these celebrations the wine flowed freely, as is common at banquets, especially in the land of Moab, rich in vineyards. This sheds additional light on the curses which the prophet foretells will befall Moab: tears and wailing, and the silencing of cries of *hedad*, a phrase that served both as a cry of victory and as a call to set the rhythm while stomping grapes to make wine.[30]

It is possible that the prophecy in Isaiah was originally spoken by Elisha at the time of the war of revenge against Moab, as it is written in the prophecy: "That is the word that the Lord spoke concerning Moab long ago" (16:13). Isaiah added to it only the last line: "And now the Lord has spoken: In three years, fixed like the years of a hired laborer, Moab's population, with all its huge multitude, shall shrink. Only a remnant shall be left, of no consequence" (16:14). This prophecy was not fulfilled at the time of Mesha, for the reason given at the time of the war of Jehoram: "A great wrath came upon Israel, so they withdrew from him and went back to [their own] land" (2 Kings 3:27). Nonetheless, this final verse explains that the prophecy was not invalidated but would be fulfilled in the time of Hezekiah and was therefore repeated, at that time, by Isaiah.

* * *

Science, in all its branches, is a resource. It is similar to water, food, money, and other things that we use. Each of us, in the choices we make according to our system of belief, decides whether to use these resources for good or for evil, for faith or for heresy, to draw closer to holiness or to distance ourselves from it. The study of documents and ancient sources from the time of the Bible, or any other period, is not inherently different from other branches of science. If we are worthy, the use of academic research in Torah study will be an elixir of life, not a poison.

Endnotes

1. It is my understanding that Rabbi Tau prefers not to be referred to by the title *Rosh Yeshivah* and his wish must be respected.
2. Tsvi Israel Tau, *Tzadik be-Emunato Yeḥyeh* (Jerusalem: N. B. Elyashiv, 2002).
3. I will not refrain from stating that in my opinion the rabbi's opinions are worthy of a better organized and better written forum than the pamphlet in which they appear. I will not elaborate here.
4. The idea of the "two floors" appears in several places in the writings of Rav Abraham Isaac ha-Kohen Kook. See *Iggrot ha-Ra'aya* [The letters of Rav Kook] (Jerusalem: Mosad Harav Kook, 1985), 1:135; "Rosh Davar" 11 (Mussar ha-Kodesh), in *Orot ha-Kodesh* (Jerusalem: Mosad Harav Kook, 1964), 3:27, inter alia.
5. "U-Nishmat Mi Yatza Mimekh," in *Tzadik be-Emunato Yeḥyeh*, 32.
6. "Al Plishat Ha-Ḥol el ha-Kodesh," in *Tzadik be-Emunato Yeḥyeh*, 37.
7. "Ke-she-Niknasu Yivanim le-Heichal," in *Tzadik be-Emunato Yeḥyeh*, 47.
8. Rav Kook made salient points on this subject as well in his introduction to "Mussar Ha-Kodesh" mentioned above. See "Rosh Davar" 9, 26; 6, 24; 14, 31.

9. This section is based on material that I learned in my youth from my teacher, Rabbi Yoel Bin Nun. However, I am unaware of his current position on these matters and the responsibility for the content is entirely my own.
10. Deut. 11:29–30; 27:2–8.
11. This is according to the *peshat* meaning of the verses in Joshua 8, and the commentaries of Isaac Abravanel and the Malbim on these verses. The Babylonian Talmud, tractate *Sotah* 36a records a controversy among the sages of the Mishnah on the question of when the covenant was made. Rabbi Shimon was of the opinion that the People of Israel made the covenant on the day they crossed the Jordan. This can also be understood from the simple meaning of the Mishnah (*Sotah* 7:5) and the Tosefta (*Sotah* 8:7). See also the opinion of Rabbi Yehudah in the Jerusalem Talmud, tractate *Sotah* 7:3; *Seder Olam Rabbah*, 11. The opinion of Rabbi Ishmael is that the People of Israel arrived at Mount Ebal only after fourteen years of conquest and the division of the land, while Rabbi Elazar argues that in this context "Gerizim and Ebal" refer to two small slopes on the banks of the Jordan, not the hills near Shechem.
12. M. Greenberg, "Ḥ'bru (Ḥ'fru)—Ivrim" [Habiru [Apiru]—Hebrews], in *Ha-Historia shel Am Yisrael* [The history of the Jewish people], ed. Benjamin Mazar (Jerusalem: Am Oved, 1982), 2:95–102. Greenberg argues, in brief, on the basis of a previous, longer article, that the Apiru were the Israelites. Nadav Na'aman, in *Ha-Historia shel Eretz Yisrael* [The history of the Land of Israel], ed. Yaacov Shavit (Jerusalem: Keter, 1982), 1:233–240, rejected this approach and explained the verse in another way. My teacher Rabbi Yoel Bin Nun ("Ha Ivrim ve-Eretz ha-Ivrim" [The Hebrews and the land of the Hebrews], *Megadim* 15 [1992]: 9–26) took the best from both approaches to create a third approach.
13. The academic world is divided on the question of the relative chronologies of the Amarna documents and the Exodus. For the purposes of this article I have followed the opinion of Professor Immanuel Velikovsky and the many other scholars who agree with him. The more current opinion reverses the chronological order. The scope of this article does not allow me to explain these approaches in depth or my reasons for preferring one over the other. My opinions on the subject are not conclusive.
14. For a translation of the documents and their history see William L. Moran, ed. and trans., *The Amarna Letters* (Baltimore: Johns Hopkins University Press, 1992). The quote from letter 287 in on page 328.
15. Ibid., 332–333.
16. Ibid., 334.
17. This midrash appears also as "Milḥemet Ya'akov u-Banav" [The war of Jacob and his sons], in *Sefer Ha-Yasher*, ed. Joseph Dan (Jerusalem: Mosad Bialik, 1986), 168–186.
18. See Gen. 34:2.
19. See the quotes above from Chron. See also Ps. 78:9–10, and the *Jerusalem Targum* (*Targum Pseudo-Jonathan*) to Ex. 13:17: "And so it was that when Pharaoh had freed the people, the Lord did not lead them by the way of the land of the Philistines, though that was near, for the Lord said, 'Lest the people be frightened by seeing their brethren who were killed in war'—two hundred thousand strong men of the tribe of Ephraim, who took shields, and lances, and other weapons, and went down to Gat to carry off the flocks of the Philistines. Because they transgressed against the decree of the Lord, and left Egypt three years before the end, they were delivered into the hand of the Philistines, who killed them. These are the dry bones which the word of the Lord restored to life through Ezekiel the prophet, in the valley of Dura. However, if they saw them, they would be afraid, and return to Egypt."
20. There are many midrashim on this subject. I will provide two examples. First from the Babylonian Talmud, tractate *Sanhedrin* 92b: "Now, who were they whom Ezekiel revived?—

Rav said: 'They were the children of Ephraim, who counted to the end but erred, as it is written, "And the sons of Ephraim; Shuthelah, and Bared his son, and Tahath his son, and Eladah his son, and Tahath his son. And Zabad his son, and Shuthelah his son, and Ezzer, and Elead, whom the men of Gath that were born in that land slew" (1 Chron. 7:20–21), and "And Ephraim their father mourned many days, and his brethren came to comfort him" (7:22).'" Secondly, from the *Mekhilta de-Rabbi Yishmael*, Beshalaḥ: "This refers to the war of the sons of Ephraim, as it is said, 'And the sons of Ephraim: Shuthelah—and Bered was his son . . . whom the men of Gath that were born in the land slew' (1 Chron. 7:20–21)—two hundred thousand children of Ephraim. And it also says: 'The children of Ephraim were archers, handling the bow, they turned back in the day of battle' (Ps. 78:9). Why? Because 'they keep not the covenant of God and refused to walk in his law' (78:10), that is because they ignored the stipulated term, because they violated the oath."

21. *Esther Rabbah* 1.
22. In his commentary on this verse, Rashi, justifiably, identifies the 7,000 that were left in the Ahab's army during his war with Ben-hadad with the 7,000 mentioned in the prophecy that Elijah received on Mount Horeb.
23. For further information on these findings, see: Hayim Tadmor, *Asshur, Bavel ve-Yehudah: Mekharim be-Toldot Ha-Mizraḥ Ha-Kadum* [Assyria, Babylonia, and Judah: Studies in the history of the ancient Near East] (Jerusalem: Mosad Bialik, 2006), 1–2.
24. The deciphering was done primarily by A. K. Grayson in Canada and Riekele Borger and his students in Germany.
25. See William W. Hallo, "Mesopotamia," in *Entzeklopedia Mikrait* [Encyclopaedia biblica] (Jerusalem: Mosad Bialik, 1968), 5:59–130 (esp. page 90); A. Malamat, "Milhamot Yisrael ve-Ashur" [The wars between Israel and Assyria], in *Ha-Historia Ha-Tzva'it shel Eretz Yisrael Be-Yimei Ha-Mikra* [The military history of Israel in the time of the Bible], ed. Jacob Liver (Tel Aviv: Maarachot, 1964), 241–260, esp. 246–247. It is possible that partial invasions in remote areas occurred in the time of Jehu.
26. I heard a similar explanation from my revered teacher Rabbi Yoel Bin Nun, upon which my arguments here are based.
27. This is the interpretation of Radak (Rabbi David Kimḥi).
28. This is the interpretation of Radak and Ralbag (Gersonides) on this verse. Rashi, following the midrash, explains that according to the Torah itself the prohibition is to be lifted in the case of a war against Moab or Ammon.
29. "The Moabite Stone," in W. F. Albright, "Palestinian Inscriptions," in *Ancient Near Eastern Texts*, ed. James B. Pritchard (Princeton: Princeton University Press, 1969), 320.
30. Yehudah Elitzur analyzed the proclamation of Moab along the lines presented here. I have expressed my thoughts here in a slightly different manner. His ideas are seminal and should be read in the original. See Yehuda Elitzur, "Masa Moav u-Ketovet Mesha" [The proclamation of Moab and the Mesha Stele], in *Yisrael ve-ha-Mikra: Meḥkarim Geografi'im, Histori'im u-Haguti'im* [Israel and the Bible: Geographic, historical, and philosophical studies], ed. Yoel Elitzur and Amos Frisch (Ramat Gan: Bar Ilan University, 1999), 175–182.

Archaeology and the Bible

Haggai Misgav

In 1967, an inscription was discovered in Tel Deir ʿAlla in Jordan (identified by some with the biblical Sukkot). The inscription was written on plaster in black and white ink on the walls of a structure, apparently used for ritual purposes, dating from the eighth century BCE. Its translation reads: "The Book of Balaam, son of Beor. A divine seer was he. The gods came to him at night. And he beheld a vision in accordance with El's utterance. . . . Balaam arose on the morrow; he summoned the heads of the assembly to him."[1]

The inscription describes none other than the biblical magician Balaam son of Beor, the beholder of visions, and tells his story in language very similar to that used in Numbers 22–24. Though the two stories are not identical, the discovery of the inscription was a cause of great excitement for my late father, Dr. Yehiel Tzvi Moshkovitz, who devoted several years to writing the *Da'at Mikra* commentary to the book of Numbers. He felt that the inscription gives form and substance to the image of the biblical magician, regarded by the sages as a counterpart to Moses and authenticates the existence of prophecy amongst non-Jews. I remember an incident in which my father enthusiastically described the discovery to my uncle, a Haredi Jew who had studied at the Pressburg Yeshiva. My uncle shook his head skeptically and said, "Why are you so excited about this?" After my father's emotional attempts to explain the importance of the discovery, my uncle again shook his head and said, "And if there wasn't such an inscription, you wouldn't believe that the story was real?"

This anecdote illustrates the essence of the dilemma facing the religious student when he makes use of archeological data to understand the Bible. In my opinion, the expression of scorn, or at least indifference, described in this anecdote, a very common reaction, is camouflage for fear. The possibility of using external data to verify the authenticity of the Bible also raises the possibility of using external data to *disprove* its authenticity. Is this a legitimate way to study the Bible? What is the significance of these external proofs for one who seeks to discover the holiness of the text and his or her own personal commitment to it?

Moreover, even if we set aside the possibility of disproving the authenticity of the Bible (we will return to this subject later), we are proceeding on a path that was unknown to our forefathers, the classical biblical commentators. They were the creators of the intellectual path that Judaism has followed throughout the generations, and these new approaches have not been subjected to their scrutiny. Are the insights that might arise from this new approach consistent with Orthodox thought? Principles of faith are not factual matters; the conceptual structure of Judaism rests on the authority of rabbinic scholars and their instructions. If we expand our conceptual basis to include new information, what will happen to the ancient, preexisting sources of authority? Who will be able to provide spiritual guidance to a generation for whom the conceptual foundations are completely new?

It appears that in the present generation the prevalent religious approach in both the public and private spheres is one of "simple faith." The intention is not necessarily to the Breslov understanding of the term, but rather to a belief that is not grounded in theological analysis and does not accept the authority of reason in matters of faith. This approach sanctifies naïveté not only with respect to issues of thought and philosophy, but also in literary matters. The Bible is not a subject for research and inquiry. Its words are true and just according to their simple, literal meaning. Even ideas like the position expressed by Maimonides in *Guide of the Perplexed* (3:3) that certain biblical passages are metaphorical have no place in the intellectual world of those who adhere to this approach. This school of thought perceives the use of new information, especially from external sources, and all the more so from nonreligious and non-Jewish sources, as a danger. The more enlightened adherents to this approach are aware of this "dangerous" information, but call its veracity into question and often deride attempts to interpret it.

Among students of the Bible and archaeology within religious Jewish, non-Haredi society, there are those who are less hesitant in their approach to science and secular knowledge and are familiar with academic terminology. However, this relative openness does not change their worldview, nor will they allow it to do so. It is a source of pride for them that their familiarity with external concepts has not damaged their pure faith in the simple meaning of the Torah, and its chronology and stories as they appear. They view all difficulties and challenges as the product of intellectual limitations. For this reason, they favor approaches like that of Professor Immanuel Velikovsky (1895–1979), a psychologist and one of the founders of the Hebrew University, who believed that the Bible, as well as the folklore of other peoples, preserved historical truth.[2] He therefore believed that it was correct to erase hundreds of years from accepted historical chronologies and even to use natural catastrophes to corroborate biblical chronology, according to its simple meaning.

However, such an approach is not suitable for a person who considers himself to be a member of the scientific community and wants to be accepted as a scholar within the academic world. Even if the Bible is not the subject of one's research, when one takes the first step along this path, one must do some soul-searching and ask: "Who am I? What is my worldview? How far can I allow external concepts and information to penetrate the interpretation of the sources that are the foundation of my life?" This path, of this new type of scholar, is not paved. Earlier scholars did not confront this problem and thus did not address it. Later scholars usually ignored it for the same reason, namely the lack of earlier opinions to follow. Thus, necessarily, the scholar develops new exegetical methods and non-simplistic understandings of the text. Perhaps, at the end of the process, rather than a new interpretation of the Bible, he will have a new formulation of the principles of faith.

In this article, I will attempt to survey the history of archaeology, a relatively new science (not yet 150 years old), and its aims in order to comprehend the network of interrelationships that have formed between it, the Bible, and biblical studies (also a new field, although older than archaeology).

It is current practice to divide the development of archaeology (as far as it relates to periods that impact the Bible) into three stages: classical, new, and postmodern.[3] The classical approach, called "biblical archaeology," was established in the first half of the previous century. It emphasized important and dramatic historical events—meaning, military campaigns and destructions—and the politics of the ancient world. This school coined the basic terminology of the archaeology of the Land of Israel, which it correlated with historical events and the establishment of political frameworks. Thus, "Iron Age I" signified the period of settlement following the Exodus from Egypt, "Iron Age II" the period of the monarchy, and the preceding Bronze Age is still referred to in museums in Israel as the "Canaanite Period."

For instance, Yigal Yadin identified a layer in his excavations at Hazor as the vestiges of a large fire, indicating destruction, which he dated to the thirteenth century BCE. Sections of this layer included the city's temples, in one of which were found shattered and decapitated idols, deliberately destroyed.

Its date, determined by independent archeological criteria, corresponds to the time of the conquest of the Land of Israel under the leadership of Joshua son of Nun. Hazor was one of the cities destroyed in the conquest, and one of the three described in the book of Joshua as having been burnt to the ground. Yadin, predictably, identified the remains with the biblical narrative and saw in it proof of the authenticity of part of that narrative: an Israelite invasion that utterly destroyed Hazor, burnt it to the ground, razed its temples, and shattered its idols.

However, other scholars disagreed with the connection he made between the site and the biblical story. They found holes and contradictions in his argument, and inconsistencies between the story and the archeological findings. One of the more famous examples of such a contradiction is the story of Ai. For many years it has been accepted to identify Ai with Et-Tell in the Binyamin region, near the city of Ramallah, both because of the similar meaning of the names and because Et-Tell's location corresponds to the topography described in the Bible. The conquest of Ai and the sins of Achan lie at the center of one of the longer and more traumatic stories in the book of Joshua. Nevertheless, no archeological evidence of a settlement in the relevant time period, the Late Bronze Age, can be found there. Even archeologists such as Yadin were aware of the problem. They conceded that not every biblical story is exact in all its details and that some stories are etiological legends intended to explain actual historical phenomena. Other scholars, however, tended to give little credence to the accuracy of the biblical narrative and rejected the initial premise that it reflects historical truth.

It must be noted that the specific solution to the problem of Ai is very simple: it involves rejecting the identification of that particular location with the biblical Ai, with or without proposing an alternative location. It is similarly possible to find individual solutions to almost all of the contradictions and inconsistencies that have arisen. However, the very existence of constant tension between each new discovery and the biblical story, in a kind of eternal ping-pong game of questions and answers, has undoubtedly eroded belief in the Bible as an exact and straightforward historical record.

This school of thought found support in the field of biblical studies. Beginning at the end of the nineteenth century, biblical scholars have assigned most of the biblical narrative a very late date, viewing them as reconstructions of history with varying degrees of accuracy and reliability. This perception of the Bible as an ideological work not bound by historical truth correlated with skeptical perspectives within biblical archaeology.

Still, proponents of both sides of this controversy defined themselves as biblical archeologists. In other words, every finding and each new theory was inevitably and immediately viewed in the context of one or the other defining biblical narrative. Politics remained the major area of interest, and the central questions revolved around major historical events.

However, in the last quarter of the twentieth century, more in England and the United States than in Israel, a new approach developed that abandoned the "revolving sword" of the Bible and grounded archaeology on a scientific rather than a literary basis. This approach advocates the use of tools drawn from the natural sciences and statistics to analyze findings, and the construction of models of archeological development that do not constantly revert to the Bible for verification. In short, its aim is to transform archaeology from an auxiliary of history into an independent science. It is possible that in those countries, where historical literature from ancient times is relatively scarce, it was easier to implement these changes. The methodology of the study of prehistory also influenced this process. In any case, biblical archeological research published outside of Israel also followed this new trend.

The questions of the "new archaeology" (as it is called by its opponents) are also different. Long term cultural processes and the development of cultural phenomena have replaced historical events and political changes as the focus of interest. Processes examined in this light can impact classical historical conceptions, and shift emphasis from political events to internal developments, social, and otherwise. The period of time examined by this new approach is longer, because a particular historical event, which was seen before as having changed the face of the region with the thrust of a sword, is no longer the focus of research. It has been replaced by slow social developments, which can be detected only through the collection of maximal amounts of data by all methods available to researchers.

While the impact of the new archelogy in Israel would appear to be minor, in the last generation every published archeological report has included various scientific appendices—including physical, chemical, petro-chemical, anthropological, statistical, and other reports—in addition to the standard ceramic and stratigraphic analyses. Because of the rich history of the Land of Israel, and the potential significance of every social, cultural, and historical conclusion, the overarching historical questions still dominate Israeli archaeology. Nonetheless, Israeli archeologists have attempted to interpret findings not only through the lens of ancient literature, but also by means of models based on other branches of science.

The continuing debate about the historical accuracy of the biblical narrative has recently been ignited by a new/old attempt to explain a finding from the Iron Age I according to sociological models, and to view the characteristic settlement pattern in the Land of Israel in this period as the product of internal developments in Canaanite society. To clarify the matter, I will explain some basic concepts and information.

Iron Age I is characterized by the wide distribution of a new type of settlement in Judea and Samaria. These settlements, called "conquest settlements" on the basis of the biblical story, include a small number of residential units, about twenty rooms, each of which apparently housed one family, attached to each other in a circular structure so that the back walls of all the units together formed an exterior wall. In the center of the circle was a large courtyard used for cooking and other daily tasks. The ceramic remains at the sites are typical of the period, and are poorly manufactured relative to those of the preceding late Bronze Age culture. Many hundreds of such settlements are scattered across the central highland region of the Land of Israel. They reflect a nonurban society based on clans, lacking centralized leadership, and poor in resources and technology. The Canaanite cities, most of which still existed in this period in the plains and valleys, were much larger, richer, and better fortified.

These data can be interpreted in one of two ways. On the one hand, there are many parallels between these findings and the books of Joshua and Judges: a fragmented, leaderless, tribal society, subject to relentless political pressure from its neighbors. On the other hand, it is hard to believe that the weak, nomadic society represented by these archaeological discoveries invaded and overcame Canaanite culture in a swift, decisive war as described in Joshua—especially as Canaanite culture was not in any way defeated, as we have seen. Part of the problem lies with understanding the biblical narrative itself. It is difficult to reconcile the idyllic picture of the first part of the book of Joshua with the scattered and besieged tribes of Israel described in the second part and in the beginning of Judges. It is no wonder then that many scholars have tried to construct an independent explanation for this archeological phenomenon. They have demonstrated that the same process was repeated in different periods in the history of the Land of Israel: the decline and fall of an extensive urban culture that, after a dark age of some two centuries, was replaced by a new culture. In most of these cases, the reasons are internal: climatic catastrophes or demographic changes. The new scholars argued that this explanation could be adopted in this situation as well, because these are similar phenomena that occurred in the same region.

Therefore, the conquest settlements are a "dark age," the product of internal developments that led to a change in the lifestyle of part of the Canaanite population and the adoption of more convenient social frameworks suited to the new conditions of the region, and, ultimately, to the development of a new identity and consciousness. Support for this opinion can also be found in the similarities between the settlement period ceramics and Canaanite ceramics, as well as the similarity of the houses in both periods and even perhaps in their architectural development. Therefore, according to this approach, there was no conquest and settlement as described in the Bible, but instead a local culture that changed its character and created a new culture.

The controversy between these two schools of thought continues even today. As is to be expected, there are also intermediary positions. There are those who advocate a more complex model: the peaceful penetration of tribes from outside the Land of Israel who settled alongside the Canaanite cities. On the basis of an analysis of the regional spoken languages and the types of tools they used, it may be conjectured that these tribes came from the east bank of the Jordan River. Over the course of time, as a result of demographic and economic pressures, conflicts erupted between the old and new cultures. The Israelite kingdom that had coalesced from the settler tribes emerged from these conflicts. The process of settlement itself would have taken a long time, certainly more than the few years depicted in Joshua.

Because the founders of classical biblical archaeology were either learned religious Christians or ardent Zionist Israeli scholars, the new archaeology was perceived as "post-Zionist" and intended to undermine Jewish nationalistic, if not necessarily religious, values. Although the new scholars themselves for the most part strongly object to these labels, this image was easily adopted by the opponents of the new approach, and, as a result, the debate has shifted from the professional to the ideological realm. Reference to the worldview of a scholar makes it easier to ridicule his views by revealing, as it were, his destructive, hidden, and politically motivated agenda. In my opinion, those who have chosen to defend the classical position in this way need to work harder. The other side's arguments are legitimate and cannot be dismissed with irrelevancies.

To reconcile the biblical picture with these new theories, one must go back to the Bible itself and attempt to read it from a new perspective. It will soon become clear that, in discussing the settlement period, one can in fact begin with the wanderings of the family of the Patriarchs, and see their three hundred years in the Land of Israel, during which they settled, traded, multiplied, and even intermingled with the local inhabitants, as the beginning of a long process that came to its conclusion in the days of Joshua and the judges. Various references in less commonly read biblical books, for example, the evidence in Chronicles of Israelite settlements at the time of the subjugation to Egypt (1 Chron. 7:20–29), hint at ambiguity in the settlement process. The book of Judges describes a non-chronological development, and, in fact, the settlement process was long and drawn out, with ups and downs, and the gap between Israelites and Canaanites was not so great. Intermittent wars accompanied this process, from the war of the sons of Jacob in the story of Dinah, to the wars of Joshua, and up until the scattered and decentralized wars of the judges. Perhaps the social and cultural process depicted by archaeology is not so far from the simple meaning of the biblical text.

It must be noted that many important scholars call attention to the fact that, in general, when all is said and done, the historical and archeological information at our disposal correlates with the general outline of the biblical narrative. The social structure of the Middle Bronze Age corresponds to the stories of the Patriarchs; the period of settlement, however, as we define it, corresponds to the period of the consolidation of the nation of Israel; there is strong proof for Israelite monarchy, despite disagreement about the existence of the united monarchy. The campaign of Shishak, the rise of Assyria, and the destruction of Samaria and Judah all left a clear mark in the archeological remains.

Moreover, several findings reveal an impressive correspondence with the biblical narrative. I will discuss three of these. Firstly, the altar on Mount Ebal, a defined square structure dated by its excavator to the beginning of the settlement period, is reminiscent of the Israelite altar described in the Bible. Remains of kosher animals were found surrounding the altar; the remains include that of the fallow deer (*yaḥmor*), which while not itself a sacrificial animal, could have served other purposes for those performing the sacrifices. The location of the altar corresponds closely to the details of the story of the altar erected by Joshua on Mount Ebal (Josh. 8). Although many have challenged this identification, no convincing alternate has yet been proposed.

The excavator of this altar, Adam Zertal, also discovered a city in Tel El-Ahwat in Wadi Ara that was built according to a plan not found anywhere else in the Land of Israel, but which has parallels in Sardinia, the home of the one of the tribes of the Sea Peoples called the "Shardana." (The Sea Peoples were known in the Bible as the Philistines, after the name of one of their other tribes.) The site was apparently a storage area for war chariots. Many factors connect these findings to the biblical story of Deborah: Sisera (his name is not

Semitic, and there are similar place names in Sardinia) set out from this area to wage chariot warfare against Barak son of Abinoam (Judg. 4). The identification of this city with Harosheth-goiim (4:2) is plausible.

The third example, the Tel Dan inscription, is more complicated. The inscription, discovered in the early 1990s, describes the victory of a king of Aram over a coalition that included Joram son of Ahab, the king of Israel, and Ahaziah son of Joram, the king of Judah. The inscription is written in Aramaic, and was discovered piece by piece, over the course of time. The scientists in the laboratories of the Israel Museum reconstructed the text by finding points of connection between the fragments. In the following translation, the words and letters within square brackets are additions made, as far as possible, on the basis of internal similarities within the inscription and the linguistic rules of ancient Aramaic. On the evidence of its location and archeological considerations, the inscription was dated to the second half of the ninth century BCE. The following translation of the inscription is based on the reconstructed text:

(1) [...] and cut [...]

(2) [...] my father went up against him in war at [...]

(3) And my father lay down and he went to his fathers. Now the king of

(4) Israel had gone formerly into the land of my father. But, then, as for me, Hadad made me king.

(5) And Hadad went before me, and I departed from the seven [...]

(6) [...] my kingdom and I killed [seve]nty kings who harnessed [thousands of]

(7) chariots and thousands of horsemen. [I killed Jeho]ram son of [Ahab]

(8) King of Israel, and I killed [Ahaz]iahu son of [Jehoram]

(9) king of the house of David. And I made [their towns into ruins and turned]

(10) their land into [...][4]

(11) other [...]

(12) over Israel [...]

(13) siege upon [...][5]

Based on the names of the kings of Israel and Judah, which are reconstructed with reasonable certainty, it is the universally accepted opinion that the author of the inscription was Hazael, the king of Aram-Damascus, who, according to both the Bible and contemporary Assyrian records, reigned at the same time as these kings. In the inscription, Hazael apparently claims that he killed both kings. Thus, alongside an impressive verification of the biblical narrative's description of the contemporary political constellation and the joint death of the kings, there is also an apparent contradiction: the Bible ascribes their deaths, at the hand of Jehu, to internal Israelite upheavals, and does not connect them in any way to the king of Aram-Damascus (see 2 Kings 9).

It is not difficult to resolve this contradiction. Certain words in the inscription can be read in a way that weakens the connection between Hazael and the deaths of the kings. It is possible to cast doubt on the historical value of the inscription as a typical self-glorifying text. Clever ways can be found to combine the biblical text with the inscription by raising the possibility of a secret conspiracy between Hazael and Jehu, in which Hazael arranged a temporary calm and a lull in the fighting between Aram and Israel out of a common cause with the rebel king anointed by Elisha.

However, these three proposed solutions raise a fundamental problem that illustrates the dilemma sketched out at the beginning of this essay. Reading the words differently (*qtalu* instead of *qitelti* in lines 7–8) does not solve the problem because the biblical narrative does not connect the death of the kings to the battles of Hazael at all; the injury of Joram described in 2 Kings 9:15 is not a sufficient explanation. Casting doubt on the historical value of the inscription because its author might have glorified himself is spurious, and raises the question of what internal criteria can be used to access sources' reliability. Is it possible to pinpoint an independent gauge for establishing the reliability of a text? Is the meticulous detail of the biblical text truly an indicator of its reliability? Perhaps the fact that the author (Jeremiah according to rabbinic tradition and, in any case, someone from the generation of the destruction of the Temple) wrote long after the time of the events casts doubt on the Bible's reliability. Is the fact that the inscription was written for the purpose of self-adulation a reason to reject it? Perhaps the fact that its author lived at the time of the events described, combined with the fact that a description of the death of two kings was not part of the usual template for these inscriptions, enhances its credibility? If so, perhaps this is the beginning of a new approach to assessing the reliability of a biblical story from a critical perspective?

The third solution raises an even more interesting problem. If we deduce from the inscription that there was a conspiracy between Hazael and Jehu, we are not merely closing a gap. Closing gaps is not a particular problem for the religious student of the Bible. The sages themselves in many places filled in missing details, sometimes even when the story could be understood without them. However, in this case, we return to a biblical story that lacks any apparent holes, and find within it new meaning because of an archeological discovery. This implies that before the discovery our comprehension of the story was impaired by the absence of important information. What does this say about all the other cases in which we lack external information?

It seems to me that this example teaches an important message: not to content oneself with the traditional interpretations of the great commentators, because the traditional method of learning is no longer the only way to discover the truth. "Rabbi Joshua son of Levi said in the name of Bar Kafra, 'One who knows how to calculate time periods and constellations and does not do so, Scripture says of him: "[those] who never give a thought to the plan of the Lord, and take no note of what He is designing" (Isa. 5:12).'"[6] In this vein it can be said, "One who studies the Bible and does not make use of archeological research, Scripture says of him: '[those] who never give a thought to the plan of the Lord.'" Because the modern world gives us tools that we never had before to understand the background of the Bible, we must make use of them. We have no right to reject or ignore them by arguing that they are irrelevant to the eternal meaning of the Bible, or that if the Bible did not provide historical details it is a sign that there is no need for them. The example before us clearly demonstrates that this is not the case, and that the meaning of the Bible is different from what it appeared to be without the external information.

Another, very different, problem is the role of the prophet. If in fact Jehu prepared his rebellion in advance, with careful political strategy, Elisha the prophet did not anoint a surprise candidate, but took advantage of a political process taking shape without his intervention and infused it with his own urgency. If so, what can we conclude about the prophet's knowledge, about his ability to see that which is concealed, the degree of initiative in his actions, or his relation to the world around him? He tried to manipulate reality, but was himself manipulated to no less an extent, perhaps more. What can be learnt from this about the phenomenon of prophecy, its function and aims?

Our use of archeological information—and we must use it because it is here to stay—should not only push us to blaze new trails in interpreting the straightforward meaning of the Bible, but should also force us to reformulate our beliefs, and perhaps even the principles of belief themselves.

In recent years a new trend with postmodern characteristics has developed within archaeology. Scholars began to pay attention to the cultural interpretation of discoveries, the ideas and outlooks that can be identified behind the buildings and artifacts. In this vein, there are those who are searching their excavations for information about those people who, until now, have not been at the center of scholarly attention: women, villagers, and inhabitants of frontier communities, desert cultures, and political and cultural borders. This third stage in archeological research reflects a new postmodern understanding. In place of the hubris of attempting to fully understand the past that motivated the early excavators, and led to the formation of the "new archaeology" and its expansion into other scientific areas, there is a growing awareness that the information at our disposal is not only a function of the perspective of the excavator, but is also based upon connections and interpretations. The methods of researching the past at our disposal do not lead us to the past itself, nor do they bring the past to us. They merely provide us with a peephole that is by nature limited in its direction, scope, and shape. This understanding is more than just a recognition of the limitations of scientific research. It also entails the recognition of the legitimacy of other windows on the past and its interpretation, among them the Bible.

For the religious person who wants to study archaeology, this approach is undoubtedly more comfortable than others. The intimidating confrontation between these two fields of knowledge, two methods to understand our origins, is giving way perhaps to the possibility of quiet cooperation. Perhaps this is the beginning of a new revolution. The scholar who decides to take this approach to the sources of information available to him, as he comes to discover the past through the evidence in the Bible, encounters no direct, complete, or exclusive evidence about a specific event. He encounters a text intended to reflect these events, not to describe or represent them. At the end of this long journey, we are faced with the awareness that the Bible is a story *about* past events; it is not a record of past events. We must read it as we read any other story. We must search within it for hidden literary contexts, and recognize the possibility that the actual order of events differed from the way in which the story is told (the sages preceded us in this in their realization that "there is no chronological order in the Torah"). We must be prepared to read the text synchronically as well as diachronically, or as a circular narrative, or according to other literary constructs. We must accept the possibility that perhaps certain stories are meant to be understood metaphorically (Maimonides already interpreted several stories of the prophets in this way). We must read the phrases repeated several times in the first part of the book of Joshua—"so that no one escaped or got away" (Josh 8:22), or "they crushed them, letting none escape" (11:8)—as reflections of the subjective impression of the victor, rather than an objective record of events. In short, we must regard the Bible as an interpretation of history, presented as a narrative, rather than an exclusive account. We must understand that it is not the events themselves that mold our consciousness, but our perception of them as formed by the biblical story—by the word of God and by the hand of His prophets.

I will conclude with a rabbinic debate about archaeology—specifically, paleography—at the center of which lies a dilemma, similar to those raised above, that positions the faith and knowledge of the simple believer against contradictory historical-archeological information:

> Rabbi Yose said: Ezra was worthy to have received the Torah on behalf of Israel if Moses had not preceded him. . . . And even though the Torah was not given through him, its writing was changed through him. . . . Why is it called *Ashurit*? Because it came with them from Assyria. . . . It has been taught: Rabbi said: The Torah was originally given to Israel in this [*Ashurit*] writing. When they sinned, it was changed into *ro'etz* [or *da'atz*, meaning "Hebrew"] But when they repented, the [*Ashurit* characters] were returned as it is written: "'Return to Bizzaron, you prisoners of hope.' In return [I] announce this day: I will repay you double" (Zech. 9:12). Why [then] was it named *Ashurit*? Because its script was approved [*me'usheret*].
>
> Rabbi Shimon b. Eliezer said on the authority of Rabbi Eliezer b. Parta, who spoke on the authority of Rabbi Eliezar ha-Moda'i: This writing did not change at all, as it is written: "The hooks [*vavei*] of the posts" (Exod. 26). As the posts have not changed, neither have the hooks [the letter vav]. Again, it is written, "and to the Jews in their own script and language" (Esther 8:9). As their language has not changed, neither has their writing.[7]

The question discussed by the sages in this passage, which dates to the second century CE, is an historical question with theological and halakhic implications: In which script was the Torah given? The Torah that we have now is written in a script that is universally known as *Ashurit*. At that time, the Samaritans were living in the Land of Israel, and they possessed an almost identical Torah, excepting certain fundamental changes, such as its claim for the centrality of Mount Gerizim. The Samaritan Torah was written in a different script, universally known, even by the sages, as *Ivrit* (Hebrew) script. But if their script is Hebrew and ours is not, what is the origin of our script, the *Ashurit*? And what does this imply about the sanctity of the script and of the text itself, and about the authenticity of our faith as opposed to that of the Samaritans?

Three perspectives are represented in this debate. The most radical opinion is ascribed to the earliest of them all, Eliezer ha-Moda'i, a priest and the uncle of Bar Kokhba, who lived in the first half of the second century. He argued that the Torah was given in our script, which was never replaced or changed in any way. This is an approach that refuses to recognize the existence of any development in the Jewish religion. "What has been is what will be, and what has been done is what will be done, and there is nothing new under the sun" (Eccles. 1:9). It is not far removed from the view that says, "Anything new is forbidden by the Torah."

Rabbi, who lived at the end of the century and on whose shoulders rested the fate of the entire People of Israel, decided to cooperate with the world rather than fight against it. He was the first for whom the title *Nasi* (prince) became part of his name—Rabbi Yehuda HaNasi—and, in this respect, he was the heir of the previous holder of the title, Bar Kokhba. Rabbi was prepared to acknowledge that a change had occurred in the script of the Torah. Evidence exists, even if its origin is foreign. All agree that the alternative script is called *Ivrit*. He respected the historical tradition of Rabbi Yose, the first speaker in the discussion, who lived in the previous generation. However, the halakhic and historical tradition compelled him to only partially accept the opinion of Eliezer ha-Moda'i, and to thus create an intermediary position: the Torah was given in this script but it was forgotten. The authority of the sages to innovate, including the legitimacy for his own numerous halachic innovations, was grounded in the fact that they were, in fact, restoring authority to the Torah. The world has a system, but it is circular.

Rabbi Yose was the historian of the group. Rabbi asked Rabbi Yose's son, Rabbi Ishmael, to share with him the historical traditions of his father. On one occasion, Rabbi Yose refused to take a preliminary fundamental position concerning Roman culture, either positive or negative, although he ran the risk of severe punishment.[8] He could not close his eyes to historical information, and was prepared to reexamine his positions in view of reality. As opposed to his two colleagues, the earlier and the later, he was prepared to recognize the implications of his understanding and to accept the existence of process and development: "This was true once, but is no longer." The Torah was not given in our holy script. The Samaritans actually possess this ancient script, but it is no longer holy because Ezra had the authority to change it.

This debate is not only historical or political, and concerns more than rabbinic authority. The debate is about what is perhaps the most important concept in Jewish thought: holiness. Both Rabbi Eliezer ha-Moda'i and Rabbi equate antiquity with holiness. Holiness is objective, an integral part of something that cannot be changed. For this purpose, Rabbi was prepared to create new conceptual frameworks, but not to forfeit the basic principle.

Rabbi Yose defined the concept of holiness differently. Antiquity does not convey holiness. Whatever is consecrated by the people, the leaders, the sages, and the *halakhah* is holy. Rabbi Yose, the historian, was prepared to redefine his beliefs in light of new information from an external source, from his observation of the surrounding situation. Holiness does not determine the *halakhah*; *halakhah* determines holiness.

Luckily this debate does not concern a halakhic question. Halakhic decisions are universally binding. In this case there is no authoritative judgment, and all three opinions remain valid. Everyone and every generation can, and perhaps must, choose its own path, according to its worldview, according to the truth, and according to its understanding.

"Common sense is the fundamental principle. The Torah was not intended for someone lacking reason. Intellect is the angel that mediates between man and his God."[9]

Endnotes

1. "Deir 'Alla Inscription," *Livius.org: Articles on Ancient History*, 20 March 2016, http://www.livius.org/sources/content/deir-alla-inscription.
2. His two major works were *Worlds in Collision* (1950) and *Ages in Chaos* (1952), both translated into Hebrew.
3. The new archaeology developed in the 1970s. Postmodern archaeology originated in the 1980s, and gathered strength toward the end of the twentieth century. For further information see S. Bonimovich, "Parshanut tarbutitit vetekes mikrai: ha'arkeologia hamikrait be-edan ha-postmoderni" [Cultural interpretation and biblical ceremony: biblical archaeology in the postmodern era], *Cathedra* 100 (2001): 27–46.
4. The word "destruction" should be added here.
5. Christopher Rollston, "The Tel Dan Inscription," *Bible Odyssey*, 25 June 2017, http://www.bibleodyssey.org/en/people/related-articles/tel-dan-inscription.
6. Babylonian Talmud, tractate *Shabbat* 75a.
7. Babylonian Talmud, tractate *Sanhedrin* 21b–22a.
8. Babylonian Talmud, tractate *Shabbat* 33b.
9. Rabbi Abraham Ibn Ezra, *Introduction to the Commentary on the Torah*.

The Book of Daniel and the Twenty-First-Century Religious Bible Student

Rivka Raviv

The ways of Providence are mysterious, and for this reason I have difficulty explaining how I first came to study the book of Daniel. Nonetheless, for over a decade I have found myself returning repeatedly to this fascinating book and finding within it issues that continue to seize my attention. I believe that the study of the Bible, especially the book of Daniel, mandates reference to all the various branches of modern biblical scholarship, in the spirit of the search for "new contextual interpretations that emerge daily."[1] This scholarship, however, poses a formidable challenge to a reader connected to the world of traditional Jewish exegesis.

I shall begin with a survey of several central themes in the study of the book of Daniel where the religious approach is in conflict with the conclusions of biblical criticism. I will then present the ways in which I have chosen to utilize this encounter and what I ultimately gleaned from it.

A. The Conclusions of Biblical Scholarship on the Book of Daniel

Chronology and Literary Framework of the Book

Let us begin with the premise, accepted in biblical scholarship, that the work at hand is not one book, but two: the "Book of Tales" (chap. 1–6) and the "Book of Visions" (chap. 7–12),[2] the former of which predates the latter. The literary differences between these two books have given rise to the widespread assumption that several authors of different periods contributed to the formation of this work.[3] The chapters of the "Book of Tales," which bear a literary similarity to the literature of the early Second Temple period,[4] are believed to predate the "Book of Visions." Scholars are divided as to when the texts were written, who combined them, and for what purpose.

The documents discovered in the Judean Dessert, which include passages from the book of Daniel as well as additional texts with similar content, such as *Tefillat Nabunaid* (The Prayer of Nabunaid) (4Q242)[5] and *Sefer ha-Anakim* (The Book of Giants) (4Q530),[6] as well as scholarship on postbiblical literature such as *1 Enoch*, pose challenges of their own to the traditional perception of the book. The pronounced mix of parallels and contrasts between these texts has brought scholars to regard them collectively as "Daniel literature" from which the canonical work ultimately emerged.[7]

Studies of postbiblical literature led to a deeper understanding of the apocalyptic genre, a collection of works authored beginning in the third century BCE to which the book of Daniel typically is assigned. This categorization reinforces the conclusion that the book is far removed from the Babylonian period that is its setting.

Many scholars have applied linguistic evidence in efforts to date the book, which is written in Hebrew and Aramaic with an assortment of Persian and Greek loanwords. However, scholars who have attempted such an approach have reached differing conclusions. There are those who have concluded from the study of the Aramaic passages that the language used is an early form of Aramaic, while others have concluded that it is a later dialect.[8] Studies of the Persian and Greek loanwords have similarly led to disparate conclusions.[9]

The general scholarly consensus is that the book of Daniel was written before the Hasmonean revolt and completed no later than 164 BCE. There is evidence from the *1 Maccabees* that the content of the book—including the Hebrew names of Hananiah, Mishael, and Azariah (chap. 1), the story of their salvation from the fiery furnace (chap. 3), and the story of the salvation of Daniel from the lions' den (chap. 6)—was well-known to the authors.[10]

Notwithstanding, scholars differ concerning the number of years by which the book of Daniel predates the reign of Antiochus Epiphanes.[11] Many scholars have concluded that the book was redacted in its entirety just before the outbreak of the Hasmonean revolt against Antiochus. Among these is J. J. Collins, one of the greatest contemporary scholars of the book, who has voiced unalloyed confidence in this conclusion, writing that "as we have noted, there is no doubt that Daniel 7 is describing the persecution of the

Jews under Antiochus Epiphanes."[12] This view is based on the historical information that emerges from the "Book of Visions," and especially from chapter 11,[13] from which scholars have inferred that the "Book of Visions" was written against the background of Antiochus's persecution of the Jews. By the same token, scholars view the historical information evinced by the "Book of Tales" as indicative that its authors were far removed from the Babylonian period, as we shall see below.

The book of Daniel poses a relatively large number of chronological difficulties, some of which arise from a comparison to other biblical writings while others are suggested by a comparison of factual information emerging from the book and extrabiblical historical evidence.[14] The most significant problem regarding the historical knowledge of the author of the book is his reference to Darius the Mede. He appears once in the "Book of Tales," immediately following the murder of King Belshazzar[15] of Babylon,[16] as well as twice in the "Book of Visions." Once at the beginning of chapter 9, where he is presented as the son of Ahasuerus and the newly appointed king of Babylon: "In the first year of Darius son of Ahasuerus, of Median descent, who was made king over the kingdom of the Chaldeans" (Dan. 9:1). That year is regarded as the seventieth year of "Jerusalem's desolation" (9:2). He is mentioned for the second time at the opening of the final vision of the book, at the beginning of chapter 11.

As early as 1935, H. H., Rowley, in *Darius the Mede and the Four World Empires in the Book of Daniel*, argued that the book contained historical inaccuracies.[17] The most significant of these is that Cyrus conquered the Median kingdom in 550 BCE, and when he conquered Babylon eleven years later, in 539 BCE, Media no longer existed. In 538 BCE, Cyrus published his edicts allowing the rebuilding of temples.[18] Rowley, and many other scholars who followed in his footsteps, argued that the fact that the author of the book wrote that Darius the Mede reigned after the death of Belshazzar, the last king of Babylon, indicates that the author of the book was very far removed from the time of the events he depicted and made errors as a result.

Also in question is the place of the book of Daniel in the Hebrew Bible. It is well known that in the Septuagint and Vulgate, Daniel appears among the books of the Prophets. Recently the argument has been raised that this was the case in the Hebrew Bible as well until the sages of the Babylonian Talmud, because of the defeat of the Bar Kokhba revolt, decided to move it to the Writings and declared that Daniel had not been a prophet, in contradiction of early Palestinian postbiblical traditions that viewed Daniel as a prophet.[19]

Theological Questions

The Book of Daniel also poses a range of complex theological difficulties. Jerome recommended reading the book because "no other prophet spoke of Jesus with as much clarity as Daniel."[20] Over the course of time, and especially in the Middle Ages, the meaning of the book stood at the center of Jewish-Christian polemics, with a frequent focus on the vision of the "one like a human being" (Dan. 7:3–14).

During the last century, numerous scholars have deepened our understanding of the theological roots of the visions of Daniel and many of them have made connections between them and Canaanite myths. Daniel Boyarin made an important contribution when he argued that the editor of the material in chapter 7 had been well aware of its mythical significance and purposely edited its content to suppress this meaning and adapt it to the monotheistic outlook of the Bible.[21]

The final topic I would like to consider in this essay is the ongoing scholarly deliberation over the visions of the four kingdoms, in chapters 2 and 7. In the first vision, in chapter 2, Nebuchadnezzar, in the second year of his reign, dreams of a statue comprised of four types of metal. In the second vision, set in the first year of the reign of Belshazzar, Daniel dreams of four predatory animals rising from the sea. Modern scholarship has demonstrated the existence of foreign, extrabiblical traditions common to many civilizations (such as Persia, Greece, and Rome) in which the concept of four kingdoms or epochs forms the basis for the description of the structure of history. The dating of the book to the late Hellenistic period has given rise to the conclusion that its authors used these traditions, which they presented as true prophecy.[22]

Scholarly Conclusions and the Religious Approach to Bible Study

The examples cited above, which are part of a larger and more pervasive system of dilemmas that confront religious students of the book of Daniel today, are accompanied by other weighty questions that the book raises even when not read with a modern perspective. Together, these challenges compel us to ask how the contemporary religious reader can cope with such polarized approaches to the study of this book.[23]

Yet both the content of the book and the lessons derived from it by the sages are so important to the spiritual world of the man of faith[24] that it would be difficult to accede to the book's relegation, even if temporary, to obscurity. Suffice to say that it contains the only example in biblical narrative of Jews who are prepared to sacrifice their lives to spurn idol-worship, as reflected in a rabbinic homily in the Babylonian Talmud about the self-sacrifice of Hananiah, Mishael, and Azariah: "The holy One, Blessed be He, wanted to turn the entire world to blood, but when He beheld Hananiah, Mishael, and Azariah, His temper cooled, as it is written: 'standing among the myrtles in the Deep'" (Zech. 1:8).[25]

According to this midrash, the continued existence of our world is owed to an event reported in the book of Daniel! Is it conceivable for a modern man of faith to repudiate a book that offers so existential an insight?

Between Religious and Academic Study

Both the questions raised in modern biblical scholarship and the conclusions reached penetrate the very core of our being as religious students of the Bible.[26] I shall illustrate this reality with two examples.

First, in approaching the composition and editing of Scripture, the religious reader adheres to the belief that it is of divine origin and considers it a holy text. Meanwhile, according to the modern perspective, the Bible emerged in the same way as many other literary works, developing out of traditions that coalesced over time. Modern scholars attempt to arrive at conclusions regarding the genesis of the book by examining the literary and intellectual context of the period when it came about, asking: Who contributed to its composition and editing? When did these developments take place?

The religious approach, in contrast, ties the sanctity of the Bible to the phenomenon of prophecy, making it difficult to stretch the time of a biblical book's composition beyond the age of prophecy as described in rabbinic literature. The second-century *Seder Olam*, the first rabbinical work of chronography, indicates that in the view of the Rabbis, prophecy ended with the beginning of the Hellenistic era: "Alexander the Great reigned twelve years and died. Until this point there were prophets who prophesied under divine inspiration. From here onward, 'Incline your ear and listen to the words of the sages'" (Prov. 22:17).[27] In any case, the creation of the books of the Bible came to an end in this period.[28]

The second subject to which I would point is the historical veracity of Scripture. It is uncommon for religious exegesis to cast doubt on the historical veracity of the biblical text. Modern biblical scholarship, meanwhile, sees the text as literature based on a kernel of historical truth at the most.

It follows that the encounter of religious study based on traditional Jewish commentary with the products of modern biblical scholarship obligates the religious student both to thoroughly examine his basic assumptions and to search for means of resolving the tension between these different points of view. In the following pages, I shall present several methods that I have discovered for resolving the contradictions between religious beliefs and modern scholars' assumptions and conclusions regarding the book of Daniel. These tools, I would argue, also enable us to draw conclusions concerning the overarching conflict between these approaches to the Bible.

B. Confronting Questions Relating to the Composition and Editing of the Text

The Composition and Redaction of the Book of Daniel

On examination of texts from the classical rabbinic literature and beyond, it becomes evident that the discrepancy between these approaches is not particularly great as it concerns the book of Daniel. The sages also traced the book to several authors, some of whom lived in the Persian period and perhaps even the beginning of the Hellenistic era, far later than the Babylonian period.[29] In the words of the sages, "the men of the Great Assembly wrote Ezekiel and the Twelve Minor Prophets, Daniel, and Esther."[30] Though modern scholars extend the period of composition to the middle of the Hellenistic period, the point of conflict between the religious and scholarly perspectives is relatively small.

In his commentary to chapter 7, Malbim (Rabbi Meir Leibush Wisser) similarly opines that the book underwent editing:

> "In the first year of King Belshazzar of Babylon"—The end of the days of Belshazzar and the kingdom of Darius having been described, here begins the second section of this book. The first section told of the life of Daniel, and from here begins the telling of his prophecies, and his words (aside from the first verse, which was written by the men of the Great Assembly, who wrote the book of Daniel, as the sages said) are expressed in the first person, for he himself wrote everything in its present state.

Malbim thus distinguishes between what later scholarship would identify as the "Book of Tales" and the "Book of Visions," and distinguishes between the words of Daniel and the words of the editors, the men of the Great Assembly.

The fact is that Jewish commentators throughout the ages discussed the editing of the text of other biblical books as well by the men of the Great

Assembly, especially the Prophets and Writings. Two examples are the comments of Rashi regarding the first prophecy in the book of Ezekiel[31] and those of Rashbam (Rabbi Samuel ben Meir) on the editing of the opening and closing of Ecclesiastes.[32] Also relevant to the present discussion are several lines from the commentary of Elijah of Vilna (known as the Vilna Ga'on) to Proverbs 24:23:[33]

> The men of the Great Assembly redacted the Prophets and Writings. In Psalms—as it is written: "and David established with divine inspiration"—they also arranged words of praise and thanksgiving to God, may He be blessed, that had been written with divine inspiration by others, and at the beginning of these materials they added the name of the author, as in "A psalm of Asaph," "A prayer of Moses," etc.

In my assessment, traditional Jewish commentators considered the process of editing to be not an exclusively human endeavor, but an activity dependent upon revelation, as explained by Rashi:

> "In the thirtieth year, on the fifth day of the fourth month, when I was in the community of exiles by the Chebar Canal, the heavens opened and I saw visions of God" (Ezek. 1:1)—The prophet wrote elliptically, neither revealing his name or identity nor explaining from what point he reckoned [the years]. The divine spirit therefore interrupted his words with the two verses immediately following this one to explain who the prophet is and from what point he reckoned, as it is said: "On the fifth day of the month—it was the fifth year of the exile of King Jehoiachin" (1:2).[34]

Although Rashi does not refer specifically to the men of the Great Assembly, he does make a clear reference to editing, positing that the actual words of the prophet are interrupted by the insertion of two explanatory verses (2–3) between the first verse of the book and the continuation of the prophecy in verse 4.[35]

We thus see that the religious approach to the composition of the Bible is more complex than generally thought. The Bible is the product of divine revelations to the prophets, but it does not follow that its text did not undergo redaction and adaptation after the time of a given prophet.

The Original Place of Daniel in the Hebrew Bible

We saw above that several scholars have questioned the authenticity of the conventional placement of Daniel among the Writings, arguing that its rightful place is preserved in the Septuagint, where the book is included among the books of the Prophets. This position is based on evidence from Jewish and Christian post-biblical literature of the first and second centuries: Qumran literature,[36] Josephus Flavius in *Judean Antiquities* and *Against Apion*,[37] and the New Testament, in all of which Daniel is considered a prophet.[38] Attestations of Daniel's status as a prophet also exists in classical rabbinical literature beginning with *Seder Olam*[39] and continuing throughout the works of the Palestinian sages through late midrashic literature. We thus find Daniel identified as a prophet in *Bereshit Rabbah*,[40] *Va-yikra Rabbah*,[41] *Midrash Tanhuma*,[42] and *Aggadat Bereshit*,[43] proving that Daniel was long considered a prophet by Jews and Christians alike. The first indication that the book of Daniel is included in the Writings and that Daniel was not a prophet appears in the Babylonian Talmud.[44]

I have discovered several ways to respond to the question of the place of the book of Daniel in the Bible. First, there appear to be several indirect indications within classical rabbinic literature and postbiblical literature that the book was included among the Writings as early as the consolidation of the canon and throughout the mishnaic period.

According to the Mishnah, the book of Daniel figured in a list of the Writings even before the destruction of the Second Temple and the revolts. In describing how the High Priest kept himself awake on the night of Yom Kippur, the Mishnah states: "If he is learned, he studies, and if he is not learned, sages study with him; if he is used to reading, he reads, and if not, others read to him. What do they read him? Job, Ezra, and Chronicles. Zechariah b. Kvutal said: I often read to him from the book of Daniel."[45] These stories seem to have captured the interest of the high priest and kept him awake. The first three books listed—Job, Ezra, and Chronicles—are without doubt among the Writings in the Hebrew Bible, and in my opinion, the reference to Daniel in this list implies, at least indirectly, its inclusion among the books of the Writings as early as the time of the Second Temple.

There also is evidence from the second generation of Palestinian *amoraim* that Daniel was placed among the Writings. This is reflected in the words of Samuel b. Naḥman in *Bereshit Rabbah*: "'Laban named it Yegar-sahadutha' (Gen. 31:47)—Rabbi Shemuel bar Naḥman said: Do not disparage the *Sursi* [i.e., Aramaic][46] language, because the Holy One, blessed be He, gave it honor in the Torah, the Prophets, and the Writings. In the Torah, *Yegar-sahadutha*; in the Prophets, *kidnah te'merun lehom* (Jer. 10:11); and in the Writings, it is written, 'The Chaldeans spoke to the king in Aramaic'" (Dan. 2:4).[47]

A critical literary analysis of the following passage in the Babylonian Talmud similarly suggests that its redactors assumed Daniel to be part of the Writings:

> "I, Daniel, alone saw the vision; the men who were with me did not see the vision, yet they were seized with a great terror and fled into hiding" (Dan. 10:7)—Who were these men? Rabbi Jeremiah (some say Rabbi Ḥiyya b. Abba) said: "They were Haggai, Zechariah, and Malachi." They are superior to him and he is superior to them. They are superior to him because they are prophets and he is not a prophet. He is superior to them because he saw and they did not see.[48]

This passage is comprised of two parts. The first is written in a combination of Hebrew and Aramaic, and the second, only in Aramaic. The first section quotes a verse in Daniel that explains that the apparition of the angel clothed in linen described in the previous verses (5–6) was seen only by Daniel, and identifies the men who were with Daniel but did not see the angel, whom Rabbi Jeremiah (according to another tradition, Rabbi Ḥiyya b. Abba) identifies as the Second Temple era prophets: Haggai, Zechariah, and Malachi. Daniel may thus be inferred to have seen visions too sublime for the others to perceive.

The Aramaic section of the Talmudic passage compares Daniel to the three prophets of the Second Temple period, positing that although Daniel is superior to them, as intimated by the Hebrew section of the passage, they nonetheless are superior to him because he is not considered to be a prophet.

One need not conclude from this passage that the book was moved from the Prophets to the Writings. On the contrary, the change in attitude toward Daniel may have come about precisely because the book was among the Writings. The assumption that the sages were influenced by the fact that Daniel was included in the Writings clearly explains the connection between the two parts of the passage. It also resolves the contradiction between the opening of the Aramaic section ("he is superior to them") and the Hebrew section (Daniel saw more than the Second Temple era prophets), as well as the statement that Daniel was not a prophet. This provides a means of resolving the contradiction: although Daniel saw more than the others (as stated in the Hebrew section), they are superior to him (as related in the Aramaic section) first and foremost because their books, unlike that of Daniel, are included in the Prophets.

This example illustrates how the methods of modern scholarship of rabbinic literature can in fact assist the religious reader in confronting contradictions between his religious perspective and scholarly opinion.

The Vision of the Four Kingdoms: The Connection between Biblical and Extrabiblical Traditions

As we have seen, there is an affinity between ancient extrabiblical traditions describing the structure of history in terms of four kingdoms and the vision of the four kingdoms in Daniel 2:7.[49] Scholars have thus concluded that the authors of the book of Daniel used these traditions and adapted them to Jewish audiences of the Hellenistic period. This conclusion contradicts the way in which the book itself presents the subject at the beginning of chapter 7: "Daniel saw a dream and a vision of his mind in bed; afterward he wrote down the dream. Beginning the account, Daniel related the following . . ." The problem is that in chapter 2, the biblical narrative first reveals the rubric of the four kingdoms in the dream of King Nebuchadnezzar of Babylon (Dan. 2:31–45). Although Nebuchadnezzar needs Daniel to remind him of the dream and explain it, the origin of the dream is Nebuchadnezzar, a gentile.

In my opinion, the way in which the biblical narrative reveals the idea of the four kingdoms to the reader is compatible with scholarly findings. God revealed the concept of the four kingdoms to the nations of the world and it is therefore not surprising that such extrabiblical traditions exist. Nonetheless, to be fully understood, these traditions must be studied in their biblical version, as presented in Daniel.[50]

We may conclude from this example that revisiting verses and carefully analyzing their diction can be a means of confronting the contradictions between the religious perspective and scholarly opinion. In this example, we distinguished between the data, or facts, and scholarly conclusions. In my opinion, while it is impossible to reject or ignore the facts, their interpretation and the conclusions derived are not unequivocal, and this allows the religious reader flexibility in confronting the challenges that they pose.

Historical Accuracy of the Bible

Our perception of the historical accuracy of the events described in the Bible also requires more thorough clarification in light of modern biblical scholarship. We shall examine several basic ways of confronting this issue before looking at an example from the book of Daniel.

First, the reader can reexamine or reinterpret historical data. There are religious students of the Bible who try to contend with the contradictions between historical truth as reflected by the Bible and extrabiblical findings through a "critique of the critique"—that is, a reexamination[51] or reinterpretation[52] of the extrabiblical findings.

Second, not all scriptural passages reflect historical truth. A study of traditional Jewish exegesis reveals occasional objections to simple readings that assume the literal historical correctness of the text. One example is the way in which Se'adyah Ga'on and Gersonides understand the conversation between Eve and the snake.[53] This approach is rarely exhibited and cannot in my opinion serve as the primary means of resolving difficulties. Nonetheless, its existence is evidence of the ongoing discussion of this issue throughout Jewish history.

Finally, the historical meaning of the text is dynamic. According to the audacious approach to historical meaning in the Bible proposed by Abraham Isaac Kook in the early twentieth century, the biblical story be seen as dynamic, changing throughout time:

> The sacred impressions that all those events that the supreme, divine wisdom decided should be written in the Torah, and the way in which they are intended to be impressed upon us, are precisely measured according to divine standards. When this meaning of the story, its inner essence, which is intended to be impressed upon the soul, is described according to its literal meaning, we are sometimes unable, from a distance in time, to understand the essence of its truth. We must then evaluate, by means of divine standards, following the all-knowing God, what external form the story should take, so that when it reaches us, its fundamental principle will be exactly the same principle that was intended to be impressed upon us.[54]

According to Rav Kook, the aim of the Bible is ethical; the historical story within it is worded so as to achieve this purpose. When the reader is removed in time from the period in which the events occurred, he must tell the story anew, sometimes in a different way, so that its original ethical meaning is expressed. The midrashim of the sages thus serve as intermediaries and retell the biblical story, turning it into a vibrant parable whose external form changes over time.

This radical approach is based to a large extent on the interpretation of midrash, which often reconstructs biblical stories. Rav Kook calls upon the religious student of the Bible to attempt a new understanding of the historical layer of the biblical text.

An illustration of the attempt to grapple with the historical accuracy of the Bible can be found in the identification of Darius the Mede.[55] Some scholars have explained the perplexing historical evidence of the reign of Darius by identifying Darius with a historical figure. Josephus (*Antiquities*, book 10, 11:4) identifies Darius as a relative of Cyrus. According to him, King Cyrus of Persia conquered Babylon and destroyed it in cooperation with Darius. Several scholars followed this approach and suggested identifying Darius the Mede with Ugbaro, the ruler of Gutium who in actuality conquered Babylon and was appointed to govern it.[56] This identification enables the reader to see historical truth in the verses of chapter 6 of Daniel: "and Darius the Mede received the kingdom, being about sixty-two years old" (Dan. 6:1). To be precise, Darius the Mede, not the king of Media, was appointed king of Babylon.

In fact, when we examine the way in which the sages understood Darius, it appears that none of them perceived him as the king of Media. Based on the tradition in *Seder Olam*, he was understood to be the king of Babylon: "Seventy years since Nebuchadnezzar had begun his reign, seventy years less one since he had subdued Jehoiakim, and then Darius came and completed one more year for Babylon."[57]

In other traditions within classical rabbinic literature, Darius was considered to be a Persian king. For example, in a midrash in *Mekhilta* that discusses the four kingdoms, the kingdom of Darius is called Media, although it is clear that the reference is to Persia:[58]

> Concerning the kings of Babylon, what does it say? "The nation or kingdom that does not serve him—King Nebuchadnezzar of Babylon" (Jer. 27:8). About the kingship of Media, what does it say? "Then King Darius wrote to all peoples" (Dan. 6:26). Regarding the kings of Greece, what does it say? "The beast had four heads, and dominion was given to it" (7:6). Concerning the fourth kingdom, what does it say? It says, "It will devour the whole earth, tread it down, and crush it" (23).[59]

The midrash in *Mekhilta* uses a verse from chapter 6 of Daniel that discusses the kingship of Darius the Mede as representing the kingdom of Persia.

The example of Darius the Mede illustrates that when facing arguments against the historical veracity of the biblical text, the religious reader has strategies at his disposal, including both reexamination of extrabiblical data and occasional use of exegetical traditions in the classical rabbinic literature that reconstruct the meaning of the biblical text and are surprisingly similar to conclusions presented in scholarly literature.

Conclusion

Methods of confronting difficulties within the biblical text have been developed throughout the generations, and remain effective today. They include linguistic analysis and the use of exegetical traditions that address similar challenges. Moreover, the method of critiquing the critique—that is, reexamining and reinterpretating extrabiblical findings—should produce effective results in confronting these challenges. Above all, the basic foundations of Bible study in religious circles must be revaluated, while at the same time deepened and expanded.

From a personal perspective, as someone who studies the classical rabbinical commentaries to Daniel, I find that the conflict between the different perspectives raises challenging questions. It inspires a thorough search for answers, and consequently a deeper understanding of the biblical text and classical rabbinic interpretations of it. Moreover, modern findings have more than once led me to reevaluate both the biblical text and *midrashim*. It was the encounter between the modern questions and the biblical text that made me realize that the sages themselves searched for new meanings for the biblical material and that they thus can provide us with answers to modern questions. The religious reader's encounter with biblical scholarship is fraught with complications and liable, as we know, to weaken him religiously, and therefore requires great caution. However, it also can empower us and enable us to glean new understandings from both the book of books and traditional Jewish biblical commentary.

Endnotes

1. Rashbam, Gen. 37:2.
2. Some include chapter 7 in the "Book of Tales"; see: J. J. Collins, *Daniel: A Commentary on the Book of Daniel*, ed. F. M. Cross (Minneapolis: Fortress, 1993), 24–29.
3. Hartman and DiLella argue that four different authors wrote the four visions, the last of whom, the author of chapter 9, left his mark on all the visions. In contrast, Haran argues that

one author wrote all of the visions and reedited the "Book of Tales." See L. F. Hartman and A. A. DiLella, *The Book of Daniel* (New York: Doubleday, 1978), 13–14; M. Haran, *Ha-Asufah ha-Mikra'it* [The biblical collection] (Jerusalem: Mosad Bialik, 1996), 1:116.
4. For example, Esther and Tobit. See Michael V. Fox, *Character and Ideology in the Book of Esther* (Columbia: University of South Carolina Press, 1991), 145–148.
5. For a discussion of the subject, see: E. Eshel, "Possible Sources of the Book of Daniel," in *The Book of Daniel: Composition and Reception*, ed. J. J. Collins and P.W. Flint (Leiden: Brill, 2001), 387–393.
6. For a discussion of the connection between this passage and the throne vision in chapter 7, see: Ryan E. Stokes, "The Throne Visions of Daniel 7, 1 Enoch 14, and the Qumran Book of Giants (4Q530): An Analysis of Their Literary Relationship," *Dead Sea Discoveries* 15 (2008): 340–358.
7. See L. T. Stuckenbruck, "Daniel and Early Enoch Traditions in the Dead Sea Scrolls," in *The Book of Daniel: Composition and Reception*, 368–386.
8. See H. H. Rowley, *The Aramaic of the OT* (London: Oxford University Press, 1929), 138; Haran, *Ha-Asufah*, 106.
9. The "Book of Tales" contains twenty Persian words, most of which are titles of royal bureaucrats or articles of clothing. There are two Persian words in the "Book of Visions." See Haran, *Ha-Asufah*, 106–108. Some scholars see the Greek words scattered throughout the "Book of Tales" as further proof that the book was written in the Hellenistic period, while others have argued that as these words are few and mostly from the field of music (such as *psanterin, somphonia*, denoting psaltery and the bagpipe, in 3:5), they cannot be seen as evidence for a late dating of the "Book of Tales." See Haran, *Ha-Asufah*, 120; S. R. Driver, *Daniel* (Cambridge: Cambridge University Press, 1922), 118–119.
10. See 1 Maccabees 1:59–60. The First Book of Maccabees is dated to approximately 100 BCE. The argument that the author of that book knew the Daniel tales but not his visions was refuted by the findings in Qumran. See Collins, *Daniel*, 72–73; Haran, *Ha-Asufah*, 51–121.
11. The debate regarding the dating of the book of Daniel continues until today. In any case, almost all scholars agree that parts of the book are linked to the period of Antiochus Epiphanes. The exceptions, Kitchen and Wiseman, argue that the entire book predates the time of Antiochus. See: H. L. Ginsberg, "Daniel," *Entzeklopedia Mikrait* [Encyclopaedia biblica], ed. Umberto Casutto (Jerusalem: Mosad Bialik, 1954), 2:686–697; D. J. Wiseman, "Some Historical Problems in the Book of Daniel," in *Notes on Some Problems in the Book of Daniel*, ed. D. J., Wiseman (London: Tyndale, 1965), 35–44; Collins, *Daniel*, 18–19; Haran, *Ha-Asufah*, 103–124.
12. J. J. Collins, *The Apocalyptic Imagination: An Introduction to Jewish Apocalyptic Literature* (Grand Rapids: Eerdmans, 1998), 102.
13. See Haran, *Ha-Asufah*, 117.
14. See Collins's survey of scholarly attempts to resolve some of these contradictions: Collins, *Daniel*, 29–33.
15. The historical identity of Belshazzar also presents a dilemma. The name Belshazzar does not appear among the kings of Babylon. See Y. Avishur, "The Royal Court of the Last Kings of Babylon, Nabonid and Belshazzar, and the Function of Daniel and Other Provincials According to the Bible and Other Sources," *Transeuphratène* 37 (2009): 21–36.
16. Cf. Daniel 5:30, 6:1.
17. H. H., Rowley, *Darius the Mede and the Four World Empires in the Book of Daniel: A Historical Study of Contemporary Theories* (Cardiff: University of Wales Press, 1935).
18. See Collins, *Daniel*, 30.

19. See K. Koch, "Is Daniel Also among the Prophets?," in *Interpreting the Prophets*, ed. J. L. Mays and P. J. Achtemeier (Philadelphia: Fortress, 1987), 237–248.
20. Jerome's preface to the book of Daniel.
21. See D. Boyarin, "Daniel 7, Intertextuality, and the History of Israel's Cult," *Harvard Theological Review* 105 (2012): 139–162.
22. For many years there has been ongoing scholarly debate on the relationship between these traditions. The first to point out the connection between the Judaeo-Christian division of the four kingdoms and ancient Persian sources was Eduard Meyer, *Ursprung und Anfänge des Christentums* (Stuttgart: J. G. Cotta, 1921), 2:189. Several subsequent studies proved that this was an accepted conceptual framework throughout the ancient world, beginning in the eighth century BCE. See J. W. Swain, "The Theory of the Four Monarchies: Opposition History under the Roman Empire," *Classical Philology* 35 (1940): 1–21, and the extension of the discussion in D. Flusser, "The Four Empires in the Fourth Sibyl and in the Book of Daniel," *Israel Oriental Studies* 2 (1972): 148–172.
23. It is interesting to note that classical rabbinic literature reflects a desire to hide the contents of the book of Daniel from its readers, albeit for different reasons. There are several indications that Daniel was considered problematic in the reality of life under the rule of the kingdoms. Criticism focused primarily on the problem of using the book to calculate the end of days. See tractates *Sanhedrin* 97b and *Megillah* 3a.
24. Daniel is the only biblical source (at least in the simple meaning of the text) for many ideas such as the belief in the resurrection of the dead, the schematization of history according to the four kingdoms, the chronography of the Second Temple period in rabbinic literature, the dedication required to maintain a Jewish existence in the Diaspora, the dates of the End of Days, the guardian angels of the nations, and understanding the experience of prophecy.
25. *Sanhedrin* 93a.
26. For an explanation of the essential differences between modern and (both Jewish and Christian!) religious interpretations of the Bible, see B. S. Childs, "Critical Reflections on Barr's Understanding of the Literal and the Allegorical," *Journal for the Study of the Old Testament* 46 (1990): 3–9; J. Barr, "The Literal, the Allegorical, and Modern Biblical Scholarship," *Journal for the Study of the Old Testament* 44 (1989): 3–17.
27. *Seder Olam: Mahadurah Madda'it, Perush u-Mavo* [Seder Olam: Critical edition, commentary, and introduction], ed. Chaim Milikowsky (Jerusalem: Yad Ben-Zvi, 2013), 322 (chap. 30).
28. The sages considered prophecy a necessary condition for the continued composition of biblical books. On the dating of the cessation of this phenomenon, see Chaim Milikowsky, "Sof ha-Nevuah ve-Sof ha-Mikra be-Einei Seder Olam, Sifrut Ḥazal ve-ha-Sifrut mi-Saviv Lah" [The end of prophecy and the end of the period of canonization as viewed by Seder Olam, classical rabbinic literature, and contemporary literature], *Sidra* 10 (1994): 83–94. See also contrasting discussion in Ephraim Urbach, "Matai Pasekah ha-Nevuah?" [When did prophecy cease?], *Me-Olamam shel Ḥakhamim: Kovetz Ma'ovetz* [From the world of the sages: A collection of articles] (Jerusalem: Magnes, 1988), 9–20.
29. Simeon the Righteous, described as one of the "last surviving members of the Great Assembly" (*Avot* 1:1), is described by the Talmud as having lived in the time of Alexander the Great: "When the Samaritans requested the house of our God from Alexander the Great in order to destroy it, he gave it to them. Simeon the Righteous was informed" (*Yoma* 69a). On scholarly opinion about the source material on the historical background of Simeon the Righteous, see Amram Tropper, *Simeon the Righteous in rabbinic Literature* (Leiden: Brill, 2013).

30. *Bava Batra* 15a.
31. See Rashi, Ezek. 1:1.
32. See Rashbam, Eccles. 1:1, 12:8.
33. The verse reads: "These also are by the sages: It is not right to be partial in judgment."
34. Rashi, Ezek. 1:1.
35. For further examples, see Israel Ta-Shma, "Mashehu al Bikkoret ha-Mikra be-Ashkenaz bi-Yemei ha-Beinayim" [A note on biblical criticism in Ashkenaz in the Middle Ages], in *Ha-Mikra bi-Re'i Mefareshav* [The Bible in the eyes of its exegetes], ed. Sara Japhet (Jerusalem: Magnes, 1994), 453–459; R. Harris, "Muda'ut la-'Arikhat ha-Mikra' etzel Parshanei Tzefon Tzarefat" [Awareness of the redaction of the Bible among the exegetes of northern France], *Shnaton: An Annual for Biblical and Near Eastern Studies* 12 (2000): 289–310.
36. Fragments of eight Daniel scrolls were found in Qumran, while three other Qumran documents quote it and describe Daniel as a prophet. See L. T. Stuckenbruck, "Daniel and Early Enoch Traditions," 368 n1.
37. *Judean Antiquities*, books 8–10, trans. Christopher T. Begg and Paul Spilsbury (Leiden: Brill, 2005), vol. 5 of Steve Mason, ed., *Josephus Flavius: Translation and Commentary* (Leiden: Brill, 2000), book 10, sec. 194, 275, sec. 203, 280; *Against Apion*, trans. John M. G. Barclay (Leiden: Brill, 2007), vol. 10 of Steve Mason, ed., *Josephus Flavius: Translation and Commentary* (Leiden: Brill, 2000), book 1, sec. 40, 30.
38. For a more thorough discussion, see Rivka Raviv, "Al Mekomo shel Sefer Daniyyel ba-Tanakh ha-Ivri" [On the original position of the book of Daniel in the Jewish Bible], *Jewish Studies Internet Journal* 6 (2007): 1–12.
39. *Seder Olam*, chap. 20.
40. *Bereshit Rabbah*, 27:1.
41. *Va-yikra Rabbah*, 13:5.
42. *Midrash Tanhuma*, Bo´ 5.
43. *Aggadat Bereshit*, chap. 14.
44. *Megillah* 3a; *Sanhedrin* 93b–94a. It is clear from examination of the manuscripts that there are no meaningful differences between the text of printed editions and that of the manuscripts, with the exception of MS Firenze of *Sanhedrin*, whose text apparently was used by Rashi.
45. Mishnah, tractate *Yoma* 1:3.
46. Bracketed clarification is per Arukh.
47. *Bereshit Rabbah*, 74:14.
48. *Megillah* 3a.
49. See note 27 above.
50. Abraham Isaac Kook addressed the subject of extrabiblical findings predating the Bible which are also revelations in the Torah: "It is not well-known that among the early generations there were those with knowledge of the Divine, prophets, men of a high spiritual level, such as Methuselah, Enoch, Shem and Eber, and others. Is it possible that they did not in any way influence the people of their generations, even if their efforts were not as well known as the outstanding work of Ethan the Ezrahite, our father Abraham, may his memory be for a blessing? How is it possible that they would have had no impact on their contemporaries? Moreover, their teachings must have been similar to those of the Torah." *Eder ha-Yekar* (Jerusalem: Mosad Harav Kook, 1982), 42–44.
51. See the recent book by Amnon Bazak, *Ad ha-Yom ha-Zeh: She'elot Yesod be-Limmud Tanakh* [Until this day: Fundamental questions in Bible teaching] (Jerusalem: Yediot, 2013), 247–316.

52. See, e.g., the prescient words of Yoel Elitzur in "Al Ofnot be-Ḥeker Toledot Yisrael" [Trends in Jewish historical research], *Al Atar* 7 (2001): 23–41.
53. See their comments to Gen. 3.
54. Rav Kook, *Ein Ayah* B (Jerusalem: Mosad Harav Kook, 1999), 43.
55. For a complete discussion, see Rivka Raviv, "Daryavesh ha-Madi al pi Sifrut Ḥazal" [Darius the Mede according to classical rabbinic literature], *Sidra* 27–28 (2013): 245–257.
56. Cyrus was recognized as king of Babylon only about one year after its conquest. See R. D. Wilson, *Studies in the Book of Daniel* (New York: Revell, 1938), 263; Collins, *Daniel*, 31n299–303.
57. *Seder Olam*, chap. 28.
58. The phrase "Media and Persia" appears four times in Daniel: 5:28; 6:9,13; 8:20. The book of Esther appears to indicate that its author regarded Media as part of the kingdom of Persia, rather than an independent kingdom. Cook and Tuplin have proven that non-Jews as well as Jews referred to Persia as Media during the Hellenistic period. See C. Tuplin, "Persians as Medes," *Achaemenid History* 8 (1994): 235–256.
59. *Mekhilta de-Rabbi Yishmael*, Be-shallaḥ, A, 87.

Index of Sources

Hebrew Bible

Gen

1:1; 55, 313
1:2; 148
1:5; 19
1:6; 347
1:27; 375
1:31; 18-20, 130
2:2; 20
2:8–9; 18
3:21; 129-130
4:1; 346
5:1; 177, 180
5:1-2; 493
6:2; 156
6:5; 199
6:11; 199
7:11; 347
8:4; 485
8:21; 199
8:22; 19
9:1–6; 200
10:5 307
11:5; 246
12:1; 228
12:3; 155
12:4; 46
12:6; 45, 48, 51, 315, 352
12:33; 155
14:14; 351
18:20; 53
18:21; 130
18:22; 52-53
19:15; 2
22:14; 47
22:2; 389
22:3; 234
24:7; 130
25:2; 96
25:6; 134

25:27; 374
26:5; 173, 374
27:2; 130
28:10–22; 253
30:14; 402
31:32; 163
31:39; 175
31:47; 537
32:29; 159
32:33; 19
35:5; 502
36:5; 130
36:10; 130
36: 22; 402
36:24; 401
36:31; 44-45
36:39; 49
37:2; 20
38:24; 162
42:37; 163
43:15; 130
45:8; 129-130
46:8; 160
46:23; 103, 129
46:26; 11
48:20; 50
48:22; 503
49:1; 12
50:23; 391

Exod

1:1;160
3:14–15; 160
3:16; 9
4:10; 26, 31, 32
5:22; 9
5:6,9; 8
6:3; 431, 436
6:10; 311
7:20–21; 231
10:1–2; 18

12:36; 157, 177, 484
12:38; 195
13:13; 249
15:1; 313-314
15:11; 435
15:16; 313
15:17; 313
15:25–26; 491
16:34–35; 352
16:4–5; 491
16:5; 18
17:14; 113-114
17:16; 490
18:13; 177
18:21; 180
19:6; 174
19:9; 136
19:11; 363
19:11–18; 361
19:19; 315
19:20; 371
20:1; 306, 324, 372
20:2; 158, 307, 340
20:2–3; 306
20:7; 69
20:8, 11; 18
20:8; 354
20:8–11; 19
20:11; 20
20:15–16; 324
20:18; 413
20:19; 309, 371
21:1; 180
21:2; 181
21:7; 391
21:13; 181
21:14; 181
21:24; 181, 211
21:37; 455-456
22:11; 175
22:12; 175
22:17; 167
22:19; 174
22:21–22; 11
22:24; 181
23:26; 406
24:3; 11, 181
24:4–8; 365
24:5; 120
24:7; 309

24:9–10; 362
24:12; 335
25:8; 174
28:41; 158
30:13; 306
33:20; 405
34:7; 33
34:27; 17

Lev

1:1; 308, 317
1:2; 174
2:13; 50
5:5; 167
10:16; 135
11:42; 135
13:33; 135
15:33; 418
16:10; 51
16:8; 353
16:21; 167
17:7; 172
18:3–4; 165
19:24; 169
19:27; 168
20:3; 169
20:23; 171
21:9; 162, 341
24:15; 342
25:18; 173
26:3; 24
26:14; 24
26:19; 24
27:34; 114

Num

3:45; 245
5:6; 330
7:1; 1, 134
9:10; 127
10:29–31; 492
10:35; 53-54
10:35–36; 53
11:1; 54
11:15; 52
12:7; 17
13:16; 436
15:31; 29, 46, 218, 302
15:32–36; 330
16:3; 350

18:14–18; 443
18:15; 249
21:13; 147
21:14; 56, 147-148
21:17; 33, 54
23:5; 486
23:16; 486
26:31; 160
33:2; 21, 22
33:36; 49
35:9–34; 348
36:13; 31

Deut

1:1; 26, 31, 34-35, 314, 317, 372
1:2; 46, 47
1:3; 27, 45, 48
1:6; 32, 36
1:13; 134
1:33–39; 331
2:5–6; 27
2:8; 49
2:24; 26, 34, 148
2:26; 34
2:37; 48
3:1; 48, 51
3:11; 45
3:23; 311
4:2; 332
4:6; 176
4:7; 405
4:8; 173
4:9; 367
4:9–13; 368
4:10; 326, 369
4:10–14; 368
4:10–15; 367
4:11; 367
4:12; 326
4:32; 231
4:36; 371
4:41; 181
4:44; 28
4:44–45; 446
5:1; 446
5:2-3; 331
5:5; 325
5:6–18; 29
5:12; 69, 354
5:19; 368

5:19–23; 327
5:20–23; 369
5:21; 332, 367
6:7; 369
6:8; 345
8:1; 310
9:10; 310
10:22; 20
11:13–21; 304
11:22; 377
12:2; 167
12:15; 355
12:21; 446
12:31; 386
13:1; 46
15:2; 129
15:14; 341-342
15:19; 444
15:19–23; 444
18:2; 446
18:9; 146
18:10; 169
18:10–11; 155
20:10; 34
21:11; 347
22:5; 168
22:11; 168
23:19; 166
24:8; 446
24:16; 33, 165
28:15; 24
28:23; 24
28:69; 167, 332
29:9; 332
29:11; 50
29:28; 124
30:12; 220
31:22; 28, 48
31:26; 1, 303, 352
31:9; 43, 48, 76
31:9–13; 369
32:1; 309
32:10; 371
32:4; 413
32:44; 28
33:18; 403
33:27; 120
33:4; 12
33:4; 56
34:1; 44, 51

34:1–12; 48
34:10; 486
34:12; 29
34:5; 42, 216, 352
34:6; 44

Prophets

Josh

1:5;196
1:8; 372
5:12; 352
7:7; 28
7:26; 75
8:3–9; 197
8:22; 527
9:4; 125
9:7; 503
9:27; 75
10:8; 197
10:9; 197
10:11; 197
10:12; 197
10:28–39; 197
14:14; 75
15:14; 72
15:31; 72
15:63; 75
16:10; 75
19:45; 75
24:19; 500
24:26; 46
24:29; 72, 75
24:33 ; 72

Judg

5:30; 347
8:21; 159
9:2; 501
9:4; 501
9:23; 501
9:27; 501
9:28; 501
9:46; 501
16:31; 130
18:13; 435
19:6; 28

1. Sam

1:1–2; 236
2:8; 347
2:24 69
5:5; 77
6:8; 78
6:18; 77
9:9; 77
9:18; 77
13:1; 125
25:1; 82
27:6; 72, 74, 77
28:3; 77
30:17; 344

2. Sam

3:27; 349
8:10; 436
12:1–4; 455
12:5–6; 455
21:19; 231

1. Kgs

5:1; 505
5:12; 97
5:13 95
20:15; 506
20:27; 505

2. Kgs

3:4–7; 507
3:5; 508
3:27; 512
7:6; 437
14:6; 34, 166
17:6; 100, 102
18:11; 102
18:18; 92
20:6; 406
20:20; 232
21:2; 398
21:16; 405
23:12; 399
23:26; 399
23:34; 437

Isa

1:4; 155
2:11; 483
5:12; 525
6:1; 405, 437

6:5; 407
8:19; 82
13:6; 431
14:9; 347
16: 6–14; 511
16:13; 512
19:4; 437
33:6; 65
39:6–7; 82
40:1; 82
42:16; 77
42:21; 335, 338
49:4; 172
49:7; 83
54:9; 83
55:6; 405
63:9; 65

Jer

7:29–31; 380
7:31; 380
9:23; 414
10:11; 538
15:4; 399
19:5; 380
23:28; 44
27:8; 541
36:18; 311

Ezek

1:1; 84, 466
1:1-2; 534
1:1–4; 86
1:3; 466
8:17; 52
24:24; 84
38:17; 54
40:1; 466
40:5; 467
42:15–20; 467-468
46:21; 472

Joel

1:3; 18
1:15; 431

Amos

7:7; 437
9:1; 437

Mic

6:6–7; 380

Zech

1:8; 534
2:12; 52
9:12; 527

Mal

1:6; 437
2:6; 485
3:22; 31

Writings

Ps

1:1; 373
14:1; 91
19:8; 31, 485
19:11; 485
25:8; 343
29:4; 371
40:8: 1; 2
51:20; 89
55:24; 147
62:12; 218
68:15; 432
75:1; 89
89:21; 2
106:22; 309
111:6; 9
115:16; 362
119:18; 234
120:1; 89
120:2; 89
123:1; 90
130:7–8; 90
136:25; 54
137:9; 391
145:18; 186

Prov

1:1; 93, 96
1:7; 93
2:10; 65
3:18; 372
3:35; 43
8:30; 481
22:17; 534

22:20; 113
24:23; 96
25:1; 46, 92, 93-95, 113
25:11; 233
25:13; 29
26:5; 407
30:1; 92, 94
31:1; 92

Job

1:1–3; 236
2:11; 96
3:12; 391
9:13; 148
26:12; 148
37:2; 372
37:16; 65
42:8; 189
42:9–12; 414

Song

1:1; 96-97
1:2; 125
1:8; 494
4:4; 88
6:11; 70

Ruth

1: 21; 431
4:10; 162

Lam

1:1; 306

Eccl

1:1; 96-97
1:3; 112
1:9; 528
5:8; 310
12:7; 183
12:8; 97
12:11; 372

Esth

6:1 100
8:9; 527
9:32; 114

Dan

2:4; 538
2:31–45; 539

6:1; 540
6:26; 541
7:3–14; 533
7:8; 541
9:1-2; 532
10:7; 538
10:21; 65

Ezra

4:17; 103
7:12; 103

Neh

10:35–37; 446
11:3; 101

1 Chr

2:3; 103
2:7; 102
3:19–24; 82
6:24; 89
7:13; 100
7:14; 160
7:20–24; 500
8:29; 100
9:1–3; 101
12:33; 403, 404
14:17; 505
18:10; 436
20:1–3; 231
28:17; 104
28:9; 186
29:29; 78

2 Chr

8:17; 49
9:29; 80
20:36; 104
33:12–13; 399
36:3; 125

Mishnah

Pesḥ.

93b; 127

Sanh.

10; 301

Mid.

2:5; 472

Yad.
3:5; 110

Jerusalem Talmud

y. *Meg.*
1:5 (70d); 114

y. *B. Bat.*
(8:2); 56

Babylonian Talmud

b. *Ber.*
5a; 335
12a; 304

b. *Sabb.*
115b–116a; 53
30b; 112
63a 343
b. *Pesaḥ*
49b; 56
116b; 273

b. *Yoma*
28b; 162, 374

b. *Sukkah*
42a; 12

b. *Meg.*
7a; 114
 31b; 24

b. *Ḥag.*
13a; 110

b. *Giṭ.*
60a; 1
70a; 310

b. *Qidd.*
21b; 347
30a; 136, 139

b. *B. Bat.*
14b; 20, 22, 55, 31, 43
15a; 32, 43, 72, 99, 359

b. *Sanh.*
38a; 376
4b; 345
56a; 188
71a; 418
89a; 476
100a; 114
106b; 147

b. *Mak.*
11a; 43

Targum

Tg. Ps.-J.
18:14; 9

Midrashic Literature

Gen. Rab.
55:3; 383
64; 374
67–74 (§ 9); 129
1171–1185 (§ 94); 129
196 (§ 20:21); 129

Exod. Rab.
5:18; 8
5:22; 9
13:4; 18
30:15; 52
47:9; 17

Num. Rab.
14:19; 486

Deut. Rab.
1:1; 26
1:7a; 26

Esth. Rab.
1; 510

Mid. Prov.
100, 26:24; 54

Be-reishit Rabbati
2:34–35; 12

Mid. Tanḥ
Be-shallaḥ 16; 52
Tetsaveh 9; 43

Sipre Deut.
170; 146

Pesiq. Rab. Kah.
8:1; 112

Mek. de-R. Yishmael
Be-shallaḥ, A, 87; 541

Abot R. Nat.
1:4; 113
34; 124

Later Collections and Commentaries

Abraham ben Mordecai
Responsa Ginat Veradim to Oraḥ Ḥayyim
2:6; 139

Abravanel, Isaac
Commentaries on
Exod. 23:19; 172
Num. 21:10; 148

Perush al Nevi'im Aḥaronim
Preface to the book of Kings, 428; 79
Preface to the book of Samuel, 163–164; 100; 163–164; 99
Preface to the book of Jeremiah, 298–300; 120
Preface to the Former Prophets 7–8; 76, 78
Commentary to 1 Kgs 10:22; 543–544; 104; 550–551; 79

Abulafia, Meir (Ramah)
Preface to *Sefer Masoret Seyag la-Torah* 3a; 137

al-Fayyumi, Nathanel, Beirav
Gan ha-Sekhalim 1114–1122 (chap. 6); 183

Barzillai al-Bargeloni, Judah ben (attributed)
Ginze Mitsrayim: Hilkhot Sefer Torah, 37; 54

Baumol, Joshua b. Nahum
She'elot u-Teshuvot Emek Halakhah, 2:34; 26

Benamozegh, Elia
Sefer Torat Hashem ve-Nosaf alav Em la-Mikra va Em la-Masoret
1:16a-b (Gen 3:24); 157
3a; 34
4:90b (Num 29:11); 158
5:33a–b; 176
10 5:151b–152a (Exod 4:10); 11

ben Solomon, Menahem
Midrash Sekhel Tov, 210; 44

Bonfils, Joseph ben Samuel
Perush al Raba al ha-Torah
1:91–93; 47
1:112; 47
2:65–66, Commentary on Deut. 1:2; 49

Borenstein, Samuel b. Rabbi Abraham
Shem mi-Shemuel, Exodus, parashat Va-'era' (1911); 32

David ben Levi of Narbonne
Sefer ha-Mikhtam al Masekhet Megillah, 485; 44

Einhorn, Ze'ev Wolf
Commentary to *Exod. Rab.* 5:22, 33; 9

Eliezer b. Nathan
Even ha-Ezer, Responsa sec. 34; 25

Elijah of Vilnius
Be'ur ha-Gera: Proverbs
283 (24:23); 90
288; 91
328–329; 96-97

Engel, Joseph b. Judah
Sefer Beit ha-Otzar 1:3; 8

Gersonides
Commentary on Exod 40:2; 156

Gunzberg, Aryeh Leib
Gevurat Ari commentary to *b. Yoma* 54a; 100
Responsa *Sha'agat Aryeh*, responsum 36; 140

Ḥai Ga'on
Teshuvot ha-Ge'onim Responsum 3; 132
Responsum 78; 132

Ḥalawa, Moses ben David
Shut Maharam Ḥalawa, Responsum 144; 134

ha-Me'iri, Menaḥem
Beit ha-Beḥirah to *b. Qid.* 30a; 137
Preface to *Kiryat Sefer*; 117

Ḥatam Sofer. See Sofer, Moses (Ḥatam Sofer)

Hirschensohn, Chaim
Eleh Divre ha-Berit 2:34–35; 12

Seder la-Mikra 2:133–135. 182

Sefer Malki ba-Kodesh
5–6: 203–208; 79, 85
responsa 6:1–32:450–475; 128
responsa 6:4, 2:478–488; 69
responsa 6:6, 2:496–504; 71
responsa 6:6 2:497–498; 180

Sefer Nimuke Rashi
1:83b (274,Gen. 46:8); 12
2:166b (593); 159
4:120a; 23

Index of Sources

Sefer Yamim mi-Kedem
192–194; 86
28–35; 161

Hoffmann, David Zvi
Gen, 1:199–204n40; 150
Lev, 2:247; 151

Ibn Adret, Solomon
Shut ha-Rashba ha-Meyuḥasot le-Ramban, responsum 232; 133

Ibn Attar, Ḥayyim b. Moshe
Or ha-Ḥayyim; 21, 31

Ibn Balaam, Judah
Commentary on Deut. 5:6–21; 125

Ibn Ezra, Abraham
Long commentary to Exod 25:29; 104
Long recension to Exod 2:10; 153
Commentary on Deut 1:2; 45
First commentary on Ps; 89

Ibn Kaspi, Joseph
Commentary to 1 Chron. 1:5; 104

Ibn Mansur al-Damari
Midrash Ner ha-Sekhalim; 175

Ibn Naḥmias, Joseph
Perush al Sefer Mishle, 179 (30:1); 95

Isserles, Moses (Rema)
Gloss to Shulḥan Arukh, Oraḥ Ḥayyim, 143:4; 138

Jacob ben Meir of Ramerupt (Rabbenu Tam)
Laws of Torah scrolls and superior technique for Torah scrolls § 517; 136

Joseph of Orleans (Yosef Bekhor Shor)
Commentary on Gen. 38:13, 24; 162

Judah the Pious
Perushe ha-Torah
64–65; 51
138; 50
184–185; 55
198; 50

Kimḥi, David
Commentary on Prov 1:6; 90
Preface to his commentary on Josh 115
Preface to the commentary on Chr; 97

Kimḥi, Joseph
Commentary to Prov 25:1–2; 91

Kimḥi, Moses
Commentary on Prov 30:1; 91

Kook, Abraham Isaac
Ein Ayah B 43; 540

"Ra'yonot le-Toledot ha-Ga'on Aderet,"
42–43; 180, 188

Li-Nevukhe ha-Dor
99–105 (chap. 14a); 186
167–169 (chap. 32); 187
170–172 (chap. 33); 153
215–220; 64
259 (chap. 53); 124–126 (chap. 2); 1
Pinkas "Rishon le-Yafo," in Kevatzim mi-Ketav Yad Kodsho §91a; 64
Pinkas mi-Tekufat Boisk 2:118–119 (chap. 32); 179
Pinkas 4 in Pinkese ha-Re'ayah chap. 87a, 1:250–252; 64

Kranz, Jacob (the Maggid of Dubno)
Ohel Ya'akov al ha-Torah 236–237, on Lev. 4:34; 134

Lerner, Mayer
Hadar ha-Karmel 1:26–27; 188

Levi ben Gershom. See **Gershonides**

Loew, Rabbi Judah b. Rabbi Betzalel (Maharal)
Tiferet Israel, chap. 43; 31

Maggid of Dubno. See **Kranz, Jacob (the Maggid of Dubno)**

Maharal. See **Loew, Rabbi Judah b. Rabbi Betzalel (Maharal)**

Maimonides, Abraham
Perush Rabbenu Avraham ben ha-Rambam z"l al Be-reishit u-Shemot
144 (Gen. 38:11–12); 163
100b; 175

Maimonides, Moses
The Guide of the Perplexed (Moreh Nevukhim)
3:29; 155, 167
3:32; 173, 358, 474-475
3:37; 171

3:49; 172-173
3:54; 415
The Eight Chapters of Ethics (*Shemonah Perakim*)
35–36; 407-408

Malbim. *See* **Wisser, Meir Leibush**

Moses ben Nachman. *See* **Nachmanides**

Nachmanides
Commentary on Genesis 34:13; 184
Commentary on Deuteronomy 1:1–3; 27
31:24–25; 28

Perfet, Isaac
Shut ha-Rivash, Responsum 284; 126

Rabbenu Tam. *See* Jacob ben Meir of Ramerupt (Rabbenu Tam)

Ramah. *See* **Abulafia, Meir (Ramah)**

Rashbam
Commentary on Gen 1:1–2; 19
Commentary on Ps 130–138; 90

Rashban. *See* **Schück, Salamon (Rashban)**

Rashi
Commentary to Ps 144:2; 125
Commentary to *b. Git.* 60a; 8
Commentary to *b. Ḥul.* 100b; 19

Tosafot
b. Shab. 55b; 132
b. Yad., 2:14; 111

Zohar
3:210b; 486
3,149 485
3:193; 487
3:276a 419

Reicher, Saie
Torat ha-Rishonim
1:18; 189
1:26; 163

Reischer, Jacob b. Joseph
Iyun Ya'akov
78a (Bava Batra 1:16); 31
78a (Bava Batra 15); 20

Rema. *See* **Isserles, Moses (Rema)**

Samuel ben Meir. *See* **Rashbam**

Schick, Solomon Tzevi b. Nathan
Sefer Torah Shelemah 1:83a–84b; 13

Schück, Salamon (Rashban)
Sefer Torah Shelemah, Deuteronomy, parashat Devarim; 34

Shiṭah Meḳubetset
B. Bat. 15a; 43
B. Ber. 21b; 25

Sofer, Moses (Ḥatam Sofer)
Ḥatam Sofer al ha-Torah Arukh ha-Shalem, 4:181; 53

Solomon ben Samuel of Würzburg
Supercommentary to Ibn Ezra; 51

Soloveitchik, Joseph B.
The Lonely Man of Faith 7:2: 10; 71

Vital, Samuel
Responsa Be'er Mayim Ḥayyim, responsum 27, 64–65; 135

Wisser, Meir Leibush (Malbim)
Commentary on Gen 4:22; 156
Preface to the commentary on Ps; 90

Yerahmi'el b. Solomon
Seder Olam Nusaḥ Sheni
368-369; 10
382; 76

Yosef Bekhor Shor (Joseph Orleans)
Commentary to Gen 1:31; 19

Zadok (Tzadok) of Lublin
Peri Tzaddik
Exod, Yitro 4; 21, 178
Lev, Behar 1; 34
Kedushat Shabbat, article 7; 34

Index of Names

A

Aaron 74, 362, 440, 443
Abaye 24, 308
Abdi-Heba 502
Abihu 362, 440
Abimelech 26, 397, 501, 504
Abraham ben David of Posquires (Ravad) 329
Abraham Ibn Ezra vii, 3, 44–45, 51, 59–61, 83, 87, 89, 96, 104–105, 154, 203, 242, 291, 203, 293, 315, 320, 325, 328, 342, 352, 354, 358–359, 377–378, 439, 495, 529
Abravanel, Isaac 29, 40, 59, 74, 76, 78–79, 81, 99, 104, 107–108, 120, 148, 172, 226, 353, 359, 476, 480, 513,
Adam 9, 12, 15–16, 18, 64, 71, 104, 129–130, 189, 261, 288, 295, 297, 376, 493, 495
Africa 157, 223
Agur son of Jakeh 92, 95–96
Ahab son of Omri 398, 400, 409–410, 435, 505–507, 514, 523
Ahaz 94, 104, 410–411, 509, 511
Ahijah 81
Ahijah the Shilonite 80 Ahitophel 398
Akhenaten (Amenhotep IV) 502
Akhetaten 502
Albo, Joseph 320, 421, 476, 496–497
Alexander the Great 534, 544
Amalek 9, 321, 344, 490, 495, 497
Amarna 502–504, 513
Amemar 304
America xv, 4, 115, 160, 229, 242, 235, 339, 356–357, 410, 424, 450
Amram 13, 163
Anah 401
Anani 100
Apiru (Habiru) 502, 513
Aram (kingdom) 505–507, 523–524
Arama, Isaac 97, 107, 235
Aram-Damascus 524
Arnon (wadi) 34, 147–148, 508

Asaph 90, 105, 536
Asriel 159–160
Assyria 15, 101, 242, 409, 506–507, 514, 522, 527
Aster, Shawn Zelig v, xi,192, 478
Aviner, Shlomo 107, 190, 256, 261, 386
Avivi, Yosef 254, 261
Avvim 26–27
Azariah 103, 531, 534
Azazel 51, 353
Azel 100

B

Balaam 56–58, 485
Balak 56–58, 485
Bamberger, M. L. 94
Barak son of Abinoam 312, 523
Bashan 51
Bathsheba 6, 231, 423, 454
Behemoth 349
Beit Ḥoron 500, 502–503
Bekhor Shor, Joseph 4, 20, 37, 378, 491
Ben Asher, Aaron ben Moses 117, 124, 126, 128, 141, 144
Ben Asher, Jacob 341, 348
Ben Azzai 111, 493
Ben Naftali,Moses ben David 117, 124, 126, 128, 141, 144
Benamozegh, Elia 34, 246
Ben-Asher, Aharon 411
Ben-hadad 505–507, 514
Benjamin 84–85
Bered 500, 514
Beriah 500, 502–503
Berlin, Naphtali Tzevi Judah (Netziv) 6, 83, 87, 161, 454
Berman, Joshua vi, xiii, 443
Bethel 253, 503
Bezalel son of Uri son of Hur 155
Bigman, David v, 300, 344, 360,
Bin Nun, Yoel 86, 386, 396, 426, 513–514
Birs Nimrud 465

Index of Names

Bizzaron 527
Bonfils, Joseph ben Eliezer 315, 320, 352
Bonfils, Joseph ben Samuel 47, 49
Borenstein, Avraham 35–36, 40
Borenstein, Samuel b. Rabbi Abraham 32
Borsippa xii, 465–466, 468–469, 478
Brandes, Yehuda iii, xi, 223, 386, 388, 389, 394, 468
Brettler, Marc Zvi xii, 60, 240, 241–242, 244,
Breuer, Mordechai viii, ix, xii, 39,72, 121, 122, 218, 224, 226, 246, 252–262, 285, 291, 338, 351, 353, 359–360, 426, 480
Brin, Gershon 36, 353, 359
Buber, Martin 264, 322, 333, 422
Buber, Solomon 14, 27, 39, 44, 54, 105, 319, 322
Burkert, Walter 231–232
Buzi 85, 86

C

Caleb son of Jephunneh 74–75, 101
Canaan 45, 73, 159, 194–195, 301, 307, 352, 381, 394, 429, 499, 502
Carmi 101
Carr, E. H. 196, 205
Cassuto, Umberto 224–225, 281,325, 429, 490, 494
Chaim ibn Attar 314
Cherlow, Yuval xii, 86, 288, 299, 386, 388, 389
Cohen, Adiel xii, 245, 426
Cohen, Chezi xii, 320, 358, 360
Collins, J. J. 531, 542–543, 546
Cyrus 82, 87, 90, 359, 532, 541, 546

D

Dan 75, 101, 103, 129, 222, 351
Daniel vi, xiii, 216, 530–544
Darius son of Ahasuerus 532
David ben Levi of Narbonne 44, 59
Davidson, Hannah xv
De Bono, Edward 266
De Wette, Wilhelm Martin Leberecht 39, 437
Deborah 312, 522
Deutsch, Chayuta iii, vi, xiii, 223, 380, 421
Dibon (Dhiban) 508–509, 511
Dinah 503, 522
Dothan 503
Duran, Profiat 118, 122

E

Ebal (mount) 499–501, 504, 513, 522
Egypt 8, 10–11, 20–22, 53, 55, 58, 62, 103, 143, 145, 157–160, 165, 176, 194–195, 205–206, 215, 231, 246–251, 260, 273, 281, 309, 374, 404, 429, 432, 434, 438, 483–484-497, 500, 502–504, 513, 517, 522
Eichhorn, Ze'ev Wolf 374, 437, 447
Eldad 53–54, 62
Elead 500, 514
Eleadah 500
Elhanan 231
Eliab 103
Eliakim son of Josiah 436
Eliezer 374
Eliezer b. Nathan 25, 39
Eliezer of Beaugency 3, 37, 85, 87
Elijah 70, 124, 127, 406, 411, 514
Elijah of Vilnius 90, 94, 96, 106
Elisha 398, 506, 508, 512, 524, 525
Elisha ben Abuyah 409
Elitzur, Yoel vi, xiii, 428, 439, 441, 514, 546
Elyashiv, Netanel Binyamin 498, 512
Engel, Joseph b. Judah 8, 14
Ephraim 50–51, 236, 435, 500, 502–503, 513–514
Er 163
Eshel, Hanan x, 135, 546
Esther 63, 100, 110, 216, 419, 425, 426, 430, 514, 527, 535, 543, 546
Ethan the Ezrahite 89, 103, 188, 297, 545
Ewald 447
Ezekiel vi, xiii, 37, 54, 85–87, 110, 114, 210, 216–217, 260, 350, 430–431, 433, 463–474, 476–480, 513, 535–536
Ezer 500
Ezida 465–466, 468–471, 478
Ezra vii, 76, 80, 87, 89, 98–108, 118, 126–127, 141, 213, 225, 238, 242, 430, 474, 480, 527, 529, 537

F

Fargeon, Yoshi x, 6, 108, 356, 394
Fez 246
Finkelstein, Israel 198, 205

G

Gad 76, 78, 508
Gafni, Isaiah 230–231, 242
Galilee 195
Ganzel, Tova iii, vi, xiii, 394, 478–479
Gehazi 398
Gibeon (city) 100–101, 500, 503–504
Gibeon (person) 100–101
Gilboa (mount) 503
Girona 98

Glatzer, Nahum 322, 338
Goliath 231
Gomorrah 50, 53
Gould, Stephen Jay 237, 243
Greece 208, 250- 251, 453, 533, 541
Greenberg, David xv
Greenberg, Moshe 39, 242, 245, 259, 421, 426, 480, 513
Greenberg, Uri Zvi 390
Gunzberg, Aryeh Leib 102, 109, 140

H
Hacohen, Avia 190, 243, 320, 355, 358–360, 423, 424, 495
Hadad 436
Haman 344
Hamat (kingdom) 436
Hammurabi xii, 150, 297, 446, 451–454, 482, 488
Hamor 501, 503–504
Hananiah 531, 534
Haran 434, 496, 504
Hazael 505–506, 524–525
Hazor 197, 517–518
Hebron 74–75, 503
Heinemann, Yosef 254
Heschel, Abraham Joshua 39, 264, 322, 338
Hezekiah 46, 76, 91–95, 105, 107, 110, 113–15, 141, 170, 216, 399, 401, 404–406, 408, 410–411, 473, 512
Hilkiah 39, 84–85, 118
Hirschensohn, Chaim 11–12, 15, 23, 32–33, 69, 71, 83–87, 123, 142, 159, 161, 164, 180, 182, 190, 226, 350, 358
Hivite 503
Hoffmann, David Zvi 17, 150–151, 153, 428, 438
Horeb 32, 320, 326–327, 329, 331–332, 338–339, 366–367, 372, 378, 492, 507, 514
Hur 101
Hyksos 159–160

I
Isaac Luria (Ari) 35, 420–421, 484
Isaac vi, xiii, 9, 60, 160, 183, 292, 374, 379–381, 383, 386–397
Isaiah 82–87, 95, 118, 142, 203, 206, 216, 252, 312, 359, 405–408, 410–411, 421, 437–438, 478, 480, 509, 512
Isaiah di Trani 95
Israel (kingdom) 508, 524
Issachar 402–404

Italy 15, 246
Ithiel 95–96

J
Jacob 8–9, 11, 13, 19–20, 50, 56–57, 71, 130, 159–160, 163–164, 175, 183, 205, 253, 341, 365, 374, 379, 402–403, 431, 436, 485, 496, 500, 502–503, 513, 522
Jacob ben Meir (Rabbenu Tam) 107, 135–136, 183, 187
Jacobs, Louis 264, 280, 285, 322
Jakeh 92, 95–96
Jedaiah 101
Jedo 80–81
Jehoiakim 84–85, 436, 465, 541
Jehoiarib 101
Jehoram 507
Jehu 505, 506, 514, 524–525
Jeremiah 76, 78, 84–85, 118–120, 204, 225, 311–312, 380, 399–400, 409, 411, 422, 435, 440, 476, 524
Jeroboam son of Nabat 80–81, 398, 400, 409, 440
Jethro 7, 12, 15, 83, 177, 180, 181, 182, 483–484, 490–492, 495–497
Job 20, 22–23, 42, 61, 65, 67, 71, 87–88, 96, 106, 121, 148, 177, 189, 214, 225, 235–236, 242–243, 373, 392, 394, 412–414, 421, 432, 433, 440, 483, 496, 537
Joram son of Ahab 436, 523–524
Jordan 45, 48, 75, 181, 196, 378, 499, 501, 504, 508, 511, 513, 521
Joseph 9–11, 159–160, 253, 426, 503
Joseph Ibn Megas 43
Joseph Ibn Naḥmias 94, 95, 106–107
Josephus 153, 399, 405, 409, 537, 541, 545
Joshua 9, 33, 39–44, 46–51, 56, 58–60, 108, 117, 119–120, 140, 196–198, 216, 242, 303, 352–353, 434, 438, 495, 500–504, 512–513, 518, 520–522, 525, 527
Josiah son of Amon of Judah 84–85, 359, 394, 399, 434, 436
Judah (kingdom) vi, xiii, 23, 46, 74–75, 77–80, 84, 85, 92–94, 101–102, 107, 113, 132, 163, 303, 304, 408, 409, 411, 436, 465–466, 507, 514, 522–524
Judah 100–102, 162–163, 296
Judah ben Barzillai al-Bargeloni 54, 70
Judah Ha-Chasid 315
Judah Ibn Balaam 124, 141, 166
Judah Loew of Prague (Maharal) 31, 40, 316, 320

Judah the Pious vii, 4, 49–51, 55, 60–62, 291, 293, 251, 353, 359
Judean Dessert 531

K
Kallir, Eleazar 383
Kaplan, Mordecai 243, 264, 268, 281, 285
Kara, Joseph 3, 77, 81, 97, 107–108, 125, 141
Kasher, Menachem Mendel 13–14, 39, 61, 140–141, 164, 189–190, 424
Kellner, Menachem 239, 244, 281, 285
Kierkegaard, Soren 382–384, 395–396
Kimḥi, David (Radak) 3, 75, 81, 93, 98–99, 106, 117, 234–236, 242, 478, 514
Kimhi, Joseph 95, 106
Kimḥi, Moses 92, 95, 105–106
King David 8, 14, 35, 48, 55, 77–78, 81, 88–92, 96, 104–106, 117, 215, 225, 436, 454, 505, 536
Kirchheim, Raphael 100
Kook, Abraham Isaac xiii, 4–5, 14, 40–41, 54, 64, 65, 67, 71, 86–87, 90, 94, 107, 130, 141–143, 151, 153, 179–180, 186–188, 190, 224, 226–227, 236, 243, 256, 262, 273, 283, 284, 285, 286, 299, 315, 319–320, 350, 357–359, 377, 384–386, 389, 393, 396, 421–425, 441, 479, 493, 495, 497, 512, 540–541, 545–546
Kook, Zvi Yehuda 4–5, 65, 67, 71, 179
Korah 88, 104–105, 350, 461, 497
Kranz, Jacob (Maggid of Dubno) 32, 40
Kugel, James 223, 268–270, 281, 282–283, 285, 287
Kula, Amit vi, xiii, 227, 412, 423, 426

L
Laban 21, 175, 190, 195, 484–485, 496, 537
Leibowitz, Yeshayahu 236–237, 256, 266-269, 271, 281–283, 285–286, 385, 387, 396
Leviathan 148, 349 Levin, Hanoch 389
Lindenbaum, Matthew xvi,
Livorno (Leghorn) 10, 15, 246, 259–260
Luzzatto, Samuel David (Shadal) 6, 86, 106, 161, 176, 251, 256, 259, 477

M
Mack, Hananel vi, xiii, 36, 224, 242, 398
Maimonides xv, 4–5, 62, 64, 68, 70, 80, 117, 122, 128, 138–139, 141, 152, 155, 161, 163–164, 167, 171–175, 179, 189–190, 201–202, 206, 221–222, 226–227, 233, 235, 239, 242, 245, 247, 258, 263, 265–266, 268, 270, 273, 282, 286, 296–297, 300–304, 306–307, 311, 315, 318, 320, 326, 329, 338, 342, 348–349, 356–358, 378, 384–385, 387, 396, 407, 411, 414, 420, 422, 424, 461, 471, 473–475 479–480, 482, 486, 492–494, 496–497, 516, 527
Malachi 31, 91, 108, 433, 435, 538
Manasseh vi, xiii, 11, 50, 51, 160, 194–195, 204, 301, 355, 392, 398–411
Marah 8, 491, 497
Medad 52, 54, 62
Medan, Yaakov vi, xiii, 226, 377, 423, 498
Media 100–102, 113, 419, 519, 541, 546
Meir ben Todros HaLevi Abulafia 104, 137, 145
Meir the Levite son of Rabbi Todros the Levite of Spain 136
Menaḥem b. Rabbi Simeon 3–4
Menahem ben Solomon ha-Meiri 44, 122
Menahem son of Gadi 506
Mesha 507–509, 511–512, 514
Mesopotamia 452–453, 477–478, 494, 514
Messas, Joseph 350, 359
Misgav, Haggai vi, xiii, 515
Mishael 531, 534
Moab 27, 34, 147–148, 181, 220, 309, 311, 331, 332, 354, 499, 501, 507–512, 514
Molech 169, 380–381, 385, 391
Morocco 38, 246
Moses vi, ix, xvii, 3, 5–7, 9–14, 17–39, 41–62, 64, 67–70, 72–73, 76, 82, 88, 90, 92, 95–96, 103–104, 106, 110–112, 114, 117, 122, 126, 129–130, 134, 138, 141,143–145, 150–151, 154, 156–157, 160–161, 164–166, 169, 177, 178, 180–181, 184, 186, 188, 196, 202–204, 214–218, 220–221, 224–226, 239, 247, 249–251, 258, 263, 265–267, 277, 281, 291, 293–294, 301–305, 308–314, 316–332, 335–336, 338, 352–355, 361–365, 369–370, 371, 377–378, 386, 394, 396, 402, 405–407, 413, 420, 424, 435–436, 438, 439, 446–448, 456–461, 481–488, 491–497, 515, 527, 536
Moshkovitz, Yehiel Tzvi 515

N
Nachmanides 4, 7, 28, 36, 39–40, 59, 67, 128, 133–134, 142–143, 147, 158, 159,

164, 172–173, 184, 190, 227, 242, 308,
   311–314, 319–320, 324, 352–353, 359,
   377–378, 384, 413, 421, 495
Nadab 362, 440
Narbonne 98, 105–106
Nathan 76, 78, 80, 454,
Nathan ben Yehiel of Rome 53, 61
Nebuchadnezzar 465–466, 533, 539, 541
Nebuzaradan 84
Nehardea 304, 319
Netanel son of Zoar 404
Nissim of Gerona (Ran) 40, 58
Noaḥ 8–9, 15, 46, 83, 184, 187–188,
   187–200, 232, 239, 243
Noll, Mark 240, 244

O
Og 50, 54
Oholibamah 401
Onan 103, 163
Onkelos 332
Osiris 159–160, 249, 260

P
Pallu 103
Perfet, Isaac 126
Persia 113, 250–251, 419, 533, 541, 546
Pharaoh Neco 436
Pines, Shlomo xv, 4, 161, 286, 356
Plantinga, Alvin 237, 243
Poznański, Samuel 94
Pressburg Yeshiva 515
Pseudo-Kara 101–102, 108–109
Pseudo-Rashi 3, 39, 100, 101, 108

R
Rabban Shimon ben Gamaliel 53
Rabbi Abahu 307
Rabbi Akiva 35, 111, 125–126, 128,
   143, 180, 202, 223–224, 298, 309,
   320, 325, 340–341, 400, 408, 418, 425,
   457, 493
Rabbi Avin bar Kahana 349
Rabbi Bibi Abba 381
Rabbi Bon 307
Rabbi Elazar 505, 513
Rabbi Elazar ben Azariah 145, 341–342
Rabbi Eliezer 127, 211
Rabbi Eliezer b. Parta 527
Rabbi Eliezer ben Jacob 472–473, 479
Rabbi Eliezer ha-Moda'i 529
Rabbi Ḥama bar Ḥaninah 374

Rabbi Hamnuna 13
Rabbi Ḥaninah 292, 504–505
Rabbi Ḥiyya b. Abba 538
Rabbi Ishmael 309, 325, 341, 457, 513, 528
Rabbi Jeremiah 538
Rabbi Jose 307, 513
Rabbi Joshua b. Levi 307, 310
Rabbi Joshua b. Rabbi Nehemiah 306
Rabbi Judah bar Ilai 481
Rabbi Judah the Prince (Rabbi Yehudah,
   Rabbi) 11, 19, 26, 33, 39, 42–43, 47, 54,
   60, 110–111, 141, 303, 310, 335, 352, 479
Rabbi Levi 24, 505
Rabbi Levi bar Hama 335
Rabbi Matana 305
Rabbi Meir 129, 207
Rabbi Nathan 113, 310
Rabbi Neḥemiah 32, 42–43, 47, 303,
   310, 352
Rabbi Nehemiah 33, 42–43, 310
Rabbi Samuel b. Nachman 305
Rabbi Shimon 42–43, 98, 114, 425, 495, 513
Rabbi Shimon ben Lakish 7–8, 126, 134
Rabbi Shimon ben Menasya 111
Rabbi Shimon ben Shetaḥ 131
Rabbi Shimon ben Yoḥai 374, 379
Rabbi Simon 82, 107, 307
Rabbi Tanḥuma 26
Rabbi Yehoshua bar Abba 42
Rabbi Yoḥanan b. Zakai 306
Rabbi Yoḥanan ben Zakkai 401
Rabbi Yoseph 349
Rabinowitz, Zadok Ha-Cohen of Lublin 38,
   180, 350, 459
Rachmani, Shachar 4
Rahab 148, 503
Rashi see Shlomo Yitzchaki
Rav 42, 88, 99, 112, 340, 374, 473
Rav Aḥa bar Ada 136
Rav Ashi 53, 304, 374, 408, 411, 478, 514
Rav Gidel 42
Rav Ḥisda 304
Rav Hoshaya 56
Rav Shmuel bar Sheilat 112
Rav Yehudah 99, 113–114, 133
Rav Yehudah bar Rav Shmuel bar Sheilat
   112–113
Rav Yoseph 133, 135–136, 139, 224, 260
Raviv, Rivka vi, xiii, 423, 530, 545–546
Red Sea 104, 195, 197, 210, 358, 491
Reischer, Jacob b. Joseph 20, 31
Reuben 50, 167, 402–403, 410

Rofé, Alexander 217, 223, 434, 440
Rosenfeld, Ben-Zion 143, 472, 479
Rosenzweig, Franz 264, 321
Ross, Tamar xii, 227, 277, 282, 284, 286, 344, 356–357, 360, 393, 383, 397, 423
Rowley, H. H., 532, 543
Ruth 8, 110, 114–115, 162, 238, 431, 456, 467

S
Samaria 503, 506, 507, 520, 522
Samuel 75–78, 81–82, 98–99, 141–142, 231, 236, 304, 344, 433–435, 437–438, 440, 442, 454
Samuel b. Meir (Rashbam) 3–4, 19,20, 27, 37, 39, 45, 60, 87, 90, 97, 107, 173, 223, 227, 328, 342, 377, 497, 536, 542, 545
Sardinia 522–523
Sarid, Yossi 383, 395
Schick, Solomon Tzevi b. Nathan 13, 16
Schück, Salamon (Rashban) 58, 62
Schwartz, Baruch x, 58, 281, 282
Se'adyah Ga'on 87, 100, 124, 215, 124, 439, 540
Sennacherib 92, 101–102
Shalmaneser III 506
Shammah, Avraham vi, xii, 377
Shammai 36, 111, 114, 133, 372
Shechem 205, 499–504, 513
Shemesh, Aharon 400–402, 410
Shlomo Yitzchaki (Rashi) 3, 8, 11, 14–15, 19, 23, 25, 36–37, 39, 45, 53, 61, 74, 81, 100–101, 108, 114–115, 125, 127–128, 143, 158–159, 164, 177, 182, 190, 222, 224, 239, 249, 299, 319, 325, 328, 334, 339, 346–347, 357–358, 384, 411, 434, 439, 444, 477–478, 480, 490, 495, 514, 536, 545
Shobal 101
Shuthelah 500
Sihon 32, 34, 54–55, 147–148
Silman, Yochanan 330, 333, 338
Sinai (mount) v, xii, 8, 18–19, 21, 24, 35, 55, 58, 62–63, 65, 72, 138–139, 182, 188, 193, 194, 202, 204, 220–221, 223, 225, 227, 235, 239, 265, 267, 278, 281–282, 285, 291, 294, 296, 303, 305–311, 313, 318–321, 323, 325–327, 329–331, 333–336, 338–339, 354, 360–363, 371–373, 378–379, 424, 429, 456–458, 460, 491–492, 501, 504
Sisera 522
Sodom 8, 50, 53, 380, 388, 393
Sofer, Moses 32, 41
Solomon 46, 49, 80, 88–89, 92–97, 104, 106–107, 111–113, 115–116, 216, 312, 435, 440–441, 466–468, 473, 478, 505
Solomon ben Samuel of Würzburg 51, 61
Solomon, Norman 10, 270–271, 287
Soloveitchik, J. B. 71–72, 266–267, 282, 286–287, 277, 423
Sommer, Benjamin D. xii, 287, 397
Sperling, D. S. 245, 259
Spinoza, Baruch 210, 223, 421, 447
Staiman, Avi xv
Stalybridge 196
Stout, Jeffrey 276
Sukkot 172, 515
Sura 304
Susa 451, 480
Syria 170, 189, 208, 247–248

T
Tahath 500
Talmage, Frank 38, 233–235, 242
Tamar 103, 162–164, 296
Tau, Tsvi Israel 498–499, 512
Tel Deir 'Alla 515
Tel El-Ahwat 522
Thrope, Samuel xv Timna 401–403, 410
Toi 436
Tzadok ha-Kohen vi, xiii, 21, 38, 395, 424, 481–490, 492–497

U
Ucal 95–96
Uzzah 78
Uzziah 410–411, 437

V
Vainstub, Daniel 381, 394
Velikovsky, Immanuel 513, 517
Veyne, Paul 230

W
Wadi Ara 522
Weiss, Hillel 389, 390, 397
Weiss, Meir 255, 265,
Wellhausen, Julius 150, 153, 245–246, 428, 439
Werblowsky, R. J. Zwi 256, 262
Wisser, Meir Leibush (Malbim) 40, 90–92, 96, 101,105–106, 109, 156, 161, 189, 464, 477, 535

Y
Yegar-sahadutha 537–538
Yehoshua, A.B. 382, 395–397

Yerah.m i'el b. Solomon 10
Yeshivat Har Hamor 498
Yoḥanan HaKohen 383
Yonatan (translator) 332

Z
Zabad 500, 514
Zaidman, Yaakov 255
Zebulun 101, 403

Zechariah 108, 438, 538
Zedekiah 84, 85, 91, 465
Zelophehad 330, 355
Zerahiah of Barcelona 235
Zertal, Adam 204, 522, 204
Zerubbabel 83, 99, 100
Zibeon 401
Zimri 103, 485
Zuckermandel, Moses Samuel 111, 204

www.ingramcontent.com/pod-product-compliance
Lightning Source LLC
Chambersburg PA
CBHW070740020526
44114CB00042B/2038